Hybrid and Alternative Fuel Vehicles

Third Edition

James D. Halderman

PEARSON

Boston   Columbus   Indianapolis   New York   San Francisco   Upper Saddle River   Amsterdam
Cape Town   Dubai   London   Madrid   Milan   Munich   Paris   Montreal   Toronto   Delhi
Mexico City   São Paulo   Sydney   Hong Kong   Seoul   Singapore   Taipei   Tokyo

Vice President and Executive Publisher: Vernon Anthony
Senior Acquisitions Editor: Lindsey Prudhomme Gill
Development Editor: Dan Trudden
Project Manager: Jessica H. Sykes
Editorial Assistant: Yvette Schlarman
Media Project Manager: Karen Bretz
Director of Marketing: David Gesell
Marketing Manager: Harper Coles
Senior Marketing Coordinator: Alicia Wozniak
Production Manager: Holly Shufeldt
Creative Director: Jayne Conte
Cover Designer: Bruce Kenselaar
Image Permission Coordinator: Mike Lackey
Full-Service Project Management/Composition: Abinaya Rajendran,
   Integra Software Services, Ltd.
Printer/Binder: Webcom
Cover Printer: Webcom
Cover Photos: LAforet Aurelien / Fotolia.com, Boca / Fotolia.com,
   andrea lehmkuhl / Fotolia.com, ferkelraggae / fotolia.com, LPETTET /
   iStockphoto.com, powerofforever / iStockphoto.com

Library of Congress Cataloging-in-Publication Data
Halderman, James D.,
   Hybrid and alternative fuel vehicles/James D. Halderman. — 3rd ed.
      p. cm.
   ISBN-13: 978-0-13-278484-9
   ISBN-10: 0-13-278484-X
   1. Hybrid electric vehicles.   2. Alternative fuel vehicles.   I. Title.
TL221.15.H35 2013
629.22'9 — dc23

                                                                   2012003326

10 9 8 7 6 5 4 3 2

ISBN-10:   0-13-278484-X
ISBN-13: 978-0-13-278484-9

PREFACE

Professional Technician Series Part of Pearson Automotive's Professional Technician Series, the second edition of *Hybrid and Alternative Fuel Vehicles* represents the future of automotive textbooks. The series includes textbooks that cover all 8 areas of ASE certification plus additional titles covering common courses.

Current revisions are written by a team of very experienced writers and teachers. The series is also peer reviewed for technical accuracy.

NEW TO THIS EDITION

The third edition of *Hybrid and Alternative Fuel Vehicles* was updated and expanded:

1. Full color used throughout to help bring the subject alive.
2. Over 140 new color line Drawings and photos.
3. Two chapters have been moved in response to suggestions from instructors and reviewers. The chapters on service procedures and first responders are now Chapters 17 and 18.
4. Updated content includes:
   - Chevrolet VOLT description and operation
   - Buick LaCrosse mild hybrid

- Two-mode operation and transmission operation
- Auxiliary battery location chart
- High-voltage battery location chart
- SAE J1772 electric vehicle plug
- Level 1, 2, and 3 charging stations

A COMPLETE INSTRUCTOR AND STUDENT SUPPLEMENTS PACKAGE

All Professional Technician textbooks are accompanied by a full set of instructor and student supplements. Please see page vi for a detailed list of supplements.

A FOCUS ON DIAGNOSIS AND PROBLEM SOLVING

The Professional Technician Series has been developed to satisfy the need for a greater emphasis on problem diagnosis. Automotive instructors and service managers agree that students and beginning technicians need more training in diagnostic procedures and skill development. To meet this need and demonstrate how real-world problems are solved, "Real World Fix" features are included throughout and highlight how real-life problems are diagnosed and repaired.

The following pages highlight the unique core features that set the Professional Technician Series book apart from other automotive textbooks.

chapter 1

CARBON-BASED FUELS AND THE ENVIRONMENT

OBJECTIVES: After studying Chapter 1, the reader will be able to: • Describe the role of hybrid and alternative fuel vehicles in today's society. • Identify carbon-based fuels. • Describe how organic materials decompose into carbon-based fuels. • Explain the difference between carbon-based and non-carbon-based energy sources. • Explain the federal and California Air Resources Board emission standards. • List alternatives to carbon-based fuels. • List the factors that will be needed to reduce the carbon footprint.

KEY TERMS: • AT-PZEV 4 • Bin number 4 • CAA 3 • CARB 3 • Carbohydrates 1 • Carbon 1 • Carbon dioxide 2 • Carbon footprint 9 • Carbon monoxide 2 • EPA 3 • Global warming 11 • Greenhouse gas (GHG) 7 • Hydrocarbons 2 • ILEV 4 • IPCC 7 • Irradiance 6 • Kyoto protocol 7 • LEV 3 • Nitrogen 2 • NLEV 4 • ODS 8 • Organic 1 • Oxygen 2 • Ozone 6 • Peak oil 10 • pH 9 • PM 8 • PZEV 4 • Smog 2 • Soot 3 • Stratosphere 6 • SULEV 3 • Tier 3 • TLEV 3 • Troposphere 6 • ULEV II 3 • Ultraviolet (UV) radiation 6 • UVA 6 • UVB 6 • UVC 6 • VOC 8 • ZEV 4

THE PURPOSE OF HYBRID AND ALTERNATIVE-FUEL VEHICLES

The purpose of manufacturing and selling hybrid and alternative-fuel vehicles is to provide an alternative vehicle to the buyer who wishes to reduce the use of our natural resources. The cost of fuel is continuously increasing, and the fuel being used is mostly nonrenewable and produced from crude oil. Some alternative fuels come from renewable sources, such as from corn for the manufacture of ethanol, but most of the other fuels used for motor vehicles are petroleum based. Most of the current choices of fuel contain carbon and, as a result of combustion, release carbon dioxide gas, which is thought to contribute to global warming. The use of hybrid and alternative-fuel vehicles will help the environment and reduce the production of carbon dioxide by reducing the amount of fuel used.

CARBON-BASED SOCIETY

The term **organic** is applied to anything that was alive at one time. Throughout history most of the energy used in the world is generated by burning organic fuel that contains **carbon** (abbreviated **C**). An economy that uses only carbon-based fuels is often referred to as a *carbon-based society*. Carbon is formed from materials that were once alive on the earth, including:

■ Plants that die and eventually are turned into coal, oil, and natural gas
■ Animal life of all types that also dies and decays to form carbon fuels

The source of carbon-based fuels is limited to the remains of dead plants and animals and is therefore not a limitless resource.

CHEMICAL FUNDAMENTALS OF CARBON-BASED SOCIETY

All life-forms are able to collect, store, and use energy from their environment. In carbon-based biology, the basic energy storage compounds are in **carbohydrates**, where the carbon atoms are linked by single bonds into a chain. For example, carbon dioxide (CO_2) plus water (H_2O), when combined with chlorophyll in the plant and sunlight, produces glucose and oxygen (O_2). A carbohydrate is oxidized (combined with oxygen) to release energy (and waste products of water and carbon dioxide).

Plants release oxygen during photosynthesis, and animals, including humans, release carbon dioxide when they exhale.

CARBON-BASED FUELS AND THE ENVIRONMENT 1

OBJECTIVES AND KEY TERMS appear at the beginning of each chapter to help students and instructors focus on the most important material in each chapter. The chapter objectives are based on specific ASE and NATEF tasks.

SAFETY TIP

How to Depower the Honda HV System

To turn off the 144 volts for safety or compression testing, remove the ignition key, then take out the rear seat cushions, and remove a small access panel (one with two bolts—in the center of the top aluminum plate). **SEE FIGURE 12–24.** Remove the red switch cover and turn the switch to off. Replace the red switch cover. A resistor is hard-wired to the positive post of each capacitor in case of a failure of the ignition switch system because it is designed to drain the capacitors of high voltage at each key cycle to off. After five minutes, check the orange cables for low voltage using a CAT III voltmeter while wearing rubber linesman's gloves. If it is at 12 volts or less, the vehicle is now safe to work on.

SAFETY TIP alert students to possible hazards on the job and how to avoid them.

REAL WORLD FIX

A Bad Day Changing Oil

A shop owner was asked by a regular customer who had just bought a Prius if the oil could be changed there. The owner opened the hood, made sure the filter was in stock (it is a standard Toyota filter used on other models), and said yes. Not hearing the engine running, the technician hoisted the vehicle into the air, removed the drain bolt, and drained the oil into the oil drain unit. When the filter was removed, oil started to fly around the shop. When the voltage level dropped, the onboard computer started the engine so that the HV battery could recharge. The technician should have removed the key to keep this from happening. Be sure that the "ready" light is off before changing the oil or doing any other service work that may cause personal harm or harm to the vehicle if the engine starts.

REAL WORLD FIX present students with actual automotive service scenarios and show how these common (and sometimes uncommon) problems were diagnosed and repaired.

TECH TIP

Do Not Overfill the Fuel Tank

Gasoline fuel tanks have an expansion volume area at the top. The volume of this expansion area is equal to 10% to 15% of the volume of the tank. This area is normally not filled with gasoline, but rather is designed to provide a place for the gasoline to expand into, if the vehicle is parked in the hot sun and the gasoline expands. This prevents raw gasoline from escaping from the fuel system. A small restriction is usually present to control the amount of air and vapors that can escape the tank and flow to the charcoal canister.

TECH TIP feature real-world advice and "tricks of the trade" from ASE-certified master technicians.

❓ FREQUENTLY ASKED QUESTION

When Do I Need to De-Power the High-Voltage System?

During routine service work, there is no need for a technician to de-power the high-voltage system. The only time when this process is needed is if service repairs or testing is being performed on any circuit that has an orange cable attached. These include:

- AC compressor if electrically powered
- High-voltage battery pack or electronic controllers

The electric power steering system usually operates on 12 volts or 42 volts and neither is a shock hazard. However, an arc will be maintained if a 42-volt circuit is opened. Always refer to service information if servicing the electric power steering system or any other system that may contain high voltage.

FREQUENTLY ASKED QUESTION are based on the author's own experience and provide answers to many of the most common questions asked by students and beginning service technicians.

NOTE: Capacitors are also called **condensers**. This term developed because electric charges collect, or condense, on the plates of a capacitor much like water vapor collects and condenses on a cold bottle or glass.

NOTE provide students with additional technical information to give them a greater understanding of a specific task or procedure.

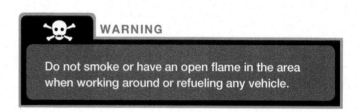

CAUTION: If a push-button start is used, remove the key fob at least 15 feet (5 meters) from the vehicle to prevent the vehicle from being powered up.

CAUTION alert students about potential damage to the vehicle that can occur during a specific task or service procedure.

☠ WARNING

Do not smoke or have an open flame in the area when working around or refueling any vehicle.

WARNING alert students to potential dangers to themselves during a specific task or service procedure.

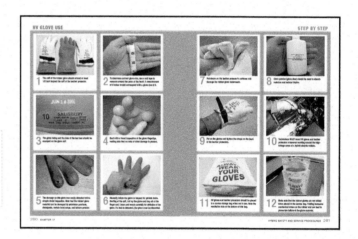

STEP-BY-STEP photo sequences show in detail the steps involved in performing a specific task or service procedure.

THE SUMMARY, REVIEW QUESTIONS, AND CHAPTER QUIZ at the end of each chapter help students review the material presented in the chapter and test themselves to see how much they've learned.

RESOURCES IN PRINT AND ONLINE

NAME OF SUPPLEMENT	PRINT	ONLINE	AUDIENCE	DESCRIPTION
Instructor Resource Manual 0132785307		✓	Instructors	Contains solutions and answers from problems found in the textbook.
TestGen 0132785277		✓	Instructors	Test generation software and test bank for the text.
Test Item File in BB 0132785390		✓	Instructors	Upload the test bank into your BlackBoard course using this cartridge.
PowerPoint Presentation 0132784858		✓	Instructors	Slides include chapter learning objectives, lecture outline of the test, and graphics from the book.
Image Bank 0132785390		✓	Instructors	All of the images and graphs from the textbook to create customized lecture slides.
Instructors Resource CD-ROM 0132865823	✓			Contains a variety of instructor support material including PowerPoints, crossword puzzles, chapter quizzes and review questions and English and Spanish Glossary,
NATEF Correlated Task Sheets – for instructors 0132953412		✓	Instructors	Downloadable NATEF task sheets for easy customization and development of unique task sheets.
NATEF Task Sheets – For Students 0132685382	✓		Students	Study activity manual that correlates NATEF Automobile Standards to chapters and pages numbers in the text. Available to students at a discounted price when packaged with the text.
CourseSmart eText 0132989492		✓	Students	An alternative to purchasing the print textbook, students can subscribe to the same content online and save up to 50% off the suggested list price of the print text. Visit **www.coursesmart.com**
Companion Website		✓	Instructors and Students	Online package of practice tests, flashcards and more. Visit **www.pearsonhighered.com/autostudent**

All online resources can be downloaded from the Instructor's Resource Center: **www.pearsonighered.com/irc**

ACKNOWLEDGMENTS

A large number of people and organizations have cooperated in providing the reference material and technical information used in this text. The author wishes to express sincere thanks to the following persons for their special contributions:

Stephen Ellis–Honda
Ford Motor Company
General Motors Corporation
Curt Henriott–Ford
Tim Jones–Honda Training Center
Chris Karr–Ford
Andy Knevel–Toyota
Lloyd Koppes–Toyota
NEDRA
Adam Pietrzak–General Motors
Craig Van Batenburg–ACDC
Toyota Motor Sales–USA, Inc.
Dick Krieger
Jeff Rehkopf
Dan Avery
John Kershaw
Steve Cartwright–Federal Mogul Training Center
Elizabeth Rickard–Honda
Tim Jones–Honda
Kevin Boden–Consulab
Steve Ash–Sinclair Community College
Chuck Taylor–Sinclair Community College
Jimmy Dinsmore–Cox Media
Tom Birch
David Norman–San Jacinto College
Jim Linder–Linder Technical Services
Joe Palazzolo–GKN Driveline
Nathan BankeConsulab
Tom Freels–Sinclair Community College

TECHNICAL AND CONTENT REVIEWERS The following people reviewed the manuscript before production and checked it for technical accuracy and clarity of presentation. Their suggestions and recommendations were included in the final draft of the manuscript. Their input helped make this textbook clear and technically accurate while maintaining the easy-to-read style that has made other books from the same author so popular.

Jim Anderson
Greenville High School

Rankin E. Barnes
Guilford Technical Community College

Victor Bridges
Umpqua Community College

Darrell Deeter
Saddleback College

Matt Dixon
Southern Illinois University

Dr. Roger Donovan
Illinois Central College

A.C. Durdin
Moraine Park Technical College

Herbert Ellinger
Western Michigan University

Al Engledahl
College of DuPage

Patrick English
Ferris State University

Robert M. Frantz
Ivy Tech Community College, Richmond

Michael R. Francis
Owens Community College

Christopher Fry
Harry S Truman College

Dr. David Gilbert
Southern Illinois University

Joseph P Gumina
City College Of San Francisco

Larry Hagelberger
Upper Valley Joint Vocational School

Oldrick Hajzler
Red River College

Gary F. Ham
South Plains College

Blaine M. Heisner
Southern Illinois University Carbondale

Betsy Hoffman
Vermont Technical College

Marty Kamimoto
Fresno City College

Richard Krieger
Michigan Institute of Technology

Carlton H. Mabe, Sr.
Virginia Western Community College

Roy Marks
Owens Community College

Tony Martin
University of Alaska Southeast

Kerry Meier
San Juan College

Clifford Meyer
Saddleback College

Kevin Murphy
Stark State College of Technology

Teresa L. Noto, M.S.
Farmingdale State College

Paul Pate
College of Southern Nevada

Fritz Peacock
Indiana Vocational Technical College

Dennis Peter
NAIT (Canada)

Eric Pruden
Pennsylvania College of Technology

Jeff Rehkopf
Florida State College

Kenneth Redick
Hudson Valley Community College

Matt Roda
Mott Community College

Omar Trinidad
Southern Illinois University

Mitchell Walker
St. Louis Community College at Forest Park

Jennifer Wise
Sinclair Community College
Special thanks to instructional designer
Alexis I. Skriloff James.

SPECIAL THANKS   I wish to thank Blaine Heeter, Mike Garblik, and Chuck Taylor of Sinclair Community College in Dayton, Ohio, and James (Mike) Watson, who helped with many of the photos. A special thanks to Dick Krieger for his detailed and thorough reviews of the manuscript before publication. Most of all, I wish to thank Michelle Halderman for her assistance in all phases of manuscript preparation.

—James D. Halderman

JIM HALDERMAN brings a world of experience, knowledge, and talent to his work. His automotive service experience includes working as a flat-rate technician, a business owner, and a professor of automotive technology at a leading U.S. community college for more than 20 years.

He has a Bachelor of Science degree from Ohio Northern University and a Master's degree in Education from Miami University in Oxford, Ohio. Jim also holds a U.S. patent for an electronic transmission control device. He is an ASE-certified Master Automotive Technician and Advanced Engine Performance (L1) ASE-certified. Jim is the author of many automotive textbooks, all published by Pearson Prentice Hall Publishing Company. He has presented numerous technical seminars to national audiences, including the California Automotive Teachers (CAT) and the Illinois College Automotive Instructor Association (ICAIA). He is also a member and presenter at the North American Council of Automotive Teachers (NACAT). Jim was also named Regional Teacher of the Year by General Motors Corporation and outstanding alumni of Ohio Northern University. Jim and his wife, Michelle, live in Dayton, Ohio. They have two children.

jim@jameshalderman.com

BRIEF CONTENTS

CONTENTS

chapter 1

CARBON-BASED FUELS AND THE ENVIRONMENT

OBJECTIVES: After studying Chapter 1, the reader will be able to: • Describe the role of hybrid and alternative fuel vehicles in today's society. • Identify carbon-based fuels. • Describe how organic materials decompose into carbon-based fuels. • Explain the difference between carbon-based and non-carbon-based energy sources. • Explain the federal and California Air Resources Board emission standards. • List alternatives to carbon-based fuels. • List the factors that will be needed to reduce the carbon footprint.

KEY TERMS: • AT-PZEV 4 • Bin number 4 • CAA 3 • CARB 3 • Carbohydrates 1 • Carbon 1 • Carbon dioxide 2 • Carbon footprint 9 • Carbon monoxide 2 • EPA 3 • Global warming 11 • Greenhouse gas (GHG) 7 • Hydrocarbons 2 • ILEV 4 • IPCC 7 • Irradiance 6 • Kyoto protocol 7 • LEV 3 • Nitrogen 2 • NLEV 4 • ODS 8 • Organic 1 • Oxygen 2 • Ozone 6 • Peak oil 10 • pH 9 • PM 8 • PZEV 4 • Smog 2 • Soot 3 • Stratosphere 6 • SULEV 3 • Tier 3 • TLEV 3 • Troposphere 6 • ULEV II 3 • Ultraviolet (UV) radiation 6 • UVA 6 • UVB 6 • UVC 6 • VOC 8 • ZEV 4

THE PURPOSE OF HYBRID AND ALTERNATIVE-FUEL VEHICLES

The purpose of manufacturing and selling hybrid and alternative-fuel vehicles is to provide an alternative vehicle to the buyer who wishes to reduce the use of our natural resources. The cost of fuel is continuously increasing, and the fuel being used is mostly nonrenewable and produced from crude oil. Some alternative fuels come from renewable sources, such as from corn for the manufacture of ethanol, but most of the other fuels used for motor vehicles are petroleum based. Most of the current choices of fuel contain carbon and, as a result of combustion, release carbon dioxide gas, which is thought to contribute to global warming. The use of hybrid and alternative-fuel vehicles will help the environment and reduce the production of carbon dioxide by reducing the amount of fuel used.

CARBON-BASED SOCIETY

The term **organic** is applied to anything that was alive at one time. Throughout history most of the energy used in the world is generated by burning organic fuel that contains **carbon** (abbreviated **C**). An economy that uses only carbon-based fuels is often referred to as a *carbon-based society*. Carbon is formed from materials that were once alive on the earth, including:

- Plants that die and eventually are turned into coal, oil, and natural gas
- Animal life of all types that also dies and decays to form carbon fuels

The source of carbon-based fuels is limited to the remains of dead plants and animals and is therefore not a limitless resource.

CHEMICAL FUNDAMENTALS OF CARBON-BASED SOCIETY

All life-forms are able to collect, store, and use energy from their environment. In carbon-based biology, the basic energy storage compounds are in **carbohydrates,** where the carbon atoms are linked by single bonds into a chain. For example, carbon dioxide (CO_2) plus water (H_2O), when combined with chlorophyll in the plant and sunlight, produces glucose and oxygen (O_2). A carbohydrate is oxidized (combined with oxygen) to release energy (and waste products of water and carbon dioxide).

Plants release oxygen during photosynthesis, and animals, including humans, release carbon dioxide when they exhale.

CHEMISTRY OF THE ATMOSPHERE

When carbon is burned, it combines with the oxygen in the air. The atmosphere on earth has about 21% **oxygen,** abbreviated O_2 (pronounced "O two"), about 78% **nitrogen,** abbreviated N_2 (pronounced "N two"), and 1% of many other gases. It is these two main elements in our atmosphere that can combine to form other gases that are the source of most of the concerns regarding the use of carbon-based fuels. In the atmosphere, two oxygen atoms combine naturally to form a molecule of oxygen, O_2. Two atoms of nitrogen are naturally combined to form one molecule of nitrogen, N_2. If nitrogen and oxygen molecules are exposed to high heat and/or pressure, they can combine to form oxides of nitrogen (NO and NO_2).

CHEMISTRY OF CARBON-BASED FUELS

The science of carbon-based fuels is called *organic chemistry*. Organic chemistry names chemicals according to the number of carbon atoms that are in the molecule.

The name and number of the most commonly used carbon molecules include:

Methane = one carbon atom

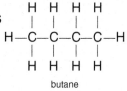
methane

Ethane = two carbon atoms

ethane

Propane = three carbon atoms

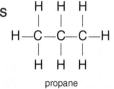
propane

Butane = four carbon atoms

butane

Pentane = five carbon atoms

pentane

Hexane = six carbon atoms

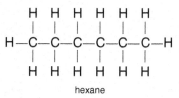
hexane

Heptane = seven carbon atoms

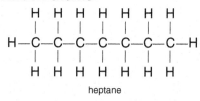
heptane

Octane = eight carbon atoms

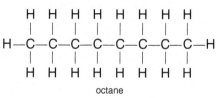
octane

The carbon atoms are attached to hydrogen atoms to form **hydrocarbons** (abbreviated **HC**). There are literally thousands of hydrocarbons, and they differ not only by the number of carbon atoms, but also by the way they are attached to each other. The various bonds by which the molecule is constructed results in a change in the physical characteristics of the hydrocarbon.

Molecules that have a high number of carbon atoms release more energy when they burn, which translates into more power from the fuel and from the engine.

Gasoline is composed of hundreds of different hydrocarbons that are blended together to create the specified volatility and other physical characteristic for use in an engine.

CHEMISTRY OF CARBON-BASED EMISSIONS

When carbon-based fuels are burned, the carbon and the hydrogen from the fuel combine with the oxygen and the nitrogen in the air to create many new and often dangerous compounds, including:

- **Carbon monoxide (CO)** — A colorless, odorless poisonous gas.
- **Carbon dioxide (CO_2)** — An inert greenhouse gas, which is thought to cause global warming.
- **Hydrocarbons (HC)** — This is simply unburned fuel and is one of the components of smog. (**Smog** is a term used to describe a condition that looks like smoke and/or fog.)

Which States Are "Green States"?

States that have adopted the California emission standards are usually called *green states*. Other states that have adopted the California emission standards include Connecticut, Maine, Massachusetts, New Jersey, New York, Rhode Island, Vermont, Pennsylvania, Oregon, and Washington.

THE CLEAN AIR ACT ESTABLISHES THE FRAMEWORK

The federal **Clean Air Act (CAA)** was established in 1970 to create nationwide air quality standards to protect public health. Recognizing the large contribution motor vehicles make to air pollution, the Clean Air Act also set the first federal tailpipe standards.

The CAA also granted California, which has some of the worst air quality in the nation, the authority to set its own vehicle emission standards. Other states began adopting the stricter California standards beginning in 1990.

Federal and California tailpipe standards limit exhaust emissions of five pollutants:

■ **Hydrocarbons (HC)**—a component of smog.
■ **Nitrogen oxides (NO_x)**—a lung irritant and a component of smog.
■ **Carbon monoxide (CO)**—a colorless, odorless poisonous gas.
■ **Particulate matter (PM)**—for diesel vehicles only; also called **soot.**
■ **Formaldehyde (HCHO)**—thought to be a cancer-causing gas.

Beginning in 2007, SUVs and other light-duty trucks, even the largest passenger vehicles, are subject to the same national pollution standards as passenger cars.

NOTE: Carbon dioxide is not directly regulated. Because it is a by-product of fuel economy, one gallon of gasoline creates about 19 pounds of carbon dioxide. It is indirectly regulated as part of fuel economy.

EMISSION STANDARDS IN THE UNITED STATES

In the United States, emission standards are managed by the **Environmental Protection Agency (EPA)** as well as some U.S. state governments. Some of the strictest standards in the world are formulated in California by the **California Air Resources Board (CARB).**

TIER 1 AND TIER 2 Federal emission standards set by the clean air act amendments (CARB) of 1990 are grouped by **tier.** All vehicles sold in the United States must meet **Tier 1** standards that went into effect in 1994 and are the least stringent. Additional **Tier 2** standards have been optional since 2001, and are currently being phased-in to be fully adopted by 2009. The current Tier 1 standards are different between automobiles and light trucks (SUVs, pickup trucks, and minivans), but Tier 2 standards will be the same for both types.

There are several ratings that can be given to vehicles, and a certain percentage of a manufacturer's vehicles must meet different levels in order for the company to sell its products in affected regions. Beyond Tier 1, and in order by stringency, are the following levels:

■ **TLEV—Transitional Low-Emission Vehicle**—More stringent for HC than Tier 1.
■ **LEV** (also known as: **LEV I**)—**Low-Emission Vehicle**—An intermediate California standard about twice as stringent as Tier 1 for HC and NO_x.
■ **ULEV—Ultra-Low-Emission Vehicle**—(also known as **ULEV I**) A stronger California standard emphasizing very low HC emissions.
■ **ULEV II—Ultra-Low-Emission Vehicle**—A cleaner-than-average vehicle certified under the Phase II LEV standard. Hydrocarbon and carbon monoxide emissions levels are nearly 50% lower than those of a LEV II-certified vehicle. ● **SEE FIGURE 1–1.**
■ **SULEV—Super-Ultra-Low-Emission Vehicle**—A California standard even tighter than ULEV, including much lower HC and NO_x emissions; roughly equivalent to Tier 2, Bin 2 vehicles.

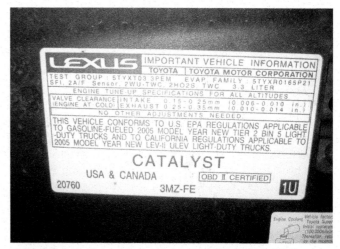

FIGURE 1–1 The underhood decal showing that this Lexus RX-330 meets both National (Tier 2; BIN 5) and California LEV-II (ULEV) regulation standards.

- **ZEV—Zero-Emission Vehicle**—A California standard prohibiting any tailpipe emissions. The ZEV category is largely restricted to electric vehicles and hydrogen-fueled vehicles. In these cases, any emissions that are created are produced at another site, such as a power plant or hydrogen reforming center, unless such sites run on renewable energy.

NOTE: A battery-powered electric vehicle charged from the power grid will still be up to 10 times cleaner than even the cleanest gasoline vehicles over their respective lifetimes.

The current California ZEV regulation allows manufacturers a choice of two options for meeting the ZEV requirements:

1. Vehicle manufacturers can meet the ZEV obligations by meeting standards that are similar to the ZEV rule as it existed in 2001. This means using a formula allowing a vehicle mix of 2% pure ZEVs, 2% AT-PZEVs (vehicles earning advanced technology partial ZEV credits), and 6% PZEVs (extremely clean conventional vehicles). The ZEV obligation is based on the number of passenger cars and small trucks a manufacturer sells in California.

2. Manufacturers may also choose a new alternative ZEV compliance strategy of meeting part of the ZEV requirement by producing the sales-weighted market share of approximately 250 fuel-cell vehicles by 2008. The remainder of the ZEV requirements could be achieved by producing 4% AT-PZEVs and 6% PZEVs. The required number of fuel-cell vehicles will increase to 2,500 from 2009 to 2011, 25,000 from 2012 through 2020, and 50,000 from 2015 through 2017. Manufacturers can substitute battery electric vehicles for up to 50% of the fuel-cell vehicle requirements.

   - **PZEV—Partial Zero-Emission Vehicle**—Compliant with the SULEV standard; additionally has near-zero evaporative emissions and a 15-year/150,000-mile warranty on its emission control equipment.

Tier 2 standards are even more stringent. Tier 2 variations are appended with "II," such as *LEV II* or *SULEV II*. Other categories have also been created:

- **ILEV—Inherently Low-Emission Vehicle**

- **AT-PZEV—Advanced Technology Partial Zero Emission Vehicle**—If a vehicle that meets the PZEV standards and is using high-technology features, such as an electric motor or high-pressure gaseous fuel tanks for compressed natural gas, it qualifies as an AT-PZEV. Hybrid electric vehicles such as the Toyota Prius can qualify, as can internal combustion engine vehicles that run on natural gas (CNG), such as the Honda Civic GX. These vehicles are classified as "partial" ZEV because they receive partial credit for the number of ZEV vehicles that automakers would otherwise be required to sell in California.

- **NLEV—National Low-Emission Vehicle**—All vehicles nationwide must meet this standard, which started in 2001. ● **SEE CHARTS 1–1 AND 1–2.**

		NMOG GRAMS/MILE	CO GRAMS/MILE	NO$_X$ GRAMS/MILE
LEV I (Cars)	LEV	0.125/0.156	3.4/4.2	0.4/0.6
	LEV	0.075/0.090	3.4/4.2	0.2/0.3
	ULEV	0.040/0.055	1.7/2.1	0.2/0.3
LEV II (Cars and Trucks less than 8,500 Lbs)	LEV	0.075/0.090	3.4/4.2	0.05/0.07
	ULEV	0.040/0.055	1.7/2.1	0.05/0.07
	SULEV	–/0.010	–/1.0	–/0.02

CHART 1–1

LEV Standard Categories

NOTE: Are 100,000-mile standards for LEV I, and 120,000-mile standards for LEV II. NMOG means non-methane organic gases, which includes alcohol. CO means carbon monoxide. NO$_X$ means oxides of nitrogen. PM means particulate matter, also known as soot.
Source: Data compiled from California Environmental Protection Agency—Air Resource Board (CARB) documents.

CERTIFICATION LEVEL	NMOG (g/mi)	CO (g/mi)	NO$_X$ (g/mi)
LEV-2	0.090	4.2	0.07
ULEV-2	0.055	2.1	0.07
SULEV	0.010	1.0	0.02

CHART 1–2

California LEV II 120,000-Mile Tailpipe Emissions Limits

NOTE: Are 100,000-mile standards for LEV I, and 120,000-mile standards for LEV II. NMOG means non-methane organic gases, which includes alcohol. CO means carbon monoxide. NO$_X$ means oxides of nitrogen. PM means particulate matter, also known as soot. The specification is in grams per mile (g/mi).
Source: Data compiled from California Environmental Protection Agency—Air Resource Board (CARB) documents.

FEDERAL EPA BIN NUMBER The higher the tier number, the newer the regulation; the lower the **bin number,** the cleaner the vehicle. The 2004 Toyota Prius is a very clean Bin 3, while the Hummer H2 is a dirty Bin 11. Examples include:

- Tier 1: The former federal standard; carried over to model year 2004 for those vehicles not yet subject to the phase-in.

- Tier 2, Bin 1: The cleanest federal Tier 2 standard, a zero-emission vehicle (ZEV).

- Tier 2, Bins 2–4: Cleaner than the average standard.

- Tier 2, Bin 5: "Average" of new Tier 2 standards, roughly equivalent to a LEVII vehicle.

- Tier 2, Bins 6–9: Not as clean as the average requirement for a Tier 2 vehicle.

- Tier 2, Bin 10: Least-clean Tier 2 bin applicable to passenger vehicles.

NOTE: After January 1, 2007, the highest Bin Number allowed is Bin 8.

● **SEE CHARTS 1–3 THROUGH 1–5.**

After January 1, 2007, the highest Bin Number allowed is Bin 8.

CERTIFICATION LEVEL	NMOG (g/mi)	CO (g/mi)	NO$_X$ (g/mi)
Bin 1	0.0	0.0	0.0
Bin 2	0.010	2.1	0.02
Bin 3	0.055	2.1	0.03
Bin 4	0.070	2.1	0.04
Bin 5	0.090	4.2	0.07
Bin 6	0.090	4.2	0.10
Bin 7	0.090	4.2	0.15
Bin 8a	0.125	4.2	0.20
Bin 8b	0.156	4.2	0.20
Bin 9a	0.090	4.2	0.30
Bin 9b	0.130	4.2	0.30
Bin 9c	0.180	4.2	0.30
Bin 10a	0.156	4.2	0.60
Bin 10b	0.230	6.4	0.60
Bin 10c	0.230	6.4	0.60
Bin 11	0.230	7.3	0.90

CHART 1–3

EPA Tier 2 120,000-Mile Tailpipe Emission Limits

NOTE: The bin number is determined by the type and weight of the vehicle. After January 1, 2007, the highest Bin Number allowed is Bin 8.
Source: Data compiled from the Environmental Protection Agency (EPA).

SMOG EMISSION INFORMATION
New vehicles are equipped with a sticker that shows the relative level of smog-causing emissions created by the vehicle compared to others

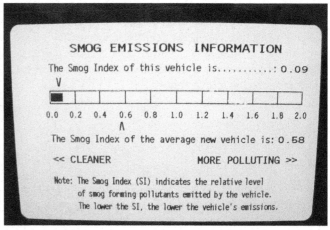

FIGURE 1–2 This label on a Toyota Camry hybrid shows the relative smog-producing emissions, but this does not include carbon dioxide (CO_2), which may increase global warming.

on the market. Smog-causing emissions include unburned hydrocarbons (HC) and oxides of nitrogen (NO$_X$). ● **SEE FIGURE 1–2.**

CALIFORNIA STANDARDS
The pre-2004 California Air Resources Board (CARB) standards as a whole were known as LEV I. Within that, there were four possible ratings: Tier 1, TLEV, LEV, and ULEV. The newest CARB rating system (since January 1, 2004) is known as LEV II. Within that rating system there are three primary ratings: LEV, ULEV, and SULEV. States other than California are given the option to use the federal EPA standards, or they can adopt California's standards. ● **SEE CHARTS 1–5.**

SELECTED EMISSIONS STANDARDS	SCORE
Bin 1 and ZEV	10
PZEV	9.5
Bin 2	9
Bin 3	8
Bin 4	7
Bin 5 and LEV II cars	6
Bin 6	5
Bin 7	4
Bin 8	3
Bin 9a and LEV I cars	2
Bin 9b	2
Bin 10a	1
Bin 10b and Tier 1 cars	1
Bin 11	0

CHART 1–4

Air Pollution Score U.S. EPA Vehicle Information Program (The higher the score, the lower the emissions.)
Source: Courtesy of EPA.

	MINIMUM FUEL ECONOMY (MPG) COMBINED CITY-HIGHWAY LABEL VALUE				
SCORE	GASOLINE	DIESEL	E85	LPG	CNG*
10	44	50	31	28	33
9	36	41	26	23	27
8	30	35	22	20	23
7	26	30	19	17	20
6	23	27	17	15	18
5	21	24	15	14	16
4	19	22	14	12	14
3	17	20	12	11	13
2	16	18	–	–	12
1	15	17	11	10	11
0	14	16	10	9	10

CHART 1–5

Greenhouse Gas Score

*CNG assumes a gallon equivalent of 121.5 cubic feet.
Source: Courtesy of EPA.

EUROPEAN STANDARDS

Europe has its own set of standards that vehicles must meet, which includes the following tiers:

- Euro I (1992–1995)
- Euro II (1995–1999)
- Euro III (1999–2005)
- Euro IV (2005–2008)
- Euro V (2008+)

Vehicle emission standards and technological advancements have successfully reduced pollution from cars and trucks by about 90% since the 1970s. Unfortunately, there currently are more vehicles on the road and they are being driven more miles each year, partially offsetting the environmental benefits of individual vehicle emissions reductions.

OZONE

Ozone is composed of three atoms of oxygen and is abbreviated O_3. Ozone occurs naturally in the atmosphere and can be detected by smell after a thunderstorm. Ozone has a strong clean smell, and in high concentrations it can be a lung and respiratory irritant. Ozone can be created by lightning, which breaks the molecular structure of oxygen (O_2) into atoms (O), which then combine back into oxygen or combine to create ozone.

Upper-level ozone: Ozone located in the upper atmosphere (called the ozone layer) is helpful because it helps to block harmful ultraviolet rays from the sun from entering the lower atmosphere. Therefore, ozone is not a health concern when it is located in the upper regions of the atmosphere.

Ground-level ozone: Ozone that is located at ground level or in the atmosphere close to the earth is a health concern to humans because it causes health problems, including:

- Eye irritation
- Asthma
- Shortness of breath
- Chest tightness
- Wheezing

Vehicles and ozone: Exhaust from vehicles causes ground-level-ozone levels to increase because unburned hydrocarbons (HC) and oxides of nitrogen (NO_X) in the presence of sunlight combine to create ozone, also called smog, which is a term used to describe the smoky or fog-like appearance of ground-level ozone.

ULTRAVIOLET RADIATION ABSORPTION

Ultraviolet (UV) radiation is divided into three designations based on its impact on living organisms. The designations include:

- Designation "A," abbreviated **UVA,** is not absorbed by the ozone layer and generally is not damaging to biological organisms.
- Designation "B," abbreviated **UVB,** is only partially absorbed by the ozone layer and can cause damage to biological organisms.
- Designation "C," abbreviated **UVC,** is almost completely absorbed by the ozone layer and represents little, if any, health concerns.

INTENSITY OF RADIATION Another consideration in evaluating the effects of UV radiation is the intensity at the earth's surface—that is, how much radiation is reaching the earth's surface. For example, consider the difference in radiation between a 20-watt lightbulb and a 100-watt bulb. There is a large difference in intensity and thus in the amount of light or radiation. The term used to define the amount of solar radiation is **irradiance.** The solar irradiance at the earth's surface varies greatly depending on factors such as:

- Latitude
- Time of day
- Time of year
- Cloud cover
- Haze

In the case of the UV irradiance, additional factors are ozone density and elevation above sea level.

OZONE CONTROL OF UVB IRRADIANCE The protection of the earth's living systems from UVB and UVC radiation is a result of the absorption of this radiation by ozone. While there is some ozone in the lower atmosphere, called the **troposphere,** it is small compared to the amount in the upper atmosphere, called the **stratosphere.**

The most important factor is the total amount of ozone that solar radiation encounters before reaching the earth's surface. This is referred to as *column ozone* since it is the total amount of ozone in a column between the earth's surface and the top of the stratosphere.

GREENHOUSE GASES **Greenhouse gases** are those gases in our atmosphere that if in too great a concentration can prevent heat from escaping the surface, which leads to an increase in the temperature on earth. In a nursery greenhouse, the glass panes are painted white to reflect the heat back into the greenhouse. The ultraviolet light can penetrate through the paint and warms the

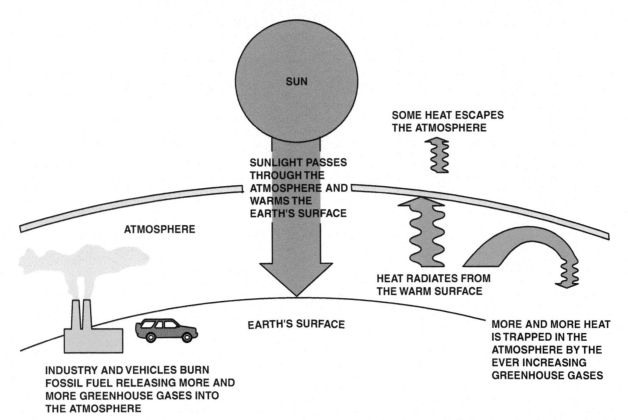

FIGURE 1–3 The atmosphere allows radiation to pass through to the earth's surface and blocks the release of heat back into space if there is too high a concentration of greenhouse gases.

interior so plants can be grown in colder periods of the year or in colder climates. Therefore, the gases in our atmosphere that act like the white paint on the glass panes of a greenhouse are called greenhouse gases, abbreviated **GHG.** ● **SEE FIGURE 1–3.**

Greenhouse gases tend to absorb this infrared radiation as it is reflected back toward space, trapping the heat in the atmosphere. Atmospheric concentrations of several important greenhouse gases (carbon dioxide, methane, nitrous oxide, and most man-made gases) have increased by about 25% since large-scale industrialization began some 150 years ago. The growth in the concentration of these gases is believed to be caused by human activity. Carbon dioxide that is generated as a result of human activity is known an *anthropogenic greenhouse gas*. In particular, anthropogenic carbon dioxide emissions have greatly increased since the beginning of the industrial age due largely to the burning of fossil fuels and cutting down of forests for timber and other uses, such as paper and chemicals. ● **SEE FIGURE 1–4.**

KYOTO PROTOCOL

A meeting in Kyoto, Japan, on December 11, 1997, the **Kyoto Protocol,** asked that countries voluntarily agree to reduce their overall emissions of greenhouse gases by at least 5% below 1990 levels in the commitment period 2008 to 2012. The United States and Australia signed this agreement but did not ratify it, so these countries are not accountable for reducing the amount of greenhouse gases produced.

LOW-CARBON DIET   Whether in coal, oil, or gas, carbon is the essential ingredient of all fossil fuels. When these fuels are burned to provide energy, carbon dioxide (CO_2), a greenhouse gas, is released to the earth's atmosphere. The goal today is to reduce the use of carbon-based fuels and try to live on a "low-carbon diet" by using alternative energy sources that do not result in the release of CO_2.

As society has become more dependent on carbon-based fuels, there has been a rapid increase in the atmospheric concentration of CO_2—from around 280 parts per million (ppm) before the Industrial Revolution to 370 ppm today. If current trends of fossil fuel use continue, the concentration of CO_2 is likely to exceed 700 ppm by the end of this century. According to the **Intergovernmental Panel on Climate Change (IPCC),** this could lead to global warming of between 1.4 and 5.8°C, more frequent severe weather conditions, and damage to many natural ecosystems.

Most experts recommend that atmospheric CO_2 concentrations be held at around 500 to 550 ppm. This could be difficult because the global energy demand is expected to double between 2000 and 2050.

Depletion of the earth's upper ozone layer due to the release of man-made chemicals threatens human health and damages plant life.

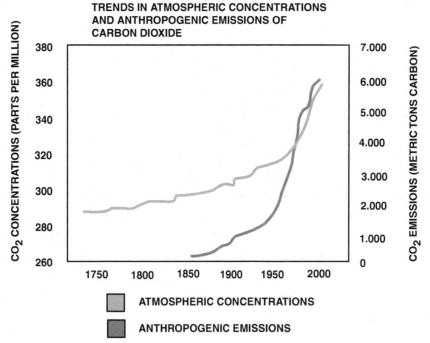

FIGURE 1–4 The chart shows that the atmospheric concentration of greenhouse gases due to human sources (anthropogenic) such as the burning of carbon-based fuel is increasing. *(Courtesy of Oakridge Labs)*

 **TECH TIP**

Watch for Sunburn When at High Altitude

When at a location that is above 1,000 feet, and especially if above 5,000 feet, consider that there is much less atmosphere above to block the UV radiation. This means that sunburn and eye damage, such as cataracts, can more easily occur at high altitude compared to areas that are at or near sea level.

Certain man-made chemicals used in refrigeration, air conditioning, fire and explosion prevention, and as solvents can trigger reactions in the atmosphere that destroy the ozone layer.

Ozone-depleting substances (ODS) include:

- Chlorofluorocarbons (CFCs)
- Hydrochlorofluorocarbons (HCFCs)
- Halons
- Methyl bromide

HEALTH EFFECTS OF AIR POLLUTION

According to medical experts, almost every disease has an environmental element, either minor or major. Skin cancer is largely thought to be caused by severe sunburn, often in childhood. Unburned hydrocarbon (HC) emissions along with oxides of nitrogen (NO_X) combine in the atmosphere in the presence of sunlight to generate ground-level ozone (O_3). High levels of ozone, a respiratory irritant, can cause respiratory problems, including inflammation of the lungs.

Ozone exposure may lead to the following conditions:

- Premature death (due to long-term exposure to high levels of ozone)
- Shortness of breath
- Chest pain when inhaling deeply
- Wheezing and coughing

Another health concern involves **particulate matter (PM),** also called **soot,** which is found in the exhaust of diesel engines. Particulate matter has been linked to respiratory disease and cancer.

 FREQUENTLY ASKED QUESTION

What Are Volatile Organic Compounds?

Volatile organic compounds, abbreviated VOC, are gases emitted by paints, solvents, aerosol sprays, cleaners, glues, permanent markers, pesticides, and fuels. Health effects of VOC emissions into the atmosphere include:

- Eye, nose, and throat irritation
- Headaches
- Nausea

To reduce the levels of volatile organic compounds released, always follow the manufacturer's directions for use of household and industrial products.

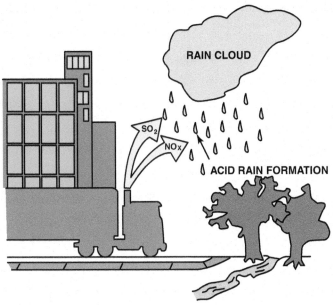

FIGURE 1–5 Acid rain is formed when sulfur dioxide (SO_2) and oxides of nitrogen (NO_X) combine with rain, forming acids.

FIGURE 1–6 The sidewalk section at the top is about 20 years old and shows the effects of acid rain, as compared to the lower section, which is about 5 years old. Notice that the acid rain has eroded the cement, leaving the aggregate (stones) exposed on the upper section.

ACID RAIN

Acid rain refers to rain that has a **pH** lower than 7, indicating that it is acidic. Normal rain is pure water that is neither acidic (a pH of less than 7) nor alkaline (a pH greater than 7). Acid rain usually has a pH of 5.5 but can be as low as 4.3, according to the EPA. The rain becomes acidic due to gases in the atmosphere, such as sulfur dioxide (SO_2) and oxides of nitrogen (NO_X). Sulfur dioxide combines with the rain water to form mild sulfuric acid; oxides of nitrogen combine with rain water to form nitric acid. ● **SEE FIGURE 1–5.**

Both acids are harmful to the environment and can cause the following problems:

- Damage to forests and soils
- Damage to fish because the acid rain makes lakes and streams more acidic
- Damage to buildings and paint on vehicles
- Damage to roads and sidewalks (● **SEE FIGURE 1–6**)

Acid rain can be reduced by limiting exhaust emissions of NO_X and using low-sulfur fuels.

CARBON FOOTPRINT

Total **carbon footprint** includes energy-related emissions from human activities, including heat, light, power, refrigeration, and all transport-related emissions from vehicles, freight, and distribution.

The carbon footprint is a representation of the effect a person or organization has on the climate in terms of the total volume of greenhouse gases (mostly carbon dioxide) produced.

Many actions generate carbon emissions, which contribute to accelerating global warming and climate change.

For example, when gasoline is burned in a vehicle, it produces carbon in the form of carbon dioxide. Depending on the fuel efficiency of the vehicle and the miles traveled, a gasoline-powered vehicle can easily generate its own weight in carbon dioxide each year. The average American is responsible for about 20 tons of carbon dioxide emissions each year, a far greater per-capita number than that of any other industrialized country. The United States produces more than 20% of the world's total greenhouse gas emissions.

Home energy use and transportation represent approximately 40% of all emissions, with the other 60% being produced at work or through work-related activities.

GUIDE TO CARBON DIOXIDE AND OTHER GREENHOUSE GASES
Carbon dioxide (CO_2) is not the only man-made greenhouse gas—it is simply the one that has accumulated the most in the atmosphere and is presently having the greatest cumulative warming effect on our planet. Human sources of carbon dioxide primarily include the burning of fossil fuels (coal, oil, and natural gas), and deforestation. It has been estimated that 15,000 pounds (6,800 kg) of carbon dioxide is created by each vehicle every year. The amount of carbon dioxide in the atmosphere has increased 30% since preindustrial times.

OTHER GREENHOUSE GASES PRODUCED BY HUMAN ACTIVITIES

- **Methane (CH_4)**—emitted by agriculture, ranching, landfills, and energy exploration. Human activities have increased the concentration of methane in the atmosphere by about 145%.
- **Nitrous Oxide (N_2O)**—produced by various agricultural and industrial practices, including the use of nitrogen

How Can CO₂ Exhaust Emissions be Reduced?

To reduce CO_2 exhaust emissions, the total amount of fuel consumed must be reduced. Therefore, the best way to reduce CO_2 emissions is to do any or all of the following:

- Drive a small vehicle that achieves excellent fuel economy.
- Drive a hybrid electric vehicle (HEV) that uses the electric motor to help the gasoline engine and uses less fuel.
- Reduce driving.

---

fertilizers, nylon production, and the burning of organic material and fossil fuels. Human activities have increased the level of nitrous oxide in the atmosphere by about 15% above natural levels.

- **Tropospheric (ground level) Ozone (O_3)**—ozone in the lower part of the atmosphere, created by the reaction of sunlight with human-produced pollutants from vehicles and power plants. Tropospheric ozone has probably doubled in the northern hemisphere since preindustrial times. This lower-level ozone is a smog and is an irritant to the nose and throat.

- **Chlorofluorocarbons (CFCs) and hydrofluorocarbons (HFCs)**—chemicals used in refrigeration, air conditioning, and other industrial processes. The production of chlorofluorocarbons is rapidly being eliminated because of their destructive effect on the ozone layer. Yet other halocarbons, such as HFC-134a (used in automotive air conditioning systems), are now being produced as substitutes, many of which are also greenhouse gases.

All of these gases, aside from the halocarbons, are also produced by natural causes, but it is the rapid build-up in the atmosphere over the past few centuries, due to human activities, that is now causing global warming.

REDUCING THE CARBON FOOTPRINT The following is a list of simple things you can do immediately that will start to reduce your contribution to global warming. The items in this list will cost you no money at all and will in fact save you money.

1. Turn electrical devices off when not in use, such as lights, television, DVD player, stereo, and computer.
2. Turn down the central heating slightly (try just 1 to 2 degrees).
3. Turn down the water heating setting (just 2 degrees will make a significant saving).
4. Check the central heating timer setting—there is no point in heating the house if everyone is gone to work during the day.
5. Fill the dishwasher and washing machine with a full load—this will save you water and electricity, as well as detergent.
6. Unplug your cell phone as soon as it has finished charging.

7. Defrost the freezer regularly; if not done automatically, consider disabling the automatic function to save electricity.
8. Do shopping in a single trip.
9. Walk, rather than drive, to the gym, store, whenever possible.
10. Sign up with a green energy supplier, who will supply electricity from renewable sources (e.g., wind and hydroelectric power). This will reduce the carbon footprint contribution from energy sources that use carbon-based fuels.

The following is a list of items that may take an initial investment, but should pay for themselves over the course of 1 to 4 years through savings on your energy bills.

1. Install energy-saving light bulbs, such as compact fluorescent bulbs, instead of incandescent bulbs.
2. Install thermostatic valves on your radiators, if not equipped.
3. Insulate the hot water tank.
4. Insulate the walls and ceiling of the house.

NOTE: Thirty-five percent of heat generated in the house is lost through the walls. Installing cavity wall insulation to a medium-size house should reduce heating bills by up to $100 per year. Also, installing 6-inch thick insulation could reduce about 25% of the heat escaping through the roof.

5. Replace an old freezer, if it is over 15 years old, with a new one with a higher energy-efficiency rating.
6. Replace an older furnace with an energy-efficient unit.
7. Travel less and travel more carbon-footprint-friendly.
8. Carpool to work or school.

What Is Meant By "Peak Oil"?

Peak oil is a term used to define when the worldwide crude oil production peaks and starts to decline. Are we near peak oil? Some experts think that we are at or near peak oil, and that from now on the oil supply for energy use is on the decline. Why is this important? If the earth is approaching a period of decreasing oil production and is still using oil at an increasing rate, the earth will run out of this resource in less than 100 years. The first oil production started in the late 1880s and has continued to increase as motor vehicles have continued to use gasoline and other petroleum-based fuels. Even though vehicles now have better fuel economy, there are many more vehicles today than ever before. Therefore, we will run out of oil eventually, so the more that people conserve, the longer the oil will last. In the meantime, the world needs to find and start using alternative energy sources.

9. Use the bus or a train rather than your vehicle.

10. See if your employer will allow you to work from home one day a week.

11. While on vacation, rent a bicycle to explore locally rather than use a rental vehicle.

12. When staying in a hotel, turn the lights and air conditioning off when you leave your hotel room.

13. Ask for your room towels to be washed every other day, rather than every day.

In addition to the primary carbon footprint, there is also a secondary carbon footprint that has an indirect effect and is caused by buying habits.

1. Buying foods out of season at the supermarket means that these will have to be shipped in from far away, adding to your carbon footprint.

2. Buy local wine rather from European countries, Australia, or South Africa.

3. Buy local fruit and vegetables, or grow a garden.

4. Try to buy clothes and products from closer to home (avoid items that are made in distant lands such as China and India).

5. Do not leave the computer and monitor on when not in use.

6. Try to avoid printing unnecessary documents.

To further decrease your carbon footprint, consider doing the following:

- Plant trees.
- Avoid cutting down trees.
- Drive less.
- Drive a more fuel-efficient vehicle, such as a hybrid electric vehicle (HEV).

GLOBAL WARMING

In the past 300 billion years the earth's climate has fluctuated between warm periods and cold periods. The ice age started 3 million years ago. Glaciers advanced and retreated 20 times, and they covered all of North America. We are in a warm period between glaciations, which peaked about 20,000 years ago. Heat is trapped in the earth's atmosphere. As the gases increase, so does the heat, therefore the term **global warming.**

The greenhouse gases in the atmosphere include:

1. Water vapor (H_2O)

2. Carbon dioxide (CO_2)

3. Methane (CH_4)

4. Nitrous oxide (N_2O)

5. Chlorofluorocarbons (CFCs)

Carbon dioxide increased 30% in the last 100 years and methane doubled; nitrous oxide has increased by 15%, enhancing the heat-trapping capability of the earth's atmosphere. Global temperatures have increased 0.5°F to 1.0°F since the late nineteenth century.

In the twentieth century, the 10 warmest years occurred in last 15 years of the century, with 1998 being the warmest year on record. This increased global temperature has caused hurricanes due to the warmer ocean water, plus El Niño events, which are caused by the warming of the equatorial Pacific Ocean. ● **SEE FIGURE 1–7.**

POTENTIAL ADVERSE AND BENEFICIAL EFFECTS

Over the next 50 years temperatures could increase 1.0°F to 4.5°F (1.7°C to 3.5°C), and over the next 100 years temperatures could increase 2.2°F to 10.0°F (2°C to 7°C).

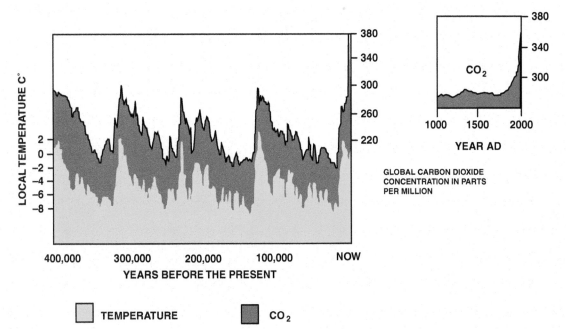

FIGURE 1–7 Notice that the temperature has risen and fallen over time, but the levels of CO_2 in the atmosphere have never been higher and are thought to be the cause of global warming. *(Courtesy of the EPA)*

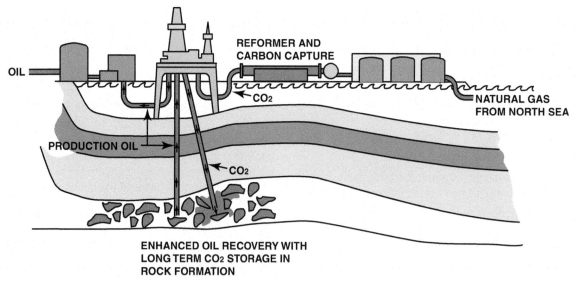

FIGURE 1–8 Pumping carbon dioxide back into the earth not only reduces the amount released to the atmosphere but also helps force more crude oil to the surface, thereby increasing the efficiency of existing wells.

To prevent these conditions from occurring, greenhouse gases must be reduced by 60%, or a method must be used where CO_2 can be stored below the earth's surface. The process of storing carbon dioxide underground is called *sequestration*. ● **SEE FIGURE 1–8.**

Possible ideas include the following:

- Inject carbon dioxide into the Strait of Gibraltar.
  - Make a giant vat of "salty seltzer."
- Underground injection of CO_2 can be used to force oil out from old wells. This could consume 20 million tons of CO_2 per year.
- Inject CO_2 into porous rock beneath oceans.
  - Norway injects 1 million tons/year.
  - CO_2 could increase pressure within an aquifer, widen fissures, and escape.
- React CO_2 with crushed serpentine or olivine rocks— form carbonate solids.
- Retrofit power plants to capture CO_2.
  - The drawback is that this is very expensive.
- Retire old power plants—build new plants that capture CO_2.
- Suck CO_2 out of the atmosph ere into chemical enclosures that absorb CO_2.
- Plant trees.
  - We would need an area as large as Australia of newly planted trees.

Is global warming a reality? Is it part of a 1-million-year ice-age warming trend? Only time will tell. Purchasing hybrid

FIGURE 1–9 Carbonated water is usually the most common (first listed) ingredient in s oft drinks and other carbonated beverages.

electric or alternative-fuel vehicles that consume less carbon-based fuel is one way that vehicle owners can reduce the global warming effect due to CO_2 exhaust emissions.

? FREQUENTLY ASKED QUESTION

What Is Carbonated Water?

Carbonated water is water that has had carbon dioxide dissolved in it to give it a fizz. Carbonated water is usually the number-one ingredient in soda pop. While the consumption of this carbon dioxide is normally not a health concern, frequent consumers of soft drinks may also be at a higher risk of kidney stones and a slightly higher risk of heart disease. The role of carbon dioxide in these beverages may be a contributing factor. ● **SEE FIGURE 1–9.**

1. Hybrid electric vehicles (HEVs) are capable of providing better fuel economy than a comparable size vehicle that uses an internal combustion engine (ICE) alone.

2. Today's society is based on the use of carbon-based fuels, which are made from the remains of living plants and animals.

3. Carbon atoms are attached to hydrogen atoms to form hydrocarbons, abbreviated HC.

4. The Clean Air Act (CAA) was created to establish standards to protect public health. The CAA established the Environmental Protection Agency (EPA), which in turn emission standards.

5. Anthropogenic (man-made) greenhouse gases are causing an increase in the concentration of CO_2 in the atmosphere.

6. The Kyoto Protocol calls for countries to voluntarily reduce the formation of greenhouse gases by at least 5% below 1990 levels. To help reduce the generation of greenhouse gases, reduce the total amount of fuel burned.

7. Global warming is thought to be occurring and is likely caused by the increased production of greenhouse gases.

REVIEW QUESTIONS

1. What is the purpose or the need for hybrid electric vehicles in today's society?

2. What is meant by the term "carbon-based society"?

3. What are hydrocarbons? List eight hydrocarbons.

4. What are the meanings of the following terms: TLEV, LEV, ULEV, SULEV, ZEV, NLEV, PZEV, and AT-PZEV?

5. Which type of ultraviolet radiation is the most harmful to living organisms on earth?

6. What are six things people can do to reduce their individual carbon footprint?

CHAPTER QUIZ

1. The major greenhouse gas from gasoline-powered vehicles is _____.
   a. Carbon monoxide (CO)
   b. Carbon dioxide (CO_2)
   c. Oxides of nitrogen (NO_X)
   d. Unburned hydrocarbons (HCs)

2. Particulate matter (PM) is also called _____.
   a. Soot
   b. HC
   c. CO_2
   d. Smog

3. The earth's atmosphere contains _____; _____.
   a. 78% hydrogen; 21% oxygen
   b. 21% nitrogen; 78% oxygen
   c. 78% nitrogen; 21% oxygen
   d. 21% inert gases; 78% oxygen

4. Which hydrocarbon (HC) molecule contains seven carbon atoms?
   a. Methane
   b. Ethane
   c. Pentane
   d. Heptane

5. Which of the following result in smog when exposed to sunlight?
   a. Unburned hydrocarbon (HC)
   b. Oxides of nitrogen (NO_X)
   c. Carbon dioxide (CO_2)
   d. Both a and b

6. Which of the California emission standards has the tightest requirements?
   a. SULEV
   b. ULEV
   c. LEV
   d. TLEV

7. Which of the following ultraviolet radiation types is the most harmful to living organisms?
   a. UVA
   b. UVB
   c. UVC
   d. None of the above

8. Why is sunburn more likely to occur at high altitudes as compared to sea level?
   a. There is less ozone above to block the UV rays
   b. You are closer to the sun
   c. There is less oxygen
   d. It is colder at high altitudes and sunburn is therefore less likely

9. To reduce your carbon footprint, what action(s) can be performed?
   a. Drive a hybrid electric vehicle instead of a conventional gasoline-engine vehicle
   b. Drive fewer miles
   c. Insulate homes
   d. All of the above

10. Peak oil means _____.
    a. The oil that is closest to the surface of the earth
    b. When worldwide oil production peaks and then starts to decline
    c. When the use of oil peaks and starts to decline
    d. Good crude oil that burns without creating greenhouse gases

INTRODUCTION TO HYBRID VEHICLES

OBJECTIVES: **After studying Chapter 2, the reader will be able to:** • Describe the different types of hybrid electric vehicles. • Explain how a hybrid vehicle is able to achieve an improvement in fuel economy compared to a conventional vehicle design. • Discuss the advantages and disadvantages of the various hybrid designs. • Describe HEV components, including motors, energy sources, and motor controllers. • Discuss the operation of a typical hybrid electric vehicle.

KEY TERMS: • Assist hybrid 22 • BAS 19 • BEV 14 • EV 14 • Full hybrid 22 • HEV 14 • HOV lane 20 • Hybrid 21 • ICE 14 • Idle stop mode 21 • Medium hybrid 22 • Micro-hybrid drive 20 • Mild hybrid 21 • Motoring mode 19 • Parallel-hybrid design 17 • Power-assist mode 21 • Quiet mode 21 • Series-hybrid design 16 • Series-parallel hybrid 18 • Strong hybrid 22 • ZEV 15

HYBRID VEHICLE

DEFINITION OF TERMS A hybrid vehicle is one that uses two different methods to propel the vehicle. A hybrid electric vehicle, abbreviated **HEV** uses both an internal combustion engine and an electric motor to propel the vehicle. Most hybrid vehicles use a high-voltage battery pack and a combination electric motor and generator to help or assist a gasoline engine. The **internal combustion engine (ICE)** used in a hybrid vehicle can be either gasoline or diesel, although only gasoline-powered engines are currently used in hybrid vehicles. An electric motor is used to help propel the vehicle, and in some designs, is capable of propelling the vehicle alone without having to start the internal combustion engine.

BACKGROUND In the early years of vehicle development, many different types of propulsion systems were used, including:

- steam engine powered
- gasoline engine powered
- electric motor powered

Early electric vehicles (**EVs**) were also called **battery electric vehicles (BEV).** These early electric vehicles used lead–acid batteries, an electric traction motor, and a mechanical controller. A traction motor is an electric motor used to rotate the drive wheels and propel vehicle. The vehicle moves as a result of the traction between the wheel and the road surface to transmit the torque needed to move the vehicle.

ELECTRIC VEHICLES

EARLY ELECTRIC VEHICLES The controller was operated by the driver and allowed different voltages to be applied to the electric motor, depending on the needs of the driver. For an example, assume that an early electric vehicle used six 6-volt batteries. If the batteries are connected in series, the negative terminal of one battery is connected to the positive terminal of the second battery. Two 6-volt batteries connected in series result in 12 volts, but the same current as one of the batteries. If two 6-volt 500-amp hour batteries were connected in series, then the output would be 12 volts and 500-amp hours. If the batteries were connected in parallel, the current of each battery is increased, but the voltage remains the same. If two 6-volt 500-amp hour batteries were connected in parallel, then the voltage would be six volts, but the capacity would be 1,000 amp hours.

The old electric vehicle mechanical controller was able to switch all six batteries in various combinations of series and parallel configurations to achieve lower voltage for slow speeds and higher voltages for higher speeds.

Electric vehicles did not have a long range and needed to have the batteries charged regularly, which meant that electric vehicles could only be used for short distances. In fact electric vehicles were almost more popular than steam power in 1900 when steam had 40% of the sales and electric had 38% of the sales. The gasoline-powered cars represented only 22% of the vehicles sold.

NOTE: Due to the oil embargo of 1973 and increased demand for alternative energy sources, Congress enacted Public Law 94-413, the *Electric and Hybrid Vehicle Research, Development, and Demonstration Act of 1976*, which was designed to promote new technologies.

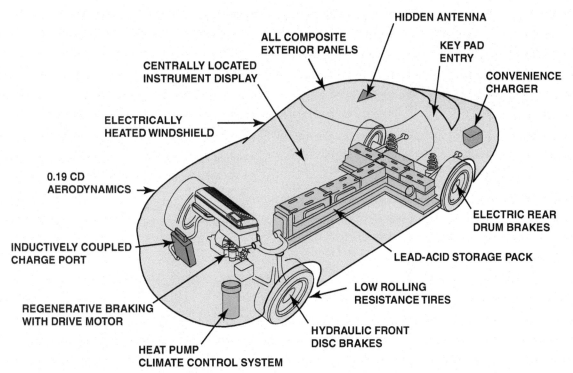

FIGURE 2–1 View of the components of the General Motors electric vehicle (EV1). Many of the features of this vehicle, such as regenerative braking, currently used on hybrid vehicles were first put into production on this vehicle.

NEWER ELECTRIC VEHICLES In the late 1990s, several vehicle manufacturers produced electric vehicles, using electronic controllers to meet the demands for zero emission vehicles as specified by law in California at the time. Electric vehicles were produced by Ford, Toyota, Nissan, and General Motors. Legislation was passed in California that included the following revisions within the **zero emissions vehicle (ZEV)** mandate.

As a direct result of the California zero-emission vehicle mandate originally calling for 10% ZEV, General Motors developed the Electric Vehicle 1, known as EV1, and it was leased to customers in California and Arizona. ● **SEE FIGURE 2–1 and 2–2.**

By 2010, there were several electric vehicles for sale although often in limited parts of the country and in limited numbers. Electric vehicles include the Tesla, Nissan Leaf, and Chevrolet VOLT as well as plug-in hybrid electric vehicles such as the Toyota Prius.

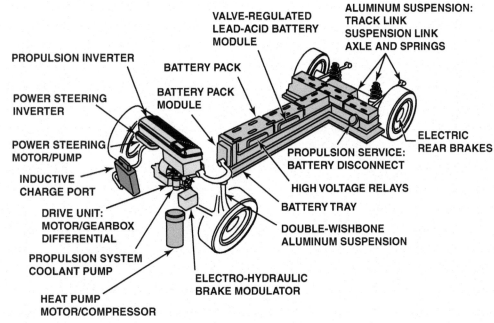

FIGURE 2–2 General Motors EVI without the body.

DRIVING A HYBRID VEHICLE   Driving a hybrid electric vehicle is the same as driving any other conventional vehicle. In fact, many drivers and passengers are often not aware they are driving or riding in a hybrid electric vehicle. Some unique characteristics that the driver may or may not notice include:

- After the internal combustion engine has achieved normal operating temperature and other conditions are met, the engine will stop when the vehicle slows down and stops. This condition may cause some concern to some drivers who may think that the engine has stalled and then may try to restart it.

- The brake pedal may feel different, especially at slow speeds of about 5 mph and 15 mph when slowing to a stop. It is at about these speeds that the brake system switches from regenerative braking to actually applying brake force to the mechanical brakes. A slight surge or pulsation may be felt at this time. This may or may not be felt and is often not a concern to drivers.

- The power steering works even when the engine stops because all hybrid electric vehicles use an electric power steering system.

- Some hybrid electric vehicles are able to propel the vehicle using the electric motor alone, resulting in quiet, almost eerie operation.

- If a hybrid electric vehicle is being driven aggressively and at a high rate of acceleration, there is often a feeling that the vehicle is not going to slow down when the accelerator pedal is first released. This is caused by two factors:

  1. The inertia of the rotor of the electric motor attached to the crankshaft of the ICE results in the engine continuing to rotate after the throttle has been closed.

  2. The slight delay that occurs when the system switches the electric motor from powering the vehicle to generating (regenerative braking). While this delay would rarely be experienced, and is not at all dangerous, for a fraction of a second it gives a feeling that the accelerator pedal did not react to a closed throttle.

OWNING A HYBRID ELECTRIC VEHICLE

- The fuel economy will be higher compared to a similar-type vehicle, especially if driven in city-type driving conditions where engine stop and regenerative braking really add to the efficiency of a hybrid electric vehicle. However, the range of the hybrid version may be about the same as the conventional version of the same vehicle because the hybrid version usually has a smaller fuel tank capacity.

- A hybrid electric vehicle will cost and weigh more than a conventional vehicle. The increased cost is due to the batteries, electric motor(s), and controllers used plus the additional components needed to allow operation of the heating and air conditioning systems during idle stop periods. The cost is offset in part by returning improved fuel economy as well as government energy credits awarded at the time of purchase for some new-technology vehicles. It may take many years of operation before the extra cost is offset by cost savings from the improved fuel economy. However, many owners purchase a hybrid electric vehicle for other reasons besides fuel savings, including a feeling that they are helping the environment and love of the high technology involved.

SERIES HYBRID   The types of hybrid electric vehicles include series, parallel, and series-parallel designs. In a **series-hybrid design,** sole propulsion is by a battery-powered electric motor, but the electric energy for the batteries comes from another on-board energy source, such as an internal combustion engine. In this design, the engine turns a generator and the generator can either charge the batteries or power an electric motor that drives the transmission. The internal combustion engine never powers the vehicle directly. ● **SEE FIGURES 2–3 AND 2–4.**

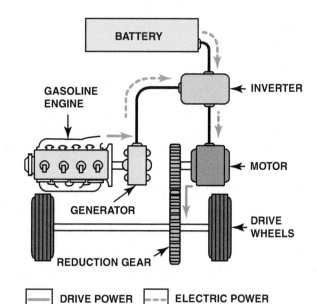

FIGURE 2–3 A drawing of the power flow in a typical series-hybrid vehicle.

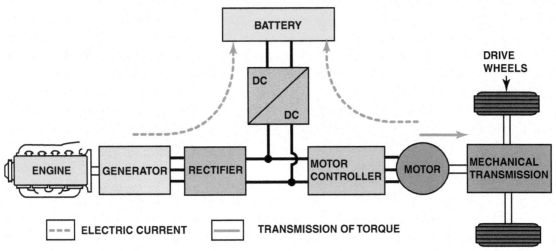

ELECTRIC CURRENT --- TRANSMISSION OF TORQUE ──

FIGURE 2–4 This diagram shows the components included in a typical series-hybrid design. The solid-line arrow indicates the transmission of torque to the drive wheels. The dotted-line arrows indicate the flow of electrical current.

The engine is only operated to keep the batteries charged. Therefore, the vehicle could be moving with or without the internal combustion engine running. Series-hybrid vehicles also use regeneration braking to help keep the batteries charged. The Chevrolet VOLT is an example of a series-hybrid design.

The engine is designed to just keep the batteries charged, and therefore, is designed to operate at its most efficient speed and load. An advantage of a series-hybrid design is that no transmission, clutch, or torque converter is needed.

A disadvantage of a series-hybrid design is the added weight of the internal combustion engine to what is basically an electric vehicle. The engine is actually a heavy on-board battery charger. Also, the electric motor and battery capacity have to be large enough to power the vehicle under all operating conditions, including climbing hills.

All power needed for heating and cooling must also come from the batteries so using the air conditioning in hot weather and the heater in cold weather reduces the range that the vehicle can travel on battery power alone.

PARALLEL HYBRID In a **parallel-hybrid design,** multiple propulsion sources can be combined, or one of the energy sources alone can drive the vehicle. In this design, the battery and engine are both connected to the transmission.

The vehicle using a parallel-hybrid design can be powered by the internal combustion engine alone, by the electric motor alone (full hybrids only), or by a combination of engine and electric motor propulsion. In most cases, the electric motor is used to assist the internal combustion engine. One of the advantages of using a parallel-hybrid design is that by using an electric motor or motors to assist the internal combustion engine, the engine itself can be smaller than would normally be needed. ● **SEE FIGURES 2–5 AND 2–6.**

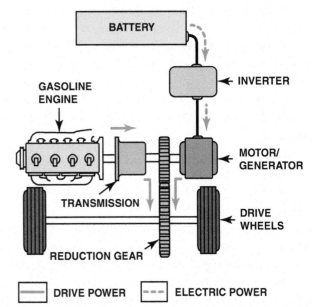

DRIVE POWER ── ELECTRIC POWER ---

FIGURE 2–5 The power flow in a typical parallel-hybrid vehicle.

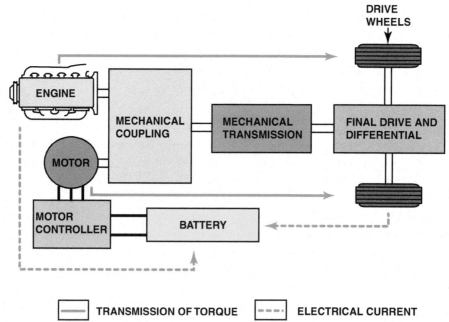

| TRANSMISSION OF TORQUE | ---- ELECTRICAL CURRENT |

FIGURE 2–6 Diagram showing the components involved in a typical parallel-hybrid vehicle. The solid-line arrows indicate the transmission of torque to the drive wheels, and the dotted-line arrows indicate the flow of electrical current.

? FREQUENTLY ASKED QUESTION

Is a Diesel-Hybrid Electric Vehicle Possible?

Yes, using a diesel engine instead of a gasoline engine in a hybrid electric vehicle is possible. While the increased efficiency of a diesel engine would increase fuel economy, the extra cost of the diesel engine is the major reason this combination is not currently in production.

NOTE: A parallel-hybrid design could include additional batteries to allow for plug-in capability, which could extend the distance the vehicle can travel using battery power alone.

One disadvantage of a parallel-hybrid design is that complex software is needed to seamlessly blend electric and ICE power. Another concern about the parallel-hybrid design is that it had to be engineered to provide proper heating and air-conditioning system operation when the ICE stops at idle.

SERIES-PARALLEL HYBRID The Toyota and Ford hybrids are classified as **series-parallel hybrids** because they can operate using electric motor power alone or with the assist of the ICE. Series-parallel hybrids combine the functions of both a series and a parallel design.

The internal combustion engine may be operating even though the vehicle is stopped if the electronic controller

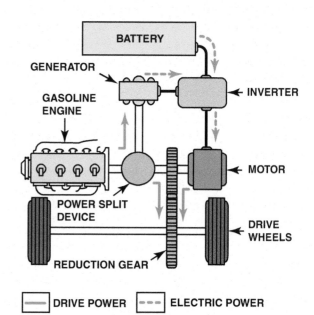

| DRIVE POWER | ---- ELECTRIC POWER |

FIGURE 2–7 A series-parallel hybrid design allows the vehicle to operate in electric motor mode only or in combination with the internal combustion engine.

has detected that the batteries need to be charged. ● **SEE FIGURE 2–7.**

NOTE: The internal combustion engine may or may not start when the driver starts the vehicle depending on the temperature of the engine and other conditions. This can be confusing to some who are driving a hybrid electric vehicle for the first time and sense that the engine did not start when they tried to start the engine.

BELT ALTERNATOR STARTER SYSTEMS

PARTS AND OPERATION The belt system, commonly called the **belt alternator starter (BAS),** is the least expensive system that can be used and still claim that the vehicle is a hybrid. For many buyers, cost is a major concern and the BAS system allows certain hybrid features without the cost associated with an entire redesign of the engine and powertrain. Consumers will be able to upgrade from conventional models to BAS hybrids at a reasonable cost and will get slightly better fuel economy.

The BAS concept is to replace the belt-driven alternator with an electric motor that serves as a generator and a motor. When the engine is running the motor, acting as a generator, it will charge a separate 36-volt battery (42-volt charging voltage). When the engine needs to be started again after the engine has been stopped at idle to save fuel (idle stop), the BAS motor is used to crank the engine by taking electrical power from the 36-volt battery pack and applies its torque via the accessory belt, and cranks the engine instead of using the starter motor.

NOTE: A BAS system uses a conventional starter motor for starting the ICE the first time, and only uses the high-voltage motor-generator to start the ICE when leaving idle stop mode.

The motor-generator is larger than a standard starter motor so more torque can be generated in the cranking mode, also referred to as the **motoring mode.** The fast rotation of the BAS allows for quicker starts of the engine, and makes the start/stop operation possible. Having the engine shut off when the vehicle is at a stop saves fuel. Of course, the stopping of the engine does create a sense that the engine has stalled, which is a common concern to drivers unfamiliar with the operation of hybrid vehicles.

A typical BAS system will achieve a 8% to 15% increase in fuel economy, mostly affecting the city mileage with little, if any, effect on the highway mileage. On extremely small vehicles, the belt alternator starter might nudge a vehicle into the mild hybrid category. The BAS system is the type used in the Saturn VUE hybrid SUV. ● **SEE FIGURES 2–8 AND 2–9.**

MICRO-HYBRID DRIVE SYSTEM One of the major fuel-saving features of a hybrid electric vehicle is the idle stop mode, in which the internal combustion engine is stopped, instead of idling, while in traffic.

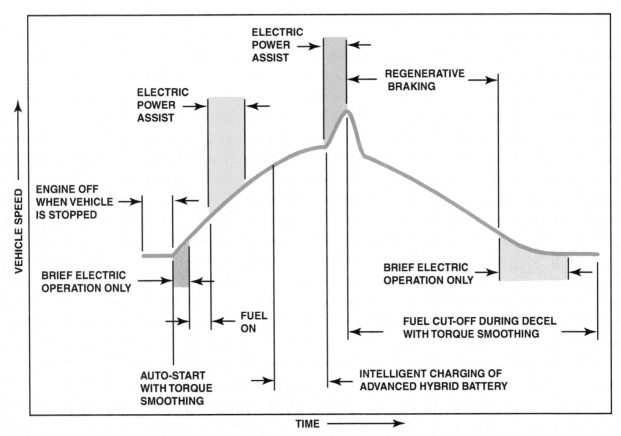

FIGURE 2–8 This chart shows what is occurring during various driving conditions in a BAS-type hybrid.

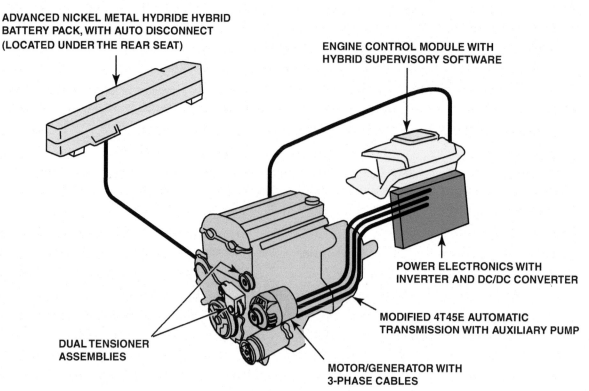

ADVANCED NICKEL METAL HYDRIDE HYBRID
BATTERY PACK, WITH AUTO DISCONNECT
(LOCATED UNDER THE REAR SEAT)

ENGINE CONTROL MODULE WITH
HYBRID SUPERVISORY SOFTWARE

POWER ELECTRONICS WITH
INVERTER AND DC/DC CONVERTER

MODIFIED 4T45E AUTOMATIC
TRANSMISSION WITH AUXILIARY PUMP

MOTOR/GENERATOR WITH
3-PHASE CABLES

DUAL TENSIONER
ASSEMBLIES

FIGURE 2–9 The components of a typical belt alternator starter (BAS) system.

? FREQUENTLY ASKED QUESTION

Can Hybrids Use the HOV Lane?

In most locations the answer is yes, but it depends on the type of hybrid vehicle. The **high-occupancy vehicle (HOV) lane** in many cities is reserved for use by vehicles that are carrying more than one occupant as a way to encourage carpooling and the use of public transportation. In California, only those hybrids classified as being high-fuel-economy models and those meeting certain emission ratings qualify. Those that do qualify, such as the Toyota Prius, are issued stickers that show that they are entitled to be in the HOV lane even if there is just the driver in the vehicle. High-performance hybrids, such as the Honda Accord hybrid, do not meet the specified fuel economy rating to allow the owners to be issued HOV stickers, which are also limited as to how many in the entire state can be issued.
● **SEE FIGURE 2–10.**

One simple system developed by Valeo uses a starter/alternator that is used as a conventional alternator when the engine is running, and as a starter to start the engine by transmitting power through the drive belt system. This type of system is often called a **micro-hybrid drive** system.
● **SEE FIGURE 2–11.**

The only mechanical addition needed is a special belt tensioner that allows two-directional belt travel and can be fitted to almost any existing gasoline or diesel engine. The fuel and exhaust emission savings are proportional to the amount of idle time and can save up to 6% during city driving conditions.

FIGURE 2–10 This sticker on a hybrid vehicle allows the driver to use the high-occupancy vehicle (HOV) lanes even if there is only one person in the vehicle as a way to increase demand for hybrid vehicles in California.

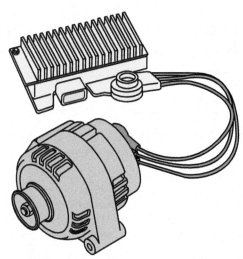

FIGURE 2–11 A combination starter/alternator is used to provide idle stop function to conventional vehicles. This very limited and low cost system is called a micro-hybrid drive.

COMMON FEATURES OF MOST HYBRIDS

The following are the most common features of hybrids that improve fuel economy:

Idle stop. The **idle stop mode** turns off the engine when the vehicle is stopped. When the brake is released, the engine immediately starts. This ensures that the vehicle is not using fuel, nor creating CO_2 emissions, when the engine is not required to propel the vehicle.

Regenerative braking. When decelerating, the braking system captures the energy from the vehicle's inertia and converts it to electrical energy which is stored in the battery or other device for later use. Regenerative braking helps keep the batteries charged.

Power assist. The electric motor provides extra power using electrical current drawn from the battery to assist the internal combustion engine during acceleration. This **power-assist mode** enables the vehicle to use a smaller, more fuel-efficient engine without giving up vehicle performance.

Engine-off drive-electric vehicle mode. The electric motor propels the vehicle at lower speeds. This mode is often called the motoring mode. Because the internal combustion engine is not being used during acceleration, no fuel is being used and no emissions are being released. When the hybrid is in this mode, it is essentially an electric vehicle.

LEVELS OF HYBRID VEHICLES

The term **hybrid** refers to a type of vehicle. However, there are different levels of "hybridization" among hybrids on the market. Different vehicle manufacturers use various hybrid technologies.

MILD HYBRID A **mild hybrid** will incorporate idle stop and regenerative braking but is not capable of using the electric motor to propel the vehicle on its own without help from the

 **TECH TIP**

Watch Out for Motoring Mode

When a hybrid electric vehicle is operating at low speeds, it is often being propelled by the electric motor alone, sometimes called motoring mode. As a result, the vehicle is very quiet and is said to be operating in **quiet mode.**

During this time, the driver should be aware that the vehicle is not making any sound and should be careful when driving in congested areas. Service technicians should also be extremely careful when moving a hybrid electric vehicle around the shop due to the silence of the vehicle.

Hybrid Features by Make/Model

Make/Model	Idle Stop	Regen-erative Braking	Motor Assist	Engine-Off Drive—EV Mode
2004–2007 Chevrolet Silverado 1500/GMC Sierra Hybrid	✓	✓		
Ford Escape and Mercury Mariner Hybrid	✓	✓	✓	✓
Honda Accord Civic Hybrid	✓	✓	✓	
Honda Insight	✓	✓	✓	
Toyota Prius	✓	✓	✓	✓
Saturn VUE	✓	✓	✓	
Toyota Highlander/ Lexus RX hybrids	✓	✓	✓	✓

internal combustion engine. A mild hybrid system has the advantage of costing less, but saves less fuel compared to a full hybrid vehicle and usually uses a 42-volt electrical motor and battery package (36-volt batteries, 42-volt charging). An example of this type of hybrid is the General Motors Silverado pickup truck and the Saturn VUE. The fuel savings for a mild type of hybrid design is about 8% to 15%.

MEDIUM HYBRID   A **medium hybrid** uses 144- to 158-volt batteries that provide for engine stop/start, regenerative braking, and power assist. Like a mild hybrid, a typical medium hybrid is not capable of propelling the vehicle from a stop using battery power alone. Examples of a medium hybrid vehicle include the Honda Insight, Civic, and Accord. The fuel economy savings are about 20% to 25% for medium hybrid systems.

FULL HYBRID   A **full hybrid,** also called a **strong hybrid,** uses idle stop regenerative braking, and is able to propel the vehicle using the electric motor(s) alone.

Each vehicle manufacturer has made its decision on which hybrid type to implement based on its assessment of the market niche for a particular model. Examples of a full or strong

hybrid include the Ford Escape SUV, Toyota Highlander, Lexus RX400h, Lexus GS450h, Toyota Prius, and Toyota Camry. The fuel economy savings are about 30% to 50% for full hybrid systems.

EFFICIENCIES OF ELECTRIC MOTORS AND INTERNAL COMBUSTION ENGINES

- An electric motor can have efficiency (including controller) of over 90%, while a gasoline engine only has efficiency of 35% or less.
- An ICE does not have the overload capability of an electric motor. That is why the rated power of an internal combustion engine is usually much higher than required for highway cruising. Operating smoothly at idle speed produces a much lower efficiency than operating at a higher speed.
- Maximum torque of an internal combustion engine is reached at intermediate speed and the torque declines as speed increases further.
- There is a maximum fuel efficiency point in the speed range for the ICE, and this speed is optimized by many hybrid vehicle manufacturers by using a transmission that keeps the engine speed within the most efficient range.

ELECTRIC MOTORS   Electric motors offer ideal characteristics for use in a vehicle because of the following factors:

- Constant power over all speed ranges
- Constant torque at low speeds needed for acceleration and hill-climbing capability
- Constant torque below base speed
- Constant power above base speed
- Only single gear or fixed gear is needed in the electric motor transmission.

SUMMARY

1. Hybrids use two different power sources to propel the vehicle.

2. A mild hybrid with a lower voltage system (36-50 volts) is capable of increasing fuel economy and reducing exhaust emissions but is not capable of using the electric motor alone to propel the vehicle.

3. A medium hybrid uses a higher voltage than a mild hybrid (140-150 volts) and offers increased fuel economy over a mild hybrid design but is not capable of operating using the electric motor alone.

4. A full or strong hybrid uses battery voltages of about 200 to 300 volts, is capable of operating using the electric motor(s) alone, and achieves the highest fuel economy improvement of all types of hybrids.

5. Early in vehicle history, electric vehicles were more popular than either steam- or gasoline-powered vehicles.

6. Legislation passed in California in 1998, which mandated zero-emission vehicles (ZEVs), caused the vehicle manufacturers to start producing electric vehicles. When the law was changed to allow the substitution of other vehicles that produced lower emissions, but not zero, it helped promote the introduction of hybrid electric vehicles (HEVs).

7. A hybrid vehicle is defined as having two power sources to propel the vehicle.

8. Electric motors are perfect for vehicle use because they produce torque at lower speed, whereas internal combustion engines need to have an increased speed before they produce maximum power and torque.

1. What are the advantages and disadvantages of a series-hybrid design?

2. What type of hybrid electrical vehicle is a Toyota Prius and Ford Escape hybrid?

3. What are the advantages and disadvantages of mild, medium, and full hybrid vehicles?

4. Why does a BAS system cost less than the other types of hybrid vehicles?

5. What are the four modes of operation of a typical hybrid vehicle?

CHAPTER QUIZ

1. The GM EV1 was what type of vehicle?
   a. Totally electric powered
   b. A first-generation hybrid electric vehicle (HEV)
   c. A series-type HEV
   d. A parallel-type HEV

2. Which type of hybrid uses 36 to 42 volts?
   a. Mild hybrid
   b. Medium hybrid
   c. Full hybrid
   d. Strong hybrid

3. Which type of hybrid is capable of propelling the vehicle using just the electric motor?
   a. BAS type
   b. Strong (full) hybrid
   c. Medium hybrid
   d. Mild hybrid

4. About how fast does a motor-generator crank the internal combustion engine?
   a. About 1000 RPM
   b. About 2000 RPM
   c. About 150–300 RPM
   d. About 400–600 RPM

5. Which type of hybrid electric design costs the least?
   a. Strong hybrid design
   b. Series-hybrid design
   c. Parallel-hybrid design
   d. BAS design

6. Which type of hybrid electric vehicle has idle stop operation?
   a. Strong hybrids only
   b. Strong, mild, and medium hybrids
   c. Mild hybrids only
   d. Medium hybrids only

7. Technician A says that most hybrids require that they be plugged into an electrical outlet at night to provide the electrical power to help propel the vehicle. Technician B says that the internal combustion engine in an HEV will often stop running when the vehicle is stopped. Which technician is correct?
   a. Technician A only
   b. Technician B only
   c. Both Technicians A and B
   d. Neither Technician A nor B

8. Technician A says that most hybrids use the series-hybrid design. Technician B says that some hybrids have 42-volt batteries. Which technician is correct?
   a. Technician A only
   b. Technician B only
   c. Both Technicians A and B
   d. Neither Technician A nor B

9. Electric motors are better than an internal combustion engine to propel a vehicle because _____.
   a. They produce high torque at low speeds
   b. They do not burn fuel and therefore do not release carbon dioxide into the environment
   c. They are quiet
   d. All of the above are correct

10. All of the following are characteristic of a hybrid electric vehicle (HEV), *except* _____.
   a. High voltages (safety issue)
   b. Lower fuel economy
   c. Lower amount of carbon dioxide released to the atmosphere
   d. Quiet

HYBRID ENGINE SYSTEMS

OBJECTIVES: **After studying Chapter 3, the reader will be able to:** • Explain how a four-stroke cycle gasoline engine operates. • Explain the Atkinson cycle and how it affects engine efficiency. • List the various methods by which vehicle engines are classified and measured. • Describe the importance of using the specified oil in the engine of a hybrid electric vehicle. • Describe how the fuel injection and ignition systems work on hybrid gasoline engines. • Explain how active control engine mounts function. • Describe how wide-band oxygen sensors work. • Explain how variable valve timing is able to improve engine power and reduce exhaust emissions.

KEY TERMS: • 720° cycle 26 • ACM 36 • Active fuel management 35 • ANC 36 • APP 38 • APS 38 • Atkinson cycle 26 • BHP 29 • Compression ratio (CR) 28 • COP 37 • Cylinder deactivation 35 • Displacement 27 • Drive-by-wire 38 • Electronic throttle control (ETC) 38 • EMI 37 • ERFS 43 • Four-stroke cycle 24 • GDI 45 • Horsepower 29 • ICE 24 • Major thrust surface 29 • Miller cycle 26 • MRFS 43 • Nernst cell 40 • Offset crankshaft 31 • Power 29 • Pumping losses 27 • PVV 44 • Servomotor 38 • TDC 24 • Torque 28 • VTEC 35 • Wide-band oxygen sensor 39 • Work 29

HYBRID INTERNAL COMBUSTION ENGINES (ICE)

The engine converts a portion of the energy contained in the fuel into useful power. This power is used to move the vehicle. The **internal combustion engine (ICE)** used in hybrid electric vehicles (HEV) differs from those used in conventional vehicles. These differences can include:

- Smaller engine displacement than most similar vehicles of the same size and weight.
- Use of the Atkinson cycle to increase efficiency.
- Crankshaft offset to reduce internal friction.
- Often do not use a conventional starter motor.
- Some use spark plugs that are indexed so the open side of the spark is pointed toward the intake valve for maximum efficiency.
- Engine mounts are computer controlled to counteract and eliminate undesirable engine vibration.
- The use of low-viscosity engine oil, such as SAE 0W-20.

The engines used in hybrid vehicles are also similar to those used in non-hybrid vehicles and share the following features:

1. Conventional fuel injection system.
2. Conventional engine layout and number of cylinders (except for the Honda Insight, which uses a three-cylinder engine).

3. Uses the same engine parts as conventional engines, except for those using compressed natural gas (CNG) as a fuel. These engines use stronger internal parts, such as pistons and connecting rods, to better withstand the high compression used in these engines.
4. Same ignition system.
5. Same or similar engine lubrication system, including the oil filter but with a lighter-viscosity oil than that used in similar conventional vehicles.

ENGINE FUNDAMENTALS

FOUR-STROKE CYCLE OPERATION Most automotive engines use the **four-stroke cycle** of events, begun by the starter motor, which rotates the engine. The four-stroke cycle is repeated for each cylinder of the engine. ● **SEE FIGURE 3–1.**

- **Intake stroke.** The intake valve is open and the piston inside the cylinder travels downward, drawing a mixture of air and fuel into the cylinder.
- **Compression stroke.** As the engine continues to rotate, the intake valve closes and the piston moves upward in the cylinder, compressing the air–fuel mixture.
- **Power stroke.** When the piston gets near the top of the cylinder, called **top dead center (TDC),** the spark at the spark plug ignites the air–fuel mixture, which forces the piston downward.

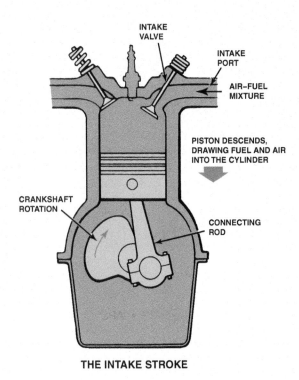

THE INTAKE STROKE

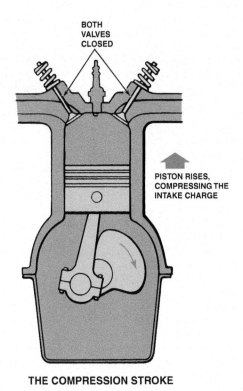

THE COMPRESSION STROKE

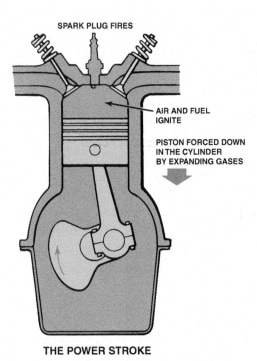

THE POWER STROKE

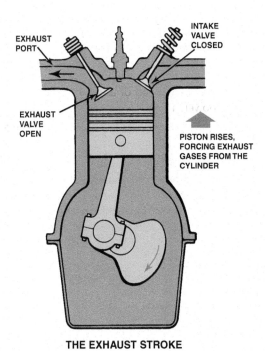

THE EXHAUST STROKE

FIGURE 3–1 The downward movement of the piston draws the air–fuel mixture into the cylinder through the open intake valve on the intake stroke. On the compression stroke, the mixture is compressed by the upward movement of the piston with both valves closed. Ignition occurs at the beginning of the power stroke, and combustion drives the piston downward to produce power. On the exhaust stroke, the upward-moving piston forces the burned gases out the open exhaust valve.

FIGURE 3–2 Cutaway of an engine showing the cylinder, piston, connecting rod, and crankshaft.

- **Exhaust stroke.** The engine continues to rotate, and the piston again moves upward in the cylinder. The exhaust valve opens, and the piston forces the residual burned gases past the exhaust valve and into the exhaust manifold and exhaust system.

This sequence repeats as the engine rotates. To stop the engine, the electricity to the ignition system is shut off by the ignition switch. A piston that moves up and down, or reciprocates, in a cylinder can be seen in ● **FIGURE 3–2.**

The piston is attached to a crankshaft with a connecting rod. This arrangement allows the piston to reciprocate (move up and down) in the cylinder as the crankshaft rotates. The combustion pressure developed in the combustion chamber at the correct time will push the piston downward to rotate the crankshaft.

THE 720° CYCLE Each cycle of events requires that the engine crankshaft make two complete revolutions or 720° (360° × 2 = 720°), and is therefore called a **720° cycle.** The greater the number of cylinders, the closer together the power strokes occur. To find the angle of rotation between engine power strokes of an engine, divide 720° by the number of cylinders.

Angle with three cylinders = 720°/3 = 240°

Angle with four cylinders = 720°/4 = 180°

Angle with five cylinders = 720°/5 = 144°

Angle with six cylinders = 720°/6 = 120°

Angle with eight cylinders = 720°/8 = 90°

Angle with ten cylinders = 720°/10 = 72°

This means that in a four-cylinder engine, a power stroke occurs at every 180° of the crankshaft rotation (every 1/2 rotation). A V-8 engine operates much more smoothly because a power stroke occurs twice as often (every 90° of crankshaft rotation).

Engine cycles are identified by the number of piston strokes required to complete the cycle. A piston stroke is a one-way piston movement between the top and bottom of the cylinder (and vice versa). During one stroke, the crankshaft revolves 180° (1/2 revolution). A cycle is a complete series of events that continually repeat. All currently produced automobile engines use a four-stroke cycle.

ATKINSON CYCLE

BACKGROUND In 1882, James Atkinson, a British engineer, invented an engine that achieved a higher efficiency than the Otto cycle but produced lower power at low engine speeds. The **Atkinson cycle** engine was produced in limited numbers until 1890, when sales dropped, and the company that manufactured the engines finally went out of business in 1893.

OPERATION However, the one key feature of the Atkinson cycle that remains in use today is that the intake valve is held open longer than normal to allow a reverse flow into the intake manifold. This reduces the effective compression ratio and engine displacement and allows the expansion to exceed the compression ratio while retaining a normal compression pressure. This is desirable for good fuel economy because the compression ratio in a spark ignition engine is limited by the octane rating of the fuel used, while a high expansion delivers a longer power stroke and reduces the heat wasted in the exhaust. This increases the efficiency of the engine because more work is being achieved. ● **SEE FIGURE 3–3.**

NOTE: Four-stroke engines of this type with forced induction, such as an engine-driven supercharger, are known as Miller cycle engines. At present, no hybrid engine uses a supercharger or the Miller cycle.

- The Toyota Prius (front-wheel drive) and Ford Escape hybrid (front- and four-wheel drive) vehicles use the Atkinson cycle engine.
- The Atkinson cycle's low output is compensated for by the power produced by the electric motor.
- The Ford ZETEC gasoline engine is also designed for economy, using the Atkinson cycle for its operation.

Sometimes called a "five-stroke" cycle, the Atkinson cycle uses a normal intake stroke, but as the compression stroke is about to start, the intake valve is left open to reduce pumping losses. See Frequently Asked Question, "What Is Meant by 'Pumping Losses'"?

The open intake valve allows a "backflow stroke" of air from the cylinder into the intake manifold. As the piston moves up the cylinder, the intake valve closes and the compression

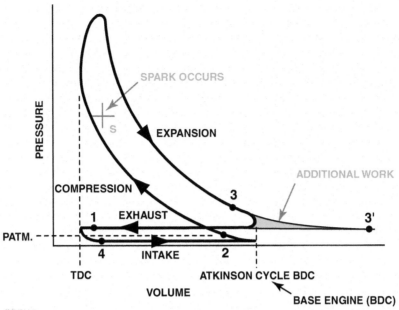

FIGURE 3-3 A pressure volume diagram showing where additional work is generated by the delayed closing of the intake valve. Point "S" is where the spark occurs.

? FREQUENTLY ASKED QUESTION

What Is Meant by "Pumping Losses"?

Pumping losses refer to the energy required to overcome the restriction in the intake system to fill the cylinders with air during the intake stroke. Pumping losses are created by the throttle valve that restricts the flow of air into the cylinders. Diesel engines do not have this concern because they are un-throttled, meaning that there is no restriction to airflow entering a diesel engine. To reduce pumping losses several methods are used, including:

1. Introduce a high percentage (over 30%) of exhaust gas recirculation (EGR) into the intake. Because the exhaust gases do not burn, but rather occupy space, the power of the engine is reduced. To achieve the original power from the engine, the throttle must be opened farther than normal, thereby reducing pumping losses due to the closed throttle.

2. The use of an electronic throttle allows the power train engineer to program the PCM to open the throttle at highway speeds to reduce pumping losses, and at the same time introduce additional exhaust gas recirculation to maintain engine speed.

3. Reduce engine speed by using overdrive transmissions/transaxles. The slower the engine speed, the easier it is to increase its efficiency. The most efficient engines are huge ship diesel engines that operate at about 100 RPM and can achieve an efficiency of about 50%, or twice that of a conventional gasoline or diesel engine.

stroke begins. A 12.3-to-1 compression ratio ensures there is sufficient cylinder pressure for good performance. The power stroke begins as the air–fuel mixture is ignited by the spark plug, and the cycle is completed as the piston forces the exhaust gases out the exhaust valve on the exhaust stroke.

The Atkinson cycle is up to 10% more efficient than a conventional four-stroke gasoline engine, and produces more torque than a conventional engine at high engine speeds, but it does reduce low-end engine torque. A typical hybrid electric vehicle can take advantage of this by using an electric motor to propel the vehicle at lower speeds. Electric motors excel at low RPM torque, so the hybrid transaxle makes up for the low-speed losses of the Atkinson cycle gasoline engine.

ENGINE SPECIFICATIONS

DISPLACEMENT Engine size is described as displacement. **Displacement** is the cubic inch (cu. in.) or cubic centimeter (cc) volume displaced or swept by all of the pistons. The diameter of a cylinder is called the *bore*. The distance the piston travels down in the cylinder is called the *stroke*. ● **SEE FIGURE 3–4.**

A liter (L) is equal to 1,000 cubic centimeters; therefore, most engines today are identified by their displacement in liters.

1 L = 1,000 cc

1 L = 61 cu. in.

1 cu. in. = 16.4 cc

The formula to calculate the displacement of an engine is basically the formula for determining the volume of a cylinder multiplied by the number of cylinders. However, because the formula has been publicized in many different forms, it seems somewhat confusing. The volume of a cylinder is determined by

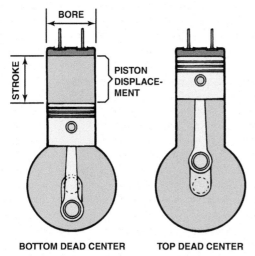

FIGURE 3–4 The bore and stroke of pistons are used to calculate an engine's displacement.

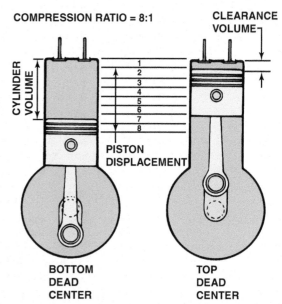

FIGURE 3–5 Compression ratio is the ratio of the total cylinder volume (when the piston is at the bottom of its stroke) to the clearance volume (when the piston is at the top of its stroke).

multiplying the area of a circle by the stroke. The area of a circle is determined by the radius (half the diameter) times Pi (3.14).

Then, multiply that by the stroke in inches followed by the number of cylinders. The formula is:

Cubic Inches = $\pi \times R^2 \times$ stroke $\times$ number of cylinders

For example, a six cylinder engine with a bore of 4 in. and a stroke of 3 in. would have according to the formula:

Cu. In. = 3.14×2^2 (4) $\times 3 \times 6 = 226$ cu. in.

Because 1 cubic inch equals 16.4 cubic centimeters, this engine displacement equals 3,706 cubic centimeters or, rounded to 3,700 cubic centimeters, 3.7 liters. Most hybrid engines use the same size or smaller displacement engine as used in the non-hybrid version of the same vehicle.

Some vehicles, such as the Prius, use a unique engine that is based on a regular production engine that has been modified for maximum efficiency.

COMPRESSION RATIO Compression ratio (CR) is the ratio of the volume in the cylinder above the piston when the piston is at the bottom of the stroke to the volume in the cylinder above the piston when the piston is at the top of the stroke. ● **SEE FIGURE 3–5.**

$$CR = \frac{\text{Volume in cylinder with piston at bottom of cylinder}}{\text{Volume in cylinder with piston at top center}}$$

Compression ratio is always expressed as "to one." Therefore, if the cylinder volume with the piston at bottom dead center (BDC) is 9 times greater than volume with the piston at top dead center (TDC), then the compression ratio is 9:1 (read as 9 to 1). ● **SEE FIGURE 3–6.**

Most hybrid engines, except for the Chevrolet Volt, are designed to operate on regular 87-octane gasoline. While the static compression ratio may be higher than normal, the late closing of the intake valve allows for normal dynamic compression.

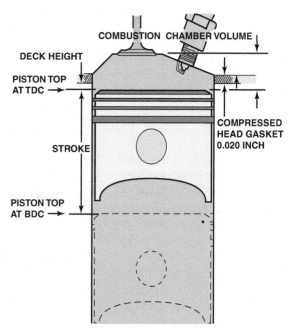

FIGURE 3–6 Combustion chamber volume is the volume above the piston with the piston is at top dead center.

TORQUE, WORK, AND POWER

TORQUE Torque is the term used to describe a rotating (twisting) force that may or may not result in motion. Torque is measured as the amount of force multiplied by the length of the lever through which it acts. If 10 pounds of force is applied

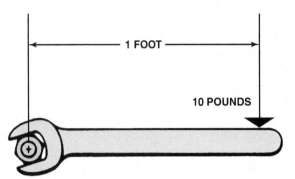

FIGURE 3–7 Torque is a twisting force equal to the distance from the pivot point times the force applied expressed in units called pound-feet (lb-ft) or Newton-meters (N-m).

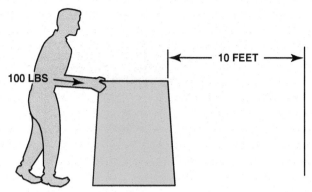

FIGURE 3–8 Work is calculated by multiplying force times distance. If you push 100 pounds 10 feet, you have done 1,000 foot-pounds of work.

to the end of a one-foot-long wrench to turn a bolt, then 10 pound-feet of torque is being exerted. ● **SEE FIGURE 3–7.**

The metric unit for torque is Newton-meters because Newton is the metric unit for force and the distance is expressed in meters.

One pound-foot = 1.3558 Newton-meters

One Newton-meter = 0.7376 pound-foot

WORK **Work** is defined as actually accomplishing movement when torque or a force is applied to an object. A service technician can apply torque to a bolt in an attempt to loosen it, yet no work is done until the bolt actually moves. Work is calculated by multiplying the applied force (in pounds) by the distance the object moves (in feet). Applying 100 pounds of force to move an object 10 feet accomplishes 1,000 foot-pounds of work (100 pounds × 10 feet = 1,000 foot-pounds). ● **SEE FIGURE 3–8.**

POWER The term **power** means the rate of doing work. Power equals work divided by time. Work is achieved when a certain amount of mass (weight) is moved a certain distance by a force. Whether the object is moved in 10 seconds or 10 minutes does not make a difference in the amount of work accomplished, but it does affect the amount of power needed. Power is expressed in units of foot-pounds per minute.

HORSEPOWER The power an engine produces is called horsepower (hp). One **horsepower** is the power required to move 550 pounds one foot in one second, or 33,000 pounds one foot in one minute (550 lb × 60 sec = 33,000 lb). This is expressed as 500 foot-pounds (ft-lb) per second or 33,000 foot-pounds per minute. ● **SEE FIGURE 3–9.**

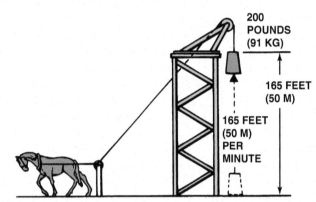

FIGURE 3–9 One horsepower is equal to 33,000 foot-pounds (200 lbs ×165 ft) of work per minute.

The actual horsepower produced by an engine is measured with a dynamometer. A dynamometer (often abbreviated as *dyno* or *dyn*) places a load on the engine and measures the amount of twisting force the engine crankshaft places against the load. The load holds the engine speed, so it is called a brake. The horsepower derived from a dynamometer is called **brake horsepower (BHP).** The dynamometer actually measures the torque output of the engine. The horsepower is calculated from the torque readings at various engine speeds (in revolutions per minute, or RPM).

Horsepower is torque times RPM divided by 5,252.

$$\text{Horsepower} = \frac{\text{Torque} \times \text{RPM}}{5,252}$$

Torque is what the driver "feels" as the vehicle is being accelerated. A small engine operating at a high RPM may have the same horsepower as a large engine operating at a low RPM.

FREQUENTLY ASKED QUESTION

Is It Lb-Ft or Ft-Lb of Torque?

The unit for torque is expressed as a force times the distance (leverage) from the object. Therefore, the official unit for torque is lb-ft (pound-feet) or Newton-meters (a force times a distance). However, it is commonly expressed in ft-lb and even some torque wrenches are labeled with this unit.

HYBRID ENGINE DESIGN FEATURES

PISTON PIN OFFSET The piston pin holes are usually not centered in the piston. They are located toward the **major thrust surface,** approximately 0.062 in. (1.57 millimeters) from the piston centerline, as shown in ● **FIGURE 3–10.**

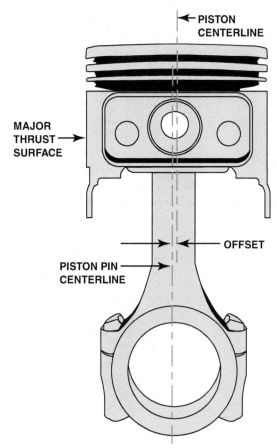

MAJOR THRUST SURFACE →

← **PISTON CENTERLINE**

← **OFFSET**

PISTON PIN CENTERLINE →

FIGURE 3–10 Piston pin offset toward the major thrust surface.

Pin offset is designed to reduce piston slap and noise that can result as the large end of the connecting rod crosses over top dead center. The minor thrust side of the piston head has a greater area than does the major side. This is caused by the *pin offset*. The action includes the following steps:

- As the piston moves up in the cylinder on the compression stroke, it rides against the minor thrust surface.
- When compression pressure becomes high enough, the greater head area on the minor side causes the piston to cock slightly in the cylinder.
- This keeps the *top* of the minor thrust surface on the cylinder.
- It forces the *bottom* of the major thrust surface to contact the cylinder wall.
- As the piston approaches top center, both thrust surfaces are in contact with the cylinder wall.
- When the crankshaft crosses over top center, the force on the connecting rod moves the entire piston toward the major thrust surface.
- The lower portion of the major thrust surface has already been in contact with the cylinder wall. The rest of the piston skirt slips into full contact just after the crossover point, thereby controlling piston slap. This action is illustrated in ● **FIGURE 3–11.**

Offsetting the piston toward the minor thrust surface would provide a better mechanical advantage. It also would cause less piston-to-cylinder friction. For these reasons, the offset is often placed toward the minor thrust surface in racing engines. Noise and durability are not as important in racing engines as is maximum performance.

NOTE: Not all piston pins are offset. In fact, many engines operate without the offset to help reduce friction and improve power and fuel economy.

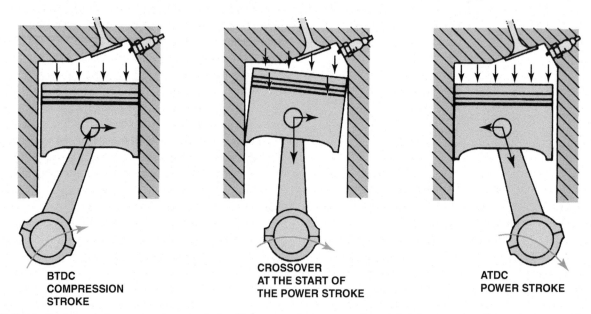

BTDC COMPRESSION STROKE

CROSSOVER AT THE START OF THE POWER STROKE

ATDC POWER STROKE

FIGURE 3–11 Engine rotation and rod angle during the power stroke cause the piston to press harder against one side of the cylinder, called the major thrust surface.

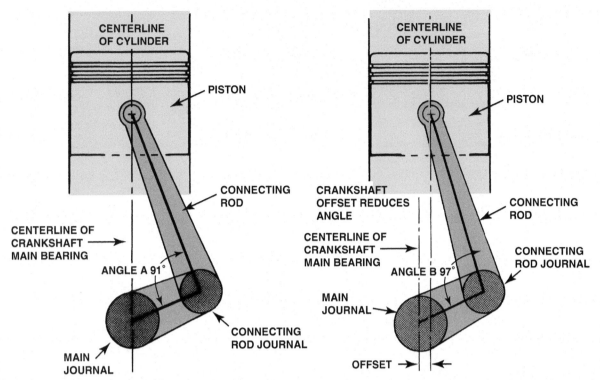

FIGURE 3–12 The crank throw is halfway down on the power stroke. The piston on the left without an offset crankshaft has a sharper angle than the engine on the right with an offset crankshaft.

OFFSET CRANKSHAFT The thrust side is the side of the cylinder that the connecting rod points to when the piston is on the power stroke. Most V-block engines (V-6 or V-8) rotate clockwise as viewed from the front of the engine. The left-bank piston thrust side faces the inside (center) of the engine. The right-bank piston thrust side faces the outside of the block. This rule is called the *left-hand rule* and states:

- Stand at the rear of the engine and point your left hand toward the front of the engine.
- Raise your thumb straight up, indicating the top of the engine.
- Point your middle finger toward the right. This represents the major thrust side of the piston.

To reduce side loads, some vehicle manufacturers offset the crankshaft from center. This is called an **offset crankshaft**. For example, if an engine rotates clockwise as viewed from the front, the crankshaft may be offset to the left to reduce the angle of the connecting rod during the power stroke. The offset usually varies from 1/16 in. to 1/2 in., depending on make and model. Some inline gasoline engines used in hybrid gasoline/electric vehicles use an offset crankshaft. ● **SEE FIGURE 3–12.**

VARIABLE VALVE TIMING

PURPOSE AND FUNCTION Variable valve timing is used to improve engine efficiency over the entire engine speed range to improve fuel economy and reduce exhaust emissions.

Conventional camshafts are permanently synchronized to the crankshaft so that they operate the valves at a specific point in each combustion cycle. In an engine, the intake valve opens slightly before the piston reaches the top of the cylinder and closes about 60° after the piston reaches the bottom of the stroke on every cycle, regardless of the engine speed or load. On newer engines, the camshaft can have the capability of a variable valve-timing feature that changes the camshaft specifications during different operating modes.

TYPES OF VARIABLE VALVE TIMING Many vehicle manufacturers use three basic types of variable valve timing.

1. Exhaust camshaft variable action only on overhead camshaft engines, such as on many inline 4- and 6-cylinder engines.
2. Intake and exhaust camshaft variable action on both camshafts used in many engines.
3. Changing the relationship of the camshaft to the crankshaft, in overhead valve cam-in-block engines.

Variable cam timing allows the valves to be operated at different points in the combustion cycle, to improve performance. ● **SEE CHART 3–1.**

Variable camshaft timing is used on engines from the following vehicle manufacturers.

- General Motors
- BMW
- Chrysler
- Ford

DRIVING CONDITION	CHANGE IN CAMSHAFT POSITION	OBJECTIVE	RESULT
Idle	No change	Minimize valve overlap	Stabilize idle speed
Light engine load	Retard valve timing	Decrease valve overlap	Stable engine output
Medium engine load	Advance valve timing	Increase valve overlap	Better fuel economy with low emissions
Low/medium speed/heavy load	Advance valve timing	Advance intake valve closing	Improve low and midrange torque
High RPM heavy load	Retard valve timing	Retard intake valve closing	Improve engine output

CHART 3–1

The purpose for varying the cam timing includes providing for more engine torque and power over a wide engine speed and load range.

- Nissan/Infiniti
- Hyundai/Kia
- Toyota/Lexus
- VW/Audi

On a system that controls the intake camshaft only, the camshaft timing is advanced at low engine speed, closing the intake valves earlier to improve low RPM torque. At high engine speeds, the camshaft is retarded by using engine oil pressure against a helical gear to rotate the camshaft. When the camshaft is retarded, the intake valve closing is delayed, improving cylinder filling at higher engine speeds. Variable cam timing can be used to control exhaust cam timing only. Engines that use this system can eliminate the exhaust gas recirculation (EGR) valve because the computer can close the exhaust valve sooner than normal, trapping some exhaust gases in the combustion chamber and therefore eliminating the need for an EGR valve. Some engines use variable camshaft timing on both intake and exhaust cylinder cams.

PARTS AND OPERATION   The camshaft position actuator oil control valve (OCV) directs oil from the oil feed in the head to the appropriate camshaft position actuator oil passages. There is one OCV for each camshaft position actuator. The OCV is sealed and mounted to the front cover. The ported end of the OCV is inserted into the cylinder head with a sliding fit. A filter screen protects each OCV oil port from any contamination in the oil supply. The camshaft position actuator is mounted to the front end of the camshaft, and the timing notch in the

nose of the camshaft aligns with the dowel pin in the camshaft position actuator to ensure proper cam timing and camshaft position actuator oil hole alignment. ● **SEE FIGURE 3–13.**

Varying the exhaust and/or the intake camshaft position allows for reduced exhaust emissions and improved performance. ● **SEE CHART 3–2.**

By varying the exhaust cam phasing, vehicle manufacturers are able to meet newer oxides of nitrogen (NOx) reduction standards and eliminate the exhaust gas recirculation (EGR) valve. Also by using exhaust cam phasing, the powertrain control module (PCM) can close the exhaust valves sooner than usual, thereby trapping some exhaust gases in the combustion chamber. Manufacturers use one or two actuators that allow

CAMSHAFT PHASING CHANGE	IMPROVES
Exhaust cam phasing	Reduces exhaust emissions
Exhaust cam phasing	Increases fuel economy (reduces pumping losses)
Intake cam phasing	Increases low-speed torque
Intake cam phasing	Increases high-speed power

CHART 3–2

Changing the exhaust cam timing mainly helps reduce exhaust emissions, whereas changing the intake cam timing mainly helps the engine produce increased power and torque.

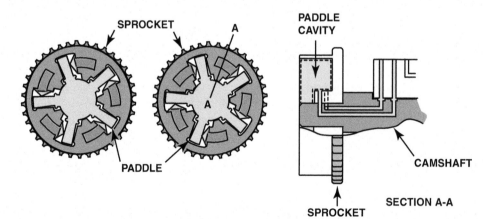

FIGURE 3–13 Camshaft rotation during advance and retard.

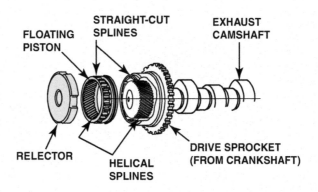

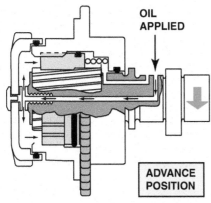

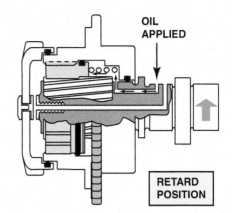

FIGURE 3–14 A spline phaser assembly.

the camshaft piston to change by up to 50° in relation to the crankshaft position. The two types of cam phasing devices commonly used are

1. **Spline phaser.** Used on overhead camshaft (OHC) engines and

2. **Vane phaser.** Used on OHC and overhead valve (OHV) cam-in-block engines.

SPLINE PHASER SYSTEM OPERATION On most engines, the pulse-width-modulated (PWM) control valve is located on the front of the cylinder head. Oil pressure is regulated by the control valve and then directed to the ports in the cylinder head leading to the camshaft and cam phaser position. The cam phaser is located on the exhaust cams and is part of the exhaust cam sprocket. When the PCM commands an increase in oil pressure, the piston is moved inside the cam phaser and rides along the helical splines, which compresses the coil spring. This movement causes the cam phaser gear and the camshaft to move in an opposite direction, thereby retarding the cam timing. ● **SEE FIGURE 3–14.**

VANE PHASER SYSTEM The vane phaser system used on overhead camshaft (OHC) engines uses a camshaft piston (CMP) sensor on each camshaft. Each camshaft has its own actuator and its own *oil control valve* (OCV). Instead of using a piston along a helical spline, the vane phaser uses a rotor with four vanes, which is connected to the end of the camshaft. The rotor is located inside the stator, which is bolted to the cam sprocket. The stator and rotor are not connected. Oil pressure

is controlled on both sides of the vanes of the rotor, which creates a hydraulic link between the two parts. The oil control valve varies the balance of pressure on either side of the vanes and thereby controls the position of the camshaft. A return spring is used under the reluctor of the phaser to help return it to the home or zero degrees position. ● **SEE FIGURE 3–15.**

MAGNETICALLY CONTROLLED VANE PHASER On this type, the PCM controls a magnetically controlled vane phaser by using a 12 volt pulse-width-modulated (PWM) signal

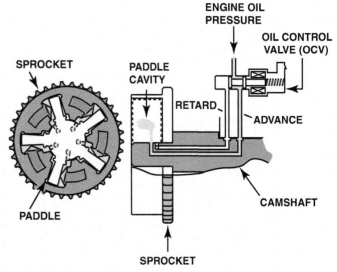

FIGURE 3–15 A vane phaser is used to move the camshaft, using changes in oil pressure from the oil control valve.

FIGURE 3–16 The screen(s) protect the solenoid valve from dirt and debris that can cause the valve to stick. This fault can set a P0017 diagnostic trouble code (crankshaft position/camshaft position correlation error).

 TECH TIP

Check the Screen on the Control Valve If There Are Problems

If an NOx emission failure at a state inspection occurs or a diagnostic trouble code is set related to the cam timing, remove the control valve and check for a clogged oil screen. A lack of regular oil changes can cause the screen to become clogged, thereby preventing proper operation. A rough idle is a common complaint because the spring may not be able to return the camshaft to the idle position after a long highway trip. ● **SEE FIGURE 3–16.**

to an electromagnet, which operates the OCV. A magnetically controlled vane phaser is used on many double overhead camshaft engines on both the intake and exhaust camshafts. The OCV directs pressurized engine oil to either advance or retard chambers of the camshaft actuator to change the camshaft position in relation to the crankshaft position.

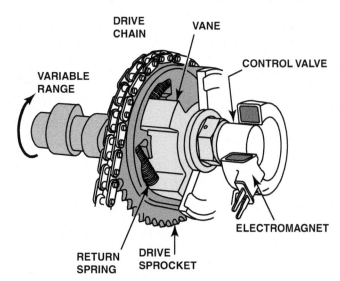

FIGURE 3–17 A magnetically controlled vane phaser.

The following occurs when the pulse width is changed. The cam phasing is continuously variable with a range from 40° for the intake camshaft to 50° for the exhaust camshaft. ● **SEE FIGURE 3–17.**

CAM-IN-BLOCK ENGINE CAM PHASER Overhead valve engines that use a cam-in-block design use a magnetically controlled cam phaser to vary the camshaft in relation to the crankshaft. This type of phaser is not capable of changing the duration of valve opening or valve lift. Inside the camshaft actuator is a rotor with vanes that are attached to the camshaft. Oil pressure is supplied to the vanes, which causes the camshaft to rotate in relation to the crankshaft. The camshaft actuator solenoid valve directs the flow of oil to either the advance or retard side vanes of the actuator. ● **SEE FIGURE 3–18.**

The ECM sends a PWM signal to the camshaft actuator magnet. The movement of the pintle is used to direct oil flow to the actuator. The higher the duty cycle, the greater the movement in the valve position and change in camshaft timing.

NOTE: When oil pressure drops to zero when the engine stops, a spring-loaded locking pin is used to keep the camshaft locked to prevent noise at engine start. When the engine starts, oil pressure releases the locking pin.

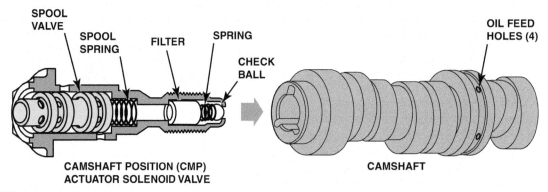

FIGURE 3–18 A camshaft position actuator used in a cam-in-block engine.

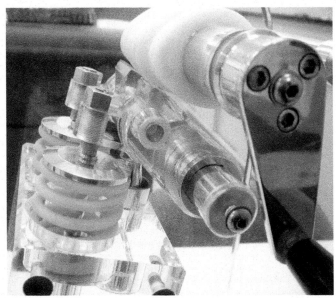

FIGURE 3–19 A plastic mockup of a Honda VTEC system that uses two different camshaft profiles—one for low-speed engine operation and the other for high speed.

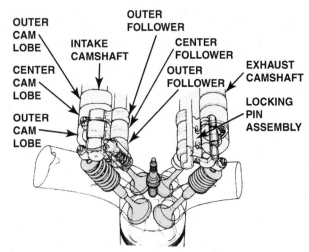

FIGURE 3–20 Engine oil pressure is used to switch cam lobes on a VTEC system.

VARIABLE LIFT SYSTEM

HONDA VTEC SYSTEM Variable camshafts include the system used by Honda/Acura, called **variable valve timing and lift electronic control (VTEC).** This system uses two different camshafts for low and high RPM. When the engine is operating at idle and speeds below about 4000 RPM, the valves are opened by camshafts that are optimized by maximum torque and fuel economy. When engine speed reaches a predetermined speed, depending on the exact make and model, the computer turns on a solenoid, which opens a spool valve. When the spool valve opens, engine oil pressure pushes against pins that lock the three intake rocker arms together. With the rocker arms lashed, the valves must follow the profile of the high RPM cam lobe in the center. This process of switching from the low-speed camshaft profile to the high-speed profile takes about 100 milliseconds (0.1 sec). ● **SEE FIGURES 3–19 AND 3–20.**

CYLINDER DEACTIVATION SYSTEMS

PURPOSE AND FUNCTION Some engines are capable of **cylinder deactivation.** They are designed to be operated on four of eight cylinders during low-load conditions to improve fuel economy. The power train computer monitors

TECH TIP

Always Use the Specified Oil in a Hybrid Electric Vehicle

Most hybrid electric vehicle engines require a low viscosity engine oil such as SAE 0W-20 or SAE 5W-20. There are three major reasons why this low viscosity oil is used:

1. Lower viscosity oil improves fuel economy by reducing drag inside the engine.
2. During starting after idle stop has occurred, the oil has to flow quickly to get oil to all of the moving parts especially in cold weather.
3. Most hybrid electric vehicle engines use a type of variable valve timing or displacement deactivation system that requires the rapid flow of oil to function as designed.

Therefore, for best overall performance and economy, always use the specified oil in all engines.

engine speed, coolant temperature, throttle position, and load and determines when to deactivate cylinders. The General Motors two-mode hybrid SUV and pickup trucks use variable displacement systems called **active fuel management.**

PARTS AND OPERATION The key to this process is the use of two-stage hydraulic valve lifters. In normal operation, the inner and outer lifter sleeves are held together by a pin and operate as an assembly. When the computer determines that the cylinder can be deactivated, oil pressure is delivered to a passage, which depresses the pin and allows the outer portion of the lifter to follow the contour of the cam while the inner portion remains stationary, keeping the valve closed. The electronic operation is achieved through the use of lifter oil manifold, which is located in the valley between the banks of cylinders and contains solenoids to control the oil flow used to activate or deactivate the cylinders. ● **SEE FIGURES 3–21 AND 3–22.**

■ Engine speed input is used to maintain a steady idle speed so the driver is not aware of a change in the number of cylinders that are working.

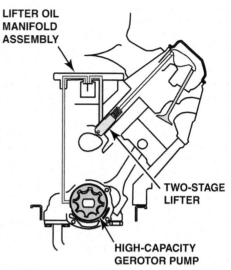

FIGURE 3–22 Active fuel management includes many different components and changes to the oiling system, which makes routine oil changes even more important on engines equipped with this system.

■ Crankshaft position sensors are used primarily as the spark timing input sensor. The crankshaft position (CKP) sensor is also used as an input to the PCM to determine when to activate or deactivate cylinders.

? **FREQUENTLY ASKED QUESTION**

How Are Engine Vibrations Controlled During Cylinder Deactivations?

When a Honda V-6 equipped with cylinder deactivation is running only on three cylinders, there is a natural imbalance, which can produce drumming sounds and vibrations. To counteract this, the engine is mounted on special **active control engine mounts (ACM)** that electronically adjust themselves to counteract engine vibrations. The ACM vacuum solenoid valve (VSV) is controlled by a pulse signal transmitted from the engine control module (ECM). In normal operation, the frequency of this pulse signal is matched with engine speed to effectively dampen engine vibration. ● **SEE FIGURE 3–23.**

Further booming sounds are reduced by an **active noise control (ANC)** system that automatically sends an out-of-phase sound through the loudspeaker system to cancel out engine noises. This system also works when the engine is idling and the counter sounds are produced by the speakers in the vehicle even if the radio is off. This technology is often called *noise cancelation.*

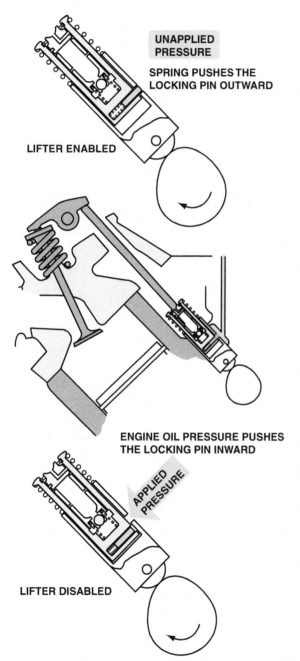

FIGURE 3–21 Oil pressure applied to the locking pin causes the inside of the lifter to freely move inside the outer shell of the lifter, thereby keeping the valve closed.

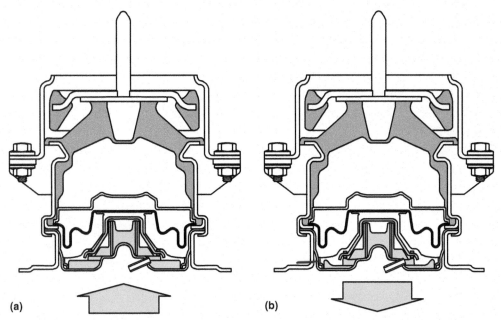

FIGURE 3–23 (a) A Ford Escape hybrid engine mount in the rigid position. (b) At idle speed, the engine mount passages are opened, allowing more movement of the engine to reduce vibration.

(a)   (b)

HYBRID IGNITION SYSTEMS

COIL-ON-PLUG IGNITION All hybrid electric vehicles use coil-on-plug-type ignition system. ● **SEE FIGURE 3–24.**

The coil-on-plug system eliminates the spark plug wires that are often sources of **electromagnetic interference (EMI),** which can cause problems to some computer signals. The vehicle computer controls the timing of the spark. Ignition timing also can be changed (retarded or advanced) on a cylinder-by-cylinder basis for maximum performance and to respond to knock sensor signals.

TYPES OF COP IGNITION There are two basic types of **coil-on-plug (COP)** ignition:

1. **Two-wire.** This design uses the vehicle computer to control the firing of the ignition coil. The two wires include:
   - Ignition voltage feed.
   - Pulse ground wire which is controlled by the computer.
   All ignition timing and dwell control are handled by the computer.

2. **Three-wire.** This design includes an ignition module at each coil. The three wires include:

   - Ignition voltage
   - Ground
   - Pulse from the computer to the built-in module

   Each coil is controlled by the PCM, which can vary the ignition timing separately for each cylinder based on signals the PCM receives from the knock sensor(s). For example, if the

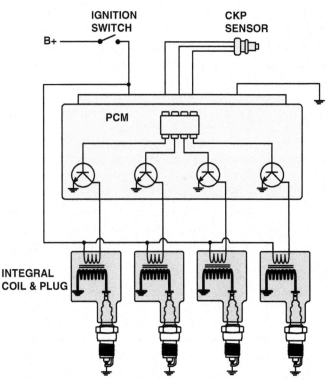

FIGURE 3–24 A typical coil-on-plug ignition system showing the triggering and the switching being performed by the PCM via input from the crankshaft position sensor.

knock sensor detects that a spark knock has occurred after firing cylinder 3, then the PCM will continue to monitor cylinder 3 and retard timing on just this one cylinder if necessary to prevent engine-damaging detonation.

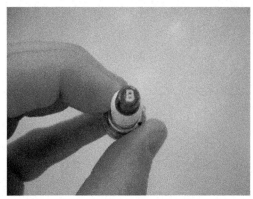

FIGURE 3–25 The letter printed on the top of the center electrode indicates that this spark plug is designed to fit into a spark plug opening that is stamped with a "B," so the open side of the side electrode is pointing toward the intake valve for best combustion of the air–fuel mixture in the cylinder.

INDEXED SPARK PLUGS

One hybrid engine, the three-cylinder 2000–2009 Honda Insight, uses indexed spark plugs. Indexed spark plugs mean that the side electrode is facing away from the intake valve. With normal spark plugs, the side electrode may or may not block the spark (electrical arc). Honda has four different spark plugs available for this engine, labeled A, B, C, and D. The specified plug for each cylinder is stamped next to the spark plug opening. The spark plugs also have a letter marked on the top. ● **SEE FIGURE 3–25.**

The service technician has to remove the coil from each cylinder to determine the letter for the plug needed. The indexed spark plugs usually have to be purchased from a Honda dealer to assure that the correct indexed plug is used.

ELECTRONIC THROTTLE CONTROL

PURPOSE AND FUNCTION An **electronic throttle control (ETC)** system does not use a direct mechanical link between the accelerator pedal and the throttle plate. In the place of the linkage, an electric motor is used to move the throttle plate. The electronic throttle system has the following advantages over the conventional throttle cable design:

- Eliminates the mechanical throttle cable, thereby reducing the number of moving parts.
- Helps reduce pumping losses by using the electronic throttle to open at highway speeds with greater fuel economy.

The electronic throttle can be called **drive-by-wire,** but most hybrid vehicle manufacturers use the term electronic throttle control (ETC), including General Motors, Ford, Honda, and Toyota.

The ETC is used for the following functions:

1. Opens the throttle for cold-start fast idle.
2. Controls the throttle opening while the driver is using the cruise control.

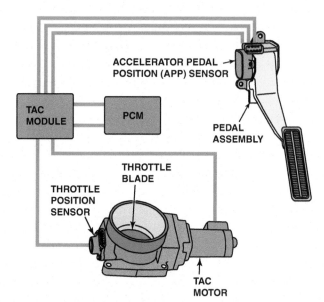

FIGURE 3–26 The throttle pedal is connected to the accelerator pedal position (APP) sensor. The electronic throttle body includes a throttle position sensor to provide throttle angle feedback to the vehicle computer. Some systems use a Throttle Actuator Control (TAC) module to operate the throttle blade (plate).

3. Closes the throttle as needed to provide torque reduction for traction control.
4. Limits throttle opening for engine speed control.
5. Opens the throttle to maintain engine and vehicle speed as the powertrain control module (PCM) leans the air–fuel ratio, retards ignition timing, and introduces additional exhaust gas recirculation (EGR) to reduce pumping losses.

PARTS AND OPERATION The typical ETC system includes the following components:

1. **Accelerator pedal position (APP)** sensor, also called **accelerator pedal sensor (APS).**
2. The electronic throttle actuator (servomotor), which is part of the electronic throttle body.
3. A throttle position (TP) sensor.
4. An electronic control unit, usually the vehicle PCM. ● **SEE FIGURE 3–26.**

The accelerator pedal position sensor uses two and sometimes three separate sensors, which act together to give accurate accelerator pedal position information to the controller, but also are used to check that the sensor is working properly. They function just like a throttle position sensor, and two are needed for proper system function. One APP sensor output signal increases as the pedal is depressed and the other signal decreases. The controller compares the signals with a look-up table to determine the pedal position. Using two or three signals improves redundancy should one sensor fail, and it allows quick recognition and diagnosis of a malfunction. When three sensors are used, the third signal can either decrease or increase with pedal position, but its voltage range will still be different from the other two.

The actuator, often referred to as a **servomotor,** is a DC electric motor. The voltage received by the servomotor is in the

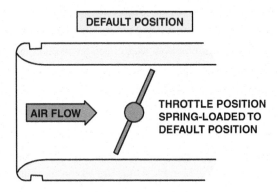

DEFAULT POSITION

AIR FLOW →

THROTTLE POSITION
SPRING-LOADED TO
DEFAULT POSITION

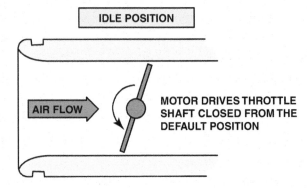

IDLE POSITION

AIR FLOW →

MOTOR DRIVES THROTTLE
SHAFT CLOSED FROM THE
DEFAULT POSITION

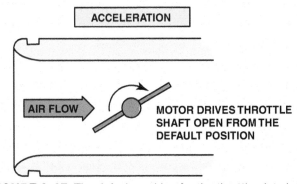

ACCELERATION

AIR FLOW →

MOTOR DRIVES THROTTLE
SHAFT OPEN FROM THE
DEFAULT POSITION

FIGURE 3–27 The default position for the throttle plate is in slightly open position. The servomotor then is used to close it for idle and open it during acceleration.

form of a square wave whose voltage and frequency remain the same. The servomotor responds to the change in duty cycle, which is the percentage reading between the on and off time. ● **SEE FIGURE 3–27.**

WIDE-BAND OXYGEN SENSORS

TERMINOLOGY **Wide-band oxygen sensors** were first used in 1992 on some Hondas. Today, they are used by most vehicle manufacturers to ensure that the exhaust emissions can meet the current standard. Wide-band oxygen sensors

have various names, depending on the vehicle and/or oxygen sensor manufacturer, including:

- Wide-band oxygen sensor
- Broadband oxygen sensor
- Wide-range oxygen sensor
- Air–fuel ratio (AFR) sensor
- Wide-range air–fuel (WRAF) sensor
- Lean air–fuel (LAF) sensor
- Air–fuel (AF) sensor

Most hybrid electric vehicles use a wide-band oxygen sensor and they are manufactured in dual cell and single cell designs.

INTRODUCTION A conventional zirconia oxygen sensor reacts to an air–fuel mixture that is either richer or leaner than 14.7:1. This means that the sensor cannot be used to detect the exact air–fuel mixture. ● **SEE FIGURE 3–28.**

The need for more stringent exhaust emission standards such as the natural low emission vehicle (NLEV), plus the ultra-low emission vehicle (ULEV) and the super ultra-low emission vehicle (SULEV), requires more accurate fuel control than can be provided by a traditional oxygen sensor.

PURPOSE AND FUNCTION A wide-band oxygen sensor is capable of supplying air–fuel ratio information to the PCM over a much broader range. Compared with a conventional zirconia oxygen sensor, the wide-band oxygen sensor has the following features:

1. The ability to detect exhaust air–fuel ratio from as rich as 10:1 to as lean as 23:1 in some cases.

2. Allows the engine to achieve improved fuel economy by allowing the engine to operate using a leaner-than-normal air–fuel ratio.

3. Cold start activity within as little as 10 seconds.

PLANAR DESIGN In 1998, Bosch introduced a wide-band oxygen sensor that is flat and thin (1.5 mm or 0.006 in.), known as a planar design and not in the shape of a thimble as previously constructed. Now several manufacturers produce a similar *planar* design wide-band oxygen sensor. Its thin design makes it easier to heat than older styles of oxygen sensors and,

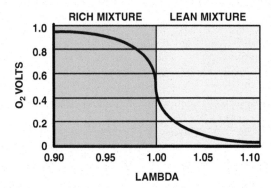

FIGURE 3–28 A conventional zirconia oxygen sensor can only reset to exhaust mixtures that are richer or leaner than 14.7:1 (lambda 1.00).

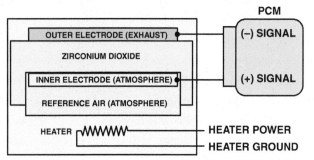

FIGURE 3–29 A planar design zirconia oxygen sensor places all of the elements together, which allows the sensor to reach operating temperature quickly.

 FREQUENTLY ASKED QUESTION

How Quickly Can a Wide-Band Oxygen Sensor Achieve Closed Loop?

In a Toyota Highlander hybrid electric vehicle, the operation of the gasoline engine is delayed for a short time when the vehicle is first driven. During this time of electric operation, the oxygen sensor heaters are turned on in readiness for the gasoline engine starting. The gasoline engine often achieves closed-loop operation during *cranking* because the oxygen sensors are fully warm and ready to go at the same time the engine is started. Having the gasoline engine achieve closed loop quickly, allows it to meet the stringent SULEV standards.

as a result, it can achieve closed loop in less than 10 seconds. The sandwich-type designs of the planar style of oxygen sensor have the same elements and operate the same, but are stacked in the following way from the exhaust side to the ambient air side.

- Exhaust stream
- Outer electrode
- Zirconia (Zr_2) (electrolyte)
- Inner electrode (reference or signal)
- Outside (ambient) air`
- Heater

   ● **SEE FIGURE 3–29.**

Another name for a conventional oxygen sensor is a **Nernst cell,** named for Walther Nernst, 1864–1941, a German physicist known for his work in electrochemistry.

DUAL CELL PLANAR WIDE-BAND OXYGEN SENSOR

CONSTRUCTION A dual cell planar-type wide-band oxygen sensor is made like a conventional planar O2S, or Nernst cell. Above the Nernst cell is another zirconia layer with two electrodes, called the *pump cell.* The two cells share a common ground, called the *reference.* There are two internal chambers.

- The air reference chamber is exposed to ambient air.
- The diffusion chamber is exposed to the exhaust gases.

Platinum electrodes are on both sides of the zirconia electrolyte elements, which separate the air reference chamber and the exhaust-exposed diffusion chamber.

OPERATION In a conventional zirconia oxygen sensor, a bias or reference voltage can be applied to the two platinum electrodes, and then oxygen ions can be forced (pumped) from the ambient reference air side to the exhaust side of the sensor. If the polarity is reversed, the oxygen ion can be forced to travel in the opposite direction.

The basic principle of operation of a typical wide-band oxygen sensor is that it uses a positive or negative voltage signal to keep a balance between two sensors. Oxygen sensors do not measure the quantity of free oxygen in the exhaust. Instead, oxygen sensors produce a voltage that is based on the ion flow between the platinum electrodes of the sensor to maintain a stoichiometric balance.

For example,

- If there is a lean exhaust, there is oxygen in the exhaust and the ion flow from the ambient side to the exhaust side is low.
- If there is rich exhaust, the ion flow is increased to help maintain balance between the ambient air side and the exhaust side of the sensor.

The PCM pumps O_2 ions in and out of the diffusion chamber to bring the voltage back to 0.45 V, using the pump cell. The operation of a wide-band oxygen sensor is best described by looking at what occurs when the exhaust is stoichiometric, rich, and lean. ● **SEE FIGURE 3–30.**

STOICHIOMETRIC When the exhaust is at stoichiometric (14.7:1 air–fuel ratio), the voltage of the Nernst cell is 450 mV (0.45 V). The voltage between the diffusion chamber and the air reference chamber changes from 0.45 V. This voltage will be

- Higher if the exhaust is rich
- Lower if the exhaust is lean

The reference voltage remains constant, usually at 2.5 V, but can vary depending on the year, make, and model of vehicle and the type of sensor.

RICH EXHAUST When the exhaust is rich, the voltage between the common (reference) electrode and the Nernst cell electrode that is exposed to ambient air is higher than 0.45 V. The PCM applies a negative current in milliamperes to the pump cell electrode to bring the circuit back into balance.

LEAN EXHAUST When the exhaust is lean, the voltage between the common (reference) electrode and the Nernst cell electrode is lower than 0.45 V. The PCM applies a positive current in milliamperes to the pump cell to bring the circuit back into balance.

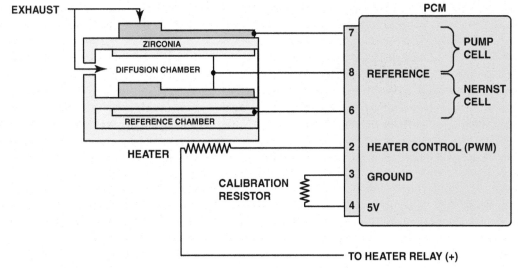

FIGURE 3–30 The reference electrodes are shared by the Nernst cell and the pump cell.

SCAN TOOL DIAGNOSIS Most service information specifies that a scan tool be used to check the wide-band oxygen sensor, because the PCM performs tests of the unit and can identify faults. However, even wide-band oxygen sensors can be fooled if there is an exhaust manifold leak or other fault which could lead to false or inaccurate readings. If the oxygen sensor reading is false, the PCM will command an incorrect amount of fuel. The scan data shown on a global (generic) OBD-II scan tool will often be different than the reading on the factory scan tool.

SCAN TOOL DATA (PID) The following information will be displayed by a scan tool when looking at data for a wide-band oxygen sensor.

- If the current is positive, this means that the PCM is pumping current in the diffusion gap due to a rich exhaust.

- If the current is negative, the PCM is pumping current out of the diffusion gap due to a lean exhaust.

- Air–fuel ratio is usually expressed in lambda. One means that the exhaust is at stoichiometric (14.7:1 air–fuel ratio) and numbers higher than one indicate a lean exhaust and numbers lower than one indicate a rich exhaust.

DIGITAL METER TESTING When testing a wide-band oxygen sensor for proper operation, perform the following steps:

STEP 1 Check service information and determine the circuit and connector terminal identification.

STEP 2 Measure the calibration resistor. While the value of this resistor can vary widely, depending on the type of sensor, the calibrating resistor should still be checked for opens and shorts.
- If open, the ohmmeter will read OL (infinity ohms).
- If shorted, the ohmmeter will read zero or close to zero.

NOTE: The calibration resistor is usually located within the connector itself.

STEP 3 Measure the heater circuit for proper resistance or current flow.

STEP 4 Measure the reference voltage relative to ground. This can vary but is generally 2.4 to 2.6 V.

STEP 5 Using jumper wires connect an ammeter and measure the current in the pump cell control wire.

RICH EXHAUST When the exhaust is rich (lambda less than 1.00), the Nernst cell voltage will move higher than 0.45 V. The PCM will pump oxygen from the exhaust into the diffusion gap by applying a negative voltage to the pump cell.

LEAN EXHAUST When the exhaust is lean (lambda higher than 1.00), the Nernst cell voltage will move lower than 0.45 V. The PCM will pump oxygen out of the diffusion gap by applying a positive voltage to the pump cell. A pump cell is used to pump oxygen into the diffusion gap when the exhaust is rich. The pump cell applies a negative voltage to do this.

- Positive current = lean exhaust
- Negative current = rich exhaust
  - **SEE FIGURE 3–31.**

SINGLE-CELL WIDE-BAND OXYGEN SENSOR

CONSTRUCTION A typical single-cell wide-band oxygen sensor looks similar to a conventional four-wire zirconia oxygen sensor. The typical single-cell wide-band oxygen sensor, usually called an *air–fuel ratio sensor,* has the following construction features:

- It can be made using the cup or planar design.
- Oxygen (O_2) is pumped into the diffusion layer similar to the operation of a dual cell wide-band oxygen sensor.
  - **SEE FIGURE 3–32.**

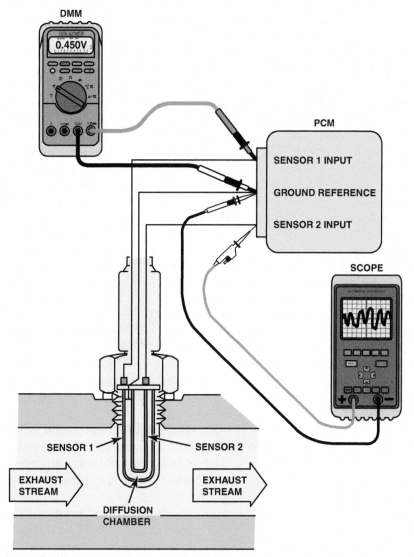

FIGURE 3–31 Testing a dual cell wide-band oxygen sensor can be done using a voltmeter or a scope. The meter reading is attached to the Nernst cell and should read stoichiometric (450 mV) at all times. The scope is showing activity to the pump cell with commands from the PCM to keep the Nernst cell at 14.7:1 air–fuel ratio.

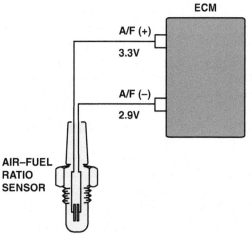

FIGURE 3–32 A single cell wide-band oxygen sensor has four wires with two for the heater and two for the sensor itself. The voltage applied to the sensor is 0.4 V (3.3 − 2.9 = 0.4) across the two leads of the sensor.

- Current flow reverses positive and negative.
- There are two cell wires and two heater wires (power and ground).
- The heater usually requires 6 amperes and the ground side is pulse-width modulated.

MILLIAMMETER TESTING The PCM controls the single-cell wide-band oxygen sensor by maintaining a voltage difference of 300 mV (0.3 V) between the two sensor leads. The PCM keeps the voltage difference constant under all operating conditions by increasing or decreasing current between the elements of the cell.

- Zero (0 mA) represents lambda or stoichiometric air–fuel ratio of 14.7:1
- +10 mA indicates a lean condition
- −10 mA indicates a rich condition

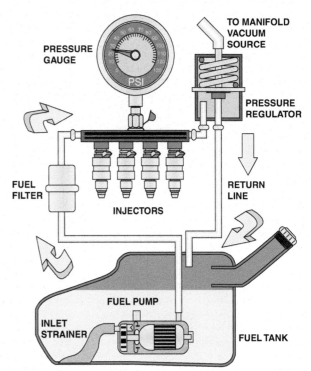

FIGURE 3–33 A typical port fuel-injected system showing a vacuum-controlled fuel-pressure regulator.

SCAN TOOL TESTING A scan tool will display a voltage reading but can vary depending on the type and maker of the tool.

Wide-band oxygen sensors have a long life, but they can fail. Most of the failures will cause a diagnostic trouble code (DTC) to set, usually causing the malfunction indicator (check engine) lamp to light.

FUEL INJECTION SYSTEMS

INTRODUCTION Most hybrid engines use the same or similar port fuel injection system that is used in non-hybrid engines.

FUEL SYSTEM PARTS AND OPERATION Electronic fuel injection systems use a solenoid-operated injector to spray atomized fuel in timed pulses into the manifold or near the intake valve. ● **SEE FIGURE 3–33.**

Sequential firing of the injectors according to engine firing order is the most accurate and desirable method of regulating port fuel injection.

RETURNLESS FUEL INJECTION SYSTEMS

PURPOSE AND FUNCTION Most hybrid engines, have used a returnless-type fuel delivery system for the following reasons:

1. In a return-type fuel system, hot fuel is returned to the fuel tank, which can add to the evaporative emissions.

2. The fuel flows through the fuel filter many times requiring that the fuel filter be replaced on a regular basis thereby increasing maintenance costs.

3. The added return line and fittings adds cost and weight to the vehicle.

The use of a returnless-type fuel system does require a slightly higher fuel pump pressure than used in a return-type system.

TYPES OF SYSTEMS The types of returnless systems include the following:

- **Mechanical returnless fuel system (MRFS).**
  This system has a bypass regulator to control rail pressure that is located in close proximity to the fuel tank. Fuel is sent by the in-tank pump to a chassis-mounted inline filter, with excess fuel returning to the tank through a short return line. ● **SEE FIGURE 3–34.**

  The inline filter may be mounted directly to the tank, thereby eliminating the shortened return line. Supply pressure is regulated on the downstream side of the inline filter to accommodate changing restrictions throughout the filter's service life.

- **Electronic returnless fuel system (ERFS).**
  This system is unique because it does not use a mechanical valve to regulate rail pressure. Fuel pressure at the rail is sensed by a pressure transducer, which sends a low-level signal to a controller. The controller contains logic to calculate a signal to the pump power driver. The power driver contains a high-current transistor that controls the pump speed using pulse width modulation (PWM).

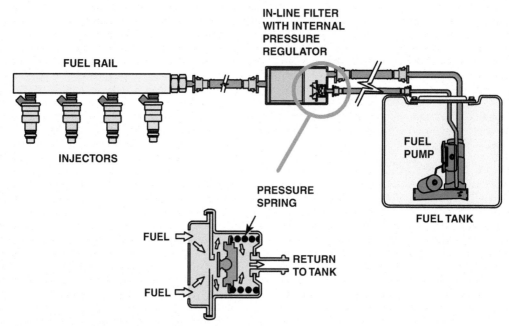

FIGURE 3–34 A mechanical returnless fuel system. The bypass regulator in the fuel filter controls fuel line pressure.

A **pressure vent valve (PVV)** is employed at the tank to relieve overpressure due to thermal expansion of fuel. ● **SEE FIGURE 3–35.**

■ **Demand Delivery system.** A demand pressure regulator mounts at the head or port entry and regulates the pressure downstream at the injectors by admitting the precise quantity of fuel into the rail as consumed by the engine. A fuel pump and a bypass regulator are used within the fuel sender assembly.

The supply pressure is higher than the required rail set pressure to accommodate dynamic line and filter pressure losses. Electronic pump speed control is accomplished using a smart regulator as an integral flow sensor. ● **SEE FIGURE 3–36.**

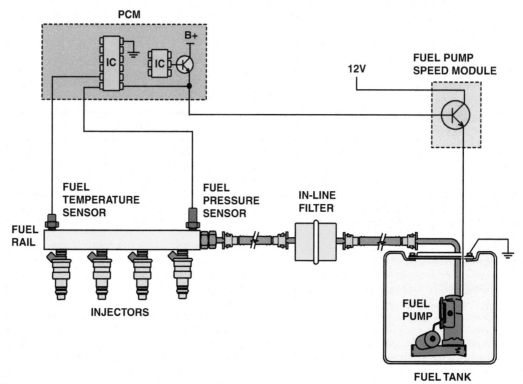

FIGURE 3–35 The fuel-pressure sensor and fuel-temperature sensor are often constructed together in one assembly to help give the PCM the needed data to control the fuel-pump speed.

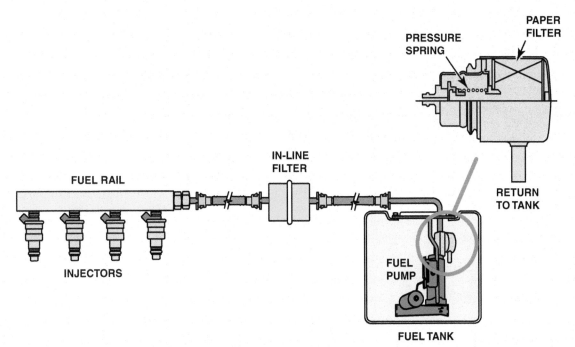

FIGURE 3–36 A demand delivery system uses a fuel pressure regulator attached to the fuel pump assembly.

GASOLINE DIRECT INJECTION (GDI)

Gasoline direct injection (GDI) systems inject fuel directly into the combustion chamber just before the spark. Currently the Lexus LS 600h hybrid electric vehicle uses gasoline direct injection to increase engine power and efficiency. The fuel, under very high pressure of 500 to 2,900 PSI (3,440 to 15,200 kPa),

is injected in a fine mist into the closely packed air molecules. When ignition occurs, the fuel is moving, under pressure, throughout the cylinder. The flame front moves quickly through the compressed, combustible swirling mixture.

Gasoline direct injection systems, like diesel systems, require very high fuel pressures to overcome the combustion chamber pressures during injection. ● **SEE FIGURE 3–37.**

Some hybrid vehicle engines today use gasoline direct injection and some use both direct and port injectors together in the same engine to provide superior power with reduced exhaust emissions.

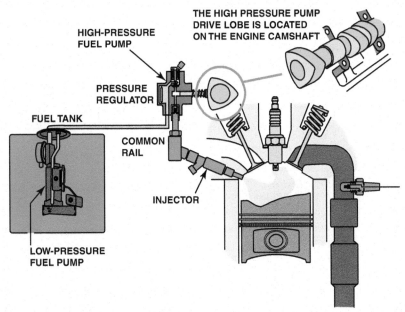

FIGURE 3–37 A typical direct injection system uses two pumps—one low-pressure electric pump in the fuel tank and the other a high-pressure pump driven by the camshaft. The high pressure fuel system operates at a pressure as low as 500 PSI during light load conditions and as high as 2,900 PSI under heavy loads.

SUMMARY

1. The four strokes of the four-stroke cycle are intake, compression, power, and exhaust.

2. Engines are classified by number and arrangement of cylinders and by number and location of valves and camshafts, as well as by type of mounting, fuel used, cooling method, and induction pressure.

3. Engine size is called displacement and represents the volume displaced or swept by all of the pistons.

4. Engine power is expressed in horsepower, which is a calculated value based on the amount of torque or twisting force the engine produces.

5. The Atkinson cycle is used on most hybrid engines due to its greater efficiency.

6. Many inline hybrid engines use an offset crankshaft and low-friction pistons to reduce internal friction.

7. All hybrid engines use coil-on-plug ignition systems and the Honda Insight uses indexed spark plugs.

8. All hybrid engines use electronically controlled port fuel injection and some use gasoline direct injection.

9. Most hybrid electric vehicle use a wide-band oxygen sensor to help the engine achieve the lowest possible exhaust emissions.

REVIEW QUESTIONS

1. How does the Atkinson cycle differ from a conventional (Otto) four-stroke cycle?

2. What features are different between an engine used in a hybrid vehicle and the engine used in a conventional vehicle?

3. What is an indexed spark plug?

4. How does the changing of the valve timing or opening affect the engine?

5. What is the difference between port fuel injection and gasoline direct fuel injection?

6. What is the difference between a conventional oxygen sensor and a wide-band oxygen sensor?

CHAPTER QUIZ

1. Which is a characteristic of many hybrid electric vehicle (HEV) gasoline engines?
   a. Smaller in displacement
   b. Offset crankshaft
   c. Variable valve timing and/or displacement
   d. All of the above

2. A hybrid electric vehicle (HEV) gasoline engine usually uses what viscosity of engine oil?
   a. SAE 0W-20 or SAE 5W-20   b. SAE 5W-30
   c. SAE 10W-30   d. SAE 20W-50

3. Brake horsepower is calculated using which of the following?
   a. Torque times RPM
   b. 2π times stroke
   c. Torque times RPM divided by 5,252
   d. Stroke times bore times 3,300

4. Torque is expressed in units of _____.
   a. Pound-feet   b. Foot-pounds
   c. Foot-pounds per minute d. Pound-feet per second

5. Horsepower can also be expressed in units of _____.
   a. Pound-feet   b. Foot-pounds
   c. Foot-pounds per minute d. Pound-feet per second

6. Hybrid electric vehicle gasoline engines often use what systems to achieve maximum fuel economy?
   a. Returnless fuel delivery system
   b. Wide-band oxygen sensors
   c. Variable valve timing
   d. All of the above

7. The Atkinson cycle engine design _____.
   a. Requires special fuel and oil designed for this type of engine
   b. Operates differently than the normal four stoke cycle gasoline engine
   c. Uses the same four stroke cycle but delays the closing of the intake valve
   d. Both a and b are correct

8. A wide-band oxygen sensor is used to _____.
   a. Help the engine achieve a super ultra-low emission vehicle (SULEV) rating
   b. Help improve fuel economy by allowing the engine to operate at a lean air–fuel ratio
   c. Help the engine meet achieve ultra-low emission vehicle (ULEV) rating
   d. All of the above

9. The use of an offset crankshaft is used to _____.
   a. Improve power output of the engine
   b. To improve the fuel economy by reducing internal engine friction
   c. To reduce engine noise
   d. All of the above

10. One key way to improve fuel economy is to reduce pumping losses. What methods is used in many hybrid's to reduce pumping losses?
   a. Use the Atkinson cycle
   b. Use electronic throttle control (ETC)
   c. Use variable valve timing
   d. All of the above

chapter 4

GASOLINE

OBJECTIVES: **After studying Chapter 4, the reader will be able to:** • Describe how the proper grade of gasoline affects engine performance. • List gasoline purchasing hints. • Discuss how volatility affects driveability. • Explain how oxygenated fuels can reduce CO exhaust emissions. • Discuss safety precautions when working with gasoline.

KEY TERMS: • Air–fuel ratio 51 • Antiknock index (AKI) 52 • ASTM 49 • British thermal unit (BTU) 50 • Catalytic cracking 48 • Cracking 48 • Detonation 51 • Distillation 47 • Distillation curve 49 • Driveability index (DI) 49 • E10 54 • Ethanol 54 • Fungible 48 • Gasoline 47 • Hydrocracking 48 • Octane rating 51 • Oxygenated fuels 54 • Petroleum 47 • Ping 51 • Reformulated gasoline (RFG) 55 • RVP 49 • Spark knock 51 • Stoichiometric 51 • Tetraethyl lead (TEL) 52 • Vapor lock 49 • Volatility 49 • WWFC 57

GASOLINE

DEFINITION **Gasoline** is a term used to describe a complex mixture of various hydrocarbons refined from crude petroleum oil for use as a fuel in engines. Gasoline and air burns in the cylinder of the engine and produces heat and pressure which is transferred to rotary motion inside the engine and eventually powers the drive wheels of a vehicle. When combustion occurs, carbon dioxide and water are produced if the process is perfect and all of the air and all of the fuel are consumed in the process.

CHEMICAL COMPOSITION Gasoline is a combination of hydrocarbon molecules that have between five and 12 carbon atoms. The names of these various hydrocarbons are based on the number of carbon atoms and include:

- **Methane**—one carbon atom
- **Ethane**—two carbon atoms
- **Propane**—three carbon atoms
- **Butane**—four carbon atoms
- **Pentane**—five carbon atoms
- **Hexane**—six carbon atoms
- **Heptane**—seven carbon atoms (Used to test octane rating—has an octane rating of zero)
- **Octane**—eight carbon atoms (A type of octane is used as a basis for antiknock rating)

REFINING

TYPES OF CRUDE OIL Refining is a complex combination of interdependent processing units that can separate crude oil into useful products such as gasoline and diesel fuel. As it comes out of the ground, **petroleum** (meaning "rock oil") crude can be as thin and light colored as apple cider or as thick and black as melted tar. A barrel of crude oil is 42 gallons, not 55 gallons as commonly used for industrial barrels. Typical terms used to describe the type of crude oil include:

- Thin crude oil has a high American Petroleum Institute (API) gravity, and therefore, is called *high-gravity* crude.
- Thick crude oil is called *low-gravity* crude. High-gravity-type crude contains more natural gasoline and its lower sulfur and nitrogen content makes it easier to refine.
- Low-sulfur crude oil is also known as "sweet" crude.
- High-sulfur crude oil is also known as "sour" crude.

DISTILLATION In the late 1800s, crude was separated into different products by boiling, in a process called **distillation.** Distillation works because crude oil is composed of hydrocarbons with a broad range of boiling points.

In a distillation column, the vapor of the lowest-boiling hydrocarbons, propane and butane, rises to the top.

The straight-run gasoline (also called naphtha), kerosene, and diesel fuel cuts are drawn off at successively lower positions in the column.

CRACKING Cracking is the process where hydrocarbons with higher boiling points could be broken down (cracked) into lower-boiling hydrocarbons by treating them to very high temperatures. This process, called *thermal cracking*, was used to increase gasoline production starting in 1913.

Instead of high heat, today cracking is performed using a catalyst and is called **catalytic cracking.** A catalyst is a material that speeds up or otherwise facilitates a chemical reaction without undergoing a permanent chemical change itself. Catalytic cracking produces gasoline of higher quality than thermal cracking.

Hydrocracking is similar to catalytic cracking in that it uses a catalyst, but the catalyst is in a hydrogen atmosphere. Hydrocracking can break down hydrocarbons that are resistant to catalytic cracking alone, and it is used to produce diesel fuel rather than gasoline.

Other types of refining processes include:

- Reforming
- Alkylation
- Isomerization
- Hydrotreating
- Desulfurization

● **SEE FIGURE 4–1.**

SHIPPING The gasoline is transported to regional storage facilities by tank railway car or by pipeline. In the pipeline method, all gasoline from many refiners is often sent through the same pipeline and can become mixed. All gasoline is said to be **fungible,** meaning that it is capable of being interchanged because each grade is created to specification so there is no reason to keep the different gasoline brands separated except for grade. Regular grade, mid-grade, and premium grades are separated in the pipeline and the additives are added at the regional storage facilities and then shipped by truck to individual gas stations.

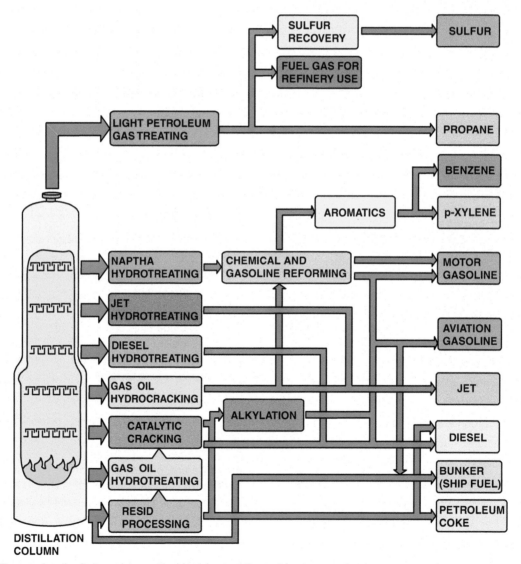

FIGURE 4–1 The crude oil refining process showing most of the major steps and processes.

VOLATILITY

DEFINITION OF VOLATILITY **Volatility** describes how easily the gasoline evaporates (forms a vapor). The definition of volatility assumes that the vapors will remain in the fuel tank or fuel line and will cause a certain pressure based on the temperature of the fuel.

REID VAPOR PRESSURE (RVP) **Reid vapor pressure (RVP)** is the pressure of the vapor above the fuel when the fuel is at 100°F (38°C). Increased vapor pressure permits the engine to start in cold weather. Gasoline without air will not burn. Gasoline must be vaporized (mixed with air) to burn in an engine. ● **SEE FIGURE 4–2.**

SEASONAL BLENDING Cold temperatures reduce the normal vaporization of gasoline; therefore, winter-blended gasoline is specially formulated to vaporize at lower temperatures for proper starting and driveability at low ambient temperatures. The **American Society for Testing and Materials (ASTM)** standards for winter-blend gasoline allow volatility of up to 15 pounds per square inch (PSI) RVP.

At warm ambient temperatures, gasoline vaporizes easily. However, the fuel system (fuel pump, carburetor, fuel-injector nozzles, etc.) is designed to operate with liquid gasoline. The volatility of summer-grade gasoline should be about 7.0 PSI RVP. According to ASTM standards, the maximum RVP should be 10.5 PSI for summer-blend gasoline.

DISTILLATION CURVE Besides Reid vapor pressure, another method of classifying gasoline volatility is the **distillation curve.** A curve on a graph is created by plotting the temperature at which the various percentage of the fuel evaporates. A typical distillation curve is shown in ● **FIGURE 4–3.**

DRIVEABILITY INDEX A distillation curve shows how much of a gasoline evaporates at what temperature range. To predict cold-weather driveability, an index was created called the **driveability index,** also called the *distillation index,* and abbreviated **DI.**

The DI was developed using the temperature for the evaporated percentage of 10% (labeled T10), 50% (labeled T50), and 90% (labeled T90). The formula for DI is:

$$DI = 1.5 \times T10 + 3 \times T50 + T90$$

The total DI is a temperature and usually ranges from 1000°F to 1200°F. The lower values of DI generally result in good cold-start and warm-up performance. A high DI number is less volatile than a low DI number.

NOTE: Most premium-grade gasoline has a higher (worse) DI than regular-grade or midgrade gasoline, which could cause poor cold-weather driveability. Vehicles designed to operate on premium-grade gasoline are programmed to handle the higher DI, but engines designed to operate on regular-grade gasoline may not be able to provide acceptable cold-weather driveability.

VOLATILITY-RELATED PROBLEMS At higher temperatures, liquid gasoline can easily vaporize, which can cause **vapor lock.** Vapor lock is a *lean* condition caused by vaporized fuel in the fuel system. This vaporized fuel takes up space normally occupied by liquid fuel. Bubbles that form in the fuel cause vapor lock, preventing proper operation of the fuel-injection system.

Heat causes some fuel to evaporate, thereby causing bubbles. Sharp bends cause the fuel to be restricted at the bend. When the fuel flows past the bend, the fuel can expand to fill the space after the bend. This expansion drops the pressure, and bubbles form in the fuel lines. When the fuel is full of bubbles, the engine is not being supplied with enough fuel and the engine runs lean. A lean engine will stumble during acceleration, will run rough, and may stall. Warm weather and alcohol-blended fuels both tend to increase vapor lock and engine performance problems.

If winter-blend gasoline (or high-RVP fuel) is used in an engine during warm weather, the following problems may occur:

1. Rough idle
2. Stalling
3. Hesitation on acceleration
4. Surging

FIGURE 4–2 A gasoline testing kit, including an insulated container where water at 100°F is used to heat a container holding a small sample of gasoline. The reading on the pressure gauge is the Reid vapor pressure (RVP).

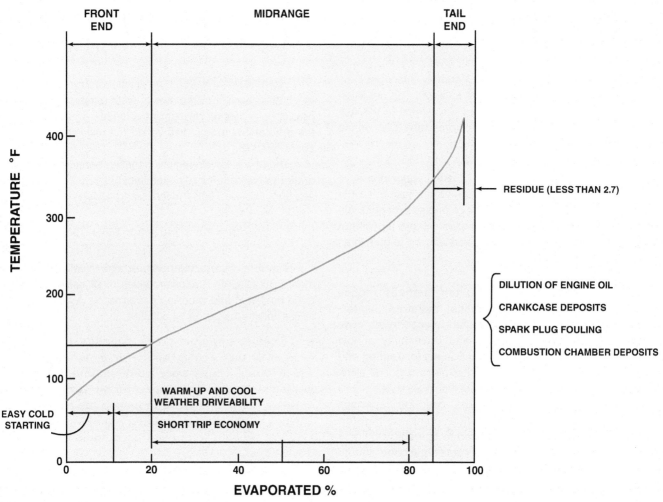

FIGURE 4–3 A typical distillation curve. Heavier molecules evaporate at higher temperatures and contain more heat energy for power, whereas the lighter molecules evaporate easier for starting.

 FREQUENTLY ASKED QUESTION

Why Do I Get Lower Gas Mileage in the Winter?

Several factors cause the engine to use more fuel in the winter than in the summer, including:

- Gasoline that is blended for use in cold climates is designed for ease of starting and contains fewer heavy molecules, which contribute to fuel economy. The heat content of winter gasoline is lower than summer-blended gasoline.
- In cold temperatures, all lubricants are stiff, causing more resistance. These lubricants include the engine oil, as well as the transmission and differential gear lubricants.
- Heat from the engine is radiated into the outside air more rapidly when the temperature is cold, resulting in longer run time until the engine has reached normal operating temperature.
- Road conditions, such as ice and snow, can cause tire slippage or additional drag on the vehicle.

GASOLINE COMBUSTION PROCESS

CHEMICAL REACTIONS The combustion process involves the chemical combination of oxygen (O_2) from the air (about 21% of the atmosphere) with the hydrogen and carbon from the fuel. In a gasoline engine, a spark starts the combustion process, which takes about 3 ms (0.003 sec) to be completed inside the cylinder of an engine. The chemical reaction that takes place can be summarized as follows: hydrogen (H) plus carbon (C) plus oxygen (O_2) plus nitrogen (N) plus spark equals heat plus water (H_2O) plus carbon monoxide (CO) (if incomplete combustion) plus carbon dioxide (CO_2) plus hydrocarbons (HC) plus oxides of nitrogen (NO_X) plus many other chemicals. In an equation format it looks like this:

$$H + C + O_2 + N + Spark = Heat + CO_2 + HC + NO_x$$

HEAT ENERGY The heat produced by the combustion process is measured in **British thermal units (BTUs).** One BTU is the amount of heat required to raise one pound of water

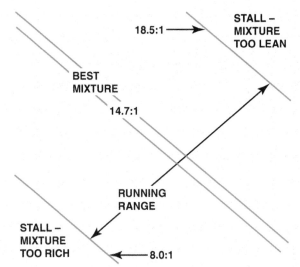

FIGURE 4–4 An engine will not run if the air–fuel mixture is either too rich or too lean.

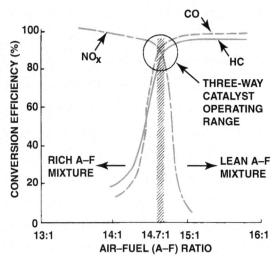

FIGURE 4–5 With a three-way catalytic converter, emission control is most efficient with an air–fuel ratio between 4.65 to 1 and 14.75 to 1.

one Fahrenheit degree. The metric unit of heat is the *calorie* (cal). One calorie is the amount of heat required to raise the temperature of one gram (g) of water one Celsius degree.

Gasoline—About 114,000 BTUs per gallon

AIR–FUEL RATIOS
Fuel burns best when the intake system turns it into a fine spray and mixes it with air before sending it into the cylinders. In fuel-injected engines, the fuel becomes a spray and mixes with the air in the intake manifold. There is a direct relationship between engine airflow and fuel requirements; this is called the **air–fuel ratio.**

The air–fuel ratio is the proportion by weight of air and gasoline that the injection system mixes as needed for engine combustion. The mixtures, with which an engine can operate without stalling, range from 8 to 1 to 18.5 to 1. ● SEE FIGURE 4–4.

These ratios are usually stated by weight, such as:

- 8 parts of air by weight combined with 1 part of gasoline by weight (8:1), which is the richest mixture that an engine can tolerate and still fire reliably.

- 18.5 parts of air mixed with 1 part of gasoline (18.5:1), which is the leanest practical ratio. Richer or leaner air–fuel ratios cause the engine to misfire badly or not run at all.

STOICHIOMETRIC AIR–FUEL RATIO
The ideal mixture or ratio at which all of the fuel combines with all of the oxygen in the air and burns completely is called the **stoichiometric** ratio, a chemically perfect combination. In theory, this ratio for gasoline is an air–fuel mixture of 14.7 to 1. ● SEE FIGURE 4–5.

In reality, the exact ratio at which perfect mixture and combustion occurs depends on the molecular structure of gasoline, which can vary. The stoichiometric ratio is a compromise between maximum power and maximum economy.

NORMAL AND ABNORMAL COMBUSTION

The **octane rating** of gasoline is the measure of its antiknock properties. *Engine knock* (also called **detonation, spark knock,** or **ping**) is a metallic noise an engine makes, usually during acceleration, resulting from abnormal or uncontrolled combustion inside the cylinder.

Normal combustion occurs smoothly and progresses across the combustion chamber from the point of ignition. ● SEE FIGURE 4–6.

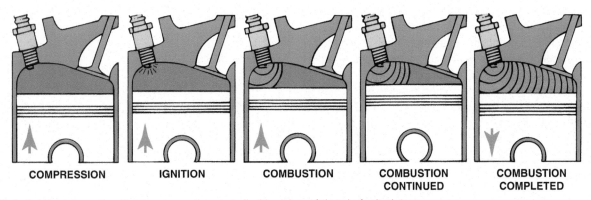

| COMPRESSION | IGNITION | COMBUSTION | COMBUSTION CONTINUED | COMBUSTION COMPLETED |

FIGURE 4–6 Normal combustion is a smooth, controlled burning of the air–fuel mixture.

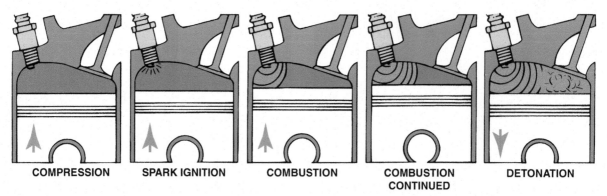

| COMPRESSION | SPARK IGNITION | COMBUSTION | COMBUSTION CONTINUED | DETONATION |

FIGURE 4–7 Detonation is a secondary ignition of the air–fuel mixture. It is also called spark knock or pinging.

Normal flame-front combustion travels between 45 and 90 mph (72 and 145 km/h). The speed of the flame front depends on air–fuel ratio, combustion chamber design (determining amount of turbulence), and temperature.

During periods of spark knock (detonation), the combustion speed increases by up to 10 times to near the speed of sound. The increased combustion speed also causes increased temperatures and pressures, which can damage pistons, gaskets, and cylinder heads. ● **SEE FIGURE 4–7.**

One of the first additives used in gasoline was **tetraethyl lead (TEL).** TEL was added to gasoline in the early 1920s to reduce the tendency to knock. It was often called ethyl or high-test gasoline.

OCTANE RATING

The antiknock standard or basis of comparison was the knock-resistant hydrocarbon isooctane, chemically called trimethyl-pentane (C_8H_{18}), also known as 2-2-4 trimethylpentane. If a gasoline tested had the exact same antiknock characteristics as isooctane, it was rated as 100-octane gasoline. If the gasoline tested had only 85% of the antiknock properties of isooctane, it was rated as 85 octane. Remember, octane rating is only a comparison test.

The two basic methods used to rate gasoline for antiknock properties (octane rating) are the *research method* and the *motor method*. Each uses a model of the special cooperative fuel research (CFR) single-cylinder engine. The research method and the motor method vary as to temperature of air, spark advance, and other parameters. The research method typically results in readings that are 6 to 10 points higher than those of the motor method. For example, a fuel with a research octane number (RON) of 93 might have a motor octane number (MON) of 85.

The octane rating posted on pumps in the United States is the average of the two methods and is referred to as (R + M) ÷ 2, meaning that, for the fuel used in the previous example, the rating posted on the pumps would be

$$\frac{RON + MON}{2} = \frac{93 + 85}{2} = 89$$

The pump octane is called the **antiknock index (AKI).**

FIGURE 4–8 A pump showing regular with a pump octane of 87, plus rated at 89, and premium rated at 93. These ratings can vary with brand as well as in different parts of the country.

GASOLINE GRADES AND OCTANE NUMBER The posted octane rating on gasoline pumps is the rating achieved by the average of the research and the motor methods. ● **SEE FIGURE 4–8.**

Except in high-altitude areas, the grades and octane ratings are as follows:

Grades	Octane rating
Regular	87
Midgrade (also called Plus)	89
Premium	91 or higher

? **FREQUENTLY ASKED QUESTION**

What Grade of Gasoline Does the EPA Use When Testing Engines?

Due to the various grades and additives used in commercial fuel, the government (EPA) uses a liquid called indolene. Indolene has a research octane number of 96.5 and a motor method octane rating of 88, which results in an R + M ÷ 2 rating of 92.25.

Horsepower and Fuel Flow

To produce 1 hp, the engine must be supplied with 0.50 lb of fuel per hour (lb/hr). Fuel injectors are rated in pounds per hour. For example, a V-8 engine equipped with 25 lb/hr fuel injectors could produce 50 hp per cylinder (per injector) or 400 hp. Even if the cylinder head or block is modified to produce more horsepower, the limiting factor may be the injector flow rate.

The following are flow rates and resulting horsepower for a V-8 engine:

30 lb/hr: 60 hp per cylinder or 480 hp
35 lb/hr: 70 hp per cylinder or 560 hp
40 lb/hr: 80 hp per cylinder or 640 hp

Of course, injector flow rate is only one of many variables that affect power output. Installing larger injectors without other major engine modification could decrease engine output and drastically increase exhaust emissions.

HIGH-ALTITUDE OCTANE REQUIREMENTS

As the altitude increases, atmospheric pressure drops. The air is less dense because a pound of air takes more volume. The octane rating of fuel does not need to be as high because the engine cannot take in as much air. This process will reduce the combustion (compression) pressures inside the engine. In mountainous areas, gasoline (R + M) ÷ 2 octane ratings are two or more numbers lower than normal (according to the SAE, about one octane number lower per 1,000 ft or 300 m in altitude). ● **SEE FIGURE 4–9.**

FIGURE 4–9 The posted octane rating in most high-altitude areas shows regular at 85 instead of the usual 87.

A secondary reason for the lowered octane requirement of engines running at higher altitudes is the normal enrichment of the air–fuel ratio and lower engine vacuum with the decreased air density. Some problems, therefore, may occur when driving out of high-altitude areas into lower-altitude areas where the octane rating must be higher. Most computerized engine control systems can compensate for changes in altitude and modify air–fuel ratio and ignition timing for best operation.

Because the combustion burn rate slows at high altitude, the ignition (spark) timing can be advanced to improve power. The amount of timing advance can be about 1 degree per 1,000 ft over 5,000 ft. Therefore, if driving at 8,000 ft of altitude, the ignition timing can be advanced 3 degrees.

High altitude also allows fuel to evaporate more easily. The volatility of fuel should be reduced at higher altitudes to prevent vapor from forming in sections of the fuel system, which can cause driveability and stalling problems. The extra heat generated in climbing to higher altitudes plus the lower atmospheric pressure at higher altitudes combine to cause vapor lock problems as the vehicle goes to higher altitudes.

GASOLINE ADDITIVES

DYE Dye is usually added to gasoline at the distributor to help identify the grade and/or brand of fuel. In many countries, fuels are required to be colored using a fuel-soluble dye. In the United States and Canada, diesel fuel used for off-road use and not taxed is required to be dyed red for identification. Gasoline sold for off-road use in Canada is dyed purple.

OCTANE IMPROVER ADDITIVES When gasoline companies, under federal EPA regulations, removed tetraethyl lead from gasoline, other methods were developed to help maintain the antiknock properties of gasoline. Octane improvers (enhancers) can be grouped into three broad categories:

1. Aromatic hydrocarbons (hydrocarbons containing the benzene ring) such as xylene and toluene
2. Alcohols such as ethanol (ethyl alcohol), methanol (methyl alcohol), and tertiary butyl alcohol (TBA)
3. Metallic compounds such as methylcyclopentadienyl manganese tricarbonyl (MMT)

NOTE: MMT has been proven to be harmful to catalytic converters and can cause spark plug fouling. However, MMT is currently one of the active ingredients commonly found in octane improvers available to the public and in some gasoline sold in Canada. If an octane boost additive has been used that contains MMT, the spark plug porcelain will be rust colored around the tip.

Propane and butane, which are volatile by-products of the refinery process, are also often added to gasoline as octane improvers. The increase in volatility caused by the added propane and butane often leads to hot-weather driveability problems.

Can Regular-Grade Gasoline Be Used If Premium Is the Recommended Grade?

Maybe. It is usually possible to use regular-grade or midgrade (plus) gasoline in most newer vehicles without danger of damage to the engine. Most vehicles built since the 1990s are equipped with at least one knock sensor. If a lower octane gasoline than specified is used, the engine ignition timing setting will usually cause the engine to spark knock, also called detonation or ping. This spark knock is detected by the knock sensor(s), which sends a signal to the computer. The computer then retards the ignition timing until the spark knock stops.

NOTE: Some scan tools will show the "estimated octane rating" of the fuel being used, which is based on knock sensor activity.

As a result of this spark timing retardation, the engine torque is reduced. While this reduction in power is seldom noticed, it will reduce fuel economy, often by 4 to 5 miles per gallon. If premium gasoline is then used, the PCM will gradually permit the engine to operate at the more advanced ignition timing setting. Therefore, it may take several tanks of premium gasoline to restore normal fuel economy. For best overall performance, use the grade of gasoline recommended by the vehicle manufacturer.

FIGURE 4–10 This fuel tank indicates that the gasoline is blended with 10% ethanol (ethyl alcohol) and can be used in any gasoline vehicle. E85 contains 85% ethanol and can only be used in vehicles specifically designed to use it.

FIGURE 4–11 A container with gasoline containing alcohol. Notice the separation line where the alcohol–water mixture separated from the gasoline and sank to the bottom.

OXYGENATED FUEL ADDITIVES **Oxygenated fuels** contain oxygen in the molecule of the fuel itself. Examples of oxygenated fuels include methanol, ethanol, methyl tertiary butyl ether (MTBE), tertiary-amyl methyl ether (TAME), and ethyl tertiary butyl ether (ETBE).

Oxygenated fuels are commonly used in high-altitude areas to reduce carbon monoxide (CO) emissions. The extra oxygen in the fuel itself is used to convert harmful CO into carbon dioxide (CO_2). The extra oxygen in the fuel helps ensure that there is enough oxygen to convert all CO into CO_2 during the combustion process in the engine or catalytic converter.

METHYL TERTIARY BUTYL ETHER (MTBE). MTBE is manufactured by means of the chemical reaction of methanol and isobutylene. Unlike methanol, MTBE does not increase the volatility of the fuel, and is not as sensitive to water as are other alcohols. The maximum allowable volume level, according to the EPA, is 15% but is currently being phased out due to health concerns, as well as MTBE contamination of drinking water if spilled from storage tanks.

TERTIARY-AMYL METHYL ETHER. Tertiary-amyl methyl ether (TAME) contains an oxygen atom bonded to two carbon atoms and is added to gasoline to provide oxygen to the fuel. It is

slightly soluble in water, very soluble in ethers and alcohol, and soluble in most organic solvents including hydrocarbons.

ETHYL TERTIARY BUTYL ETHER. ETBE is derived from ethanol. The maximum allowable volume level is 17.2%. The use of ETBE is the cause of much of the odor from the exhaust of vehicles using reformulated gasoline.

ETHANOL. **Ethanol,** also called *ethyl alcohol* is drinkable alcohol and is usually made from grain. Adding 10% ethanol (ethyl alcohol or grain alcohol) increases the $(R + M) \div 2$ octane rating by three points. The alcohol added to the base gasoline, however, also raises the volatility of the fuel about 0.5 PSI. Most automobile manufacturers permit up to 10% ethanol if driveability problems are not experienced.

The oxygen content of a 10% blend of ethanol in gasoline, called **E10**, is 3.5% oxygen by weight. ● **SEE FIGURE 4–10.**

Keeping the fuel tank full reduces the amount of air and moisture in the tank. ● **SEE FIGURE 4–11.**

What Is Meant by "Phase Separation"?

All alcohols absorb water, and the alcohol–water mixture can separate from the gasoline and sink to the bottom of the fuel tank. This process is called *phase separation*. To help avoid engine performance problems, try to keep at least a quarter tank of fuel at all times, especially during seasons when there is a wide temperature span between daytime highs and nighttime lows. These conditions can cause moisture to accumulate in the fuel tank as a result of condensation of the moisture in the air.

GASOLINE BLENDING

Gasoline additives, such as ethanol and dyes, are usually added to the fuel at the distributor. Adding ethanol to gasoline is a way to add oxygen to the fuel itself. Gasoline containing an addition that has oxygen is called *oxygenated fuel*. There are three basic methods used to blend ethanol with gasoline to create E10 (10% ethanol, 90% gasoline).

1. **In-line blending**—Gasoline and ethanol are mixed in a storage tank or in the tank of a transport truck while it is being filled. Because the quantities of each can be accurately measured, this method is most likely to produce a well-mixed blend of ethanol and gasoline. ● **SEE FIGURE 4–12.**

2. **Sequential blending**—This method is usually performed at the wholesale terminal and involves adding a measured amount of ethanol to a tank truck followed by a measured amount of gasoline. ● **SEE FIGURE 4–13.**

3. **Splash blending**—Splash blending can be done at the retail outlet or distributor and involves separate purchases of ethanol and gasoline. In a typical case, a distributor can purchase gasoline, and then drive to another supplier and purchase ethanol. The ethanol is then added (splashed) into the tank of gasoline. This method is the least-accurate method of blending and can result in ethanol concentration for E10 that should be 10% to range from 5% to over 20% in some cases. ● **SEE FIGURE 4–14.**

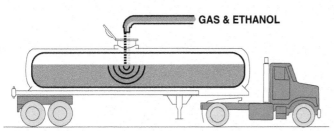

FIGURE 4–12 In-line blending is the most accurate method for blending ethanol with gasoline because computers are used to calculate the correct ratio.

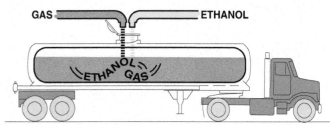

FIGURE 4–13 Sequential blending uses a computer to calculate the correct ratio as well as the prescribed order in which the products are loaded.

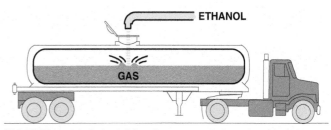

FIGURE 4–14 Splash blending occurs when the ethanol is added to a tanker with gasoline and is mixed as the truck travels to the retail outlet.

REFORMULATED GASOLINE

Reformulated gasoline (RFG) is manufactured to help reduce emissions. The gasoline refiners reformulate gasoline by using additives that contain at least 2% oxygen by weight and reducing the additive benzene to a maximum of 1% by volume. Two other major changes done at the refineries are as follows:

1. **Reduce light compounds.** Refineries eliminate butane, pentane, and propane, which have a low boiling point and evaporate easily. These unburned hydrocarbons are released into the atmosphere during refueling and through the fuel tank vent system, contributing to smog formation. Therefore, reducing the light compounds from gasoline helps reduce evaporative emissions.

2. **Reduce heavy compounds.** Refineries eliminate heavy compounds with high boiling points such as aromatics and olefins. The purpose of this reduction is to reduce the amount of unburned hydrocarbons that enter the catalytic converter, which makes the converter more efficient, thereby reducing emissions.

Because many of the heavy compounds are eliminated, a drop in fuel economy of about 1 mpg has been reported in areas where reformulated gasoline is being used. Formaldehyde is formed when RFG is burned, and the vehicle exhaust has a unique smell when reformulated gasoline is used.

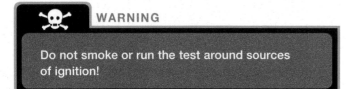
Is Water Heavier Than Gasoline?

Yes. Water weighs about 8 pounds per gallon whereas gasoline weighs about 6 pounds per gallon. The density as measured by specific gravity includes:

Water = 1.000 (the baseline for specific gravity)

Gasoline = 0.730 to 0.760

This means that any water that gets into the fuel tank will sink to the bottom.

TESTING GASOLINE FOR ALCOHOL CONTENT

Take the following steps when testing gasoline for alcohol content.

> ☠ **WARNING**
>
> Do not smoke or run the test around sources of ignition!

1. Pour suspect gasoline into a graduated cylinder.
2. Carefully fill the graduated cylinder to the 90-mL mark.
3. Add 10 mL of water to the graduated cylinder by counting the number of drops from an eyedropper.

4. Put the stopper in the cylinder and shake vigorously for 1 minute. Relieve built-up pressure by occasionally removing the stopper. Alcohol dissolves in water and will drop to the bottom of the cylinder.
5. Place the cylinder on a flat surface and let it stand for 2 minutes.
6. Take a reading near the bottom of the cylinder at the boundary between the two liquids.
7. For percent of alcohol in gasoline, subtract 10 from the reading and multiply by 10.

For example,

The reading is 20 mL: 20 − 10 = 10% alcohol

If the increase in volume is 0.2% or less, it may be assumed that the test gasoline contains no alcohol. ● **SEE FIGURE 4–15.** Alcohol content can also be checked using an electronic tester. See the step-by-step sequence at the end of the chapter.

GENERAL GASOLINE RECOMMENDATIONS

The fuel used by an engine is a major expense in the operation cost of the vehicle. The proper operation of the engine depends on clean fuel of the proper octane rating and vapor pressure for the atmospheric conditions.

To help ensure proper engine operation and keep fuel costs to a minimum, follow these guidelines:

1. Purchase fuel from a busy station to help ensure that it is fresh and less likely to be contaminated with water or moisture.

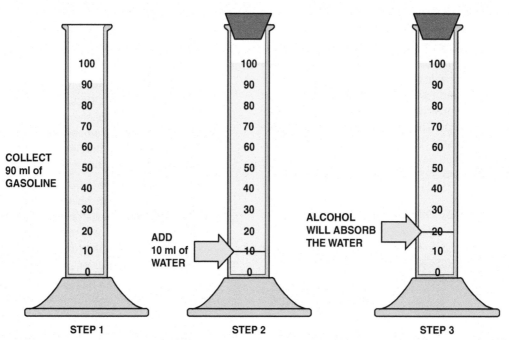

FIGURE 4–15 Checking gasoline for alcohol involves using a graduated cylinder and adding water to check if the alcohol absorbs the water.

How Does Alcohol Content in the Gasoline Affect Engine Operation?

In most cases, the use of gasoline containing 10% or less of ethanol (ethyl alcohol) has little or no effect on engine operation. However, because the addition of 10% ethanol raises the volatility of the fuel slightly, occasional rough idle or stalling may be noticed, especially during warm weather. The rough idle and stalling may also be noticeable after the engine is started, driven, then stopped for a short time. Engine heat can vaporize the alcohol-enhanced fuel causing bubbles to form in the fuel system. These bubbles in the fuel prevent the proper operation of the fuel injection system and result in a hesitation during acceleration, rough idle, or in severe cases repeated stalling until all the bubbles have been forced through the fuel system, replaced by cooler fuel from the fuel tank.

What Is "Top-Tier" Gasoline?

Top-tier gasoline is gasoline that has specific standards for quality, including enough detergent to keep all intake valves clean. Four automobile manufacturers, including BMW, General Motors, Honda, and Toyota, developed the standards. Top-tier gasoline exceeds the quality standards developed by the World Wide Fuel Charter (**WWFC**) that was established in 2002 by vehicle and engine manufacturers. The gasoline companies that agreed to make fuel that matches or exceeds the standards as a top-tier fuel include ChevronTexaco, Shell and ConocoPhillips. Ford has specified that BP fuel, sold in many parts of the country, is the recommended fuel to use in Ford vehicles. ● **SEE FIGURE 4–16.**

2. Keep the fuel tank above one-quarter full, especially during seasons in which the temperature rises and falls by more than 20°F between daytime highs and nighttime lows. This helps to reduce condensed moisture in the fuel tank and could prevent gas line freeze-up in cold weather.

FIGURE 4–16 The gas cap on a Ford vehicle notes that BP fuel is recommended.

NOTE: Gas line freeze-up occurs when the water in the gasoline freezes and forms an ice blockage in the fuel line.

3. Do not purchase fuel with a higher octane rating than is necessary. Use midgrade (plus) or premium if specified and required by the vehicle manufacturer. Most newer engines are equipped with a detonation (knock) sensor that signals the vehicle computer to retard the ignition timing when spark knock occurs. Therefore, an operating difference may not be noticeable to the driver when using a low-octane fuel, except for a decrease in power and fuel economy. In other words, the engine with a knock sensor will tend to operate knock free on regular fuel, even if premium, higher-octane fuel is specified.

4. Avoid using gasoline with alcohol in warm weather, even though many alcohol blends do not affect engine drive-ability. If warm-engine stumble, stalling, or rough idle occurs, change brands of gasoline.

5. Do not purchase fuel from a retail outlet when a tanker truck is filling the underground tanks. During the refilling procedure, dirt, rust, and water may be stirred up in the underground tanks. This undesirable material may be pumped into your vehicle's fuel tank.

6. Do not overfill the gas tank. After the nozzle clicks off, add just enough fuel to round up to the next dime. Adding additional gasoline will cause the excess to be drawn into the charcoal canister. This can lead to engine flooding and excessive exhaust emissions.

7. Be careful when filling gasoline containers. Always fill a gas can on the ground to help prevent the possibility of static electricity buildup during the refueling process. ● **SEE FIGURE 4–17.**

Why Should I Keep the Fuel Gauge Above One-Quarter Tank?

The fuel pickup inside the fuel tank can help keep water from being drawn into the fuel system unless water is all that is left at the bottom of the tank. Over time, moisture in the air inside the fuel tank can condense, causing liquid water to drop to the bottom of the fuel tank (water is heavier than gasoline—about 8 lb per gallon for water and about 6 lb per gallon for gasoline). If alcohol-blended gasoline is used, the alcohol can absorb the water and the alcohol–water combination can be burned inside the engine. However, when water combines with alcohol, a separation layer occurs between the gasoline at the top of the tank and the alcohol–water combination at the bottom. When the fuel level is low, the fuel pump will draw from this concentrated level of alcohol and water. Because alcohol and water do not burn as well as pure gasoline, severe driveability problems can occur such as stalling, rough idle, hard starting, and missing.

FIGURE 4–17 Many gasoline service stations have signs posted warning customers to place plastic fuel containers on the ground while filling. If placed in a trunk or pickup truck bed equipped with a plastic liner, static electricity could build up during fueling and discharge from the container to the metal nozzle, creating a spark and possible explosion. Some service stations have warning signs not to use cell phones while fueling to help avoid the possibility of an accidental spark creating a fire hazard.

 **TECH TIP**

Do Not Overfill the Fuel Tank

Gasoline fuel tanks have an expansion volume area at the top. The volume of this expansion area is equal to 10% to 15% of the volume of the tank. This area is normally not filled with gasoline, but rather is designed to provide a place for the gasoline to expand into, if the vehicle is parked in the hot sun and the gasoline expands. This prevents raw gasoline from escaping from the fuel system. A small restriction is usually present to control the amount of air and vapors that can escape the tank and flow to the charcoal canister.

This volume area could be filled with gasoline if the fuel is slowly pumped into the tank. Since it can hold an extra 10% (2 gallons in a 20-gallon tank), some people deliberately try to fill the tank completely. When this expansion volume is filled, liquid fuel (rather than vapors) can be drawn into the charcoal canister. When the purge valve opens, liquid fuel can be drawn into the engine, causing an excessively rich air–fuel mixture. Not only can this liquid fuel harm vapor recovery parts, but overfilling the gas tank could also cause the vehicle to fail an exhaust emission test, particularly during an enhanced test when the tank could be purged while on the rollers.

 **TECH TIP**

The Sniff Test

Problems can occur with stale gasoline from which the lighter parts of the gasoline have evaporated. Stale gasoline usually results in a no-start situation. If stale gasoline is suspected, sniff it. If it smells rancid, replace it with fresh gasoline.

NOTE: If storing a vehicle, boat, or lawnmower over the winter, put some gasoline stabilizer into the gasoline to reduce the evaporation and separation that can occur during storage. Gasoline stabilizer is frequently available at lawnmower repair shops or marinas.

1 A fuel composition tester (SPX Kent-Moore J-44175) is the recommended tool, by General Motors, to use to test the alcohol content of gasoline.

2 This battery-powered tester uses light-emitting diodes (LEDs), meter lead terminals, and two small openings for the fuel sample.

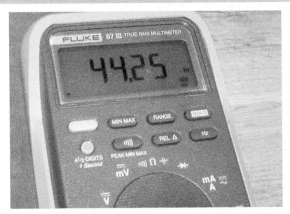

3 The first step is to verify the proper operation of the tester by measuring the air frequency by selecting AC hertz on the meter. The air frequency should be between 35 Hz and 48 Hz.

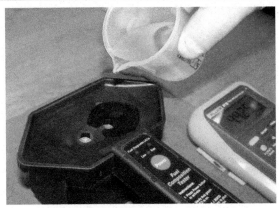

4 After verifying that the tester is capable of correctly reading the air frequency, gasoline is poured into the testing cell of the tool.

5 Record the AC frequency as shown on the meter and subtract 50 from the reading (e.g., 60.50 − 50.00 = 10.5). This number (10.5) is the percentage of alcohol in the gasoline sample.

6 Adding additional amounts of ethyl alcohol (ethanol) increases the frequency reading.

SUMMARY

1. Gasoline is a complex blend of hydrocarbons. Gasoline is blended for seasonal usage to achieve the correct volatility for easy starting and maximum fuel economy under all driving conditions.

2. Winter-blend fuel used in a vehicle during warm weather can cause a rough idle and stalling because of its higher Reid vapor pressure (RVP).

3. Abnormal combustion (also called detonation or spark knock) increases both the temperature and the pressure inside the combustion chamber.

4. Most regular-grade gasoline today, using the (R + M) ÷ 2 rating method, is 87 octane; midgrade (plus) is 89; and premium grade is 91 or higher.

5. Oxygenated fuels contain oxygen to lower CO exhaust emissions.

6. Gasoline should always be purchased from a busy station, and the tank should not be overfilled.

REVIEW QUESTIONS

1. What is the difference between summer-blend and winter-blend gasoline?

2. What is Reid vapor pressure?

3. What is vapor lock?

4. What does the (R + M) ÷ 2 gasoline pump octane rating indicate?

5. What are the octane improvers that may be used during the refining process?

6. What is stoichiometric?

CHAPTER QUIZ

1. Winter-blend gasoline _____.
   a. Vaporizes more easily than summer-blend gasoline
   b. Has a higher RVP
   c. Can cause engine driveability problems if used during warm weather
   d. All of the above

2. Vapor lock can occur _____.
   a. As a result of excessive heat near fuel lines
   b. If a fuel line is restricted
   c. During both a and b
   d. During neither a nor b

3. Technician A says that spark knock, ping, and detonation are different names for abnormal combustion. Technician B says that any abnormal combustion raises the temperature and pressure inside the combustion chamber and can cause severe engine damage. Which technician is correct?
   a. Technician A only
   b. Technician B only
   c. Both Technicians A and B
   d. Neither Technician A nor B

4. Technician A says that the research octane number is higher than the motor octane number. Technician B says that the octane rating posted on fuel pumps is an average of the two ratings. Which technician is correct?
   a. Technician A only
   b. Technician B only
   c. Both Technicians A and B
   d. Neither Technician A nor B

5. Technician A says that in going to high altitudes, engines produce lower power. Technician B says that most engine control systems can compensate the air–fuel mixture for changes in altitude. Which technician is correct?
   a. Technician A only
   b. Technician B only
   c. Both Technicians A and B
   d. Neither Technician A nor B

6. Which method of blending ethanol with gasoline is the most accurate?
   a. In-line
   b. Sequential
   c. Splash
   d. All of the above are equally accurate methods

7. What can be used to measure the alcohol content in gasoline?
   a. graduated cylinder
   b. electronic tester
   c. scan tool
   d. either a or b

8. To avoid problems with the variation of gasoline, all government testing uses _____ as a fuel during testing procedures.
   a. MTBE (methyl tertiary butyl ether)
   b. Indolene
   c. Xylene
   d. TBA (tertiary butyl alcohol)

9. Avoid topping off the fuel tank because _____.
   a. It can saturate the charcoal canister
   b. The extra fuel simply spills onto the ground
   c. The extra fuel increases vehicle weight and reduces performance
   d. The extra fuel goes into the expansion area of the tank and is not used by the engine

10. Using ethanol-enhanced or reformulated gasoline can result in reduced fuel economy.
    a. True
    b. False

chapter 5

ALTERNATIVE FUELS

OBJECTIVES: **After studying Chapter 5, the reader will be able to:** • Describe how alternative fuels affect engine performance. • List alternatives to gasoline. • Discuss how alternative fuels affect fuel economy. • Discuss how to identify a flex fuel vehicle. • Discuss safety precautions when working with alternative fuels.

KEY TERMS: • AFV 63 • Anhydrous ethanol 62 • Biomass 67 • Cellulose ethanol 62 • Cellulosic biomass 62 • Coal to liquid (CTL) 71 • Compressed natural gas (CNG) 68 • E85 62 • Ethanol 61 • Ethyl alcohol 61 • FFV 63 • Fischer-Tropsch 71 • Flex Fuels 63 • FTD 71 • Fuel compensation sensor 63 • Gas to liquid (GTL) 71 • Grain alcohol 61 • Liquid petroleum gas (LPG) 67 • LP-gas 67 • M85 67 • Methanol 67 • Methanol to gasoline (MTG) 71 • NGV 68 • Propane 67 • Switchgrass 62 • Syncrude 71 • Syn-gas 67 • Synthetic fuel 71 • Underground coal gasification (UCG) 71 • V-FFV 64 • Variable fuel sensor 63

ETHANOL

ETHANOL TERMINOLOGY **Ethanol** is also called **ethyl alcohol** or **grain alcohol,** because it is usually made from grain and is the type of alcohol found in alcoholic drinks such as beer, wine, and distilled spirits like whiskey. Ethanol is composed of two carbon atoms and six hydrogen atoms with one added oxygen atom. ● **SEE FIGURE 5–1.**

ETHANOL PRODUCTION Conventional ethanol is derived from grains, such as corn, wheat, or soybeans. Corn, for example, is converted to ethanol in either a dry or wet milling process. In dry milling operations, liquefied cornstarch is produced by heating cornmeal with water and enzymes. A second enzyme converts the liquefied starch to sugars, which are fermented by yeast into ethanol and carbon dioxide. Wet milling operations separate the fiber, germ (oil), and protein from the starch before it is fermented into ethanol.

 FREQUENTLY ASKED QUESTION

Does Ethanol Production Harm the Environment?

The production of ethanol is referred to as being *carbon neutral* because the amount of CO_2 released during production is equal to the amount of CO_2 that would be released if the corn or other products were left to decay.

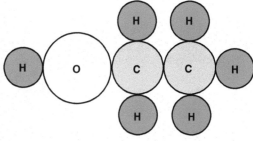

FIGURE 5–1 The ethanol molecule showing two carbon atoms, six hydrogen atoms, and one oxygen atom.

The majority of the ethanol in the United States is made from:

- Corn
- Grain
- Sorghum
- Wheat
- Barley
- Potatoes

In Brazil, the world's largest ethanol producer, it is made from sugarcane. Ethanol can be made by the dry mill process in which the starch portion of the corn is fermented into sugar and then distilled into alcohol.

The major steps in the dry mill process include:

1. **Milling.** The feedstock passes through a hammer mill that turns it into a fine powder called *meal*.

2. **Liquefaction.** The meal is mixed with water and then passed through cookers where the starch is liquefied. Heat is applied at this stage to enable liquefaction. Cookers use

a high-temperature stage of about 250°F to 300°F (120°C to 150°C) to reduce bacteria levels and then a lower temperature of about 200°F (95°C) for a holding period.

3. **Saccharification.** The mash from the cookers is cooled and a secondary enzyme is added to convert the liquefied starch to fermentable sugars (dextrose).

4. **Fermentation.** Yeast is added to the mash to ferment the sugars to ethanol and carbon dioxide.

5. **Distillation.** The fermented mash, now called beer, contains about 10% alcohol plus all the nonfermentable solids from the corn and yeast cells. The mash is pumped to the continuous-flow, distillation system where the alcohol is removed from the solids and the water. The alcohol leaves the top of the final column at about 96% strength, and the residue mash, called *silage*, is transferred from the base of the column to the co-product processing area.

6. **Dehydration.** The alcohol from the top of the column passes through a dehydration system where the remaining water will be removed. The alcohol product at this stage is called **anhydrous ethanol** (pure, no more than 0.5% water).

7. **Denaturing.** Ethanol that will be used for fuel must be denatured, or made unfit for human consumption, with a small amount of gasoline (2% to 5%), methanol, or denatonium benzoate. This is done at the ethanol plant.

CELLULOSE ETHANOL

TERMINOLOGY   **Cellulose ethanol** can be produced from a wide variety of cellulose biomass feedstock, including:

- Agricultural plant wastes (corn stalks, cereal straws)
- Plant wastes from industrial processes (sawdust, paper pulp)
- Energy crops grown specifically for fuel production.

These nongrain products are often referred to as **cellulosic biomass.** Cellulosic biomass is composed of cellulose and lignin, with smaller amounts of proteins, lipids (fats, waxes, and oils), and ash. About two-thirds of cellulosic materials are present as cellulose, with lignin making up the bulk of the remaining dry mass.

REFINING CELLULOSE BIOMASS   As with grains, processing cellulose biomass involves extracting fermentable sugars from the feedstock. But the sugars in cellulose are locked in complex carbohydrates called polysaccharides (long chains of simple sugars). Separating these complex structures into fermentable sugars is needed to achieve the efficient and economic production of cellulose ethanol.

Two processing options are employed to produce fermentable sugars from cellulose biomass:

- Acid hydrolysis is used to break down the complex carbohydrates into simple sugars.
- Enzymes are employed to convert the cellulose biomass to fermentable sugars. The final step involves microbial fermentation, yielding ethanol and carbon dioxide.

NOTE: Cellulose ethanol production substitutes biomass for fossil fuels. The greenhouse gases produced by the combustion of biomass are offset by the CO_2 absorbed by the biomass as it grows in the field.

E85

WHAT IS E85?   Vehicle manufacturers have available vehicles that are capable of operating on gasoline plus ethanol or a combination of gasoline and ethanol called **E85.** E85 is composed of 85% ethanol and 15% gasoline.

Pure ethanol has an octane rating of about 113. E85, which contains 35% oxygen by weight, has an octane rating of about 100 to 105. This compares to a regular unleaded gasoline which has a rating of 87. ● **SEE FIGURE 5–2.**

NOTE: The octane rating of E85 depends on the exact percent of ethanol used, which can vary from 81% to 85%. It also depends on the octane rating of the gasoline used to make E85.

HEAT ENERGY OF E85   E85 has less heat energy than gasoline.

Gasoline = 114,000 BTUs per gallon
E85 = 87,000 BTUs per gallon

This means that the fuel economy is reduced by 20% to 30% if E85 is used instead of gasoline.

FIGURE 5–2 Some retail stations offer a variety of fuel choices, such as this station in Ohio where E10 and E85 are available.

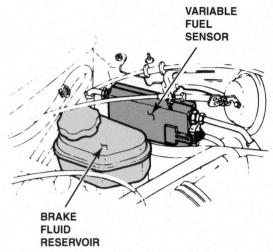

FIGURE 5–3 The location of the variable fuel sensor can vary, depending on the make and model of vehicle, but it is always in the fuel line between the fuel tank and the fuel injectors.

Example: A Chevrolet Tahoe 5.3-liter V-8 with an automatic transmission has an EPA rating of 15 mpg in the city and 20 mpg on the highway when using gasoline. If this same vehicle was fueled with E85, the EPA fuel economy rating drops to 11 mpg in the city and 15 mpg on the highway.

ALTERNATIVE-FUEL VEHICLES

The 15% gasoline in this blend helps the engine start, especially in cold weather. Vehicles equipped with this capability are commonly referred to as **alternative-fuel vehicles (AFVs)**, **Flex Fuels,** and **flexible fuel vehicles,** or **FFVs.** Using E85 in a flex-fuel vehicle can result in a power increase of about 5%. For example, an engine rated at 200 hp using gasoline or E10 could produce 210 hp if using E85.

NOTE: E85 may test as containing less than 85% ethanol if tested in cold climates because it is often blended according to outside temperature. A lower percentage of ethanol with a slightly higher percentage of gasoline helps engines start in cold climates.

These vehicles are equipped with an electronic sensor in the fuel supply line that detects the presence and percentage of ethanol. The PCM then adjusts the fuel injector on-time and ignition timing to match the needs of the fuel being used.

E85 contains less heat energy, and therefore will use more fuel, but the benefits include a lower cost of the fuel and the environmental benefit associated with using an oxygenated fuel.

General Motors, Ford, Chrysler, Mazda, and Honda are a few of the manufacturers offering E85 compatible vehicles. E85 vehicles use fuel system parts designed to withstand the

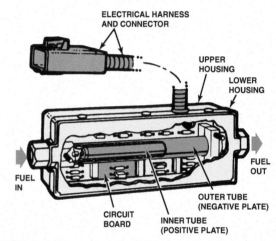

FIGURE 5–4 A cutaway view of a typical variable fuel sensor.

additional alcohol content, modified driveability programs that adjust fuel delivery and timing to compensate for the various percentages of ethanol fuel, and a **fuel compensation sensor** that measures both the percentage of ethanol blend and the temperature of the fuel. This sensor is also called a **variable fuel sensor.** ● SEE FIGURES 5–3 AND 5–4.

E85 FUEL SYSTEM REQUIREMENTS Most E85 vehicles are very similar to non-E85 vehicles. Fuel system components may be redesigned to withstand the effects of higher concentrations of ethanol. In addition, since the stoichiometric point for ethanol is 9:1 instead of 14.7:1 as for gasoline, the air–fuel mixture has to be adjusted for the percentage of ethanol present in the fuel tank. In order to determine this percentage of ethanol in the fuel tank, a compensation sensor is used. The fuel compensation sensor is the only additional piece of hardware required on some E85 vehicles. The fuel compensation sensor provides both the ethanol percentage and the fuel temperature to the PCM.

Purchase a Flex-Fuel Vehicle

If purchasing a new or used vehicle, try to find a flex-fuel vehicle. Even though you may not want to use E85, a flex-fuel vehicle has a more robust fuel system than a conventional fuel system designed for gasoline or E10. The enhanced fuel system components and materials usually include:

- Stainless steel fuel rail
- Graphite commutator bars instead of copper in the fuel pump motor (ethanol can oxidize into acetic acid, which can corrode copper)
- Diamond-like carbon (DLC) corrosion-resistant fuel injectors
- Alcohol-resistant O-rings and hoses

The cost of a flex-fuel vehicle compared with the same vehicle designed to operate on gasoline is a no-cost or a low-cost option.

FIGURE 5–5 A pump for E85 (85% ethanol and 15% gasoline). E85 is available in more locations every year.

FREQUENTLY ASKED QUESTION

How Does a Sensorless Flex-Fuel System Work?

Many General Motors flex-fuel vehicles do not use a fuel compensation sensor and instead use the oxygen sensor to detect the presence of the lean mixture and the extra oxygen in the fuel.

The Powertrain Control Module (PCM) then adjusts the injector pulse-width and the ignition timing to optimize engine operation to the use of E85. This type of vehicle is called a **virtual flexible fuel vehicle,** abbreviated **V-FFV.** The virtual flexible fuel vehicle can operate on pure gasoline or blends up to 85% ethanol.

The benefits of E85 vehicles are less pollution, less CO_2 production, and less dependence on oil. ● **SEE FIGURE 5–5.**

Ethanol-fueled vehicles generally produce the same pollutants as gasoline vehicles; however, they produce less CO and CO_2 emissions. While CO_2 is not considered a pollutant, it is thought to lead to global warming and is called a greenhouse gas.

FLEX-FUEL VEHICLE IDENTIFICATION   Flexible fuel vehicles (FFVs) can be identified by:

- Emblems on the side, front, and/or rear of the vehicle
- Yellow fuel cap showing E85/gasoline (● **SEE FIGURE 5–6**)
- Vehicle emission control information (VECI) label under the hood (● **SEE FIGURE 5–7**)
- Vehicle identification number (VIN)

Vehicles that are flexible fuel include:

Chrysler

2004+

- 4.7L Dodge Ram Pickup 1500 Series
- 2.7L Dodge Stratus Sedan
- 2.7L Chrysler Sebring Sedan
- 3.3L Caravan and Grand Caravan SE

2003–2004

- 2.7L Dodge Stratus Sedan
- 2.7L Chrysler Sebring Sedan

2003

- 3.3L Dodge Cargo Minivan

The PCM uses this information to adjust both the ignition timing and the quantity of fuel delivered to the engine. The fuel compensation sensor uses a microprocessor to measure both the ethanol percentage and the fuel temperature. This information is sent to the PCM on the signal circuit. The compensation sensor produces a square wave frequency and pulse width signal. The normal frequency range of the fuel compensation sensor is 50 hertz, which represents 0% ethanol and 150 hertz, which represents 100% ethanol. The pulse width of the signal varies from 1 millisecond to 5 milliseconds. One millisecond would represent a fuel temperature of –40°F (–40°C), and 5 milliseconds would represent a fuel temperature of 257°F (125°C). Since the PCM knows both the fuel temperature and the ethanol percentage of the fuel, it can adjust fuel quantity and ignition timing for optimum performance and emissions.

2000–2003

- 3.3L Chrysler Voyager Minivan
- 3.3L Dodge Caravan Minivan 3.3L Chrysler Town and Country Minivan

1998–1999

- 3.3L Dodge Caravan Minivan
- 3.3L Plymouth Voyager Minivan
- 3.3L Chrysler Town & Country Minivan

Ford Motor Company

*Ford offers the flex fuel capability as an option on select vehicles—see the owner's manual.

2004+

- 4.0L Explorer Sport Trac
- 4.0L Explorer (4-door)
- 3.0L Taurus Sedan and Wagon

2002–2004

- 4.0L Explorer (4-door)
- 3.0L Taurus Sedan and Wagon

2002–2003

- 3.0L Supercab Ranger Pickup 2WD

2001

- 3.0L Supercab Ranger Pickup 2WD
- 3.0L Taurus LX, SE, and SES Sedan

1999–2000

- 3.0L Ranger Pickup 4WD and 2WD

General Motors

*Select vehicles only—see your owner's manual.

2005+

- 5.3L Vortec-Engine Avalanche
- 5.3L Vortec-Engine Police Package Tahoe

2003–2005

- 5.3L V8 Chevy Silverado* and GMC Sierra* Half-Ton Pickups 2WD and 4WD
- 5.3L Vortec-Engine Suburban, Tahoe, Yukon, and Yukon XL

2002

- 5.3L V8 Chevy Silverado* and GMC Sierra* Half-Ton Pickups 2WD and 4WD
- 5.3L Vortec-Engine Suburban, Tahoe, Yukon, and Yukon XL
- 2.2L Chevy S10 Pickup 2WD

2000–2001

- 2.2L Chevy S10 Pickup 2WD
- 2.2L GMC Sonoma Pickup 2WD

Isuzu

2000–2001

- 2.2L Hombre Pickup 2WD

Mazda

1999–2003

- 3.0L Selected B3000 Pickups

Mercedes-Benz

2005+

- 2.6L C240 Luxury Sedan and Wagon

2003

- 3.2L C320 Sport Sedan and Wagon

Mercury

2002–2004

- 4.0L Selected Mountaineers

2000–2004

- 3.0L Selected Sables

Nissan

2005+

- 5.6L DOHC V8 Engine

*Select vehicles only—see the owner's manual or VECI sticker under the hood.

 **TECH TIP**

Avoid Resetting Fuel Compensation

Starting in 2006, General Motors vehicles designed to operate on E85 do not use a fuel compensation sensor, but instead use the oxygen sensor and refueling information to calculate the percentage of ethanol in the fuel. The PCM uses the fuel level sensor to sense that fuel has been added and starts to determine the resulting ethanol content by using the oxygen sensor. However, if a service technician were to reset fuel compensation by clearing long-term fuel trim, the PCM starts the calculation based on base fuel, which is gasoline with less than or equal to 10% ethanol (E10). If the fuel tank has E85, then the fuel compensation cannot be determined unless the tank is drained and refilled with base fuel. Therefore, avoid resetting the fuel compensation setting unless it is known that the fuel tank contains gasoline or E10 only.

FIGURE 5–6 A flex-fuel vehicle often has a yellow gas cap, which is labeled E85/gasoline.

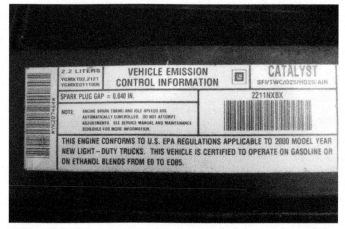

FIGURE 5–7 A vehicle emission control information (VECI) sticker on a flexible fuel vehicle indicating that it can use ethanol from 0 to 85%.

HOW TO READ A VEHICLE IDENTIFICATION NUMBER

The vehicle identification number (VIN) is required by federal regulation to contain specific information about the vehicle. The following chart shows the character in the eighth position of the VIN number from Ford Motor Company, General Motors, and Chrysler that designates their vehicles as flexible fuel vehicles.

Ford Motor Company

Vehicle	8th Character
Ford Crown Victoria	V
Ford F-150	V
Ford Explorer	K
Ford Ranger	V
Ford Taurus	2
Lincoln Town Car	V
Mercury Mountaineer	K
Mercury Sable	2
Mercury Grand Marquis	V

General Motors

Vehicle	8th Character
Chevrolet Avalanche	Z
Chevrolet Impala	K
Chevrolet Monte Carlo	K
Chevrolet S-10 Pickup	5
Chevrolet Sierra	Z
Chevrolet Suburban	Z
Chevrolet Tahoe	Z
GMC Yukon and Yukon XL	Z
GMC Silverado	Z
GMC Sonoma	5

Chrysler

Vehicle	8th Character
Chrysler Sebring	T
Chrysler Town & Country	E, G or 3
Dodge Caravan	E, G or 3
Dodge Cargo Minivan	E, G or 3
Dodge Durango	P
Dodge Ram	P
Dodge Stratus	T
Plymouth Voyager	E, G or 3

Mazda

Vehicle	8th Character
B3000 Pickup	V

Nissan

Vehicle	4th Character
Titan	B

Mercedes Benz

Check owner's manual or the VECI sticker under the hood.

NOTE: For additional information on E85 and for the location of E85 stations in your area, go to www.e85fuel.com.

 FREQUENTLY ASKED QUESTION

How Long Can Oxygenated Fuel Be Stored Before All of the Oxygen Escapes?

The oxygen in oxygenated fuels, such as E10 and E85, is not in a gaseous state like the CO_2 in soft drinks. The oxygen is part of the molecule of ethanol or other oxygenates and does not bubble out of the fuel. Oxygenated fuels, just like any fuel, have a shelf life of about 90 days.

METHANOL

METHANOL TERMINOLOGY   **Methanol,** also known as *methyl alcohol, wood alcohol,* or *methyl hydrate,* is a chemical compound formula that includes one carbon atom and four hydrogen atoms and one oxygen. ● **SEE FIGURE 5–8.**

Methanol is a light, volatile, colorless, tasteless, flammable, poisonous liquid with a very faint odor. It is used as an antifreeze, a solvent, and a fuel. It is also used to denature ethanol. Methanol burns in air, forming CO_2 (carbon dioxide) and H_2O (water). A methanol flame is almost colorless. Because of its poisonous properties, methanol is also used to denature ethanol. Methanol is often called wood alcohol because it was once produced chiefly as a by-product of the destructive distillation of wood. ● **SEE FIGURE 5–9.**

PRODUCTION OF METHANOL   The biggest source of methanol in the United States is coal. Using a simple reaction between coal and steam, a gas mixture called **syn-gas** (*synthesis gas*) is formed. The components of this mixture are carbon monoxide and hydrogen, which, through an additional chemical reaction, are converted to methanol.

Natural gas can also be used to create methanol and is re-formed or converted to synthesis gas, which is later made into methanol.

Biomass can be converted to synthesis gas by a process called partial oxidation, and later converted to methanol. **Biomass** is organic material, such as:

- Urban wood wastes
- Primary mill residues
- Forest residues
- Agricultural residues
- Dedicated energy crops (e.g., sugarcane and sugar beets) that can be made into fuel

Electricity can be used to convert water into hydrogen, which is then reacted with carbon dioxide to produce methanol.

Methanol is toxic and can cause blindness and death. It can enter the body by ingestion, inhalation, or absorption through the skin. Dangerous doses will build up if a person is regularly exposed to fumes or handles liquid without skin protection. If methanol has been ingested, a doctor should be contacted immediately. The usual fatal dose is 4 fl oz (100 to 125 mL).

M85   Some flexible fuel vehicles are designed to operate on 85% methanol and 15% gasoline called **M85.** Methanol is very corrosive and requires that the fuel system components be constructed of stainless steel and other alcohol-resistant rubber and plastic components. The heat content of M85 is about 60% of that of gasoline.

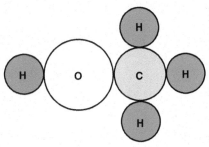

FIGURE 5–8 The molecular structure of methanol showing the one carbon atom, four hydrogen atoms, and one oxygen atom.

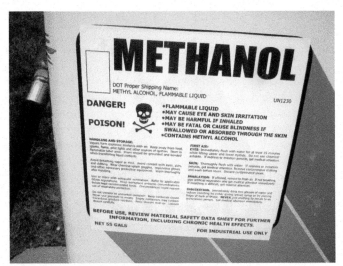

FIGURE 5–9 Sign on methanol pump shows that methyl alcohol is a poison and can cause skin irritation and other personal injury. Methanol is used in industry as well as being a fuel.

PROPANE

Propane is the most widely used of all of the alternative fuels. Propane is normally a gas but is easily compressed into a liquid and stored in inexpensive containers. When sold as a fuel, it is also known as **liquefied petroleum gas (LPG)** or **LP-gas** because the propane is often mixed with about 10% of other gases such as butane, propylene, butylenes, and mercaptan to give the colorless and odorless propane a smell. Propane is nontoxic, but if inhaled can cause asphyxiation through lack of oxygen. Propane is heavier than air and lays near the floor if released into the atmosphere. Propane is commonly used in forklifts and other equipment used inside warehouses and factories because the exhaust from the engine using propane is not harmful. Propane is a by-product of petroleum refining of natural gas. In order to liquefy the fuel, it is stored in strong tanks at about 300 PSI (2,000 kPa). The heating value of propane is less than that of gasoline; therefore, more is required, which reduces the fuel economy. ● **SEE FIGURE 5–10.**

FIGURE 5–10 Propane fuel storage tank in the trunk of a Ford taxi.

FIGURE 5–11 The blue sticker on the rear of this vehicle indicates that it is designed to use compressed natural gas.

COMPRESSED NATURAL GAS

CNG VEHICLE DESIGN Another alternative fuel that is often used in fleet vehicles is **compressed natural gas, or CNG,** and vehicles using this fuel are often referred to as **natural gas vehicles (NGVs).** Look for the blue CNG label on vehicles designed to operate on compressed natural gas. ● **SEE FIGURE 5–11.**

Natural gas has to be compressed to about 3,000 PSI (20,000 kPa) or more, so that the weight and the cost of the storage container is a major factor when it comes to preparing a vehicle to run on CNG. The tanks needed for CNG are typically constructed of 0.5-inch-thick (3 mm) aluminum reinforced with fiberglass. ● **SEE FIGURE 5–12.** The octane rating of CNG is about 130 and the cost per gallon is about half of the cost of gasoline. However, the heat value of CNG is also less, and therefore more is required to produce the same power and the miles per gallon is less.

CNG COMPOSITION Compressed natural gas is made up of a blend of:

- Methane
- Propane
- Ethane
- N-butane
- Carbon dioxide
- Nitrogen

Once it is processed, it is at least 93% methane. Natural gas is nontoxic, odorless, and colorless in its natural state. It is odorized during processing, using ethyl mercaptan ("skunk"), to allow for easy leak detection. Natural gas is lighter than air and will rise when released into the air. Since CNG is already a vapor, it does not need heat to vaporize before it will burn,

FIGURE 5–12 A CNG storage tank from a Honda Civic GX shown with the fixture used to support it while it is being removed or installed in the vehicle. Honda specifies that three technicians be used to remove or install the tank through the rear door of the vehicle due to the size and weight of the tank.

which improves cold start-up and results in lower emissions during cold operation. However, because it is already in a gaseous state, it does displace some of the air charge in the intake manifold. This leads to about a 10% reduction in engine power as compared to an engine operating on gasoline. Natural gas also burns slower than gasoline; therefore, the ignition timing must be advanced more when the vehicle operates on natural gas. The stoichiometric ratio, the point at which all the air and fuel is used or burned is 16.5:1 compared to 14.7:1 for gasoline. This means that more air is required to burn one pound of natural gas than is required to burn one pound of gasoline. ● **SEE FIGURE 5–13.**

The CNG engine is designed to include:

- Increased compression ratio
- Strong pistons and connecting rods
- Heat-resistant valves
- Fuel injectors designed for gaseous fuel instead of liquid fuel

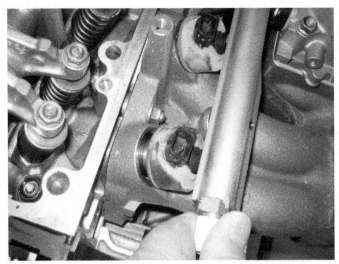

FIGURE 5–13 The fuel injectors used on this Honda Civic GX CNG engine are designed to flow gaseous fuel instead of liquid fuel and cannot be interchanged with any other type of injector.

FIGURE 5–14 This CNG pump is capable of supplying compressed natural gas at either 3,000 PSI or 3,600 PSI. The price per gallon is higher for the higher pressure.

 FREQUENTLY ASKED QUESTION

What Is the Amount of CNG Equal to in Gasoline?

To achieve the amount of energy of one gallon of gasoline, 122 cubic feet of compressed natural gas (CNG) is needed. While the octane rating of CNG is much higher than gasoline (130 octane), using CNG instead of gasoline in the same engine would result in a reduction 10% to 20% of power due to the lower heat energy that is released when CNG is burned in the engine.

CNG FUEL SYSTEMS When completely filled, the CNG tank has 3,600 PSI of pressure in the tank. When the ignition is turned on, the alternate fuel electronic control unit activates the high-pressure lock-off, which allows high-pressure gas to pass to the high-pressure regulator. The high-pressure regulator reduces the high-pressure CNG to approximately 170 PSI and sends it to the low-pressure lock-off. The low-pressure lock-off is also controlled by the alternate fuel electronic control unit and is activated at the same time that the high-pressure lock-off is activated. From the low-pressure lock-off, the CNG is directed to the low-pressure regulator. This is a two-stage regulator that first reduces the pressure to approximately 4 to 6 PSI in the first stage and then to 4.5 to 7 inches of water in the second stage. Twenty-eight inches of water is equal to 1 PSI, therefore, the final pressure of the natural gas entering the engine is very low. From here, the low-pressure gas is delivered t`o the gas mass sensor/mixture control valve. This valve controls the air–fuel mixture. The CNG gas distributor adapter then delivers the gas to the intake stream.

CNG vehicles are designed for fleet use that usually have their own refueling capabilities. One of the drawbacks to using CNG is the time that it takes to refuel a vehicle. The ideal method of refueling is the slow fill method. The slow filling method compresses the natural gas as the tank is being fueled. This method ensures that the tank will receive a full charge

of CNG; however, this method can take three to five hours to accomplish. If more than one vehicle needs filling, the facility will need multiple CNG compressors to refuel the vehicles.

There are three commonly used CNG refilling station pressures:

P24—2,400 PSI

P30—3,000 PSI

P36—3,600 PSI

Try to find and use a station with the highest refilling pressure. Filling at lower pressures will result in less compressed natural gas being installed in the storage tank, thereby reducing the driving range. ● **SEE FIGURE 5–14.**

The fast fill method uses CNG that is already compressed. However, as the CNG tank is filled rapidly, the internal temperature of the tank will rise, which causes a rise in tank pressure. Once the temperature drops in the CNG tank, the pressure in the tank also drops, resulting in an incomplete charge in the CNG tank. This refueling method may take only about five minutes; however, it will result in an incomplete charge to the CNG tank, reducing the driving range.

LIQUEFIED NATURAL GAS

Natural gas can be turned into a liquid if cooled to below –260°F (–127°C). The natural gas condenses into a liquid at normal atmospheric pressure and the volume is reduced by about 600 times. This means that the natural gas can be more efficiently transported over long distances where no pipelines are present when liquefied.

Because the temperature of liquefied natural gas (LNG) must be kept low, it is only practical for use in short haul trucks where they can be refueled from a central location.

P-SERIES FUELS

P-series alternative fuel is patented by Princeton University and is a non-petroleum- or natural gas-based fuel suitable for use in flexible fuel vehicles or any vehicle designed to operate on E85 (85% ethanol, 15% gasoline). P-series fuel is recognized by the United States Department of Energy as being an alternative fuel, but is not yet available to the public. P-series fuels are blends of the following:

- Ethanol (ethyl alcohol)
- Methyltetrahydrofuron, abbreviated MTHF
- Natural gas liquids, such as pentanes
- Butane

The ethanol and MTHF are produced from renewable feedstocks, such as corn, waste paper, biomass, agricultural waste, and wood waste (scraps and sawdust). The components used in P-type fuel can be varied to produce regular grade, premium grade, or fuel suitable for cold climates. ● **SEE CHART 5–1** for the percentages of the ingredients based on fuel grade.

● **SEE CHART 5–2** for a comparison of the most frequently used alternative fuels.

COMPOSITION OF P-SERIES FUELS (BY VOLUME)			
COMPONENT	REGULAR GRADE (%)	PREMIUM GRADE (%)	COLD WEATHER (%)
Pentanes plus	32.5	27.5	16.0
MTHF	32.5	17.5	26.0
Ethanol	35.0	55.0	47.0
Butane	0.0	0.0	11.0

CHART 5–1

P-series fuel varies in composition, depending on the octane rating and temperature.

 FREQUENTLY ASKED QUESTION

What Is a Tri-Fuel Vehicle?

In Brazil, most vehicles are designed to operate on ethanol or gasoline or any combination of the two. In this South American country, ethanol is made from sugarcane, is commonly available, and is lower in price than gasoline. Compressed natural gas (CNG) is also being made available so many vehicle manufacturers in Brazil, such as General Motors and Ford, are equipping vehicles to be capable of using gasoline, ethanol, or CNG. These vehicles are called tri-fuel vehicles.

ALTERNATIVE FUEL COMPARISON CHART					
CHARACTERISTIC	PROPANE	CNG	METHANOL	ETHANOL	REGULAR UNLEADED GAS
Octane	104	130	100	100	87–93
BTU per gallon	91,000	N.A.	70,000	83,000	114,000–125,000
Gallon equivalent	1.15	122 cubic feet—1 gallon of gasoline	1.8	1.5	1
On-board fuel storage	Liquid	Gas	Liquid	Liquid	Liquid
Miles/gallon as compared to gas	85%	N.A.	55%	70%	100%
Relative tank size required to yield driving range equivalent to gas	Tank is 1.25 times larger	Tank is 3.5 times larger	Tank is 1.8 times larger	Tank is 1.5 times larger	
Pressure	200 PSI	3,000–3,600 PSI	N.A.	N.A.	N.A.
Cold weather capability	Good	Good	Poor	Poor	Good
Vehicle power	5–10% power loss	10–20% power loss	4% power increase	5% power increase	Standard
Toxicity	Nontoxic	Nontoxic	Highly toxic	Toxic	Toxic
Corrosiveness	Noncorrosive	Noncorrosive	Corrosive	Corrosive	Minimally corrosive
Source	Natural gas/petroleum refining	Natural gas/crude oil	Natural gas/coal	Sugar and starch crops/biomass	Crude oil

CHART 5–2

The characteristics of alternative fuels compared to regular unleaded gasoline shows that all have advantages and disadvantages.

SYNTHETIC FUELS

Synthetic fuels can be made from a variety of products, using several different processes. Synthetic fuel must, however, make these alternatives practical only when conventional petroleum products are either very expensive or not available.

FISCHER-TROPSCH   Synthetic fuels were first developed using the **Fischer-Tropsch** method and have been in use since the 1920s to convert coal, natural gas, and other fossil fuel products into a fuel that is high in quality and clean-burning. The process for producing Fischer-Tropsch fuels was patented by two German scientists, Franz Fischer and Hans Tropsch, during World War I. The Fischer-Tropsch method uses carbon monoxide and hydrogen (the same synthesis gas used to produce hydrogen fuel) to convert coal and other hydrocarbons to liquid fuels in a process similar to hydrogenation, another method for hydrocarbon conversion. The process using natural gas, also called **gas-to-liquid (GTL)** technology, uses a catalyst, usually iron or cobalt, and incorporates steam re-forming to give off the by-products of carbon dioxide, hydrogen, and carbon monoxide. ●**SEE FIGURE 5–15.**

Whereas traditional fuels emit environmentally harmful particulates and chemicals, namely sulfur compounds, Fischer-Tropsch fuels combust with no soot or odors and emit only low levels of toxins. Fischer-Tropsch fuels can also be blended with traditional transportation fuels with little equipment modification, as they use the same engine and equipment technology as traditional fuels.

The fuels contain a very low sulfur and aromatic content and they produce virtually no particulate emissions. Researchers also expect reductions in hydrocarbon and carbon monoxide emissions. Fischer-Tropsch fuels do not differ in fuel performance from gasoline and diesel. At present, Fischer-Tropsch fuels are very expensive to produce on a large scale, although research is under way to lower processing costs. Diesel fuel created using the Fischer-Tropsch diesel (**FTD**) process is often called *GTL diesel*. GTL diesel can also be combined with petroleum diesel to produce a GTL blend. This fuel product is currently being sold in Europe and plans are in place to introduce it in North America.

COAL TO LIQUID (CTL)   Coal is very abundant in the United States and coal can be converted to a liquid fuel through a process called **coal to liquid (CTL).** The huge cost is the main obstacle to these plants. The need to invest $1.4 billion per plant before it can make product is the reason no one has built a CTL plant yet in the United States. Investors need to be convinced that the cost of oil is going to remain high in order to get them to commit this kind of money.

A large plant might be able to produce 120,000 barrels of liquid fuel a day and would consume about 50,000 tons of coal per day. However, such a plant would create about 6,000 tons of CO_2 per day. These CO_2 emissions, which could contribute to global warming, and the cost involved make CTL a technology that is not likely to expand.

Two procedures can be used to convert coal-to-liquid fuel:

1. **Direct**—In the direct method, coal is broken down to create liquid products. First the coal is reacted with hydrogen (H_2) at high temperatures and pressure with a catalyst. This process creates a synthetic crude, called **syncrude,** which is then refined to produce gasoline or diesel fuel.

2. **Indirect**—In the indirect method, coal is first turned into a gas and the molecules are reassembled to create the desired product. This process involves turning coal into a gas called syn-gas. The syngas is then converted into liquid, using the Fischer-Tropsch (FT) process.

Russia has been using CTL by injecting air into the underground coal seams. Ignition is provided and the resulting gases are trapped and converted to liquid gasoline and diesel fuel through the Fischer-Tropsch process. This underground method is called **underground coal gasification (UCG).**

METHANOL TO GASOLINE   Exxon Mobil has developed a process for converting methanol (methyl alcohol) into gasoline in a process called **methanol-to-gasoline (MTG).** The MTG

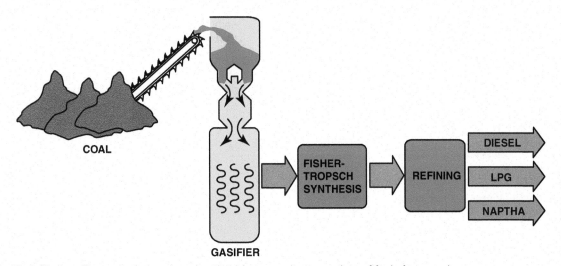

FIGURE 5–15 A Fischer-Tropsch processing plant is able to produce a variety of fuels from coal.

process was discovered by accident when a gasoline additive made from methanol was being created. The process instead created olefins (alkenes), paraffins (alkenes), and aromatic compounds, which in combination are known as gasoline. The process uses a catalyst and is currently being produced in New Zealand.

FUTURE OF SYNTHETIC FUELS Producing gasoline and diesel fuels by other methods besides refining from crude oil has usually been more expensive. With the increasing cost of crude oil, alternative methods are now becoming economically feasible. Whether or not the diesel fuel or gasoline is created from coal, natural gas, or methanol, or created by refining crude oil, the transportation and service pumps are already in place. Compared to using compressed natural gas or other similar alternative fuels, synthetic fuels represent the lowest cost.

SAFETY PROCEDURES WHEN WORKING WITH ALTERNATIVE FUELS

All fuels are flammable and many are explosive under certain conditions. Whenever working around compressed gases of any kind (CNG, LNG, propane, or LPG), always wear personal protective equipment (PPE), including at least the following items:

1. Safety glasses and/or face shield.
2. Protective gloves.
3. Long-sleeved shirt and pants to help protect bare skin from the freezing effects of gases under pressure in the event that the pressure is lost.
4. If any fuel gets on the skin, the area should be washed immediately.
5. If fuel spills on clothing, change into clean clothing as soon as possible.
6. If fuel spills on a painted surface, flush the surface with water and air dry. If simply wiped off with a dry cloth, the paint surface could be permanently damaged.
7. As with any fuel-burning vehicle, always vent the exhaust to the outside. If methanol fuel is used, the exhaust contains *formaldehyde*, which has a sharp odor and can cause severe burning of the eyes, nose, and throat.

WARNING

Do not smoke or have an open flame in the area when working around or refueling any vehicle.

SUMMARY

1. Flexible fuel vehicles (FFVs) are designed to operate on gasoline or gasoline-ethanol blends up to 85% ethanol (E85).
2. Ethanol can be made from grain, such as corn, or from cellulosic biomass, such as switchgrass.
3. E85 has fewer BTUs of energy per gallon compared with gasoline and will therefore provide lower fuel economy.
4. Older flexible fuel vehicles used a fuel compensation sensor but newer models use the oxygen sensor to calculate the percentage of ethanol in the fuel being burned.
5. Methanol is also called methyl alcohol or wood alcohol and, while it can be made from wood, it is mostly made from natural gas.
6. Propane is the most widely used alternative fuel. Propane is also called liquefied petroleum gas (LPG).

7. Compressed natural gas (CNG) is available for refilling in several pressures, including 2,400 PSI, 3,000 PSI, and 3,600 PSI.
8. P-series fuel is recognized by the United States Department of Energy as being an alternative fuel. P-series fuel is a non-petroleum-based fuel suitable for use in a flexible fuel vehicle. However, P-series fuel is not commercially available.
9. Synthetic fuels are usually made using the Fischer-Tropsch method to convert coal or natural gas into gasoline and diesel fuel.
10. Safety procedures when working around alternative fuel include wearing the necessary personal protective equipment (PPE), including safety glasses and protective gloves.

REVIEW QUESTIONS

1. Ethanol is also known by what other terms?
2. The majority of ethanol in the United States is made from what farm products?
3. How is a flexible fuel vehicle identified?
4. Methanol is also known by what other terms?
5. What other gases are often mixed with propane?

6. Why is it desirable to fill a compressed natural gas (CNG) vehicle with the highest pressure available?
7. P-series fuel is made of what products?
8. The Fischer-Tropsch method can be used to change what into gasoline?

1. Ethanol can be produced from what products?
   a. Switchgrass   b. Corn
   c. Sugarcane   **d. Any of the above**

2. E85 means that the fuel is made from _____.
   a. 85% gasoline, 15% ethanol
   b. 85% ethanol, 15% gasoline
   c. Ethanol that has 15% water
   d. Pure ethyl alcohol

3. A flex-fuel vehicle can be identified by _____.
   a. Emblems on the side, front, and/or rear of the vehicle
   b. VECI
   c. VIN
   d. Any of the above

4. Methanol is also called _____.
   a. Methyl alcohol   b. Wood alcohol
   c. Methyl hydrate   **d. All of the above**

5. Which alcohol is dangerous (toxic)?
   a. Methanol
   b. Ethanol
   c. Both ethanol and methanol
   d. Neither ethanol nor methanol

6. Which is the most widely used alternative fuel?
   a. E85   b. Propane
   c. CNG   d. M85

7. Liquefied petroleum gas (LPG) is also called _____.
   a. E85   b. M85
   c. Propane   d. P-series fuel

8. How much compressed natural gas (CNG) does it require to achieve the energy of one gallon of gasoline?
   a. 130 cubic feet   **b. 122 cubic feet**
   c. 105 cubic feet   d. 91 cubic feet

9. When refueling a CNG vehicle, why is it recommended that the tank be filled to a high pressure?
   a. The range of the vehicle is increased
   b. The cost of the fuel is lower
   c. Less of the fuel is lost to evaporation
   d. Both a and c

10. Producing liquid fuel from coal or natural gas usually uses which process?
    a. Syncrude   b. P-series
    c. Fischer-Tropsch   d. Methanol to gasoline (MTG)

DIESEL AND BIODIESEL FUELS

OBJECTIVES: **After studying Chapter 6, the reader will be able to:** • Explain diesel fuel specifications. • List the advantages and disadvantages of biodiesel. • Discuss API gravity. • Explain E-diesel specifications.

KEY TERMS: • API gravity 75 • ASTM 74 • B20 77 • Biodiesel 76 • Cetane number 74 • Cloud point 74 • Diesohol 78 • E-diesel 78 • Petrodiesel 77 • PPO 77 • SVO 77 • UCO 77 • ULSD 76 • WVO 77

DIESEL FUEL

FEATURES OF DIESEL FUEL Diesel fuel must meet an entirely different set of standards than gasoline. Diesel fuel contains 12% more heat energy than the same amount of gasoline. The fuel in a diesel engine is not ignited with a spark, but is ignited by the heat generated by high compression. The pressure of compression (400 to 700 PSI or 2,800 to 4,800 kilopascals) generates temperatures of 1200°F to 1600°F (700°C to 900°C), which speeds the preflame reaction to start the ignition of fuel injected into the cylinder.

DIESEL FUEL REQUIREMENTS All diesel fuel must have the following characteristics:

- **Cleanliness.** It is imperative that the fuel used in a diesel engine be clean and free from water. Unlike the case with gasoline engines, the fuel is the lubricant and coolant for the diesel injector pump and injectors. Good-quality diesel fuel contains additives such as oxidation inhibitors, detergents, dispersants, rust preventatives, and metal deactivators.

- **Low-temperature fluidity.** Diesel fuel must be able to flow freely at all expected ambient temperatures. One specification for diesel fuel is its "pour point," which is the temperature below which the fuel would stop flowing.

- **Cloud point** is another concern with diesel fuel at lower temperatures. Cloud point is the low-temperature point when the waxes present in most diesel fuels tend to form crystals that can clog the fuel filter. Most diesel fuel suppliers distribute fuel with the proper pour point and cloud point for the climate conditions of the area.

CETANE NUMBER The cetane number for diesel fuel is the opposite of the octane number for gasoline. The **cetane number** is a measure of the ease with which the fuel can be ignited. The cetane rating of the fuel determines, to a great extent, its ability to start the engine at low temperatures and to provide smooth warm-up and even combustion. The cetane rating of diesel fuel should be between 45 and 50. The higher the cetane rating, the more easily the fuel is ignited.

SULFUR CONTENT The sulfur content of diesel fuel is very important to the life of the engine. Sulfur in the fuel creates sulfuric acid during the combustion process, which can damage engine components and cause piston ring wear. Federal regulations are getting extremely tight on sulfur content to less than 15 parts per million (PPM). High-sulfur fuel contributes to acid rain.

DIESEL FUEL COLOR Diesel fuel intended for use on the streets and highways is clear or green in color. Diesel fuel to be used on farms and off-road use is dyed red. ● **SEE FIGURE 6–1.**

GRADES OF DIESEL FUEL **American Society for Testing Materials (ASTM)** also classifies diesel fuel by volatility (boiling range) into the following grades:

GRADE #1 This grade of diesel fuel has the lowest boiling point and the lowest cloud and pour points, as well as a lower BTU content—less heat per pound of fuel. As a result, grade #1 is suitable for use during low-temperature (winter) operation. Grade #1 produces less heat per pound of fuel compared to grade #2 and may be specified for use in diesel engines involved in frequent changes in load and speed, such as those found in city buses and delivery trucks.

(a)

(b)

FIGURE 6–1 (a) Regular diesel fuel on the left has a clear or greenish tint, whereas fuel for off-road use is tinted red for identification. (b) A fuel pump in a farming area that clearly states the red diesel fuel is for off-road use only.

GRADE #2 This grade has a higher boiling point, cloud point, and pour point as compared with grade #1. It is usually specified where constant speed and high loads are encountered, such as in long-haul trucking and automotive diesel applications. Most diesel is Grade #2.

DIESEL FUEL SPECIFIC GRAVITY TESTING The density of diesel fuel should be tested whenever there is a driveability concern. The density or specific gravity of diesel fuel is measured in units of **API gravity.** API gravity is an arbitrary scale expressing the gravity or density of liquid petroleum products devised jointly by the American Petroleum Institute and the National Bureau of Standards. The measuring scale is calibrated in terms of degrees API. Oil with the least specific gravity has the highest API gravity. The formula for determining API gravity is as follows:

Degrees API gravity = (141.5 ÷ specific gravity at 60°F) − 131.5

FIGURE 6–2 Testing the API viscosity of a diesel fuel sample using a hydrometer.

The normal API gravity for #1 diesel fuel is 39 to 44 (typically 40). The normal API gravity for #2 diesel fuel is 30 to 39 (typically 35). A hydrometer calibrated in API gravity units should be used to test diesel fuel. ● **SEE FIGURE 6–2.**

● **SEE CHART 6–1** for a comparison among specific gravity, weight density, pounds per gallon, and API gravity of diesel fuel.

DIESEL FUEL HEATERS Diesel fuel heaters, either coolant or electric, help prevent power loss and stalling in cold weather. The heater is placed in the fuel line between the tank

? FREQUENTLY ASKED QUESTION

How Can You Tell If Gasoline Has Been Added to the Diesel Fuel by Mistake?

If gasoline has been accidentally added to diesel fuel and is burned in a diesel engine, the result can be very damaging to the engine. The gasoline can ignite faster than diesel fuel, which would tend to increase the temperature of combustion. This high temperature can harm injectors and glow plugs, as well as pistons, head gaskets, and other major diesel engine components. If contaminated fuel is suspected, first smell the fuel at the filler neck. If the fuel smells like gasoline, then the tank should be drained and refilled with diesel fuel. If the smell test does not indicate a gasoline smell (or any rancid smell), then test a sample for proper API gravity.

NOTE: Diesel fuel designed for on-road use should be green in color. Red diesel fuel (high sulfur) should only be found in off-road or farm equipment.

API GRAVITY COMPARISON CHART
Values for API Scale Oil

API GRAVITY SCALE	SPECIFIC GRAVITY	WEIGHT DENSITY, LB/FT	POUNDS PER GALLON
0			
2			
4			
6			
8			
10	1.0000	62.36	8.337
12	0.9861	61.50	8.221
14	0.9725	60.65	8.108
16	0.9593	59.83	7.998
18	0.9465	59.03	7.891
20	0.9340	58.25	7.787
22	0.9218	57.87	7.736
24	0.9100	56.75	7.587
26	0.8984	56.03	7.490
28	0.8871	55.32	7.396
30	0.8762	54.64	7.305
32	0.8654	53.97	7.215
34	0.8550	53.32	7.128
36	0.8448	52.69	7.043
38	0.8348	51.06	6.960
40	0.8251	50.96	6.879
42	0.8155	50.86	6.799
44	0.8030	50.28	6.722
46	0.7972	49.72	6.646
48	0.7883	49.16	6.572
50	0.7796	48.62	6.499
52	0.7711	48.09	6.429
54	0.7628	47.57	6.359
56	0.7547	47.07	6.292
58	0.7467	46.57	6.225
60	0.7389	46.08	6.160
62	0.7313	45.61	6.097
64	0.7238	45.14	6.034
66	0.7165	44.68	5.973
68	0.7093	44.23	5.913
70	0.7022	43.79	5.854
72	0.6953	43.36	5.797
74	0.6886	42.94	5.741
76	0.6819	42.53	5.685
78	0.6754	41.12	5.631
80	0.6690	41.72	5.577
82	0.6628	41.33	5.526
84	0.6566	40.95	5.474
86	0.6506	40.57	5.424
88	0.6446	40.20	5.374
90	0.6388	39.84	5.326
92	0.6331	39.48	5.278
94	0.6275	39.13	5.231
96	0.6220	38.79	5.186
98	0.6116	38.45	5.141
100	0.6112	38.12	5.096

CHART 6–1

The API gravity scale is based on the specific gravity of the fuel.

FIGURE 6–3 An electrical resistance heater coil in the air inlet on a General Motors 6.5-liter V-8 diesel engine used to warm the air entering the engine.

and the primary filter. Some coolant heaters are thermostatically controlled, which allows fuel to bypass the heater once it has reached operating temperature. ● **SEE FIGURE 6–3.**

ULTRA-LOW-SULFUR DIESEL FUEL Diesel fuel is used in diesel engines and is usually readily available throughout the United States, Canada, and Europe, where many more cars are equipped with diesel engines. Diesel engines manufactured to 2007 or newer standards must use ultra-low-sulfur diesel fuel containing less than 15 parts per million (PPM) of sulfur compared to the older, low-sulfur specification of 500 PPM. The purpose of the lower sulfur amount in diesel fuel is to reduce emissions of sulfur oxides (SO_x) and particulate matter (PM) from heavy-duty highway engines and vehicles that use diesel fuel. The emission controls used on 2007 and newer diesel engines require the use of **ultra-low-sulfur diesel (ULSD)** for reliable operation.

Ultra-low-sulfur diesel (ULSD) will eventually replace the current highway diesel fuel, low-sulfur diesel, which can have as much as 500 PPM of sulfur. ULSD is required for use in all model year 2007 and newer vehicles equipped with advanced emission control systems. ULSD looks lighter in color and has less smell than other diesel fuel.

BIODIESEL

DEFINITION OF BIODIESEL **Biodiesel** is a domestically produced, renewable fuel that can be manufactured from vegetable oils, animal fats, or recycled restaurant greases. Biodiesel is safe, biodegradable, and reduces serious air pollutants such as particulate matter (PM), carbon monoxide, and hydrocarbons. Biodiesel is defined as mono-alkyl esters of long-chain fatty acids derived from vegetable oils or animal fats which conform to A STM D6751 specifications for use in diesel engines. Biodiesel refers to the pure fuel before blending with diesel fuel. ● **SEE FIGURE 6–4.**

FIGURE 6–4 A pump decal indicating that the biodiesel fuel is ultra-low-sulfur diesel (ULSD) and must be used in 2007 and newer diesel vehicles.

BIODIESEL BLENDS Biodiesel blends are denoted as "BXX" with "XX" representing the percentage of biodiesel contained in the blend (i.e., **B20** is 20% biodiesel, 80% petroleum diesel). Blends of 20% biodiesel with 80% petroleum diesel (B20) can generally be used in unmodified diesel engines; however, users should consult their OEM and engine warranty statement. Biodiesel can also be used in its pure form (B100), but it may require certain engine modifications to avoid maintenance and performance problems and may not be suitable for wintertime use. Most diesel engine or vehicle manufacturers of diesel vehicles allow the use of B5 (5% biodiesel). For example, Cummins, used in Dodge trucks, allows the use of B20 only if the optional extra fuel filter has been installed. Users should consult their engine warranty statement for more information on fuel blends of greater than 20% biodiesel.

In general, B20 costs 30 to 40 cents more per gallon than conventional diesel. Although biodiesel costs more than regular diesel fuel, often called **petrodiesel,** fleet managers can make the switch to alternative fuels without purchasing new vehicles, acquiring new spare parts inventories, rebuilding refueling stations, or hiring new service technicians.

FEATURES OF BIODIESEL Biodiesel has the following characteristics:

1. Purchasing biodiesel in bulk quantities decreases the cost of fuel.
2. Biodiesel maintains similar horsepower, torque, and fuel economy.
3. Biodiesel has a higher cetane number than conventional diesel, which increases the engine's performance.

I Thought Biodiesel Was Vegetable Oil?

Biodiesel is vegetable oil with the glycerin component removed by means of reacting the vegetable oil with a catalyst. The resulting hydrocarbon esters are 16 to 18 carbon atoms in length, almost identical to the petroleum diesel fuel atoms. This allows the use of biodiesel fuel in a diesel engine with no modifications needed. Biodiesel-powered vehicles do not *need* a second fuel tank, whereas vegetable-oil-powered vehicles do.

There are three main types of fuel used in diesel engines. These are:

- Petroleum diesel, a fossil hydrocarbon with a carbon chain length of about 16 carbon atoms.
- Biodiesel, a hydrocarbon with a carbon chain length of 16 to 18 carbon atoms.
- Vegetable oil is a triglyceride with a glycerin component joining three hydrocarbon chains of 16 to 18 carbon atoms each, called straight vegetable oil **(SVO)**. Other terms used when describing vegetable oil include:
- Pure plant oil **(PPO)**—a term most often used in Europe to describe SVO
- Waste vegetable oil **(WVO)**—this oil could include animal or fish oils from cooking
- Used cooking oil **(UCO)**—a term used when the oil may or may not be pure vegetable oil

Vegetable oil is not liquid enough at common ambient temperatures for use in a diesel engine fuel delivery system designed for the lower-viscosity petroleum diesel fuel. Vegetable oil needs to be heated to obtain a similar viscosity to biodiesel and petroleum diesel. This means that a heat source needs to be provided before the fuel can be used in a diesel engine. This is achieved by starting on petroleum diesel or biodiesel fuel until the engine heat can be used to sufficiently warm a tank containing the vegetable oil. It also requires purging the fuel system of vegetable oil with petroleum diesel or biodiesel fuel prior to stopping the engine to avoid the vegetable oil thickening and solidifying in the fuel system away from the heated tank. The use of vegetable oil in its natural state does, however, eliminate the need to remove the glycerin component. Many vehicle and diesel engine fuel system suppliers permit the use of biodiesel fuel that is certified as meeting testing standards. None permit the use of vegetable oil in its natural state.

4. It is nontoxic, which makes it safe to handle, transport, and store. Maintenance requirements for B20 vehicles and petrodiesel vehicles are the same.
5. Biodiesel acts as a lubricant and this can add to the life of the fuel system components.

NOTE: For additional information on biodiesel and the locations where it can be purchased, visit www .biodiesel.org.

E-DIESEL FUEL

DEFINITION OF E-DIESEL   **E-diesel,** also called **diesohol** outside of the United States, is standard No. 2 diesel fuel that contains up to 15% ethanol. While E-diesel can have up to 15% ethanol by volume, typical blend levels are from 8% to 10%.

CETANE RATING OF E-DIESEL   The higher the cetane number, the shorter the delay between injection and ignition.

Normal diesel fuel has a cetane number of about 50. Adding 15% ethanol lowers the cetane number. To increase the cetane number back to that of conventional diesel fuel, a cetane-enhancing additive is added to E-diesel. The additive used to increase the cetane rating of E-diesel is ethylhexylnitrate or ditertbutyl peroxide.

E-diesel has better cold-flow properties than conventional diesel. The heat content of E-diesel is about 6% less than conventional diesel, but the particulate matter (PM) emissions are reduced by as much as 40%, 20% less carbon monoxide, and a 5% reduction in oxides of nitrogen (NO_X).

Currently, E-diesel is considered to be experimental and can be used legally in off-road applications or in mass-transit buses with EPA approval. For additional information, visit www.e-diesel.org.

SUMMARY

1. Diesel fuel produces 12% more heat energy than the same amount of gasoline.
2. Diesel fuel requirements include cleanliness, low-temperature fluidity, and proper cetane rating.
3. Emission control devices used on 2007 and newer engines require the use of ultra-low-sulfur diesel (ULSD) that has less than 15 parts per million (PPM) of sulfur.
4. The density of diesel fuel is measured in a unit called API gravity.
5. The cetane rating of diesel fuel is a measure of the ease with which the fuel can be ignited.
6. Biodiesel is the blend of vegetable-based liquid with regular diesel fuel. Most diesel engine manufacturers allow the use of a 5% blend, called B20 without any changes to the fuel system or engine.
7. E-diesel is a blend of ethanol with diesel fuel up to 15% ethanol by volume.

REVIEW QUESTIONS

1. What is meant by the cloud point?
2. What is ultra-low-sulfur diesel?
3. Biodiesel blends are identified by what designation?

CHAPTER QUIZ

1. What color is diesel fuel dyed if it is for off-road use only?
   - **a.** Red
   - **b.** Green
   - **c.** Blue
   - **d.** Yellow
2. What clogs fuel filters when the temperature is low on a vehicle that uses diesel fuel?
   - **a.** Alcohol
   - **b.** Sulfur
   - **c.** Wax
   - **d.** Cetane
3. The specific gravity of diesel fuel is measured in what units?
   - **a.** Hydrometer units
   - **b.** API gravity
   - **c.** Grade number
   - **d.** Cetane number
4. What rating of diesel fuel indicates how well a diesel engine will start?
   - **a.** Specific gravity rating
   - **b.** Sulfur content
   - **c.** Cloud point
   - **d.** Cetane rating
5. Ultra-low-sulfur diesel fuel has how much sulfur content?
   - **a.** 15 PPM
   - **b.** 50 PPM
   - **c.** 500 PPM
   - **d.** 1,500 PPM
6. E-diesel is diesel fuel with what additive?
   - **a.** Methanol
   - **b.** Sulfur
   - **c.** Ethanol
   - **d.** Vegetable oil
7. Biodiesel is regular diesel fuel with vegetable oil added.
   - **a.** True
   - **b.** False
8. B20 biodiesel has how much regular diesel fuel?
   - **a.** 20%
   - **b.** 40%
   - **c.** 80%
   - **d.** 100%
9. Most diesel fuel is what grade?
   - **a.** Grade #1
   - **b.** Grade #2
   - **c.** Grade #3
   - **d.** Grade #4
10. Most manufacturers of vehicles equipped with diesel engines allow what type of biodiesel?
    - **a.** B100
    - **b.** B80
    - **c.** B20
    - **d.** B5

HYBRID AUXILIARY AND HIGH-VOLTAGE BATTERIES

OBJECTIVES: **After studying Chapter 7, the reader will be able to:** • Prepare for ASE Electrical/Electronic Systems (A6) certification test content area "B" (Battery Diagnosis and Service). • Describe how auxiliary 12-volt and high-voltage hybrid vehicle batteries work. • List battery ratings. • Describe deep cycling. • List the safety precautions necessary when working with batteries. • Explain how to safely charge a battery. • Describe how to perform a battery load test. • Explain how to perform a conductance test. • Discuss how to jump start a vehicle safely. • Discuss hybrid electric vehicle auxiliary batteries. • Explain the types of high-voltage batteries used in most hybrid electric vehicles.

KEY TERMS: • AGM 82 • alkaline 96 • Ampere hour 83 • Battery electrical drain test 87 • battery module 92 • CA 83 • CCA 83 • Cells 80 • Deep cycling 83 • Electrolyte 81 • Flooded cell batteries 82 • Gassing 80 • Gel battery 82 • Grid 80 • lithium-ion (Li-ion) 93 • IOD 87 • Load test 85 • metal hydride 91 • MCA 83 • Parasitic load test 87 • Recombinant battery 82 • Reserve capacity 83 • solid state 98 • SLA 82 • SLI 80 • SVR 82 • thermistors 93 • VRLA 82 • Zinc-air 98

INTRODUCTION TO HYBRID AUXILIARY BATTERIES

PURPOSE AND FUNCTION Every electrical component in a vehicle is supplied current from the battery. The battery is one of the most important parts of a vehicle because it is the heart or foundation of the electrical system. The primary purpose of an automotive battery is to provide a source of electrical power for all of the vehicle electrical needs. In a hybrid electric vehicle (HEV), the 12-volt auxiliary battery is used to

- Power all of the 12-volt accessories
- Power the electronic controller for the high-voltage system

TECH TIP

The Hybrid Electric Vehicle Will Not Start If the Auxiliary Battery Is Discharged

If the 12-volt auxiliary battery is discharged or defective, it cannot power the electronic controller used to start the vehicle. The gasoline engine will not start nor will the vehicle move under high-voltage battery power. If "nothing happens" when the vehicle is attempted to be started, always start the diagnosis with the state-of-charge and condition of the auxiliary 12-volt battery.

WHY BATTERIES ARE IMPORTANT The battery also acts as a stabilizer to the voltage for the entire electrical system. The battery *must* be in good (serviceable) condition to assure correct hybrid vehicle operation. The battery must be confirmed to be in serviceable condition before performing any electrical system testing.

12-VOLT AUXILIARY BATTERY CONSTRUCTION

CASE Most automotive battery cases (container or covers) are constructed of polypropylene, a thin (approximately 0.08 in., or 0.02 mm, thick), strong, and lightweight plastic. In contrast, containers for industrial batteries and some truck batteries are constructed of a hard, thick rubber material. Inside the case are six cells (for a 12-volt battery). ● **SEE FIGURE 7–1.**

Each cell has positive and negative plates. Built into the bottom of many batteries are ribs that support the lead-alloy plates and provide a space for sediment to settle, called the *sediment chamber.* This space prevents spent active material from causing a short circuit between the plates at the bottom of the battery. A **maintenance-free battery** uses little water during normal service because of the alloy material used to construct the battery plate grids. Maintenance-free batteries are also called **low-water-loss batteries.**

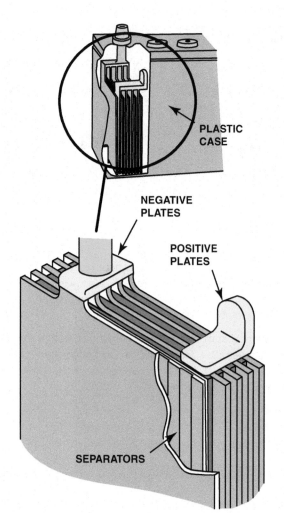

FIGURE 7–1 Batteries are constructed of plates grouped into cells and installed in a plastic case.

GRIDS Each positive and negative plate in a battery is constructed on a framework, or **grid,** made primarily of lead. Lead is a soft material and must be strengthened for use in an automotive battery grid. Adding antimony or calcium to the pure lead adds strength to the lead grids. ● SEE FIGURE 7–2.

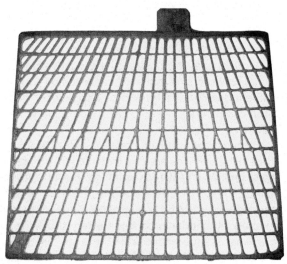

FIGURE 7–2 A grid from a battery used in both positive and negative plates.

 FREQUENTLY ASKED QUESTION

What Is an SLI Battery?

Sometimes the term *SLI* is used to describe a type of battery. **SLI** means starting, lighting, and ignition, and describes the use of a typical automotive battery. The auxiliary battery used in hybrid electric vehicles is an SLI-type battery compared to the high-voltage battery used to help propel the vehicle, which is sometimes called a *traction battery*.

Battery grids hold the active material and provide the electrical pathways for the current created in the plate. Maintenance-free batteries use calcium instead of antimony, because 0.2% calcium has the same strength as 6% antimony. A typical lead-calcium grid uses only 0.09% to 0.12% calcium. Using low amounts of calcium instead of higher amounts of antimony reduces **gassing.** Gassing is the release of hydrogen and oxygen from the battery that occurs during charging and discharging, which results in water usage. Low-maintenance batteries use a low percentage of antimony (about 2% to 3%), or use antimony only in the positive grids and calcium for the negative grids. *The percentages that make up the alloy of the plate grids constitute the major difference between standard and maintenance-free batteries.* The chemical reactions that occur inside each battery are identical regardless of the type of material used to construct the grid plates.

POSITIVE PLATES The positive plates have *lead dioxide (peroxides),* in paste form, placed onto the grid framework. This process is called *pasting*. This active material can react with the sulfuric acid of the battery and is dark brown in color.

NEGATIVE PLATES The negative plates are pasted to the grid with a pure *porous lead,* called *sponge lead* and are gray in color.

SEPARATORS The positive and the negative plates must be installed alternately next to each other without touching. Nonconducting *separators* are used, which allow room for the reaction of the acid with both plate materials, yet insulate the plates to prevent shorts. These separators are porous (with many small holes) and have ribs facing the positive plate. Separators must be made from insulting material such as resin-coated paper, porous rubber, fiberglass, or expanded plastic.

CELLS **Cells** are constructed of positive and negative plates with insulating separators between each plate. Most batteries use one more negative plate than positive plate in each cell; however, many newer batteries use the same number of positive and negative plates. A cell is also called an *element*. Each cell is actually a 2.1-volt battery, regardless of the number of positive or negative plates used. The greater the number of plates used in each cell, the greater the amount of current (amperes) that can be produced. Typical batteries

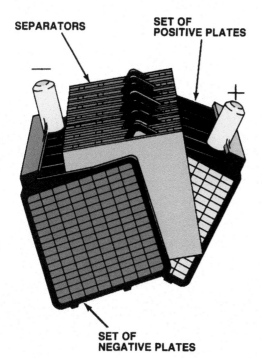

FIGURE 7–3 Two groups of plates are combined to form a battery element.

contain four positive plates and five negative plates per cell. A 12-volt battery contains six cells connected in series, which produce 12.6 volts ($6 \times 2.1 = 12.6$) and have 54 plates (9 plates per cell $\times$ 6 cells). If the same 12-volt battery had five positive plates and six negative plates, for a total of 11 plates per cell (5×6), or 66 plates (11 plates $\times$ 6 cells), then it would have the same voltage, but the amount of current that the battery could produce would be increased. ● **SEE FIGURE 7–3.**

The amperage capacity of a battery is determined by the amount of active plate material in the battery and the area of the plate material exposed to the electrolyte in the battery.

PARTITIONS Each cell is separated from the other cells by *partitions* which are made of the same material as that used for the outside case of the battery. Electrical connections between cells are provided by lead connectors that loop over the top of the partition and connect the plates of the cells together. Many batteries connect the cells directly through the partition connectors, which provide the shortest path for the current and the lowest resistance. ● **SEE FIGURE 7–4.**

ELECTROLYTE **Electrolyte** is the term used to describe the acid solution in a battery. The electrolyte used in automotive batteries is a solution (liquid combination) of 36% sulfuric acid and 64% water. This electrolyte is used for both lead-antimony and lead calcium (maintenance-free) batteries. The chemical symbol for this sulfuric acid solution is H_2SO_4.

- H_2 = Symbol for hydrogen (the subscript 2 means that there are two atoms of hydrogen)
- S = Symbol for sulfur
- O_4 = Symbol for oxygen (the subscript 4 indicates that there are four atoms of oxygen)

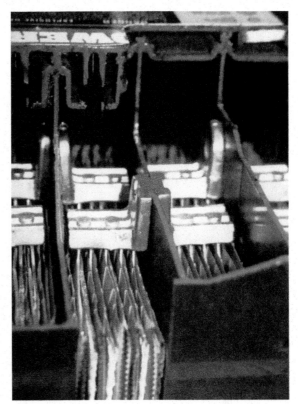

FIGURE 7–4 A cutaway battery showing the connection of the cells to each other through the partition.

Electrolyte is sold premixed in the proper proportion and is factory installed or added to the battery when the battery is sold. Additional electrolyte must *never* be added to any battery after the original electrolyte fill. It is normal for some water (H_2O) in the form of hydrogen and oxygen gases to escape during charging as a result of the chemical reactions. The escape of gases from a battery during charging or discharging is called gassing. Only pure distilled water should be added to a battery. If distilled water is not available, clean drinking water can be used.

HOW A BATTERY WORKS

PRINCIPLE INVOLVED How a battery works is based on a scientific principle discovered years ago that states:

- When two dissimilar metals are placed in an acid, electrons flow between the metals if a circuit is connected between them.
- This can be demonstrated by pushing a steel nail and a piece of solid copper wire into a lemon. Connect a voltmeter to the ends of the copper wire and nail, and voltage will be displayed.

A fully-charged lead-acid battery has a positive plate of lead dioxide (peroxide) and a negative plate of lead surrounded by a sulfuric acid solution (electrolyte). The difference in potential (voltage) between lead peroxide and lead in acid is approximately 2.1 volts.

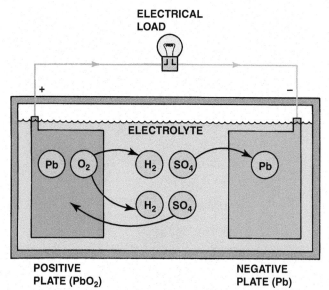

FIGURE 7–5 Chemical reaction for a lead-acid battery that is fully charged being discharged by the attached electrical load.

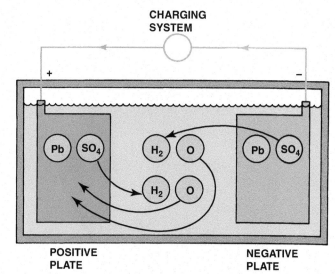

FIGURE 7–6 Chemical reaction for a lead-acid battery that is fully discharged being charged by the attached alternator.

DURING DISCHARGING The positive plate lead dioxide (PbO_2) combines with the SO_4, forming $PbSO_4$ from the electrolyte and releases its O_2 into the electrolyte, forming H_2O. The negative plate also combines with the SO_4 from the electrolyte and becomes lead sulfate ($PbSO_4$). ● **SEE FIGURE 7–5.**

FULLY DISCHARGED STATE When the battery is fully discharged, both the positive and the negative plates are $PbSO_4$ (lead sulfate) and the electrolyte has become water (H_2O). As the battery is being discharged, the plates and electrolyte approach the completely discharged state. When a battery is completely discharged, there are no longer dissimilar metals submerged in an acid. The plates have become the same material ($PbSO_4$) and the electrolyte becomes water (H_2O). This is a chemical reaction that can be reversed during charging.

CAUTION: Never charge or jump start a frozen battery because the hydrogen gas can get trapped in the ice and ignite if a spark is caused during the charging process. The result can be an explosion.

DURING CHARGING During charging, the sulfate that was deposited on the positive and negative plates returns to the electrolyte, where it becomes normal-strength sulfuric acid solution. The positive plate returns to lead dioxide (PbO_2), the negative plate is again pure lead (Pb), and the electrolyte becomes H_2SO_4. ● **SEE FIGURE 7–6.**

VALVE-REGULATED LEAD–ACID BATTERIES

TERMINOLOGY There are two basic types of **valve-regulated lead-acid (VRLA),** also called **sealed valve-regulated (SVR)** or **sealed lead-acid (SLA),** batteries. These batteries use a low-pressure venting system that releases excess gas and automatically reseals if a buildup of gas is created due to overcharging. The two types include the following:

- **Absorbed glass mat.** The acid used in an **absorbed glass mat (AGM)** battery is totally absorbed into the separator, making the battery leak-proof and spill-proof. The battery is assembled by compressing the cell about 20%, then inserting it into the container. The compressed cell helps reduce damage caused by vibration and helps keep the acid tightly against the plates. The sealed maintenance-free design uses a pressure release valve in each cell. Unlike conventional batteries that use a liquid electrolyte, called **flooded cell batteries,** most of the hydrogen and oxygen given off during charging remains inside the battery. The separator or mat is only 90% to 95% saturated with electrolyte, thereby allowing a portion of the mat to be filled with gas. The gas spaces provide channels to allow the hydrogen and oxygen gases to recombine rapidly and safely. Because the acid is totally absorbed into the glass mat separator, an AGM battery can be mounted in any direction. AGM batteries also have a longer service life, often lasting 7–10 years. Absorbed glass mat batteries are used as standard equipment in some vehicles such as the Chevrolet Corvette and in most Toyota hybrid electric vehicles. ● **SEE FIGURE 7–7.**

- **Gelled electrolyte batteries.** In a gelled electrolyte battery, silica is added to the electrolyte, which turns the electrolyte into a substance similar to gelatin. This type of battery is also called a **gel battery.** Both types of valve-regulated, lead-acid batteries are also called **recombinant battery** design. A recombinant-type battery means that the oxygen gas generated at the positive plate travels through the dense electrolyte to the negative plate. When the oxygen reaches the negative plate, it reacts with the lead, which consumes the oxygen gas and prevents the formation of hydrogen gas. It is because of this oxygen recombination that VRLA batteries do not use water.

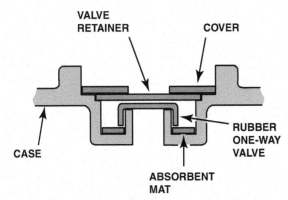

FIGURE 7–7 Pressure relief valve from a VRLA battery. This valve stays closed during normal operating conditions and prevents gases from entering or leaving the battery case.

FIGURE 7–8 This battery has a rating of 1,000 cold amperes (CA) and 900 amperes using the cold-cranking amperes (CCA) rating system.

BATTERY RATINGS

Batteries are rated according to the amount of current they can produce under specific conditions.

COLD-CRANKING AMPERES Every automotive battery must be able to supply electrical power to crank the engine in cold weather and still provide battery voltage high enough to operate the ignition system for starting. The cold-cranking ampere rating of a battery is the number of amperes that can be supplied by a battery at 0°F (–18°C) for 30 seconds while the battery still maintains a voltage of 1.2 volts per cell or higher. This means that the battery voltage would be 7.2 volts for a 12-volt battery and 3.6 volts for a 6-volt battery. The cold-cranking performance rating is called **cold-cranking amperes (CCA).** Try to purchase a battery with the highest CCA for the money. See the vehicle manufacturer's specifications for recommended battery capacity.

CRANKING AMPERES The designation **CA** refers to the number of amperes that can be supplied by a battery at 32°F (0°C). This rating results in a higher amperage rating than the more stringent CCA rating. ● **SEE FIGURE 7–8.**

MARINE CRANKING AMPERES **Marine cranking amperes (MCA)** is similar to the cranking amperes (CA) rating and is tested at 32°F (0°C).

RESERVE CAPACITY The **reserve capacity** rating for batteries is *the number of minutes* for which the battery can produce 25 amperes and still have a battery voltage of 1.75 volts per cell (10.5 volts for a 12-volt battery). This rating is actually a measurement of the time for which a vehicle can be driven in the event of a charging system failure.

AMPERE HOUR **Ampere hour** is an older battery rating system that measures how many amperes of current the battery

FREQUENTLY ASKED QUESTION

What Is Meant by "Deep Cycling" a Battery?

Deep cycling is almost fully discharging of a battery and then completely recharging it. Golf cart batteries are an example of lead-acid batteries that must be designed to be deep cycled. A golf cart must be able to cover two 18-hole rounds of golf and then be fully recharged overnight. Charging is hard on batteries because the internal heat generated can cause plate warpage, so these specially designed batteries use thicker plate grids that resist warpage. Normal automotive batteries are not designed for repeated deep cycling.

can produce over a period of time. For example, a battery that has a 50 amp-hour (A-H) rating can deliver 50 amperes for one hour or 1 ampere for 50 hours or any combination that equals 50 amp-hours.

BATTERY SERVICE SAFETY PRECAUTIONS

HAZARDS Batteries contain acid and release explosive gases (hydrogen and oxygen) during normal charging and discharging cycles.

SAFETY PROCEDURES To help prevent physical injury or damage to the vehicle, always adhere to the following safety procedures.

1. When working on any electrical component on a vehicle, disconnect the negative battery cable from the battery. When the negative cable is disconnected, all electrical circuits in the vehicle will be open, which will prevent accidental electrical contact between an electrical component and ground. Any electrical spark has the potential to cause explosion and personal injury.

2. Wear eye protection (goggles preferred) when working around any battery.

3. Wear protective clothing to avoid skin contact with battery acid.

4. Always adhere to all safety precautions as stated in the service procedures for the equipment used for battery service and testing.

5. Never smoke or use an open flame around any battery.

6. Never stand near a battery that is being jump started, especially in cold weather because the battery could explode.

AUXILIARY BATTERY VOLTAGE TEST

STATE OF CHARGE Testing the battery voltage with a voltmeter is a simple method for determining the state of charge of any battery. ● **SEE FIGURE 7–9.**

The voltage of a battery does not necessarily indicate whether the battery can perform satisfactorily, but it does indicate to the technician more about the battery's condition than a simple visual inspection. A battery that "looks good" may not be good. This test is commonly called a *terminal voltage test* or an *open circuit battery voltage test* because it is conducted with an open circuit, no current flowing, and no load applied to the battery.

1. If the battery has just been charged or the vehicle has recently been driven, it is necessary to remove the surface charge from the battery before testing. A surface charge is a charge of higher-than-normal voltage that is just on the surface of the battery plates. The surface charge is quickly removed when the battery is loaded and therefore does not accurately represent the true state of charge of the battery.

2. To remove the surface charge, turn the headlights on high beam (brights) for one minute, then turn the headlights off and wait two minutes. With the engine and all electrical accessories off, and the doors shut (to turn off the interior lights), connect a voltmeter to the battery posts. Connect the red positive lead to the positive post and the black negative lead to the negative post.

NOTE: If the meter reads negative (–), the battery has been reverse charged (has reversed polarity) and should be replaced, or the meter has been connected incorrectly.

3. Read the voltmeter and compare the results with the state-of-charge (SOC) shown in Chart 7–1. The voltages shown are for a battery at or near room temperature (70°F to 80°F, or 21°C to 27°C). ● **SEE CHART 7–1.**

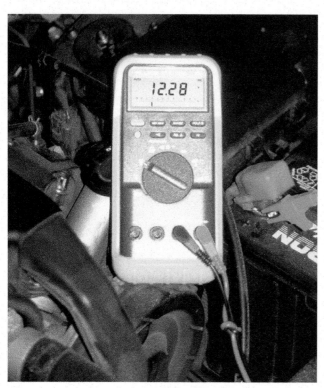

(a)

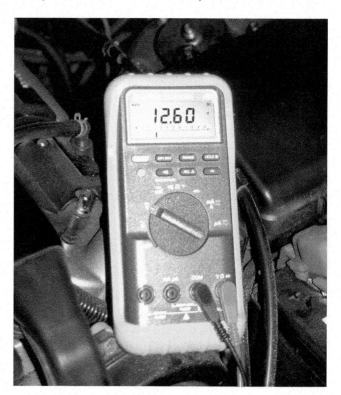

(b)

FIGURE 7–9 (a) A voltage reading of 12.28 volts indicates that the battery is not fully charged and should be charged before testing. (b) A battery that measures 12.6 volts or higher after the surface charge has been removed is 100% charged.

STATE-OF-CHARGE (SOC)	BATTERY VOLTAGE
Fully charged	12.6 volts or higher
75% charged	12.4 volts
50%	12.2 volts
25%	12.0 volts
Discharged	11.9 volts or lower

CHART 7–1

A comparison showing the relationship between battery voltage and state-of-charge.

AUXILIARY BATTERY LOAD TESTING

TERMINOLOGY One test to determine the condition of any battery is the **load test.** Most automotive starting and charging testers use a carbon pile to create an electrical load on the battery. The amount of the load is determined by the original CCA rating of the battery, which should be at least 75% charged before performing a load test.

TEST PROCEDURE To perform a battery load test, take the following steps:

STEP 1 **Determine the CCA rating of the battery.** The proper electrical load used to test a battery is one-half of the CCA rating or three times the ampere-hour rating, with a minimum 150 ampere load. ● **SEE FIGURE 7–10.**

STEP 2 **Connect the load tester to the battery.** Follow the instructions for the tester being used.

STEP 3 **Apply the load for a full 15 seconds.** Observe the voltmeter during the load testing and check the voltage at the end of the 15-second period while the battery is still under load. A good battery should indicate above 9.6 V.

FIGURE 7–10 This battery has cold-cranking amperes (CCA) of 550 A, cranking amperes (CA) of 680 A, and load test amperes of 270 A listed on the top label. Not all batteries have this complete information.

FIGURE 7–11 An alternator regulator battery starter tester (ARBST) automatically loads the battery with a fixed load for 15 seconds. to remove the surface charge, then removes the load for 30 seconds. to allow the battery to recover, and then reapplies the load for another 15 sec. The results of the test are then displayed.

STEP 4 **Repeat the test.** Many battery manufacturers recommend performing the load test twice, using the first load period to remove the surface charge on the battery and the second test to provide a more true indication of the condition of the battery. Wait 30 seconds between tests to allow time for the battery to recover.**Results**: If the battery fails the load test, recharge the battery and retest. If the load test is failed again, the battery needs to be replaced. ● **SEE FIGURE 7–11.**

AUXILIARY BATTERY CONDUCTANCE TESTING

TERMINOLOGY General Motors, Chrysler, Honda and Ford specify that an electronic conductance tester be used to test batteries in vehicles still under factory warranty. Conductance is a measure of how well a battery can create current. This tester sends a small signal through the battery and then measures a part of the AC response. As a battery ages, the plates can become sulfated and shed active materials from the grids, reducing the battery capacity. Conductance testers can be used to test flooded or AGM-type batteries. The unit can determine the following information about a battery:

- Tested CCA
- State of charge
- Voltage of the battery
- Defects such as shorts and opens
- Most conductance testers also display an internal resistance value

FIGURE 7–12 A conductance tester is very easy to use and has proved to accurately determine battery condition if the connections are properly made. Follow the instructions on the display exactly for best results.

However, a conductance tester is not designed to accurately determine the state of charge or CCA rating of a new battery. Unlike a battery load test, a conductance tester can be used on a battery that is discharged. This type of tester should only be used to test batteries that have been in service. ● **SEE FIGURE 7–12.**

TEST PROCEDURE To test a battery using an electronic conductance tester, perform the following steps.

STEP 1 Connect the unit to the positive and negative terminals of the battery. If testing a side post battery, always use the lead adapters and *never* use steel bolts as these can cause an incorrect reading.

> NOTE: Test results can be incorrectly reported on the display if proper, clean connections to the battery are not made. Also be sure that all accessories and the ignition switch are in the off position.

STEP 2 Enter the CCA rating (if known).

STEP 3 The tester determines and displays the measured CCA of the battery as well as state of charge and the voltage, plus one of the following:

- **Good battery.** The battery can return to service.
- **Charge and retest.** Fully recharge the battery and return it to service.
- **Replace the battery.** The battery is not serviceable and should be replaced.
- **Bad cell—replace.** The battery is not serviceable and should be replaced.

Some conductance testers can check the charging and cranking circuits, too.

AUXILIARY BATTERY CHARGING

CHARGING PROCEDURE If the state-of-charge of a battery is low, it must be recharged. It is best to slow charge any battery to prevent possible overheating damage to the battery. Perform the following steps.

STEP 1 **Determine the charge rate.** The charge rate is based on the current state-of-charge (SOC) and charging rate. ● **SEE CHART 7–2** for the recommended charging rate.

STEP 2 **Connect a battery charger to the battery.** Be sure the charger is not plugged in when connecting to a battery. Always follow the battery charger's instructions for proper use.

STEP 3 **Set the charging rate.** The initial charge rate should be about 35 A for 30 minutes to help start the charging process. Fast charging a battery increases the temperature of the battery and can cause warping of the plates inside the battery. Fast charging also increases the amount of gassing (release of hydrogen and oxygen), which can create a health and fire hazard. The battery temperature should not exceed 125°F (hot to the touch).

- Fast charge: 15 A maximum
- Slow charge: 5 A maximum

● **SEE FIGURE 7–13.**

OPEN CIRCUIT VOLTAGE	STATE-OF-CHARGE (SOC) (%)	@60 A (MIN.)	@50 A (MIN.)	@40 A (MIN.)	@30 A (MIN)	@20 A (MIN.)	@20 A (MIN.)
12.6	100	N.A. (Fully charged)	N.A. (Fully charged)	N.A. (Fully charged)	N.A. (Fully charged)	N.A. (Fully charged)	N.A. (Fully charged)
12.4	75	15	20	27	35	48	90
12.2	50	35	45	55	75	95	180
12.0	25	50	65	85	115	145	260
11.8	0	65	85	110	150	195	370

CHART 7–2

Battery charging guidelines based on the state-of-charge of the battery and the charging rate.

FIGURE 7–13 A typical industrial battery charger. Be sure that the ignition switch in the vehicle is in the off position before connecting any battery charger. Connect the cables of the charger to the battery before plugging the charger into the outlet. This helps prevent a voltage spike and spark that could occur if the charger happened to be accidentally left on. Always follow the battery charger manufacturer's instructions.

CHARGING AGM BATTERIES Charging an absorbed glass mat (AGM) battery requires a different charger than is used to recharge a flooded-type battery. The differences include:

- The AGM can be charged with high current, up to 75% of the ampere-hour rating due to lower internal resistance.
- The charging voltage has to be kept at or below 14.4 volts to prevent damage.

Because most conventional battery chargers use a charging voltage of 16 volts or higher, a charger specifically designed to charge AGM batteries must be used. AGM batteries are often used as auxiliary batteries in hybrid electric vehicles when the battery is located inside the vehicle.

BATTERY CHARGE TIME The time needed to charge a completely discharged battery can be estimated by using the reserve capacity rating of the battery in minutes divided by the charging rate.

Hours needed to charge the battery = Reserve capacity/ Charge current

For example, if a 10 A charge rate is applied to a discharged battery that has a 90-minute reserve capacity, the time needed to charge the battery will be 9 hours.

90 minutes/10 A = 9 hours

HYBRID AUXILIARY BATTERY LOCATIONS

The location of the 12-volt auxiliary battery varies according to the make, model, and year of hybrid electric vehicle. As a general rule, the type of battery used is determined by the location such as

- An AGM battery is used when the battery is located in the trunk or near the passenger compartment area.
- A flooded-type battery is used if the battery is located under the hood.

● **SEE CHART 7–3** for a summary of the locations and type of 12-volt auxiliary battery.

AUXILIARY BATTERY ELECTRICAL DRAIN TESTING

TERMINOLOGY The **battery electrical drain test** determines if any component or circuit in a vehicle is causing a drain on the battery when everything is off. This test is also called the **ignition off draw (IOD)** or **parasitic load test.** Many electronic components draw a continuous, slight amount of current from the battery when the ignition is off. These components include the following:

1. Electronically tuned radios for station memory and clock circuits.
2. Computers and controllers, through slight diode leakage.
3. The alternator, through slight diode leakage.

These components may cause a voltmeter to read full battery voltage if it is connected between the negative battery terminal and the removed end of the negative battery cable. Because of this fact, voltmeters should not be used for battery drain testing. This test should be performed when one of the following conditions exists:

1. When a battery is being charged or replaced (a battery drain could have been the cause for charging or replacing the battery).
2. When the battery is suspected of being drained.

NOTE: Battery electrical draw can only be tested on the auxiliary 12-volt battery. It is not possible for the service technician to test the high-voltage battery pack for electrical drain.

PROCEDURE FOR BATTERY ELECTRICAL DRAIN TEST There are many different testers that can be used for battery electrical drain testing, but an inductive ammeter is one of the most commonly used.

- **Inductive DC ammeter.** The fastest and easiest method to measure battery electrical drain is to connect an inductive DC ammeter that is capable of measuring low current (10mA) around either battery cable. ● **SEE FIGURE 7–14.**
- **DMM set to read milliamperes.** The following is the procedure for performing the battery electrical drain test using a DMM set to read DC amperes.

MAKE/MODEL/YEAR	AUXILIARY 12-V BATTERY LOCATION	TYPE OF BATTERY
Buick LaCrosse (2012+)	Under the hood	Flooded lead-acid
Cadillac Escalade (2008+) (two mode)	Under the hood; driver's side	Flooded lead-acid
Chevrolet Malibu (2008+)	Under the hood driver's side	Flooded lead-acid
Chevrolet Silverado (2004–2008) (PHT)	Under the hood; driver's side	Flooded lead-acid
Chevrolet Silverado (2011+) Two-Mode	Under the hood; driver's side	Flooded lead-acid
Chevrolet Tahoe (2008+) (two mode)	Under the hood; driver's side	Flooded lead-acid
Chevrolet Volt (2011+)	Behind the rear seat under the floor in the center	Absorbed glass mat (AGM)
Chrysler Aspen (2009)	Under driver's side door, under vehicle	Flooded lead-acid
Dodge Durango (2009)	Under driver's side door, under vehicle	Flooded lead-acid
Ford Escape (2005+)	Under the hood; driver's side	Flooded lead-acid
GMC Sierra (2004–2008) (PHT)	Under the hood; driver's side	Flooded lead-acid
GMC Sierra (2011+) Two-mode	Under the hood; driver's side	Flooded lead-acid
GMC Yukon (2008+) (two mode)	Under the hood; driver's side	Flooded lead-acid
Honda Accord (2005–2007)	Under the hood; driver's side	Flooded lead-acid
Honda Civic (2003+)	Under the hood; driver's side	Flooded lead-acid
Honda Insight (1999–2005)	Under the hood; center under windshield	Flooded lead-acid
Honda Insight (2010+)	Under the hood; driver's side	Flooded lead-acid
Lexus GS450h (2007+)	In the trunk; driver's side, behind interior panel	Absorbed glass mat (AGM)
Lexus LS 600h (2006+)	In the trunk; driver's side, behind interior panel	Absorbed glass mat (AGM)
LexusRX400h/RX 450h (2006+)	Under the hood; passenger side	Flooded lead-acid
Mercury Mariner (2005–2011)	Under the hood; driver's side	Flooded lead-acid
Nissan Altima (2007–2011)	In the trunk; driver's side	Absorbed glass mat (AGM)
Nissan Leaf (2011+)	Under the hood	Flooded lead-acid
Saturn AURA Hybrid (2007–2010)	Under the hood; driver's side	Flooded lead-acid
Saturn VUE Hybrid (2007–2010)	Under the hood; driver's side	Flooded lead-acid
Toyota Camry Hybrid (2007+)	In the trunk; passenger side	Absorbed glass mat (AGM)
Toyota Highlander Hybrid (2006+)	Under the hood; passenger side	Flooded lead-acid
Toyota Prius (2001–2003)	In the trunk; driver's side	Absorbed glass mat (AGM)
Toyota Prius (2004–2009)	In the trunk; driver's side	Absorbed glass mat (AGM)
Toyota Prius (2010+)	In the trunk; driver's side	Absorbed glass mat (AGM)

CHART 7–3

A summary chart showing where the 12-volt auxiliary batteries are located. Only the auxiliary 12-volt batteries can be serviced or charged.

FIGURE 7–14 This mini clamp-on digital multimeter is being used to measure the amount of battery electrical drain that is present. In this case, a reading of 20 mA (displayed on the meter as 00.02 A) is within the normal range of 20 to 30 mA. Be sure to clamp around all of the positive battery cable or all of the negative battery cable, whichever is easiest to get the clamp around.

STEP 1 Make certain that all lights, accessories, and ignition are off.

STEP 2 Check all vehicle doors to be certain that the interior courtesy (dome) lights are off.

STEP 3 Disconnect the *negative* (−) battery cable and install a parasitic load tool, as shown in ● **FIGURE 7–15.**

STEP 4 Start the engine and drive the vehicle about 10 minutes, being sure to turn on all the lights and accessories, including the radio.

STEP 5 Turn the engine and all accessories off, including the under-hood light.

STEP 6 Connect an ammeter across the parasitic load tool switch and wait 20 minutes for all computers and circuits to shut down.

STEP 7 Open the switch on the load tool and read the battery electrical drain on the meter display.

NOTE: Using a voltmeter or test light to measure battery drain is *not* recommended by most vehicle manufacturers. The high internal resistance of the voltmeter results in an irrelevant reading that does not provide the technician with adequate information about a problem.

Results:

- Normal = 20 to 30 mA (0.02 to 0.03 A)
- Maximum allowable = 50 mA (0.05 A)

FINDING THE SOURCE OF THE DRAIN If there is a drain, check and temporarily disconnect the following components.

1. Under-hood light
2. Glove compartment light
3. Trunk light

FIGURE 7–15 After connecting the shut-off tool, start the engine and operate all accessories. Stop the engine and turn off everything. Connect the ammeter across the shut-off switch in parallel. Wait 20 minutes. This time allows all electronic circuits to "time out" or shut down. Open the switch—all current now will flow through the ammeter. A reading greater than specified (usually greater than 50 mA, or 0.05 A) indicates a problem that should be corrected.

If after disconnecting these three components, the battery drain draws more than 50 mA (0.05 A), disconnect one fuse at a time from the fuse box until the excessive drain drops to normal.

NOTE: Do not reinsert fuses after they have been removed as this action can cause modules to "wake up," leading to an inconclusive test.

If the excessive battery drain stops after one fuse is disconnected, the source of the drain is located in that particular circuit, as labeled on the fuse box. Continue to disconnect the *power-side* wire connectors from each component included in that particular circuit until the test light goes off. The source of the battery drain can then be traced to an individual component or part of one circuit. If all fuses have been removed and the drain is still in excess of 50mA, disconnect fusible links one at a time while observing the ammeter.

JUMP STARTING

To jump start another vehicle with a dead battery, connect good-quality copper jumper cables or a jump box to the good battery and the dead battery. Some auxiliary batteries are located in the rear of the vehicle and/or under a panel. ● **SEE FIGURE 7–16.**

When using jumper cables or a battery jump box, the last connection made should always be on the engine block or an engine bracket on the dead vehicle as far from the battery as possible. It is normal for a spark to be created when the jumper cables finally complete the jumping circuit, and this spark could cause an explosion of the gases around the battery. Many

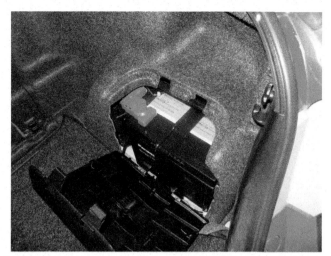

FIGURE 7–16 The 12-volt auxiliary AGM battery for this Camry hybrid was located in the trunk under a covering panel.

FIGURE 7–17 The high-voltage battery and motor controls are located behind the rear passenger's seat in a Honda Civic.

newer vehicles have special ground and/or positive power connections built away from the battery just for the purpose of jump starting. Check the owner's manual or service information for the exact location.

HYBRID AND ELECTRIC VEHICLE HIGH-VOLTAGE BATTERIES

PURPOSE AND FUNCTION Most hybrid electric vehicles use dual-voltage electrical systems. The high-voltage (HV) system is used to power the electric drive (traction) motor, while a conventional 12-volt system is used to power all other aspects of vehicle operation. One advantage to using this system is that the vehicle can use any conventional electrical accessories in its design.

NOTE: It is possible for an HEV to have three separate voltage systems. The Toyota Highlander HEV has a 12-volt auxiliary system, a 42-volt system for the electric power assist steering, and a 288-volt system for the hybrid drive.

ELECTRIC MOTOR REQUIREMENTS HEVs use high-output electric motors to drive and assist vehicle movement. These motors are rated anywhere from 10 to 50 kW, so they consume large amounts of electrical power during operation. If a conventional 12-volt electrical system was used to power these motors, the amount of current flow required would be extremely large and the cables used to transmit this energy would also be so large as to be impractical. Also, the motors used in these systems would have large gauge windings and would be big and heavy relative to their power output.

Automotive engineers overcome this problem by increasing the voltage provided to the motors, thus decreasing the amount of current that must flow to meet the motor's wattage requirements. (see Frequently Asked Question, "Why Do Higher Voltage Motors Draw Less Current?"). Smaller amounts of current flowing in the cables mean that the cables can be sized smaller, making it much more practical to place a battery in the rear of the vehicle and run cables from there to the drive motor in the engine compartment. ● **SEE FIGURE 7–17.**

The motors can also be made much smaller and more powerful when they are designed to operate on higher voltages.

NICKEL-METAL HYDRIDE BATTERIES

USES Most current production HEVs use nickel-metal hydride (NiMH) battery technology for the high-voltage battery. NiMH batteries are being used for these applications because of their performance characteristics such as specific energy,

Why Do Higher Voltage Motors Draw Less Current?

Keep in mind that an electric motor is powered by wattage. Every electric motor is rated according to the amount of power (in watts) it consumes. Power is calculated using the following formula:

$$P = I \times E$$

or

Power (in watts) = Current (in amperes) × Voltage (in volts)

An electric motor rated at 144 watts will consume 12 amperes at 12 volts of applied voltage (12 volts × 12 amperes = 144 watts). If this same motor was powered with 6 volts, it would draw 24 amperes to achieve the same power output. This increase in current draw would require a much bigger cable to efficiently transmit the electric current and minimize voltage drop. The motor windings would also have to be much heavier to handle this increased current. Imagine that we power this same motor with a 144-volt battery. Now we require only 1 ampere of electrical current to operate the motor (144 volts × 1 ampere = 144 watts). The cable required to transmit this current could be sized much smaller and it will now be much easier to run the cables over the length of the car without significant power loss. Also, the electric motor can be made much smaller and more efficient when less current is needed to power it. Some hybrid systems have motors that operate at up to 650 volts in an effort to increase system efficiency.

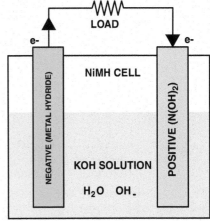

FIGURE 7–18 An NiMH cell. The unique element in a nickel-metal hydride cell is the negative electrode which is a hydrogen absorbing alloy. The positive electrode is nickel hydroxide. The electrolyte does not enter into the chemical reaction and is able to maintain a constant conductivity regardless of the state-of-charge of the cell.

battery achieve high power performance and excellent cycle life. ● **SEE FIGURE 7–18.**

OPERATION DURING CHARGING During battery charging, hydrogen ions (protons) travel from the positive electrode to the negative electrode, where they are absorbed into the metal hydride material. The electrolyte does not participate in the reaction and acts only as a medium for the hydrogen ions to travel through.

OPERATION DURING DISCHARGING When the battery is discharged, this process reverses, with the hydrogen ions (protons) traveling from the negative electrode back to the positive electrode. The density of the electrodes changes somewhat during the charge–discharge process, but this is kept to a minimum as only protons are exchanged during battery cycling. Electrode stability due to minimal density changes is one of the reasons why the NiMH battery has very good cycle life. ● **SEE FIGURE 7–19.**

ADVANTAGES Nickel-based alkaline batteries have a number of advantages over other battery designs. These include the following:

- High specific energy.
- The nickel electrode can be manufactured with large surface areas, which increase the overall battery capacity.
- The electrolyte does not react with steel, so NiMH batteries can be housed in sealed steel containers that transfer heat reasonably well.
- The materials used in NiMH batteries are environmentally friendly and can be recycled.
- Excellent cycle life.
- Durable and safe.

cycle life, and safety. From a manufacturing perspective, the NiMH battery is attractive because the materials used in its construction are plentiful and recyclable.

DESCRIPTION AND OPERATION Nickel-Metal Hydride (NiMH) uses a positive electrode made of nickel hydroxide and potassium hydroxide electrolyte. The nominal voltage of an NiMH battery cell is 1.2 volts. The negative electrode is unique, however, in that it is a hydrogen-absorbing alloy, also known as a **metal hydride.**

ELECTROLYTE NiMH batteries are known as alkaline batteries due to the alkaline (pH greater than 7) nature of the electrolyte. The electrolyte is aqueous potassium hydroxide. Potassium hydroxide works very well for this application because it does not corrode the other parts of the battery and can be housed in a sealed steel container. Also, potassium hydroxide does not take part in the chemical reaction of the battery, so the electrolyte concentration stays constant at any given state-of-charge (SOC). These factors help the NiMH

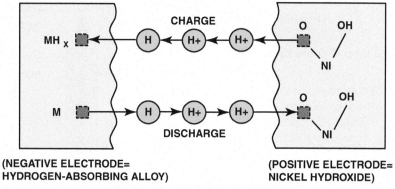

(NEGATIVE ELECTRODE=
HYDROGEN-ABSORBING ALLOY)

(POSITIVE ELECTRODE=
NICKEL HYDROXIDE)

FIGURE 7–19 Chemical reactions inside an NiMH cell. Charging and discharging both involve an exchange of hydrogen ions (protons) between the two electrodes.

DISADVANTAGES   Disadvantages of the NiMH battery include the following:

- High rate of self-discharge, especially at elevated temperatures.
- Moderate levels of memory effect, although this seems to be less prominent in newer designs.
- Moderate to high cost.

NiMH BATTERY DESIGNS   There are two primary designs for an NiMH battery cell. These are:

1. **Cylindrical type.** The cylindrical type has the active materials made in long ribbons and arranged in a spiral fashion inside a steel cylinder (case). The negative electrode is wound alongside the positive electrode, and the separator material holding the electrolyte is placed between them. The negative electrode is attached to the steel battery case, while the positive electrode is attached to the (−) terminal at the top of the battery. There is a self-resealing safety vent located at the top of the battery case, which will relieve internal pressure in case of overcharge, short circuiting, reverse charge, or other abuse. Cylindrical cells are often constructed very similar to a conventional "D" cell. Cylindrical cells are most often incorporated into modules with a group of six cells connected in series. This creates a single **battery module** with a 7.2-volt output. Groups of these modules can then be connected in series to create higher voltage battery packs. ● **SEE FIGURE 7–20.**

2. **Prismatic type.** The prismatic type is a rectangular or boxlike design with the active materials formed into flat plates, much like a conventional lead-acid battery. The positive and negative plates are placed alternately in the battery case, with tabs used to connect the plate groups. Separator material is placed between the plates to prevent them from touching but still allow electrolyte to circulate freely. ● **SEE FIGURE 7–21.**

BATTERY CELLS ARE CONNECTED IN SERIES   Each cell of an NiMH battery produces only 1.2 volts. In order to create a battery pack that is capable of producing high

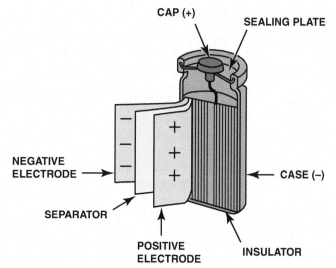

FIGURE 7–20 Cylindrical type NiMH batteries are made with stainless steel housing.

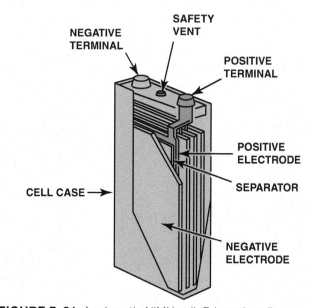

FIGURE 7–21 A prismatic NiMH cell. Prismatic cells are built with flat plates and separators similar to conventional lead–acid batteries.

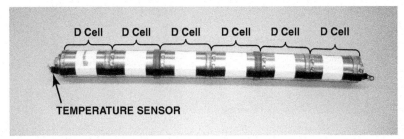

D Cell   D Cell   D Cell   D Cell   D Cell   D Cell

TEMPERATURE SENSOR

FIGURE 7–22 Each cell has 1.25 volts and a group of six as shown has 7.5 volts. These sections are then connected to other sections to create the high-voltage battery pack.

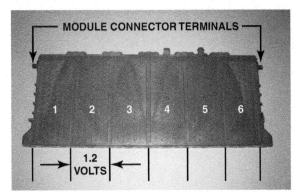

MODULE CONNECTOR TERMINALS

1   2   3   4   5   6

1.2 VOLTS

FIGURE 7–23 A prismatic NiMH module from a Toyota Prius HV battery pack. The battery posts are located on the left and right sides of the module. A self-resealing vent is located on the top right for venting hydrogen gas if the module overheats.

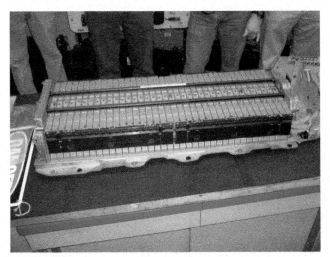

FIGURE 7–24 A Toyota Camry Hybrid high-voltage battery pack with a total of 34 battery modules connected in series. Each module was rated at 7.2 volts, making 7.2 × 34 = 244 volts of battery output.

voltage, many individual NiMH cells must be connected in series. **SEE FIGURE 7–22.**

Battery designers are limited by the nominal cell voltage of the battery technology. In the case of NiMH batteries, each cell is capable of producing only 1.2 volts. A high-voltage battery based on NiMH technology must be built using

multiples of 1.2 volts. In order to build a 144-volt battery, 114 individual NiMH cells must be connected together in series (144 × 1.2 volts). Obviously, the higher the voltage output of the battery, the greater the number of individual battery cells that must be used to achieve the necessary voltage. **SEE FIGURES 7–23 AND 7–24.**

 FREQUENTLY ASKED QUESTION

How Is SOC of an NiMH Battery Determined?

The state-of-charge (SOC) of an NiMH battery cannot be measured using cell voltage alone. Instead, SOC is determined using a complex calculation based on battery temperature, output current, and cell voltage. Accurate SOC measurements are critical for maximizing NiMH battery performance and service life.

HIGH-VOLTAGE BATTERY COOLING High operating temperatures can lower performance and cause damage to an NiMH battery pack. All current production HEVs use air cooling to control HV battery pack temperature. Cabin air is circulated over the battery cells using an electric fan and ducting inside the vehicle. **SEE FIGURE 7–25.**

Temperature sensors (**thermistors**) are mounted in various locations in the battery pack housing to send data to the module responsible for controlling battery temperature. These inputs are used to help determine battery charge rate and cooling fan operation. In the case of the Ford Escape Hybrid, the air conditioning system has an extra zone that cools the air being circulated over the HV battery pack. **SEE FIGURE 7–26.**

LITHIUM-ION HIGH-VOLTAGE BATTERIES

USES A battery design that shows a great deal of promise for electric vehicles (EV) and hybrid electric vehicles (HEV) applications is **lithium-ion (Li-ion)** technology. Lithium-ion

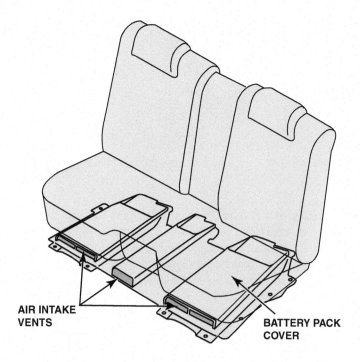

AIR INTAKE VENTS

BATTERY PACK COVER

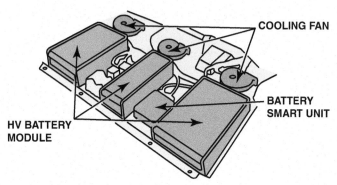

COOLING FAN

HV BATTERY MODULE

BATTERY SMART UNIT

FIGURE 7–25 The battery cooling system for a Toyota hybrid SUV. All production hybrid HV battery packs are air cooled. Note the air intake vents located under the seats.

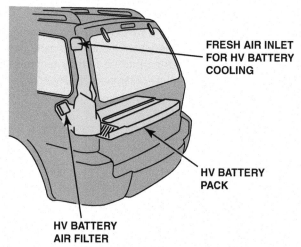

FRESH AIR INLET FOR HV BATTERY COOLING

HV BATTERY PACK

HV BATTERY AIR FILTER

FIGURE 7–26 The HV battery cooling system from a Ford Escape Hybrid. Ford uses outside air to cool the battery pack, then increases cooling with a separate zone in the A/C system when necessary.

ACCESS DOOR TO CHARGE PORT

FIGURE 7–27 The Tesla roadster uses 6,800 small Li-ion cells that are slightly larger than an AA battery to power this high-performance sports car. The 375-volt battery pack can supply up to 900 amperes of current to the 3-phase AC induction motor to deliver 295 lbs-ft of torque to the rear drive wheels.

batteries have been used extensively in consumer electronics since 1991 and are currently used in the following vehicles:

- Chevrolet Volt
- Nissan Leaf
- Tesla (● **SEE FIGURE 7–27**)

? FREQUENTLY ASKED QUESTIONS

How Many Types of Lithium-ion Batteries Are There?

There are numerous types of lithium-ion batteries, and the list is growing. While every component of the battery is under development, the primary difference between the various designs is the materials used for the positive electrode or *cathode*. The original Li-ion cell design used lithium cobalt oxide for its cathode, which has good energy storage characteristics but suffers chemical breakdown at relatively low temperatures. This failure results in the release of heat and oxygen, which often leads to a fire or explosion as the electrolyte ignites.

In order to make lithium-ion batteries safer and more durable, a number of alternative cathode materials have been formulated. One of the more promising cathode designs for automotive applications is lithium iron phosphate ($LiFePO_4$), which is stable at higher temperatures and releases less energy when it does suffer breakdown. Other lithium-ion cathode designs include the following:

- Lithium nickel cobalt oxide (LNCO)
- Lithium metal oxide (LMO)
- Nickel cobalt manganese (NCM)
- Nickel cobalt aluminum (NCA)
- Manganese oxide spinel (MnO)

Research and development continues on not only cathode design but also anodes, separator materials, and electrolyte chemistry.

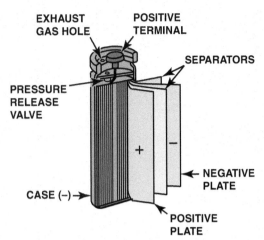

FIGURE 7–28 Construction of a cylindrical lithium-ion cell. Note the pressure relief valve and exhaust gas hole that will relieve internal battery pressure if it gets too hot.

DESCRIPTION A lithium-ion cell is named so because during battery cycling, lithium ions move back and forth between the positive and negative electrodes. Lithium-ion has approximately twice the specific energy of nickel-metal hydride (NiMH).

CONSTRUCTION The positive electrode in a conventional lithium-ion battery has lithium cobalt oxide as its main ingredient, with the negative electrode being made from a specialty carbon. The electrolyte is an organic solvent, and this is held in a separator layer between the two electrode plates. To prevent battery rupture and ensure safety, a pressure release valve is built into the battery's housing that will release gas if the internal pressure rises above a preset point. ● **SEE FIGURE 7–28.**

OPERATION The lithium-ion cell is designed so that lithium ions can pass back and forth between the electrodes when the battery is in operation.

1. During battery discharge, lithium ions leave the anode (negative electrode) and enter the cathode (positive electrode).

2. The reverse takes place when the battery is charging.

ADVANTAGES Lithium-ion batteries have the following advantages:

- High specific energy
- Good high temperature performance
- Low self-discharge
- Minimal memory effect
- High nominal cell voltage. The nominal voltage of a lithium-ion cell is 3.6 volts, which is three times that of nickel-based alkaline batteries. This allows for fewer battery cells being required to produce high voltage from an HV battery. ● **SEE FIGURE 7–29**

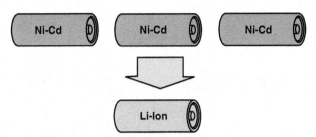

FIGURE 7–29 One advantage of a lithium-ion cell is that it produces 3.6 volts, whereas an NiMH cell produces only 1.2 volts.

DISADVANTAGES Disadvantages of the lithium-ion battery include:

- High cost
- Issues related to battery overheating

NOTE: Early lithium-ion battery designs have experienced problems with thermal runaway, which has led to fire and even explosions. Li-ion battery packs in automotive applications must be designed with cooling and safety systems that will prevent overheating and isolate cell failures.

? FREQUENTLY ASKED QUESTION

What Were the Causes of Lithium-ion Battery Failure?

Three major factors are responsible for failure of lithium-ion batteries.

- Operating the cells outside their required voltage range (2 to 4 volts)
- Operating the cells outside their required temperature range of 32° to 176°F (0° to 80° C)
- Short circuits (internal or external)

For these reasons, lithium-ion battery packs in automotive applications require precise battery management using specialized cooling and safety systems.

STATE-OF-CHARGE MANAGEMENT The HV battery in a hybrid electric vehicle is subjected to constant charging and discharging during normal operation. The battery can overheat under the following conditions:

1. The battery state-of-charge (SOC) rises above 80%.

2. The battery is placed under a load when its SOC is below 20%. In order to prevent overheating and maximize service life, the battery SOC must be carefully managed. In most hybrid electric vehicle applications, a target SOC of 60% is used, and the battery is then cycled so its SOC varies no more than 20% higher or lower than the target. ● **SEE FIGURE 7–30.**

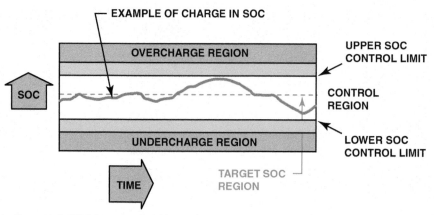

FIGURE 7–30 The HV battery pack SOC is maintained in a relatively narrow range to prevent overheating and maximize service life.

NOTE: The Chevrolet Volt is designed to allow the state-of-charge to drop to 25% to 35% before the gasoline engine is started to maintain that level of state-of-charge. The cooling system and software are designed to allow this reduced SOC so that the vehicle can be driven for an extended distance without having to start the engine.

HIGH-VOLTAGE BATTERY AND DISCONNECT LOCATION

PURPOSE AND FUNCTION Most hybrid electric vehicles are equipped with a high-voltage disconnect switch or connector that is used to cut off high voltage from the rest of the system beyond the battery pack. This disconnect does not need to be removed or switched unless service work is being performed on the high-voltage circuits in the vehicle. Always follow the exact safety instruction as stated in service information before working around any of the high-voltage components or wiring.

BATTERY TYPE AND SAFETY SWITCH/PLUG LOCATION ● **SEE CHART 7–4** for the location and type of batteries used for the high-voltage system and the location of the high-voltage disconnect switch.

OTHER HIGH-VOLTAGE BATTERY TYPES

There are many different types of batteries that are not currently being used in electric or hybrid electric vehicles but may find other applications in future vehicles. These types of batteries include the following types:

NICKEL-CADMIUM The nickel-cadmium design is known as an **alkaline** battery, because of the alkaline nature of its **electrolyte.** Alkaline batteries generate electrical energy through the chemical reaction of a metal with oxygen in an alkaline electrolyte. A nickel-cadmium battery uses the following materials:

- Nickel hydroxide for the positive electrode
- Metallic cadmium for the negative electrode
- Potassium hydroxide (an alkaline solution) for the electrolyte

The nominal voltage of a Ni-Cd battery cell is 1.2 volts.

- **Advantages of Ni-Cd batteries** include:
  - good low-temperature performance
  - long life
  - excellent reliability
  - low maintenance requirements.
- **Disadvantages of Ni-Cd batteries** include:
  - Ni-Cd batteries have a specific energy that is only slightly better than lead-acid technology
  - suffers from toxicity related to its cadmium content.

? FREQUENTLY ASKED QUESTIONS

How Is an Alkaline Battery Different from a Lead-Acid Battery?

Lead-acid batteries use sulfuric acid as the electrolyte, which acts as the medium between the battery's positive and negative electrodes. Acids have a pH that is below 7, and pure water has a pH of exactly 7. If electrolyte from a lead-acid battery is spilled, it can be neutralized using a solution of baking soda and water (an alkaline solution).

Alkaline batteries use an electrolyte such as potassium hydroxide, which has a pH greater than 7. This means that the electrolyte solution is basic, which is the opposite of acidic. If an alkaline battery's electrolyte is spilled, it can be neutralized using a solution of vinegar and water (vinegar is acidic). Both nickel-cadmium (Ni-Cd) and nickel-metal hydride (NiMH) batteries are alkaline battery designs.

MAKE/MODEL/YEAR	HIGH-VOLTAGE BATTERY TYPE AND VOLTAGE	HIGH-VOLTAGE BATTERY LOCATION	HIGH-VOLTAGE SAFETY SWITCH/PLUG LOCATION
Buick LaCrosse (2012+)	115 volts Li-ion	Behind rear seat	Located on the side of the battery pack behind the rear seat
Cadillac Escalade (2008+) (two mode)	300 volts NiMH	Under second row seat	Under second row seat; passenger side
Chevrolet Malibu (2008–2011)	36 volts NiMH	Mounted behind rear seat under vehicle	Located on the side of the battery pack behind the rear seat
Chevrolet Malibu (2012+)	115 volts Li-ion	Behind rear seat	Located on the side of the battery pack behind the rear seat
Chevrolet Silverado (2004–2008) (PHT)	36 volts AGM lead-acid batteries	Under second row seat	Rear passenger side behind cover
Chevrolet Tahoe (2008+) (two mode)	300 volts NiMH	Under second row seat	Under second row seat; passenger side
Chevrolet Volt (2011+)	346 volts Li-ion	Under the center of the vehicle and under the rear seat	In the center console (remove inner tray to get access)
Chrysler Aspen (2009)	288 volts NiMH	Under rear seat; Driver's side	Under the front of the rear seat; driver's side
Dodge Durango (2009)	288 volts NiMH	Under rear seat; Driver's side	Under the front of the rear seat; driver's side
Ford Escape (2005+)	300 volts NiMH	Cargo area in the rear under carpet	Under rear carpet; round orange switch on passenger side
GMC Sierra (2004–2008) (PHT)	36 volts AGM lead-acid batteries	Under second row seat	Rear passenger side behind cover
GMC Yukon (2008+) (two mode)	300 volts NiMH	Under second row seat	Under second row seat; passenger side
Honda Accord (2005–2007)	144 volts NiMH	Behind rear seat	Switch on battery pack behind rear seat
Honda Civic (2003+)	144 volts–158 volts depending on model year. NiMH	Behind rear seat	Switch on battery pack behind rear seat
Honda Insight (1999–2005)	144 volts NiMH	Under the hatch floor in rear	Under the hatch carpet; remove small plate in center
Honda Insight (2010+)	144 volts NiMH	Under the floor behind rear seat	Switch on battery pack behind rear seat
Lexus GS450h (2007+)	288 volts NiMH	Trunk behind rear seat	No high-voltage disconnect; disconnect 12-volt battery to de-power the high-voltage system
Lexus LS 600h (2006+)	288 volts NiMH	Trunk behind rear seat	No high-voltage disconnect; disconnect 12-volt battery to de-power the high-voltage system
LexusRX400h/RX 450h (2006+)	288 volts NiMH	Under the second row seat	Under the second row seat; driver's side behind an access panel
Mercury Mariner (2005–2011)	300 volts NiMH	Cargo area in the rear under carpet	Under rear carpet; round orange switch on passenger side
Nissan Altima (2007–2011)	245 volts NiMH	Behind rear seat	Trunk area; passenger side of high-voltage battery pack

CHART 7–4

Hybrid electric vehicle high-voltage battery type location and location of the disconnect switch/plug.

CONTINUED

MAKE/MODEL/YEAR	HIGH-VOLTAGE BATTERY TYPE AND VOLTAGE	HIGH-VOLTAGE BATTERY LOCATION	HIGH-VOLTAGE SAFETY SWITCH/PLUG LOCATION
Nissan Leaf (2011+)	360 volts Li-ion	Under the vehicle	Under rear floor
Saturn AURA Hybrid (2007–2010)	36 volts NiMH	Behind the rear seat; under the vehicle floor	Located on the side of the battery pack behind rear seat
Saturn VUE Hybrid (2007–2010)	36 volts NiMH	Behind the rear seat	Located on the side of the battery pack behind rear seat
Toyota Camry Hybrid (2007+)	245 volts NiMH	Behind the rear seat	Orange disconnect with integral fuse on left side of battery pack
Toyota Highlander Hybrid (2006+)	288 volts NiMH	Under the second row seat	Under the second row seat; driver's side behind an access panel
Toyota Prius (2001–2003)	274 volts NiMH	Behind rear seat	Orange disconnect with integral fuse on left side of battery pack
Toyota Prius (2004–2009)	201 volts NiMH	Behind rear seat	Orange disconnect with integral fuse on left side of battery pack
Toyota Prius (2010+)	201 volts NiMH	Behind rear seat	Orange disconnect with integral fuse on left side of battery pack

CHART 7–4 (CONTINUED)

LITHIUM POLYMER The **lithium-polymer (Li-poly)** battery design came out of the development of solid state electrolytes in the 1970s. Solid state electrolytes are solids that can conduct ions but do not allow electrons to move through them. Since lithium-polymer batteries use solid electrolytes, they are known as **solid-state** batteries. Solid polymer is much less flammable than liquid electrolytes and is able to conduct ions at temperatures above 140°F (60°C).

- **Advantages.** Li-poly batteries show good promise for EV and HEV applications for a number of reasons, including the following:

  - The lithium in the battery is in ionic form, making the battery safer because it is much less reactive than pure lithium metal.

  - The Li-poly battery cell can be made in many different shapes and forms, so they can be made to fit into the available space in the vehicle chassis.

  - Li-Poly batteries have good cycle and calendar life, and have the potential to have the highest specific energy and power of any battery technology.

- **Disadvantages.** The major disadvantage with the Li-poly battery is that it is a high-temperature design and must be operated between 176°F and 248°F (80°C and 120°C).

H2/ZINC-AIR The **Zinc-air** design is a mechanically rechargeable battery. This is because it uses a positive electrode of gaseous oxygen and a sacrificial negative electrode made of zinc. The negative electrode is spent during the discharge cycle, and the battery is recharged by replacing the zinc electrodes. Zinc-air is one of several metal–air battery

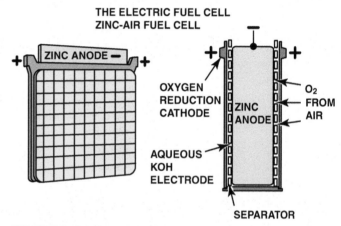

THE ELECTRIC FUEL CELL
ZINC-AIR FUEL CELL

FIGURE 7–31 Zinc-air batteries are recharged by replacing the zinc anodes. These batteries are also considered to be a type of fuel cell, because the positive electrode is oxygen taken from atmospheric air.

designs (others include aluminum-air and iron-air) that must be recharged by replacement of the negative electrode (anode).
● **SEE FIGURE 7–31.**

- **Advantages.** Zinc-air has a very high specific energy and efficiency, and the potential range of an EV vehicle equipped with a zinc-air battery is up to 600 km. Zinc-air batteries can be recharged very quickly, since a full recharge is achieved through replacement of the zinc electrodes.

- **Disadvantages.** The primary disadvantage with this design is the level of infrastructure required to make recharging practical.

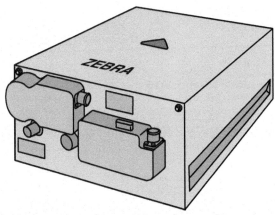

FIGURE 7–32 Sodium-metal-chloride batteries are also known as ZEBRA batteries. These batteries are lightweight (40% of the weight of lead-acid) and have a high energy density.

ZEBRA BATTERY

- **Construction.** The ZEBRA battery is a sodium-metal-chloride battery. This battery was invented in 1985 by the *Zeolite Battery Research Africa* (ZEBRA) project. This type of battery uses two different electrolytes; first, the beta alumina similar to the sodium-sulfur design, then another layer of electrolyte between the beta alumina and the positive electrode. ● **SEE FIGURE 7–32.**

- **Advantage.** This design has been used successfully in various applications and has proven to be safe under all operating conditions. Sodium-metal-chloride technology is considered to have very good potential for EV and HEV applications.

- **Disadvantage.** A disadvantage of the sodium-metal-chloride design is high operating temperatures.

BATTERY COMPARSION

● **CHART 7–5** shows a comparison of specific energy and nominal voltage for the various battery technologies.

HIGH-VOLTAGE BATTERY SERVICE

During normal vehicle operation, the charge and discharge cycles of the high-voltage battery in an HEV are monitored and controlled by a separate battery module. This module monitors battery temperature, current, and voltage to calculate SOC and determine at what rate the battery should be charged. While dealerships sometimes have a special high-voltage battery charger for recharging HEV battery packs, the best charger is the vehicle itself. If the HV battery in an HEV becomes discharged, the first step ought to be getting the vehicle started to recharge the battery pack. The procedure will vary depending on the model in question. Always follow the manufacturer's specified procedures when starting a disabled hybrid vehicle.

HIGH-VOLTAGE BATTERY SAFETY PRECAUTIONS

Always keep in mind that the high-voltage batteries for an HEV can produce sufficient voltage and current to severely injure or kill. Always wear appropriate personal protective equipment

BATTERY TYPE COMPARISON CHART				
BATTERY TYPE	NOMINAL VOLTAGE (V) PER CELL	THEORETICAL SPECIFIC ENERGY (WH/KG*)	PRACTICAL SPECIFIC ENERGY (WH/KG*)	MAJOR ISSUES
Lead-Acid	2.1	252	35	Heavy, low cycle life, toxic materials
Nickel-Cadmium	1.2	244	50	Toxic materials, cost
Nickel-Metal Hydride	1.2	278–800	80	Cost, high self-discharge rate, memory effect
Lithium-Ion	3.6	766	120	Safety issues, calendar life, cost
Zinc-Air	1.1	1320	110	Low power, limited cycle life, bulky
Sodium-Sulfur	2.0	792	100	High-temperature battery, safety, low power electrolyte
Sodium-Metal-Chloride (ZEBRA)	2.5	787	90	High temperature operation, low power

*Specific energy is measured in watt-hours/kilogram

CHART 7–5

Secondary type battery comparison showing specifications and limitations.

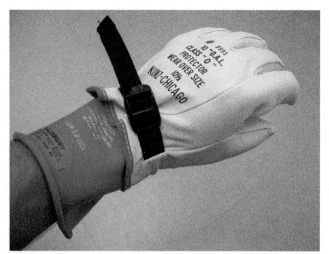

FIGURE 7–33 Appropriate personal protective equipment (PPE) must be worn whenever working on or around a hybrid vehicle high-voltage system.

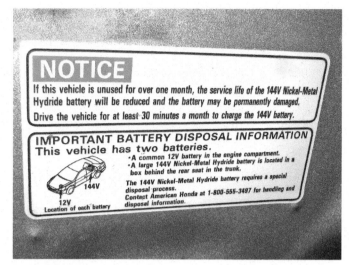

FIGURE 7–34 A battery service warning label from a Honda hybrid electric vehicle.

(PPE) and use approved safety procedures when working around these batteries. ● **SEE FIGURE 7–33.** Precautions include the following steps:

- Do not work on the vehicle if moisture is present on the skin or anywhere on or near the vehicle.
- If service must be performed on the hybrid system, be sure to disconnect the HV battery and allow enough time for system capacitors to discharge before proceeding.
- If an electrical fire occurs, do not attempt to extinguish it using water. Use an ABC fire extinguisher or wait for firefighters to deal with it.
- ALWAYS refer to the service manual for approved safety procedures when handling the HV battery pack.

- The battery case contains liquid potassium hydroxide, a strong alkali solution. Any liquid around the battery should be checked with litmus paper to determine if it is an electrolyte spill. If an electrolyte spill has occurred, be sure to disable the HV system, and then use a mixture of vinegar and water to neutralize the solution before cleaning up with soap and water.
- Remove any clothing that has come into contact with electrolyte and flush any exposed skin with large amounts of water. If electrolyte comes in contact with the eyes, flush with large amounts of water, but do not use a neutralizing solution. Be sure to seek medical advice to prevent further injury from electrolyte contact.
- Read all warning labels and always follow the vehicle manufacturer's instructions. ● **SEE FIGURE 7–34.**

SUMMARY

1. When a flooded-type lead-acid battery is being discharged, the acid (SO_4) is leaving the electrolyte and being deposited on the plates. When the battery is being charged, the acid (SO_4) is forced off the plates and back into the electrolyte.

2. Flood-type lead acid batteries give off hydrogen and oxygen when being charged.

3. Auxiliary batteries are rated according to CCA and reserve capacity.

4. Auxiliary batteries can be tested with a voltmeter to determine the state of charge. A battery load test loads the battery to one-half of its CCA rating.

5. A good auxiliary battery should be able to maintain higher than 9.6 volts for the entire 15 seconds test period.

6. Auxiliary batteries can be tested with a conductance tester even if discharged.

7. A battery drain test should be performed if the battery runs down.

8. Be sure that a battery charger is unplugged from a power outlet when making connections to a battery.

9. NiMH batteries are the type most used in hybrid electric vehicles.

10. Lithium-ion (Li-ion) type batteries are used in some electric and plug-in electric vehicles.

1. Why can discharged batteries freeze?
2. What are the battery-rating methods?
3. What are the results of a voltmeter test of a battery and its state-of-charge?

4. What are the steps for performing a battery load test?
5. What battery types are most used in electric and hybrid electric vehicles?

CHAPTER QUIZ

1. When an auxiliary battery becomes completely discharged, both positive and negative plates become _____ and the electrolyte becomes _____.
   a. H_2SO_4/Pb
   b. $PbSO_4/H_2O$
   c. PbO_2/H_2SO_4
   d. $PbSO_4/H_2SO_4$

2. Deep cycling means _____.
   a. Overcharging the battery
   b. Overfilling or underfilling the battery with water
   c. The battery is fully discharged and then recharged
   d. The battery is overfilled with acid (H_2SO_4)

3. Which battery rating is tested at 0°F (–18°C)?
   a. Cold-cranking amperes (CCA)
   b. Cranking amperes (CA)
   c. Reserve capacity
   d. Battery voltage test

4. Which battery rating is expressed in minutes?
   a. Cold-cranking amperes (CCA)
   b. Cranking amperes (CA)
   c. Reserve capacity
   d. Battery voltage test

5. What battery rating is tested at 32°F (0°C)?
   a. Cold-cranking amperes (CCA)
   b. Cranking amperes (CA)
   c. Reserve capacity
   d. Battery voltage test

6. When load testing a battery, which battery rating is often used to determine how much load to apply to the battery?
   a. CA
   b. RC
   c. MCA
   d. CCA

7. A battery high-rate discharge (load capacity) test is being performed on a 12-volt battery. Technician A says that a good battery should have a voltage reading of higher than 9.6 volts while under load at the end of the 15 seconds test. Technician B says that the battery should be discharged (loaded) to twice its CCA rating. Which technician is correct?
   a. Technician A only
   b. Technician B only
   c. Both technicians A and B
   d. Neither technician A nor B

8. When charging a lead-acid (flooded-type) battery, _____.
   a. The initial charging rate should be about 35 amperes for 30 minutes
   b. The time is determined by the reserve capacity divided by the charge current
   c. The battery temperature should not exceed 125°F (hot to the touch)
   d. All of the above

9. Where are AGM auxiliary batteries usually located in a hybrid electric vehicle?
   a. Under the hood
   b. In the trunk/rear area
   c. Under the front fender
   d. Under the front seat

10. Which type of battery is most used in hybrid electric vehicles?
    a. Nickel-Metal Hydride
    b. Lithium-Ion
    c. Nickel-Cadmium
    d. Sodium-Nickel Chloride

OBJECTIVES: **After studying Chapter 8 this chapter, the reader will be able to:** • Describe the operation of DC and AC electric motors. • Explain how a brushless DC motor works. • Discuss the advantages and disadvantages of using electric motors in hybrid electric vehicles. • Explain how electric power steering works. • Describe how a DC-to-DC converter works. • Discuss how a DC-to-AC inverter works.

KEY TERMS: • ACIM 108 • AC Induction motor 108 • AC motor 110 • Armature 108 • Brushless motor 108 • Commutator 108 • DC motor 108 • Electrical noise 108 • Electromagnetics 104 • Electromagnetism 104 • EPS 118 • Flux 103 • hp 107 • IGBT 112 • Inverter 117 • IPM 109 • kW 107 • Lenz's law 107 • Lodestone 102 • Magnetism 102 • MOSFET 117 • PDU 111 • Permeability 104 • Pole 103 • PWM 110 • Reluctance 104 • Resolver 113 • Right-hand rule 104 • Rotor 107 • Senseless DC motor 109 • SPM 109 • Squirrel-cage rotor 108 • Stator 107

FUNDAMENTALS OF MAGNETISM

Magnetism is a form of energy that is generated by the motion of electrons and alignment of atoms in some materials. It is recognized by the attraction it exerts on other materials. Like electricity, magnetism cannot be seen. It can be explained in theory, however, because it is possible to see the results of magnetism and recognize the actions that it causes.

A type of iron ore, called **lodestone,** exists as a magnet in nature. ●**SEE FIGURE 8–1.**

Many other materials can be artificially magnetized to some degree, depending upon their atomic structure or iron content. Metals that do not contain iron, called nonferrous metals, cannot be magnetized. Metals that contain iron, called

🔧 TECH TIP

A Cracked Magnet Becomes Two Magnets

Magnets are commonly used in vehicle crankshaft, camshaft, and wheel speed sensors. If a magnet is struck and cracks or breaks, the result is two smaller-strength magnets. Because the strength of the magnetic field is reduced, the sensor output voltage is also reduced. A typical problem occurs when a magnetic crankshaft sensor becomes cracked, resulting in a no-start condition. Sometimes the cracked sensor works well enough to start an engine that is cranking at normal speeds but will not work when the engine is cold and cranks more slowly. ●**SEE FIGURE 8–2.**

FIGURE 8–1 A freely suspended natural magnet will point toward the magnetic north pole.

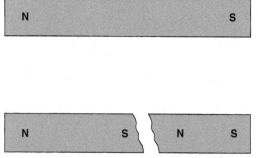

FIGURE 8–2 If a magnet breaks or is cracked, it becomes two weaker magnets.

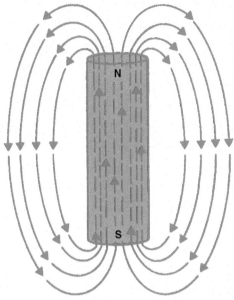

FIGURE 8–3 Magnetic lines of force leave the north pole and return to the south pole of a bar magnet.

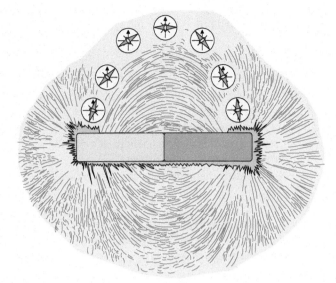

FIGURE 8–4 Iron filings or a compass can be used to observe the magnetic lines of force.

ferrous metals, can be magnetized. Soft iron, which has low carbon content, is very easy to magnetize. Nonferrous metals, such as aluminum, and nonmetals, such as glass, wood, and plastic, cannot be magnetized at all.

LINES OF FORCE The lines that create a field of force around a magnet are believed to be caused by the way groups of atoms are aligned in the magnetic material. In a bar magnet, the lines are concentrated at both ends of the bar and form closed, parallel loops in three dimensions around the magnet. Force does not flow along these lines the way electrical current flows, but the lines *do* have direction. They come out of one end, or **pole,** of the magnet and enter at the other end; they NEVER intersect. ● **SEE FIGURE 8–3.**

The opposite ends of a magnet are called its north and south poles. In reality, they should be called the "north seek-ing" and "south seeking" poles, because they seek the earth's North Pole and South Pole, respectively.

The stronger the magnet, the more magnetic lines that are formed. The magnetic lines of force, also called magnetic **flux,** or flux lines, form a magnetic field. The terms *magnetic field, lines of force, flux,* and *flux lines* are used interchangeably.

Flux density refers to the number of flux lines per unit of area. To determine flux density, divide the number of flux lines by the area in which the flux exists. For example, 100 flux lines divided by an area of 10 square centimeters equals a flux density of 10. A magnetic field can be measured using a Gauss gauge, named for German scientist Johann Carl Fredrick Gauss (1777–1855).

Magnetic lines of force can be seen by spreading fine iron filings or dust on a piece of paper laid on top of a magnet. A magnetic field can also be observed by using a compass. A compass is simply a thin magnet or magnetized iron needle balanced on a pivot. The needle will rotate to point toward the opposite pole of a magnet. It can be very sensitive to

small magnetic fields. Since it is a small magnet, a compass usually has one end marked N and the other marked S. ● **SEE FIGURE 8–4.**

ATTRACTING OR REPELLING The poles of a magnet are called north (N) and south (S) because when a magnet is suspended freely, the poles tend to point toward the North and South Poles of the earth.

Magnetic flux lines exit from the magnet's north pole and bend around to enter the south pole. An equal number of lines exit and enter, so magnetic force is equal at both poles of a magnet. Flux lines are concentrated at the poles, and therefore magnetic force (flux density) is stronger at the ends.

Magnetic poles behave like positively and negatively charged particles. When unlike poles are placed close together, the lines exit from one magnet and enter the other. The two magnets are pulled together by flux lines and the two magnetic fields join to become one large one. If like poles are placed close together, the curving flux lines meet head-on, forcing the magnets apart. Therefore, like poles of a magnet repel and the unlike poles attract. ● **SEE FIGURE 8–5.**

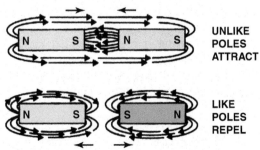

UNLIKE POLES ATTRACT

LIKE POLES REPEL

FIGURE 8–5 Magnetic poles behave like electrically charged particles—unlike poles attract and like poles repel.

Magnetize a Steel Needle

A piece of steel can be magnetized by rubbing a magnet in one direction along the steel. This causes the atoms to line up in the steel, so it acts like a magnet. The steel often won't remain magnetized, while the true magnet is permanently magnetized.

When soft iron or steel is used, such as a paper clip, it will lose its magnetism quickly. The atoms in a magnetized needle can be disturbed by heating it or by dropping the needle on a hard object, which would cause the needle to lose its magnetism. Soft iron is used inside ignition coils because it will not retain its magnetism.

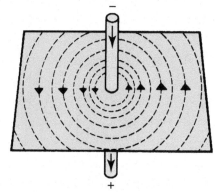

FIGURE 8–6 A magnetic field surrounds a current-carrying conductor.

PERMEABILITY Magnetic flux lines cannot be insulated. There is no known material through which magnetic force does not pass, if the force is strong enough. However, some materials allow the force to pass though more easily than others. This degree of passage is called **permeability.** Iron allows magnetic flux lines to pass through much more easily than air, so iron is very permeable.

RELUCTANCE While there is no absolute insulation for magnetism, certain materials resist the passage of magnetic force. This can be compared to resistance within an electrical circuit. Air does not allow easy passage, so air has a high **reluctance.** Magnetic flux lines tend to concentrate in permeable materials and avoid reluctant materials. As with electricity, magnetic force follows the path of least resistance.

wire and connect the ends to the terminals of a 1.5-volt dry-cell battery. When energized, the nail will become a magnet and will be able to pick up tacks or other small steel objects.

STRAIGHT CONDUCTOR The magnetic field surrounding a straight, current-carrying conductor exists along the entire length of the wire. The strength of the current determines how many flux lines there will be and how far out they extend from the surface of the wire. ● **SEE FIGURE 8–6.**

RIGHT-HAND RULE Magnetic flux cylinders have direction, just as the flux lines surrounding a bar magnet have direction.

Most automotive circuits use the conventional theory of current flow (+ to −), and therefore the **right-hand rule** is used to determine the direction of the magnetic flux lines. ● **SEE FIGURE 8–7.**

ELECTROMAGNETISM

PRINCIPLES Scientists discovered around 1820 that current-carrying conductors are also surrounded by a magnetic field. The creation of a magnetic field by the use of an electrical current is called **electromagnetism.** These fields may be made many times stronger than those surrounding conventional magnets. Also, the magnetic field strength around a conductor may be controlled by changing the current. As current increases, more flux lines are created and the magnetic field expands and becomes stronger. As current decreases, the magnetic field contracts, or collapses. These discoveries greatly broadened the practical uses of magnetism and opened an area of study known as **electromagnetics.**

CREATING AN ELECTROMAGNET A magnet can be created by magnetizing a piece of iron or steel or by using electricity to make an electromagnet. An easy way to create an electromagnet is to wrap a nail with 20 turns of insulated

TECH TIP

Electricity and Magnetism

Electricity and magnetism are closely related because whenever an electrical current is flowing through a conductor, a magnetic field is created. When a conductor is moved through a magnetic field, an electrical current is created. This relationship can be summarized as follows:

- Electricity creates magnetism.
- Magnetism creates electricity.

From a service technician's point of view, this is important because wires carrying current should always be routed as the factory intended to avoid causing interference with another circuit or electronic component. This is especially important when installing or servicing spark plug wires, which carry high voltages and can cause a lot of electromagnetic interference.

FIGURE 8–7 The right-hand rule for magnetic field direction is used with the conventional theory of electron flow.

FIGURE 8–8 Conductors with opposing magnetic fields will move apart into weaker fields.

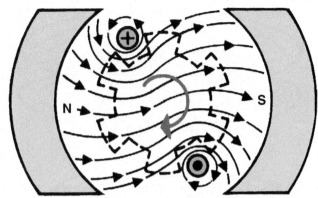

FIGURE 8–9 Electric motors use the interaction of magnetic fields to produce mechanical energy.

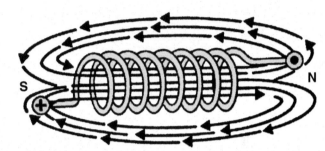

FIGURE 8–10 The magnetic lines of flux surrounding a coil look similar to those surrounding a bar magnet.

FIELD INTERACTION The cylinders of flux surrounding current-carrying conductors interact with other magnetic fields. In the following illustrations, the cross symbol (+) indicates current moving inward, or away from you. It represents the tail of an arrow. The dot symbol (•) represents an arrowhead and indicates current moving outward. If two conductors carry current in opposite directions, their magnetic fields also rotate in opposite directions. If they are placed side-by-side, the opposing flux lines between the conductors create a strong magnetic field. Current-carrying conductors tend to move out of a strong field into a weak field, so the conductors move away from each other. ● SEE FIGURE 8–8.

If the two conductors carry current in the same direction, their fields are in the same direction. The flux lines between the two conductors cancel each other out, leaving a very weak field between them. The conductors are drawn into this weak field, and they tend to move toward each other.

MOTOR PRINCIPLE Electric motors, such as automobile starter motors, use this field interaction to change electrical energy into mechanical energy. If two conductors carrying current in opposite directions are placed between strong north and south poles, the magnetic field of the conductor interacts with the magnetic fields of the poles. The clockwise field of the top conductor adds to the fields of the poles and creates a strong field beneath the conductor. The conductor then tries to move up to get out of this strong field. The counterclockwise field of the lower conductor adds to the field of the poles and creates a strong field above the conductor. The conductor then tries to move down to get out of this strong field. These forces cause the center of the motor, where the conductors are mounted, to turn clockwise. ● SEE FIGURE 8–9.

COIL CONDUCTOR If several loops of wire are made into a coil, the magnetic flux density is strengthened. Flux

lines around a coil are the same as the flux lines around a bar magnet. ● SEE FIGURE 8–10.

They exit from the north pole and enter at the south pole. The magnetic field of a coil can be strengthened by increasing the number of turns in the wire, by increasing the current through the coil, or both.

ELECTROMAGNETS The magnetic field surrounding a current-carrying coil of wire can be strengthened by using a soft iron core. Because soft iron is very permeable, magnetic flux lines pass through it easily. If a piece of soft iron is placed inside a coiled conductor, the flux lines concentrate in the iron core, rather than pass through the air, which is less permeable. The concentration of force greatly increases the strength of the magnetic field inside the coil. Coils with an iron core are called electromagnets. ● SEE FIGURE 8–11.

ELECTROMAGNETIC INDUCTION

PRINCIPLES Magnetic flux lines can create an electromotive force, or voltage, in a conductor if either the flux lines or the conductor is moving. This movement is called relative motion. In other words, there is relative

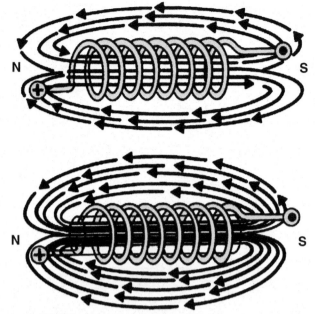

FIGURE 8–11 An iron core concentrates the magnetic lines of force surrounding a coil.

VOLTAGE STRENGTH Induced voltage depends upon magnetic flux lines being broken by a conductor. The strength of the voltage depends upon the rate at which the flux lines are broken. The more flux lines broken per unit of time, the greater the induced voltage. If a single conductor breaks one million flux lines per second, one volt is induced.

There are four ways to increase induced voltage:

- Increase the strength of the magnetic field, so there are more flux lines.
- Increase the number of conductors that are breaking the flux lines.
- Increase the speed of the relative motion between the conductor and the flux lines so that more lines are broken per time unit.
- Increase the angle between the flux lines and the conductor to a maximum of 90 degrees. There is no voltage induced if the conductors move parallel to, and do not break any, flux lines, as shown in ● **FIGURE 8–13.**

Maximum voltage is induced if the conductors break flux lines at 90 degrees and the voltage decreases when the flux lines are cut at angles between 0 and 90 degrees. ● **SEE FIGURE 8–14.**

Voltage can be electromagnetically induced, and can be measured. Induced voltage creates current. The direction of induced voltage (and the direction in which current moves) is called polarity and depends upon the direction of the flux lines, as well as the direction of relative motion.

motion between the flux lines and the conductor. This process is called induction, and the resulting electromotive force is called induced voltage. This creation of a voltage in a conductor by a moving magnetic field is called electromagnetic induction. If the conductor is in a complete circuit, current flows.

Voltage is induced when magnetic flux lines are broken by a conductor. This relative motion can be a conductor moving across a magnetic field or a magnetic field moving across a stationary conductor (as in alternators and ignition coils). In both cases, the induced voltage is generated by relative motion between the conductor and the magnetic flux lines. The highest voltage is generated when the motion is at right angles. ● **SEE FIGURE 8–12.**

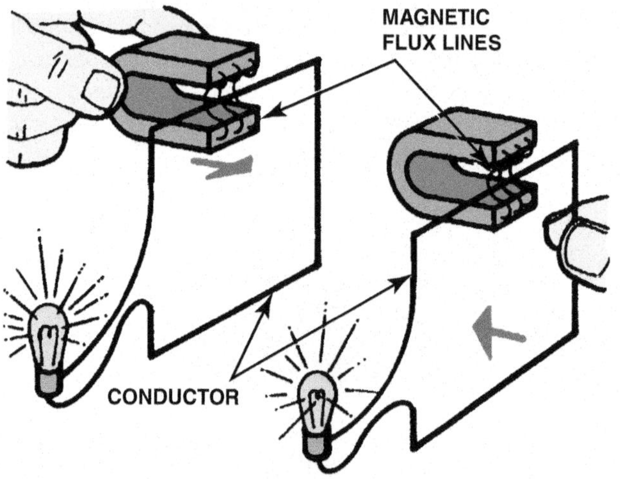

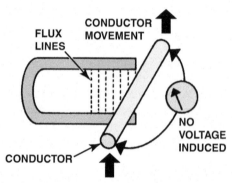

FIGURE 8–13 No voltage is induced if the conductor is moved in the same direction as the magnetic lines of force (flux lines).

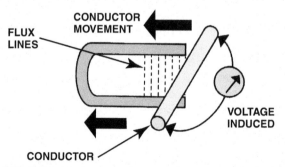

FIGURE 8–14 Maximum voltage is induced when conductors cut across the magnetic lines of force (flux lines) at a 90-degree angle.

FIGURE 8–12 Voltage can be induced by the relative motion between a conductor and magnetic lines of force.

An induced current moves so that its magnetic field opposes the motion that induced the current. This principle is called **Lenz's law.** The relative motion between a conductor and a magnetic field is opposed by the magnetic field of the current it has induced.

ELECTRIC MOTORS

ELECTRIC MOTOR POWER Electric motor power is expressed in **kilowatts (kW).** This is the preferred international standard for rating mechanical and electrical power. A 100% efficient motor would produce one kilowatt of mechanical power with an input of one kilowatt of electrical power. A kilowatt is equal to 1,000 watts. A watt is the amount of power that would lift an object weighing 3.6 ounces (102 grams) a distance of 39 inches (one meter) in one second. The watt scale of power measurement is named after the Scottish engineer James Watt. One **hp** is equal to 746 watts. The hp rating was developed by Watt in the late 1700s when horses were the main source of power. Watt wanted a way to express the amount of power available from steam engines in terms that could be easily understood. By doing some simple experiments, he determined that 550 foot-pounds per second was the power produced by an average horse. This means that the horse could lift a weight of 550 pounds one foot in one second.

Horsepower to Kilowatt Conversion Chart

Horsepower (hp)	Kilowatt (kW)
25	19
50	37
75	56
100	75
125	93
150	112
175	131
200	149

ELECTRIC MOTOR OPERATION Most electric motors work by electromagnetism and the fundamental principle that there is a mechanical force on any wire when it is conducting electricity while contained within a magnetic field. The force is described by the Lorentz force law and is perpendicular to both the wire and the magnetic field.

In an electric motor, the rotating part (usually on the inside) is called the **rotor,** and the stationary part is called the **stator.** The motor contains electromagnets that are wound on a frame. One basic principle of electromagnetism is that a magnetic field surrounds every conductor carrying a current. The strength of the magnetic field is increased as the current flow (in amperes) is increased.

Inside the starter housing is a strong magnetic field created by the field coil magnets. The armature, made up of many conductors, is installed inside this strong magnetic field, with very little clearance between the armature and the field coils.

The two magnetic fields act together, and their lines of force "bunch up" or are strong on one side of the armature loop wire and become weak on the other side of the conductor. This causes the conductor (armature) to move from the area of strong magnetic field strength toward the area of weak magnetic field strength.

This causes the armature to rotate. This rotation force (torque) is increased as the current flowing through the starter motor increases. The torque of a starter is determined by the strength of the magnetic fields. Magnetic field strength is measured in ampere-turns. If the current or the number of turns of wire is increased, the magnetic field strength is increased. ● **SEE FIGURE 8–15.**

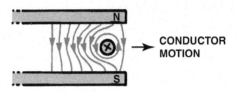

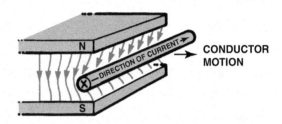

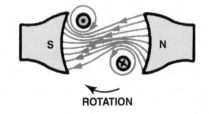

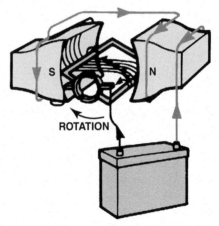

FIGURE 8–15 The armature loops rotate due to the difference in the strength of the magnetic field. The loops move from a strong magnetic field strength toward a weaker magnetic field strength.

FIGURE 8–16 A typical DC brush-type motor cutaway showing the armature, commutator, and brushes on the left side.

One of the first electromagnetic rotary motors was invented by Michael Faraday in 1821. The classic **DC motor** uses a rotating armature in the form of an electromagnet with two poles. A rotary switch called a **commutator** reverses the direction of the electric current twice every cycle, to flow through the **armature** so that the poles of the electromagnet push and pull against the permanent magnets on the outside of the motor. As the poles of the armature electromagnet pass the poles of the permanent magnets, the commutator reverses the polarity of the armature electromagnet. During that instant of switching polarity, inertia keeps the motor going in the proper direction. A typical DC motor today uses four poles, as shown in ● **FIGURE 8–16.**

When the coil is powered in a simple electric motor, a magnetic field is generated around the armature. The left side of the armature is pushed away from the left magnet and drawn toward the right, causing rotation. The armature continues to rotate. When the armature becomes horizontally aligned, the commutator reverses the direction of current through the coil, reversing the magnetic field. The process then repeats.

DC motor speed generally depends on a combination of the voltage and current flowing in the motor coils and the motor load or braking torque. The following are the basic principles of a typical DC motor:

- The speed of the motor is proportional to the applied voltage.
- The torque is proportional to the applied current.
- The speed is typically controlled by altering the voltage or current flow by using taps in the motor windings or by using a variable voltage supply.

The speed can also be controlled by using an electronic circuit that switches the supply voltage on and off very rapidly. As the "on" to "off" time is varied to alter the average applied voltage, the speed of the motor varies.

The use of brushes in an electric motor has many disadvantages, including:

1. Any arcing of the brushes also causes **electrical noise,** which can cause serious problems with the electronics in the vehicle.

2. The brushes eventually wear out and require replacement. This adds to the maintenance cost of the vehicle and could result in customer dissatisfaction due to motor failure and/or the cost involved in brush replacement.

BRUSHLESS MOTORS

There are two types of electric **brushless motors:** the AC induction motor and the AC synchronous motor.

AC INDUCTION MOTOR An **AC induction motor,** as is used in the General Motors parallel hybrid truck (PHT), uses electromagnetic induction from the stator to induce a current and therefore creates a magnetic field in the rotor without the need for brushes. An AC induction motor is also known as an AC asynchronous motor, or AC induction motor **(ACIM),** because it allows a certain amount of slip between the rotor and the changing magnetic field in the stator. The term *asynchronous* means that the speed of the motor is not necessarily related to the frequency of the current flowing through the stator windings. ACIMs include squirrel-cage and wound-rotor induction designs.

- A **squirrel-cage rotor** is composed of parallel thick copper or aluminum conductors connected to a ring of the same material at the ends. As the stator magnetic field rotates, the field interacts with the magnetic field established by the magnetic poles of the rotor, causing the rotor to turn at nearly the speed of the rotating stator magnetic field. ● **SEE FIGURE 8–17.**

- An alternate design is called the wound rotor. In this case, the rotor has the same number of poles as the stator, and the windings are made of wire. When the stator magnetic field rotates and the rotor windings are shorted, the stator magnetic field motion induces a field into the wound rotor, causing the rotor to turn at nearly the speed of the rotating stator magnetic field. ● **SEE FIGURE 8–18.**

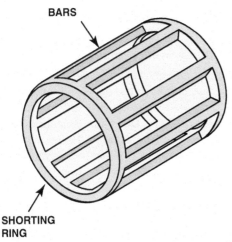

FIGURE 8-17 A squirrel-cage type rotor used in an AC induction motor.

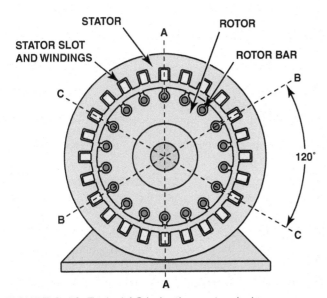

FIGURE 8-18 Typical AC induction motor design.

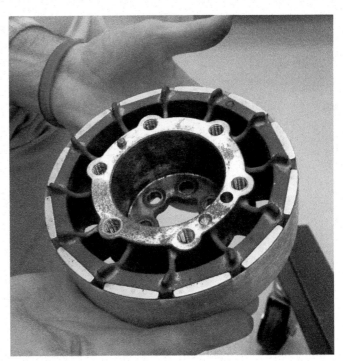

FIGURE 8-19 The rotor for the integrated motor assist (IMA) used on the Honda Insight and Civic is a surface permanent magnet (SPM) design. The magnets are made from neodymium.

AC SYNCHRONOUS MOTOR The AC synchronous motor rotates exactly at the supply frequency or a submultiple of the supply frequency. The speed is controlled by varying the frequency of the AC supply and the number of poles in the stator winding, according to the relation:

$$RPM = 120F \div p$$

where

RPM = Synchronous speed

F = AC power frequency

p = Number of poles, usually an even number but always a multiple of the number of phases

An electronic switching circuit produces commutating currents in the stator windings based on the position of the magnetic poles on the rotor. The rotor of the motor rotates at the same speed as the stator commutation. The speed of the motor is controlled by the frequency of the AC current being used.

PERMANENT MAGNET ROTORS. Brushless motors, which use permanent magnet rotors, produce high starting torque and are typically over 90% efficient. Brushless permanent magnet motors use two designs of rotors:

1. In one type, the permanent magnets are mounted on the outside surface of the rotor. These are called **surface permanent magnets (SPMs).** ● SEE FIGURE 8-19.

2. In the other type, the permanent magnets are housed inside the outer shell of the rotor and are called **interior permanent magnets (IPMs).** The Honda Accord, Ford hybrids, and Toyota hybrids use an IPM-type rotor assembly.

In both types of motors, the stator coils are stationary and the permanent magnet assembly rotates. Alternating current (AC) is fed to the various phases in the stator in order to get the permanent magnets in the rotor to "chase" the changing magnetic field. ● **SEE FIGURES 8-20 and 8-21.**

The current is fed into one of the three stator phases and flows out of a second phase. This current flows through the phases, acts as a position sensor, and helps the controller to determine when to energize which phase of the stator. This is sometimes called a **senseless DC motor** design.

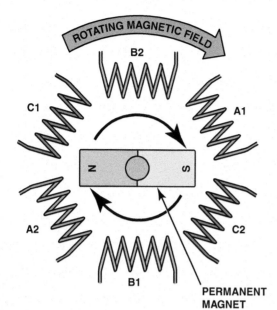

FIGURE 8-20 The rotor in most electric motors used to propel hybrid electric vehicles uses a permanent magnet design. The coils surrounding the rotor in the stator are pulsed on and off to control the speed and torque of the motor.

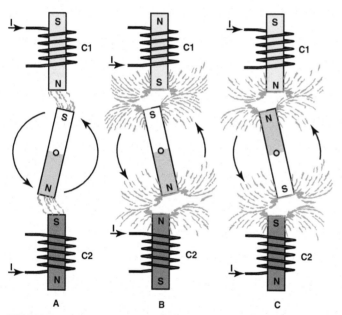

FIGURE 8-21 The rotor is forced to rotate by changing the polarity and the frequency of the coils surrounding the rotor.

Induction motors at rest draw a very high current, known as the locked rotor current. They also produce torque, which is known as the locked rotor torque (LRT). As the motor accelerates, both the torque and the current will tend to change with rotor speed if the voltage is maintained at a constant level.

Is It a DC or an AC Motor?

Honda hybrid vehicle sales-related information states that the electric motor used on a Honda to help propel the vehicle is a "DC brushless motor." However, a DC motor is usually controlled by a **pulse-width modulated (PWM)** signal from the motor controller, so it is actually an AC synchronous motor. Why is it called a DC motor? Some field engineers have stated that it is most likely due to marketing concerns. If the term *AC motor* was used, then some people would think that the vehicle has to be plugged into an AC electrical outlet. The AC is created using an inverter, which changes DC current from the batteries to AC current for use by the electric motor. Many vehicle buyers could be confused by this technical explanation, so the use of the term *DC brushless motor* or some other generic term is used in sales literature.

How Many Electric Motors Are in a Hybrid Vehicle?

There are ten electric motors, sometimes more, in most hybrid vehicles. These include:

1. One or two drive motor(s)
2. Motor to circulate the coolant during idle stop to keep the passengers warm (Toyotas/Honda Accord/Honda Civic)
3. Motor for electric power steering (EPS) (all)
4. Motor for A/C compressor (New Prius and Accord)
5. Motor for cooling CVT (Ford/Toyota/Lexus)
6. Motor for AT trans (hybrid Accord, GM PHT, Saturn Vue)
7. Motor(s) for air cooling the HV batteries (all)
8. Motor for hydroelectric power steering (GM 42/36v)
9. Motor in CVT to engage park (2004 + Prius)
10. Rear differential (Lexus RX400h/Highlander 4WD)

The starting current of a motor, with a fixed voltage, will drop very slowly as the motor accelerates and will only begin to fall when the motor has reached at least 80% full speed.

Typically, the efficiency of an induction motor is greater than 92% for high-speed motors, such as is used in electric hybrid vehicles.

Why Are Power Ratings for Internal Combustion Engines Higher Than Electric Motors?

There are two basic reasons why internal combustion engines, both gasoline and diesel, are usually rated higher in power than electric motors.

1. Internal combustion engine horsepower rating is the maximum power that can be produced.

2. The horsepower rating of an electric motor is typically given as the amount of power that can be delivered for one continuous hour without overheating.

Besides the difference in how the power rating is achieved, electric motor power is usually expressed in kilowatts. There are 1,000 watts in a kilowatt, and 746 watts is equal to one horsepower. Therefore, a 30-kW (30,000-watt) electric motor is capable of producing about 40 horsepower.

 TECH TIP

Electric Motors Are Perfect for Vehicles

A gasoline or diesel engine produces very little torque and power at low speeds and must use a transmission to multiply torque to get the vehicle moving. An electric motor, such as an AC induction motor, produces maximum torque at low speeds, making it the perfect power source to get a vehicle moving from a stop. Then, when the torque of an electric motor starts to drop off, the torque multiplied by the speed (RPM) results in power. Therefore, a typical electric motor used on a hybrid vehicle has the following characteristics:

- Delivers constant torque at low speed, typically from zero to 1500 RPM
- Delivers constant power above 1500 RPM (● **SEE FIGURE 8–22**)

For example, the rear electric motor used in a Toyota Highlander has the following specifications:

Power output: 123 kW @ 4500 RPM (167 hp)
Maximum torque: 247 lb. ft. @ 0 to 1500 RPM

MOTOR CONTROL

PRINCIPLES Most hybrid electric vehicles use an AC synchronous AC motor and is controlled as follows:

1. To change the speed of the motor the frequency of the applied current is changed. The speed is synchronized to the frequency so when the frequency is changed, the speed changes.

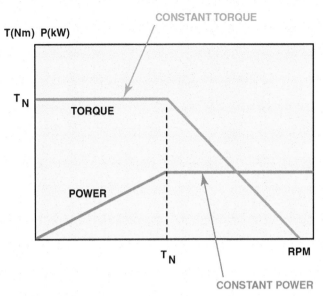

FIGURE 8–22 Notice on the graph that at lower motor speeds the torque produced by the motor is constant and at higher motor speeds the power is constant. Power is equal to torque times RPM; therefore, as the torque decreases the speed increases, keeping the power constant.

2. The pulse-width and voltage is adjusted to change the power output to match the demands of the vehicle for electric assist or propulsion.

EXAMPLES An example of traction motor control is the motor control module (MCM) used on Honda hybrid electric vehicles, which is typical of the controller used in most hybrid electric vehicles. The MCM has three inputs from three rotor position sensors, A, B, and C. They send digital information to the MCM to indicate rotor angular position. The MCM is programmed to use this information to determine which driver circuits in the **power drive unit (PDU)** be turned on. The PDU controls all functions of the motor, whether it is producing torque to drive the vehicle or is being used as a generator to charge the batteries during regenerative braking. ● **SEE FIGURE 8–23.**

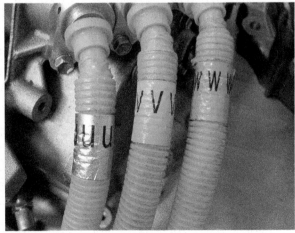

FIGURE 8–23 The power cables for a motor-generator in a Toyota hybrid transaxle.

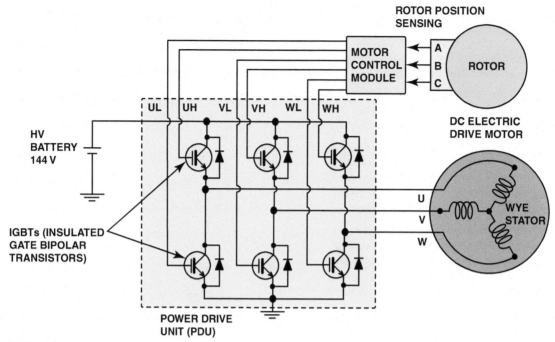

FIGURE 8–24 The drive control unit on a Honda hybrid electric vehicle controls the current and voltage through the stator windings of the motor.

The MCM has three outputs: U, V, and W. Each winding sends control information (digital high-low) to the PDU.

These three inputs tell the PDU which of the power transistors to turn on to drive current through the stator windings and continue rotation of the rotor.

A typical Honda PDU schematic is shown in ● **FIGURE 8–24.**

MOTOR CONTROL IGBTS The arrangement of transistors and diodes results in three-phase control of the electric motor for both moving the vehicle (assist) and recharging the battery pack. The current flow through the PDU is controlled by six **insulated gate bipolar transistors (IGBTs).** Three of these transistors control the voltage side of the circuit and are called positive or high-side IGBTs. The other three transistors are negative or low-side IGBTs because they are on the negative (ground) side of the stators coils. The base of each IGBT connects to an input terminal in the connector to the PDU. The IGBTs are current drivers that send current from the battery pack through the stator windings to energize the stator coils and move the rotor to power the drive wheels. Most motor controllers include Hall-effect current sensors. ● **SEE FIGURE 8–25.**

Each IGBT has a diode connected in parallel between the collector and the emitter. These six diodes work together to rectify stator AC to pulsating DC to charge the high-voltage batteries when the DC electric drive motor becomes a generator during regenerative braking. At that time, the IGBTs are instantly shut off by the motor control module (MCM) to stop powering the DC electric drive motor. Because the HEV is still moving forward, the crankshaft is rotating, which rotates the permanent magnet rotor

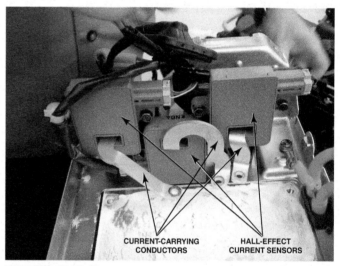

FIGURE 8–25 The three legs of the brushless motor run through three Hall-effect-type current sensors. The conductors used in the Honda unit are flat aluminum and attach to the motor controller terminals.

(armature) in the DC electric drive motor. The rotation of the rotor causes the lines of flux from the powerful permanent magnets to induce an AC current in the stator coils. The six diodes are forward biased and turn on to rectify the AC current induced in the stator coils to pulsating DC to recharge the battery pack.

Rotor position information is sent to the MCM, which is programmed to turn on the correct IGBTs to keep the rotor turning. It is critical that the controller know the exact position of the rotor.

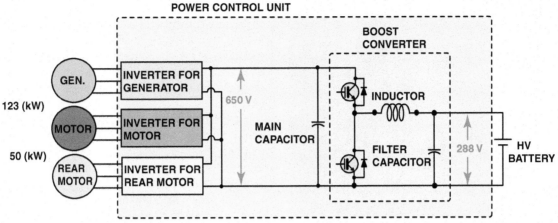

FIGURE 8-26 A schematic showing the motor controls for a Lexus RX 400h. Note the use of the rear motor to provide 4WD capability.

The IGBTs process drive current to the electric drive motor. The diodes form a rectifier bridge to change the AC generated in the electric drive motor to pulsating DC to charge the battery pack. ● **SEE FIGURE 8-26.**

Honda, Toyota, and Lexus use a speed sensor called a **resolver** to detect the rotor position. ● **SEE FIGURES 8-27 and 8-28.**

COOLING THE ELECTRONICS The current flow and the electronic devices in hybrid electric control units generate a lot of heat. Toyota, Ford, and GM hybrids use a liquid cooling method to control the temperature of the electronics. ● **SEE FIGURE 8-29.**

SPEED SENSOR RESOLVER

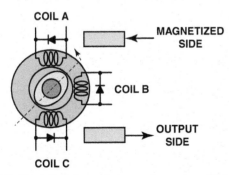

FIGURE 8-27 A Toyota motor speed sensor called a resolver.

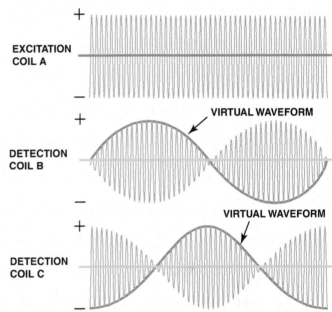

FIGURE 8-28 Each coil in the speed sensor (resolver) generates a unique waveform, allowing the motor controller to determine the position of the rotor in the motor. The top waveform is coil A, the middle waveform is coil B, and the bottom waveform is coil C. The controller uses the three waveforms to determine the position of the rotor.

CAPACITORS IN HYBRID CONTROLLERS

PRINCIPLES Capacitance is the ability of an object or surface to store an electrical charge. In 1745, Ewald Christian von Kliest and Pieter van Musschenbroek independently discovered capacitance in an electric circuit. While engaged

FIGURE 8–29 The underside of the Toyota Prius controller showing the coolant passages used to cool the electronic control unit.

in separate studies of electrostatics, they discovered that an electric charge could be stored for a period of time.

A capacitor consists of two conductive plates with an insulating material between them. The insulating material is commonly called a dielectric. It may be air, mica, ceramic, glass, paper, plastic, or any similar nonconductive material. The higher the dielectric constant number of a material, the better it is as an insulator. ● **SEE FIGURE 8–30.**

Material	Dielectric Constant
Vacuum	1.0
Air	1.00059
Polystyrene	2.5
Paper	3.5
Mica	5.4
Flint glass	9.9
Methyl alcohol	35
Glycerin	56.2
Pure water	81

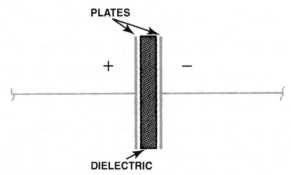

FIGURE 8–30 This simple capacitor, made of two plates separated by an insulating material, is called a dielectric.

OPERATION When a capacitor is placed in a closed circuit, the voltage source, such as a battery, forces electrons around the circuit. Because electrons cannot flow through the dielectric of the capacitor, excess electrons collect on what becomes the negatively charged plate. At the same time the other plate loses electrons, and therefore becomes positively charged.

Current continues until the voltage charge across the capacitor plates becomes the same as the source voltage. At that time, the negative plate of the capacitor and the negative terminal of the battery are at the same negative potential. ● **SEE FIGURE 8–31.**

The positive plate of the capacitor and the positive terminal of the battery are also at equal positive potentials. There is then a voltage charge across the battery terminals and an equal voltage charge across the capacitor plates. The circuit is in balance, and there is no current. An electrostatic field now exists between the capacitor plates because of their opposite charges. It is this field that stores energy. ● **SEE FIGURE 8–32.**

PRECAUTIONS If the circuit is opened, the capacitor will hold its charge until it is connected into an external circuit through which it can discharge. When the charged capacitor is connected to an external circuit, it discharges. After discharging, both plates of the capacitor are neutral because all the energy from a circuit stored in a capacitor is returned when it is discharged. ● **SEE FIGURES 8–33 and 8–34.**

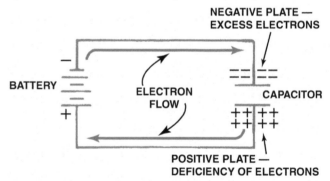

FIGURE 8–31 As the capacitor is charging, the battery forces electrons through the circuit.

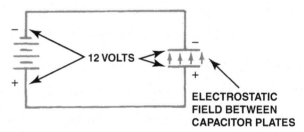

FIGURE 8–32 When the capacitor is charged, there is equal voltage across the capacitor and the battery. An electrostatic field exists between the capacitor plates. No current flows in the circuit.

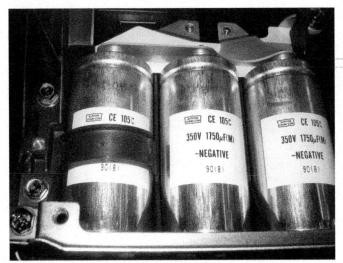

FIGURE 8–33 The three large capacitors in this Honda hybrid absorb voltage spikes that occur when the voltage level is changed in the DC-DC converters.

FIGURE 8–35 Using a CAT III-rated digital meter and wearing rubber lineman's gloves, this technician is checking for voltage at the inverter to verify that the capacitors have discharged.

FIGURE 8–34 The dark cylinders are capacitors that are part of the electronic control unit of this Toyota hybrid.

Theoretically, a capacitor can hold its charge indefinitely. Actually, the charge slowly leaks off the capacitor through the dielectric. The better the dielectric, the longer the capacitor holds its charge. When the ignition of an HEV is turned off, vehicle manufacturers warn that you must wait 5 to 10 minutes for the capacitors to discharge before servicing the high-voltage system. While these capacitors often discharge in less than five minutes, it is wise to wait the amount of time specified by the vehicle manufacturer. ● **SEE FIGURE 8–35.**

CAUTION: To avoid an electrical shock, any capacitor should be treated as if it were charged until it is proven to be discharged.

NOTE: Capacitors are also called *condensers*. This term developed because electric charges collect, or condense, on the plates of a capacitor much like water vapor collects and condenses on a cold bottle or glass.

FARAD RATING Capacitance is measured in farads, which is named after Michael Faraday (1791–1867). The symbol for farads is F. If a charge of 1 coulomb is placed on the plates of a capacitor and the potential difference between them is 1 volt, the capacitance is then defined to be 1 farad. One coulomb is equal to the charge of 6.25×10^{18} electrons. One farad is an extremely large quantity of capacitance. Microfarads (0.000001 farad), abbreviated μF, are more commonly used.

The capacitance of a capacitor is proportional to the quantity of charge that can be stored in it for each volt difference in potential between its plates:

$$C = Q \div V$$

Where C is capacitance in farads, Q is the quantity of stored electrical charge in coulombs, and V is the difference in potential in volts.

Therefore, stored electric charge can be calculated using the formula:

$$Q = CV$$

SNUBBERS Snubbers are capacitors and resistors arranged in a circuit to control the high-voltage surges that can occur when circuits containing coils are switched on and off. Snubbers are also called *flyback, freewheeling, suppressor,* or *catch diodes.* Because the switch is being protected, this results in higher reliability, higher efficiency, higher

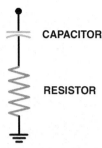

CAPACITOR

RESISTOR

FIGURE 8–36 A typical snubber circuit showing a capacitor and a resistor in series and connected to ground.

FIGURE 8–37 The snubber circuit from a Honda hybrid showing the six capacitors used to control voltage spikes in the switching circuits.

switching frequency, smaller size, lower weight, and lower electromagnetic interference (EMI). ● **SEE FIGURES 8–36 and 8–37.**

CONVERTERS AND INVERTERS

CONVERTERS DC-to-DC converters (usually written DC-DC converter) are electronic devices used to transform DC voltage from one level of DC voltage to another higher or lower level. They are used to distribute various levels of DC voltage throughout a vehicle from a single power bus (or voltage source).

One example of a DC-DC converter circuit is the circuit the PCM uses to convert 14 V to 5 V. The 5 volts is called the reference voltage, abbreviated V-ref, and is used to power many sensors in a computer-controlled engine management system. The schematic of a typical 5-volt V-ref interfacing with the TP sensor circuit is shown in ● **FIGURE 8–38.**

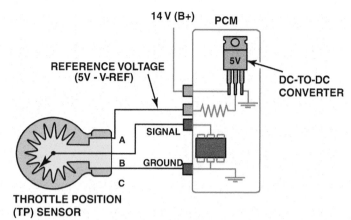

THROTTLE POSITION (TP) SENSOR

FIGURE 8–38 A DC-to-DC converter is built into most powertrain control modules (PCM) and is used to supply the 5-volt reference, called V-ref, to many sensors used to control the internal combustion engine.

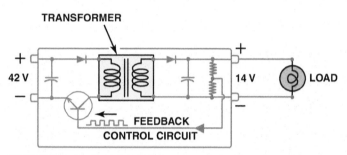

FIGURE 8–39 This DC-DC converter is designed to convert 42 volts to 14 volts to provide 14 V power to accessories on a hybrid electric vehicle operating with a 42-volt electrical system.

The PCM operates on 14 volts and uses the principle of DC conversion to provide a constant 5-volt sensor reference voltage to the TP sensor and other sensors. The TP sensor demands little current, so the V-ref circuit is a low-power DC-voltage converter in the range of one watt. The PCM uses a DC-DC converter that is a small semiconductor device called a voltage regulator and is designed to convert battery voltage to a constant 5 volts regardless of changes in the charging voltage.

Hybrid electric vehicles use DC-DC converters to provide higher or lower DC voltage levels and current requirements.

A high-power DC-DC converter schematic is shown in ● **FIGURE 8–39**, this represents how a DC-DC converter works.

The central component of a converter is a transformer that physically isolates the input (42 V) from the output (14 V). The power transistor pulses the high-voltage coil of the transformer; the resulting changing magnetic field induces a voltage in the coil windings of the lower-voltage side of the transformer. The diodes and capacitors help control and limit the voltage and frequency of the circuit.

DC-DC CONVERTER CIRCUIT TESTING Usually a DC control voltage is used that is supplied by a digital logic circuit to shift the voltage level to control the converter. A voltage test can indicate if the correct voltages are present when the converter is on and off.

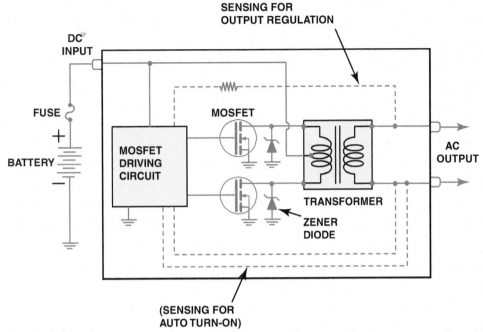

FIGURE 8-40 A typical circuit for an inverter designed to change DC current from a battery to AC current for use by the electric motors used in a hybrid electric vehicle.

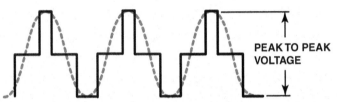

FIGURE 8-41 The switching (pulsing) MOSFETs create a waveform called a modified sine wave (solid lines) compared to a true sine wave (dotted lines).

Voltage measurements are usually specified to diagnose a DC-DC converter system. A digital multimeter (DMM) that is CAT III–rated should be used.

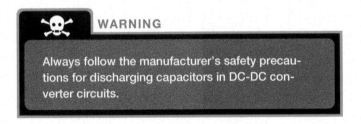

WARNING

Always follow the manufacturer's safety precautions for discharging capacitors in DC-DC converter circuits.

1. Always follow the manufacturer's safety precautions when working with high-voltage circuits. These circuits are usually indicated by orange wiring.
2. Never tap into wires in a DC-DC converter circuit to access power for another circuit.
3. Never tap into wires in a DC-DC converter circuit to access a ground for another circuit.
4. Never block airflow to a DC-DC converter heat sink.
5. Never use a heat sink for a ground connection for a meter, scope, or accessory connection.

6. Never connect or disconnect a DC-to-DC converter while the converter is powered up.
7. Never connect a DC-to-DC converter to a larger-voltage source than specified.

INVERTERS An **inverter** is an electronic circuit that changes direct current (DC) into alternating current (AC). In most DC-AC inverters, the switching transistors—usually **metal oxide semiconductor field-effect transistors (MOSFETs)**—are turned on alternately for short pulses. As a result the transformer produces a modified sine wave output, rather than a true sine wave. ● **SEE FIGURE 8-40.**

The waveform produced by an inverter is not the perfect sine wave of household AC current, but is rather more like a pulsing DC current that reacts similar to sine wave AC in transformers and in induction motors. ● **SEE FIGURE 8-41.**

AC motors are powered by inverters. An inverter converts DC power to AC power at the required frequency and amplitude. The inverter consists of three half-bridge units and the output voltage is mostly created by a pulse width modulation (PWM) technique. The three-phase voltage waves are shifted 120° to each other to power each of the three phases.

WARNING

Do not touch the terminals of a battery that are being used to power an inverter. There is always a risk those battery terminals could deliver a much greater shock than from batteries alone, if a motor or inverter should develop a fault.

ELECTRIC POWER STEERING

Most electric power steering units use a brush-type DC electric motor that operates on 12 volts. Some operate from 42 volts and use an electronic controller and a brushless DC motor as an actuator.

The **electric power steering (EPS),** also called electric power-assisted steering (EPAS), system includes the following components and inputs/outputs:

- A DC motor
- Reduction gear
- Torque sensor

● **SEE FIGURE 8–42** for an example of an EPS used on a Toyota Highlander hybrid SUV.

The electric power steering (EPS) is controlled by the EPS ECU, which calculates the amount of needed assist based on the input from the steering torque sensor. The steering torque sensor is a noncontact sensor that detects the movement and torque applied to the torsion bar. The torsion bar twists when the driver exerts torque to the steering wheel, and the more torque applied causes the bar to twist further. This generates a higher-voltage signal to the EPS ECU. ● **SEE FIGURE 8–43.**

The steering shaft torque sensor and the steering wheel position sensor are not serviced separately from each other or from the steering column assembly. The steering column assembly does not include the power steering motor and module assembly. The detection ring 1 and detection ring 2 are mounted on the input shaft, and detection ring 3 is mounted on the output shaft. The input shaft and the output shaft are connected by a torsion bar. When the steering wheel is turned, the difference in relative motion between detection rings 2 and 3 is sensed by the detection coil and sends two signals to the EPS ECU. These two signals are called Torque Sensor Signal 1 and

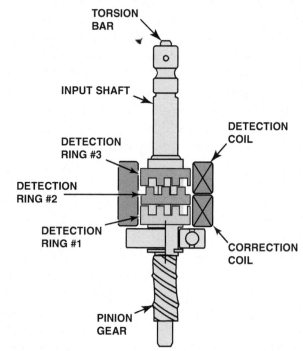

FIGURE 8–43 The torque sensor converts the torque the driver is exerting to the steering wheel into a voltage signal. *(Courtesy of University of Toyota and Toyota Motor Sales, U.S.A., Inc.)*

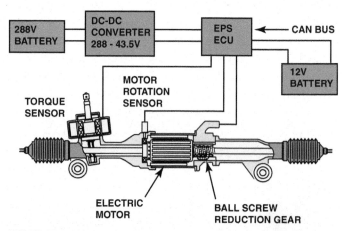

FIGURE 8–44 The electric power steering used in the Toyota/Lexus SUVs use a brushless DC (labeled BLDC) motor around the rack of the unit and operates on 42 volts. *(Courtesy of University of Toyota and Toyota Motor Sales, U.S.A., Inc.)*

Torque Signal 2. The EPS ECU uses these signals to control the amount of assist and also uses the signals for diagnosis.

NOTE: If the steering wheel, steering column, or the steering gear is removed or replaced, the zero point of the torque sensors must be reset using a scan tool.

The Toyota Highlander and Lexus RX 400h use a different electric power steering unit due to the larger size of the vehicles. This unit uses a concentric brushless DC motor on the steering rack. ● **SEE FIGURES 8–44 and 8–45.**

FIGURE 8–42 A Toyota Highlander hybrid EPS assembly.

FIGURE 8–45 Photo of the electric power steering gear on a Lexus 400h taken from underneath the vehicle.

The Honda electric power steering uses an electric motor to provide steering assist and replaces the need for a hydraulic pump, hoses, and gear. A torque sensor is used to measure road resistance and the direction that the driver is turning the steering wheel. The torque sensor input and the vehicle speed is used by the EPS controller to supply the EPS motor with the specified current to help assist the steering effort. ● SEE FIGURE 8–46.

The motor turns the pinion shaft using a worm gear. The worm gear is engaged with the worm wheel so that the motor turns the pinion shaft directly when providing steering assist. The steering rack is unique because the tie rods are mounted to the center of the rack rather than at the ends of the rack as in a conventional Honda power steering arrangement. ● SEE FIGURE 8–47.

If a major fault were to occur, the control module will first try to maintain power-assisted steering even if some sensors have failed. If the problem is serious, then the vehicle can be driven and steered manually. The EPS control unit will turn on the EPS dash warning light if a fault has been detected. A fault in the system will not cause the malfunction indicator light to come on because that light is reserved for emission-related faults only. Fault codes can be retrieved by using a scan tool, and the codes will be displayed by the flashing of the EPS warning lamp.

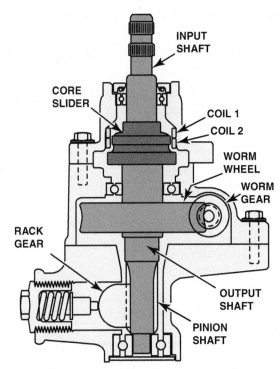

FIGURE 8–46 A cross-sectional view of a Honda electric power steering (EPS) steering gear showing the torque sensor and other components.

FIGURE 8–47 Honda electric power steering unit cutaway.

SUMMARY

1. Magnetic lines of force leave the north pole and enter the south pole of a magnet.
2. Magnetic lines of force are called flux lines.
3. Any conductor carrying an electrical current generates a magnetic field around the conductor, and a moving magnetic field across a conductor creates electricity.
4. Like poles repel and unlike poles attract.
5. A brushless DC motor is also known as an AC synchronous motor.
6. Powerful permanent magnets are used in the rotors of DC brushless motors.
7. The operation of motors is performed by the controller, which is capable of switching the voltage and/or the frequency of the current flowing through the stationary windings of the motor.
8. DC-DC converters are used in hybrid electric vehicles to convert the high-voltage battery current into a lower voltage used by the accessories and lighting systems.

1. How is an electrical current induced in a wire?
2. How does an AC synchronous motor work?
3. How does an AC induction motor work?
4. How is the operation of a brushless DC motor controlled?
5. What is a DC-DC converter, and why is it needed in a hybrid electric vehicle?

CHAPTER QUIZ

1. All of the following statements are true, except _____.
   a. The magnetic lines of force leave the south pole and enter the north pole
   b. Around every conductor carrying a current is a magnetic field
   c. Magnetic lines of force never intersect
   d. The higher the current through a conductor the stronger the magnetic flux

2. Technician A says that some DC motors use brushes. Technician B says that an AC synchronous motor uses a permanent magnet rotor. Which technician is correct?
   a. Technician A only
   b. Technician B only
   c. Both technicians A and B
   d. Neither technician A nor B

3. The power of most electric motors is expressed in _____.
   a. Horsepower
   b. kW
   c. Watts
   d. Amperes

4. AC synchronous motors used in hybrid electric vehicles use how many windings in the stationary part of the motor?
   a. One
   b. Two
   c. Three
   d. Four

5. Technician A says that a traction (AC synchronous) motor used in a hybrid electric vehicle is controlled by varying the voltage to the motor. Technician B says that the frequency of the current is controlled. Which technician is correct?
   a. Technician A only
   b. Technician B only
   c. Both technicians A and B
   d. Neither technician A nor B

6. Technician A says that a DC-to-DC converter is used to convert 12 volts from the battery to a higher voltage to run the electric motor(s) in a hybrid electric vehicle. Technician B says that a DC-to-DC converter is used to convert the voltage from the motor/generator to a higher voltage to charge the high-voltage batteries. Which technician is correct?
   a. Technician A only
   b. Technician B only
   c. Both technicians A and B
   d. Neither technician A nor B

7. What type of electric motor is used for the traction motor in most hybrid electric vehicles?
   a. DC brush-type motor
   b. AC induction-type motor
   c. Brushless DC motor
   d. Both b and c are used

8. The _____ are used to rectify AC to DC current.
   a. Transistors
   b. Diodes
   c. Capacitors
   d. Condensers

9. What is the most common type of rotor used in an AC synchronous motor?
   a. Wire wound
   b. Permanent magnet
   c. Squirrel-cage
   d. Both b and c

10. Current sensors are commonly used by the motor controller to help with the tasks of motor management. What type of sensor is usually used for this task?
    a. Hall-effect
    b. Potentiometer
    c. Wheatstone bridge
    d. Piezoelectric

chapter 9

REGENERATIVE BRAKING SYSTEMS

OBJECTIVES: **After studying Chapter 9, the reader will be able to:** • Describe how regenerative braking works. • Explain the principles involved in regenerative braking. • Discuss the parts and components involved in regenerative braking systems. • Describe the servicing precautions involved with regenerative brakes.

KEY TERMS: • Base brakes 122 • Brake pedal position (BPP) 125 • Electrohydraulic brake (EHB) 123 • F = ma 121 • Force 121 • G 128 • Inertia 121 • Kinetic energy 121 • Mass 121 • Regen 122 • Regeneration 122 • Torque 121

INTRODUCTION

When test driving a hybrid vehicle the driver may notice that there is a slight surge or pulsation that occurs at lower speeds usually about 5 to 20 mph (8 to 32 km/h). The brakes may also be touchy and seem to be very sensitive to the brake force applied to the brake pedal. This is where the regenerative braking system stops regenerating electricity for charging the batteries and where the mechanical (friction) brakes take over. This chapter describes how this system works and how the various components of a hybrid electric vehicle (HEV) work together to achieve the highest possible efficiency.

PRINCIPLES OF REGENERATIVE BRAKING

INERTIA, FORCE, AND MASS If a moving object has a mass, it has **inertia**. Inertia is the resistance of an object to change its state of motion. In other words, an object in motion tends to stay in motion and an object at rest tends to stay at rest unless acted on by an outside force.

A hybrid electric vehicle reclaims energy by converting the energy of a moving object, called **kinetic energy,** into electric energy. According to basic physics:

A **force** applied to move an object results in the equation:

$$F = ma$$

where:

F = force

m = mass

a = acceleration

The faster an object is accelerated, the more force that has to be applied. Energy from the battery (watts) is applied to the coil windings in the motor. These windings then produce a magnetic force on the rotor of the motor, which produces torque on the output shaft. This torque is then applied to the wheels of the vehicle by use of a coupling of gears and shafts. When the wheel turns, it applies a force to the ground, which due to friction between the wheel and the ground, causes the vehicle to move along the surface.

All vehicles generate **torque** to move the wheels to drive the vehicle down the road. During this time, it is generating friction and losses. When standard brakes are applied, it is just another friction device that has specially designed material to handle the heat from friction, which is applied to the drums and rotors that stop the wheel from turning. The friction between the wheel and the ground actually stops the vehicle. However, the energy absorbed by the braking system is lost in the form of heat and cannot be recovered or stored for use later to help propel the vehicle.

 FREQUENTLY ASKED QUESTION

What Is the Difference Between Mass and Weight?

Mass is the amount of matter in an object. One of the properties of mass is inertia. Inertia is the resistance of an object to being put in motion and the tendency to remain in motion once it is set in motion. The weight of an object is the force of gravity on the object and may be defined as the mass times the acceleration of gravity.

Therefore, mass means the property of an object and weight is a force.

RECLAIMING ENERGY IN A HYBRID

On a hybrid vehicle that has regenerative brakes, the kinetic energy of a moving vehicle can be reclaimed that would normally be lost due to braking. Using the inertia of the vehicle is the key. Inertia is the kinetic energy that is present in any moving object. The heavier the object, and the faster it is traveling, the greater the amount of energy and therefore, the higher the inertia. It is basically what makes something difficult to start moving and what makes something hard to stop moving. Inertia is the reason energy is required to change the direction and speed of the moving object.

TRANSFERRING TORQUE BACK TO THE MOTOR

Inertia is the fundamental property of physics that is used to reclaim energy from the vehicle. Instead of using 100% friction brakes (**base brakes**), the braking torque is transferred from the wheels back into the motor shaft. One of the unique things about most electric motors is that electrical energy can be converted into mechanical energy and also mechanical energy can be converted back into electrical energy. In both cases, this can be done very efficiently.

Through the use of the motor and motor controller, the force at the wheels transfers torque to the electric motor shaft. The magnets on the shaft of the motor (called the rotor—the moving part of the motor) move past the electric coils on the stator (the stationary part of the motor), passing the magnetic fields of the magnets through the coils, producing electricity. This electricity becomes electrical energy, which is directed to and recharges the high-voltage battery. This process is called **regeneration, regen,** or simply "reclaiming energy."

PRINCIPLES INVOLVED

Brakes slow and stop a vehicle by converting kinetic energy, the energy of motion, into heat energy, which is then dissipated to the air. Fuel is burned in the internal combustion engine to make heat, which is then converted to mechanical energy and finally this is used to create kinetic energy in the moving vehicle. The goal of regenerative braking is to recover some of that energy, store it, and then use it to put the vehicle into motion again. It is estimated that regenerative braking can eventually be developed to recover about half the energy wasted as braking heat. Depending on the type of vehicle, this would reduce fuel consumption by 10% to 25% below current levels.

Regenerative braking can be extremely powerful and can recover about 20% of the energy normally wasted as brake heat. Regenerative braking has the following advantages:

- Reduces the drawdown of the battery charge
- Extends the overall life of the battery pack
- Reduces fuel consumption

All production hybrid electric vehicles use regenerative braking as a method to improve vehicle efficiency, and this feature alone provides the most fuel economy savings.

FIGURE 9–1 This Honda Insight hybrid electric vehicle is constructed mostly of aluminum to save weight.

FIGURE 9–2 A Toyota Prius hybrid electric vehicle. This sedan weighs more and therefore has greater kinetic energy than a smaller, lighter vehicle.

How much energy is reclaimed depends on many factors, including weight of the vehicle, speed, and the rate of deceleration. ●**SEE FIGURE 9–1**.

The amount of kinetic energy in a moving vehicle increases with the square of the speed. This means that at 60 mph, the kinetic energy is four times the energy of 30 mph. The speed is doubled (times 2) and the kinetic energy is squared (2 times 2 equals 4). ●**SEE FIGURE 9–2**.

The efficiency of the regenerative braking is about 80%, which means that only about 20% of the inertia energy is wasted to heat. There are losses when mechanical energy is converted to electrical energy by the motor/generator(s) and then some energy is lost when it is converted into chemical energy in the high-voltage batteries.

TYPES OF REGENERATIVE BRAKING SYSTEMS

Two different regeneration designs include:

- **Series regeneration.** In series regenerative braking systems, the amount of regeneration is proportional to the brake pedal position. As the brake pedal is depressed further, the controller used to regulate the regenerative braking system computes the torque needed to slow the vehicle as would occur in normal braking. As the brake pedal is depressed even further, the service brakes are blended into the regenerative braking to achieve the desired braking performance based on brake pedal force and travel. Series regenerative braking requires active brake management to achieve total braking to all four wheels. This braking is more difficult to achieve if the hybrid electric vehicle uses just the front or rear wheels to power the vehicle. This means that the other axle must use the base brakes alone, whereas the drive wheels can be slowed and stopped using a combination of regenerative braking and base brake action. All series regenerative braking systems use an **electrohydraulic brake (EHB)** system, which includes the hydraulic control unit that manages the brake cylinder pressures, as well as the front-rear axle brake balance. Most hybrid vehicles use this type of regenerative braking system. ●**SEE FIGURE 9–3**.

  The regenerative braking system mainly uses the regenerative capability, especially at higher vehicle speeds, and then gradually increases the amount of the base braking force at low vehicle speeds.

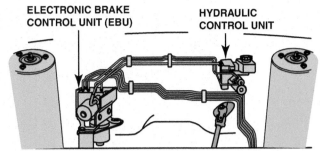

FIGURE 9–3 The electronic brake control unit (EBU) is shown on the left (passenger side) and the brake hydraulic unit is shown on the right (driver's side) on this Ford Escape system.

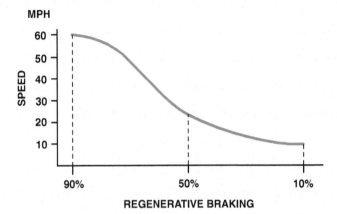

FIGURE 9–4 A typical brake curve showing the speed on the left and the percentage of regenerative braking along the bottom. Notice that the base brakes are being used more when the vehicle speed is low.

 FREQUENTLY ASKED QUESTION

Are the Friction Brakes Used During Regenerative Braking?

Yes. Most hybrid vehicles make use of the base (friction) brakes during stopping. The amount of regenerative braking compared to the amount of friction braking is determined by the electronic brake controller. It is important that the base brakes be used regularly to keep the rotors free from rust and ready to be used to stop the vehicle. A typical curve showing the relative proportion of brake usage is shown in ●**FIGURE 9–4.**

- **Parallel regeneration.** A parallel regenerative braking system is less complex because the base (friction) brakes are used along with energy recovery by the motors becoming generators. The controller for the regenerative braking system determines the amount of regeneration that can be achieved based on the vehicle speed. Front and rear brake balance is retained because the base brakes are in use during the entire braking event. The amount of energy captured by a parallel regenerative braking system is less than from a series system. As a result, the fuel economy gains are less.

BATTERY CHARGING DURING REGENERATION

BACKGROUND Kinetic energy can be converted into electrical energy with a generator and it can be returned to the high-voltage batteries and stored for later use. Electric regenerative braking has its roots in the "dynamic brakes" used on electric trolley cars in the early Twentieth Century.

 FREQUENTLY ASKED QUESTION

How Does the Computer Change a Motor to a Generator So Quickly?

The controller of the drive motors uses a varying frequency to control power and speed. The controller can quickly change the frequency, and can therefore change the operation of a typical AC synchronous motor from propelling the vehicle (called motoring) to a generator. ●**SEE FIGURE 9–5.**

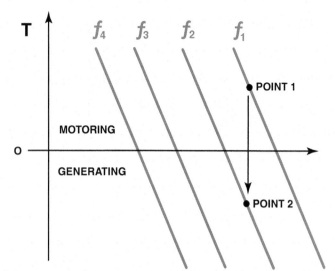

FIGURE 9–5 The frequency ("f") applied to the stator windings of an AC synchronous motor can be varied to create either forward torque ("T") or regenerative braking. If the frequency is changed from point 1 to point 2 as shown on the chart, the torque is changed from motoring (powering the vehicle) to generating and this change can be made almost instantly by the controller.

In the early electric trolley cars, the driver's control handle had a position that cut power to the electric motors and supplied a small, finely controlled excitation current to the motors' field windings. This turned the motors into generators that were driven by the motion of the trolley car. Increasing the magnetic field current increased the generating load, which slowed the trolley car, and the current being generated was routed to a set of huge resistors. These resistors converted the current to heat, which was dissipated through cooling fins. By the 1920s, techniques had been developed for returning that current to the power grid, making it available to all the other trolley cars in the system, reducing the load on the streetcar system's main generator by as much as 20%.

Regenerative braking systems are still being used in cities around the world. It is relatively easy to feed the current generated from braking into an on-board high-voltage battery system. The challenge was to make those components small enough to be practical, but still have enough storage capacity to be useful. A big breakthrough came with the development of the electronically controlled permanent-magnet motors.

PARTS AND OPERATION Motors work by activating electromagnets in just the right position and sequence. A conventional DC motor has groups of wire windings on the armature that act as electromagnets. The current flows through each winding on the armature only when the brushes touch its contacts located on the commutator. Surround the armature with a magnetic field and apply current to just the windings that are in the right position, and the resulting magnetic attraction causes the armature to rotate. The brushes lose contact with that set of windings just as the next set comes into the right position. Together, the brushes and rotation of the armature act like a mechanical switch to turn on each electromagnet at just the right position.

Another way to make a motor, instead of using electromagnets on the armature, is to use permanent magnets. Because it is impossible to switch the polarity of permanent magnets, the polarity of the field windings surrounding them needs to be switched. This is a brushless, permanent-magnet motor and the switching is only possible with the help of electronic controls that can switch the current in the field windings fast enough. The computer-controlled, brushless, permanent-magnet motor is ideal for use in electric vehicles. When connected to nickel-metal hydride (NiMH) batteries that can charge and discharge very quickly, the package is complete.

LIMITATIONS OF REGENERATIVE BRAKES There are some limitations that will always affect even the best regenerative braking systems including:

- It only acts on the driven wheels.
- The system has to be designed to allow for proper use of the antilock braking system.
- The batteries are commanded to be kept at a maximum of about 60%, plus or minus 20%, which is best for long battery life and to allow for energy to be stored in the batteries during regenerative braking. If the batteries were allowed to be fully charged, then there would be no place for the electrical current to be stored and the conventional friction brakes alone have to be used to slow and stop the vehicle. Charging the batteries over 80% would also overheat the batteries.

So far its use is limited to electric or hybrid electric vehicles, where its contribution is to extend the life of the battery pack, as well as to save fuel.

REGENERATIVE BRAKING SYSTEMS

DASH DISPLAY The Toyota Prius is equipped with a center dash LCD that shows how many watt-hours of regeneration have occurred every 5 minutes. These are indicated by small "suns" that appear on the display and each sun indicates 50 watt-hours. When a sun appears, enough power has been put back into the battery to run a 50-watt lightbulb for an hour. Depending on the driver and the traffic conditions, some drivers may not be seeing many suns on the display, which indicates that the regeneration is not contributing much energy back to the batteries. The battery level also gives an indication of how much regeneration is occurring. The battery state-of-charge (SOC) is also displayed.

REGENERATIVE BRAKE COMPONENTS

It is the ABS ECU that handles regenerative braking, as well as ABS functions, sending a signal to the hybrid ECU how much regeneration to impose. But how does the ABS ECU know what to do?

Rather than measuring brake pedal travel, which could vary with pad wear, the system uses pressure measuring sensors to detect master cylinder pressure. Some systems use a **brake pedal position (BPP)** sensor as an input signal to the brake ECU. The higher the master cylinder pressure, the harder the driver is pushing on the brake pedal.

If the driver is pushing only gently, the master cylinder piston displacement will be small and the hydraulic brakes will be only gently applied. In this situation, the ECU knows that the driver wants only gentle deceleration and instructs the hybrid ECU to apply only a small amount of regeneration. However, as master cylinder pressure increases, so does the amount of regeneration that can automatically be applied.

There are four pressure sensors in the braking system and two pressure switches. However, it is the master cylinder pressure sensor that is most important. ● **SEE FIGURES 9–6 AND 9–7** on page 127.

● **SEE FIGURES 9–6 AND 9–7** on page 127.

TECH TIP

"B" Means Braking

All Toyota hybrid vehicles have a position on the gear selector marked "B." This position is to be used when descending steep grades and the regenerative braking is optimized. This position allows the safe and controlled descent without having the driver use the base brakes. Having to use the base brakes only wastes energy that could be captured and returned to the batteries. It can also cause the brakes to overheat. ● **SEE FIGURE 9–8.**

HOW THE REGENERATION SYSTEM WORKS

To keep the hybrid electric vehicles feeling as much like other vehicles as possible, the hybrids from Toyota and Honda have both the regeneration and conventional brakes controlled by the one brake pedal. In the first part of its travel, the brake pedal operates the regenerative brakes alone, and then as further pressure is placed on the pedal, the friction brakes come into play as well. The current Honda Civic Hybrid mixes the two brake modes together imperceptibly, whereas the first model Toyota Prius, for example, has more of a two-stage pedal.

Regeneration also occurs only when the throttle has been fully lifted. In the Hybrid Civic, it is like decelerating in fourth gear (in a five- or six-speed transaxle), while in the Prius models it feels less strong.

The wear of the hydraulic brakes and pads will also be reduced. The base brakes are still used when descending long hills, though as the battery becomes more fully charged, regeneration progressively reduces its braking action and the hydraulic brakes then do more and more of the work. Regeneration switches off at low speeds, so the disc brake pads and rotors stay clean and fully functional.

NOTE: One of the major concerns with hybrid vehicles is rust and corrosion on the brake rotors and drums. This occurs on hybrids because the base brakes are usually only used at low vehicle speeds.

The amount of regeneration that occurs is largely dictated by the output of the master cylinder pressure sensor. The ECU looks at the brake pressure signal from the sensor when the brake pedal switch is not triggered and uses this as the starting value. When the brake pedal is pushed, it then checks the difference between the starting value and the "brake pedal on" value and sets the regeneration value, according to this difference.

The voltage output of the pressure sensor ranges from about 0.4 to 3.0 volts, rising with increasing pressure. Service information states that a fault will be detected if the voltage from the sensor is outside of the range of 0.14V to 4.4V, or if the voltage output of the sensor is outside a certain ratio to its nominally 5V supply voltage. ● **SEE FIGURE 9–9** on page 127.

FREQUENTLY ASKED QUESTION

Can an On-Vehicle Brake Lathe be Used on a Hybrid Electric Vehicle?

Yes. When a brake rotor needs to be machined on a hybrid electric vehicle, the rotor is being rotated. On most hybrids, the front wheels are also connected to the traction motor that can propel the vehicle and generate electricity during deceleration and braking. When the drive wheels are being rotated, the motor/generator is producing electricity. However, unless the high-voltage circuit wiring has been disconnected, no harm will occur.

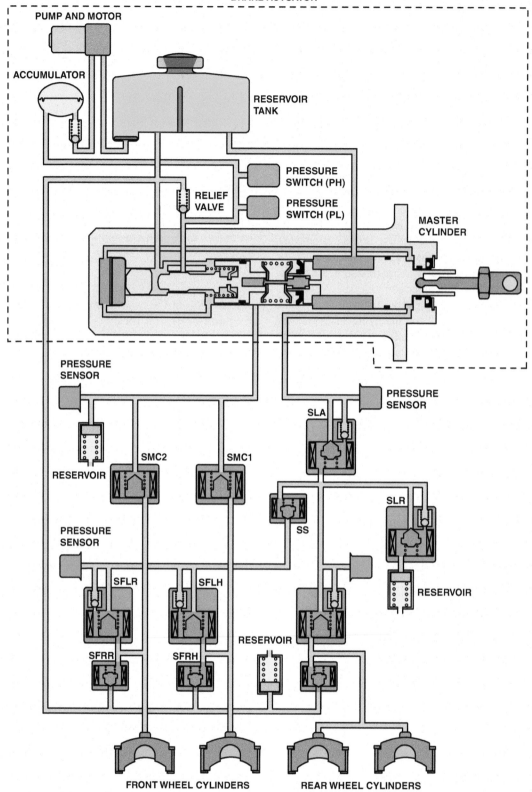

FIGURE 9–6 The Toyota Prius regenerative braking system component showing the master cylinder and pressure switches.

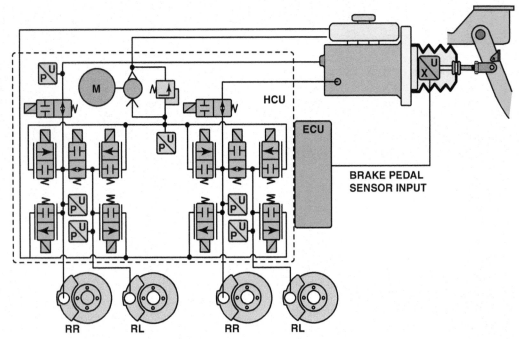

FIGURE 9–7 The Ford Escape regenerative braking system, showing all of the components. Notice the brake pedal position sensor is an input to the ECU, which controls both the brake and traction control systems.

FIGURE 9–8 The "B" position on the shift display on this Lexus RX 400h means braking. This shifter position can be selected when descending long hills or grades. The regenerative braking system will be used to help keep the vehicle from increasing in speed down the hill without the use of the base brakes.

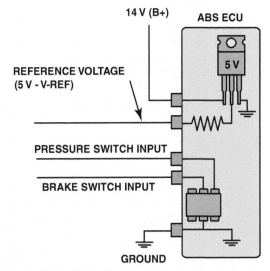

FIGURE 9–9 The ABS ECU on a Toyota Prius uses the brake switch and pressure sensor inputs to control the regenerative braking system. The circuit includes a voltage signal from the sensor, the regulated 5V supply to it, the input from the brake light switch (12V when the brakes are on), and the ground connection.

ELECTRIC MOTOR BECOMES A GENERATOR When a motor is used for regenerative braking, it acts as a generator and produces an alternating current (AC). The AC current needs to be rectified (converted) to DC current to go into the batteries. Each of the three main power wires coming out of the motor needs two large diodes. The two large diodes on each main wire do the job of converting the AC into DC.

Regenerative braking is variable. In the same way as the accelerator pedal is used to adjust the speed, the braking is varied by reducing the speed.

There are deceleration programs within the Powertrain Control Module (PCM), which varies the maximum deceleration rates according to vehicle speed and battery state-of-charge (SOC).

DECELERATION RATES

Deceleration rates are measured in units of "feet per second per second." What it means is that the vehicle will change in velocity during a certain time interval divided by the time interval. Deceleration is abbreviated "ft/sec^2" (pronounced "feet per second, per second" or "feet per second squared") or meters per sec^2 (m/s^2) in the metric system. Typical deceleration rates include the following.

- Comfortable deceleration is about 8.5 ft/sec^2 (3 m/s^2).

- Loose items in the vehicle will "fly" above 11 ft/sec^2 (3.5 m/s^2).

- Maximum deceleration rates for most vehicles and light trucks range from 16 to 32 ft/sec^2 (5 to 10 m/s^2).

An average deceleration rate of 15 ft/sec^2 (FPSPS) (3 m/s^2) can stop a vehicle traveling at 55 mph (88 km/h) in about 200 ft (61 m) and in less than 4 seconds. Deceleration is also expressed in units called a **g.** One g is the acceleration of gravity, which is 32 feet per second per second.

With a conventional hydraulic braking system, the driver can brake extremely gently, thereby only imperceptibly slowing the vehicle. A typical hybrid using regenerative braking will normally indicate a 0.1 g (about 3 ft/sec^2) deceleration rate when the throttle is released and the brake pedal has not been applied. This rate is what a driver would normally expect to occur when the accelerator pedal is released. This slight deceleration feels comfortable to the driver, as well as the passengers, because this is what occurs in a nonhybrid vehicle that does not incorporate regenerative braking. When the brake pedal is pressed, the deceleration increases to a greater value than 0.1 g, which gives the driver the same feeling of deceleration that would occur in a conventional vehicle. Maximum deceleration rates are usually greater than 0.8 g and could exceed 1 g in most vehicles. ● SEE FIGURE 9–10.

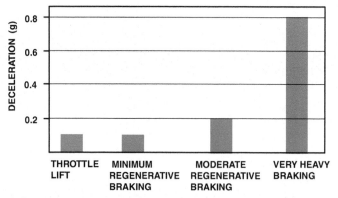

FIGURE 9–10 This graph compares the figures: at the far left a throttle lift typically giving about 0.1 g deceleration; second from the left a minimum regenerative braking of about 0.1 g; second from the right, a moderate regenerative braking is about 0.2 g; and on the far right a hard emergency stop resulting in braking of (at least) 0.8 g, which uses both the regenerative braking system, as well as the base hydraulic brake system.

FIGURE 9–11 This Honda valve train photo shows the small spring used to absorb the motion of the rocker arm when the cam is switched to a lobe that has zero lift. This action causes the valves to remain closed thereby reducing engine braking, which increases the amount of energy that can be captured by the regenerative braking system when the vehicle is slowing. The powertrain control module controls this valve action in response to inputs from the throttle position (TP) sensor and vehicle speed information.

ENGINE DESIGN CHANGES RELATED TO REGENERATIVE BRAKING

Some hybrid vehicles, such as the second-generation Honda Civic and Accord, use a variation of the VTEC valve actuation system to close all of the valves in three cylinders in both the V-6 and the inline four cylinder engines during deceleration. This traps some exhaust in the cylinders and because no air enters the pistons, the cylinders do not have anything to compress. As a result, the engine does not cause any engine braking and therefore allows more of the inertia of the moving vehicle to be converted to electrical energy due to regenerative braking. ● SEE FIGURE 9–11.

SERVICING REGENERATIVE BRAKING SYSTEMS

UNIQUE MASTER CYLINDERS Most hybrid electric vehicles use unique master cylinders that do not look like conventional master cylinders. Some use more than one brake fluid reservoir and others contain sensors and other components, which are often not serviced separately. ● SEE FIGURE 9–12.

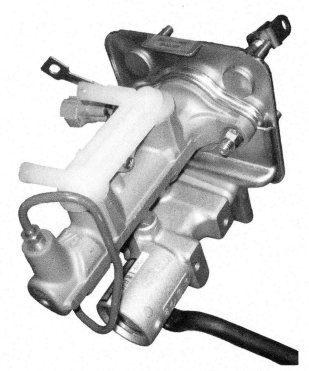

Figure 9–12 A master cylinder from a Toyota Highlander hybrid electric vehicle.

FORD ESCAPE PRECAUTIONS On the Ford Escape hybrid system, the regenerative braking system checks the integrity of the brake system as a self-test. After a certain amount of time, the brake controller will energize the hydraulic control unit and check that pressure can be developed in the system.

- This is performed when a door is opened as part of the wake-up feature of the system.
- The ignition key does not have to be in the ignition for this self-test to be performed.
- This is done by developing brake pressure for short periods of time.

CAUTION: To prevent physical harm or causing damage to the vehicle when servicing the braking system, the technician should do the following:

Frequently Asked Question

When Does Regenerative Braking Not Work?
There is one unusual situation where regenerative braking will not occur. What happens if, for example, the vehicle is at the top of a long hill and the battery charge level is high? In this situation, the controller can only overcharge the batteries. Overcharging is not good for the batteries, so the controller will disable regenerative braking and use the base brakes only. This is one reason why the SOC of the batteries is kept below 80% so regenerative braking can occur.

1. In order to change the brake pads, it is necessary to enter the "Pad Service Mode" on a scan tool and disable the self-test. This will prevent brake pressure from being applied.
2. Disconnect the wiring harness at the hydraulic control unit. ● **see Figure 9–13**
3. Check service information regarding how to cycle the ignition switch to enter the Pad Service Mode.

Figure 9–13 When working on the brakes on a Ford Escape or Mercury Mariner hybrid vehicle, disconnect the black electrical connector on the ABS hydraulic control unit located on the passenger side under the hood.

SUMMARY

1. All moving objects that have mass (weight) have kinetic energy.
2. The regenerative braking system captures most of the kinetic energy from the moving vehicle and returns this energy to high-voltage batteries to be used later to help propel the vehicle.
3. The two types of regenerative braking include parallel and series.

4. Brushless DC and AC induction motors are used in hybrid electric vehicles to help propel the vehicle and to generate electrical energy back to the batteries during braking.
5. Most hybrid electric vehicles use an electrohydraulic braking system that includes pressure sensors to detect the pressures in the system.
6. The controller is used to control the motors and turn them into a generator as needed to provide regenerative braking.

1. What is inertia?
2. What is the difference between series and parallel regenerative braking systems?
3. What happens in the regenerative braking system when the high-voltage batteries are fully charged?

4. Describe what occurs when the driver first releases the accelerator pedal and then starts to brake on a hybrid electric vehicle equipped with regenerative braking.

CHAPTER QUIZ

1. Which type of regenerative braking system uses an electrohydraulic system?
   a. Series
   b. Parallel
   c. Both series and parallel
   d. Neither series nor parallel

2. Kinetic energy is _____.
   a. The energy that the driver exerts on the brake pedal
   b. The energy needed from the batteries to propel a vehicle
   c. The energy in any moving object
   d. The energy that the motor produces to propel the vehicle

3. Inertia is _____.
   a. The energy of any moving object that has mass (weight)
   b. The force that the driver exerts on the brake pedal during a stop
   c. The electric motor force that is applied to the drive wheels
   d. The force that the internal combustion engine and the electric motor together apply to the drive wheels during rapid acceleration

4. Technician A says that the Powertrain Control Module (PCM) or controller can control the voltage to the motor(s) in a hybrid electric vehicle. Technician B says that the PCM or controller can control the electric motors by varying the frequency of the applied current. Which technician is correct?
   a. Technician A only
   b. Technician B only
   c. Both Technicians A and B
   d. Neither Technician A nor B

5. During braking on a hybrid electric vehicle equipped with regenerative braking system, what occurs when the driver depresses the brake pedal?
   a. The friction brakes are only used as a backup and not used during normal braking.
   b. The motors become generators.
   c. The driver needs to apply a braking lever instead of depressing the brake pedal to energize the regenerative braking system.
   d. The batteries are charged to 100% SOC.

6. Technician A says that a front-wheel-drive hybrid electric vehicle can only generate electricity during braking from the front wheel motor(s). Technician B says that the antilock braking (ABS) is not possible with a vehicle equipped with a regenerative braking system. Which technician is correct?
   a. Technician A only
   b. Technician B only
   c. Both Technicians A and B
   d. Neither Technician A nor B

7. In a regenerative braking system, which part of the electric motor is being controlled by the computer?
   a. The rotor
   b. The stator
   c. Both the rotor and the stator
   d. Neither the rotor nor the stator

8. In a Toyota Prius regenerative braking system, how many pressure *sensors* are used?
   a. One   b. Two
   c. Three   d. Four

9. In a Toyota Prius regenerative braking system, how many pressure *switches* are used?
   a. One   b. Two
   c. Three   d. Four

10. Two technicians are discussing deceleration rates. Technician A says that a one "g" stop is a gentle slowing of the vehicle. Technician B says that a stopping rate of 8 ft/sec^2 is a severe stop. Which technician is correct?
    a. Technician A only
    b. Technician B only
    c. Both Technicians A and B
    d. Neither Technician A nor B

chapter 10
HYBRID VEHICLE TRANSMISSIONS AND TRANSAXLES

OBJECTIVES: **After studying Chapter 10, the reader will be able to:** • Describe the function of a hybrid electric vehicle transmission. • Understand the relationship required between the ICE and electric motor(s). • Describe how the idle stop function is related to the needs of the automatic transmission operation. • Discuss modifications made to automatic transmissions installed in hybrid electric vehicles (HEVs). • Explain the operation of continuously variable transmissions (CVTs).

KEY TERMS: • Belt-and-pulley CVT 154 • Bi-directional testing 141 • Brake 136 • Creep aid 155 • Differential 131 • eCVT 152 • Electric secondary fluid pump 140 • Energy recirculation 149 • Final drive 131 • FWD 131 • Gear ratio 133 • Generator motor 152 • Kinetic energy 149 • Motor/generator 152 • Nomograph 148 • Overdrive 134 • Overrunning clutch 136 • PCM 136 • Planetary gearset 136 • PTO 132 • Reduction 134 • RWD 131 • TCC 136 • TCM 136 • Torque 132 • Traction battery 153 • Traction motor 152

TRANSMISSIONS AND TRANSAXLES

PURPOSE AND FUNCTION From the earliest days of the automobile, internal combustion engine vehicles have required the use of a transmission in order to achieve reasonable acceleration and efficiency. The transmission is responsible for providing

- Torque applied to the drive wheel to accelerate the vehicle from a stop, and
- Power at higher speeds that allow the engine to operate efficiently.

● **SEE FIGURE 10–1.**

TERMINOLOGY In **rear-wheel-drive (RWD)** applications, it is most common to utilize a transmission along with a **differential** and a **final drive** at the rear axle to transmit engine torque to the drive wheels. The Lexus GS450h and LS600h are both rear-wheel-drive hybrid electric vehicles. In a **front-wheel-drive (FWD)** vehicle, a transaxle assembly is used. A transaxle is the combination of a transmission, differential, and final drive gears built together as one assembly. Most current-production HEVs are either FWD or 4WD, and most use a transaxle for driving the front wheels. ● **SEE FIGURE 10–2.**

In a four-wheel-drive (4WD) or all-wheel-drive (AWD) vehicle, a transfer case is usually used. A transmission can also be used with a transfer case to distribute torque to all four wheels in four-wheel-drive (4WD) vehicles.

The Toyota Highlander/Lexus RX400h uses a transaxle on the front of the vehicle and an electric motor to drive the rear wheels in the 4WD model. The 4WD version of the Ford Escape

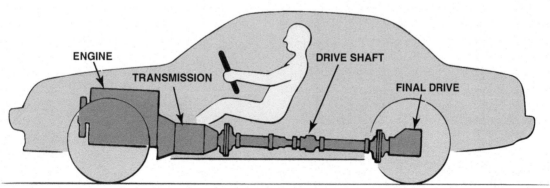

FIGURE 10–1 A vehicle transmission must adjust engine speed and torque to allow the vehicle to operate efficiently over a wide speed range.

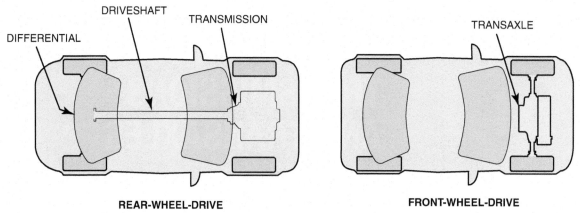

DIFFERENTIAL DRIVESHAFT TRANSMISSION TRANSAXLE

REAR-WHEEL-DRIVE **FRONT-WHEEL-DRIVE**

FIGURE 10–2 Rear-wheel-drive (RWD) vehicles use transmissions to send torque to the rear differential and final drive. Front-wheel-drive (FWD) vehicles use a transaxle, which incorporates the differential and final drive into the transaxle case.

hybrid uses a separate **power takeoff (PTO)** from the transaxle to mechanically drive the rear axle.

PRINCIPLES INVOLVED

TORQUE DELIVERY In order to move a vehicle, **torque** must be applied to the drive wheels. Torque is *twisting force*. Torque is applied to the drive wheels to make the vehicle accelerate. The vehicle transmission is responsible for increasing engine torque in the lower speed ranges when acceleration is required, and then reducing engine speed for the best fuel economy when the vehicle is cruising. Internal combustion engines (ICEs) are very different from electric motors in that they only produce torque in a relatively narrow RPM range. ● **SEE FIGURE 10–3.**

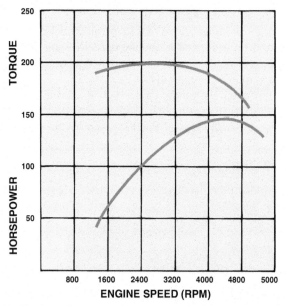

FIGURE 10–3 Graph showing engine torque vs. horsepower output for a typical internal combustion engine. ICEs produce maximum torque at high RPM, whereas electric motors produce maximum torque at low RPM.

? FREQUENTLY ASKED QUESTION

What Units of Measure Are Used to Describe Torque?

It is very common for torque to be expressed in foot-pounds. This can be confusing, however, as foot-pounds is also the unit of measure for work. To be technically accurate, torque should be expressed in terms of pound-feet. However, many service publications and tool companies still make use of the term "foot-pounds" to measure torque.

An internal combustion engine is most efficient when it is operating near its torque peak. This is the RPM when the engine is breathing most efficiently, and is typically where the engine can deliver the best fuel economy. However, it is difficult to keep the engine in this range during all phases of vehicle operation. Automotive engineers overcome this difficulty in two ways.

1. By increasing the RPM range where the engine produces torque ("flattening" the torque curve).

2. By increasing the number of speeds in the transmission. With more transmission speeds, it is easier to match the vehicle road speed with the most efficient engine RPM.

Therefore, any torque increase is generated at the expense of speed. In other words, when torque is increased in a transmission, output speed is decreased. ● **SEE FIGURE 10–4.**

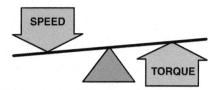

FIGURE 10–4 When output speed decreases in a transmission, output torque will increase.

What Is the Difference Between Horsepower and Torque?

Torque is twisting force. For instance, engine torque is the twisting force that is developed at the crankshaft when the engine is running. Horsepower is the rate at which work is done, and is a function of torque and engine RPM. Horsepower can be calculated using the following formula:

$$\text{Horsepower} = \frac{\text{Torque} \times \text{RPM}}{5,252}$$

Keep in mind that torque is what causes a vehicle to move and accelerate. A transmission is built to increase torque output at low vehicle speeds, and decrease it as the vehicle moves faster. A transmission can increase torque at the expense of speed and vice versa, but cannot alter engine horsepower. Horsepower is what sells a vehicle, yet it is the torque that moves a vehicle.

MULTIPLE SPEED TRANSMISSIONS/TRANSAXLES

Years ago, it was common for 2- and 3-speed automatic transmissions and 3-speed manual transmissions to be used in automotive applications. Currently, 5-, 6-, 7-, and 8-speed transmissions (automatic and manual) are becoming common. With more emphasis being placed on fuel economy and emissions, the CVT is becoming more popular as it provides infinite speed ratios and the best opportunity to maximize engine efficiency.

MANUAL TRANSAXLES

PURPOSE AND FUNCTION   Manual transaxles are used with a clutch mechanism to transmit and modify engine torque before it is sent to the front drive wheels. Engine torque is applied through the clutch assembly and into the manual transmission gearing to achieve various gear ratios. The torque then is applied to the final drive assembly, where the torque is split to the front drive wheels through drive axle shafts. ● **SEE FIGURE 10-5.**

HONDA MANUAL TRANSAXLE   The manual transaxles that have been used in the production of Honda hybrid electric vehicles (HEVs) are 5-speed designs. This means that these transaxles have five forward gear ratios and one reverse gear ratio. ● **SEE FIGURE 10-6.**

Each gear position of the transaxle has a specific **gear ratio** (or *speed ratio*), which describes how fast the input shaft will turn relative to one turn of the output shaft. ● **SEE FIGURE 10-7.**

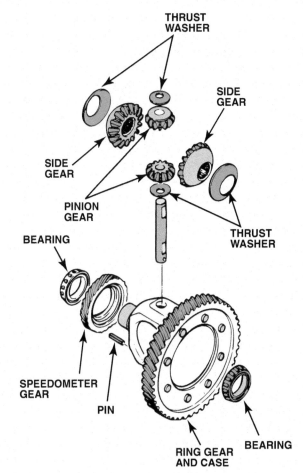

FIGURE 10-5 Components of a differential assembly. The drive shafts of a FWD vehicle are connected to the side gears.

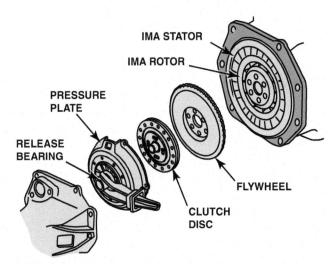

FIGURE 10-6 Manual transaxle and clutch assembly from a Honda Civic Hybrid. The flywheel is attached to the engine crankshaft through the IMA rotor.

The first and reverse gears in a manual transaxle will have numerically higher gear ratios than any of the other gears. For instance, a Honda Civic Hybrid with a 5-speed manual transaxle has a first gear ratio of 3.461:1 and a reverse gear ratio of 3.23:1. ● **SEE CHART 10-1.**

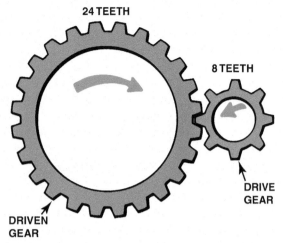

FIGURE 10–7 A gear reduction with a 3:1 gear ratio. This means that the drive gear will turn three times for each revolution of the driven gear.

GEAR	RATIO
1st	3.46:1
2nd	1.87:1
3rd	1.24:1
4th	0.91:1
5th	0.71:1
Reverse	3.23:1

CHART 10–1

Gear ratios used in a Honda 5-speed manual transaxle. Note that both 4th and 5th gears are overdrive ratios which help improve fuel economy.

These higher ratios yield lower vehicle speed but increase torque to a level that allows for easy vehicle starting from a standing stop. This arrangement is known as a **reduction,** because vehicle speed is reduced in favor of increased torque.

Both fourth and fifth gears use an **overdrive** ratio, because the transmission input shaft will turn slower than the output shaft. While the speed is increased, torque is decreased and an overdrive gear would not be selected if vehicle acceleration was required. Overdrive gear ratios are used in the higher gears in transmissions so that the internal combustion engine will turn at a relatively low speed during cruising, lowering noise levels and increasing fuel economy. ● **SEE FIGURE 10–8.**

FLUID-LEVEL CHECK The most important service procedure with any manual transaxle is fluid inspection and replacement. The fluid level and condition should be checked as part of a normal maintenance routine, and if the fluid is dirty, it should be replaced at that time. The fluid should always be

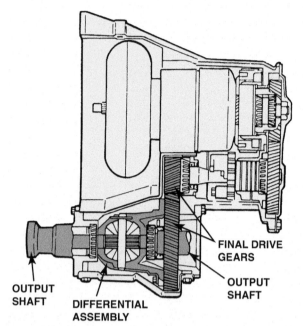

FIGURE 10–8 A transaxle final drive uses helical gears to reduce speed and increase torque. The differential assembly is attached to the final drive ring gear.

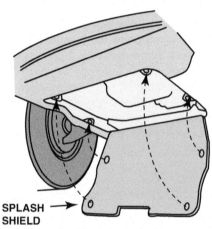

FIGURE 10–9 Lowering the splash shield to gain access to the manual transaxle fill and drain plugs.

replaced at specified intervals as recommended by the vehicle manufacturer.

In order to properly check the transaxle fluid, be sure that the vehicle is level (the vehicle should be raised on a lift) and the ignition switch is in the LOCK position. With many FWD vehicles, the splash shield must be removed to gain access to the transaxle oil level/filler plug. ● **SEE FIGURE 10–9.**

After lowering the splash shield, remove the oil filler plug (make sure the gasket is still on the plug) and check to make sure the oil is at the proper level. Note that in most manual transaxles, the fluid should be level with the bottom of the oil fill hole. ● **SEE FIGURE 10–10.**

NOTE: Some manual transaxles use dipsticks for checking fluid level.

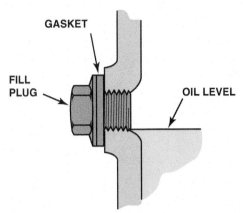

FIGURE 10–10 Remove the oil fill plug, making sure that the gasket is intact and is reinstalled with the plug after service. The oil should be level with the bottom of the fill hole.

FIGURE 10–11 Original equipment manufacturer (OEM) products are the best guarantee of using the correct fluids for a vehicle.

If the fluid is dirty, or if the specified change interval has been reached, remove the drain plug and empty the old fluid from the transaxle. Install the drain plug with a new gasket and refill the transaxle to the proper level with the manufacturer-specified fluid. Check service information for the specified fluid to use. The easiest way to be sure is to use the original equipment manufacture (OEM) fluid sold at the dealership for a specific vehicle. ● SEE FIGURE 10–11.

When draining the transmission fluid, be sure to inspect the fluid condition and look for any sign of metal content in the oil. Metallic "hair" found on a magnetic drain plug is most likely due to normal wear. However, metal pieces found in the oil indicate internal problems and may require transaxle removal and inspection.

NON-HYBRID AUTOMATIC TRANSMISSIONS

INTRODUCTION Automatic transmissions used in hybrid electric vehicles (HEVs) are usually based on existing automatic transmissions. A review of how a conventional automatic transmission works will help in understanding how automatic transmissions used in hybrid electric vehicles work.

TORQUE CONVERTER CONSTRUCTION Conventional automatic transmissions use a torque converter to couple the ICE to the transmission gear train.

- When the vehicle is starting from a standstill, the required torque from the engine is high and the output speed of the torque converter is low.
- When the vehicle speed increases and less torque is required to keep the vehicle moving, torque output decreases and output speed increases.
- The torque converter adjusts its output speed and torque to match vehicle operating conditions.

The torque converter is attached to the ICE crankshaft through a flexplate. The basic torque converter contains the following three elements:

1. Impeller,
2. Turbine, and
3. Stator

The impeller (also known as the pump) is attached to the torque converter housing and rotates with the ICE. ● SEE FIGURE 10–12.

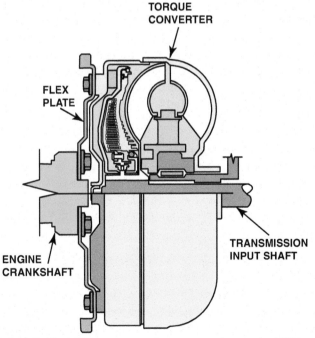

FIGURE 10–12 The torque converter attaches to the ICE crankshaft through a flexplate.

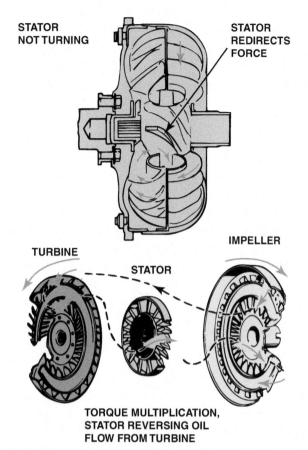

FIGURE 10–13 Torque multiplication occurs when the fluid leaving the turbine strikes the front of the stator vanes and is redirected back to the impeller. Once the turbine speed reaches 90% of the impeller speed, the torque converter enters the coupling phase.

TORQUE CONVERTER OPERATION The torque converter housing is filled with automatic transmission fluid, and the impeller moves this fluid into the turbine, which is attached to the transmission input shaft. Fluid pressure is applied to the turbine, causing it to apply torque to the transmission input shaft. As fluid exits the turbine, it is redirected into the impeller inlet by the stator, which has the net effect of increasing torque output. ● **SEE FIGURE 10–13.**

TORQUE CONVERTER CLUTCH In order to increase the efficiency of the transmission, the **torque converter clutch (TCC)** is applied and the turbine is locked to the torque converter housing. This eliminates most of the slippage (about 10%) that occurs and improves fuel economy. This results in all of the torque converter elements rotating together and the transmission input shaft being coupled directly to the ICE crankshaft. ● **SEE FIGURE 10–14.**

TCC lockup normally takes place at cruising speed under low-load conditions. Whenever greater torque is required to accelerate the vehicle, the TCC is released and the torque converter returns to a condition of vortex flow. The TCC will also normally release as a vehicle decelerates and the engine approaches idle speed. If the TCC did not release under these conditions, the engine would stall as the vehicle rolls to a stop.

PLANETARY GEARSETS Most automatic transmissions use multiple (compound) **planetary gearsets** to produce the various gear ratios for each speed range of the transmission. A planetary gearset has three members:

1. Ring gear,
2. Planet carrier with pinion gears, and
3. Sun gear
   ● **SEE FIGURE 10–15.**

In order to make a planetary gearset transmit and modify torque, one of the members must be held, one must have input torque applied to it, and one must act as the output. A direct (1:1) gear ratio can also be achieved by locking any two of the elements together. To accomplish this, apply devices are used to act as either clutches or brakes. A clutch is a device that locks two elements together so that they both rotate at the same speed and torque is transmitted through them. A **brake** holds an element stationary so that it acts as a reaction member.

APPLY DEVICES There are three types of apply devices used in most automatic transmission designs.

1. One-way clutches
2. Multiple-disc clutches
3. Bands

A one-way clutch will allow rotation in one direction but not in the other. A one-way clutch is also known as an **overrunning clutch.** This is the device that is used to operate the stator in a torque converter. ● **SEE FIGURE 10–16.**

The most common apply device used in modern automatic transmissions is the multiple-disc clutch. Multiple-disc clutches are versatile as they can also be used as brakes. Multiple-disc clutches use hydraulic pressure to squeeze alternating steel and friction plates together and lock two elements together in an automatic transmission gear train. The clutch plates are typically installed in a steel drum with the clutch apply piston underneath them. When configured as a brake, the steel clutch plates are splined to the transmission case and are thus able to hold the element solid when applied. ● **SEE FIGURE 10–17** on page 138.

TRANSMISSION PUMPS In order to shift an automatic transmission from one gear to the next, the various apply devices are applied and released by the hydraulic control circuits. These control circuits are supplied with hydraulic pressure by a pump that is located at the front of the transmission and is driven by the torque converter housing. The pump picks up fluid through an inlet pipe and strainer located in the transmission oil pan. Since the torque converter housing turns with the ICE, hydraulic pressure from this pump is available only when the ICE is running. ● **SEE FIGURE 10–18** on page 138.

TRANSMISSION CONTROLS A **powertrain control module (PCM)** or **transmission control module (TCM)** is responsible for shift points, shift quality, line pressure, and torque converter clutch lockup. Sensor data is processed by the module and control signals are sent to solenoids located

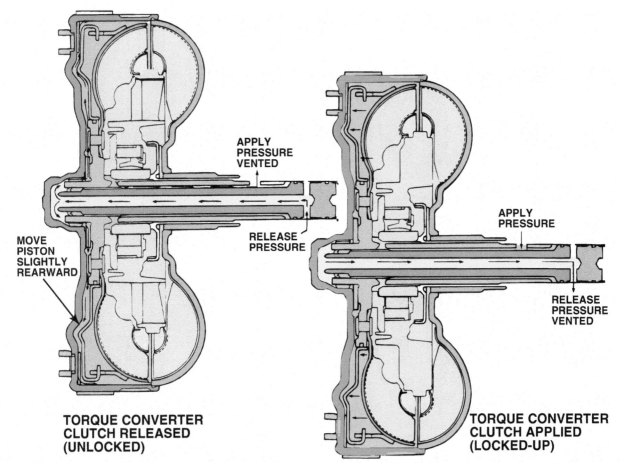

FIGURE 10–14 The torque converter clutch (TCC) is applied and released by reversing the flow of fluid through the torque converter housing.

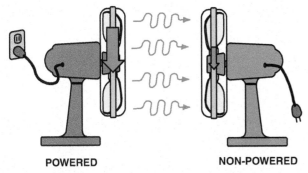

FIGURE 10–15 Planetary gearset showing the input attached to the sun gear and the output attached to the planet carrier. The ring gear would be held to make this a functional gearset.

inside the transmission case. These solenoids operate spool valves that direct hydraulic pressure to the appropriate areas and are thus able to make the transmission operate smoothly and efficiently. ● **SEE FIGURE 10–19.**

ADAPTIVE STRATEGIES One advantage of using electronic controls on an automatic transmission is that adaptive strategies can be utilized to make shifting smooth and consistent throughout the life of the transmission. As the clutches wear, it takes progressively more time for them to

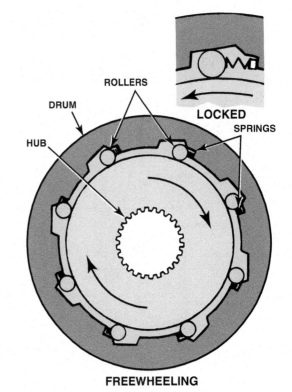

FIGURE 10–16 A one-way clutch will freewheel in one direction, but lock up if rotated in the opposite direction.

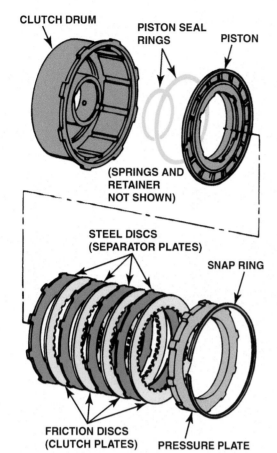

FIGURE 10-17 Multiple-disc clutches are applied by exerting hydraulic pressure on the piston. Piston seal rings are used to prevent leakage and maintain transmission fluid pressure.

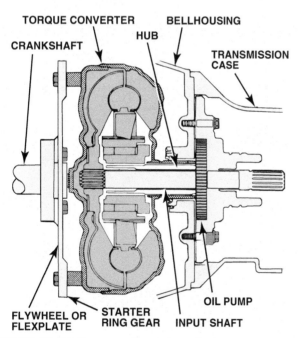

FIGURE 10-18 Cross-sectional view of a torque converter and transmission oil pump drive.

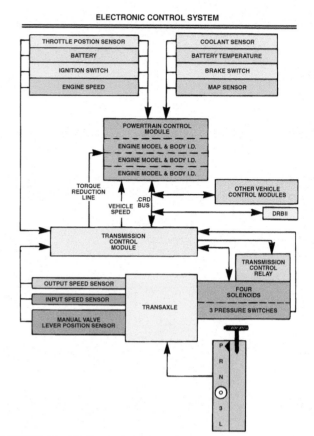

FIGURE 10-19 Control strategy for one type of electronically controlled automatic transmission.

apply as more fluid is required to move the piston to the point of clutch application. This can result in shift delays and reduced shift quality. In order to alleviate this, the transmission control module will begin to increase application pressures to worn clutches to help them apply more quickly. These new pressure values (sometimes known as transmission adaptive pressures) are then kept in the memory of the transmission control module and used in subsequent shifts.

GM PARALLEL HYBRID TRUCK AUTOMATIC TRANSMISSION

DESCRIPTION AND OPERATION The transmission in the 2004–2008 Chevrolet Silverado/GMC Sierra parallel hybrid pickup is based on the 4L60E electronically controlled automatic transmission design with minor modification to adjust for its new role in a hybrid power train. It has four forward speeds and one reverse, with the fourth speed being an overdrive. It is designed primarily for medium- and large-displacement engines and is used extensively in GM pickups and SUVs. The specific model used in the hybrid pickup is

GEAR	RATIO
1st	3.059:1
2nd	1.625:1
3rd	1.000:1
4th	0.696:1
Reverse	2.294:1

CHART 10-2

The gear ratios used in the 4L60E automatic transmission used in the General Motors parallel hybrid pickup trucks.

known as the M33. The gear ratios for the various transmission speeds are summarized in ● **CHART 10-2.**

The transmission design includes a torque converter with a lockup clutch (also known as a TCC or torque converter clutch), five multiple-disc clutches, two one-way clutches, and a single band. Two planetary gearsets are configured in a modified Simpson gear train (two separate sun gears instead of one common one). This transmission was originally designed with mechanical/hydraulic controls only, but was later modified to incorporate electronic shift control. These functions are controlled by the PCM, which receives signals from other vehicle sensors to determine load and speed and command appropriate transmission operation. ● **SEE FIGURE 10-20.**

The transmission gear selector lever can be placed in seven positions, as follows:

- P—Park
- R—Reverse
- N—Neutral
- D—Drive

- 3—Manual third
- 2—Manual second
- 1—Manual first

This transmission operates very similar to the standard 4L60E, with two exceptions. First, the transmission will upshift at lower RPMs. Second, the torque converter clutch (TCC) is programmed to lock up earlier in the RPM range than it would in the standard 4L60E transmission.

CONSTRUCTION The transmission case and bell housing is made from die-cast aluminum, the same as the conventional model. However, changes were made to accommodate the addition of the *integrated starter-generator* (*ISG*) inside the bell-housing assembly. The transmission was modified only to the extent where it was absolutely necessary, and otherwise used as much of the original design as possible.

The primary change was a decrease in the diameter of the torque converter in order for it to fit inside the rotor assembly of the ISG. ● **SEE FIGURE 10-21.**

The original torque converter is 300 mm in diameter, whereas the hybrid torque converter is 258 mm. The rotor assembly is bolted directly to the ICE crankshaft and wraps around the torque converter. A separate flexplate inside the rotor is used to drive the torque converter. The bell housing is a separate part of the most recent 4L60E transmission case design, and this was replaced with a special unit that was large enough to enclose the ISG stator assembly.

The smaller diameter of the torque converter created a new problem in that it would now generate more heat during vehicle operation and the potential existed for it to overheat under heavy load conditions. This problem is magnified by the fact that there is 2.4 quarts less fluid in the hybrid model than the standard 4L60E. To limit heat buildup in the smaller torque

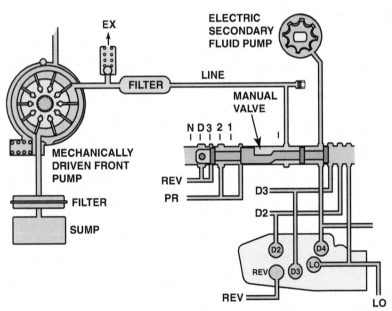

FIGURE 10-20 Hydraulic circuit diagram for a GM 4L60E Model M33 transmission. Note the inclusion of an electric secondary fluid pump in the top right of the diagram.

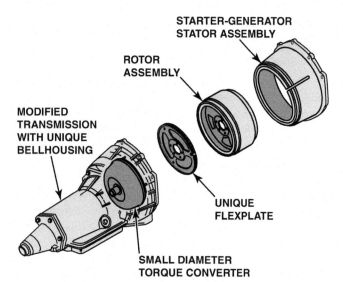

FIGURE 10–21 Integrated starter-generator (ISG) assembly adapted to a production 4L60E transmission. Note that the torque converter diameter is smaller to fit inside the rotor assembly.

converter, a different TCC control strategy was utilized so that lockup would be commanded earlier. This also necessitated the use of a torque converter with a multiplate clutch (TCC) in order to handle the torque generated by the V-8 ICE.

Use of a smaller-diameter torque converter resulted in problems accessing the bolts used to attach the torque converter to the flexplate because they were now on a smaller bolt circle. To address this problem, a small clearance notch was added to the engine block to allow access to these bolts when removing the transmission for service.

OPERATION In idle stop mode the engine stops, which will in turn stop the transmission oil pump and cause the transmission to go to "neutral." To prevent this, an **electric secondary fluid pump** is installed on the valve body inside the transmission oil pan. Whenever the engine goes into idle stop, the electric fluid pump is turned on to maintain oil pressure on the transmission forward clutch and keep the drivetrain connected to the engine. This results in a smoother transition between idle stop and engine restarting as the vehicle resumes operation. ● **SEE FIGURE 10–22.**

The conventional 4L60E transmission is made to allow the vehicle to coast or brake without any interference from the engine. This operational strategy does not work well with the hybrid configuration because it does not allow regenerative braking to take place during deceleration. This is because the ISG rotor is connected directly to the ICE and would not receive power from the drivetrain under these conditions. To enable regenerative braking, the hybrid version of the 4L60E transmission is made to apply the overrun clutch during coast or braking in the D4 range and either third or second gear. This allows power to be transmitted back through the torque converter, which can then be used to generate electric current for recharging the 42-volt battery pack.

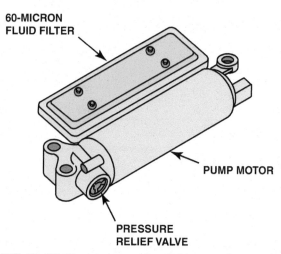

FIGURE 10–22 Electric secondary fluid pump from a 4L60E transmission in a GM hybrid pickup.

SERVICE Transmission service for the 4L60E model M33 is limited to fluid and filter changes. This transmission requires Dexron VI fluid. The filter on the electric secondary fluid pump is replaceable but is not a regular maintenance item.

Transmission pressure testing can be performed using the line pressure tap located on the transmission case. These tests are most often done by attaching a pressure gauge to the fitting on the side of the transmission and operating the transmission under various load conditions and road speeds. The test results are recorded and compared to charts to help determine what area(s) of the transmission might be malfunctioning.

? **FREQUENTLY ASKED QUESTION**

What Is Bi-Directional Testing?

Automotive scan tools often include features such as bi-directional testing (also known as *output controls*) to help diagnose electrical/electronic problems on a vehicle. Module-controlled output devices such as motors, lights, and solenoids can be commanded on and off using a scan tool, and the results of the test can be used to help determine the cause of the customer concern.

For example, with a vehicle equipped with an electronically controlled transmission that does not shift properly, the technician connects a scan tool to the vehicle and then uses the bi-directional controls to operate the transmission shift solenoids. If the scan tool can turn the shift solenoids on and off but they will not work during normal vehicle operation, the technician now knows that the solenoids, module, and power and grounds are OK. This helps narrow the diagnosis to the inputs to the module because all other parts of the circuit have been confirmed as working properly.

A scan tool can be used to access DTCs (diagnostic trouble codes) and also to perform **bi-directional testing** of the transmission solenoids. A scan tool can also be utilized for clearing the *transmission adaptive pressure* (*TAP*) values if any of the following has occurred:

1. If the transmission has been overhauled or replaced.
2. Repair or replacement of an apply or release component (band, clutch, servo, piston, etc.).
3. Repair or replacement of a component that directly affects line pressure.

TWO-MODE HYBRID TRANSMISSION

POWER TRAIN   The two-mode hybrid transmission used in General Motors hybrid trucks is labeled a 2ML70. This unit features two 60-kW motors in the hybrid drivetrain, a 300-volt battery pack, and a V-8 engine.

NOTE: The BMW 7 series two-mode hybrid uses a twin-turbocharged 4.4 liter V-8 with an 8-speed automatic transmission.

A two-mode hybrid electric vehicle is capable of increasing the fuel economy by about 25%, depending on the type of driving conditions. Like all hybrids, the two-mode combines the power of a gasoline engine with that of electric motors and includes:

- Regenerative braking that captures kinetic energy that would otherwise be lost
- Idle stop

Existing full hybrid systems have a single mode of operation, using a single planetary gearset to split engine power to drive the wheels or charge the battery.

These systems are effective at low speeds because they can move the vehicle without running the gasoline engine (ICE).

But at higher speeds, when the engine is needed, using the electric motors has much less benefit. As a result, sending power through electric motors and a variable transmission is roughly 20% less efficient than driving the vehicle through a purely mechanical power path, using gears.

COMPONENTS   This two-mode unit is called an electronically variable transmission (EVT). It includes three simple planetary gearsets with four multiplate clutches. It has four fixed gear ratios with two EV ratios for smooth, more efficient operation.

The components of the two-mode transmission include the following:

- Two 60-kW electric motor/generators assemblies.
- Three planetary gearsets (one is located in front of motor/generator A , called M/G A; another is located

FIGURE 10–23 The two-mode transmission has organge high-voltage cable entering the unit to carry electric energy from the high-volatge battery pack to propel the veicle and also to charge the battery during deceleration.

between the two motor/generators, and the last planetary gearset is located behind motor/generator B, called M/G B).

- Four wet plate clutches (two friction [rotating] and two [reaction/stationary] clutch assemblies). ● **SEE FIGURE 10–23.**

The vehicle starts moving in EV 1 with a variable ratio from infinite low to 1.7:1. If the vehicle is launched with the engine off, M/G A will spin the engine crankshaft so it can start running. EV 2 has a ratio between 1.7:1 and 0.5:1.

FIRST MODE OF OPERATION   The first mode is for accelerating from standstill to second gear. At low speed and light load, the vehicle can be propelled by:

- Either electric motor alone
- The internal combustion engine (ICE) alone
- Or a combination of the two (electric motor and/or ICE)

In this mode, the engine (if running) can be shut off under certain conditions and everything will continue to operate on electric power alone. The hybrid system can restart the ICE at any time as needed. One of the motor/generators operates as a generator to charge the high-voltage battery, and the other works as a motor to assist in propelling the vehicle.

SECOND MODE OF OPERATION   The second mode takes the vehicle from second gear through to overdrive. At higher loads and speeds, the ICE always runs. In the second mode, the motor/generators and planetary gearsets are used to keep torque and horsepower at a maximum. As the vehicle speed increases, various combinations of the four fixed ratio planetary gears engage and/or disengage to multiply engine

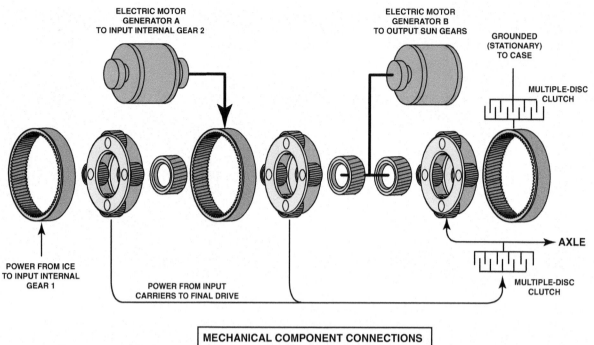

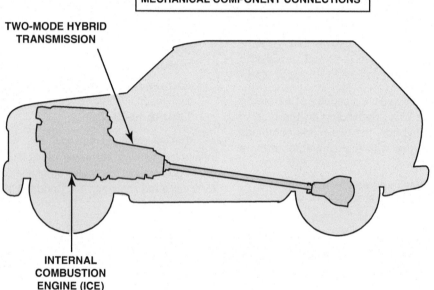

FIGURE 10–24 Using two planetary gearsets, the ICE can be maintained in the most effcient speed of about 2,000 RPM under most operating conditions.

torque, and allowing one or the other of the motor/generators to perform as a generator to charge the high-voltage battery. ● **SEE FIGURE 10–24.**

TWO-MODE SERVICE Routine service is all that is needed or required of the two-mode transmission. Fluid-level check and visual inspection should be all that is required until the first scheduled fluid change. Always use Dexron VI. Faults in the system will often set a diagnostic trouble code (DTC). Unit repair of the unit requires an engine hoist or the lift arm of a vehicle lift to remove the motor assembly. ● **SEE FIGURE 10–25.**

HONDA ACCORD HYBRID 5-SPEED AUTOMATIC TRANSMISSION

DESCRIPTION AND OPERATION Honda uses an automatic transmission (transaxle) in the 2005–2007 Accord Hybrid that is similar to the units used in its vehicles with conventional non-hybrid power trains. This transmission has five forward speeds and one reverse, and uses a standard

(a)

(b)

FIGURE 10–25 (a) Disassembly of the 2ML70 transmission requires the use of a lift or engine hoist to remove the motor assembly. (b) The motor assembly after being removed for the transmission.

torque converter with lockup clutch. There are four parallel shafts, including the main shaft, countershaft, secondary shaft, and the intermediate shaft. This design is similar to the Honda manual transaxles, as constant-mesh helical gears and a reverse idler are used to create the gear ratios. Planetary gearsets are not utilized in this design. The various speeds are selected through the application of six multiple-disc clutches and a single one-way clutch. ● **SEE FIGURE 10–26.**

The integrated motor assist (IMA) assembly is located between the ICE and the transmission. The torque converter

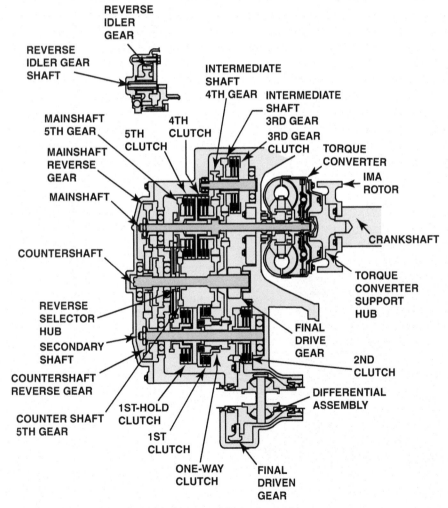

FIGURE 10–26 Cutaway view of Honda Accord Hybrid automatic transmission.

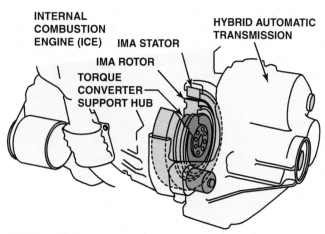

FIGURE 10–27 Honda Accord Hybrid power train, including 3.0-liter V6, IMA assembly, and 5-speed automatic transmission.

drive plate (flexplate) is attached to the IMA rotor, which in turn is driven by the ICE crankshaft. ● **SEE FIGURE 10–27.**

Most transmission control functions are performed electronically. Input signals from the sensors are processed by the PCM, which operates seven solenoid valves in the transmission to control shift points, shift quality, and torque converter lockup. In order to accommodate the hybrid power train, an electric auxiliary pump is used to maintain fluid pressure in the transmission during ICE idle stop. This pump is powered by a DC brushless (AC synchronous) motor, which requires a special controller to provide the correct operating frequency and pulse width. When the auxiliary pump is operating, it sends hydraulic pressure to the transmission regulator valve, and then on to the manual valve where it is directed to the appropriate clutches. This prevents the transmission from shifting into "neutral" when the ICE is in idle stop. Once the ICE restarts, the auxiliary pump is turned off and hydraulic pressure is again supplied by the mechanically driven transmission fluid pump. ● **SEE FIGURE 10–28.**

FIGURE 10–28 Honda Accord Hybrid auxiliary transmission fluid pump. This pump only operates when the ICE enters idle stop mode.

The vehicle gear selector has seven positions, including:

- P—Park
- R—Reverse
- N—Neutral
- D—Drive (first through fifth)
- D3—Drive (first through third)
- 2—Second
- 1—First

The gear shift linkage attaches to the manual valve lever on the transmission case. This lever incorporates a transmission range switch, which signals the PCM concerning the selected gear.

CONSTRUCTION The Honda Accord Hybrid automatic transmission is housed in an aluminum case, which attaches inline with the ICE and the IMA assembly. The various gears are engaged and disengaged through the application and release of hydraulically operated multiple-disc clutches. Since there are no planetary gears used in this transmission, there is no need for holding devices (brakes). Power is directed through the transmission by applying a clutch and locking a gear to its associated shaft. The clutches are similar in function to the synchronizers in a manual transaxle.

The torque converter clutch (TCC) is applied and released by reversing the flow of fluid through the torque converter housing. When fluid is flowing into the back (turbine) side of the torque converter, pressure is applied to back side of the clutch piston, which forces it into contact with the torque converter cover. This locks the turbine to the cover and all the elements of the torque converter rotate as one unit. ● **SEE FIGURE 10–29.**

In order to release the TCC, the flow of fluid in the torque converter housing is reversed. This causes the clutch piston to move away from the torque converter cover and the turbine is thus released. ● **SEE FIGURE 10–30.**

As with any electronically controlled transmission, the mechanical workings are relatively simple but the control strategy is complex. The PCM is responsible for the automatic transmission functions, and it receives input data from many different sensors in order to make the transmission operate smoothly and efficiently. ● **SEE FIGURE 10–31** on page 146.

SERVICE One of the roles of the PCM is to monitor transmission operation and determine if malfunctions are taking place. The PCM will run frequent self-tests of the electrical circuitry and will also analyze the sensor data to look for transmission slippage, overheating, or other problems. When a problem has been detected, the PCM will generate a DTC (diagnostic trouble code) and may also place the transmission in limp-home mode, depending on what sort of problem has been detected. Limp-home mode is when the transmission stays in one gear only (second gear is a common option) and gives the driver the ability to take the vehicle to the closest service center without having to call a tow truck.

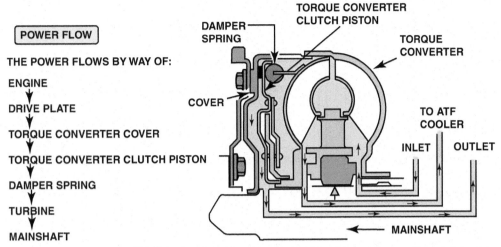

POWER FLOW

THE POWER FLOWS BY WAY OF:

ENGINE
↓
DRIVE PLATE
↓
TORQUE CONVERTER COVER
↓
TORQUE CONVERTER CLUTCH PISTON
↓
DAMPER SPRING
↓
TURBINE
↓
MAINSHAFT

FIGURE 10–29 Torque converter clutch (TCC) lockup in a Honda Accord Hybrid transmission. The clutch piston is attached to the turbine, so applying the clutch locks the turbine to the torque converter cover.

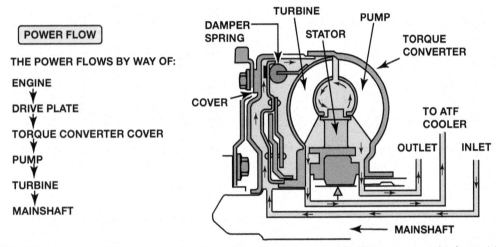

POWER FLOW

THE POWER FLOWS BY WAY OF:

ENGINE
↓
DRIVE PLATE
↓
TORQUE CONVERTER COVER
↓
PUMP
↓
TURBINE
↓
MAINSHAFT

FIGURE 10–30 The TCC is released by reversing the flow of fluid in the housing. Fluid pressure on the front side of the clutch piston causes it to move to the right, causing the turbine to be released from the torque converter housing.

There are some situations where the PCM has detected a transmission malfunction that is not noticeable by the driver, and some means must be employed to alert the driver that service is necessary. Honda does this by flashing the "D" indicator on the transmission range display on the instrument panel. ● **SEE FIGURE 10–32.**

The DTC related to the malfunction can be retrieved using a Honda or enhanced aftermarket scan tool. The scan tool is plugged into the data link connector (DLC) and the ignition switch is turned to the RUN position. The scan tool can then communicate with the PCM and identify any diagnostic trouble codes along with other sensor information that can help diagnose the problem at hand. If a scan tool is not available, Honda also makes it possible to identify the transmission DTCs by interpreting the blinking of the "D" light on the instrument panel. This can be enabled by connecting a jumper wire from the SCS (brown) wire of the DLC to a body ground with the key in the RUN position. ● **SEE FIGURE 10–33.**

TOYOTA/LEXUS POWER-SPLIT SYSTEM

APPLICATIONS The Toyota/Lexus power-split drive system is used in the following models:

- Toyota Prius
- Toyota Camry hybrid
- Lexus CT200h
- Toyota Highlander
- Lexus RX400h and RX450h

DESCRIPTION The power-split transaxle is a series–parallel hybrid technology. During most phases of vehicle operation, the system is operating as both series and parallel at the same time. While the control system is complex, the basic

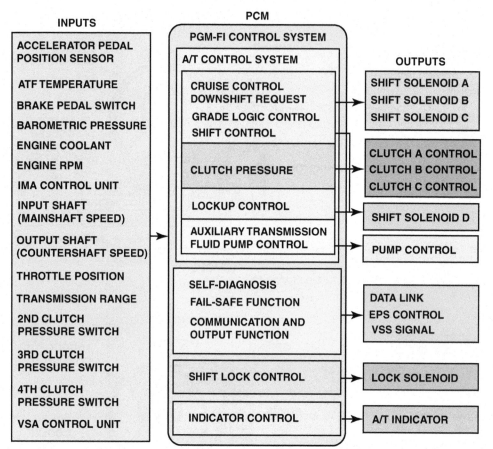

INPUTS

ACCELERATOR PEDAL
POSITION SENSOR

ATF TEMPERATURE

BRAKE PEDAL SWITCH

BAROMETRIC PRESSURE

ENGINE COOLANT

ENGINE RPM

IMA CONTROL UNIT

INPUT SHAFT
(MAINSHAFT SPEED)

OUTPUT SHAFT
(COUNTERSHAFT SPEED)

THROTTLE POSITION

TRANSMISSION RANGE

2ND CLUTCH
PRESSURE SWITCH

3RD CLUTCH
PRESSURE SWITCH

4TH CLUTCH
PRESSURE SWITCH

VSA CONTROL UNIT

PCM

PGM-FI CONTROL SYSTEM

A/T CONTROL SYSTEM

CRUISE CONTROL
DOWNSHIFT REQUEST
GRADE LOGIC CONTROL
SHIFT CONTROL

CLUTCH PRESSURE

LOCKUP CONTROL

AUXILIARY TRANSMISSION
FLUID PUMP CONTROL

SELF-DIAGNOSIS
FAIL-SAFE FUNCTION
COMMUNICATION AND
OUTPUT FUNCTION

SHIFT LOCK CONTROL

INDICATOR CONTROL

OUTPUTS

SHIFT SOLENOID A
SHIFT SOLENOID B
SHIFT SOLENOID C

CLUTCH A CONTROL
CLUTCH B CONTROL
CLUTCH C CONTROL

SHIFT SOLENOID D

PUMP CONTROL

DATA LINK
EPS CONTROL
VSS SIGNAL

LOCK SOLENOID

A/T INDICATOR

FIGURE 10–31 Control schematic for a Honda Accord Hybrid automatic transmission. Note that all sensor inputs are shown to the left of the PCM, while the output signals and actuators are shown on the right.

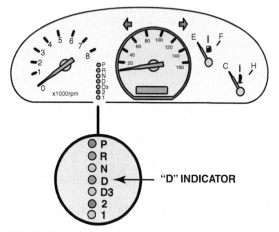

"D" INDICATOR

FIGURE 10–32 The Honda Accord Hybrid will alert the driver of a transmission malfunction by flashing the "D" indicator on the instrument panel.

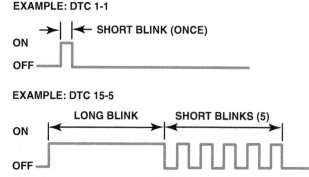

EXAMPLE: DTC 1-1

SHORT BLINK (ONCE)
ON
OFF

EXAMPLE: DTC 15-5

LONG BLINK   SHORT BLINKS (5)
ON
OFF

FIGURE 10–33 Interpreting a blinking "D" indicator to retrieve transmission DTCs from a Honda Accord Hybrid.

transaxle is very simple in design as it is built around a single planetary gearset **(power-split device)** and two electric motor/generators. ● **SEE FIGURE 10–34.**

A planetary gearset is comprised of three main components:

1. Ring gear
2. Planet carrier
3. Sun gear

In the power-split transaxle, a large electric motor/generator (MG2) is directly attached to the transaxle final drive and to the planetary ring gear. The ICE is connected to the planet carrier, and the small electric motor/generator (MG1) is connected to the sun gear. ● **SEE FIGURE 10–35.**

The planetary ring gear always turns in the same direction as the drive wheels and its speed is directly proportional to vehicle speed. In other words, if the ring gear is not moving, the vehicle is not moving.

The power-split device is so named because the ICE (attached to the planet carrier) splits it torque output

FIGURE 10–34 The Toyota Hybrid System uses two electric motor/generators (MG1 and MG2) and an ICE all connected together by a power-split device which is a simple planetary gearset.

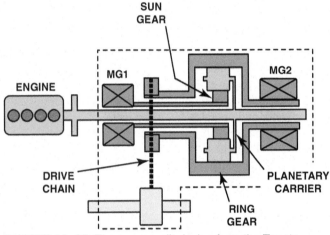

FIGURE 10–35 The power-split device from the Toyota Hybrid System. Note that the vehicle will only move when MG2 (and the ring gear) is turning.

between the sun gear (MG1) and the ring gear (MG2 and drive wheels). The gear ratio of the planetary gearset causes the ICE to send 72% of its torque to the ring gear and the remaining 28% to the sun gear. The torque split percentages remain the same regardless of what mode the transaxle is operating in because they are determined by the number of teeth on the planetary ring gear and the sun gear. ● **SEE FIGURE 10–36.**

While torque split percentages are always the same, power split percentages will vary depending on the RPM of the various components. Horsepower is the rate at which work is performed and is a function of torque and RPM. If a shaft has torque applied to it but remains at zero RPM, no work is being performed and no horsepower is transmitted through the shaft. The same principle applies to the torque-split planetary gearset. If the sun gear is stationary, it will still receive 28% of the torque of the ICE, but all of the engine horsepower will be directed through the ring gear and on to the drive wheels.

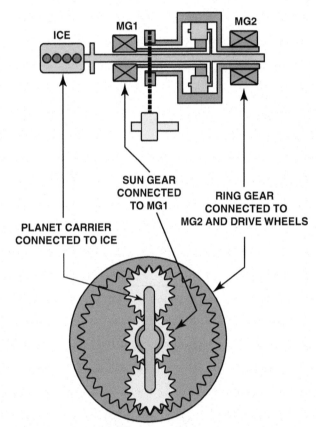

FIGURE 10–36 The planetary gearset used in the Toyota Hybrid System (THS) has 2.6 times the number of teeth in its ring gear as it has in its sun gear. This means that the ICE (attached to the planet carrier) will send 72% of its torque to the ring gear (drive wheels), and 28% of its torque to the sun gear (MG1).

OPERATION

■ **Vehicle Stopped.** When the vehicle is stopped, nothing is happening with the vehicle drive system. The ICE is shut off, and both electric motors/generators are shut off

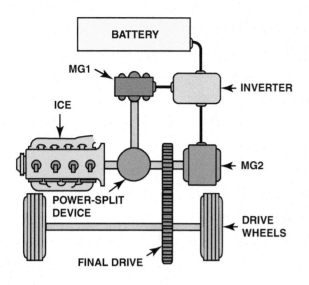

VEHICLE STOPPED

FIGURE 10–37 When the vehicle is stopped, the ICE is shut off along with both motor/generators.

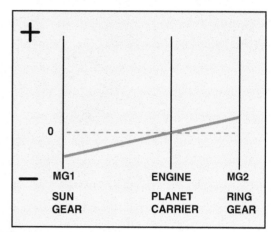

FIGURE 10–39 Light acceleration—the engine is stopped (0 RPM), MG2 is turning forward (+), and MG1 is turning backward (–).

as well. There are circuits within the vehicle that will use electrical energy from the auxiliary battery, but the drive system itself is effectively inert. ● **SEE FIGURE 10–37.**

■ **Light Acceleration.** When the vehicle is driven at low speeds and light acceleration, it is driven by MG2 alone. ● **SEE FIGURE 10–38.**

This is because the electric motor is more efficient than the ICE at low vehicle speeds. Current from the HV battery is sent through the inverter and on to MG2 to move the vehicle. A special graph, known as a **nomograph**, shows the speed relationship between the various elements. When the engine is stopped (0 RPM), MG2 is turning forward (+), and this causes MG1 to turn backward (–). ● **SEE FIGURE 10–39.**

■ **Normal Driving.** When higher vehicle speeds are required, the ICE must be started so that its output can be combined with that of MG2. The ring gear is already turning clockwise as the vehicle travels in a forward direction. Since the planet carrier (attached to the ICE) is stationary, the sun gear (driven by MG1) is used to drive the planet carrier clockwise and start the ICE. Current from the HV battery is directed through the inverter and operates MG1 as a motor, turning clockwise and spinning the ICE up to 1,000 RPM for starting. ● **SEE FIGURE 10–40.**

Once the ICE is started, MG1 operates as a generator, but turns in the counterclockwise direction. ICE output is now

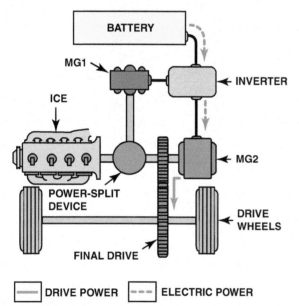

DRIVE POWER - - - ELECTRIC POWER

FIGURE 10–38 Under light acceleration, power is sent to MG2 to move the vehicle.

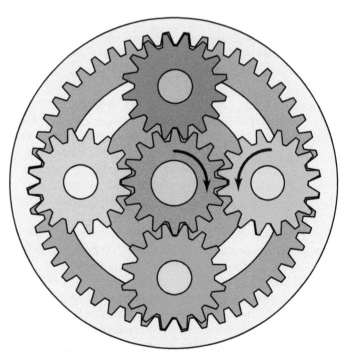

FIGURE 10–40 To start the ICE, MG1 (sun) acts as a motor and turns clockwise (CW), causing the planet carrier (attached to the ICE) to also turn CW.

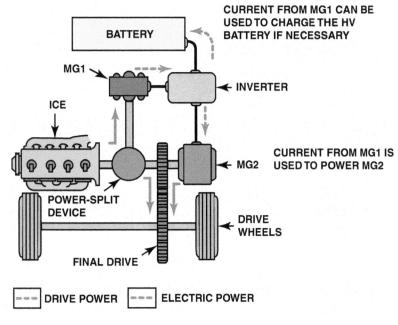

CURRENT FROM MG1 CAN BE
USED TO CHARGE THE HV
BATTERY IF NECESSARY

CURRENT FROM MG1 IS
USED TO POWER MG2

- - - DRIVE POWER   - - - ELECTRIC POWER

NORMAL DRIVING

FIGURE 10–41 Normal driving—the ICE is now running and some of its torque is used to drive MG1. Electricity generated by MG1 is used to power MG2 or recharge the HV battery.

divided or "split" between the drive wheels (ring gear) and MG1 (sun gear). Power generated by MG1 is either directed to MG2 to help move the vehicle or is used to recharge the HV battery if necessary. ● **SEE FIGURES 10–41 AND 10–42.**

■ **Full-Throttle Acceleration and High-Speed Cruise.** When greater acceleration is required, both MG2 and the ICE continue sending torque to the vehicle drive wheels, but MG2 can also receive power from the HV battery to increase its output. As demand increases further, the ICE speed is increased for more output. To enable an increase in ICE speed, the sun gear (MG1) must rotate in a clockwise direction. It is during these times that MG1 can be configured as a motor and will draw power from MG2 during a phase known as **energy recirculation**

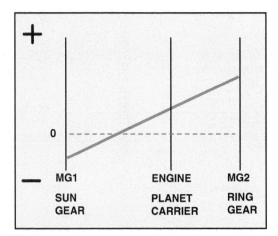

FIGURE 10–42 Normal driving—the engine is running, MG2 is turning forward +), and MG1 is turning backward (−).

(see Frequently Asked Question—"What Is Energy Recirculation?"). ● **SEE FIGURES 10–43 AND 10–44.**

■ **Deceleration and Braking.** As the vehicle is decelerating, MG2 is configured as a generator. The **kinetic energy** (energy of movement) of the vehicle is then converted into electrical energy by MG2. The ICE and MG1 are shut off, and current from MG2 is sent through the inverter and is then used to recharge the HV battery. ● **SEE FIGURE 10–45.**

 FREQUENTLY ASKED QUESTION

What Is Energy Recirculation?

In the Toyota Hybrid System, MG2 is the main traction motor. When the vehicle is running on battery power only, MG2 is the motor that is driving it. In many situations, it is MG2 that is generating torque in conjunction with the ICE to move the vehicle.

There are also times that MG2 operates as a generator. During regenerative braking, MG2 generates electric current to recharge the battery. However, there are situations aside from regenerative braking where MG2 operates as a generator and MG1 as a traction motor. Toyota calls this energy recirculation, and it is done to maximize overall system efficiency. In these situations, it is more efficient to use MG2 as a generator, with MG1 being used as a drive motor and helping to adjust the RPM of the ICE. ● **SEE FIGURES 10–46 AND 10–47** on page 151.

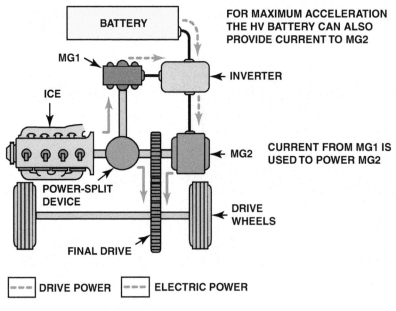

FOR MAXIMUM ACCELERATION THE HV BATTERY CAN ALSO PROVIDE CURRENT TO MG2

CURRENT FROM MG1 IS USED TO POWER MG2

╌╌╌ DRIVE POWER   ╌╌╌ ELECTRIC POWER

FULL ACCELERATION & HIGH-SPEED CRUISE

FIGURE 10–43 Full-throttle acceleration and high-speed cruise—with greater demand for acceleration, power from MG1 is combined with power from the HV battery to generate higher output from MG2. It is also possible to configure MG2 as a generator and send its power to MG1 (which then acts as a motor).

▪ **Reverse.** If reverse is selected, power is sent from the HV battery to the inverter and then on to MG2. MG2 operates in the reverse direction to back up the vehicle, but the other components in the drive system are turned off at this time. ● **SEE FIGURE 10–48** on page 152.

CONSTRUCTION The Toyota power-split transaxle is built with an aluminum case composed of two major assemblies. These are known as the MG1 assembly and the MG2 assembly, and each houses its respective motor/generator. Each of these major assemblies has its own water jacket for cooling the

motor/generator windings in the housing. There are two water jacket unions installed in each major assembly, and these send coolant to the motors from the separate inverter cooling system. ● **SEE FIGURE 10–49** on page 152.

The ICE, MG1, the power-split device, MG2, and the oil pump are all assembled on a common axis. The final drive is housed between the two major assemblies and utilizes a con-

FIGURE 10–44 Full-throttle acceleration and high-speed cruise—this graph shows MG1 acting as a motor using power from MG2. This increases the speed of the ICE, allowing it to produce higher output.

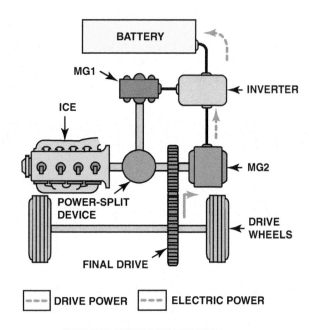

╌╌╌ DRIVE POWER   ╌╌╌ ELECTRIC POWER

DECELERATION AND BRAKING

FIGURE 10–45 Deceleration and braking—MG2 is configured as a generator and recharges the HV battery.

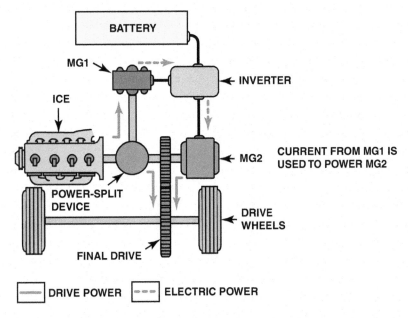

DRIVE POWER | **ELECTRIC POWER**

NORMAL ENERGY FLOW

FIGURE 10–46 During normal energy flow, MG1 acts as a generator and supplies energy to power MG2.

ventional open differential for sending torque to the front drive wheels. A chain drive attaches the ring gear of the power-split device to the counter drive gear, which drives the counter-driven gear that is meshed with the ring gear of the differential assembly.

This system does not use a conventional clutch or torque converter. With this design, there is no need to disconnect the engine from the input shaft. This is because the engine can turn

at any speed while the vehicle is stopped (ring gear is therefore stopped) by using MG1 (sun gear) as a generator. The ICE is connected directly to the transaxle input shaft using a damper disc mechanism. The transaxle oil pump is housed in the rear of the MG2 assembly and is attached to the input shaft from the ICE. This means that oil is circulated by the pump only when the ICE is running. When the vehicle is driven by MG2 only, the transaxle is splash-lubricated by the movement of the final drive gears.

The transaxle for the 2001–2003 Prius has a cable-operated parking lock mechanism. This was replaced with an electrically actuated mechanism starting with the 2004 model year.

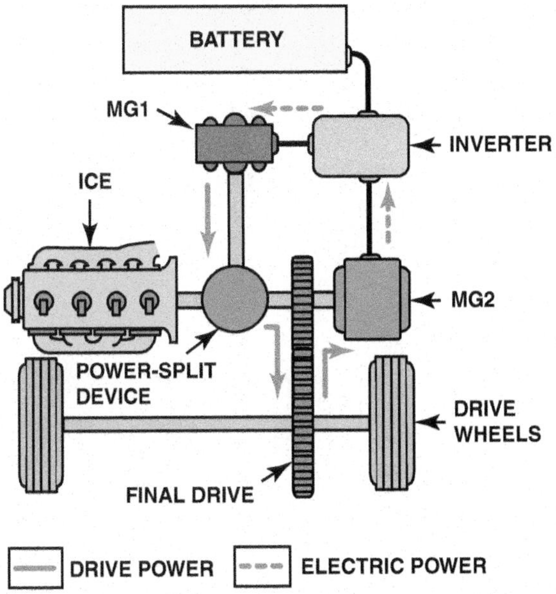

SERVICE Service procedures to be performed at specified intervals include changing the transaxle oil and the coolant for the inverter (high-voltage) system. There are drain plugs for both at the bottom of the transaxle assembly. The transaxle oil is refilled through a hole in the front of the case, with the level being brought up to a specified distance from the bottom of the hole.

The coolant is refilled at the reservoir that is located on the inverter assembly, and must be bled properly before placing the vehicle back into service. Always use the recommended fluids and procedures when servicing any vehicle.

NOTE: The fastest and most reliable way to refill the inverter cooling system is to use an airlift fluid exchange machine. This pulls the cooling system into a vacuum and then injects the coolant into the evacuated system. This method fills the system quickly and eliminates air bubbles.

DRIVE POWER | **ELECTRIC POWER**

ENERGY RECIRCULATION

FIGURE 10–47 Under certain circumstances, the hybrid system is most efficient when MG2 acts as a generator and sends its power to MG1.

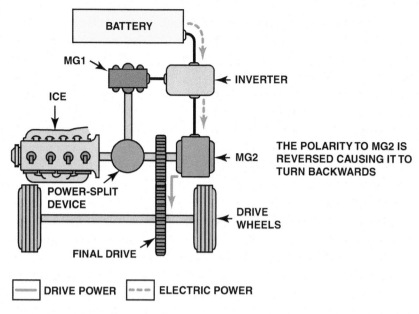

THE POLARITY TO MG2 IS REVERSED CAUSING IT TO TURN BACKWARDS

REVERSE

FIGURE 10–48 Reverse—MG2 alone is used to move the car in reverse. This is accomplished by reversing the direction of MG2.

FIGURE 10–49 Excessive heat created in the electric motors must be controlled and proper maintenance of the cooling system is important for long life to help avoid overheating motor winding as shown.

FORD ESCAPE HYBRID eCVT

PARTS AND OPERATION The Ford Escape Hybrid uses an **electronically controlled continuously variable transmission (eCVT)** that is very similar in operation to the Toyota power-split transaxle. It is built differently, however, in that the **traction motor** is on a different axis and is placed above the **generator motor**. This was done to keep the length

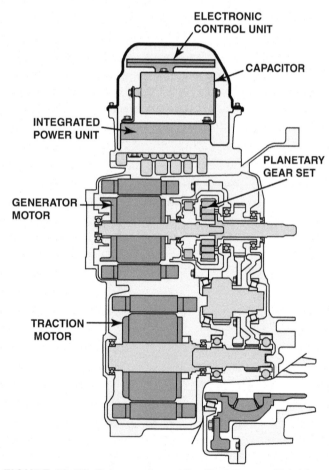

FIGURE 10–50 Cutaway view of the Ford Escape Hybrid transaxle.

of the transaxle similar to that of a conventional automatic transaxle. ● **SEE FIGURES 10–50 AND 10–51.**

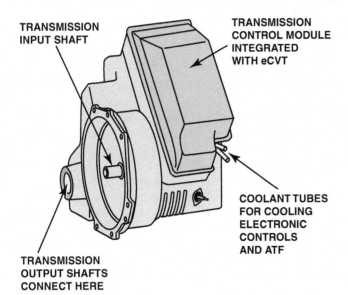

TRANSMISSION INPUT SHAFT

TRANSMISSION CONTROL MODULE INTEGRATED WITH eCVT

COOLANT TUBES FOR COOLING ELECTRONIC CONTROLS AND ATF

TRANSMISSION OUTPUT SHAFTS CONNECT HERE

FIGURE 10–51 The Ford Escape Hybrid transaxle operates very similar to the one used in the Toyota Hybrid System, but is constructed very differently.

HIGH-VOLTAGE CABLE CONNECTORS

COOLANT CONNECTOR

FIGURE 10–52 A Ford eCVT transaxle assembly showing the electrical connectors on the top of the assembly.

Another difference is that the *transmission control module* (*TCM*) is an integral part of the eCVT. This encloses the high-voltage cables and also makes it possible to cool the motors and the electronics with one heat exchanger. ● **SEE FIGURE 10–52.**

Coolant in the transaxle/electronic cooling system is sent through the water channel and absorbs heat from the ATF channel below and the heat sink for the electronic control unit above.

A small oil pump inside the eCVT circulates ATF for lubricating the gear train and for cooling the two electric motors. This oil pump is driven directly by the ICE through the planet carrier of the planetary gearset. Like the Toyota system, the oil pump will not circulate ATF unless the ICE is running. This means that the gear train is splash-lubricated when the vehicle is in electric-only operation.

The traction motor in the eCVT can be used to accelerate the vehicle from a standstill. If more power is required, the ICE is started. The starting function is performed by the generator motor, which in most cases acts as a generator to provide current to the traction motor or to the high-voltage battery when required. Like the Toyota, the Escape hybrid does not use an auxiliary starter and relies on the generator motor for starting under all circumstances.

The generator motor is also responsible for supplying all the electrical current for vehicle operation. The high voltage from the generator is sent through a DC/DC converter to provide the 12 volts necessary for powering the vehicle accessories. During vehicle braking, the traction motor becomes a generator and provides electrical current to recharge the battery (regenerative braking).

SERVICE The eCVT is lubricated-for-life with a special Mercon fluid. There is a fill plug and a drain plug located on the left side of the case, but these are used only in special service situations.

HONDA BELT-AND-PULLEY CVT

PURPOSE AND FUNCTION Internal combustion engines run most efficiently in a relatively narrow RPM range. In order to achieve the best efficiency, there must be a means of controlling the RPM of an ICE during the entire vehicle operating range. As mentioned earlier, both manual and automatic transmissions have increased the number of speeds utilized in order to keep the ICE as close as possible to its most efficient RPM at all times. The next step is to eliminate transmission speed ranges completely by using a continuously variable transmission (CVT).

DESCRIPTION AND OPERATION One CVT design being used in hybrid electric vehicles is the belt-and-pulley system as used by Honda in the Civic and Insight. Much of this system is similar to other automatic transmissions, in that it uses a planetary gearset and multiple-disc clutches with electrohydraulic controls. However, there are no distinct speed ranges (or "shifts") in this design, as variable drive and driven pulleys are used with a special steel belt to provide nonstaged speeds forward.

The pulleys used in this CVT design can vary their width by varying the hydraulic pressure applied to them. Each pulley has a movable face and a fixed face. The movable face for each pulley is attached to a piston that has hydraulic control pressure applied to it. Higher application pressure on the movable face causes the pulley to become narrow and this makes the steel belt ride closer to the outside diameter of the pulley. A lower application pressure will allow the pulley to become wider and the belt will ride closer to the pulley axis. If a low hydraulic pressure is applied to the drive pulley and a high hydraulic pressure is applied to the driven pulley, a low speed ratio is achieved. ● **SEE FIGURE 10-53.**

There is no clutch or torque converter utilized in this design. Instead, the transmission input shaft is splined directly to the ICE through the drive plate and flywheel. This assembly is built similar to a dual-mass flywheel and is designed to dampen torsional vibrations from the engine. ● **SEE FIGURE 10-55.**

TECH TIP

The Honda CVT Belt Pushes the Driven Pulley

One unique aspect of the Honda **belt-and-pulley CVT** is that the belt *pushes* the driven pulley instead of pulling it. This is in contrast to conventional automotive belt drive systems where the belt normally pulls the driven pulley. ● **SEE FIGURE 10-54.**

The drive belt is made up of 2 steel loops of 12 layers each, which are held together by approximately 280 steel belt links, also known as *elements.* These elements are compressed when placed under a load as the drive pulley pushes the driven pulley. This also increases friction on the steel pulleys and prevents slipping.

DRIVE PULLEY: WIDE/SMALL DIAMETER

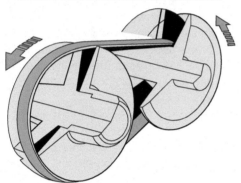

DRIVEN PULLEY: NARROW/LARGE DIAMETER
LOW RATIO, ABOUT 2.5:1

(a)

DRIVE PULLEY: NARROW/LARGE DIAMETER

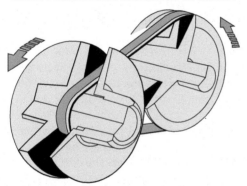

DRIVEN PULLEY: WIDE/SMALL DIAMETER
HIGH RATIO, ABOUT 0.5:1

(b)

FIGURE 10-53 (a) The vehicle speed increases, the drive pulley will have progressively higher pressure applied to it, while the driven pulley application pressure is lowered. (b) This results in a higher speed ratio, allowing the engine to operate at a lower RPM.

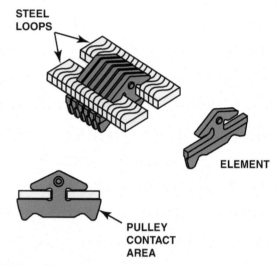

FIGURE 10-54 Honda CVT drive belt construction.

FIGURE 10-55 The Honda CVT is connected directly to the ICE through a drive plate and flywheel mechanism.

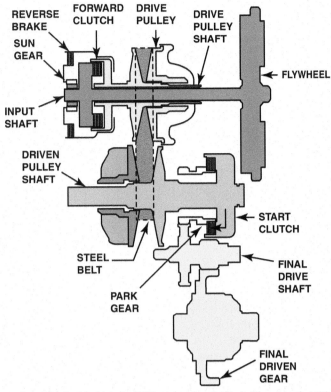

FIGURE 10–56 Honda CVT power flow in Park (P) or Neutral (N).

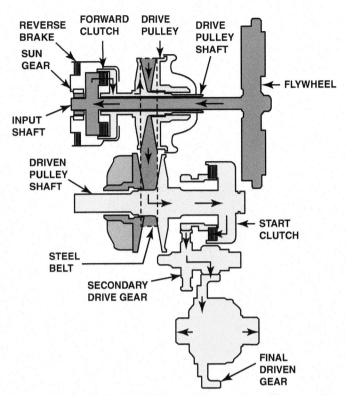

FIGURE 10–57 Honda CVT power flow in Drive (D) or Low (L).

There are three multiple-disc clutches used in the internal gear train.

1. One for the forward clutch,

2. One for the reverse brake, and

3. The third for the start clutch.

In Park (P) or Neutral (N), none of the clutches have hydraulic pressure applied to them, which prevents engine torque from being applied to the drive pulley shaft. ● SEE FIGURE 10–56.

The forward clutch and the start clutch are in operation whenever the transmission is placed in a forward gear position (D or L). ● SEE FIGURE 10–57.

The start clutch has multiple responsibilities, including the following:

1. The start clutch is engaged whenever the vehicle is moving, either in forward or reverse.

2. It must help the vehicle accelerate from a standstill by slipping and then fully engaging once the vehicle is moving, similar to a manually operated clutch.

3. The start clutch also operates in conjunction with the vehicle brakes when the **creep aid** function is activated. Creep aid operates whenever the vehicle is stopped with the ICE in idle stop (for example, at a stop light) and the driver is about to resume operation. When the driver releases the brake pedal, the brakes are held on briefly until the ICE restarts and the start clutch begins its engagement. This allows for smooth acceleration from

FIGURE 10–58 Location of the Honda CVT start clutch.

a stop and prevents the vehicle from rolling backward when the driver attempts to start off up a hill. ● SEE FIGURE 10–58.

For the reverse function, a planetary gearset is used in conjunction with the reverse brake. When the reverse brake is applied, the planet carrier is held and the sun gear (splined to the input shaft) causes the ring gear to turn backward. The ring gear is attached to the drive pulley through the forward clutch drum, so the drive pulley also turns backward. This torque is sent through the start clutch and the vehicle moves in reverse. ● SEE FIGURE 10–59.

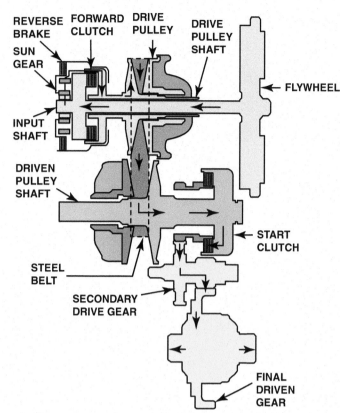

FIGURE 10–59 Honda CVT power flow in Reverse (R).

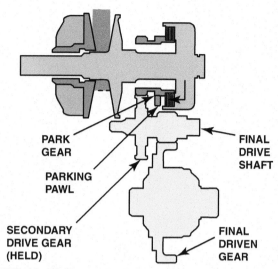

FIGURE 10–60 The parking pawl mechanism on a Honda CVT.

The Honda CVT, like any other automatic transmission, relies on hydraulic pressure to perform its various functions. The belt drive, the multiple-disc clutches, and the control system would all cease to function without hydraulic pressure. This pressure is supplied by a chain-driven pump that is driven by the transmission input shaft. Since the input shaft is driven directly by the ICE, hydraulic pressure is only present when the ICE is running. Automatic transmission fluid (ATF) is held in a pan that is bolted to the bottom of the transmission case. The ATF pump draws fluid through a strainer that is located in the pan and sends this fluid on to the system through a pressure regulator valve.

CONSTRUCTION The Honda CVT is constructed very similar to other electronically controlled transaxles, with the primary difference being the use of a belt-and-pulley system instead of multiple planetary gearsets or meshed helical gears.

The transmission has a total of four parallel shafts: the input shaft, drive pulley shaft, driven pulley shaft, and the secondary gear shaft. The secondary gear shaft is comprised of the secondary driven gear and the final drive gear. The final drive gear is meshed with the final driven gear, which is attached to a conventional open differential assembly. When the transmission is placed in Park, the parking pawl interlocks with the park gear, which then holds the secondary drive gear stationary. ● **SEE FIGURE 10–60.**

The lower valve body assembly, ATF strainer, and an ATF pan are located on the bottom of the transmission case and can be serviced readily from underneath the vehicle.

While the basic belt-and-pulley CVT is simple in design, the control system used to make it work is complex. A transmission control module (TCM), sensors, switches, and solenoid valves are utilized to make the transmission operate smoothly and efficiently. ● **SEE FIGURE 10–61.**

The TCM itself is located in the passenger compartment. The TCM takes input data from multiple vehicle sensors and modules (such as the engine control module), calculates output commands, and sends these to the appropriate solenoids. Most of the solenoids are located in the transmission assembly itself, except for the creep-aid solenoids, which are built into the brake hydraulic circuits and are mounted elsewhere in the engine compartment.

SERVICE The Honda CVT can be pressure tested and stall tested just like any other automatic transaxle when diagnosing transmission malfunctions. These tests must be performed according to manufacturer-approved procedures, and test results compared to charts published by the manufacturer.

One service item that is unique and very important is the start clutch calibration. Check service information for the exact procedure to follow. This procedure must be performed whenever any of the following vehicle components is replaced or removed:

1. Battery
2. Backup fuse
3. TCM
4. Transmission assembly
5. Lower valve body assembly
6. Engine assembly replacement or overhaul

TRANSMISSION CONTROL MODULE

	A/T CONTROL SYSTEM	
ENGINE CONTROL MODULE		**TRANSMISSION RANGE SWITCH SIGNAL**
INPUTS	SHIFT CONTROL	**START CLUTCH PRESSURE CONTROL SIGNAL**
ACCELERATOR PEDAL POSITION SENSOR		
BRAKE PEDAL SWITCH	PULLEY PRESSURE CONTROL	**DRIVEN PULLEY PRESSURE CONTROL SIGNAL**
BAROMETRIC PRESSURE		
ENGINE COOLANT		
ENGINE RPM	START CLUTCH CONTROL	**DRIVE PULLEY PRESSURE CONTROL SIGNAL**
INTAKE AIR TEMPERATURE		
THROTTLE POSITION		
TRANSMISSION RANGE	REVERSE INHIBITOR CONTROL	**REVERSE INHIBITOR CONTROL SIGNAL**
CVT INPUT SHAFT (DRIVE PULLEY)		
CVT OUTPUT SHAFT (DRIVEN PULLEY)	CREEP AID CONTROL	**CREEP AID CONTROL SIGNAL**
CVT SPEED SENSOR		
CVT SPEED SENSOR (SECONDARY)		

FIGURE 10–61 Honda CVT transmission control module (TCM), with input (sensor) information on the left and outputs shown on the right.

Fluid-level checks are performed with the vehicle level, transmission up to the operating temperature, but with the *engine turned off.*

CAUTION: Wipe off the dipstick before removing it to prevent any dirt from falling into the fill tube when checking the level of the fluid. Any dirt in the fluid can cause severe damage to the CVT transaxles.

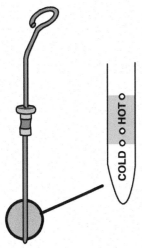

FIGURE 10–62 The Honda CVT has a dipstick for checking fluid level in the transmission case. The oil level should be maintained between the low (cold) and the high (hot) marks on the dipstick.

A dipstick is used to check the level, and fluid may be poured into the dipstick pipe to bring the level up if it is low. ● **SEE FIGURE 10–62.**

When replacing the ATF in a Honda CVT, make sure that the specified CVT fluid is used. There is a drain plug on the transmission pan, and also a filler hole located on the transmission case. In some cases, the air cleaner housing must be removed to access the filler hole. When refilling the CVT, be sure to check the dipstick regularly to make sure it is not being overfilled. Both the drain and filler plugs should have their gaskets replaced before installing them in their respective holes. Be certain to observe torque specifications when tightening these plugs to prevent damage to the threads in the transmission case and oil pan.

HONDA HYBRID AUTOMATIC TRANSAXLE

SYSTEM OVERVIEW Honda Accord hybrids (2005–2007) used a conventional automatic Honda transaxle and added the integrated starter/generator between the engine and the transaxles. The unit used a torque converter and a small electric motor mounted on the side of the unit to provide hydraulic pressure during idle stop mode operation. ● **SEE FIGURE 10–63.**

FIGURE 10-63 The Honda Accord V-6 hybrid electric vehicles used a Honda non-planetary gear type automatic transaxle equipped with a small electric pump motor to maintain hydraulic fluid pressure during idle stop operation.

SUMMARY

1. Manual transmissions are the simplest transmission design and use a driver-operated clutch mechanism to connect the ICE (internal combustion engine) to the transmission input shaft.

2. Torque converters can be described as infinitely variable transmissions that constantly adjust output speed and torque depending on vehicle operating conditions.

3. Hybrid electric vehicles (HEVs) with automatic transmissions use a modified torque converter lockup schedule to enhance regenerative braking.

4. Most automatic transmissions use planetary gearsets and hydraulically operated apply devices to achieve multiple gear ratios.

5. Automatic transmissions used in HEVs incorporate an electric auxiliary pump to provide transmission fluid pressure at engine idle stop.

6. Continuously variable transmissions (CVTs) utilize an infinite number of speed ratios to allow the ICE to operate in its most efficient RPM range during all phases of vehicle operation.

7. The two major types of CVTs include the belt-and-pulley system and the power-split system.

8. The power-split CVT utilizes two electric motor/generators and a planetary gearset to create infinite speed ratios.

9. The belt-and-pulley CVT uses a special steel belt and two variable-diameter pulleys to create infinite speed ratios.

REVIEW QUESTIONS

1. What is the difference between torque and horsepower?

2. What are the three elements in a torque converter?

3. What are the differences in the operation of an automatic transmission that has been modified for use in a hybrid electric vehicle?

4. Why does a CVT maximize the efficiency of an internal combustion engine?

1. A 5-speed manual transaxle has a fifth gear ratio of 0.95:1. Technician A says that the transaxle output speed will be greater than the input speed in fifth gear. Technician B says that fifth gear is an overdrive gear ratio. Which technician is correct?
   a. Technician A only
   b. Technician B only
   c. Both technicians A and B
   d. Neither technician A nor B

2. In a GM two-mode hybrid electric vehicle, when can the vehicle be powered by electric power alone?
   a. During the first mode
   b. During the second mode
   c. During either the first or second mode
   d. During heavy load conditions regardless of mode

3. The period of torque converter operation where the turbine is turning at 90% of the impeller (pump) speed is known as _____.
   a. Coupling Phase
   b. Vortex flow
   c. Torque converter lockup
   d. Torque multiplication

4. Technician A says that a torque converter clutch reduces slippage. Technician B says that an auxiliary fluid pump is needed for the transmission to function during idle stop mode. Which technician is correct?
   a. Technician A only
   b. Technician B only
   c. Both technicians A and B
   d. Neither technician A nor B

5. Modifications to automatic transmissions used in hybrid vehicles include _____.
   a. Electric auxiliary transmission fluid pumps
   b. Modified torque converter lockup schedule
   c. Increased number of plates in multiple-disc clutches
   d. Both a and b are correct

6. Technician A says that power-split CVTs use a torque converter. Technician B says that power-split CVTs use an electric transmission fluid pump. Which technician is correct?
   a. Technician A only
   b. Technician B only
   c. Both technicians A and B
   d. Neither technician A nor B

7. All of the following statements concerning power-split CVTs are true, *except* _____.
   a. The ICE and motor/generators are all connected through a planetary gearset
   b. One of the planetary members must be held to make the power-split CVT work
   c. The power-split CVT can operate in electric mode only
   d. Power-split CVT systems do not use a separate starter motor

8. The Honda CVT is connected to the ICE with a _____.
   a. Torque converter
   b. Manually operated clutch mechanism
   c. Drive plate and flywheel
   d. None of the above

9. In a Toyota/Lexus hybrid electric vehicle, how is reverse achieved?
   a. The ICE reverses direction and powers the drive wheels.
   b. MG2 is used to power the vehicle in reverse
   c. MG1 is used to power the vehicle in reverse
   d. Either b or c depending on exact model and year

10. Technician A says that all automatic transmissions use planetary gearsets. Technician B says that all CVTs use torque converters. Which technician is correct?
    a. Technician A only
    b. Technician B only
    c. Both technicians A and B
    d. Neither technician A nor B

chapter
11

HYBRID VEHICLE HEATING AND AIR CONDITIONING

OBJECTIVES: After studying Chapter 11, the reader will be able to: • Explain the operation of the ICE cooling system. • Explain the operation of the motor/electronics cooling system in a hybrid electric vehicle. • Explain the operation of a coolant heat storage system. • Describe the function of a vehicle's heating and A/C system. • Discuss the operation and unique service procedures for electric-drive A/C compressors.

KEY TERMS: • Accumulator 180 • Antifreeze 162 • Barrier hose 184 • Blend door 172 • Blower motor 177 • Bypass tube 161 • Cabin filter 177 • Change of state 175 • Compressor 175 • Condenser 175 • Coolant heat storage system 168 • Coolant recovery reservoir 165 • Crossflow 166 • Downflow 166 • Ethylene glycol 162 • Evaporator 175 • Evaporator drain 182 • Fan clutch 167 • Heat exchanger 165 • Heater core 161 • Helper pump 163 • HOAT 162 • Hygroscopic 179 • IAT 162 • Impeller 162 • Low-grade heat 168 • OAT 162 • OT 180 • PAG 179 • Phase-change liquid 175 • Plenum chamber 172 • Pressure cap 164 • Pressure drop 176 • PTC 172 • PTC heater 172 • R-134a 175 • Radiator 160 • Radiator hose 168 • Receiver-drier 180 • Refrigerant 175 • Scroll compressor 177 • Surge tank 165 • Thermoelectric switch 167 • Thermostat 161 • TXV 180 • Water jacket 160 • Water pump 160 • Water valve 169 • Zone valve 182

INTRODUCTION

Heating, ventilation, and air conditioning (HVAC) systems play a vital role in the operation of a hybrid electric vehicle. Passenger comfort is a primary responsibility for these systems, but HEVs also require cooling of major hybrid components, such as the high-voltage battery and the inverter electronics. A solid understanding of HVAC system operation and diagnosis is vital for any hybrid electric vehicle technician.

HYBRID ICE COOLING SYSTEMS

ENGINE COOLING The purpose of the ICE (internal combustion engine) cooling system is to bring the ICE up to an optimum temperature as quickly as possible and then to maintain that temperature under all operating conditions.

Coolant temperature for the ICE cooling system is maintained in a narrow range for a number of reasons:

1. The ICE is able to run at its highest efficiency and lowest emissions when it is at an operating temperature of 195°F to 215°F (90°C to 101°C). ICEs that run cold require richer air–fuel mixtures and suffer from reduced fuel economy. This also causes the ICE to produce increased emissions.

2. Vehicle driveabilty (engine performance) is enhanced. The ICE will have better throttle response and produce greater output when it is at operating temperature.

3. Engines that run cold tend to wear out much faster. A cold ICE will condense crankcase fumes and thus its motor oil will become contaminated more quickly.

4. The ICE cooling system is also responsible for providing heat to the vehicle's passenger compartment. The coolant temperature must be maintained at an optimum level to allow the heating system to work properly and to maximize passenger comfort.

5. Overheating the ICE can lead to reduced efficiency and possible catastrophic failure of internal mechanical components.

Temperatures in the ICE combustion chamber can exceed 6,000°F (3,300°C). A portion of this heat energy (approximately one-third) is converted into mechanical energy to move the vehicle, but the vast majority is released as waste heat. Half of this waste heat is sent out the exhaust system, and the other half is absorbed by the ICE cooling system. The heat that is absorbed by the cooling system is then dissipated into the outside air by the vehicle's radiator. ●**SEE FIGURE 11–1.**

BASIC OPERATION All automotive ICEs are liquid-cooled. This means that the cooling systems are sealed and liquid coolant is circulated through the **water jacket** (internal passages) by a **water pump** to absorb excess heat. The heated coolant is sent through a **radiator** to dissipate the heat

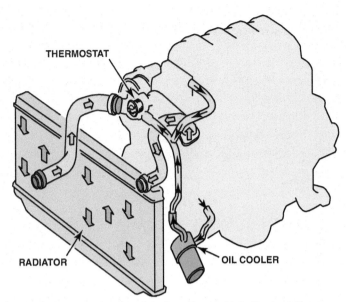

FIGURE 11-1 Coolant flow in a Toyota V-8. Coolant flows through the water jacket in the block and upward into the cylinder head to remove excess heat. The heat is then dissipated to the atmosphere at the radiator.

and lower its temperature. The coolant then returns to the ICE internal passages to continue the cycle.

The water pump is the "heart" of the ICE cooling system. It is most often driven by the ICE accessory drive belt, so it will circulate coolant whenever the ICE is running. When the ICE is first started, the cooling system must enable it to reach operating temperature as quickly as possible. To achieve this, the coolant is not circulated through the radiator until the correct temperature has been attained. A **thermostat** is used to confine coolant flow to the ICE water jacket and **heater core** until the coolant reaches approximately 195°F (91°C). At this point, the thermostat begins to open and allow coolant to flow to the radiator. ● SEE FIGURE 11-2.

When the thermostat first starts to open, some coolant will flow to the radiator and some will continue to circulate in the ICE water jacket. Coolant that does not flow through the

thermostat will enter an internal **bypass tube** and return to the water pump inlet. As the coolant temperature continues to rise, the thermostat will open wider until it is fully open at around 215°F. Most of the coolant is now flowing through the radiator and the cooling system is dissipating maximum heat from the ICE. If the coolant temperature continues to rise past this point, the electric fan will turn on and circulate air over the radiator to increase the amount of heat that can be dissipated.

When engine temperature decreases, the electric fan will turn off and the thermostat will start to close. This causes progressively more coolant to be recirculated through the water jacket and less to enter the radiator. The electric fan and thermostat work together to stabilize coolant temperature, and enable the ICE to operate at maximum efficiency and performance.

COOLING SYSTEM COMPONENTS

A number of components are common to most ICE cooling systems. These include water jackets, coolant, water pump, thermostat, pressure cap, coolant recovery reservoir, surge tank, heat exchange cooling fans, and hoses, as discussed next.

WATER JACKETS The ICE block and cylinder heads have internal passages that are designed to allow coolant to flow through and remove excess heat from critical components. The hottest areas of the ICE are around the combustion chambers, so coolant is directed into these areas and the absorbed heat is transported to cooler areas of the ICE as well as the radiator. ● SEE FIGURE 11-3. The net effect is that the ICE assembly is kept at a consistent temperature, which improves its durability and service life.

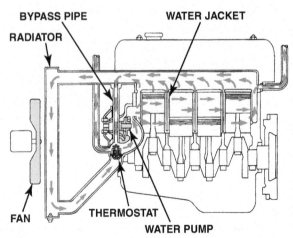

FIGURE 11-2 Major components and coolant flow in a typical ICE cooling system. Note that the heater core also dissipates heat from the coolant.

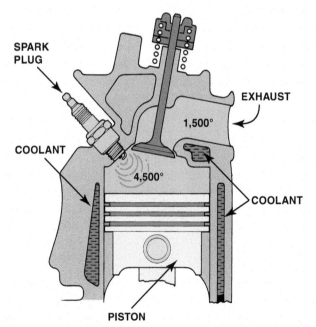

FIGURE 11-3 Approximately one-third of the total heat released by the fuel must be absorbed by the ICE cooling system.

COOLANT The coolant used in an ICE cooling system is critical to its performance. While pure water performs well in its ability to absorb and dissipate heat, it will also tend to corrode the components of the cooling system. Water also has a relatively low boiling point and a high freeze point. If coolant was allowed to freeze in an ICE's water jacket, the expansion of the coolant as it reaches its freeze point would likely result in a cracked block or cylinder head. In order to overcome these deficiencies, water is mixed 50/50 with **ethylene-glycol**-based **antifreeze.**

Ethylene glycol is a colorless, water-soluble liquid that is the primary component in most automotive antifreeze. A mixture of ethylene glycol and water will have a higher boiling point and a lower freeze point than water by itself. The one serious downside of ethylene glycol is that it is highly toxic. For this reason, propylene glycol is promoted as a less toxic alternative to ethylene glycol. Despite this advantage, there are performance differences between the two coolants and most vehicle manufacturers specify the use of ethylene-glycol-based antifreeze in their vehicle cooling systems.

Other chemicals are added to ethylene glycol to reduce foaming and cavitation and to prevent corrosion. The final component in antifreeze is a dye to provide color. This makes it easier to locate leaks, and helps to identify the coolant type.

There are a number of different kinds of automotive antifreeze, with the major difference between them being the type of corrosion inhibitor that is utilized. The green antifreeze that was used for decades across vehicle lines was based on **inorganic additive technology (IAT),** which often used silicates as its primary corrosion inhibitor. Silicates are abrasive in nature and can cause damage to water pump seals and cooling system components if they drop out of solution. Deposits formed in the water jacket by silicate dropout can also cause hot spots in the ICE cooling system as they inhibit coolant flow in those areas. IAT coolants also suffer from a relatively short service life, and have to be replaced every two to three years. Much research was conducted to find an alternative to IAT, and this led to the development of **organic acid technology (OAT)** and **hybrid organic acid technology (HOAT)** coolants.

OAT coolants utilize an organic acid to prevent corrosion in the cooling system, while HOAT coolants use both silicates and an organic acid. Most OAT and HOAT coolants are dyed a color other than green. The most recognizable OAT-based coolant is DEX-COOL, which is orange in color and has been used in all General Motors vehicles since 1996. ● **SEE FIGURE 11–4.** Newer Ford and Chrysler vehicles both use HOAT-based coolants, despite the fact that they are different colors (Ford is yellow; Chrysler is a pink/orange). ● **SEE FIGURE 11–5.** OAT and HOAT are both extended-life coolants, meaning that they have a typical service life of five years and anywhere from 100,000 to 150,000 miles.

WATER PUMP In order for the coolant to transfer heat in the ICE cooling system, it must be circulated using a water pump. Most ICEs have a water pump that is mechanically

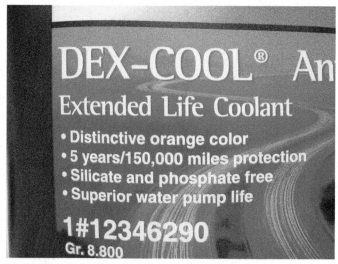

FIGURE 11–4 DEX-COOL uses organic acid technology (OAT) as a corrosion inhibitor.

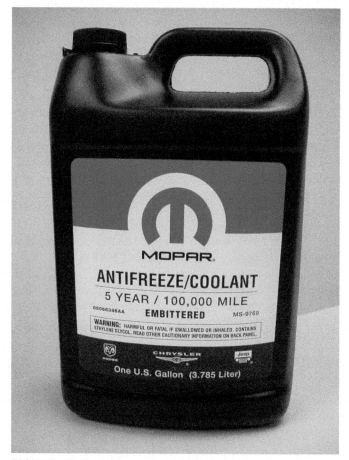

FIGURE 11–5 Ethylene-glycol-based coolants are sweet to the taste but also highly toxic. Some manufacturers "embitter" their coolant to prevent animals from drinking it.

driven, whether that is by the accessory drive belt or the timing belt. ● **SEE FIGURE 11–6.** Some HEVs now use electric drive water pumps and have eliminated the accessory drive belt completely. The ICE water pump is a non-positive displacement design, meaning that the **impeller** can turn without any coolant

FIGURE 11–6 A water pump that is driven by the ICE timing belt.

FIGURE 11–7 This water pump impeller will turn CCW (as shown) and will take coolant from the center of the impeller and "throw" it outward. The coolant then flows to the right, where it is directed into the ICE block.

being pumped if a blockage exists in the system. Coolant always enters at the center of the impeller and is "thrown" outward as the water pump is turned. ● **SEE FIGURE 11–7.** The coolant is then directed into the water jacket, where it absorbs excess heat and transfers it to lower-temperature areas of the system.

 FREQUENTLY ASKED QUESTION

Can Green Antifreeze Be Used to Top Up Systems Using Extended-Life Coolant?

Vehicle manufacturers state only the specified coolant should be used during normal maintenance. Adding green (IAT) antifreeze to a system with extended-life coolant will cause the change interval to be reduced to that of the green coolant, which is typically two to three years.

 FREQUENTLY ASKED QUESTION

Will the Heater in My Hybrid Vehicle Still Work when the ICE Is in Idle Stop Mode?

The ICE water pump is responsible for circulating coolant through the ICE water jacket, as well as the vehicle's heater core. Since the water pump is belt-driven by the ICE, there is no circulation of the coolant when the ICE is in idle stop mode. If the cabin heater is on, this will result in cold air coming out of the vents. To prevent this from happening, many hybrid electric vehicles utilize an electrically driven **helper pump** that continues to circulate coolant when the ICE enters idle stop. ● **SEE FIGURE 11–8.**

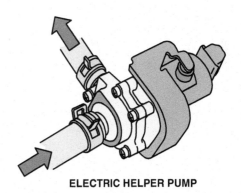

ELECTRIC HELPER PUMP

FIGURE 11–8 The electric helper pump is turned on whenever cabin heating is requested and the ICE is in idle stop mode. The pump is plumbed in series with the hoses running to the vehicle heater core.

THERMOSTAT Coolant temperature in the ICE cooling system is primarily controlled by a thermostat. Most thermostats are a poppet-type valve that utilizes a wax pellet to expand and open the valve when the coolant reaches a certain temperature. When the thermostat opens, coolant is allowed to enter the radiator and dissipate excess heat to the outside air. ● **SEE FIGURE 11–9.**

Thermostats are rated according to the temperature at which they first start to open. For instance, a 195°F (90°C) thermostat would start to open at 195°F, but would be fully open at 215°F (101°C). As the temperature of the coolant decreases, the thermostat will slowly close and prevent the coolant from entering the radiator. This "cycling" of the thermostat keeps the ICE coolant temperature within a narrow range. Thermostats are most often located near the cylinder heads, but they are sometimes located on the block as well.

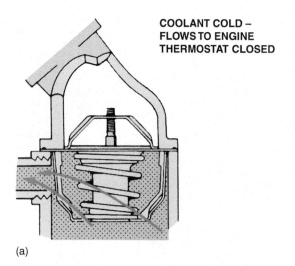

**COOLANT COLD –
FLOWS TO ENGINE
THERMOSTAT CLOSED**

(a)

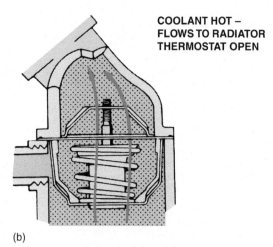

**COOLANT HOT –
FLOWS TO RADIATOR
THERMOSTAT OPEN**

(b)

FIGURE 11–9 Coolant returns to the water pump inlet via the bypass tube (a) until the thermostat starts to open (b) and allows it to flow to the radiator.

PRESSURE CAP The purpose of the **pressure cap** (also known as *radiator cap*) is to maintain pressure in the cooling system in order to maximize cooling efficiency. Pure water boils at 212°F (100°C), which is very close to the normal operating temperature of the ICE. If the coolant starts to boil, steam pockets form in the water jacket and heat transfer is curtailed. Left unchecked, this can lead to overheating and severe damage to the ICE.

The boiling point of the coolant is increased by using a pressure cap to raise the pressure in the cooling system. For every 1 PSI that the system pressure is raised, the boiling point of the coolant rises 3°F. Therefore, a 16-PSI pressure cap will increase the coolant boiling point by 48°F. As ICE temperature increases, the coolant expands and system pressure rises. If cooling system pressure rises above the pressure cap's rating, the pressure valve in the cap opens and allows some coolant to flow to the coolant recovery reservoir. This limits maximum system pressure and prevents damage to the hoses and other cooling system components.

When the ICE is shut off, its temperature decreases and the coolant contracts (decreases in volume). This causes pressure to drop in the cooling system, which can lead to collapsed hoses as a vacuum forms in the water jacket. To prevent this from happening, a vacuum valve in the pressure cap opens and allows coolant to flow from the coolant recovery reservoir back into the cooling system. ● **SEE FIGURE 11–10.**

NOTE: There is a "hot" and a "cold" level marked in most coolant recovery reservoirs. When checking the coolant level, be sure that the coolant is at the "cold" line when the vehicle has sat overnight. Once the ICE is at operating temperature, the coolant level will rise to the "hot" line as the pressure cap allows expanding coolant to flow into the coolant recovery reservoir.

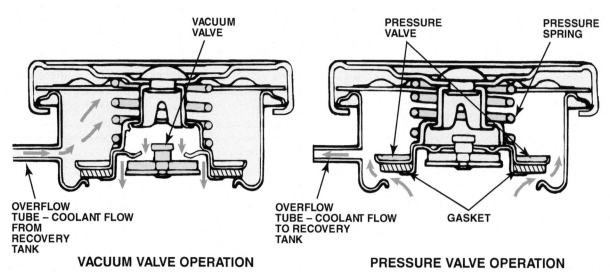

VACUUM VALVE OPERATION

PRESSURE VALVE OPERATION

FIGURE 11–10 The pressure cap is responsible for maintaining pressure as well as making sure the system is always full of liquid coolant.

COOLANT RECOVERY RESERVOIR Cooling systems on earlier vehicles were designed so that extra space was available in the radiator for coolant expansion. As the coolant increased in temperature, its level rose inside the radiator and only vapor exited when system pressure increased past the pressure cap rating. This approach allowed air to be present in the cooling system at all times, which led to greater potential for air to be trapped in the coolant. This also allowed coolant to spill on the ground if the ICE overheated.

These problems led engineers to include a **coolant recovery reservoir** in cooling system designs. The reservoir is connected to a hose that leads to a port under the pressure cap. When the pressure cap allows coolant to exit the system, the coolant flows through the hose and increases the level in the reservoir. As the temperature in the cooling system decreases, coolant is allowed to flow from the reservoir back into the cooling system. This means that the cooling system is always completely full of liquid, making it better able to transfer heat. ● **SEE FIGURE 11–11.**

SURGE TANK Some vehicles use a **surge tank** instead of a coolant recovery reservoir. The surge tank is located at the highest point in the cooling system, and is connected to the remainder of the system through a hose at the bottom of the tank. There may also be a bleed line that connects the side of the tank to the highest point on the radiator. The system pressure cap is located on the surge tank and functions similar to one that is on the radiator itself. Like the coolant recovery reservoir, the purpose of the surge tank is to make certain that the cooling system components always have liquid coolant in them to maximize cooling system efficiency. ● **SEE FIGURE 11–12.**

HEAT EXCHANGER Excess heat that is absorbed by the coolant must be dissipated to prevent ICE overheating and damage. In automotive applications, this heat can be

FIGURE 11–12 The surge tank has a pressure cap and is located at the highest point in the cooling system.

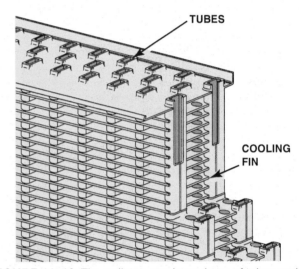

FIGURE 11–13 The radiator core is made up of tubes and fins that maximize the surface area for heat rejection.

transferred either to the outside air or to the passenger compartment. In either case, a liquid-to-air **heat exchanger** is utilized that dissipates the heat from the coolant to the air passing through it. A radiator is a heat exchanger that is located ahead of the ICE and transfers excess heat from the coolant to the outside air. A heater core is a heat exchanger that is located in the cabin air distribution system and transfers excess heat from the coolant to the air entering the passenger compartment.

Coolant flows into the inlet tank and is then directed into dozens of thin tubes that form the core of the heat exchanger. These tubes are designed with cooling fins located between them so that maximum surface area is available to dissipate heat to the outside air. ● **SEE FIGURE 11–13.** The coolant dissipates its heat as it passes through these tubes and is then gathered at the outlet tank, where it is then sent back to the ICE water jacket.

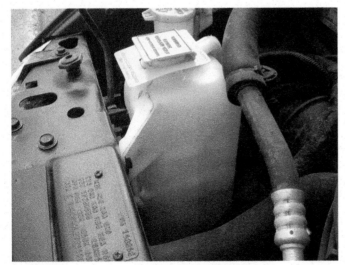

FIGURE 11–11 A coolant recovery reservoir does not have a pressure cap. Note that the coolant is currently on the "cold" line in this photo, but will rise to the "hot" line as the ICE warms up.

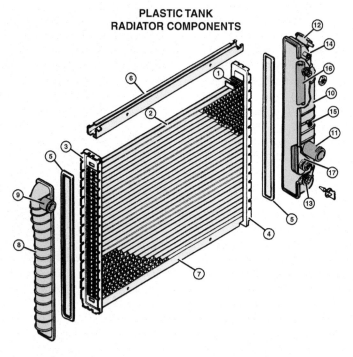

**PLASTIC TANK
RADIATOR COMPONENTS**

1 SERPENTINE LOUVERED FIN	10 OUTLET (BOTTOM) TANK
2 CORE TUBE	11 OUTLET HOSE CONNECTION
3 INLET (TOP) HEADER-TABBED TYPE (b)	12 FILLER NECK/OVERFLOW TUBE
4 OUTLET (BOTTOM)-TABBED TYPE (b)	13 DRAIN FITTING
5 GASKET SEAL (b)	14 HEATER RETURN LINE CONNECTION
6 SIDE PIECE	15 COOLANT LEVEL INDICATOR FITTING OR
7 SIDE PIECE	TEMPERATURE SENSOR SWITCH
8 INLET TANK	16 CONCENTRIC OIL COOLER
9 INLET HOSE CONNECTION	17 PLATE OIL COOLER

FIGURE 11–14 An aluminum radiator has plastic tanks that are crimped in place with a gasket to seal them.

It was most common years ago for heat exchangers to be made of copper or brass, but most are now made with aluminum. The newest designs are constructed with plastic tanks attached to an aluminum core. ●**SEE FIGURE 11–14.**

There are two major designs of radiators: **downflow** and **crossflow.** Downflow radiators have vertical tubes with tanks at the top and bottom of the core. ●**SEE FIGURE 11–15.** Crossflow radiators are made to be installed in vehicles with lower hood lines and have horizontal tubes with tanks attached to each end. ●**SEE FIGURE 11–16.**

If the vehicle is equipped with an automatic transmission, there will often be a transmission oil cooler installed in the outlet tank of the radiator. ● **SEE FIGURE 11–16.** Hot transmission fluid is pumped through the cooler element, and excess heat is removed from the fluid by the coolant flowing around it. The outlet tank will often have a drain fitting installed in it for draining the coolant during service procedures.

COOLING FANS In order for a heat exchanger to remove excess heat from the coolant, there must be sufficient airflow across it. The radiator is located at the front of the vehicle and has good airflow at highway speeds, but this decreases as the vehicle slows down. If the vehicle is moving slowly or is stopped, the ICE could overheat unless some additional

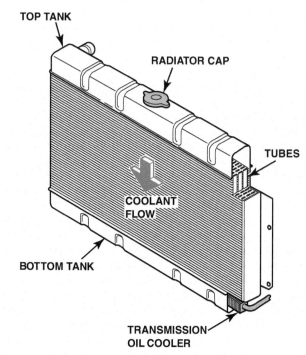

FIGURE 11–15 Coolant flows from top to bottom in a downflow radiator. Note that in most cases the radiator cap is located on the upper tank.

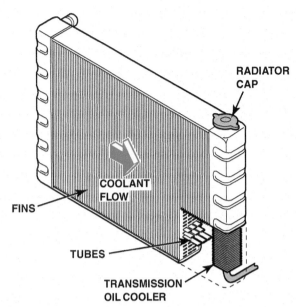

FIGURE 11-16 Coolant flows horizontally in a crossflow radiator.

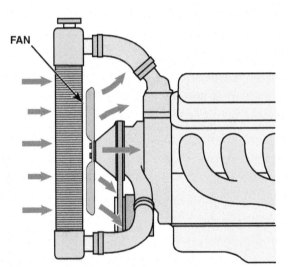

FIGURE 11-17 The fan is needed to move air across the radiator when the vehicle is moving slowly or stopped with the ICE running.

means of moving air across the radiator is provided. ● SEE FIGURE 11-17.

It was once very common for a belt-driven mechanical fan to be used to move air across the radiator. While this was a very simple and reliable approach, it was noisy and wasted a lot of energy because it ran at times when it was not needed. Accessories that are driven by the ICE crankshaft will draw a certain amount of horsepower, which leads to a reduction in fuel efficiency.

A number of different approaches have been developed to turn the fan on only when the coolant temperature rises to a certain point. One method is the use of a thermostatic **fan clutch** that is designed to slip when cold. The fan itself is still belt-driven, but the fan only engages when it is needed and otherwise reduces the noise and energy consumption associated with a fixed mechanical fan. ● SEE FIGURE 11-18.

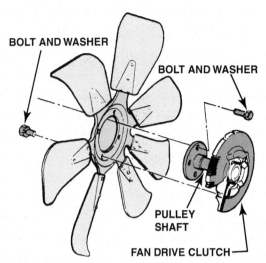

FIGURE 11-18 A thermostatic fan clutch forms the hub of this fan assembly.

Another approach is to eliminate the belt drive and use a fan driven by an electric motor. This is used in all vehicles where the ICE is mounted transversely (sideways) because there is no simple means of using the accessory drive belt to operate a fan located behind the radiator. An electric fan can be mounted either behind or in front of the vehicle radiator, depending on how much space is available in the ICE compartment. The fan can be turned on and off through the use of a **thermoelectric switch** mounted on the radiator tank, or by electronic means using the powertrain control module (PCM). ● SEE FIGURE 11-19.

One major advantage of using an electric drive for the ICE fan is the ability to accurately control airflow across the radiator regardless of the RPM of the ICE. This can be accomplished by using two separate fan motors and turning on either one or both to vary airflow. Other approaches include using a multiple-speed fan motor, or controlling the current to the motor using pulse-width modulation (PWM). The operation of the air conditioning system is also enhanced with an electric fan, as the fan can be turned on with the A/C system to ensure adequate airflow across the condenser.

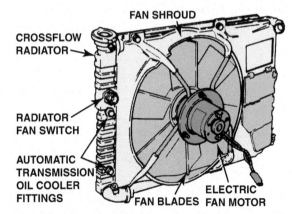

FIGURE 11-19 An electric fan can be located either in front of or behind the radiator. The fan shroud helps direct airflow toward the fan to enhance cooling efficiency.

Low-Grade Heat Requires Larger Heat Exchangers

Most ICE-powered vehicles are able to use a radiator (heat exchanger) with a moderate cross-sectional area. This is because the coolant temperature is much higher than the temperature of the surrounding air, and heat transfer takes place quickly under these conditions. However, a vehicle that is powered by a PEM (Proton Exchange Membrane) fuel cell must have a much larger heat exchanger because its coolant temperature typically runs very close to that of the surrounding air. This is known as **low-grade heat,** and this creates challenges for engineers because the frontal area of the vehicle is limited in terms of the size of the radiator that can be installed there. To maximize surface area, the radiator is sometimes installed at a rearward-tilting angle to allow it to fit into the allotted space. In some cases, supplemental heat exchangers are installed under the vehicle to increase the fuel cell's cooling capacity.

HOSES   Many sections of the cooling system utilize rigid pipes to circulate coolant. However, some sections must use flexible hoses due to normal movement between major components. The ICE itself will move on its mounts a certain amount during vehicle operation due to torque reaction. Since the vehicle's radiator and heater core stay stationary at all times, flexible hoses must be used to connect the ICE to these components.

Radiator hoses have an inner lining made from synthetic rubber. A number of textile plies are woven over top of the inner lining as reinforcements, and then an outer layer of rubber is placed on top of the reinforcing plies. The rubber outer layer must be capable of resisting damage due to leaking oil or extreme temperatures. ● **SEE FIGURE 11–20.**

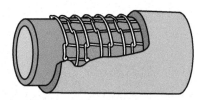

LOCKSTITCH REINFORCEMENT

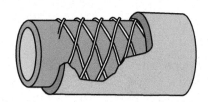

SPIRAL REINFORCEMENT

FIGURE 11–20 Radiator hose construction showing two types of reinforcement using woven textile.

COOLANT HEAT STORAGE SYSTEM (2004–2009 PRIUS)

Internal combustion engines produce increased emissions during a cold start. This is because fuel has a tendency to condense on cold air intake manifold and cylinder walls, requiring a richer air–fuel mixture to compensate. The cold surfaces in the combustion chamber also exhibit a phenomenon known as quench, where the flame along those surfaces is extinguished and the air–fuel mixture is only partially burned. These issues diminish significantly once the ICE is up to operating temperature.

In order to meet ever-increasing emissions standards, engineers strive to limit the impact that cold starts have on emissions and driveability. One approach is to utilize a **coolant heat storage system** where heated coolant is stored during normal vehicle operation and is then used to warm the engine intake ports prior to a cold start. Toyota uses this system in the second-generation Prius (2004 to 2009).

COMPONENTS   The coolant heat storage system is part of the ICE cooling system, but adds the major components described on the following page. ● **SEE FIGURE 11–21.**

The coolant heat storage tank is built very similar to a Thermos® bottle. The tank is built with an inner and outer casing, and a vacuum is formed between them. This is done to prevent heat transfer from the inner casing. Approximately 3 liters of coolant is stored inside the inner casing, and the coolant can be kept warm for up to three days. There is a standpipe that extends

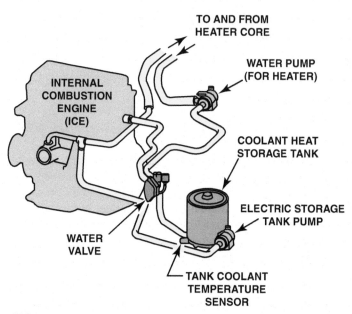

FIGURE 11–21 Toyota's coolant heat storage system. Note that the electric storage tank pump is located behind the coolant storage tank.

The Outside of a Radiator Hose Is Not the Best Indicator of its Condition

Even though the outside of a radiator hose may look fine, this is not the best indicator of the hose's overall condition. Hoses that look OK on the outside can have extensive damage on the inner lining. When inspecting a radiator hose, be sure to squeeze it within 2 inches of each end of the hose. Compare this to how the hose feels in the middle. If the hose feels soft at the ends, it is time to replace the hose.

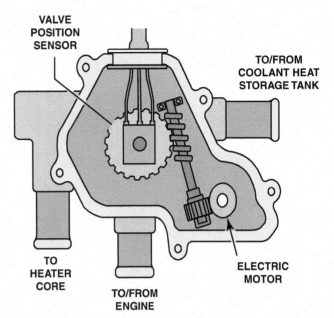

FIGURE 11–23 The valve position sensor in the water valve provides feedback to the ECM concerning the position of the water valve.

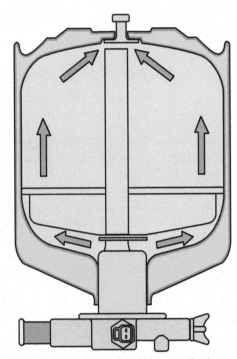

FIGURE 11–22 A vacuum exists between the inner and outer casing of the coolant heat storage tank. The outlet temperature sensor and the drain plug are located in the manifold at the bottom of the tank.

FIGURE 11–24 The storage tank and pump as seen from under the vehicle. This pump is energized when coolant must be moved through the tank but the ICE is shut off.

inside of the inner casing, so coolant must rise in order to exit the tank through the standpipe. ●**SEE FIGURE 11–22.**

The **water valve** is responsible for directing the coolant flow between the coolant storage tank, the ICE, and the vehicle's heater core. The water valve is controlled by the ECM and consists of an electric motor, drive gears, a rotary valve, and a valve position sensor. ●**SEE FIGURE 11–23.**

The storage tank pump is used to move coolant through the heat storage tank at times when the ICE is shut off. This pump is located on the side of the coolant heat storage tank and is plumbed in series with the tank inlet. ●**SEE FIGURE 11–24.**

MODES OF OPERATION The coolant heat storage system has four modes of operation. These are:

1. Preheat
2. Engine warm-up
3. Storage during driving
4. Storage during ignition off

The preheat mode is enabled prior to the starting of the ICE. The ECM turns on the electric storage tank pump and directs the water valve to send hot coolant from the

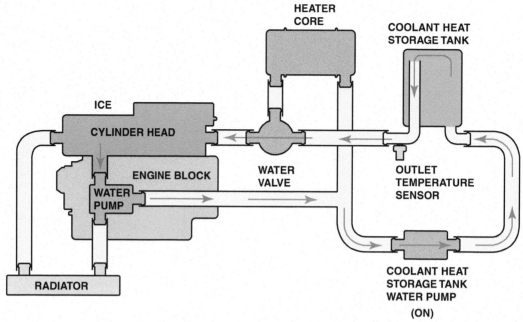

FIGURE 11–25 During preheat mode, the ICE remains off while the coolant heat storage pump is turned on. The water valve directs hot coolant from the storage tank to the ICE cylinder head.

storage tank into the cylinder head. The heat from the coolant warms the cylinder head ports and minimizes fuel condensation on the port walls. This allows for easier starting and minimizes emissions during a cold start. ● **SEE FIGURE 11–25.**

Once the preheat cycle is completed, the ICE is started and the coolant heat storage system enters the engine warm-up mode. The storage water pump is turned off and the water valve directs coolant from the ICE into the heater core, bypassing the coolant heat storage tank. ● **SEE FIGURE 11–26.** Coolant continues to circulate in this manner until the ICE reaches operating temperature.

Once the ICE has reached operating temperature, an opportunity is created to store a fresh charge of hot coolant in the storage tank. The water valve is moved to allow coolant from the ICE to flow into both the heater core and the coolant heat storage tank. This process replaces the cold coolant in the storage tank with heated coolant,

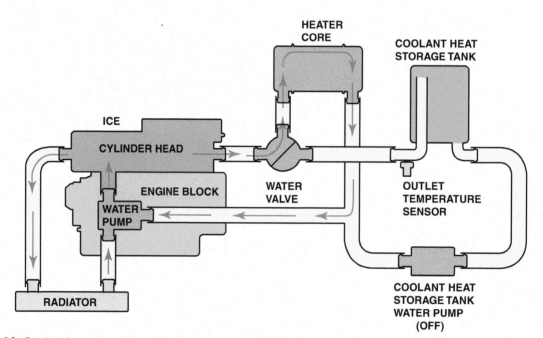

FIGURE 11–26 Coolant bypasses the coolant heat storage tank during engine warm-up mode.

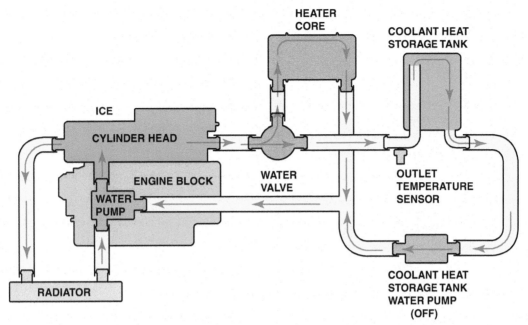

FIGURE 11–27 The coolant heat storage tank is filled with hot coolant when the ICE reaches operating temperature. This coolant is then used to warm the engine before the next cold start.

and is known as storage operation (driving). The coolant heat storage water pump remains off during this phase and coolant is moved through the system using only the ICE mechanical water pump. ● **SEE FIGURE 11–27.** Once the tank is filled with hot coolant, the water valve moves back to the engine warm-up position. This directs coolant from the ICE into the heater core, and bypasses the coolant heat storage tank.

If the ICE is shut off while the coolant heat storage tank is being filled, the water valve stays in the storage position and the storage tank pump is turned on to finish filling the tank. This phase is known as storage operation (ignition off). ● **SEE FIGURE 11–28.** Note that the flow through the tank is reversed in this mode, but that the storage tank is still able to be filled with hot coolant. This operation will not take place if the ICE has not reached operating temperature.

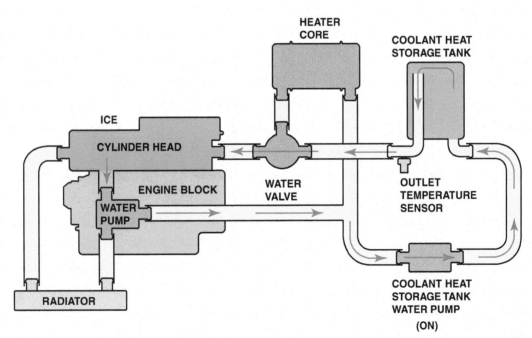

FIGURE 11–28 Storage operation (ignition off) mode. This takes place if the ICE is shut off while the coolant tank is being filled.

CABIN HEATING SYSTEMS

PRINCIPLES   Some of the waste heat absorbed by the ICE cooling system can also be dissipated by the heater core in the passenger compartment heating system. Hot coolant is pumped through the heater core and air is circulated over it to raise its temperature.

PARTS AND OPERATION   Heater cores are built similar to radiators, but are much smaller and often have the inlet and outlet pipes located at the same end of the assembly. The heater core is located in the passenger compartment, inside the **plenum chamber** (air distribution box) for the vehicle's heater and air conditioning components. ● **SEE FIGURE 11–29.**

In many systems, coolant is continually circulated through the heater core so it remains hot at all times. Air entering the plenum chamber must first pass through the A/C evaporator core, and then is directed either through or around the heater core by the **blend door** (*air mix valve*). The temperature of the air can be adjusted by changing the position of the blend door and the percentage of air that is sent through the heater core.

Once the air leaves the heater core, it is blended with any air that has bypassed it and then is sent to its destination through a series of mode valves. These direct the air to specific areas of the vehicle, depending on the mode that is selected at the time. For instance, the defrost mode will require that the air be directed toward the windshield outlets. In the heat mode, however, the air can be sent to the instrument panel outlets and/or the floor vents depending on the driver's preference.

HEV HEATING SYSTEMS   The amount of heat generated by the heating system is dependent on the temperature of the coolant that is circulated through the heater core. When the ICE is first started, it takes some time for the coolant to reach sufficient temperature for heat to be sent to the passenger compartment. This is further complicated with hybrid electric vehicles as the ICE coolant temperature is more difficult to maintain when the ICE enters into idle stop or the vehicle is operating in electric-only mode.

One other complication is that newer ICE designs are increasing in efficiency and are generating progressively less waste heat. In order to overcome this, some vehicles are using the electrical system to boost the heat to the passenger compartment when the ICE coolant tempera-ture is low. One approach is to use **PTC heaters** built into the heater core itself. **Positive temperature coefficient (PTC)** refers to the tendency of a conductor to increase its electrical resistance as its temperature increases. PTC heaters convert electrical energy into heat, and this is used to boost heat to th e passenger compartment. ● **SEE FIGURE 11–30.**

PTC heaters can also be located in the air ducts in the form of a honeycomb-shaped grid. Air that is leaving the plenum chamber passes through these heaters before it enters the passenger compartment. ● **SEE FIGURE 11–31.**

The Toyota Prius uses PTC heaters located in the heater core, as well as the footwell air ducts. The A/C electronic control unit turns on the PTC heaters when the coolant temperature is low and MAX HOT is requested.

NOTE: PTC heaters are sometimes referred to as "glow plugs."

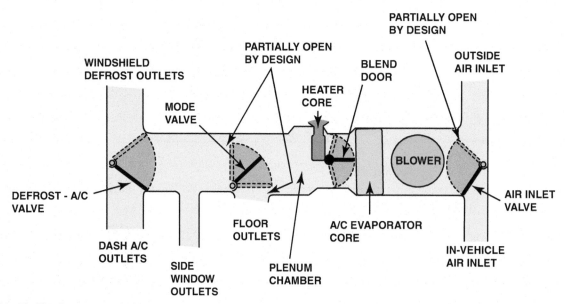

FIGURE 11–29 The heater core is located in the plenum chamber. Air temperature in this system is controlled by the position of the air mix valve (blend door).

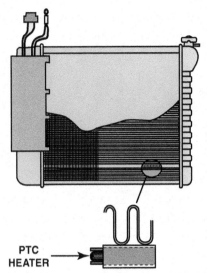

FIGURE 11–30 PTC heaters can be located on the heater core itself to help boost heat to the passenger compartment when coolant temperature is low.

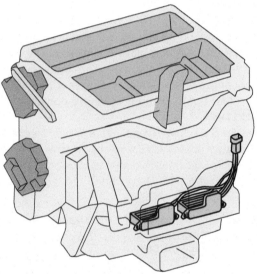

FIGURE 11–31 Two PTC heaters are located in the footwell air ducts in the Toyota Prius. These are energized when the coolant temperature is low and MAX HOT is requested in the FOOT or FOOT/DEF modes.

HYBRID ELECTRICAL SYSTEM COOLING

NEED FOR COOLING Hybrid electric vehicles are unique in that they have electric motors and electronic controls that are not found in vehicles with conventional drivetrains. These components are designed to operate under heavy load with high current and voltage demands, so they tend to generate excessive heat during vehicle operation. Special auxiliary cooling systems are incorporated into hybrid electric vehicles to prevent overheating of these critical components.

EFFECTS OF HEAT ON THE ELECTRICAL/ ELECTRONIC SYSTEM Generally speaking, electronic components operate more efficiently as their temperature decreases, but can suffer permanent damage if they overheat. All hybrid electric vehicles have cooling systems for their motors and motor controls, and some utilize air-cooling to remove excess heat from these components. ● **SEE FIGURE 11–32.**

Many hybrid electric vehicles use a liquid cooling system for their motors and motor controls. These systems are often separate from the ICE's cooling system and typically operate at lower temperatures.

SYSTEM CONSTRUCTION The liquid cooling systems used for the motors and motor controls on hybrid electric vehicles have much in common with conventional ICE cooling systems. There is a separate expansion tank that acts as a coolant reservoir for the system, and the coolant is often the same type that is used for the ICE cooling system. A radiator is used to dissipate excess heat, and is located at the front of the vehicle. Some designs may have the radiator incorporated into the ICE radiator, or it may be separate. ● **SEE FIGURE 11–33.**

A low-voltage electric water pump is used to circulate the coolant, and it is often configured to run whenever the vehicle is in operation. The coolant is circulated through the various components in the system, which could include the following:

- Electric motor-generator(s)
- DC-DC converter
- Inverter
- Transmission oil cooler
- Other high-load control modules

FIGURE 11–32 The motor and HV battery electronics on Honda hybrid vehicles are air-cooled. Note the cooling fins for the modules.

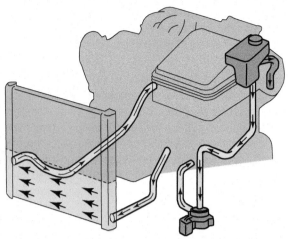

FIGURE 11–33 The electric motors and the motor controls are cooled using a separate cooling system. This Toyota Hybrid Synergy Drive (HSD) system uses a radiator that is integral with the ICE cooling system radiator.

FIGURE 11–34 This first generation Prius (01–03) transaxle has cooling passages for both of the motor-generators. Note the coolant pipes (two on each assembly) on the lower left of this photograph.

 FREQUENTLY ASKED QUESTION

Why Isn't the ICE Cooling System Used to Cool HEV Motors and Motor Controls?

Most ICE cooling systems operate at over 200°F (93°C). For maximum efficiency, it is important that the ICE operate at close to this temperature at all times. Electric motors and the motor controls, however, tend to operate more efficiently at lower temperatures. The ICE cooling system runs too hot to allow these components to operate at peak efficiency, so a separate low-temperature system is often used.

Note that a thermostat is not used in these systems. In some HEV systems the electric pump will circulate coolant whenever the key is on. In other systems, peak temperature is controlled by turning on the pump and then the fan at progressively higher speeds as the coolant temperature rises.

Toyota hybrid transaxles have cooling passages located near both of the electric motor-generators and these are part of the inverter cooling system. Coolant hoses connect to fittings on the transmission case, and these direct coolant in and out of each of the motor-generator assemblies. ● **SEE FIGURE 11–34.**

This approach is very different from the GM hybrid pickup, which circulates coolant from the ICE cooling system through the starter-generator's stator assembly.

NOTE: In the GM hybrid pickup, coolant does not circulate through the stator of the starter-generator until the ICE cooling system's thermostat opens. This is done to prevent a delay in engine warm-up.

The GM hybrid pickup utilizes a starter-generator control module (SGCM) that plays a similar role to the inverter in other hybrid control systems. This module has its own liquid cooling system, which includes a heat exchanger, electric water pump, a radiator, and a cooling fan. ● **SEE FIGURE 11–35.**

The Ford Escape Hybrid has a motor electronic (M/E) cooling system that is similar to the inverter cooling system used in the Toyota Prius. Coolant is circulated by an electric pump through the DC/DC converter and the heat exchange

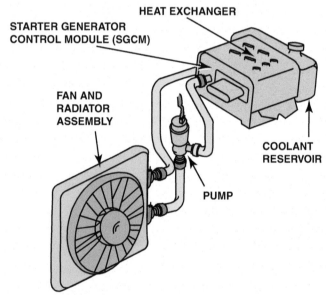

FIGURE 11–35 The SGCM on a GM hybrid pickup has its own liquid cooling system. The pump turns on when the SGCM internal temperature rises above 140°F (60°C).

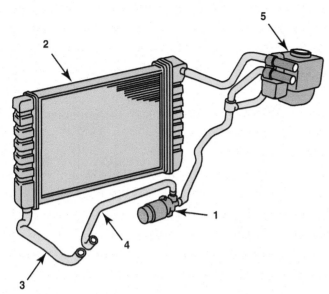

FIGURE 11–36 The motor electronics cooling system in a Ford Escape Hybrid. The electric pump (1) circulates coolant through the eCVT and the DC-DC converter and dissipates the excess heat at the radiator (2). The eCVT connects to hoses (3) and (4), and the DC-DC converter is connected to the hoses beside the coolant reservoir bottle (5).

unit mounted on top of the eCVT (hybrid transaxle). The power electronics for the hybrid drive system are located on top of the transaxle, and the coolant circulated through this unit also removes heat from the transmission fluid used for cooling the electric motors. ● **SEE FIGURE 11–36.**

TECH TIP

Phase-Change Liquid Used for Cooling Hybrid Electronics

The starter-generator control module (SGCM) on a GM hybrid pickup uses a **phase-change liquid** called Fluorinert™ inside the module to distribute heat evenly across the power electronics. This liquid will boil as the temperature of the electronic components rise, absorbing excess heat as the liquid "changes phase" and becomes a vapor.

Four sensors inside the module are used to measure the level of the phase-change liquid and determine when to enable the external cooling system pump. As system temperature rises and the liquid level decreases, the pump is turned on and coolant is circulated through the heat exchanger that is mounted on top of the SGCM. Heat is absorbed from the vapor above the phase-change liquid and is dissipated at the radiator assembly. The fan will also turn on and operate at either LO or HI speed, depending on the temperature rise in the coolant.

FREQUENTLY ASKED QUESTION

What Coolant Is Used in a Motor/Electronics Cooling System?

Most hybrid electric vehicle manufacturers specify that the same coolant used in the vehicle's ICE (engine) be used for cooling the motors and electronics. For instance, Toyota specifies that its Super Long Life Coolant be used in the 2nd generation Prius ICE cooling system as well as the inverter cooling system.

HYBRID AIR CONDITIONING SYSTEMS

BASIC OPERATION The fundamental purpose of any air conditioning system is to absorb heat in one location and then reject (dissipate) that heat in another location. There are many different methods for achieving this goal, but in automotive applications it is most common to utilize a closed-loop system where **refrigerant** goes through alternating **changes of state.**

Heat energy must be absorbed by a refrigerant (such as **R-134a**) in order for it to change from a liquid to a gas, and this property can be utilized effectively in a vehicle's **evaporator** to absorb heat from inside the passenger compartment. The gaseous refrigerant is then compressed and sent to the **condenser** (located ahead of the radiator), where the absorbed heat is then dissipated outside the vehicle. The combined effect of compressing and cooling the refrigerant causes it to return to a liquid state.

Heat is absorbed and dissipated as the refrigerant changes state. Changing the refrigerant from a gas to a liquid requires that it be compressed (by the **compressor**) and cooled (by the condenser) to remove the excess heat energy. The liquid refrigerant

FREQUENTLY ASKED QUESTION

Why Does a Propane Cylinder Get Cold When It Is Being Used?

Propane is an excellent refrigerant. When a propane cylinder is used to fuel a camp stove or a torch, the liquid in the cylinder is changing state and becoming a gas. In order for the change of state to take place, the liquid propane must absorb heat energy. The propane will absorb heat through the steel walls of the cylinder, creating a chill effect in which condensation and frost form on the outside of the cylinder. The steel cylinder is playing the same role as the evaporator in an air conditioning system. ● **SEE FIGURE 11–37.**

FIGURE 11–37 Liquid propane in this cylinder is expanding into a gas for fueling a camp stove. The liquid absorbs heat energy as it changes state, evidenced by the frost and condensation on the outside of the cylinder.

is then directed through a restriction (thermostatic expansion valve or orifice tube) in the line, where a **pressure drop** takes place. Moving from a high-pressure area to a low-pressure area allows the refrigerant to expand in the evaporator and absorb heat energy as it changes into a gas. The cycle then starts over again as the refrigerant moves out of the evaporator and into the compressor inlet. ● **SEE FIGURE 11–38.**

Control of this type of air conditioning system is accomplished through engagement of the compressor drive, as well as the airflow across the evaporator and condenser.

The compressor is most often belt-driven by the ICE accessory drive. The belt drive often uses an electrically operated clutch, which allows the compressor pulley to disconnect from the compressor and stop refrigerant flow in the system while the ICE continues to run. ● **SEE FIGURE 11–39.**

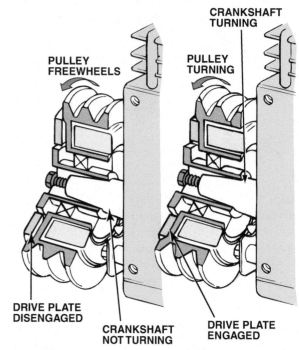

FIGURE 11–39 The A/C compressor clutch allows the compressor to engage and disengage as necessary while the ICE continues to run.

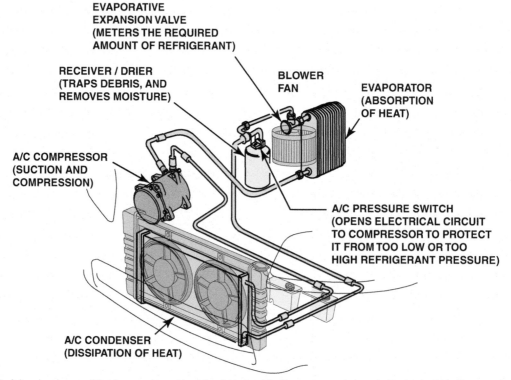

FIGURE 11–38 A basic air conditioning system. Heat is absorbed in the evaporator and dissipated by the condenser.

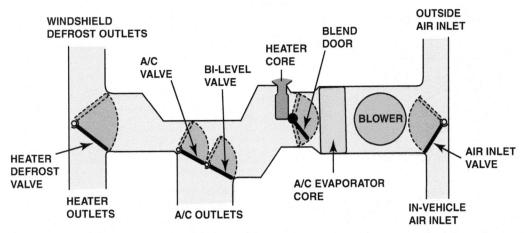

FIGURE 11–40 A basic air distribution system. Air can enter the system from outside the vehicle, or from the passenger compartment while in the recirculation mode.

Airflow into the passenger compartment is controlled by a **blower motor,** which sends the air through the evaporator and then into a series of passages and doors behind the vehicle's dashboard. ● **SEE FIGURE 11–40.** In most situations, fresh air is brought in from outside the vehicle and then is heated or cooled before being sent to the appropriate vents. It is also possible to bring the air in from the passenger compartment itself, when the system is placed in the recirculation mode.

The fresh air coming into the vehicle is sometimes sent through a **cabin filter** first, in order to remove particulate matter and prevent clogging of the vehicle's evaporator. ● **SEE FIGURE 11–57.** Note that all the incoming air must pass through the A/C evaporator core after leaving the blower motor. ● **SEE FIGURE 11–40.** In defrost mode, the A/C compressor is activated and the evaporator core is cooled to the point where any humidity in the air will condense on the evaporator and then be drained outside the vehicle. This allows for rapid clearing of the windshield and a comfortable humidity level inside the vehicle.

While in defrost mode, the air leaving the A/C evaporator core can then be sent through the heater core to raise its temperature. This warm air is now sent to the defrost outlets and is passed over the passenger side of the vehicle's windshield. The temperature of the air is controlled by the position of the air temp valve (blend door), as it either directs varying amounts of air over the heater core or bypasses it completely.

When in the *heat mode,* the A/C compressor is turned off and the evaporator operates at ambient temperature. This means that any temperature change of the incoming air is now controlled only by the air temp valve as it directs the air across the heater core. The heater core is part of the ICE cooling system, and hot coolant is circulated through it by the water pump. ● **SEE FIGURE 11–41.**

When the system is placed in the *A/C mode,* the A/C compressor is engaged and the blower motor circulates air over the evaporator. The cool, dehumidified air is then sent to the air temp valve, where it can bypass the heater core completely if maximum cooling effect is required. However, if warmer air is desirable, its temperature can be increased by changing the

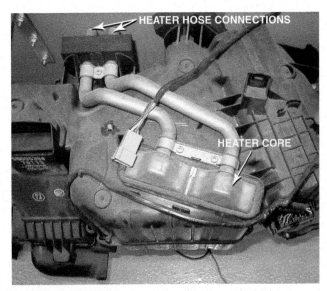

FIGURE 11–41 Coolant can circulate through the heater core when the thermostat is closed.

position of the air temp valve so that some of the air passes through the heater core on its way to the distribution ducts. The final air temperature is achieved by blending the heated air from the heater core with the unheated air.

A/C COMPONENTS

COMPRESSORS The compressor is the heart of the A/C system. It is responsible for circulating refrigerant through the system by creating high pressure in the condenser and low pressure in the evaporator. There are many different compressor designs, with most utilizing either a rotary vane or a piston-and-cylinder arrangement. However, the most commonly used compressor design in hybrid electric vehicles is the **scroll compressor.** ● **SEE FIGURE 11–42.**

The scroll compressor is a highly efficient and durable design, with very good noise, vibration, and harshness (NVH)

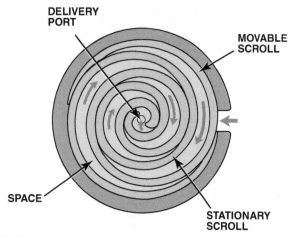

FIGURE 11–42 Basic components of a scroll compressor. Note the "pockets" of refrigerant that occupy the spaces labeled with arrows.

DELIVERY PORT

MOVABLE SCROLL

SPACE

STATIONARY SCROLL

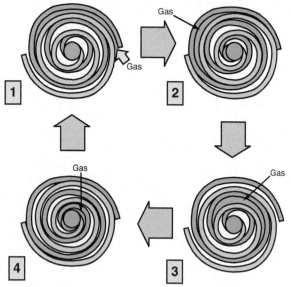

FIGURE 11–43 The movable scroll orbits inside the stationary scroll and moves the refrigerant from the outside toward the delivery port in the center.

characteristics. This is because it is a balanced unit that uses a orbiting motion rather than sliding to compress the gases. It also has very low power consumption relative to other compressor designs, making it especially attractive for hybrid applications.

A scroll compressor has two primary components: the stationary scroll and the movable scroll. The key to understanding how a scroll compressor works is remembering that the movable scroll *does not rotate*. Instead, it *orbits* inside the stationary scroll. ● SEE FIGURE 11–43. A low-pressure area is created at the inlet (outer) port of the scroll mechanism, and refrigerant enters this area and moves in a spiral pattern toward the delivery port in the center. Note that several "pockets" of refrigerant are being compressed at any one time as the movable scroll orbits inside the stationary scroll.

The compressor is on the dividing line between the high- and low-pressure sections of the air conditioning

system. Low-pressure gas enters the suction (inlet) port of the compressor, and high-pressure gas leaves the discharge (outlet) port. The temperature of the refrigerant rises as it is compressed and it is sent on for cooling in the condenser.

COMPRESSOR DRIVES Hybrid electric vehicle A/C systems are very similar to those found on vehicles with conventional powertrains. One major difference with late-model HEVs is in the design of the compressor drive mechanism. Hybrid electric vehicles increase fuel efficiency by turning the ICE off when the vehicle comes to a stop (idle stop mode). If the vehicle's A/C system is in operation (either in A/C or defrost mode), the idle stop function is often disabled and the ICE continues to run.

In order to allow idle stop to take place when the A/C system is on, compressor drives on some HEVs are modified to include an electric motor that is powered by the hybrid high-voltage battery. The electric motor can be "piggybacked" with the conventional belt drive (● SEE FIGURE 11–44), or the compressor may be electric-drive only. ● SEE FIGURE 11–45.

FIGURE 11–44 Hybrid electric vehicle A/C compressor. Note that this unit is primarily belt-driven but has a high-voltage electric motor built in to allow A/C system operation during idle stop.

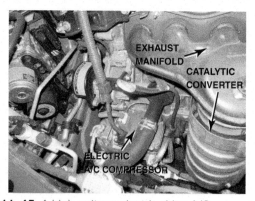

EXHAUST MANIFOLD

CATALYTIC CONVERTER

ELECTRIC A/C COMPRESSOR

FIGURE 11–45 A high-voltage electric drive A/C compressor. The compressor is mounted to the engine block in the same location as a conventional engine-driven compressor. This mounting helps reduce noise and vibration.

COMPRESSOR OIL Since the compressor has many moving parts and tight clearances, it is critical for it to receive adequate lubrication during operation. This is accomplished by circulating compressor oil throughout the system. Most vehicle manufacturers specify **polyalkylene glycol (PAG)** oil for R-134a systems. ● **SEE FIGURE 11–46.** Many different kinds of PAG oil are available, so it is important to select the correct type when servicing a vehicle's air conditioning system. This information is often available on a sticker located in the engine compartment. ● **SEE FIGURE 11–47.**

CONDENSERS The condenser is part of the high-pressure section of the air conditioning system, and is another type of heat exchanger. It receives high-temperature, high-pressure refrigerant gas from the compressor and dissipates the heat from the refrigerant to the outside air. The refrigerant leaves the outlet of the condenser as a warm, high-pressure liquid.

FIGURE 11–46 Specific AC compressor oil designed for use in Honda hybrid vehicle air conditioning systems.

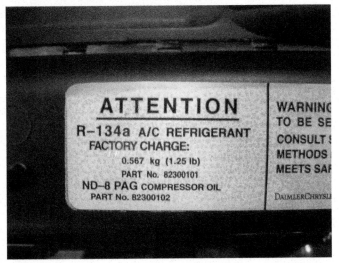

FIGURE 11–47 A label showing A/C system service information is often located under the hood on the vehicle radiator support. Note that the type and amount of refrigerant is shown, along with the specific type of compressor oil to be used.

 FREQUENTLY ASKED QUESTION

Why Should Compressor Oil be Stored in Metal Containers?

Compressor oil is **hygroscopic,** which means that it tends to absorb moisture. It should be stored in sealed containers to prevent contact with humid atmospheric air, but even plastic can allow moisture to pass through. For that reason, compressor oil should always be stored in sealed metal containers to prevent contamination.

 TECH TIP

Pay Careful Attention to the A/C Compressor Oil Required for a Hybrid Vehicle

Some late-model hybrid electric vehicles use high-voltage electric drives for their A/C compressors. This may be in conjunction with a belt drive, or the compressor may be electric drive only. These compressors often require a nonconductive oil that insulates the high-voltage motor and prevents electrical failures. ● **SEE FIGURES 11–48 AND 11–49.**

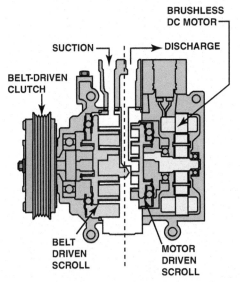

FIGURE 11–48 This hybrid vehicle A/C compressor uses two scrolls; one being belt-driven (left) and the other driven by a brushless DC motor (right).

AIR CONDITIONER SYSTEM	
REFRIGERANT: HC134e	
REC. CHARGE: MAX 0.550kg (19.4 oz.) MIN 0.500kg (17.6 oz.)	
WARNING	
IMPROPER SERVICE CAN CAUSE SHOCK AND DEATH	USE ONLY "SE-10Y" OIL ONLY

FIGURE 11–49 A/C compressors with electric drive motors require nonconductive oil. Do not use ordinary PAG oils in these systems.

The condenser can be built with one long cooling tube following a serpentine path (● **SEE FIGURE 11–50**) or may have multiple cooling tubes forming parallel paths. Surface area of the condenser is increased by the addition of thin fin material between the tubes, as well as partitioning in the tubes themselves. This ensures that sufficient air is in contact with the cooling surfaces and maximum heat is dissipated. ● **SEE FIGURE 11–51.**

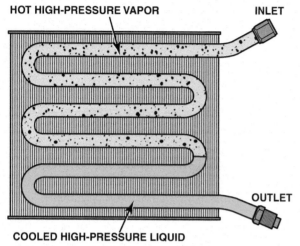

FIGURE 11–50 Refrigerant flow in a condenser.

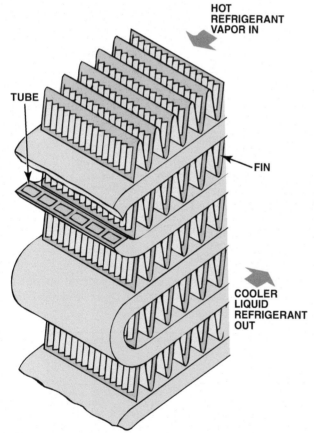

FIGURE 11–51 Condenser construction. Surface area is maximized with cooling fins and partitioned tubes to increase cooling capacity.

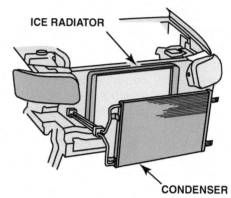

FIGURE 11–52 Condenser location on a Ford Escape Hybrid.

The condenser is typically installed ahead of the vehicle's radiator and has airflow sent through it either through vehicle movement or by the cooling fan. ● **SEE FIGURE 11–52.**

EXPANSION DEVICES In order for the refrigerant to absorb heat in the evaporator, it must go through a change of state in which it changes from a liquid to a gas. This is achieved by sending the high-pressure liquid from the condenser through an expansion device. The expansion device is most often located at the inlet to the evaporator, and is on the dividing line between the high-pressure and low-pressure sides of the air conditioning system. A pressure drop takes place across the expansion device, and lower pressure on the refrigerant allows it to expand and absorb heat energy in the evaporator.

There are two primary types of expansion devices used in automotive air conditioning systems: the **thermostatic expansion valve (TXV)** and the **orifice tube (OT).** The type of expansion device used determines the configuration of the system, as there are differences between a system that uses a TXV and one that uses an orifice tube. ● **SEE FIGURE 11–53.** Note that an expansion valve (TXV) system uses a **receiver-drier** in the high-pressure side, whereas an orifice tube system has an **accumulator** on the low-pressure side between the evaporator and the compressor suction port.

A thermostatic expansion valve uses a sensing bulb on the evaporator outlet to regulate refrigerant flow according to evaporator temperature. The sensing bulb is attached to the expansion valve diaphragm chamber by a capillary tube. ● **SEE FIGURE 11–54.** Higher evaporator temperature causes pressure to increase above the TXV diaphragm, which forces the pushrod down and opens the passage for greater refrigerant flow. A variable orifice inside the expansion valve is opened and closed to regulate refrigerant flow and adjust evaporator temperature.

The receiver-drier is located in the liquid line between the condenser and TXV. The receiver-drier is responsible for removing moisture and debris from the refrigerant, as well as ensuring that only liquid refrigerant reaches the TXV.

- HIGH-PRESSURE VAPOR
- HIGH-PRESSURE LIQUID
- LOW-PRESSURE VAPOR
- LOW-PRESSURE LIQUID

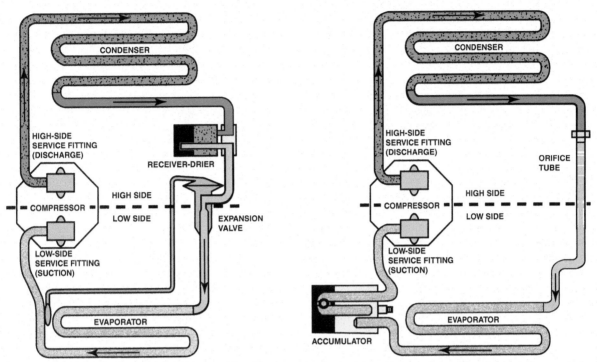

FIGURE 11–53 Basic components and refrigerant flow in an expansion-valve system and an orifice-tube system.

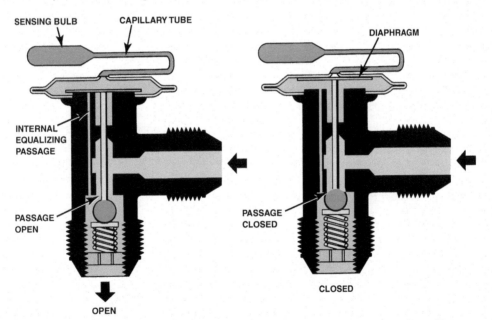

FIGURE 11–54 Operation of a thermostatic expansion valve (TXV). Higher evaporator temperature will cause refrigerant flow to increase (left), whereas lower evaporator temperature will cause the flow to decrease (right).

There are a number of different orifice tube designs, but the most common one is the fixed orifice tube. ● **SEE FIGURE 11–55.** This device has no moving parts and uses a fixed orifice (restriction) to create a pressure drop as liquid refrigerant flows into it from the condenser.

As long as the compressor is operating, refrigerant will flow through the orifice tube. This means that under low-cooling load conditions, it is possible for liquid refrigerant to leave the evaporator outlet. To prevent liquid from reaching the compressor, an accumulator is installed between the

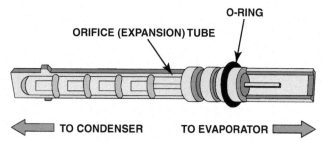

FIGURE 11–55 A fixed orifice tube has no moving parts.

evaporator and the compressor. The accumulator forms a reservoir for liquid refrigerant in the system. The accumulator is also responsible for removing moisture and debris from the refrigerant, as well as supplying oil to the compressor.

MULTIPLE ZONES It is most common for either a TXV or a fixed-orifice tube to be used in a vehicle air conditioning system. However, some A/C systems are designed to use both when multiple evaporators are being utilized. Larger vehicles, such as vans and SUVs, will sometimes use an auxiliary A/C zone to enhance cabin cooling, or in the case of some hybrid vehicles, to help cool the high-voltage battery. The auxiliary zone is connected in parallel to the primary zone, so it forms a second path for refrigerant to flow in the system. **Zone valves** can be used to control refrigerant flow for each zone in the system. ● SEE FIGURE 11–56.

A zone valve is a solenoid-operated flow control valve located in the liquid line after the condenser. It is controlled by an electronic control module (such as the PCM) as it responds to requests for vehicle cooling. Each zone can thus be controlled independently as cooling requirements change during vehicle operation.

In the case of the Ford Escape Hybrid, an orifice-tube system is used for the cooling of the passenger compartment (passenger zone), while a thermostatic expansion valve is used in the auxiliary A/C unit used to cool the high-voltage battery (battery zone).

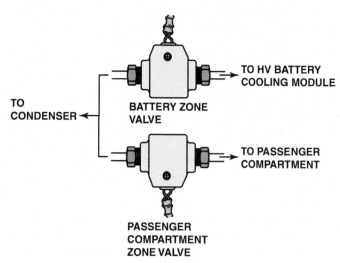

FIGURE 11–56 The battery zone valve used in the Ford Escape Hybrid will open when traction battery cooling is requested by the PCM. This can take place independent of the operation of the passenger zone valve.

EVAPORATORS The evaporator is located after the expansion device on the low-pressure side of the A/C refrigerant system. Its primary responsibility is to remove heat from the passenger compartment, but it is also tasked with reducing humidity as incoming air passes over its cool surfaces. Moisture in the air condenses on the evaporator surface, then exits the passenger compartment through a drain located beneath the evaporator housing. An added benefit is that pollen and other particulate matter will collect on the moist surface and be washed out through the **evaporator drain** with the water. Air entering the vehicle is thus conditioned for maximum passenger comfort.

An evaporator is a heat exchanger, and therefore is constructed similar to a condenser. There are two primary evaporator designs: the single pass where refrigerant flows directly from the inlet to the outlet through multiple parallel tubes, or the multipass where the tubes may weave back and forth across the evaporator. The basic design involves maximizing surface area in order to absorb as much heat as possible from the incoming air.

Many newer vehicles use cabin filters to prevent airborne particulate matter from entering the vehicle's air distribution system. This prevents the material from gathering on the evaporator and heater core, as well as removing pollen and other allergens from the passenger's breathing air. These filters need to be serviced and replaced at intervals specified by the vehicle manufacturer. ● SEE FIGURE 11–57.

NOTE: The Ford Escape Hybrid also uses a cabin filter in the auxiliary climate control (battery zone) system to prevent particulate matter from collecting on the traction battery cooling passages. ● SEE FIGURE 11–58.

REFRIGERANT LINES AND CONNECTIONS Refrigerant lines are tubes or hoses that are used to connect the various components of the A/C refrigerant system. Two major types of lines are used: rigid and flexible. Rigid lines are often made of aluminum tubing and are used to connect parts of the system that do not move relative to each other. For example,

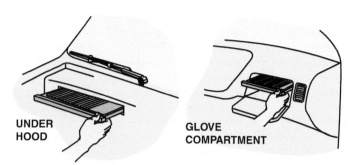

FIGURE 11–57 Cabin filters are sometimes serviced from inside the vehicle, whereas others may be accessed from under the hood.

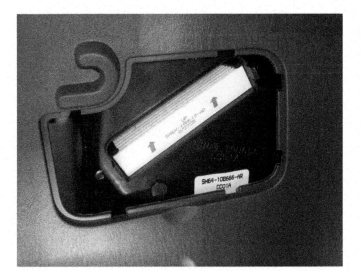

FIGURE 11–58 The battery zone filter for a Ford Escape Hybrid is located in the rear left of the vehicle's interior. This filter should be serviced regularly to prevent traction battery overheating.

? FREQUENTLY ASKED QUESTION

Does the Ford Escape Hybrid Use a Receiver-Drier for the TXV in the Battery Zone?

No. The passenger zone utilizes a fixed-orifice tube as an expansion device, as well as an accumulator at the evaporator outlet. The TXV in the battery zone does not use a receiver-drier, but does have a filter ahead of it to remove any debris from the refrigerant. This filter should be carefully inspected before replacing a suspected bad expansion valve.

the receiver-drier and the expansion valve may be connected by a rigid line because they are both mounted on the vehicle body. However, the compressor is most often mounted on the ICE, and therefore is connected to the system using flexible lines (hoses). ● SEE FIGURE 11–59.

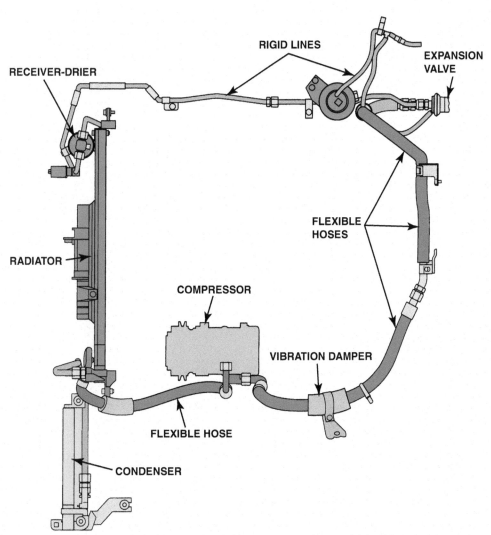

FIGURE 11–59 Flexible lines are used to attach the compressor to the remainder of the A/C system.

Flexible hoses used with R-134a systems are called **barrier hoses.** The molecules of R-134a refrigerant are smaller than those of R-12; therefore, the lining of the hose must be made of a special nylon material to prevent leakage.

When testing, recovering, or recharging the A/C system on a hybrid electric vehicle, remember that the service valves for the high and low sides of the system are different. R-134a systems use quick-disconnect fittings, with the low-side fitting made smaller than the high-side fitting to prevent the improper connection of equipment.
● **SEE FIGURE 11–60.**

FIGURE 11–60 R-134a systems use quick-disconnect fittings for the service valves. Note that this fitting is on the low side of the system and it is smaller than the fitting used on the system's high side.

SUMMARY

1. The purpose of the ICE cooling system is to bring the ICE up to optimum temperature as quickly as possible and to maintain that temperature under all operating conditions.

2. A thermostat is used to maintain the optimum coolant temperature in the ICE cooling system.

3. OAT (organic acid technology) and HOAT (hybrid organic acid technology) are two types of coolant being used in newer vehicles.

4. Electric helper pumps are used to circulate coolant in the heating system when an HEV enters idle stop mode.

5. The coolant heat storage system is used to limit vehicle emissions during cold starts.

6. The electric motors and motor electronics on a hybrid electric vehicle will often have their own liquid-cooling system.

7. Most HEVs use scroll compressors in their air conditioning systems.

8. Some HEVs use A/C compressors with electric drive or a combination belt-electric drive mechanism.

9. Nonconductive refrigeration oil is used in A/C compressors with electric drives.

10. PTC heaters are used to provide supplemental heat in HEV heating systems.

REVIEW QUESTIONS

1. What is the operation of the coolant heat storage system?

2. What is the difference between IAT and OAT/HOAT coolants?

3. Why is an HEV motor/electronics cooling system separate from that of the ICE?

4. What is the function of a PTC heater, and why is it used in an HEV heating system?

1. Coolant circulates through all of the following when the thermostat is closed, *except* _____.
   a. Heater core
   b. Radiator
   c. Water jacket
   d. Cylinder head

2. Technician A says that OAT coolants are based on propylene glycol. Technician B says that HOAT stands for hybrid organic acid technology. Which technician is correct?
   a. Technician A only
   b. Technician B only
   c. Both Technicians A and B
   d. Neither Technician A nor B

3. All of the following are examples of heat exchangers, *except* _____.
   a. Condenser
   b. Heater core
   c. Evaporator
   d. Thermostat

4. A coolant heat storage tank can keep coolant warm for a maximum of _____ day(s).
   a. One-half
   b. Two
   c. Three
   d. Four

5. The coolant heat storage system is being discussed. Technician A says that the water valve is driven by an electric motor. Technician B says that the storage tank has its own electric water pump. Which technician is correct?
   a. Technician A only
   b. Technician B only
   c. Both Technicians A and B
   d. Neither Technician A nor B

6. All of the air entering the passenger compartment must pass through the _____.
   a. Evaporator
   b. Condenser
   c. Heater core
   d. Radiator

7. Scan data indicates that the starter-generator control module (SGCM) on a GM hybrid pickup has overheated. The *least likely* cause would be _____.
   a. Low coolant level
   b. Stuck thermostat
   c. Inoperative fan
   d. Faulty electric pump

8. Technician A says that PTC heaters can be built into a conventional heater core assembly. Technician B says that a PTC heater's electrical resistance will decrease as its temperature increases. Which technician is correct?
   a. Technician A only
   b. Technician B only
   c. Both Technicians A and B
   d. Neither Technician A nor B

9. All of the following statements about hybrid electric vehicle A/C compressors are true, *except* _____.
   a. Most are reciprocating piston designs
   b. Some use a belt drive along with an electric motor
   c. Some use only an electric motor without a belt drive
   d. Nonconductive refrigeration oil must be used with A/C compressors utilizing an electric drive motor

10. A device used to turn refrigerant flow on and off in an air conditioning system with multiple evaporators is called a _____.
    a. Refrigeration switch
    b. Flow valve
    c. Zone control
    d. Zone valve

OBJECTIVES: **After studying Chapter 12, the reader will be able to:** • Identify Honda hybrid electric vehicles. • Describe how the Honda Integrated Motor Assist (IMA) system works. • Explain the precautions necessary when working on Honda hybrid electric vehicles. • Describe the features and the operational characteristics of Honda hybrid electric vehicles. • Explain the service procedures for Honda hybrid electric vehicles.

KEY TERMS: • ANC 187 • Battery module 191 • BCM 188 • CVT 187 • Generation mode 191 • Heat sink 196 • IMA 187 • IPU 189 • i-VTEC 187 • MCM 190 • MDM 189 • PCU 195 • VCM 187 • VTEC 186

BACKGROUND

2000–2006 HONDA INSIGHT The Insight prototype, by another name, was first shown to the public at the Tokyo Auto Show in 1997. It was a two-passenger sports coupe. ● **SEE FIGURE 12–1.**

It had been in development for about three years prior to that, and in 1999 it was named the Insight. First-year sales, worldwide, were limited to less than 6,000 due to lack of production capacity. Insights are made in Japan in the same small factory that builds the Acura NSX and the Honda S2000 sports vehicles. It has an all-aluminum chassis and has many high-tech features, such as low-drag aerodynamics, engine features, and hybrid software and electronics. The Insight was produced until the 2006 model year and has since been discontinued.

HONDA CIVIC HYBRID The Civic hybrid utilizes the same Civic body used for the gasoline version (also a diesel in Great Britain). Instead of building a "ground-up" chassis as in the Insight and Toyota Prius, Honda used the same unit-body with some small changes up front in motor mount locations.

The Civic hybrid uses a specially built 1.3-liter, four-cylinder gasoline engine with a chain-driven cam and Honda's **VTEC** (Variable **Valve Timing** and Lift **Electronic Control**) valve train control system. A number of different VTEC designs are used in Honda vehicles, but the version found in the 2003–2005 Civic hybrid allows three of four cylinders to be deactivated during vehicle deceleration by keeping the valves closed. This process is known as cylinder idling or valve pause. Cylinder idling reduces engine friction and pumping losses in these cylinders and thus aids in regenerative braking. Since less kinetic energy is absorbed by the ICE when the vehicle is decelerating, more energy is available for generating electricity to recharge the HV battery. ● **SEE FIGURE 12–2.**

The cylinder idling system features a two-piece rocker arm and two cam lobes for each valve. One part of the rocker arm rides on the valve-lift cam lobe and the lost motion spring, and the other part makes direct contact with the valve stem and the cylinder idle cam lobe. The cylinder idle cam lobe is not a true cam lobe as it has no lift and allows the valve to remain closed when it is being used.

During normal operation, the two pieces of the rocker arm are locked together by a piston and the valve follows the valve-lift cam lobe. The piston is moved into this default position by a return spring that is located in the cylinder idle rocker arm.

FIGURE 12–1 A first generation Honda Insight.

FIGURE 12–2 The i-VTEC on this Honda ICE is used to keep the valves closed on three of the cylinders to increase the amount of energy that can be recovered during deceleration.

During cylinder idling, oil pressure is applied to move the rocker arm piston toward the return spring and the two parts of the rocker are allowed to disconnect and operate independently. The valve then follows the cylinder idle cam lobe, which has no lift and allows the valve to remain closed. The fuel injectors are turned off to the idled cylinders, but the spark still occurs to ensure the spark plugs do not foul. ● **SEE FIGURE 12–3.**

The cylinder idling system allows the batteries to be recharged faster in stop-and-go traffic, thus contributing to greater fuel economy. Torque assist and electric power generation are both accomplished with the **Integrated Motor Assist (IMA)** motor. The IMA motor is thin and is located between the transmission and ICE. As with all hybrids, the ICE shuts off at idle and automatically starts again when the brake pedal is released.

The Civic hybrid was available with a five-speed or **CVT** transaxle until the 2005 model year. For 2006, it could only

be ordered with a CVT. Other significant changes were made for the 2006 model, including a VTEC system called **i-VTEC** (intelligent VTEC). This system allows the engine to idle on all four cylinders to allow for an all-electric cruise mode, as well as greater regenerative braking action. This system allows the engine to disengage cylinders to improve regenerative braking action. The i-VTEC system keeps both valves on three cylinders on the Accord V-6 and all four cylinders closed on the Civic four-cylinder engine. The lack of engine braking increases the amount of energy that can be captured during deceleration by the regenerative braking system. Both the Civic hybrid and the Accord hybrid use i-VTEC. This version of VTEC has great versatility as it also has a low- and high-speed valve-timing mode. ● **SEE FIGURE 12–4.**

HONDA ACCORD HYBRID The Honda Accord hybrid was released for sale in the United States in late 2004. Prior to then, all hybrids were designed to achieve high fuel economy. The Honda Accord hybrid is a V-6, which provides acceleration faster than a similar nonhybrid version and still provides increased fuel economy. The Honda Accord hybrid uses a 3.0-liter V-6 gasoline engine plus the IMA, which gives this vehicle outstanding performance.

To achieve improved fuel economy, three cylinders (the rear bank of the V-6) are deactivated by closing both valves. This is accomplished using the **Variable Cylinder Management (VCM)** system, which is another variation of VTEC. The three-cylinder mode is activated during steady-speed travel and is not noticeable to most drivers. To reduce the vibration and noise, the V-6 Accord hybrid uses two unique features:

- **Active engine mounts.** The computer-controlled engine mounts allow for engine movement without being transmitted to the body of the vehicle. The electronic mounts operate using 24 volts.

- **Active noise control (ANC).** The sound system emits sounds from the radio speakers, which are opposite in phase to the sound created by the engine when it is in the three-cylinder mode. This sound is produced whether or not the radio is on.

NOTE: A special CD to be played in the CD player is used to diagnose this system.

FIGURE 12–3 The Honda Civic hybrid engine showing the ignition and fuel system components, as well as the valve train and related components.

ROCKER ARM ASSEMBLY

CYLINDER IDLING LOBE

VALVE (CLOSED)

 **TECH TIP**

Improper Valve Clearance Can Cause a Reduction in Fuel Economy

All Honda engines use a speed-density fuel injection system to calculate airflow, called PGM-FI, or programmed fuel injection. Therefore, an improper valve clearance caused by valve and valve seat wear decreases the clearance, typically called "tight valves." This condition will cause a rich mixture as the MAP sensor voltage will be driven upward.

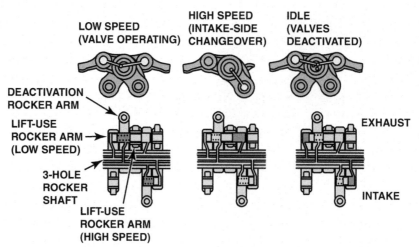

LOW SPEED (VALVE OPERATING) HIGH SPEED (INTAKE-SIDE CHANGEOVER) IDLE (VALVES DEACTIVATED)

DEACTIVATION ROCKER ARM

LIFT-USE ROCKER ARM (LOW SPEED)

3-HOLE ROCKER SHAFT

LIFT-USE ROCKER ARM (HIGH SPEED)

EXHAUST

INTAKE

FIGURE 12–4 The three modes of operation of the Civic VTEC system.

One new feature on the Honda Accord hybrid is a new air conditioning compressor that features dual scrolls. One of the scrolls is belt driven while the other has a high-voltage electric drive. During auto stop, the A/C system can now be energized without having to restart the ICE by turning on the electric drive to operate the smaller scroll in the compressor.

BODY/INTERIOR FEATURES

The dashboards on all Honda hybrids have IMA information, which shows if the system is assisting (batteries being discharged) or charging (batteries being charged). All dash displays are described in detail in the owner's manual. ● **SEE FIGURE 12–5.**

BATTERY STATE-OF-CHARGE INDICATOR. The NiMH battery state-of-charge (SOC) bar graph display represents the current state of IMA battery charge. The indicator is operated by the **battery condition monitor module (BCM),** which is responsible for calculating the battery state of charge.

The BCM maintains the IMA battery state of charge in a range of 50% to 80%, which optimizes battery life. It never allows the battery to reach 100% charge or 100% discharge. When the BCM has determined that the battery should not be charged any more, the display shows full charge. When the BCM will not let the IMA battery discharge any further, the display indicates a zero charge. The display provides the driver with information about the amount of electrical assist available at any time.

NOTE: The display is not linear. As with many fuel level gauges, the top half of the display range covers considerably more than the lower half of the capacity range.

UPSHIFT/DOWNSHIFT INDICATOR. On a manual transaxle Insight, there is an upshift indicator that will illuminate when better fuel economy can be achieved by shifting up to a higher gear.

The downshift indicator will illuminate when the Insight is unable to maintain the current speed, even with full assist. This light will sometimes illuminate when climbing steep hills at highway speeds. When driving in less hilly areas, this light may never illuminate at all.

ODOMETER/TRIP METER/FUEL EFFICIENCY METER. In the center of the instrument display, below the digital speedometer display, is the combination odometer/fuel economy meter.

Average fuel economy is shown and is updated once per minute. The dash display on an Insight also includes the odometer/trip distance display. The driver can select the lifetime odometer for the vehicle, or switch between three resetable trip meters: "Trip A," "Trip B," or "Segment." The average mileage display always shows the average for the distance that is selected. If trip meter A is selected, for example, the average mileage is shown for that trip. "Segment" mode is toggled on and off by touching the FCD button. The current segment is reset by pressing and holding the FCD button while in "Segment" mode. The normal mode display can be switched between the odometer and the two trip meters by pressing the Trip button.

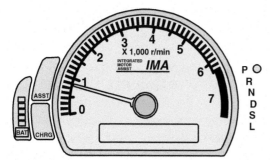

FIGURE 12–5 The dash display on a Honda Civic hybrid.

 **TECH TIP**

Online Owner's Manual

If an owner's manual is not with a Honda vehicle, go to *https://techinfo.honda.com*. Starting with model year 1990, owner's manuals are in a PDF format and are available for free. First responder information is also available at this URL.

A bar graph shows the instantaneous fuel economy, which changes in real time based on the amount of fuel that the fuel injectors are currently delivering, as well as the current vehicle speed.

When the speedometer is set to mph, odometer/trip meter distances are displayed in miles and fuel efficiency is displayed in miles per gallon. When the speedometer is set to km/h, odometer/trip meter distances are displayed in kilometers, and fuel efficiency is displayed in liters per 100 km.

Both the instantaneous bar graph and the average fuel efficiency number can be turned off. To turn off the bar graph, press and hold the FCD button until the bar and the legend disappear. To turn off the numerical average, press and hold the FCD button again, until that disappears.

ENGINE STATUS METER. The right circle on the dashboard shows information on the gasoline engine status, including gasoline engine warning lights, coolant temperature, tachometer, and idle stop indicator.

IDLE STOP INDICATOR. When the Insight goes into auto idle stop mode, a green "Auto Stop" LED at the base of the tachometer illuminates to indicate that the engine is not moving at all, and to remind the driver that the vehicle is still in the "on" mode.

SPEEDOMETER. The speedometer reads the current speed in either kilometers per hour or miles per hour. Speed is displayed both when the vehicle is moving both forward and backward. Speeds as slow as 1 mph will register on the speedometer.

DRIVING EXPERIENCE When driving a 5-speed Honda Civic for the first time, notice the silent starting of the ICE, busy dashboard readouts, and the engine shutting off at idle. Honda has tried to make its hybrid Civic work like the traditional Civic in many ways. The 5-speed shift handles very well, and with the exception of a lack of a fold-down rear seat, it handles people and cargo in an efficient way considering its size. When accelerating up a hill, the ICE usually requires third or fourth gear.

2006+ HONDA CIVIC MODES OF OPERATION

- Vehicle stationary
  - The ICE is turned off and fuel consumption is zero.

 REAL WORLD FIX

The One-Cylinder Civic Story

If a Civic hybrid will not idle, is running on only one cylinder, and that cylinder is number 1, a problem in the cylinder idling system should be considered. If the oil level in the crank case is very low (usually caused by an oil change mistake), the cylinder idling system can be "electrically stuck." To fix this problem, locate the source of the oil leak (double-gasket oil filter, perhaps?), add oil, clear any trouble codes with a scan tool, and then compression will be back in all four cylinders.

- Start-up and acceleration
  - The ICE operates in low-speed valve-timing mode with motor assist.
- Rapid acceleration
  - The ICE operates in high-speed valve-timing mode with motor assist.
- Low-speed cruising
  - The valves of all four of the engine's cylinders can be closed and combustion halted; the electric motor alone can power the vehicle.
- Gentle acceleration and high-speed cruising
  - The engine operating in low-speed valve-timing mode powers the vehicle.
- Deceleration
  - The valves of all four of the engine's cylinders are closed and combustion is halted. The IMA motor recovers a significant portion of the energy normally lost during deceleration and stores it in the battery. ●**SEE FIGURE 12–6.**

IMA OPERATION Honda's hybrid system is known as IMA (Integrated Motor Assist). IMA is a parallel-hybrid configuration that uses a motor-generator located between the ICE and the transmission. The IMA motor is an AC synchronous electric machine that can provide torque assist for moving the vehicle or generate electricity for recharging the HV battery module. All of the electronics for this system are located at the rear of the vehicle, with three power cables running between the IMA motor and the **intelligent power unit (IPU).** ●**SEE FIGURE 12–7.**

START-UP. Under most conditions, Honda hybrid engines are started by the IMA motor, which instantly spins the engine to 1,000 RPM.

Honda hybrids also use a conventional 12-volt auxiliary starter motor that is used in the following situations:

- The state of charge of the battery module is too low.
- The ambient temperature is too high or too low, usually below 0°F or over 115°F.
- There is a failure of the IMA system and the IMA light is commanded on.
- A technician has turned off the master switch in the hatch area.

When any of these conditions exist, the vehicle will not enter idle stop mode. In the last two examples, any further restarts will continue to use the 12-volt starter. In the case of the first two examples, if the HV battery SOC is raised or ambient air heats up or cools down, the IMA motor will once again be the default for start up. ●**SEE FIGURE 12–8.**

ACCELERATION. During acceleration and other high-load conditions, such as climbing a hill, current from the battery module is converted to alternating current by the **MDM (motor drive module)** and supplied to the IMA motor, which

SPEED

TIME

START-UP AND ACCELERATION	GENTLE ACCELERATION	LOW-SPEED CRUISING	ACCELERATION	RAPID ACCELERATION	HIGH-SPEED CRUISING	DECELERATION
ENGINE PLUS MOTOR	ENGINE	MOTOR	ENGINE PLUS MOTOR	ENGINE PLUS MOTOR	ENGINE	
VALVE TIMING FOR LOW ENGINE SPEED		ALL-CYLINDER DEACTIVATION	VALVE TIMING FOR LOW ENGINE SPEED	VALVE TIMING FOR HIGH ENGINE SPEED	VALVE TIMING FOR LOW ENGINE SPEED	ALL-CYLINDER DEACTIVATION
ASSIST			ASSIST	ASSIST		
CHRG ASST	CHRG ASST	CHRG ASST	CHRG ASST	CHRG ASST	CHRG ASST	CHRG ASST

FIGURE 12–6 The modes of operation of the Honda Civic hybrid and the assist and charging symbols displayed on the dash.

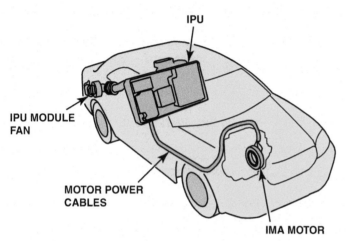

FIGURE 12–7 Major components of the Honda IMA system.

IPU

IPU MODULE FAN

MOTOR POWER CABLES

IMA MOTOR

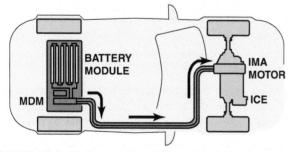

FIGURE 12–8 Under most conditions, the IMA motor is used to start the ICE.

BATTERY MODULE

MDM

IMA MOTOR

ICE

then functions as a motor. Both the gasoline engine and the electric motor work together to maximize vehicle acceleration. ● **SEE FIGURE 12–9.**

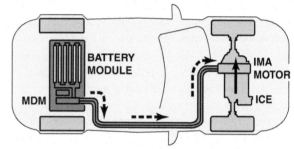

FIGURE 12–9 During acceleration, the battery module provides electrical energy to the IMA motor to help accelerate the vehicle.

BATTERY MODULE

MDM

IMA MOTOR

ICE

The amount of electric motor assist will vary depending on the load and throttle position. Under light acceleration the electric motor only operates at partial assist, while under heavy acceleration the electric motor operates at its full capacity. Maximum electric power from the motor is about 100 amps at 144 volts. After about 7 seconds, the **motor control module (MCM)** will reduce the available current to 50 amperes to reduce heat build-up of the motor. The instrument display will indicate the degree of assist on the assist/charge gauge.

During acceleration, the 12-volt electrical system is fed power from the battery module (via the DC-DC converter), and the 12-volt battery is charged as necessary.

When the HV battery state of charge (SOC) is very low, but not at the minimum level, assist will only be available during wide-open-throttle acceleration. When the remaining state of charge is reduced to the minimum level, no assist will be provided. Instead, the IMA system will generate energy to supply the 12-volt system and slow charge the NiMH battery pack. The vehicle will be low on power at this time, but on wide-open throttle, the background charging will stop to maximize the gasoline engine output available for acceleration.

CRUISE. When a Honda hybrid is cruising at a constant speed and the battery module state of charge is relatively low, some engine output is used by the IMA motor-generator being operated in **generation mode** to charge the **battery module.** Some of this energy will be delivered to the 12-volt accessories, using the DC-DC converter, as necessary. In this state, the instrument display will show partial charging on the charge/assist gauge.

When under cruise conditions, and when the high-voltage battery is sufficiently charged, the IMA motor-generator continues to turn, but only a small amount of electricity is still generated. This electricity will be used to supply the 12-volt accessories, and any excess energy will be used to slowly charge the battery module. In this state, the instrument display will show no charging on the charge/assist gauge.

During fuel-cut mode, the IMA motor-generator is operated in generation mode. In this mode, the IMA motor is driven by the wheels, generating electricity to be stored in the battery module, and slowing the vehicle in the process. **● SEE FIGURE 12–10.**

The amount that the IMA motor slows the vehicle is in proportion to the amount of regeneration being done. There are two deceleration modes:

- **Foot off the throttle, but not on the brake pedal.** In this mode, the charge/assist gauge will show partial charge, and the vehicle will slow down gradually.

- **Foot on the brake pedal.** In this mode, a higher amount of regeneration will be allowed, and the vehicle will slow more rapidly. During light brake pedal application, only the IMA motor-generator is slowing the vehicle. With heavier brake pedal application, the conventional friction brakes also come into play.

When decelerating, regeneration will continue until engine speed falls to about 1000 RPM. In many cases, the gasoline engine will now immediately enter auto idle stop mode. If vehicle speed is such that it is not clear whether the driver will most likely come to a stop, the engine may idle for a few moments before entering idle stop. If the battery state

of charge is very low, idle stop will not be entered at all, and instead the engine will continue to run at a fast idle to recharge the battery module.

During generation, the alternating current produced by the IMA motor-generator is converted by the MDM into DC, which is used to charge the battery module. The DC output of the MDM is also applied to the DC-DC converter, which reduces the voltage to 12 volts. The output of the DC-DC converter is used to supply the 12-volt needs of the vehicle electrical system and is used to charge the 12-volt battery as necessary.

When the state of charge of the battery module approaches 80%, generated electricity is only delivered to the 12-volt accessory system.

When an antilock braking event occurs, the regenerative mode is immediately canceled by the MCM (motor control module). The ABS computer communicates with the MDM during ABS events. The regeneration process is stopped immediately to prevent interference with the ABS system.

This is a different mode from idle stop mode because the engine (and by extension any engine-driven accessories, such as the air conditioning compressor) is continuing to be turned by the wheels. In idle stop mode, the engine is not operating.

Fuel-cut mode will occur when the engine speed is above 1,100 RPM. If the engine speed falls below 1,100 RPM, fuel will be supplied to prevent the engine from stalling when the driver releases the clutch.

IDLE STOP MODE. To prevent unnecessary fuel use and exhaust emissions, the gasoline engine is turned off when there is no need for propulsion or air conditioning.

When the vehicle speed drops below 19 mph (30 km/h), idle stop mode will typically be triggered, and the gasoline engine will stop turning. The engine will typically remain off until the transmission is put into first gear to begin accelerating again. Restart is performed using the IMA motor, instantly and silently.

CONDITIONS FOR ENGINE SHUTDOWN. While reducing vehicle speed, the engine stops itself automatically under these conditions:

- The vehicle speed is less than 19 mph (30 km/h) and the brake pedal is pressed.

- The transmission is in any gear, except first, before slowing down.

- The clutch is disengaged or neutral position is now selected.

- The engine speed is less than 1,000 RPM.

If the brake pedal is released while the vehicle is slowing down, the engine starts again instantly, unless vehicle speed is below a certain speed. Even in this case, the engine will be restarted if a gear is selected or the gas pedal is touched.

Idle stop will not take place during the following conditions:

- The engine has not yet had time to warm up and achieve closed loop.

- The transmission is in reverse gear.

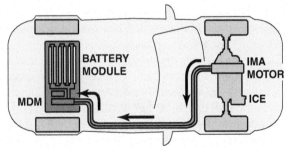

FIGURE 12–10 During deceleration, the IMA converts kinetic energy into electrical energy for recharging the HV battery pack.

When Is the Backup Starter Used?

Under normal conditions, the IMA motor acts as the starter motor for the ICE. If a failure or complete discharge of the high-voltage battery pack occurs, a backup starter is used. The backup unit is a conventional starter motor with an auxiliary 12-volt battery and is used to crank the engine when the air temperature is very cold. The starter motor rotates the engine at about 200 to 250 RPM compared to the integrated motor generator, which rotates the engine at about 1,000 RPM. The fast rotation of the internal combustion engines at cold temperatures could cause engine damage to the ICE due to a lack of lubrication.

FIGURE 12–11 Instrument display on a Civic hybrid, which shows the auto stop light.

- The battery module is not charged sufficiently to restart the engine using the IMA motor.
- If the IMA-ECU detects stop-and-go traffic conditions (for example, if the transmission has not been shifted out of first gear since the vehicle was last stopped).

Also, climate control mode will affect whether or not idle stop is performed. When "Auto mode" is selected, the engine will be allowed to continue running to operate the air conditioning compressor. If "Econ mode" is selected, idle stop may occur, possibly causing the air conditioning compressor to temporarily stop. 2006 and newer models are equipped with a dual-drive A/C compressor that enables A/C operation during idle stop.

AIR CONDITIONING INTERACTION WITH IDLE STOP MODE. The driver can control whether air conditioning or idle stop mode should be given higher priority. When the climate control system is set in full-auto mode, idle stop will not take place if the system wishes to run the air conditioning compressor. When the climate control system is set to "Econ" mode, the system will function normally, except that idle stop will only take place if the cabin temperature has stabilized at the set temperature.

In addition to choosing between Econ and Auto mode, the driver can also leave the blower fan speed set to automatic mode or set a specific fan speed. With automatic fan speed mode, the system will turn off the fan during idle stop mode. If a specific fan speed is set, the fan will continue to run at that speed during idle stop. ● **SEE FIGURE 12–11**, which shows the dash when idle stop (auto stop) has occurred.

The climate control is thermostatically controlled. The driver simply selects the desired temperature, and the climate control system will automatically adjust the mixture of cold and hot air and fan speed to maintain this temperature. To do this, the climate control system uses an interior temperature sensor located below the stereo controls, and a sunlight sensor located on the dashboard at the base of the windshield.

NOTE: Some 2000 Insights were shipped to the United States without air conditioning. Model year 2001 and newer Insights have climate control as standard equipment, because the air conditioning system helps in cooling the NiMH battery pack in hot climates.

CONDITIONS FOR ENGINE RESTART. The engine is restarted when:

- A gear is selected with the clutch disengaged.
- The brake pedal is released during deceleration.
- The accelerator pedal is depressed with the clutch disengaged and/or the transmission's neutral position is selected.
- The master brake booster vacuum becomes low.
- The battery module's remaining charge decreases to a certain level with the clutch disengaged and/or the transmission's neutral position is selected.

POWERTRAIN FEATURES

The Honda Insight was available with two transmissions:

- A conventional 5-speed manual transmission
- A continuously variable transaxle (CVT) called Honda Multimatic

The CVT transmission used in the Insight is very similar to the CVT transmission that Honda has used in other vehicles, including the Civic HX in the United States.

One of the features of the Honda Multimatic is that it does not use a torque converter, but instead uses a multilayered clutch called a Driven-Shaft-Placed Acceleration Clutch (also known as the *start clutch*). ● **SEE FIGURE 12–12.**

Honda designed a modest amount of "creep," into the operation of the Multimatic which is the slight forward movement a vehicle with an automatic transmission has in drive unless the brake pedal is depressed. Most automatic transmission users have grown accustomed to "creep," and this gives the standard

(a) **(b)**

FIGURE 12–12 (a) The Honda Civic CVT uses a metal drive chain that operates between two cones called a variator. These two cones have a very smooth surface and can be damaged if dirt gets into one of the units. (b) The Honda Civic hybrid CVT transaxle uses a start clutch rather than a torque converter. Because the torque converter, which normally drives a pump to supply hydraulic fluid to the components is not used, the Honda Civic CVT unit uses a chain-driven pump driven by the input shaft.

advantages of an automatic transmission when parking, as well as starting from a dead-stop on hills.

The Multimatic has the ability to stay in the same power band if and when needed. An example of this is the ability to remain in the high-RPM power band from a standstill to high speed. Because of this, full-throttle acceleration is equivalent to that of a manual transmission. In addition, when traveling at high speeds, because of its ability to infinitely adjust gear ratios, the Multimatic has more passing ability than the manual transmission and the conventional automatic transmission, using torque converters. The CVT unit can also be shifted to low ("L") to increase engine RPM and enhance its braking action.

GASOLINE ENGINE FEATURES The Honda three-cylinder Insight and the four-cylinder Civic use a crankshaft with an axis offset 14 mm, relative to the cylinder-bore axis, so that the crankshaft does not sit directly under the cylinder. This minimizes friction from the side thrust of the pistons against the cylinder walls, just after top-dead-center, as each piston begins its descent on the firing stroke. Honda claims this reduces internal friction by as much as 3%.

NO_X REDUCTION CATALYST SYSTEM. The Honda Insight is designed to operate at a very lean air–fuel ratio during light-throttle cruise conditions. The mixture can be as lean as 23:1 if conditions allow. This provides very good fuel economy, and low HC and CO emissions. However, the lean mixture also causes a rise in combustion temperature, and high NO_X production is the result. In order to prevent high NO_X tailpipe emissions during lean-burn operation, the Insight uses a dual-catalyst system that includes an extra NO_X storage and a special NO_X reduction catalyst. The three-way catalyst is closely coupled to the exhaust manifold to minimize light-off time, thus reducing emissions after a cold start.

The lean NO_X catalyst is in the conventional location underneath the vehicle.

The lean NO_X catalytic converter is comprised of a ceramic substrate, a platinum (Pt) catalyzing surface, and a titanium-sodium (Ti-Na) NO_X storage surface.

During lean-burn operation, the exhaust gas contains a larger percentage of oxygen (O_2) and NO_X; the NO_X is primarily nitrogen monoxide (NO). The platinum catalyzes the O_2 and NO to produce nitrogen dioxide (NO_2), which is able to be stored on the Ti-Na surface.

When the PCM determines that the Ti-Na surface is saturated, the PCM temporarily richens the air–fuel mixture, which decreases the NO_X and O_2 in the exhaust, and raises the levels of hydrocarbons (HC) and carbon monoxide (CO). The platinum is then able to use the HC and CO to reduce the NO_2 (that has been stored) into harmless nitrogen gas (N_2), carbon dioxide (CO_2), and water vapor (H_2O).

LAF (LEAN AIR–FUEL) SENSOR. A standard zirconia oxygen sensor is only capable of measuring the oxygen content of the exhaust in a narrow air–fuel mixture range, right around stoichiometric (14.7:1). However, when the engine is running in the lean-burn mode, the oxygen content of the exhaust is higher than a normal oxygen sensor is capable of measuring.

The Honda Insight and many other Honda engines use a linear air–fuel (LAF) sensor for the primary oxygen sensor that is capable of measuring air–fuel ratios as lean as 25:1. This LAF sensor is really two oxygen sensors in one. This allows the ECM to maintain precise control over the mixture during both normal and lean burn conditions. The electronic control module uses this data, along with engine speed, crankshaft angle, throttle angle, coolant temperature, and valve position, to maintain a lean air–fuel ratio below 2500 to 3200 RPM (depending on throttle position and engine load).

The VTEC-E engine can burn such a lean mixture partly because of a swirl created in the combustion chamber, created by the air–fuel entering through only one of two intake valves during low-RPM operation.

A standard zirconia oxygen sensor uses a thimble-shaped zirconia element that is exposed to the atmosphere on one side, and to the exhaust stream on the other side. If the amount of oxygen on the two sides is different, it generates a voltage. Since the amount of oxygen on the atmospheric side is fixed, the generated voltage represents the amount of oxygen in the exhaust. With the engine not running, there is atmospheric air in the exhaust, and the oxygen sensor voltage is zero since the same amount of oxygen exists on both sides of the element. When the engine is running, there is less oxygen in the exhaust, so voltage is generated up to a maximum of 1 volt.

The LAF sensor has two zirconia elements that share a diffusion chamber. There are a total of three chambers:

- Exhaust flow chamber
- Diffusion chamber
- Atmosphere reference chamber

The zirconia element that is in contact with the exhaust is the sensor element. The diffusion chamber is the space between the two zirconia elements. By applying varying voltage to the control element, the ECM can control the amount of oxygen in the diffusion chamber. Since the diffusion chamber is the reference chamber for the sensor element, this action changes the output of the sensor element.

The ECM monitors the output of the sensor element as the oxygen content of the exhaust changes, and it applies voltage to the element to try to maintain the sensor output at 0.450 volts. The ECM then monitors the control voltage to determine the actual air–fuel ratio.

Unlike a conventional sensor, the voltage can be positive or negative, and it reads the opposite direction. That is, positive voltage indicates a lean mixture, and negative voltage indicates a rich mixture. The normal operating range is about 1.5 volts.
● **SEE FIGURE 12–13**.

TECH TIP

If a LAF Sensor Code, Replace the Sensor First

The sensor will set a code when it is slow to react to a command from the PCM. When a code is set for this sensor (not the sensor circuit or a lean/rich condition), it is usually the sensor itself that has failed. This will save some time normally spent following the prescribed testing procedures.

The LAF sensor can be identified by its five-wire connectors:

- Heater positive
- Heater ground
- Sensor element positive
- Control element positive
- Sensor element ground

HIGH-VOLTAGE BATTERY MODULE. The battery pack uses nickel metal hydride (NiMH) technology for high-energy density and long service life.

The battery pack is manufactured by Panasonic EV Energy and weighs only 48 lbs (22 kg). Its operating temperature range is −22°F to +140°F (−30°C to +60°C).

The battery pack, sometimes called the *battery module,* is constructed in a modular form. ● **SEE FIGURE 12–14**. The individual NiMH cells are the same size as standard D-cell flashlight batteries. Constructing the module from standard-sized cells helped to ensure cost-effectiveness.

NOTE: The battery module is only available as a complete assembly.

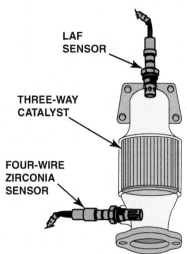

FIGURE 12–13 The upstream oxygen sensor is a lean air–fuel ratio (LAF) sensor on this Honda Accord V-6, whereas the downstream is a conventional zirconia four-wire heated oxygen sensor.

FIGURE 12–14 The view of the battery pack and the electronic assemblies after removing the rear seat and the steel panel.

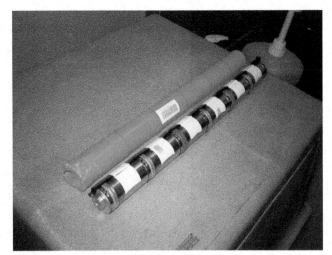

FIGURE 12–15 One six-cell segment of the battery module. The protective plastic covering has been removed. The thin strip taped alongside the batteries is a temperature sensor used by the battery condition monitor to help determine charging and discharging rate based on the temperature of the batteries. While this sensor cannot detect a failure in any one battery, it is capable of detecting a fault in a single strip of batteries.

● **SEE FIGURE 12–15,** which shows the arrangement of these cells, which are grouped together in sealed *packages of six cells each*, positioned end-to-end. The arrangement is 6 cells across by 3 cells high by 7 cells deep, with the rearmost row being only 2 cells high, for a total of 120 cells.

The cells each have a voltage of 1.2 volt, and are connected in series for a battery module terminal voltage of 144 volts. The rated capacity of the battery module is 6.5 ampere-hours (Ah), resulting in a storage capacity of 0.936 kW.

NOTE: The 2006 Honda Civic battery module operates at 158 volts. This is achieved by using 132 1.2-volt "D" NiMH batteries instead of just 120 cells and 144 volts, as used in most other Honda hybrid electric vehicles.

CAUTION: If battery module service is required, refer to the service information because serious injury or even death can occur if high-voltage safety precautions are not observed. High-voltage wires and cables are covered with orange plastic shielding or tape. Never casually handle any orange wiring or the component connected to it!

The battery module is used to supply the high voltage to the IMA motor during the assist mode and on start up in most conditions. The battery module is also used to store the regenerated power in the cruising, deceleration, and braking modes. Battery module energy is also used to charge the conventional 12-volt battery, using the DC-DC converter. The 12-volt battery is a conventional flooded-cell design and is located in the engine compartment.

The battery module cell groups are connected in series to the terminal plate, located on the side of the battery module.

The battery module contains 10 voltage sensors and 4 temperature sensors that send data to the battery condition monitor (BCM).

The battery module uses "cabin air" to dissipate the heat produced by the NiMH cells. A two-speed cooling fan is located in front of the battery module and draws air past the NiMH cells to aid in cooling of the high-voltage batteries. An inlet behind the passenger seats is the inlet for cool air.
● **SEE FIGURES 12–16 AND 12–17.**

HYBRID CONTROLS

LOCATION AND FUNCTION OF HYBRID COMPONENTS. The **power control unit (PCU)** works with the ECU to control the idle stop feature and to regulate the flow of energy between the battery pack and the electric motor. Two computerized control units, the electric motor control and charging control, are mounted on the top of the battery module box. Beneath the control units is a pack of 120 NiMH D-cells and to the left of the NiMH battery pack is the PCU and the DC-to-AC inverter, which supplies three-phase AC to the electric motor. Two fans, one for the NiMH battery and the other for cooling of the DC-DC converter and inverter, are installed. Cabin air is brought in behind the passenger seat through a vent to keep things cool. The compartment behind the seats is known as the intelligent power unit (IPU). The IPU compartment contains the following components:

FIGURE 12–16 The battery, as well as the electronics, are cooled through this vent on a Honda Civic hybrid. Blocking the airflow through this vent could cause serious damage to the hybrid system and would likely cause the setting of a diagnostic trouble code.

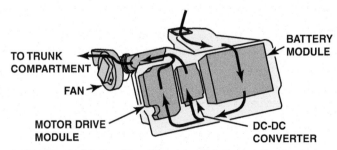

FIGURE 12–17 Cooling airflow through the intelligent power unit (IPU) of a Honda Civic hybrid.

Keep the HV Battery Module Charged

When the vehicle is stored for a long period, the IMA battery will gradually discharge and must be charged periodically (Honda says every month). If the vehicle cannot be driven (not registered), maintain the NiMH battery by following this procedure:

1. Remove the 40A EPS Fuse (No. 15) from the underhood fuse box in the engine compartment, and then start the engine. The EPS warning light on the dashboard will illuminate because the EPS fuse is missing. This does not indicate a system fault. The warning light will go off when the EPS fuse is reinstalled.
2. Run the engine at 3500 RPM for 5–10 minutes. Be careful NOT to run the vehicle in an enclosed area. Monitor the IMA battery level gauge for movement indicating its charging process.
3. The procedure is complete when the IMA battery level gauge shows a full charge. This can happen in as little as 15 minutes.
4. After shutting off the ignition, reinstall the 40A EPS fuse in its original position (No. 15).
5. Repeat monthly or as needed.

- **The motor control module (MCM).** This is the metal box located in the upper right corner, which controls when the motor operates in assist or regeneration mode, and controls the degree of assist/regeneration.
- **The battery condition module (BCM).** This is a metal box (computer) to the left of the MCM, just right of center. This tracks the battery state of charge and decides how much energy can be supplied to or delivered from the battery.
- **The battery module.** Located below the MCM and BCM, this is the Insight's 144-volt primary battery pack.
- The battery module cooling fan is located in the right rear of the IPU. This two-speed fan draws air from the cabin, behind the right seat, and pulls it through the battery pack.
- **The motor drive module (MDM).** This is the component located in the left corner of the IPU. The MDM contains the switching electronics used to bi-directionally and directionally send power between the battery module and the IMA motor based on instructions provided to it by the duel MCM.
- **Heat sink.** This is a square metal box, made of magnesium to save weight, located next to the MDM, that absorbs and dissipates heat produced by the MDM and DC-DC converter. ● **SEE FIGURE 12–18.**
- **DC-DC converter.** Located to the right of the heat sink, the DC-DC converter converts the 144-volt power

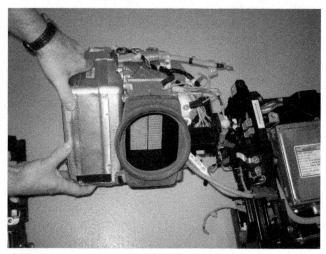

FIGURE 12–18 The heat sink can be seen through the opening where cabin air is drawn through the unit by a fan.

supplied by the IMA motor and/or battery module into 12 volts to supply the Insight's conventional 12-volt accessories.

- **Power control unit (PCU).** The MDM, heat sink, and DC-DC converter are collectively known as the power control unit.
- **PCU cooling fan.** This is located in front of the heat sink, and draws air through the heat sink to aid in cooling of the PCU.
- **Junction board.** This is a black component, located beside the DC-DC converter, and is actually part of the battery module assembly. ● **SEE FIGURE 12–19.**

Power is carried between the components in the IPU compartment behind the seats and the IMA electric motor under the hood by three orange cables that run below the floor, under the left seat.

FIGURE 12–19 The entire Honda Insight hybrid IPU assembly is shown removed and placed on the floor.

THE IMA MOTOR The 10-kilowatt, permanent magnet, brushless electric motor is mounted between the engine and the transmission. It is small and thin, measuring 2.3 inches thick and about 16 inches in diameter, but provides up to 25 pound-feet of torque. ● **SEE FIGURE 12–20.**

A power control unit (PCU) regulates the charging and conditioning of the battery pack.

The IMA motor serves a number of functions:

- It assists in vehicle propulsion when needed, allowing the use of a smaller internal combustion engine.

- It operates as a generator, allowing excess energy (such as during braking) to be used to recharge the IMA battery module, and later to be used to provide assist.

- It takes the place of the conventional alternator, providing energy that ultimately feeds the conventional 12-volt electrical system.

- It is used to start the internal combustion engine very quickly and quietly. This allows the internal combustion engine to be turned off when not needed, without any delay in restarting on demand.

- It is used to dampen crankshaft speed variations, leading to smoother idle.

The IMA motor is located between the internal combustion engine (ICE) and clutch, drive plate, or torque converter. One end of the IMA motor rotor is bolted to the ICE crankshaft, and the other end of the rotor is bolted to the flywheel.

The flywheel retains gear teeth for the backup 12-volt starter motor to mesh with when it is engaged. In manual transmission Insights, as with other manual transmission vehicles, the flywheel also serves as a surface for the clutch. The IMA motor is a permanent-magnet brushless motor. The only moving part in this type of motor, the rotor, consists of permanent magnets mounted on the circumference of the rotor assembly. The electromagnets are located around the perimeter of the stator. There are several key features of this type of motor:

- The electromagnets are located around the outside and therefore can be cooled by conduction to the motor casing, requiring no airflow inside the motor for cooling.

- Commutation (switching current between different sets of electromagnets to produce rotation) is not accomplished by a physical switching, such as brushes. Instead, the switching is accomplished by the motor drive module. This allows electronic control over torque and magnetic field slip angle, which makes it easy to operate the motor as a generator. The torque is related to the amount of current supplied to the motor and the speed is proportional to the frequency of the alternating current supplied to the motor.

12-VOLT BATTERY The 12-volt battery is located under the hood and is a conventional lead–acid design. The 12-volt battery has three functions:

1. Provide power to the onboard computers so that memory is kept alive.

2. Provide a capacitor of sorts for the DC-DC converter that allows for 12 volts (actually about 13.7 volts) of power to be available during idle stop mode.

3. Provide power to the backup 12-volt starter.

Normal jump starting procedures can be used, as well as typical charging methods. ● **SEE FIGURE 12–21**

ELECTRIC POWER STEERING The electric power steering (EPS) system on the Honda hybrid vehicle offers many advantages over conventional hydraulic systems. The pump, hydraulic fluid, and hoses are all eliminated, and because the engine is not constantly driving the pump, power losses are eliminated and fuel economy increases. The system is also simpler and more compact. ● **SEE FIGURE 12–22.**

The EPS consists of a rack-and-pinion gear with a microprocessor-controlled coaxial electric motor assisting the pinion. The microprocessor senses vehicle speed and steering torque and is programmed to vary the assist accordingly. Self-diagnosis and failure warning functions are built into the EPS system, and a factory scan tool via the OBD-II connector provides data and codes.

FIGURE 12–21 The conventional 12-volt battery is located under the hood on Honda hybrid vehicles.

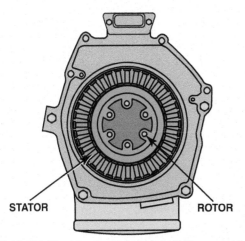

STATOR   ROTOR

FIGURE 12–20 The Honda Civic hybrid IMA assembly.

FIGURE 12–22 A cutaway of a Honda electric power steering assembly.

 FREQUENTLY ASKED QUESTION

When Was the First Honda Electric Power Steering Used?

Honda sold the Acura NSX sports vehicle with an automatic transmission in 1993, equipped with a 12-volt electric power steering (EPS). It is becoming a mainstream technology, used on many nonhybrid vehicles.

The steering rack, electric drive, and tie rods are all mounted high on the bulkhead and steer the wheels via steering links on each front suspension strut.

When replacing the rack or steering column, a scan tool must be used to reset to "zero" so that the EPS processor knows where to start providing assist.

AUXILIARY HEATER PUMP The Insight does not utilize an electric pump for circulating hot coolant. In cold weather, if the climate control is used, the gasoline engine stays running to provide circulation to the heater core. Later models of the Civic and Accord hybrid utilize "helper pumps" to circulate coolant through the heater core during auto idle stop.

SAFETY PROCEDURES

SAFETY DEVICES Honda hybrids have a computer-controlled system that will disconnect the HV battery pack from the rest of the vehicle in the event of a problem that would allow high voltage to contact anything that was unintended. To accomplish this, the hybrid computer will instantly disconnect the 12-volt power source to the two contactors in the event of an airbag deployment. By interrupting the power to the contactors,

the 144-volt supply is cut off. This same process is initiated anytime a short-to-ground is determined at a high-voltage cable or source. This is continuously monitored by the hybrid computer.

DEPOWERING THE HIGH-VOLTAGE SYSTEM There are four simple steps to ensuring that the system is safe to work on:

STEP 1 Remove the ignition key.

STEP 2 Remove the back seat cushions.

STEP 3 Remove the two bolts holding the oval cover.

STEP 4 Remove the red plastic retainer and turn the switch to off; replace the red plastic retainer on the switch.

Even though these steps have been taken, do not assume that every vehicle will power down properly. Always wear high-voltage linesman's gloves with leather protectors, as well as approved eye protection, when working around high-voltage systems. Before disconnecting a high-voltage part or connector, use a CAT III meter and test for zero volts. As long as testing for high voltage is done prior to disassembly, a high level of safety can be maintained.

SERVICE FEATURES

UNIQUE SPARK PLUGS The NGK spark plug number ILZFR5A-11 is specially built for the Insight. They are indexed, meaning the ground electrode is positioned for good intake flow. After the cylinder head is machined, a stamping with an A, B, C, or D is made near each spark plug hole to indicate which spark plug should be installed. Spark plugs have an A, B, C, or D stamped on the top of each plug that matches up to the markings on the head. ● **SEE FIGURE 12–23.** These plugs are

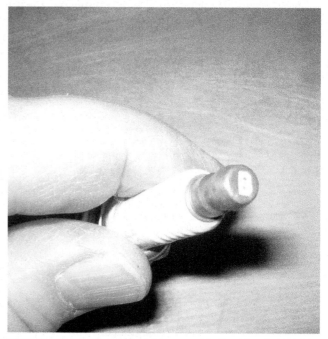

FIGURE 12–23 The spark plugs used in the Honda Insight are indexed and labeled with a letter on the top.

iridium tipped and expected life is over 100,000 miles. Gap is set at 0.040 inch. Iridium is a very soft metal, and re-gapping a used spark plug is not recommended.

 FREQUENTLY ASKED QUESTION

What Is an Electronic Balance Shaft?

A unique feature of the IMA system is the use of the electric motor to dampen engine vibration by application of reverse torque to the crankshaft. The reverse torque pulses are exactly in phase and opposite the 60-degree torque fluctuations of the gasoline engine. As a result, the Insight's IMA gasoline engine is remarkably smooth throughout its operating range. Think of this as an electronic balance shaft. If something goes wrong with this electronic balance shaft, the engine will have a vibration that may be hard to find.

 TECH TIP

Compression Test Procedure

Use the 12-volt mode, by switching off the high-voltage (HV) switch, for compression tests or any time the engine should be cranked at low RPMs. Honda hybrids have a conventional starter and a small 12-volt battery as a backup in case the Integrated Motor Assist (IMA) system fails or the 144-volt battery pack goes dead. The Insight can be jump started but NOT push started with a dead battery. Note: When in 12-volt mode, the 12-volt battery is NOT being charged by the IMA and DC-DC converter.

 REAL WORLD FIX

The Jacket Story

A DTC for an overheated inverter was retrieved when a customer arrived at the shop because the check engine light (MIL) was on. A heavy winter jacket was draped over the passenger seat and then the seat was pushed to its most rearward position. The jacket blocked the flow of air to the electrical compartment and a code was set for an overheated inverter. The jacket was removed, the code was cleared, and all was well.

 REAL WORLD FIX

Customer Complaint Is "144-Volt Battery Seems to Die Overnight"

The dash 144-volt battery indicator can be misleading. It estimates the HV battery state of charge (SOC). The HV gauge can read a close to full charge and then after a restart, it will show zero. A couple things must be kept in mind here: when the dash shows zero bars, the 144-volt battery is about 40% charged. At certain times, criteria unknown, the battery readout will reset itself, and that is why the battery seems to be losing charge rapidly while the vehicle is off. This is actually not the case as the computer is resetting its internal calculations. If the 12-volt battery goes dead or the 12-volt battery is disconnected, the dash readout for the main HV battery will read zero bars. Just drive the vehicle a few miles and the PCM and battery control module (BCM) will reset dash readouts. No scan tool is necessary for this procedure.

 REAL WORLD FIX

The Aftermarket Wheels and Tires Story

A 2005 Insight was purchased as a used vehicle in Salt Lake City. The owner bought the vehicle on the Internet. The MIL was on, but the seller said it was no big deal, so the new owner bought the shiny red hybrid. It was a long drive home, and a slow one at that. After many miles, the vehicle stalled and would not restart. It was towed to a dealership that recharged the 12-volt battery under the hood and let it run in the service bay to recharge the HV batteries, which appeared low. After a road test, the MIL lamp was on and a code was present. The code indicated "No Regen available." Some parts were tested, but all appeared to be OK. The customer picked up the vehicle, being told it may need a computer for the charging system. It was taken to another shop for a second opinion. The technician recognized that the factory wheels and tires had been replaced with aftermarket sport-type rims and tires. Suspecting that the different wheel size might have some effect, the wheels and tires were replaced with a factory set from a salvage yard. After installation, a road test was performed; it appeared that this fixed the hybrid. Apparently, accurate wheel-speed-sensor speed is critical for regenerative braking. Therefore, the incorrect wheel size resulted in a no-charging and no-assist condition.

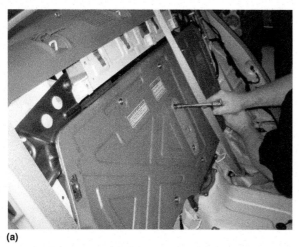
(a)

(b)

FIGURE 12–24 (a) After removing the back seat, remove the access panel to reach the shut-off switch for the high-voltage system. (b) Remove the red retainer and flip the switch to the off position. Reinstall the red retainer to prevent the switch from accidentally being moved to the on position.

 SAFETY TIP

How to Depower the Honda HV System

To turn off the 144 volts for safety or compression testing, remove the ignition key, then take out the rear seat cushions, and remove a small access panel (one with two bolts—in the center of the top aluminum plate). ● **SEE FIGURE 12–24.** Remove the red switch cover and turn the switch to off. Replace the red switch cover. The HV capacitors should be drained of high voltage by waiting five minutes. A resistor is hard-wired to the positive post of each capacitor in case of a failure of the ignition switch system because it is designed to drain the capacitors of high voltage at each key cycle to off. After five minutes, check the orange cables for low voltage using a CAT III voltmeter while wearing rubber linesman's gloves. If it is at 12 volts or less, the vehicle is now safe to work on.

CAUTION: Do not pierce the orange insulation!

SCAN TOOL DIAGNOSIS While many scan tools can be used, many generic scan tools are not able to read hybrid-specific diagnostic trouble codes (DTCs) or data. For best results, use the Honda factory scan tool. ● **SEE FIGURE 12–25.**

 **TECH TIP**

Testing the 12-Volt Starting System

To test the 12-volt auxiliary starting system, first disable the IMA starting system by removing fuse #2 from the underdash fuse box. If the 12-volt starter is engaging, the backup 12-volt system is OK. If not, test the starter as if it were in a conventional vehicle.

(a)

(b)

FIGURE 12–25 (a) For best results when diagnosing a Honda hybrid electric vehicle, use the factory scan tool. (b) A screen shot of Honda scan data as displayed on a laptop computer.

Keep the Area Clean

Whenever checking the oil level on a CVT transaxle, always clean the area around the dipstick before removing it. Even a little dirt can ruin a transaxle because the cones can be damaged by just a small amount of dirt. ● **SEE FIGURE 12–26.**

Hesitation May Be Normal

If a customer complains of a small hesitation after cruising for 30 minutes at 60 mph, and the hesitation lasts for more than 5 seconds, this may be a normal condition. When the onboard computer determines that the NO_X absorption catalyst is full of NO_X, the mixture will be temporarily enriched so that some CO can enter the NO_X absorption catalyst, react with the NO_X, and release CO_2 and N_2. After releasing the CO_2 and N_2, this special catalytic converter is now cleaned out and ready to absorb more NO_X when the engine goes back into lean burn.

A Quick and Easy Test

While cruising in a hybrid Civic, apply the brakes just enough to turn on the brake light switch. At this time, the hydraulic brakes are not engaged, but a braking effect will be noticed. Watch the dashboard readout for regeneration and release the brake pedal while watching the regeneration indicator. The brake light switch is a sensor that commands that regenerative braking begin.

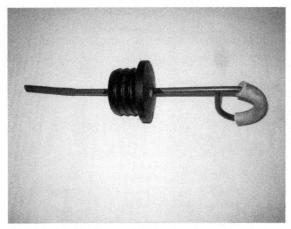

FIGURE 12–26 The dipstick from Honda hybrid CVT transaxle. Always clean around the dipstick before removing to prevent the possibility of dirt getting into and contaminating the fluid and causing serious transaxle damage.

Scan Tool Needed for Steering System Service

If replacing an electric-power steering rack or steering column, the onboard computer must be reinitialized using a scan tool. Otherwise, the EPS indicator light will illuminate after the repair and electric assist will not be available.

The Floor Mat Test

If a manual transmission Civic hybrid will not restart after idle shut down, check to make sure that the floor mat has not slid under the clutch pedal. Unless the clutch is fully disengaged and the shifter is shifted into first gear, the vehicle will not restart automatically. A floor mat under the pedal will not allow the clutch to fully disengage.

SUMMARY

1. The first production hybrid electric vehicle sold in the United States was the Honda Insight.

2. The Honda Insight used a three-cylinder gasoline engine and Integrated Motor Assist (IMA) system to provide for idle stop, regenerative braking, and power assist during acceleration.

3. The Honda Civic hybrid is based on the conventional gasoline model and provides improved fuel economy and power.

4. The i-VTEC system closes both the intake and exhaust valves of all four cylinders of a four-cylinder Civic hybrid (2006+) and three cylinders on the V6 Accord hybrid during deceleration to increase the amount of kinetic energy captured by the regenerative braking.

5. The batteries used in Honda hybrids are D-cell-size NiMHs connected in series to produce 144 volts.

6. The Honda Accord hybrid provides rapid acceleration and uses active engine mounts and active noise control to counter engine noise created during cylinder deactivation.

7. Honda hybrid engines use a linear air–fuel (LAF) sensor for fuel control.

8. The IMA battery module and the electronic modules are located behind the rear seat and are air-cooled.

9. Except for depowering the high-voltage system and some unique spark plugs used on the Insight, most service procedures are the same as for conventional vehicles.

REVIEW QUESTIONS

1. What are the differences in the engines used in Honda hybrid vehicles as compared to similar nonhybrid vehicles?

2. What features are used on the Honda Accord hybrid to reduce noise and vibration?

3. What is the difference between fuel-cut mode and idle stop mode?

4. What are the conditions that must be met for auto idle stop to occur?

5. How is the high-voltage electrical system disconnected in a Honda hybrid electric vehicle?

6. What are the safety and service procedures when working on Honda hybrid electric vehicles?

CHAPTER QUIZ

1. What is unique about the three-cylinder Insight and the four-cylinder Civic engines?
   a. Both use indexed spark plugs
   b. Offset crankshaft
   c. Direct-injection fuel injection
   d. No 12-volt starter motor

2. When the V-6 Accord hybrid engine is operating on three cylinders, what is done to reduce the noise and vibration?
   a. Retards the ignition timing to reduce noise and vibration in the cylinders
   b. Uses active engine mounts
   c. Uses active noise control
   d. Both b and c

3. Most Honda hybrid electric vehicles have a dash display that indicates _____ and _____.
   a. Assist/charging
   b. Power/economy
   c. Cruise/idle
   d. Deceleration/acceleration

4. Honda hybrids will use the 12-volt battery and conventional starter motor under what conditions?
   a. SOC of the battery module is low
   b. Ambient temperature is below 0°F (−18°C)
   c. A failure of the IMA system
   d. Any of the above

5. The state of charge of the high-voltage batteries is usually commanded to be _____.
   a. 50% to 80%   b. 10% to 50%
   c. 10% to 70%   d. 80% to 100%

6. Which of the following conditions will prevent the ICE from entering the idle stop mode?
   a. The transmission is in reverse gear
   b. The ICE has not entered closed loop
   c. Air conditioning is in "auto" mode
   d. All of the above are correct

7. The LAF sensor is capable of measuring air–fuel ratios as lean as _____.
   a. 12:1   b. 14.7:1
   c. 25:1   d. 30:1

8. The high-voltage batteries used in Honda hybrid electric vehicles are _____.
   a. One large battery module
   b. 144 one-volt batteries
   c. Made up of D-cell-size batteries
   d. 12 VRLA batteries connected in series

9. Where are the MCM and BCM located?
   a. Behind the rear seat
   b. Under the rear seat
   c. Under the hood by the passenger-side strut tower
   d. Under the passenger-side seat

10. How are the batteries in a Honda HEV cooled?
    a. Coolant cooled
    b. Air cooled
    c. Air conditioning evaporator cooled
    d. Both a and b

chapter 13

TOYOTA/LEXUS HYBRID VEHICLES

OBJECTIVES: **After studying Chapter 13, the reader will be able to:** • Identify a Toyota/Lexus hybrid electric vehicle. • Explain the operation of the various unique systems found in Toyota/Lexus hybrid electric vehicles. • List the procedures necessary to depower the high-voltage circuits in Toyota/Lexus hybrid electric vehicles. • Describe how to safely perform routine service on a Toyota/Lexus hybrid electric vehicle.

KEY TERMS: • Boost converter 212 • Coefficient of drag (Cd) 203 • ECB 215 • EPS 215 • ETC 214 • Hybrid synergy drive 203 • Inverter 212 • PID 211 • Smart key 208 • SMR 210 • THS 211 • TRAC 215 • VDIM 215 • VIN 203 • VSC 215 • VVT-i 214

TOYOTA PRIUS

BACKGROUND The Prius was first released in Japan in December of 1997 as a 1998 model. The unusual shape and hybrid emblem on the rear trunk lid makes this vehicle unique. It was a purpose-built hybrid that shared few parts with other Toyota vehicles. All Toyota hybrids are full (strong) hybrids and are capable of being propelled using battery power alone for short distances.

Prius was the world's first mass-production HEV and was designed with a very low **coefficient of drag** (abbreviated **Cd**). The Prius was modified and brought to the United States market for the 2001 model year. This first-generation Prius used the original Toyota Hybrid System, now known as THS I. The second-generation Toyota Prius was released in 2003 as a 2004 model. ● **SEE FIGURE 13–1.**

The second-generation Prius was equipped with **Hybrid Synergy Drive** (also known as THS II). Both generations of the Toyota Prius use a 1.5-liter inline four-cylinder engine that uses the Atkinson cycle to maximize fuel efficiency. Toyota HEVs do not use a separate starter motor or alternator, and all use electric power steering to increase vehicle efficiency.

The **vehicle identification number (VIN)** can be used to identify a Toyota HEV. For example, on a Prius the alphanumeric 17-character VIN is provided in the front windshield cowl and driver door post. A Prius is identified by the first six alphanumeric characters *JTDKB2*. VIN information is visible through the windshield on the driver's side and on the driver's door post, as well as on most body panels.

● **SEE FIGURE 13–2** for an overall view of the components and their location in a second-generation Toyota Prius.

FIGURE 13–1 The second-generation Prius is larger than the first generation (upper vehicle).

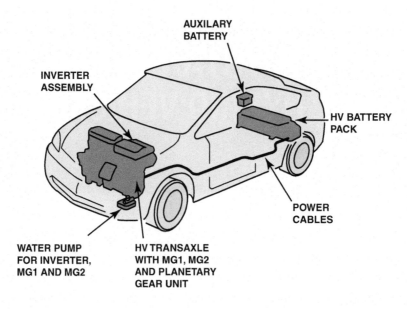

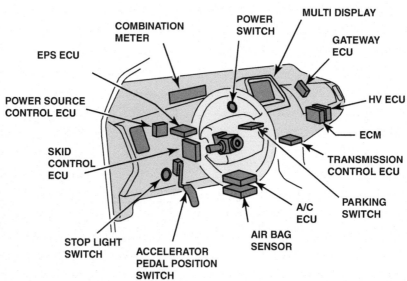

FIGURE 13–2 The major components of a second-generation Prius.

DASH DISPLAY The dashboard on the Prius is mostly digital readouts and icons. There is no tachometer, just a temperature gauge and a fuel level gauge. Near the speedometer is a "READY" light. This "READY" light, when illuminated, indicates that the Prius is ready to be driven. On many occasions, the gasoline engine will not be running, so the "READY" light is the only indication that the vehicle is on. ● **SEE FIGURE 13–3.**

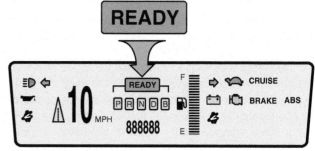

FIGURE 13–3 Dash readouts of 2001–2003 Prius. Note "Turtle" at top right. An outline of a turtle will illuminate on the right-hand side of the display when the NiMH battery pack does not have a sufficient charge to provide additional torque. There is nothing wrong with the vehicle; it just needs to be driven less aggressively so that the generator can keep up with the NiMH battery pack depletion.

 FREQUENTLY ASKED QUESTION

What Is Meant by a "Steady Ready"?

The READY light on the Prius is an indication that the vehicle is ready to be driven. When the start button is first pushed, the READY light will blink on and off. The computer is performing a self-test of the systems during this time and the vehicle cannot be driven. When the READY light is on steady, also called Ready On, it is OK to drive.

MASTER WARNING LIGHT Note the triangle-shaped indicator in Figure 13–3 with the exclamation mark in the middle. This is known as the *master warning light*. All Toyota hybrid electric vehicles use this warning indicator, which is intended to alert the driver to a vehicle condition that requires attention. If the master warning light is blinking on the instrument panel (above the steering wheel), more information related to the failure will be available on the multidisplay located on the center cluster panel.

ENERGY MONITOR The energy monitor is one of the views available on the large multidisplay. The LCD screen is interesting because it has a diagram that includes the ICE, electric motor, wheels, high-voltage NiMH battery pack, and arrows connecting these components. This indicator displays in color where the energy is flowing in the hybrid drive and regenerative braking system. ● **SEE FIGURE 13–4.**

FIGURE 13–4 The energy monitor screen indicates where the mechanical and electrical energy is flowing during vehicle operation.

The multidisplay is a touch-screen design. By pressing the "consumption" button in the lower left corner of the LCD screen, another screen will appear that shows instantaneous fuel economy. This consumption screen also shows the average fuel economy over each 5-minute period up to 30 minutes of history. ● **SEE FIGURE 13–5.** The "E" symbols shown in the bar graph each represent 50 watt-hours (Wh) of energy generated by the regenerative braking system.

SMART ENTRY AND START ELECTRONIC KEY (OPTIONAL EQUIPMENT) The second-generation Prius may be equipped with an optional smart entry and start electronic key that appears similar in function and design to the standard electronic key. However, the smart key contains a transceiver that communicates bi-directionally, enabling the vehicle to recognize the smart key when close to the vehicle. ● **SEE FIGURE 13–6.**

The system can lock or unlock doors without pushing smart key buttons and start the hybrid system without inserting the smart key into the electronic key slot.

Smart key features include:

- Passive (remote) function to lock/unlock the doors and start the vehicle
- Wireless transmitter to lock/unlock the doors
- Electronic key for starting
- Hidden metal cut key to lock/unlock the doors from the driver door lock

CAUTION: Be sure to keep the smart key at least 15 feet from the vehicle when performing repair procedures. This provides an added margin of safety as it will prevent inadvertent starting of the vehicle because the smart key range is 10 feet.

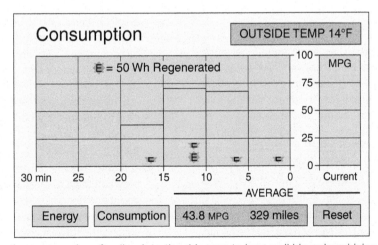

FIGURE 13–5 The consumption screen gives feedback to the driver as to how well his or her driving style is conserving fuel.

FIGURE 13–6 A Toyota smart key.

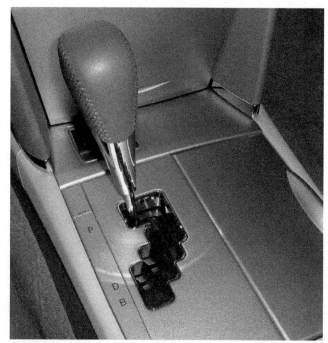

FIGURE 13–7 All Toyota hybrid vehicles have a "B" shifter position, as seen on the Camry hybrid.

DOOR (LOCK/UNLOCK) Three methods are available to lock/unlock the doors:

1. Pushing the smart key lock/unlock buttons.
2. Touching the sensor on the backside of either exterior front door handle (with the smart key close to the vehicle) unlocks the doors. Pushing the black button on the front door handle locks the doors.
3. Inserting the metal cut key in the driver's door lock and turning clockwise once unlocks the driver door, turning twice unlocks all doors. To lock all doors, turn the key counterclockwise once. Only the driver's door contains an exterior door lock.

GEAR SELECTOR On the 2001–2003 Prius, a dash-mounted shift handle is connected to the transmission via a cable. The cable is used to engage and disengage the parking pawl. No valve body is utilized in the transmission design.

The shift indicator on the dash readout uses:

- P for Park
- N for Neutral
- R for Reverse
- B for Braking

The B is often misunderstood, as some people believe it means *battery*. The B is equal to L on a conventional automatic transmission. The reason why B is used at all is to provide ICE braking when the high-voltage NiMH battery pack is fully charged and the friction brakes are the only means for slowing the vehicle. When B is selected, the transmission allows the ICE to operate at a higher RPM, causing it to absorb more of the vehicle's kinetic energy than it would at lower RPMs. Drivers looking for the best fuel economy should not shift into B unless descending a long, steep grade. ● **SEE FIGURE 13–7.**

"BY-WIRE" TECHNOLOGY Numerous systems on the Prius have been designed to incorporate *"by-wire"* technology. This is where a component that once was controlled directly by the driver, through a mechanical or hydraulic linkage, is replaced with an electrically driven and controlled component. Prius systems that utilize "by-wire" technology include:

 FREQUENTLY ASKED QUESTION

Where Is Park on the Prius?

Park on a second-generation Prius is a button rather than a position on the gear selector. ● **SEE FIGURE 13–8.**

Brake-by-wire. Stepping on the brake pedal does not necessarily mean that the friction brakes will be applied. In order to make regenerative braking work, electronic control has been utilized to act as the "decision-maker" between the brake pedal and the friction brakes. The brake system on the Prius includes a stroke simulator that provides a normal pedal stroke during regenerative braking. There is also a power source backup unit (second-generation Prius) located next to the auxiliary battery that provides electrical power to the brake system if the 12-volt battery is damaged or disconnected.

Electronic throttle control. The mechanical linkage between the ICE throttle body and the accelerator pedal has been eliminated in favor of electronic control. The ECU is now responsible for opening and closing the throttle plate according to a number of different sensor inputs aside from just accelerator pedal position.

FIGURE 13–8 To engage Park on a second-generation Prius, stop the vehicle and press the "P" button.

FIGURE 13–9 The second-generation Prius uses an electronic sensor to replace the conventional gear shift selector.

Shift-by-wire. A special electronic sensor that responds to both lateral and vertical movement is used as the driver's shift selector. ● **SEE FIGURE 13–9.**

Shift control actuator. The only mechanical shifting that takes place in a Prius transmission is the operation of the parking lock mechanism. This is performed by the shift control actuator, which includes a brushless DC motor, a special reduction mechanism, and a rotation angle sensor.

DRIVING A TOYOTA HYBRID ELECTRIC VEHICLE

If the ICE has cooled down, turning the key (2001–2003 Prius) to the crank position will cause the ICE to start when the "READY" light illuminates or shortly thereafter. If the ICE is

FIGURE 13–10 The light on the POWER button is off when the vehicle is in READY mode.

 FREQUENTLY ASKED QUESTION

How Do You Start a Second-Generation Prius?

Instead of a conventional key switch, the second-generation Prius uses a push button to start the vehicle. The electronic key is placed in its slot on the dash and the transponder key ECU checks its code. While depressing the brake pedal, press the POWER button once and Prius will go straight to READY mode. If the brake pedal is not depressed, pressing the POWER button will toggle between ACCESSORY, IGNITION ON, and OFF. ● **SEE FIGURE 13–10.**

already warmed up, the "READY" light will illuminate and the ICE will not start. When the "READY" light is lit, the vehicle is ready to drive, whether the ICE is running or not.

NOTE: In order for the Prius to start, the 12-volt battery in the trunk must be sufficiently charged.

The most unusual part of the driving experience is driving under electric power only. Not only are there zero tailpipe emissions, but the lack of ICE vibration and noise produce a new way of travel that is both quiet and smooth. It is this electric-drive feature that most hybrid enthusiasts rave about when describing a hybrid. When starting from a stop with the accelerator lightly pressed, a warmed-up Prius will be in electric-mode only. Once about 14 mph (23 km/h) is reached, the ICE that was started a few mph earlier will add power to the drive train through the planetary ring gear. This transition from electric to gasoline power is mostly seamless. At speeds over 30 mph (48 km/h), the electric drive goes to minimum assist and the ICE is its main source of power. The automobile can accelerate to over 100 mph (160 km/h) and maintain any cruising speed desired.

NOTE: The maximum ICE speed (redline) in a Prius is 4000 RPM.

Store the Smart Key Away from the Vehicle

Some vehicle manufacturers use an ignition key that is simply a short range radio transmitter. This "key" is not used in the door lock or in the ignition. Instead, the "key," often called a **smart key,** "wakes up" the vehicle if the key is within about fifteen feet (5 meters). The door will unlock when a sensor on the door handle detects a hand. Once the smart key is inside the vehicle, the vehicle will be energized, if the "start" button is depressed.

Always make sure that the owner stores the smart key at least 15 feet from the vehicle so that the system will not remain powered up, draining the battery more quickly than normal.

Do Not Wax the Door Handles

On vehicles that use a smart key for access, a sensor in the door handle is used to detect when the handle is grasped. The sensor detects the presence of a hand by the change in the electrical capacitance in the sensor circuit. Often, the sensor will not detect the hand if it has a coating of wax or polish.

NOTE: Sometimes water (rain) or ice on the door handle can also prevent proper operation.

COLD-START EMISSION CONTROLS

Internal combustion engines produce increased emissions during a cold start. In an effort to reduce these emissions, Toyota engineers have created two unique emission control systems that have been incorporated into the design of the Prius.

HC ADSORBER AND CATALYST (2001–2003 PRIUS ONLY)
When a catalytic converter is cold, it cannot oxidize HC and CO. The HC Adsorber and Catalyst (HCAC) system utilizes a special catalytic converter assembly that incorporates an HC adsorber to trap and store unburned hydrocarbons during cold starts. During these periods of operation, the bypass valve on the catalytic converter is closed and HC is held on the surface of the adsorber material. Once the catalytic converter is up to operating (light off) temperature, the HCAC bypass valve is opened and HC is purged and sent through the hot catalyst. The bypass valve is also closed during deceleration to purge any remaining HC from the adsorber. ● **SEE FIGURE 13–11.**

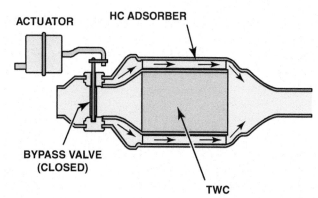

ACTUATOR   HC ADSORBER

BYPASS VALVE
(CLOSED)

TWC

FIGURE 13–11 When the bypass valve is closed, the exhaust gases are forced through the HC adsorber, which stores unburned hydrocarbons until the TWC is up to temperature.

COOLANT HEAT STORAGE SYSTEM (2004 AND LATER PRIUS ONLY)
The second-generation Prius did not use the HCAC system. Toyota engineers replaced HCAC with a coolant heat storage system in which heated coolant is stored in a specially designed tank during normal vehicle operation and is then used to warm the engine intake ports prior to a cold start. Warming the intake ports and cylinder head before a cold start helps start the ICE more quickly and reduces HC and CO emissions. See Chapter 9 for more information on this system.

What Is This Thing?

When doing exhaust repairs on a first-generation Prius, you will notice a vacuum-operated valve located in the inlet pipe of the TWC (three-way catalytic converter). This device is used to channel cold exhaust into an outer chamber of the TWC and collect unburned hydrocarbons (HCs) during cold starts. Toyota uses a MAP sensor to monitor the operation of the bypass valve. The valve itself can stick, which generates a DTC and causes the MIL to illuminate. After freeing the valve and clearing codes, restart the engine after it has cooled down to be sure it is fixed. If the code reappears, there may be more wrong than the valve itself.

FUEL SYSTEM COMPONENTS

In order to receive certification as a AT-PZEV vehicle, very strict evaporative emission standards must be met. Toyota utilizes a number of unique components as part of its evaporative emission control strategy.

BLADDER FUEL TANK Both generations of the Prius utilize a bladder fuel tank, which stores the fuel in a resin bladder enclosed in a steel shell. The resin bladder can expand and contract with the fuel, which minimizes the space into which fuel can evaporate. One challenge with this system is accurately calculating the amount of fuel left in the tank. Fuel level calculations are based on inputs from a fuel gauge sender and ambient temperature sensor (both located in the tank) plus data from two inclination sensors mounted in the combination meter ECU. The combination meter ECU is located in the vehicle instrument panel. ● **SEE FIGURE 13-12.**

NOTE: The resin bladder loses its ability to expand at low temperatures. When ambient air temperatures drop to 14°F, the capacity of the tank is reduced by approximately 5 liters.

CLOSED FUEL TANK SYSTEM The closed fuel tank system is only used on the Highlander hybrid and Lexus RX400h models. This system is unique because the fuel tank is sealed during normal vehicle operation, and the charcoal canister is only used during purge and refueling. A tank close valve (also called a vapor-containment valve) is used to seal the tank and control vapor flow during purge and refueling. An electric fuel door prevents the fuel cap from being removed until the tank pressure has been bled through the charcoal canister and the system is ready for refueling.

When refueling, the ignition switch is turned to OFF and the THS ECU waits for the fuel system to depressurize before it unlocks the fuel door. During this process, the multi-information

display reads "PLEASE WAIT NOW OPENING." When the system has finished depressurizing, it unlocks the fuel door and the display shows "REFUEL READY." If, for some reason, the fuel door does not automatically unlock, it is possible to override the lock using the emergency opener located behind the left rear quarter-panel trim.

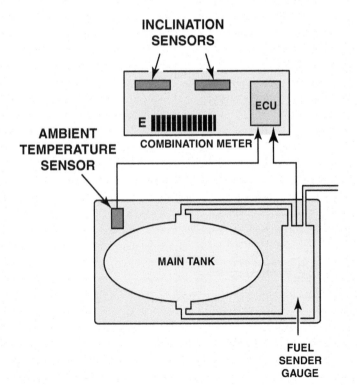

FIGURE 13-12 The Prius stores its fuel in a resin bladder located inside a steel tank.

Toyota HV Battery Specifications

Vehicle Models	Battery Construction	Raw Battery Weight	Battery Assembly Weight
2001–2003 Prius	1.2-volt cells in banks of 6 × 38 modules = 273.6 volts	93 lbs (42 kg)	115 lbs (19 kg)
2004 and later Prius	1.2-volt cells in banks of 6 × 28 modules = 201.6 volts	64 lbs (29 kg)	86 lbs (39 kg)
Highlander Hybrid Lexus RX400h	1.2-volt cells in banks of 8 × 30 modules = 288.0 volts	100 lbs (45 kg)	152 lbs (69 kg)
Camry Hybrid	1.2-volt cells in banks of 6 × 34 modules = 244.8 volts	n/a	n/a
Lexus GS450h	1.2-volt cells in banks of 6 × 40 modules = 288 volts	n/a	n/a

HIGH-VOLTAGE BATTERY PACK

FIGURE 13–13 The first-generation Prius battery pack with 38 modules. All of the battery cells are connected in series to create the HV battery.

When the Prius was refined for the U.S. market, the original battery pack used in the Japanese Prius (1998–2000) was discontinued. Toyota approached Panasonic, its supplier for NiMH battery cells, to design and manufacture a battery pack that would be considerably smaller. A partnership between Toyota and Matsushita Electric was created to design and manufacture a new NiMH battery pack. This new joint venture became known as Panasonic EV Energy. To reduce the space needed for the batteries, Panasonic EV designed a prismatic module by creating six individual NiMH cells enclosed in one rectangular casing. Each NiMH cell produces 1.2 volts; therefore, one module equals 7.2 volts. For the first-generation Prius, 38 modules were installed in series producing 273.6 volts. ● **SEE FIGURE 13–13**.

There are different high-voltage battery pack designs for the various models of Toyota HEVs. See the following chart for more information.

A first-generation Prius battery pack contains 38 modules, wiring, a **system main relay (SMR),** computer, a manual disconnect service plug, and a strong metal box to contain everything. ● **SEE FIGURE 13–14**.

HV BATTERY COOLING   The high-voltage battery pack is air cooled and utilizes a fan and ducting in the rear of the vehicle for circulating cabin air through the battery assembly. Battery pack temperature is monitored in a number of locations on the modules, and cooling fan speed is controlled based on these measurements. The cooling air can exit outside the vehicle or inside depending on the air pressure in the vehicle cabin. ● **SEE FIGURE 13–15**.

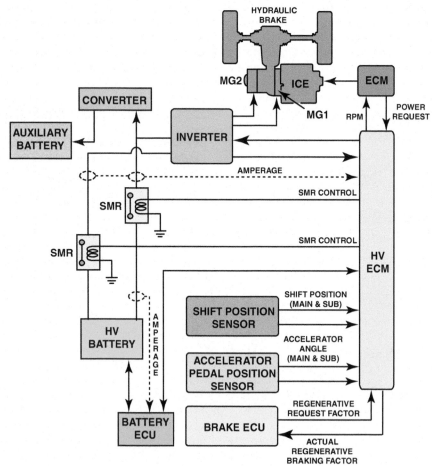

FIGURE 13–14 The electronic controls used in a Toyota hybrid vehicle. Notice the system main relays (SMR), battery ECU, and the interconnection of the various components and systems.

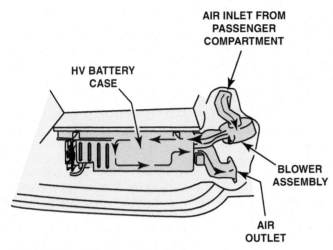

FIGURE 13-15 High-voltage battery pack cooling on a second-generation Prius.

Further information on the high-voltage battery can be found in Chapter 5.

HV BATTERY DIAGNOSIS AND SERVICE Since the battery modules are all connected in series, a poor connection at any of the modules can lead to HV battery failure. For this reason, cleanliness of the connections and proper torque on the module fasteners is critical with these battery designs.

A factory scan tool can be used for diagnosing problems that may be related to the high-voltage battery. Toyota high-voltage battery packs have a special wiring harness that allows measurement of the voltage available across pairs of battery modules. These voltage readings can be read as **parameter identification (PIDs)** on a scan tool. If the onboard computer recognizes a problem in a module, wiring, or anything that could cause a potential problem, the MIL is illuminated, a code is set, and a freeze frame is stored. The battery pack may be limited in its power output or charging capacity and, as a last resort, the vehicle may be shut down.

If the battery pack fails in service, a new one is installed. The warranty of the battery pack varies by manufacturer but typically is covered for eight years or 100,000 miles. This warranty is extended to 10 years or 150,000 miles for vehicles sold in states that have adopted California emission standards (Green states).

Environmental concerns regarding battery disposal were addressed prior to releasing hybrids in the United States by requiring a "cradle-to-grave" process. An 800 telephone number is located on the battery case or under the hood, and this number should be called when an end-of-life NiMH battery assembly needs to be recycled.

REPLACING THE HV BATTERY PACK When replacing a battery pack, the entire box is replaced as a unit. It weighs about 115 lbs (52 kg) and should be handled carefully as high voltage is contained inside. Wear high-voltage gloves

High-Voltage Battery Failures Don't Always Require Battery Replacement

Some Toyota HEVs, most notably the 2001–2003 Prius, have had problems with corrosion of the module electrical connections. Warranty repairs involved disassembling the power bus strips from the modules, applying sealant to the module cases, and cleaning all connections thoroughly. A torque wrench is then used to tighten the fasteners when reinstalling the power bus strips. Many first-generation Prius battery packs were repaired under a recall using this procedure.

with leather outer gloves, as the metal box has sharp edges. The battery box should be carefully stored or placed on an insulated bench if service is required. If a metal workbench is used, it should be covered with a rubber mat to prevent short circuits.

Caution: The high-voltage battery system must be disabled before attempting any system repairs. Be sure to wear the appropriate personal protective equipment (PPE) and follow the manufacturer-specified procedures.

 FREQUENTLY ASKED QUESTION

What Is the Life Expectancy of Hybrid HV Battery Packs?

When hybrids were first sold in Japan, the expected life of the high-voltage battery was unknown. However, after over 10 years, 98% of battery packs installed in hybrid electric vehicles are still functioning normally. Most failures (excluding collision damage) were covered under extended warranty to provide for customer satisfaction. Many problems in the battery packs were not related to the NiMH cells but to the wiring or connections external to the cells themselves.

THE TOYOTA HYBRID SYSTEM

The **Toyota Hybrid System (THS),** as used in the 1st generation Prius, consists of one planetary gearset and two electric machines. The planetary gearset is known as a power-split device, because it splits power from the ICE and uses it

FIGURE 13-16 An under hood view of the Toyota hybrid system on a Toyota Camry with all covers in place.

for moving the vehicle and for generating electrical power. ● **SEE FIGURE 13-16**.

The electric machines used in the Toyota Hybrid System are three-phase AC synchronous permanent magnet motors. There are no brushes used in this design, and the motor speed and torque is controlled by the inverter assembly. In order for each of these motors to work correctly, the exact position of its rotor is reported to the THS ECU using a resolver.

One electric machine is attached to the planetary sun gear and is called *motor-generator 1* (abbreviated *MG1*). The second electric machine is attached to the planetary ring gear and is labeled *motor-generator 2* (abbreviated *MG2*). The ICE is also connected to the planetary gearset through the planet carrier. ● **SEE FIGURE 13-17**.

During operation, each motor-generator fulfills two primary functions:

- MG1 is used to start the internal combustion engine and generate electricity for charging the high-voltage batteries, as well as driving MG2.

- MG2 is used to propel the vehicle and generate electricity during slowing and braking (regenerative braking). MG2 is connected directly to the drive wheels at all times.

NOTE: Four-wheel-drive versions of the Highlander Hybrid and Lexus RX400h use a third electric machine known as *MGR*. MGR is connected to the rear wheels and is used to propel the vehicle forward and backward as well as for regenerative braking. ● **SEE FIGURE 13-18** on page 214.

HYBRID SYNERGY DRIVE The original Toyota Hybrid System (THS I) was only used on the first-generation Prius. All Toyota hybrid electric vehicles built starting with the 2004 model year have used Hybrid Synergy Drive (HSD), also known as THS II. HSD made a number of improvements over the original, including the following:

- MG1 and MG2 operate at much higher voltages in order to increase power output. These higher voltages are generated using a **boost converter** in the inverter assembly.

- In Highlander Hybrid and RX400h, MG2 operates at much higher RPMs to increase power output and efficiency. MG2's speed is then reduced through the use of a second planetary gearset.

INVERTER ASSEMBLY Control of the motor-generators in the Toyota Hybrid System is accomplished using the **inverter** assembly located in the ICE compartment. ● **SEE FIGURE 13-19**.

The THS inverter has multiple functions, including:

1. **Inverter.** Converts high-voltage DC into three-phase AC to power MG1, MG2, and MGR.

2. **DC-DC converter.** Converts high-voltage DC to 12-VDC to power the vehicle auxiliary systems.

   NOTE: The DC-DC converter in the Camry hybrid is located in the HV battery pack assembly at the rear of the vehicle instead of with the inverter.

3. **Boost converter.** In HSD systems, DC voltage from the HV battery pack is boosted to improve motor output. These voltages range from 500 volts for Prius to 650 volts for Highlander Hybrid/RX400h, Camry Hybrid, and Lexus GS450h.

? FREQUENTLY ASKED QUESTION

Do Toyota Hybrids Charge the HV Battery in All Gear Ranges?

Toyota HEVs use a power split transmission, which does not use a torque converter or clutches. This means that when the vehicle is stopped and the ICE (planet carrier) is idling, the (sun gear) is turning while the wheels (ring gear) are stationary. Since MG1 (sun gear) is turning in this mode, it is possible to use it to charge the HV batteries. However, MG1 will charge the HV batteries when the gear selector is in Park, but not when it is in Neutral. The reason this occurs is because when the gear selector is in the Park position, the ring gear is locked in place by the parking pawl mechanism. This prevents the vehicle's wheels from turning and helps the ring gear act as a reaction member during planetary operation. However, when the gear selector is moved to the Neutral position, the ring gear is unlocked. If MG1 was used to charge the HV batteries at this time, the torque reaction would cause the ring gear (and thus the vehicle) to move. The Neutral position would then not be a neutral at all, but another forward gear.

THIS SYSTEM CONTROLS THE FOLLOWING MODES IN ORDER TO ACHIEVE THE MOST EFFICIENT OPERATION TO MATCH THE DRIVING CONDITIONS:

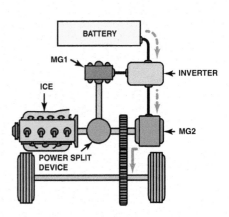

1. SUPPLY OF ELECTRICAL POWER FROM THE HV BATTERY TO MG2 PROVIDES FORCE TO DRIVE THE WHEELS.

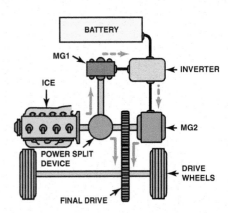

2. WHILE THE WHEELS ARE BEING DRIVEN BY THE ENGINE VIA THE PLANETARY GEARS, MG1 IS ROTATED BY THE ENGINE VIA THE PLANETARY GEARS, IN ORDER TO SUPPLY THE GENERATED ELECTRICITY TO MG2.

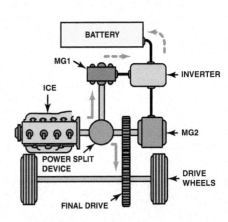

3. MG1 IS ROTATED BY THE ENGINE VIA THE PLANETARY GEARS, IN ORDER TO CHARGE THE HV BATTERY.

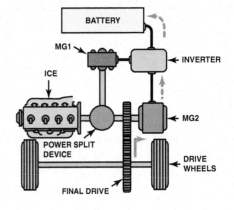

4. WHEN THE VEHICLE IS DECELERATING, KINETIC ENERGY FROM THE WHEELS IS RECOVERED AND CONVERTED INTO ELECTRICAL ENERGY AND USED TO RECHARGE THE HV BATTERY BY MEANS OF MG2.

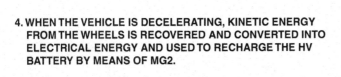

FIGURE 13–17 The Toyota Hybrid System operation.

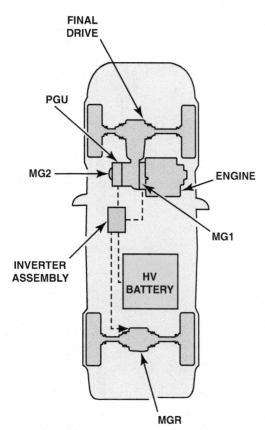

FINAL
DRIVE

PGU

MG2

ENGINE

MG1

INVERTER
ASSEMBLY

HV
BATTERY

MGR

FIGURE 13–18 Powertrain schematic for the 4WD versions of the Highlander Hybrid and RX400h. Note that MGR alone is used to drive the vehicle's rear wheels.

4. **A/C compressor inverter.** For HSD systems, the inverter assembly also converts high-voltage DC into high-voltage AC to power the A/C system's electric compressor.

5. **Cooling system.** A separate liquid cooling system is used to cool the inverter assembly, as well as MG1 and MG2.

LEXUS RX400H/TOYOTA HIGHLANDER HYBRID

The Lexus RX400h is a full (strong) hybrid, which means that it is capable of operating in electric-only or gas-engine-only mode, as well as a mode that combines the power of the gas engine and electric motor. The RX400h is built on the same platform as the Toyota Highlander Hybrid.

The RX400h uses a 3.3-liter V-6 that is based on the engine in the RX 330 but with revisions to promote smooth integration with the hybrid system. These include revised calibrations to the **Variable Valve Timing with intelligence (VVT-i)** and **Electronic Throttle Control (ETC)** systems. The ICE does not utilize an accessory drive belt. Instead, the water pump is driven by the timing belt and the A/C compressor has a high-voltage electric drive. The hybrid system uses a 288-volt DC nickel metal hydride (NiMH) battery pack that is located under the rear seat. ● **SEE FIGURE 13–20.**

NOTE: The RX400h 3.3-liter V-6 does not use the Atkinson cycle. Instead, it is based on the conventional Otto cycle.

The battery power is directed through a boost converter that raises the voltage to 650 volts DC. An inverter changes this to 650 volts AC for use by a front-mounted 123-kW electric motor that turns as high as 12,400 RPM. ● **SEE FIGURE 13–21.**

Three motor-generators are employed in the RX 400h power train, known as MG1, MG2, and MGR. Each of these has specific functions and can operate as both drive motors and generators. The engine-driven generator (MG1) can charge the battery pack or power other electric motors as needed.

The RX 400h four-wheel-drive (4WD) system uses a separate 50-kW electric motor (MGR) at the rear that provides up to 96 lb-ft of additional drive torque. MGR is integrated into the rear-drive unit with a differential in an independent

FIGURE 13–19 The inverter assembly from a first generation Prius. The inverter performs multiple functions in the THS system.

FIGURE 13–20 Air vent at the front edge of the rear seat in a Lexus RX 400h. This vent has to be kept clear to ensure proper battery operation.

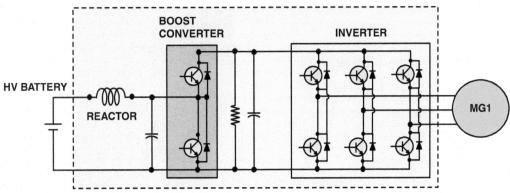

FIGURE 13–21 The boost converter is used to increase HV battery voltage to as high as 650 volts for use by the electric motors.

FIGURE 13–22 The rear-mounted electric motor (MGR) is used on four-wheel-drive versions of the Lexus RX 400h and Toyota Highlander.

rear suspension configuration. The system electronically varies front and rear torque distribution depending on traction conditions. ● **SEE FIGURE 13–22**.

The Lexus also allows extended electric-mode operation during low-speed or stop-and-go driving conditions up to and often faster than 20 MPH (32 km/h). The RX 400h uses a regenerative braking system when coasting or when the brakes are applied, capturing kinetic energy that would normally be lost as heat through the brakes and transforming it into useable electricity to recharge the batteries.

VEHICLE DYNAMIC INTEGRATED MANAGEMENT

With the RX 400h, Lexus also has a new generation of vehicle stability control systems known as **Vehicle Dynamic Integrated Management (VDIM).**

A major part of VDIM is a new **Electronically Controlled Braking (ECB)** system. The ECB system translates brake pedal stroke speed and pressure, and generates the precise amount of combined electric regeneration and hydraulic pressure needed for almost any driving condition.

The RX 400h also incorporates an antilock braking system (ABS) as well as **Vehicle Stability Control (VSC)** and **traction control (TRAC).** VDIM also interfaces with the Electronic Throttle Control (ETC) system and the **Electronic Power Steering (EPS)** system to optimize steering assist for each situation.

The EPS uses a brushless DC motor and gear reduction system built into the steering gear housing to provide steering assist. ● **SEE FIGURE 13–23**. This compact unit contributes to fuel economy by eliminating the traditional power steering pump and by providing assist only when called for by the driver. The EPS system on the RX400h is powered by 42 volts DC, which is provided by a separate DC-DC converter. The power cables to the EPS unit are colored yellow for easy identification.

VDIM constantly calculates vehicle motion based on signals from a yaw rate and deceleration sensor, speed sensor, and steering sensor. Using these inputs, VDIM controls all of the dynamic handling systems, allowing it to quickly detect the onset of instability and correct it. The corrections to vehicle attitude are fast and accurate so that the driver does not feel anything unusual.

FIGURE 13–23 The EPS unit on a Toyota Highlander hybrid is powered by 42 volts supplied by a separate DC-DC converter.

DRIVING THE RX 400H All of the comfort and luxury found inside the RX 330 is present in the RX 400h, with a few changes, including:

- In place of a traditional tachometer, the RX 400h has a power meter that displays the level of power generated by the hybrid powertrain.

- The driver can also monitor the gas-electric power distribution on the multi-information display or on the optional navigation system's 7-inch touch-panel display screen.

The RX 400h is very similar to the gasoline-engine-powered RX 330/350. However, the combination of the engine and electric motors makes the vehicle feel as if it has a V-8 engine instead of a V-6 because of the torque felt during rapid acceleration at low vehicle speeds. The RX 400h has been certified by the California Air Resources Board (CARB) as a super-ultra-low-emission vehicle (SULEV). The RX 400h is also certified as a zero evaporative emission vehicle in California and those states adopting California standards. In states not adopting California rules, the RX 400h is certified to Tier 2, Bin 3 emission levels.

TOYOTA CAMRY HYBRID

BACKGROUND The Toyota Camry Hybrid was first introduced for the 2007 model year and features a 2.4-liter inline four-cylinder ICE using the Atkinson cycle. The Camry Hybrid is a front-wheel-drive HSD (THS II) configuration. The package includes a 105-kW electric motor and a high-voltage battery pack that delivers a peak of 45 hp. Total peak power output for the vehicle adds up to 187 horsepower. The Camry Hybrid has been awarded an AT-PZEV rating by the California Air Resources Board. ● **SEE FIGURE 13–24**.

FIGURE 13–24 The Toyota Camry hybrid electric vehicle does not look any different from a regular Camry except for the emblem on the side and rear of the vehicle.

FIGURE 13–25 The Camry Hybrid battery pack as viewed from the passenger compartment. Note the cooling fan assembly on top of the battery case.

CAMRY HYBRID BATTERIES The high-voltage battery pack produces 244 volts and consists of 34 nickel metal hydride modules, each of which contains six 1.2-volt cells. The battery pack is located behind the rear passenger seat backs. ● **SEE FIGURE 13–25**.

The cooling air intake for the high-voltage battery pack is located in the center of the rear deck. The 12-volt auxiliary battery is located on the passenger side of the trunk area, and is a leakproof AGM design. The inverter assembly is more compact than previous Toyota HEVs, as the DC-DC converter has been moved to the high-voltage battery pack. The inverter incorporates a boost converter that raises the 244 volts DC from the battery pack to 650 volts DC for higher motor efficiency. ● **SEE FIGURE 13–26**.

The Camry Hybrid looks very similar to the standard Camry, including the view from inside the vehicle. The hybrid model does have an analog fuel economy meter and a console gear selector with the traditional Toyota hybrid shift positions (P-R-N-D-B).

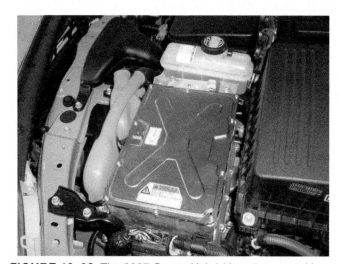

FIGURE 13–26 The 2007 Camry Hybrid inverter assembly is more compact than those found in previous Toyota HEVs.

FREQUENTLY ASKED QUESTION

Why Does the Camry Hybrid Use Two Planetaries in the Transaxle?

Similar to the Highlander Hybrid/RX400h, the Camry Hybrid uses a second planetary gearset in the transaxle to reduce the speed of MG2. Camry's MG2 is made to spin at a much higher RPM than the second-generation Prius. This is done to increase the efficiency and power output of MG2.

FIGURE 13–27 The high-voltage (HV) service plug being removed on a second-generation Prius. The handle must be lifted straight up before rotating to the left for removal.

LEXUS GS450H

The Lexus GS450h is a rear-wheel-drive sedan using a V-6 ICE and a Hybrid Synergy Drive transmission. Since the GS450h is a rear-wheel-drive vehicle, the transmission is configured very differently from other Toyota HEVs. The transmission incorporates a power-split planetary gear unit along with a two-stage motor speed reduction planetary. The second planetary can switch between two ranges and will vary the speed of MG2 according to vehicle speed and torque requirements.

MAINTENANCE AND SERVICE PROCEDURES

STEALTH OR QUIET MODE Care should be taken when driving a Toyota/Lexus hybrid in and around the shop because they can be driven using electric power only. That means it can be in a bay ready to go, with the engine ready to start up, but all the while it is perfectly silent. Known as *stealth* or *quiet* mode, this means that the vehicle can be moving yet no sound will be heard. Customers or employees can easily walk in front of the vehicle without warning due to the silence of the vehicle.

Most routine service work, such as wheel alignments, suspension work, exhaust system, and other routine under-vehicle repairs, is similar to conventional vehicles.

CAUTION: The ICE can start anytime the READY indicator is illuminated. Be sure that the READY light is out before performing any vehicle service.

DE-POWERING THE HIGH-VOLTAGE SYSTEM The high-voltage system on a Toyota hybrid electric vehicle can produce upwards of 650 volts. Incorrect handling of high-voltage circuits can cause severe burns or electric shock that could result in serious injury or death. Service on the high-voltage system should always start with steps to manually depower the system.

The following steps must be performed prior to servicing the high-voltage system on a Toyota hybrid electric vehicle:

1. Turn the ignition system OFF and secure the key on your person or in a special lock box. If the vehicle uses a smart key, secure it at least 15 feet from the vehicle to prevent inadvertent starting.

2. Disconnect the negative battery cable from the auxiliary battery. This provides an extra margin of safety when dealing with the HV system.

3. While wearing high-voltage linesman's gloves with leather outer gloves, remove the orange service plug. As an extra precaution, place a strip of electrical tape across the service plug socket in the HV battery case to prevent objects from entering the cavity. ● **SEE FIGURE 13–27.**

4. Take steps to make sure that the service plug cannot be installed by another service technician while you are servicing the vehicle. This can be done by securing the service plug on your person or in a special lock box.

5. After removing the service plug, wait five minutes before touching any part of the high-voltage system. Verify that the system is de-energized by measuring system voltage with a digital multimeter (DMM). ● **SEE FIGURE 13–28.**

NOTE: Increase the wait time to 10 minutes when servicing a Camry Hybrid or Lexus GS450h.

6. After disconnecting a high-voltage connector or terminal, be sure to wrap it with electrical tape.

Second-Generation Prius Service Plug

The 2004 and later Prius has a service plug that requires two steps to properly reinstall it in the battery pack connector. The handle (lever) on the plug must be rotated to the right as the plug is being installed. ● **SEE FIGURE 13–29.** Once the plug is inserted all the way into its connector, the handle must then be pushed downward to fully engage the service plug. Leaving out this last step can result in a no-start condition and possible generation of DTCs.

More Information Is Available in the Freeze Frame

Whenever scanning a Toyota hybrid electric vehicle for codes, be sure to look for freeze frames that are attached to any DTCs that are found. A freeze frame will have a great deal more information that can help immensely with diagnosis. Freeze frames can be used with many different types of DTCs, including those related to the hybrid high-voltage system.

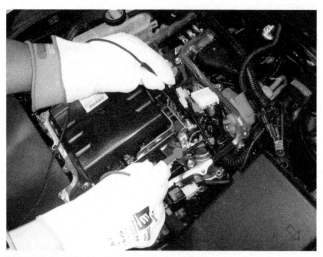

FIGURE 13–28 Verify that the system has been de-energized using a DMM before touching any part of the high-voltage system.

TESTING FOR PROPER INSULATION The Toyota Hybrid System monitors the voltage on the body and will disconnect the high-voltage source if a fault is indicated. ● **SEE FIGURE 13–30.**

A special tester, such as the Fluke model 1587, is required to test if any of the high-voltage circuits are making contact with the body or ground of the vehicle. This procedure would only be necessary in the event of a collision to be sure that there is no electrical connection between the body and the high-voltage components or circuits before restoring the high-voltage connections. ● **SEE FIGURE 13–31.**

SCAN TOOL. While some aftermarket scan tools can access hybrid PIDs and DTCs and perform some bi-directional tests, there is nothing that outperforms the factory scan tool for the specific vehicle. Toyota's Diagnostic Tester will access all available vehicle information and perform all diagnostic testing on the Toyota Hybrid System. ● **SEE FIGURE 13–32.**

NOTE: The factory scan tool can also be used to disable the ICE idle stop mode. This can come in handy when testing a Toyota hybrid's cooling system performance, tailpipe emissions, or any other procedure that requires the ICE to continue running.

SERVICE INFORMATION. The most comprehensive information available for diagnosis and repair of Toyota/Lexus vehicles is available online at the Technical Information System (TIS). This is a subscription-level service that can be purchased for 24-hour, 1-month, or 1-year periods. Toyota/Lexus service information can be accessed at http://techinfo.toyota.com.

NOTE: Be sure to disable your web browser's pop-up blockers when using TIS. Much of the linked information is accessed through pop-ups and you will not be able to view this information if your pop-up blockers are enabled.

FIGURE 13–29 Removing the service plug on a Toyota Highlander Hybrid. This service plug is located behind a plastic panel on the left side of the rear passenger seat.

Many diagnostic trouble codes found on hybrid electric vehicles are unique and often contain letters where only numbers are usually found. See the following chart for an example of selected Toyota Prius DTCs.

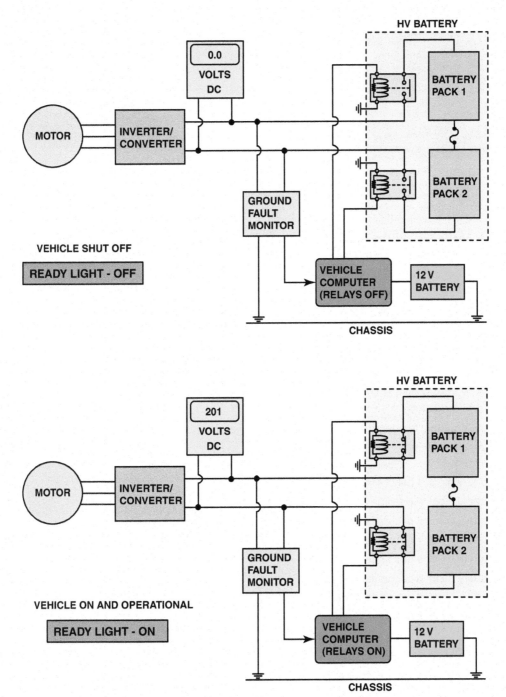

FIGURE 13–30 The Toyota computer system monitors the voltage on the chassis and stands by ready to disable the high-voltage system if a connection to ground is detected.

FIGURE 13–31 An insulation tester is used to detect any electrical connection between the high-voltage wiring and the chassis of the vehicle.

Prius Diagnostic Trouble Code Chart
Hybrid Battery System

P0560	System voltage
P0A1F	Battery energy control module
P0A7F	Hybrid battery pack deterioration
P0A80	Replace hybrid battery pack
POA81	Hybrid battery pack cooling fan 1
P0A82	Hybrid battery pack cooling fan 1
P0A85	Hybrid battery pack cooling fan 1
P0A95	High-voltage fuse
P0A9B	Hybrid battery temperature sensor circuit
P0AAC	Hybrid battery pack air temperature sensor "A" circuit
P3011	Battery block 1 becomes weak
P3012	Battery block 2 becomes weak
P3013	Battery block 3 becomes weak
P3014	Battery block 4 becomes weak
P3015	Battery block 5 becomes weak
P3016	Battery block 6 becomes weak
P3017	Battery block 7 becomes weak
P3018	Battery block 8 becomes weak
P3019	Battery block 9 becomes weak
P3020	Battery block 10 becomes weak
P3021	Battery block 11 becomes weak
P3022	Battery block 12 becomes weak
P3023	Battery block 13 becomes weak
P3024	Battery block 14 becomes weak
P3030	Disconnection between battery and ECU
P3056	Battery current sensor circuit malfunction
U0100	Lost communication with ECM/PCM "A"
U0293	Lost communication with hybrid vehicle control system

FIGURE 13–32 While some aftermarket scan tools will give some hybrid data, it is wise to use the factory tool and service information.

TOYOTA/LEXUS OIL CHANGE PROCEDURE The procedure for changing oil in a Toyota/Lexus hybrid vehicle is the same as for most other vehicles. Always be sure to check and use the specified viscosity of engine oil. If servicing a Toyota Prius, be sure that the READY light is out before hoisting the vehicle.

 **TECH TIP**

Wrong-Viscosity Oil Could Equal Big Trouble

Using engine oil with the wrong SAE viscosity rating can cause problems. Besides reducing fuel economy, the hybrid computer uses a very powerful starter motor, one so strong it could hurt the engine if it attempted to rotate a "stuck" engine. Because of this, a sensor, known as a resolver, is able to monitor cranking speed at start up and reports in milliseconds the speed that the crankshaft is being rotated. If the speed is too low, which could indicate a problem, the PCM commands the starter to shut down. A no-start with a code that has a definition of "broken crankshaft" may be the result. Therefore, the wise technician should be sure to use only the specified viscosity of engine oil.

 TECH TIP

Inverter Bleeding the Easy Way

Refilling the inverter cooling system can be a difficult task. Getting all of the air out is a challenge because of the many loops and cavities that the inverter coolant travels through. It is extremely important that this system not develop an airlock, as the inverter assembly can quickly be damaged due to overheating. To make this task easier, use an "Airlift" tool to pull a vacuum on the system before refilling it. Proper use of this tool refills the system completely and eliminates airlocks with one try.

REAL WORLD FIX

Scared to Touch!

A salvage (recycling) yard had a second-generation Toyota Prius towed in that had been hit hard in the front end. The salvage yard owner was afraid to touch it—literally. The owner had heard stories about electrocution, fires, and explosions, so being afraid was a normal response. It was in a puddle and could not be easily moved. Rule number one: Do not work in puddles. The wrecked Prius was towed inside and, using 1,000-volt rubber gloves, it was first made safe to dismantle. After looking at the front end damage, it was noted that the inverter had been ripped off the vehicle and was in the back seat, placed there by an unaware tow truck driver. Once an orange wire is dislodged, a series of events take place in milliseconds. A set of contactors, Toyota calls this the system main relay (SMR), go to their normally open positions and three large capacitors discharge. This keeps the high voltage contained to the HV battery pack. But taking no chances, rubber gloves were used to remove the large orange service plug. ● **SEE FIGURE 13–33**.

In this case, before that could be done, a jumper pack was required, as this vehicle has no hatch key, only a transmitter, and the 12-volt battery that was dead. After the hatch was opened, access to the high-voltage battery was available. The 12-volt battery was disconnected for one more measure of safety, even though it was dead. More precautions were used, such as getting out the DMM every time an orange cable was disconnected to check that there was zero or very low voltage at the cables. Disconnecting the HV cables allowed for the removal of the HV battery. Electrical tape was used to isolate any orange wire leads that were dangling and the high-voltage battery pack was carried by two technicians into the storage faculty to sit until it was sold.

FIGURE 13–33 The high-voltage disconnect plug on a second-generation Prius (2004+) includes a 125-ampere fuse. Always wear protective 1,000+ volt linesman's gloves with protective leather gloves over them when disconnecting this plug.

COOLING SYSTEM CONCERNS Flushing the coolant in the inverter can be a challenge. Toyota has a scan tool function to activate the 12-volt inverter coolant pump (it can be done manually). Getting air trapped in this system is easy and getting the air out can be difficult. See Tech Tip "Inverter Bleeding the Easy Way."

CAUTION: On a second-generation Toyota Prius, a 3-quart coolant heat storage tank is located just under the left headlight. Five hours after the vehicle is shut down, a 12-volt pump starts, a valve opens, and hot coolant is circulated into the cylinder head to keep it warm for restarts. The preheat system could burn a technician with scalding coolant. To be sure this does not happen, disconnect the pump. This can be done by removing the front of the left inner fender liner, then reaching in and disconnecting the connector from the coolant heat storage pump.

ROUTINE SERVICE The CVT requires periodic transmission fluid replacement. Be sure to use the factory-recommended fluid. Also, check the fluid level of the inverter coolant as it provides cooling for the ATF as well. The first-generation Prius used Toyota's Long Life Coolant, which was red in color. All Toyota HEVs built since 2003 have used the new Super Long Life Coolant (pink in color). ● **SEE FIGURE 13–34**.

WARNING

A small black steel pan is bolted to the bottom of the transmission on the first-generation Prius. The bolt in the pan is used for draining the ATF. Another bolt of similar size is located in the aluminum case between the transmission oil pan and the engine. Removing this bolt will drain the inverter coolant, which can be very difficult to refill.

REAL WORLD FIX

Brake Caliper Issues

On some early Toyota Prius models used in areas that use road salt, caliper failures have been reported at as little as 30,000 miles (48,000 km). One reason for this is that the regenerative braking does not require the front friction brakes to work very hard, and therefore the calipers freeze up prematurely.

FIGURE 13–34 Note that Toyota's Super Long Life Coolant is prediluted.

SUMMARY

1. The first-generation Prius was introduced in 2001 in the United States and the second generation was released in 2003 as a 2004 model.

2. The Prius engine uses the Atkinson cycle and displaces 1.5 liters.

3. The THS inverter is cooled by the same heat exchanger as the transaxle.

4. The Prius is ready to be driven when the READY light is on steady (steady ready).

5. The high-voltage battery packs on Toyota hybrids are air cooled using vents on the outside or alongside the rear seat.

6. The Lexus RX 400h has an optional rear motor, giving the vehicle four-wheel-drive capability.

7. Care should be taken when driving a Toyota hybrid in parking lots or at slow speeds in or around the shop because it operates on battery power alone under these conditions and others may not hear the vehicle approach.

REVIEW QUESTIONS

1. What is unique about starting a Prius?

2. What are the functions of the inverter in a Toyota HEV?

3. What is the procedure for disconnecting the high-voltage circuits on a Toyota HEV?

4. What are the precautions when working on Toyota hybrid vehicles?

1. Where is the 12-volt auxiliary battery located in a Toyota Prius?
   a. Under the back seat
   b. Under the hood, driver's side
   c. In the trunk
   d. Under the hood, passenger's side

2. Pressing the POWER button one time, without depressing the brake pedal, causes the HSD system to enter what mode?
   a. Accessory
   b. Ignition on
   c. Ready
   d. Vehicle started

3. On a Prius, what does the "B" mean on the shift indicator?
   a. Battery
   b. Braking
   c. Back up
   d. Booking

4. The energy monitor screen on a Toyota Prius shows the driver all of the following, *except* _____.
   a. When the gasoline engine is powering the vehicle
   b. When the electric motor is powering the vehicle
   c. When the gasoline engine is charging the high-voltage batteries
   d. When the rear motor is generating electricity during braking

5. In order for a Toyota Prius to start, what has to be OK?
   a. The high-voltage battery pack must be sufficiently charged to crank the engine.
   b. The auxiliary 12-volt battery must be sufficiently charged.
   c. The brake pedal must be depressed.
   d. All of the above

6. The Toyota Prius, Highlander, and Lexus RX 400h are all what type of hybrid electric vehicle?
   a. Full (strong)
   b. Medium
   c. Mild
   d. Plug-in

7. The Lexus RX 400h hybrid electric vehicle uses which of the follow systems?
   a. VDIM
   b. ETC
   c. EPS
   d. All of the above

8. Toyota HEV service is being discussed. Technician A says that the service plug should be removed any time the HV system is being serviced. Technician B says the service plug should be secured to prevent another technician from installing it while you are servicing the vehicle. Which technician is correct?
   a. Technician A only
   b. Technician B only
   c. Both Technicians A and B
   d. Neither Technician A nor B

9. The high-voltage batteries in Toyota hybrid electric vehicles are cooled by _____.
   a. Coolant
   b. An air conditioning evaporator
   c. Cabin air
   d. Phase-change liquid

10. Where is the high-voltage disconnect plug on a Prius?
    a. Under the hood, passenger's side
    b. To the left of the driver, next to the seat
    c. In the trunk
    d. Under the hood, driver's side

FORD/MERCURY HYBRID VEHICLES

OBJECTIVES: **After studying Chapter 14, the reader will be able to:** • Explain the operation of a Ford/Mercury hybrid electric vehicle (HEV). • Describe the features of a Ford/Mercury HEV. • Discuss the safety precautions to be followed whenever working on a Ford/Mercury HEV. • Explain how the electronically controlled continuously variable transmission (eCVT) allows the Ford/Mercury HEV to achieve maximum efficiency. • Describe the service procedures for Ford/Mercury HEVs.

KEY TERMS: • Ah 231 • BJB 234 • eCVT 225 • EPAS 231 • Floating Ground 229 • Green Zone 225 • Helper Pump 226 • HVTB 229 • RBS 232

INTRODUCTION

The Ford Escape and Mercury Mariner share most of the same components and, except for trim and other nonhybrid related features, are basically the same. ● **SEE FIGURES 14–1 AND 14–2**.

STATE-OF-THE-ART HYBRID TECHNOLOGY Full (strong) hybrid technology allows the vehicle to run exclusively on electric power or with the gasoline engine during normal operation. Actual fuel economy will vary depending on driving habits.

Exterior differences between the hybrid and nonhybrid version include:

- Unique grille
- Front and rear fascias
- Monotone body side-cladding
- Unique labels
- Standard 16-inch wheels
- Battery cooling air intake vent in the driver's side rear quarter window
- Escape/Mariner Hybrid is available with a special appearance package that features body-color door handles and silver bumper covers, body side-cladding, and wheel lip moldings.

Interior differences include:
- Center console gearshift
- Unique interior trim
- Offers seating for up to five and includes the same 60/40 split folding rear seat
- Efficient packaging of the hybrid technology, such as locating the battery pack at the rear cargo floor

FIGURE 14–1 The Ford Escape hybrid looks very similar to a conventional Ford Escape except for the hybrid emblems and several other details.

HIGH-VOLTAGE
BATTERY COOLING
AIR INLET VENT

FIGURE 14–2 The Mariner Hybrid SUV. The Ford/Mercury hybrids can be identified by the battery vent located in the left rear quarter window.

FIGURE 14-3 The dash display shows when the vehicle is being propelled using the electric motor alone, shown by the green area on the speedometer and labeled "EV." The gauge on the left of the tachometer indicates whether the electrical system is being charged by the gasoline engine or regenerative braking and when the electric motor is being used to assist the gasoline engine during acceleration.

- A unique gauge package features an economy indicator with **green zone** that shows when the vehicle is operating on battery power. ● **SEE FIGURE 14-3**.

- A hybrid hazard warning lamp, shown as a red triangle. This indicates to the driver that the vehicle should be stopped due to a hybrid system failure. A "Stop Safely Now" message will also appear in the instrument panel message center.

- A hybrid caution warning lamp, shown as a yellow wrench. This indicates to the driver that the vehicle requires service, but not immediately.

The Escape/Mariner HEVs are full (strong) hybrids, meaning they automatically switch between pure electric power, pure gasoline engine (ICE) power, or a combination of electric motor and gasoline engine operation to maximize efficiency and performance. The Escape/Mariner HEV is available as a two- or four-wheel-drive hybrid capable of towing up to 1,000 pounds when properly equipped.

FEATURES A separate gauge displays levels of charge and assist for the battery pack. An optional navigation system includes a unique energy flow diagram that displays hybrid system operation and a fuel economy screen that displays instant and average fuel economy.

Escape/Mariner Hybrid also offers a 110-volt AC power outlet, which can be used to operate a laptop computer, television, or other electrical device.

POWERTRAIN The Escape/Mariner hybrid powertrain system includes the following components:

- A 2.3-liter four-cylinder gasoline ICE featuring Atkinson-cycle combustion and producing 133 horsepower at 6,000 RPM
- A 70-kilowatt (equivalent to 93 horsepower) electric traction motor
- A generator-motor that recharges the batteries, starts the engine, and controls the CVT function of the transaxle
- A special **electronically controlled continuously variable transmission (eCVT)** used to drive the front wheels in a front-wheel-drive Escape/Mariner or all four wheels with the optional Intelligent 4WD System™
- A 330-volt nickel-metal-hydride battery pack located in the rear cargo floor

An electronic vehicle system controller manages charging, drive assist, and engine starting functions such as the idle stop function. ● **SEE FIGURE 14-4**.

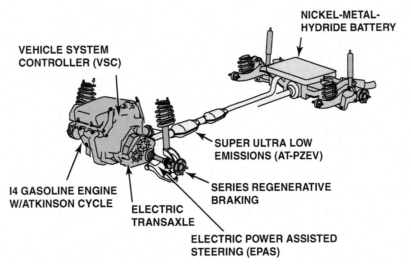

VEHICLE SYSTEM CONTROLLER (VSC)

NICKEL-METAL-HYDRIDE BATTERY

SUPER ULTRA LOW EMISSIONS (AT-PZEV)

I4 GASOLINE ENGINE W/ATKINSON CYCLE

ELECTRIC TRANSAXLE

SERIES REGENERATIVE BRAKING

ELECTRIC POWER ASSISTED STEERING (EPAS)

FIGURE 14-4 The Ford/Mercury hybrid SUV, showing the major components and where they are located.

The Ford/Mercury Hybrid uses a lightweight 2.3-liter four-cylinder ICE. The block and head are both constructed of aluminum, which saves 40 pounds. The engine also features:

- Double-overhead-cam design with four valves per cylinder
- Pent-roof combustion chambers, and centrally located spark plugs
- Direct-acting mechanical bucket tappets that require no lash adjustment during a 10-year, 150,000-mile service life
- Four orifice-type fuel injectors that provide a better spray pattern and finer atomization than is possible with more common single-orifice injectors
- Butterfly valves positioned in the intake runners that restrict airflow at low speeds to induce tumble as the fuel–air mixture enters the combustion chamber
- Counter-rotating balance weights that help eliminate vibration
  ● **SEE FIGURES 14–5 AND 14–6.**

The Ford/Mercury hybrid ICE uses a modified Atkinson combustion cycle for improved efficiency. This consists of a 12:1 compression ratio for maximum efficiency and late-closing intake valves to reduce pumping losses. Keeping the intake valve open longer yields a compression ratio below 9.0:1 at low speeds for good drivability without detonation and a much higher compression ratio at higher RPM for increased peak power. ● **SEE FIGURES 14–7 AND 14–8.**

FREQUENTLY ASKED QUESTION

What Is a Helper Pump?

The hybrid versions of the Ford Escape and the Mercury Mariner are equipped with a 12-volt-operated coolant pump. If cabin heat is needed and the ICE is off, the PCM commands the **helper pump** to turn on to circulate coolant through the heater core.

? FREQUENTLY ASKED QUESTION

What's This?

The air inlet to the Ford/Mercury hybrid ICE uses a charcoal filter to trap any hydrocarbons that may be in the intake manifold when the engine is turned off. When the engine starts, airflow through the charcoal draws out the hydrocarbons, which are then burned in the cylinders rather than being released into the atmosphere. ● **SEE FIGURE 14–9.**

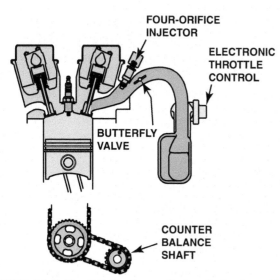

FIGURE 14–5 The 2.3-liter four-cylinder all-aluminum ICE used in the Ford Escape and the Mercury Mariner hybrids uses a modified Atkinson cycle design to achieve maximum efficiency.

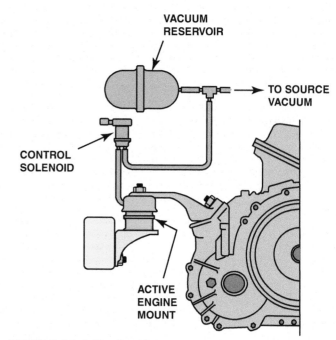

FIGURE 14–6 The Ford/Mercury 2.3-liter ICE is also equipped with an active engine mount that effectively dampens engine vibration during start/stop. The parts involved include a control solenoid, the active engine mount and a vacuum reservoir tank.

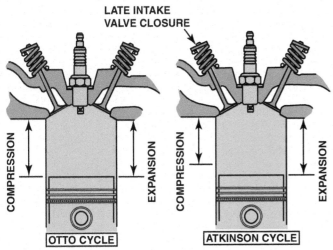

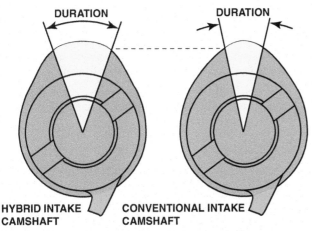

FIGURE 14–7 The Atkinson cycle delays the closing of the intake valve, which reduces the pumping losses on the compression stroke, yet results in a greater amount of expansion on the power stroke compared to a conventional (Otto cycle) gasoline engine design.

FIGURE 14–8 The cam lobe on the left is from a Ford/Mercury hybrid and shows the longer-duration intake cam lobe as compared to the intake cam lobe from a conventional gasoline engine on the right.

ELECTROMECHANICAL CVT

CONSTRUCTION The Ford/Mercury hybrid uses an electronically controlled continuously variable transmission that includes one planetary gearset, as compared to the two or more usually found in a conventional automatic. Instead of shifting from one ratio (gear) to the next in steps,

FIGURE 14–9 The air inlet to the ICE on the Ford/Mercury hybrid electric vehicle contains a charcoal filter that is used to trap and hold hydrocarbons and keep them from being released to the atmosphere.

the transaxle is designed to function smoothly, without detectable ratio changes. This is called a continuously variable transmission (CVT). This transaxle design combines the torque from the engine and traction (electric) motor. As a result, the gasoline engine can be shut down at low speeds and light loads to save fuel, while the vehicle is powered solely by the traction motor. The transaxle also routes a portion of the power produced by the engine to a generator. The transaxle includes the following components:

- 36-kW permanent magnet AC generator motor
- 70-kW permanent magnet AC traction motor
- Planetary gear set and final drive gears
- Integrated power electronics/voltage inverter
  - ● **SEE FIGURE 14–10**.

FOUR MODES OF OPERATION The transaxle operation takes place in one of four modes, as follows:

SERIES MODE.

1. Used only when the vehicle is not moving and the ICE is running. The transaxle will not enter this mode when it is placed in the "neutral" position.

NOTE: The eCVT used in the Ford Escape Hybrid operates similar to Toyota's power split transaxle. When the gear selector is in Neutral, the vehicle would tend to move if the generator motor was used to charge the HV battery. Therefore, HV battery charging takes place when the gear selector is in the Park position, but not in Neutral.

FIGURE 14-10 A cutaway of a Ford Escape/Mercury Mariner hybrid transaxle, which includes the traction motor and the generator motor.

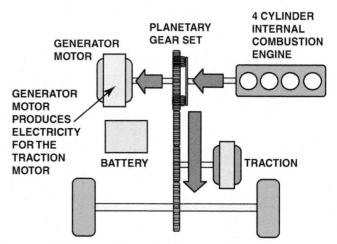

FIGURE 14-12 Positive split mode operation.

2. The ICE is running to charge the batteries or for climate control reasons. The ICE may also be running to keep the catalytic converter warm. ● **SEE FIGURE 14-11.**

POSITIVE SPLIT MODE.

1. The ICE is running and driving the generator motor to produce electricity.

2. Power from the ICE is split between the direct path to the drive wheels and the path through the generator motor.

3. This is the mode that is normally used while under cruise conditions. ● **SEE FIGURE 14-12.**

NEGATIVE SPLIT MODE.

1. The ICE is on and the generator motor is being used to consume electrical energy to reduce engine speed.

2. The traction motor can operate as a motor or a generator.

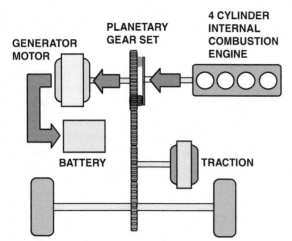

FIGURE 14-11 Series mode operation.

3. This mode is used during highway driving when the ICE has to be on but the HV battery pack does not need to be charged.

ELECTRIC MODE.

1. The vehicle is being propelled using stored electrical energy only using the traction motor.

2. This is the preferred mode whenever the required power is low enough for the electrical system to handle.

3. This mode is used in reverse because the ICE cannot deliver reverse torque through the transaxle.

ELECTRIC TRACTION MOTOR

The traction motor is a compact permanent magnet design that operates on 3-phase AC power. This power is drawn both from the generator and battery pack by using a power inverter that converts stored DC to AC. Its peak power is 70 kilowatts (equivalent to an extra 93 horsepower) at 3,000 to 4,000 RPM. During braking, the traction motor temporarily becomes a generator. The negative torque created by the generator is used to slow the vehicle, reducing the load on the base brakes and recharging the electric battery pack. The turning traction motor acts as a generator and the generated electricity is sent to the high-voltage battery.

Both the traction motor and the friction brakes are used to slow the vehicle. Regenerative braking is used in conjunction with the base brakes when possible. Regenerative braking is automatically controlled by the PCM along with the Brake System Control Module (BSCM). This electric regenerative braking represents a major part of the hybrid's efficiency advantage over conventional vehicles. ● **SEE FIGURE 14-13.**

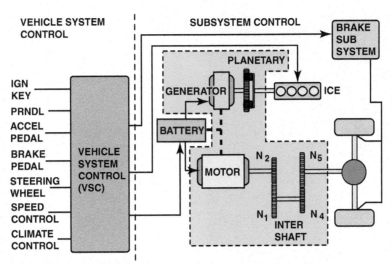

FIGURE 14–13 Ford Escape system chart showing the various sensors and components. The functions are distributed among engine, transaxle, and brake control modules. The VSC controls approximately 200 functions with about 600 signals between components.

GENERATOR MOTOR

The generator motor handles three tasks:

1. The primary responsibility is generating electric current. Most of the energy generated is used to charge the battery pack during cruising, but some of the current is sent to the traction motor during rapid acceleration.

2. The second task is starting the ICE or restarting it after shutdown, after a stop, or after coasting. In this situation, the generator acts as an AC motor and is rated at 28 kilowatts (38 horsepower).

3. The generator is also used to control the drive ratio in the transaxle's planetary gearset so that the ICE operates at its most efficient load and RPM.

● **SEE FIGURE 14–14**.

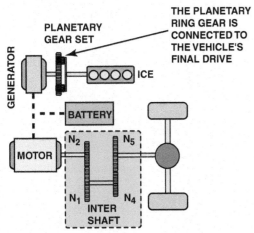

FIGURE 14–14 The transaxle is used to blend the torque from the gasoline engine and the traction motor together. The generator motor controls sun gear rotation; therefore, the effective gear ratio can vary anywhere from reduction all the way to overdrive. Thus, the eCVT is a continuously variable automatic transmission.

A fully automatic, electronically controlled 4WD system called Intelligent 4WD is available on the Ford Escape/Mercury Mariner Hybrid. In normal dry-pavement driving, torque is sent only to the front wheels. The PCM monitors wheel speeds and accelerator pedal position dozens of times per second. If slippage is detected, an electromagnetic clutch controlled by the computer applies torque to the rear wheels.

HIGH-VOLTAGE BATTERY PACK

The HV battery pack consists of 250 nickel-metal-hydride D-size cells connected in series, packaged under the cargo floor. Nickel-metal-hydride batteries have been used with excellent success in notebook computers and cell phones for years. The battery pack in the Ford/Mercury hybrid is covered by warranty for eight years or 100,000 miles. To meet AT-PZEV requirements in states that follow California's emissions standards ("Green" states), the warranty is extended to 10 years or 150,000 miles. ● **SEE FIGURE 14–15**.

The high-voltage charging system is a **floating ground** system. A floating ground system means that neither the power side nor the return side of the circuit is electrically connected to chassis or body ground. When the ICE is operating or the vehicle is moving, the high-voltage generator begins to generate high-voltage AC electricity. The high-voltage AC is changed to DC using electronics in the transmission control module (TCM). This high-voltage DC current is then supplied to the vehicle through the **high-voltage traction battery (HVTB)** cables to the high-voltage battery pack and the DC-DC converter.

BATTERY TEMPERATURE CONTROL The high-voltage (traction) battery pack works best if it is not too cold or too hot. Therefore, a traction battery cooling unit is integrated into

FIGURE 14–15 The high-voltage (traction) battery pack is located under the cargo floor area.

the driver's side of the cargo area and cooling air is brought in through a duct located on the driver's side rear window. The system is configured so that fresh air can be brought in for battery cooling, or air can be recirculated through the battery pack housing. Cooling fans are located inside the traction battery module and these circulate air over the high-voltage battery and the electronics located in the battery case. ● **SEE FIGURES 14–16 AND 14–17**.

For operation in cold climates, a battery heater is used to maintain the temperature of the high-voltage battery during cold soaks. The battery heater is powered by a 120-volt wall outlet and operates in conjunction with the ICE block heater. The heating elements are resistive element heaters mounted on printed circuit boards and located between the two layers of battery cells. When the vehicle is plugged in, the battery heater is turned on automatically if the cell temperature drops below 50°F (10°C) and then turns off if the temperature rises too high. This feature is installed on all Ford/Mercury hybrids sold in Canada and the cold-weather U.S. states, and is optional for all other areas.

 **TECH TIP**

Use the 12-Volt Battery to Charge the High-Voltage Batteries

The Ford/Mercury hybrid vehicles do not have a conventional starter motor, and therefore the ICE has to be started using the high-voltage batteries and the generator motor.

If the high-voltage batteries were to become discharged and not able to start the ICE, then it is possible for the 12-volt battery to charge the high-voltage batteries. This is achieved by sending the 12 volts to a special DC-DC converter located in the traction battery case, where the voltage is increased and then sent to the high-voltage batteries.

The switch used to start this recharging procedure is located behind a cover on the driver's side kick panel. When the switch is turned on, the 12-volt battery will charge the high-voltage batteries. To help prevent this process from discharging the 12-volt battery, an eight-minute timer is included in the circuit. The eight-minute recharge sequence can be repeated as needed to get the ICE started. After the ICE is running, both the high-voltage battery and the 12-volt battery will be charged from the motor/generator. ● **SEE FIGURE 14–18**.

NOTE: If the 12-volt battery is discharged, it can be jumped using a jump box or another vehicle, similar to jump starting a conventional vehicle.

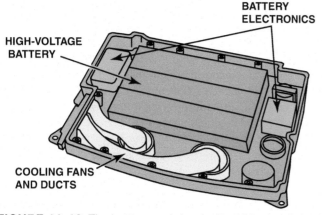

FIGURE 14–16 The battery pack from a Ford/Mercury hybrid showing the cooling ducts at the bottom.

FIGURE 14–17 The traction battery cooling unit is located on the driver's side of the cargo area and houses the battery zone A/C evaporator (labeled as "A").

FIGURE 14–18 A button is located behind a cover on the driver's side kick panel. By depressing this button, the 12-volt battery will charge the high-voltage batteries through the DC-DC converter.

NOTE: The "cold-weather states" include Alaska, Minnesota, North Dakota, South Dakota, Montana, Wisconsin, and Wyoming.

Total battery capacity is 5.5 **ampere-hours (Ah);** operating voltage varies between 216 and 397 volts. In the discharge mode, the battery pack can deliver up to 39 kilowatts of power and its maximum recharge rate is 31 kilowatts.

The high-voltage batteries are air-cooled, but could overheat in warm weather. If the temperature of the batteries increases above a predetermined level, the air-conditioning system is used to cool the batteries. The system uses a second evaporator, which is currently used to cool the rear of the conventional Escape/Mariner equipped with rear air conditioning. Because this system was already a current-production item, it was adopted to control the temperature of the batteries.

In the unlikely event that the high-voltage battery is not able to start the gasoline engine, jump starts are possible. A conventional 12-volt lead–acid battery is also provided to power the accessories such as the keyless entry system.

12-VOLT BATTERY

The 12-volt battery is a conventional lead–acid automotive battery. It is a direct-current source connected in a negative ground system. The battery has three major functions:

- Storage of electricity for later use
- Voltage stabilizer for the electrical system
- Temporary power when electrical loads exceed the DC-DC converter output current

The 12-volt battery is located under the hood. ● **SEE FIGURE 14–19**.

FIGURE 14–19 The 12-volt auxiliary battery is located under the hood on the driver's side, as shown.

ELECTRONIC CONTROLLER

The master device is a vehicle systems controller built into the powertrain control module. The engine controller is also housed within this underhood assembly.

An onboard electronic device (AC to DC converter) inside the transmission control module (TCM) converts the AC current produced by the generator motor and the traction motor to DC voltage suitable for recharging the battery pack. Power from the batteries must be inverted to AC to power the traction motor.

DC-DC CONVERTER The DC-DC converter is a liquid-cooled component that converts high-voltage (216 to 397 volts) DC power to low-voltage (12 volts) DC power while maintaining electrical isolation between the two DC power systems. The converter steps down the high voltage to 12 volts, providing power to the vehicle's low-voltage battery systems. The DC-DC converter is controlled by the PCM and is located under the hood on the passenger side of the vehicle in front of the shock tower.

Safety measures are also included to isolate high-voltage circuits in the event of tampering or a collision. ● **SEE FIGURE 14–20**.

NOTE: When the vehicle is switched off, the connection to the battery pack is opened inside the battery pack module.

ELECTRIC POWER ASSIST STEERING The **electric power assist steering (EPAS)** system consists of:

- Power steering control module
- Electric motor
- Torque sensor
- Rack-and-pinion steering gear

The electric power steering system provides power steering assist to the driver by replacing the conventional hydraulic valve system with an electric motor coupled to the

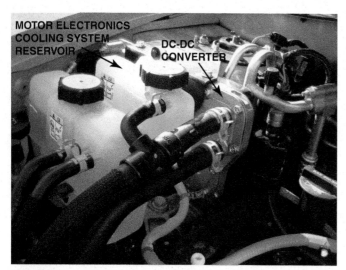

FIGURE 14–20 The cooling system for the transaxle also cools the DC-DC converter.

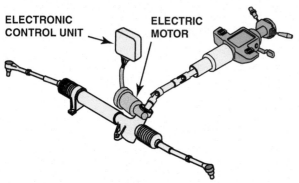

FIGURE 14–21 The Ford/Mercury hybrid uses an electric power steering assembly.

FIGURE 14–22 The electric power steering assembly partially disassembled showing the DC motor and electrical connector for the torque sensor.

FIGURE 14–23 The electric power steering torque sensor housing with connector.

steering gear. The motor is controlled by an electronic control unit that senses the steering effort through the use of a torque sensor mounted between the steering column shaft and the steering gear. Steering assist is provided in proportion to the steering input effort and vehicle speed. ● **SEE FIGURE 14–21**.

The electric power steering system requires a 12-volt, hot-at-all-times feed for fault management. The power steering control module is activated when power is applied to the hardwired ignition/run input. The power steering control module monitors the controller area network (CAN) bus. The CAN bus signal, sent by the powertrain control module (PCM) to the power steering control module, is used to indicate that power is being supplied to the DC-DC system for the power steering system. The electric power steering system powers itself down within three seconds after the key is moved to the OFF position. ● **SEE FIGURE 14–22**.

The PCM uses vehicle speed information over the CAN bus to determine the amount or level of power assist. As vehicle speed increases, the amount of power assist provided by the system is reduced to improve and enhance road feel at the steering wheel. If the vehicle speed signal is missing or out of range, the power steering control module defaults to a reduced level of assist. If the vehicle speed signal returns to the correct in-range values, the power steering control module adjusts the steering assist level accordingly. ● **SEE FIGURE 14–23**.

The power steering control module provides a periodic CAN message that indicates the operating condition of the electrical power steering system. Upon receiving an indication of a failure condition, the instrument cluster displays a text message.

The EPAS is lubricated for life and does not use a reservoir, fluid, or hoses.

REGENERATIVE BRAKING SYSTEM

The Ford Escape and Mercury Mariner are equipped with a **regenerative braking system (RBS).** The regenerative braking system is designed to recapture some of the vehicle's kinetic energy during deceleration and braking. It accomplishes this by configuring the traction motor as a generator and using the generated electricity to charge the high-voltage batteries.

The brake system used on the Ford/Mercury hybrid is a *series regenerative braking system* in which powertrain braking is used first, up to the limits of the powertrain torque capacity and battery capacity. After maximum regeneration is utilized, the friction (base) brakes are applied to supplement braking demands. The series regenerative braking system also contains the antilock brake system (ABS) module within the same unit.

The regenerative braking system (RBS) works even when the brakes are not applied. When the accelerator pedal is released, the vehicle slowly decelerates. This deceleration is caused by using the spinning motor as a generator to create electrical current. This recharges the battery pack and slows the vehicle. The RBS works only when the vehicle is traveling at 18 mph (29 km/h) or greater. When driving down hills, regenerative braking is used to maintain speed while recovering energy, similar to the way engine braking is typically used. When the battery is sufficiently charged, regenerative braking is eliminated to prevent overcharging of the batteries. Regenerative braking does not take the place of the standard friction brakes, but assists them.

SERVICE PROCEDURES

The Ford/Mercury hybrid vehicles are serviced the same as conventional vehicles except for certain precautions.

HIGH-VOLTAGE TRACTION BATTERY SYSTEMS DEPOWERING

WARNING

The nominal high-voltage traction battery (HVTB) voltage is 330 volts DC. A buffer zone must be set up and high-voltage insulated safety gloves and a face shield must be worn during HV system service. Failure to follow these instructions may result in severe personal injury or death.

1. Set up a buffer zone around the vehicle. ● **SEE FIGURE 14–24**.

FIGURE 14–24 The buffer zone is an area that should be marked with cones to warn others to avoid the area because of a high-voltage danger.

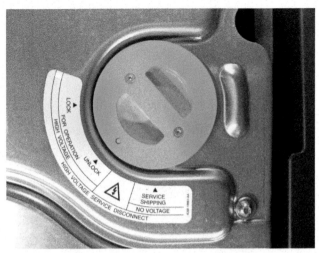

FIGURE 14–25 To depower the HV system, start by rotating the service disconnect plug CCW to the UNLOCK position.

2. Remove the service disconnect plug.
   a. Rotate the service disconnect plug CCW from the LOCK position to the UNLOCK position. ● **SEE FIGURE 14–25**.
   b. Remove the service disconnect plug and place in the SERVICE SHIPPING position.

   CAUTION: Place the service disconnect plug into the SERVICE SHIPPING position while the high-voltage traction battery (HVTB) is being removed and/or while the high-voltage system is having repairs carried out. If the service disconnect plug is left out and placed on the bench or toolbox, dirt or other contaminants may enter the HVTB, which can cause damage. ● SEE FIGURE 14–26.

3. Wear high-voltage linesman's gloves with leather gloves over them whenever working on the high-voltage circuits.

4. Always wear a face shield.

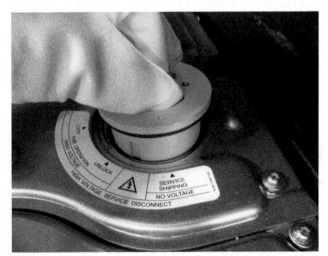

FIGURE 14–26 The service disconnect plug should be lifted and placed back in the SERVICE SHIPPING position before servicing the HV system.

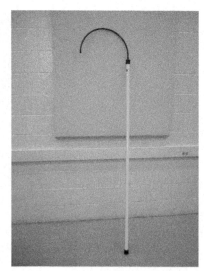

FIGURE 14–27 This fiberglass pole/steel hook assembly is required equipment for Ford dealerships that service Ford/ Mercury HEVs.

5. Have available a fiberglass hook outside the buffer zone so that a technician can be pulled to safety in the event of electrocution. ● **SEE FIGURE 14–27**.

INSPECTION AND VERIFICATION

NOTE: Verify that the service disconnect plug is properly inserted and rotated into the **LOCK** position.

1. Verify the customer concern.
2. Visually inspect for obvious signs of mechanical or electrical damage.
3. If an obvious cause for an observed or reported concern is found, correct the cause (if possible) before proceeding to the next step.
4. If the cause is not visually evident, connect the diagnostic tool to the data link connector and select the vehicle to be tested from the diagnostic tool menu.
5. Carry out the diagnostic tool data link test.

BRAKE FLUID REPLACEMENT

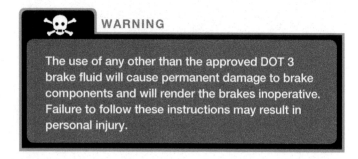

WARNING

The use of any other than the approved DOT 3 brake fluid will cause permanent damage to brake components and will render the brakes inoperative. Failure to follow these instructions may result in personal injury.

NOTE: Bleeding the hydraulic control unit (HCU) is required only when removing or installing the HCU, master cylinder, or opening the lines to the HCU.

NOTE: Make sure that the brake fluid level is above the MIN mark.

1. Adequate voltage to the HCU module is required during the system bleed. Connect the diagnostic tool.
2. Access the service bleed function on the diagnostic tool and follow the directions.

SERVICE BLEEDING

NOTE: The ignition key must be in the ON position when checking the brake fluid level.

 REAL WORLD FIX

Replacing Brake Pads Can Be a Concern

The special electrohydraulic braking system can cause personal injury. After the vehicle is parked and the key is out for approximately 15 minutes, a passive test will be conducted on the hydraulic brakes. During this test, the pump motor for the electronic brakes will operate all four brakes and check for leaks in the system. This self-test can also be initiated by opening the driver's door. The unsuspecting technician can get caught up in this small surprise and find the caliper pistons on the floor or suffer a smashed finger. There are four possible methods to prevent this during brake system service:

1. Disconnect the 12-volt battery under the hood and also remove fuses #24 (50 amp) and #31 (50 amp) from the **battery junction box (BJB)**. These are located in the underhood fuse box.
2. Disconnect the electrical connector at the brake hydraulic control unit.
3. Follow a procedure in the service manual that explains how to set the brake ECU into "Pad Service Mode" by pressing the brake pedal, cycling the ignition key, and then releasing the brake pedal.
4. Use a factory scan tool to place the system into "Brake Pad Replacement Mode."

CAUTION: Do not apply pressure to the hydraulic brake system until prompted by the diagnostic tool.

1. Connect the pressure bleeder to the vehicle. ● **SEE FIGURE 14–28**.
   ■ Do not apply pressure to the hydraulic brake system at this time.
2. Install rubber drain hoses to the brake bleeder screws and submerge the open ends of the hoses in clean brake fluid.
3. Carrying out the service bleed function drives trapped air from the HCU. Subsequent bleeding removes the air from the brake hydraulic system through the bleeder screws.

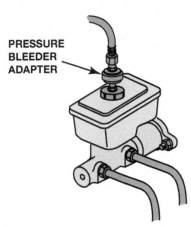

FIGURE 14–28 Using a pressure bleeder to bleed the brakes.

NOTE: Adequate voltage to the HCU module is required during the system bleed. Connect the diagnostic tool.

4. Using the pressure bleeder, apply 30 PSI (2 bars) of pressure to the brake system.

 TECH TIP

Have You Checked the Battery Air Filter Lately?

The A/C system battery zone is responsible for supplementing the cooling of the high-voltage battery. Cooling air is taken in from outside the vehicle and is filtered by a paper element located in the cooling ducts. If not serviced during the required interval, this filter could restrict airflow and cause overheating of the high-voltage battery. The filter can be serviced by removing a plastic cover located on the driver's side of the cargo area. ● **SEE FIGURE 14–29.**

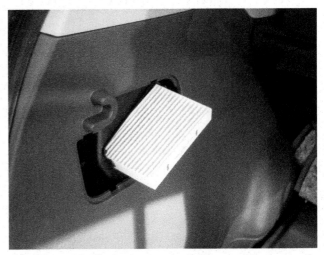

FIGURE 14–29 The battery zone air filter must be serviced regularly to prevent overheating of the high-voltage battery.

5. Access the service bleed function on the diagnostic tool.

6. The diagnostic tool indicates when the service bleed procedure is not followed correctly. Continue with the service bleed procedure after correcting the condition. While following the instructions on the diagnostic tool, apply the brake pedal one full stroke and then completely release the brake pedal.

OIL CHANGE The Ford hybrid engine requires 4.5 quarts of oil, and Ford specifies that SAE 5W-20 oil be used. The oil change procedure is the same as for a conventional vehicle, except be sure that the key is out of the ignition. ● **SEE CHART 14–1** for a summary of the components, description and their locations used in Ford and Mercury hybrid electric vehicles.

For technical service information on Ford/Mercury hybrid electric vehicles visit www.motorcraft.com.

COMPONENT	LOCATION	DESCRIPTION
Rear inertia switch	Passenger side, behind right rear trim panel.	The inertia switch disconnects high voltage and fuel in the event of a collision.
High-voltage service disconnect switch	The high-voltage service disconnect switch is located on the top, passenger side of the high-voltage battery. It has a molded plastic handle that is safety orange in color for easy identification. The high-voltage battery is located below the floor carpet in the rear of the vehicle.	Provides high-voltage battery disconnect for service. It has a molded plastic handle that is safety orange in color for easy identification.
High-voltage battery (300+ volts)	Rear of vehicle, below the carpet.	Sealed nickel-metal hydride, 300+ volts.
High-voltage wiring	Orange wire—runs along the bottom of the vehicle between the high-voltage battery and the eCVT (electronically controlled continuously variable transmission). Also connects eCVT to the DC-DC converter.	Connects high-voltage battery to eCVT. Connects eCVT to DC-DC converter. All high-voltage wires and connectors will be orange.

CHART 14–1

CONTINUED

COMPONENT	LOCATION	DESCRIPTION
12-volt battery	Driver side of the vehicle, under hood, front.	Provides 12-volt power to the vehicle. Conventional lead–acid battery.
eCVT (electronically controlled continuously variable transmission)	Same position as a conventional transaxle.	Contains the traction motor, generator motor, and hybrid electronics.
DC-DC converter	Passenger side, under hood. Located in front of the shock tower.	Provides 12-volt power to charge the battery and runs 12-volt electrical accessories.
Front inertia switch	Passenger compartment, passenger side, front seat, lower kick panel.	The inertia switch disconnects the high-voltage circuit and the electrical circuit to the gasoline fuel pump in a collision.

Note: All high-voltage wires and harnesses are wrapped in orange-colored insulation.

CHART 14–1 (CONTINUED)

SUMMARY

1. The Ford Escape and Mercury Mariner hybrids share most of the same components except for trim and other nonhybrid features.

2. The Ford/Mercury hybrids are full (strong) hybrids and are capable of propelling the vehicle using battery power alone.

3. The Ford/Mercury hybrids both use an electronically controlled continuously variable transmission (eCVT).

4. The generator motor in the eCVT has three functions: generating electric current, starting the gasoline engine, and controlling the drive ratio within the transaxle to keep the gasoline engine within its most efficient speed and load range.

5. The high-voltage battery pack is located under the floor at the rear of the vehicle. The batteries are air-cooled.

6. The 12-volt battery is a flooded lead–acid design and is located under the hood.

7. The Ford/Mercury hybrids use an electric power steering system.

8. Service procedures include setting up a buffer zone around the vehicle and depowering the high-voltage circuits.

9. Two fuses must be removed from the battery junction box (BJB) before servicing the brake system. A scan tool can also be used to place the system in "Brake Pad Replacement Mode."

REVIEW QUESTIONS

1. What are the differences between the Ford Escape hybrid and the Mercury Mariner hybrid?

2. How do the Ford/Mercury hybrids compare to other hybrid vehicles?

3. What are the features that are different about the Ford Escape and Mercury Mariner hybrids compared to the nonhybrid version of the same vehicle?

4. What safety precautions should be followed when working on the Ford Escape and Mercury Mariner hybrids?

CHAPTER QUIZ

1. The auxiliary 12-volt battery does all of the following, except _____.
   a. Powers the starter motor to crank the engine
   b. Stores electrical energy for later use
   c. Acts as a voltage stabilizer
   d. Provides temporary power

2. The vent located at the left rear of the vehicle is used to _____.
   a. Provide cool air for the gasoline engine
   b. Cool the high-voltage battery pack
   c. Cool the vehicle system controller (VSC)
   d. Both a and b

3. The Ford Escape and Mercury Mariner hybrid gasoline engines use the Atkinson cycle. This means that the engine _____.
   a. Has eight cycles instead of four cycles
   b. Has no spark plugs
   c. Uses just one valve per cylinder
   d. Delays the closing of the intake valves

4. The Ford and Mercury hybrid transaxles contain _____.
   a. A 45-kW AC generator motor
   b. A 70-kW AC traction motor
   c. Planetary gears and final drive gears
   d. All of the above

5. The Ford and Mercury hybrids are what type of hybrid?
   a. Series
   b. Full (strong)
   c. Medium
   d. Mild

6. What type of battery is used in the high-voltage system?
   a. 250 D-size batteries
   b. One large NiMH battery
   c. VRLA batteries
   d. None of the above

7. The DC-DC converter is located _____ and cooled by _____.
   a. Under the hood; a liquid cooling system
   b. Under the rear floor; a liquid cooling system
   c. Under the rear floor; air cooled
   d. Under the hood; air cooled

8. The Ford/Mercury hybrids use all of the following, *except* _____.
   a. Regenerative braking   b. Electric power-assist steering
   c. 12-volt starter   d. Idle stop capability

9. Ford and Mercury specify that the following precautions be observed when working on the high-voltage system:
   a. Create a buffer zone around the vehicle using cones.
   b. Wear linesman's gloves with leather gloves over them.
   c. Wear a face shield.
   d. All of the above.

10. What precaution(s) is/are needed before servicing the disc brakes on a Ford/Mercury hybrid vehicle?
    a. Remove the brake fluid from the master cylinder.
    b. Disable the high-voltage system.
    c. Disconnect two fuses.
    d. Unplug the electronic controller.

chapter 15

GENERAL MOTORS HYBRID VEHICLES

OBJECTIVES: **After studying Chapter 15, the reader will be able to:** • Identify General Motors hybrid electric and extended range electric vehicles. • Describe how the parallel hybrid truck system works. • Describe the features and operating characteristics of the Saturn, Chevrolet, and Buick mild hybrids, and two-mode hybrid vehicles. • Describe how the Chevrolet VOLT works. • Explain the precautions necessary when working on General Motors hybrid vehicles. • Explain the service procedures for General Motors hybrid vehicles.

KEY TERMS: • Auxiliary power outlet (APO) 240 • Belt alternator starter (BAS) 242 • Drive motor/Generator Control Module (DMCM) 247 • Electric machine (EM) 238 • Electro-hydraulic power steering (EHPS) 241 • Flywheel alternator starter (FAS) 238 • Parallel hybrid truck (PHT) 238 • Valve-regulated lead-acid (VRLA) 239

CHEVROLET/GMC PARALLEL HYBRID TRUCK

INTRODUCTION Chevrolet/GMC parallel hybrid truck is a mild hybrid that was built from 2004 until 2008. It looked like a conventional extended cab pickup and was sold throughout the United States. It used four batteries.

■ A conventional 12-volt flooded-type lead-acid battery under the hood, which is used for all of the 12-volt accessories.

■ Three 12-volt valve-regulated lead-acid (VRLA), also called absorbed glass mat (AGM), batteries connected in series located under the rear seat, which provides 36 volts for the electric traction motor.

Hybrid components in the truck are warranted for eight years/100,000 miles (160,000 km), in addition to the standard three year/60,000 km warranty. It is a mild hybrid design and is not able to be propelled using battery power alone.

BACKGROUND The overall goal of the **parallel hybrid truck (PHT)** was to maximize fuel economy on vehicles with relatively high fuel consumption and high-potential sales volume. For example, improving the fuel economy of a 15-mpg vehicle by 13% saves the same amount of fuel per mile driven as improving the total fuel economy of a 30-mpg vehicle by 30%. The more affordable hybrid system can be sold in greater numbers, increasing total fleet fuel saved.

To minimize cost, the following factors were considered:

■ Minimize the overall power level of the electrical components.

■ Minimize energy storage capacity.

■ Use low-cost energy storage (lead-acid batteries).

■ Avoid using unnecessary and costly accessories.

■ The full-size light-duty pickup truck GMC Sierra/ Chevrolet Silverado line was the most appropriate candidate. The extended-cab version, with its additional packaging space, allowed for energy (battery) storage.

The Vortec 5300 V-8 engine delivers 295 horsepower (220 kW) and 335 lb-ft (463 N-m) of torque, which is the same as its non hybrid counterpart.

Instead of a conventional starter motor and alternator, parallel hybrid pickups use a compact 14-kW electric induction motor or starter generator integrated in between the engine and transmission. The starter generator, which operates from the 36-volt battery pack, provides fast, quiet starting power and allows automatic engine stops/starts to conserve fuel. It also performs the following functions:

■ Smoothes out torsional vibrations (driveline surges).

■ Generates electrical current to charge the batteries and run auxiliary power outlets.

■ Provides coast-down regenerative braking, as an aid to fuel economy.

STARTER-ALTERNATOR The pickup trucks have what General Motors calls a **flywheel alternator starter (FAS)** hybrid system. A three-phase AC induction electric motor, called an **electric machine (EM)** by General Motors, was selected due to low cost, simple controls, and its ability to perform over the entire engine operating range. The electric machine was designed as two assemblies.

■ A rotor assembly

■ A stator assembly

The stator is located around the rotor and supported by a stamped assembly positioned by existing dowels on the rear face of the engine block and clamped between the engine and transmission. ● **SEE FIGURE 15–1.**

The rotor assembly consists of an electric rotor assembled onto a rotor hub that is bolted to the engine crankshaft and wrapped around the torque converter. ● **SEE FIGURE 15–2.**

When the trucks are slowing down or come to a stop, the fuel is shut off and the engine stops. This saves fuel and when the driver releases the brake pedal, the flywheel alternator starter, taking electrical power from the 36-volt batteries, is used to restart the engine. The electric motor is not capable of propelling the truck forward at lower speeds using battery and electric motor power alone.

BATTERIES Three **valve-regulated lead-acid (VRLA)** batteries are used in the GM parallel hybrid truck to provide a 36-volt nominal voltage and a charging voltage of 42 volts. ● **SEE FIGURE 15–3.**

A 36-volt lead-acid battery pack, three 12-volt batteries electrically connected in series, was chosen to provide the low-level power and energy storage needs at reasonable cost. By using conventional lead-acid batteries, the problems of high cost, poor low-temperature performance, and charge control issues posed by nickel-based and lithium-based batteries were eliminated. Still retaining the vehicle 12-volt battery, a dual 36-volt vehicle electrical system minimizes component changes. Fixed-rate on–off charging is based on battery state-of-charge (SOC). ● **SEE FIGURE 15–4.**

FIGURE 15–1 Stator assembly used on the General Motors parallel hybrid truck.

FIGURE 15–3 The three VRLA batteries are located under the rear seat. Note the clear plastic tubes used to the event that pressure in the batteries opens the vent valve(s).

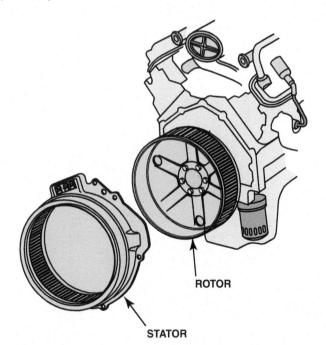

ROTOR

STATOR

FIGURE 15–2 The flywheel alternator starter assembly.

FIGURE 15–4 The decal under the hood shows the location of the 12-volt and the 36-volt (three 12-volt in series) (42 volts charging voltage) batteries.

Does the Electric Motor Smooth Out the Pulsations of the Engine?

Yes. Most hybrid electric vehicles use the computer to control the electric motor to help reduce variations in crankshaft speeds that normally occur at low speeds. This variation in crankshaft speed is due to the firing impulses and is most noticeable to a driver when the torque converter clutch is engaged at low vehicle speeds, and is often described as "chuggle" or "surge." The PCM commands the electric motor to apply a counter torque to the crankshaft to smooth out these disturbances.

Use a Laptop Computer in GM Hybrid Trucks

The 120-volt outlet in the rear seat area of the Chevrolet hybrid truck makes it convenient to use a laptop computer because the power available at the outlet does not require the use of an inverter that is needed in other vehicles that do not have 120-volt AC. ● **SEE FIGURE 15–6.**

In an emergency, the 120-volt outlet can be used to power

A refrigerator	500 watts
A television	150 watts
A microwave	over 900 watts
Five lightbulbs	500 watts
Total =	2,050 watts

IDLE STOP The engine is turned off as the vehicle slows to a stop and remains stopped until the brake pedal is released. This saves fuel and when the driver releases the brake pedal, the flywheel alternator starter, taking electrical power from the 36-volt batteries, is used to restart the engine. The vehicle may not enter idle stop mode under certain conditions, such as when the charge of the 36-volt battery pack is low.

AUXILIARY POWER OUTLET SYSTEM The parallel hybrid trucks have power outlets located under the rear seat of the cab and in the pickup bed. These two duplex power outlets are called the **Auxiliary Power Outlet (APO)** system.

The APO system provides up to 2,400 watts of 120-volt AC power. With these power outlets, most auxiliary electrical equipment and devices with a maximum limit of 2,400 watts can be plugged in.

The APO features ground-fault-protected 120-volt, 20-amp (2,400 W) outlets (a duplex outlet under the rear seat in the cab, and a duplex outlet in the truck bed), which can be used to power heavy-duty tools and equipment when used in "normal" mode. ● **SEE FIGURE 15–5.**

FIGURE 15–6A A laptop computer or other similar device can be plugged into the 120-volt AC outlet in the interior of the Chevrolet hybrid truck.

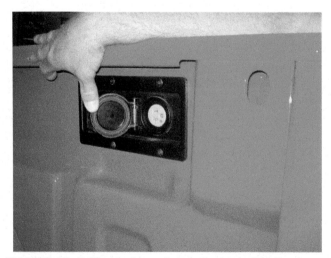

FIGURE 15–5 The double outlets in the bed of the truck are covered with a spring-loaded rubber-sealed cover to keep out water and dirt.

FIGURE 15–6B The laptop cord can be left plugged into the outlet, making it easy to use.

When the truck is parked and the key is removed from the ignition (doors locked), the APO can be placed in "continuous" mode, enabling the engine to run unattended while the truck is effectively used as a generator. The outlets are activated while the truck is running and the shifter is in Park. According to General Motors, the parallel hybrid pickups can maintain power for up to 32 hours, non-stop, before needing to fill the tank. If the truck runs low on fuel in this mode, the horn sounds to alert the owner.

NOTE: The power is shut off before the gas tank is completely drained, so the engine will start and not leave the driver stranded.

FIGURE 15–7 An electrohydraulic power steering assembly on a Chevrolet hybrid pickup truck.

GROUND-FAULT DETECTION (GFD)

PURPOSE AND FUNCTION The 120-volt AC power outlets are protected against short circuits, overloads, and ground faults. If the system detects a shorted or overloaded circuit, it will immediately shut off the outlets and the light next to the APO button will flash, while at the same time a "120-V OVERLOAD" message will appear in the Driver Information Center (DIC). After the fault condition is corrected, the system can be reset by pressing and releasing the APO button. Short circuits may occur because a defective extension cord or defective electrical device is plugged into an outlet.

RESETTING PROCEDURES Some electrical devices, such as motor-driven appliances and tools, have high start-up currents. During this start-up period, the 120-volt AC supply will attempt to start the electrical device for up to five seconds. If the current does not fall below the maximum 20-amp rating of the APO within this five-second timeframe, the system will shut off the outlets and the light next to the APO button will flash, while at the same time a "120-V OVERLOAD" message in the DIC will appear.

ELECTROHYDRAULIC POWER STEERING

PARTS AND OPERATION A 42-volt electrohydraulic power steering (**EHPS**) pump replaces the traditional belt-driven unit. This system allows the operation of the power steering when the engine is off during idle stop conditions. On the Chevrolet Silverado hybrid truck, the EHPS module controls the power steering motor, which has the function of providing hydraulic power to the brake booster and the steering gear.

A secondary function includes the ability to improve fuel economy by operating on a demand basis and the ability to provide speed-dependent variable-effort steering.

The EHPS module controls the EHPS power pack, which is an integrated assembly consisting of the following components:

- Electric motor
- Hydraulic pump
- Fluid reservoir
- Reservoir cap
- Fluid level sensor
- Electronic controller
- Electrical connectors
  - ● **SEE FIGURE 15–7.**

PARALLEL HYBRID TRUCK SYSTEMS

HVAC SYSTEM Passenger compartment cooling needs during typical engine auto stop events (statistically, 90% of stops are less than 30 seconds) are met by careful management of refrigerant capacity already in the system prior to the stop. Longer stops result in automatic engine restarts. Passenger compartment heating during auto stop periods is accomplished by a simple electric auxiliary coolant pump plumbed in series with the heater core. The auxiliary pump maintains the flow of hot coolant through the heater core during engine idle stop mode.

ELECTRIC MACHINE COOLING Coolant for the electric machine (electric motor) is taken from the engine water jacket, and is routed around the stator through a water channel created by the two stampings used as a carrier for the stator, and returned to the suction side of the engine coolant system. This plumbing blocks the flow of coolant through the electric machine until the engine thermostat opens so as not to delay engine warm up.

DRIVING THE GM PARALLEL HYBRID TRUCK

HILL CONTROL On the road, the Sierra/Silverado hybrid vehicles drive like any other V-8-powered GM pickup. One initially unnerving effect of the idle stop feature is that on a grade, the truck will roll backward in the time it takes between depressing the brake and automatically restarting of the engine. This can be avoided by pressing the "tow/haul" button at the end of the column-mounted gear shift, which prevents the engine from entering idle stop mode.

AUTOMATIC ENGINE START/STOP OVERRIDE The automatic engine start/stop override feature may cause the engine to remain running at a complete stop or may start the engine at a complete stop.

The engine will stay running at a complete stop or will automatically start from a complete stop if

- The outside temperature is high—usually above 95°F (35°C). The climate control system is working to cool the cabin in AUTO mode.
- The climate control system is in front defrosting mode.
- The brake pedal is released in Drive (D) or Third (3).
- The shift lever is in Neutral, Reverse (R), Second (2), or First (1).
- The battery pack charge is low.
- The tow/haul mode is active.
- The transfer case is in the 4LO position.
- Any door is opened while the vehicle is in Park (P).
- It is necessary to maintain 120-volt APO operation for loads greater than 1 kW.
- The hood is not fully closed.

CAUTION: Personal injury can occur if the vehicle is in the auto stop mode and the shift lever is in Drive (D). Because the vehicle has the automatic engine start/stop feature, the engine might be shut off at a complete stop. However, if the driver were to exit the vehicle, the engine will start again and the vehicle can move forward as soon as force is removed from the brake pedal. Therefore, if exiting the vehicle, first shift to Park (P) and turn the ignition to LOCK.

GENERAL MOTORS MILD (ASSIST) HYBRIDS

PURPOSE AND FUNCTION The purpose of the mild hybrid design used in mid-size General Motors vehicles is to provide many of the benefits of a hybrid electric vehicle with the least amount of changes to the base vehicle as possible.

APPLICATIONS The mild (assist) GM hybrid system is found on the following vehicles:

- Saturn VUE and Aura (2007–2010)
- Chevrolet Malibu (2007+)
- Buick LaCrosse (2012+)

PARTS AND OPERATION The Saturn VUE and Aura and the Chevrolet Malibu hybrid systems include:

- Idle stop feature (start-stop)
- Regenerative braking

These functions are made possible by using a **Belt Alternator Starter (BAS)** system. ● **SEE FIGURE 15–8.**

The large alternator which is also used to start the gasoline engine during restarts after idle stop, is driven by a wider-than-normal accessory drive belt. A dual-tensioner assembly for the motor/generator allows for the transfer of a small amount of torque to the drive system for very brief periods of time. The assembly combines a hydraulic strut tensioner and a friction-damped rotary tensioner on a common pivoting arm to control the bi-directional loads (motoring and generating). ● **SEE FIGURE 15–9.**

OPERATION The gasoline engine is started using the conventional starter motor when first started. After the engine is running, the hybrid assist system can then provide the following:

1. Electrically motored creep at startup
2. Light power assist during acceleration
3. Light regenerative mode during deceleration

The system consists of the following six elements:

1. The electric motor/generator unit that replaces the alternator, and is capable of 115 lb-ft (156 N-m) of auto-start torque.
2. Engine coolant-cooled power electronics that control the motor/generator unit and provide 12-volt vehicle accessory power.
3. A 36-volt NiMH hybrid battery pack capable of delivering and receiving more than 10 kW of peak power. The battery pack is behind the rear seat.
4. An engine control module.
5. An engine accessory drive using a dual-tensioner assembly and aramid cord belt that enables transfer of starting/propelling and generating torque. (● **SEE FIGURE 15–10.**)

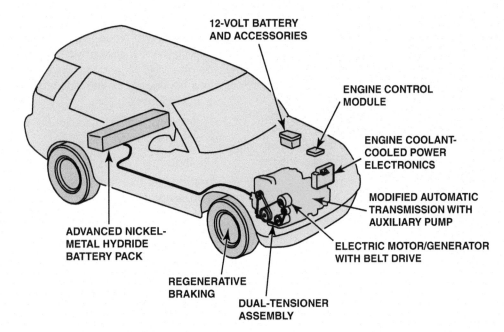

FIGURE 15–8 An overall view of the components and their locations in a Saturn VUE hybrid electric vehicle.

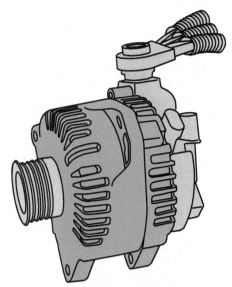

FIGURE 15–9 The motor/generator assembly used in the Saturn VUE and Chevrolet Malibu hybrid vehicle.

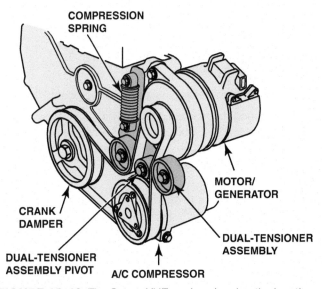

FIGURE 15–10 The Saturn VUE engine showing the location of the accessories and the motor/generator. The dual-tensioner assembly that controls the motoring (help to power the vehicle) and generating loads.

6. Hybrid-enabled Hydra-Matic 4T45-E electronically controlled four-speed automatic transaxle that includes an auxiliary oil pump and unique hybrid controls.

The mild hybrid enables early fuel cutoff to the engine during deceleration and shuts off the engine at idle (idle stop mode). Regenerative braking and optimized charging combined with an energy storage system further enhance fuel economy while maintaining all vehicle accessories and air conditioning systems during the periods when the engine is temporarily shut off.

The BAS systems indicate a range of improvement in fuel economy of around 10% to 12%.

BUICK/CHEVROLET eASSIST MILD HYBRID The BAS system used in the Chevrolet and Saturn mild hybrids was

updated in 2011 to include the following changes used in the 2012+ Chevrolet Malibu and Buick LaCrosse:

1. Uses a 15-kW electric motor-generator up from 10 kW.

2. Uses a 115-volt lithium-ion battery pack instead of a 36-volt NiMH battery.

3. The motor-generator can provide up to 15 horsepower and 79 lb-ft of torque to the 2.4 liter Ecotech four-cylinder engine.

The use of the higher voltage and more powerful motor-generator allows the archive a boost to acceleration and an improvement in fuel economy.

GENERAL MOTORS TWO-MODE HYBRID

BACKGROUND The two-mode system is under joint development by General Motors, Chrysler, and BMW. The two-mode hybrid system is a full (strong) hybrid and is capable of propelling the vehicle on battery power alone. The two-mode system is used in the following vehicles:

- BMW 7 series hybrid (2011+)
- Cadillac Escalade (2008+) ● **SEE FIGURE 15–11.**
- Chevrolet Tahoe (2008+)
- Chrysler Aspen (2009)
- Dodge Durango (2009)
- GMC Yukon (2008+)
    ● **SEE FIGURE 15–12.**

The first mode provides fuel-saving capability in low-speed, stop-and-go driving with a combination of full electric propulsion and engine power. In the first mode, the vehicle can operate in three ways:

- Electric power only
- Engine power only
- Any combination of engine and electric power

The second mode is used primarily at highway speeds to optimize fuel economy, while providing full engine power when conditions demand it, such as trailer towing or climbing steep grades. ● **SEE FIGURE 15–13.**

POWERTRAIN The two-mode hybrid features two 60-kW motors in the hybrid drivetrain, a 300-volt battery pack, and a V-8 engine. The BMW 7 series two-mode hybrid uses a twin-turbocharged 4.4 liter V-8 with an 8-speed automatic transmission. A two-mode hybrid electric vehicle is capable of increasing the fuel economy by about 25%, depending on the type of driving conditions. Like all hybrids, the two-mode combines the power of a gasoline engine with that of electric motors and includes:

- Regenerative braking that captures kinetic energy that would otherwise be lost
- Idle stop

Existing full hybrid systems have a single mode of operation, using a single planetary gearset to split engine power to drive the wheels or charge the battery. ● **SEE FIGURE 15–14.**

These systems are effective at low speeds because they can move the vehicle without running the gasoline engine. ● **SEE FIGURE 15–15.**

At higher speeds, when the engine is needed, using the electric motors has much less benefit. As a result, sending power through electric motors and a variable transmission is roughly 20% less efficient than driving the vehicle through a purely mechanical power path, using gears.

COMPONENTS The components of the two-mode transmission include the following:

- Two 60-kW electric motor/generators assemblies.
- Three planetary gearsets (one is located in front of motor/generator A; another is located between the two motor/generators, and the last is located behind motor/generator B).
- Four wet plate clutches (two friction [rotating] and two mechanical [stationary] clutch assemblies).
    ● **SEE FIGURE 15–16**

FIGURE 15–11 This Cadillac Escalade, like many hybrids built by General Motors have many emblems showing that it is a hybrid electric vehicle.

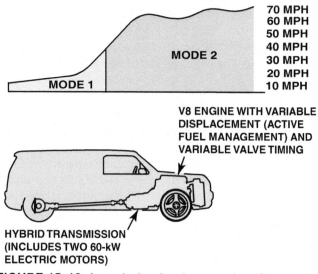

FIGURE 15–12 A graph showing the operation of the two-mode hybrid vehicle. At lower speeds, the vehicle is capable of being propelled using electrical power alone and assist at higher speeds.

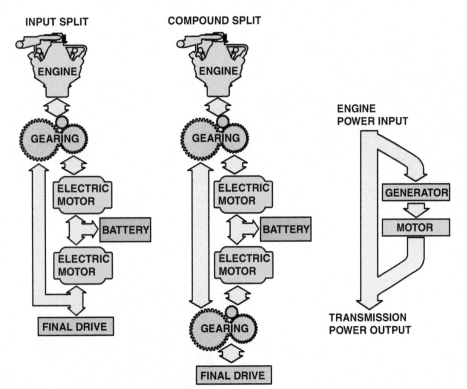

FIGURE 15–13 The two modes of the GM two-mode hybrid vehicle.

FIGURE 15–14 The two-mode General Motors hybrid encloses both electric motor-generators inside the transmission case.

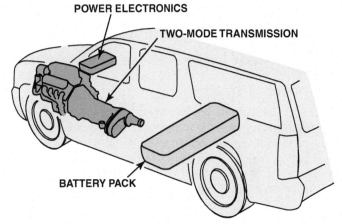

FIGURE 15–15 The two-mode General Motors vehicle is a full (strong) hybrid capable of propelling the vehicle using battery power alone.

TWO MODES OF OPERATION

- The *first mode* is for accelerating from standstill to second gear. At low speed and light load, the vehicle can move with

  - Either of the two electric motors alone

  - The internal combustion engine (ICE) alone

  - Or a combination of the two (electric motor and/or ICE)

In this mode, the engine (if running) can be shut off under certain conditions and everything will continue to operate on electric power alone. The hybrid system can restart the ICE at any time as needed. One of the motor/generators operates as a generator to charge the high-voltage battery and the other works as a motor to assist in propelling the vehicle.

The *second mode* takes the vehicle from second gear through to overdrive. At higher loads and speeds, the ICE always runs. In the second mode, the motor/generators and planetary gearsets are used to keep torque and horsepower at a maximum. As the vehicle speed increases, various combinations of the four fixed ratio planetary gears engage and/or disengage to multiply engine torque, allowing one or the other of the motor/generators to perform as a generator to charge the high-voltage battery.

FIGURE 15-16 Cutaway view of the two-mode General Motors transmission.

power source). This arrangement provides two operating modes for the electric motors. ● **SEE FIGURES 15-18 THROUGH 15-21.**

The system adds two clutches, which can engage different gear combinations to provide an overlay of four fixed (not variable) gear ratios. To the driver, the gear ratios feel and function like the stepped gear changes of an automatic transmission. Because the torque is multiplied by the gears, the electric motors can be much smaller and fit in the same housing as the transmission. ● **SEE FIGURE 15-22** on page 248.

SERVICE Besides the normal routine service that any vehicle requires, the two-mode hybrid uses a separate cooling system that may require service. This cooling is for the

BATTERIES Two-mode hybrid electric vehicles use two batteries.

1. **Auxiliary Battery** A conventional 12-volt flooded-type lead-acid battery located under the hood. The BMW uses an absorbed glass mat (AGM) 12-volt battery located under the hood. This auxiliary battery is used to power the electronics and the accessories in the vehicle. The 12-volt battery is kept charged by the use of a DC-to-DC converter that converts the 300 volts DC from the high-voltage battery pack to 12 volts DC for the auxiliary battery.

2. **High-Voltage Battery** A 300-volt nickel-metal halide (NiMH) battery pack located under the rear seat. ● **SEE FIGURE 15-17.**

The high-voltage battery is charged by the motor/generators inside the transmission. The motors are used to propel the vehicle and to charge the high-voltage battery during regenerative braking.

TWO-MODE OPERATION The two-mode system also has an electrically variable transmission but adds two planetary gearsets (which multiply the torque from the

FIGURE 15-17 The high voltage NiMH battery pack is located underneath rear seat in the GM two-mode hybrid vehicle. The high voltage disconnect plug is located on the passenger side of the battery pack.

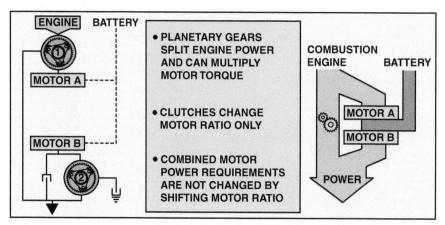

FIGURE 15-18 The gasoline engine can power motor A to charge the batteries and help propel the vehicle.

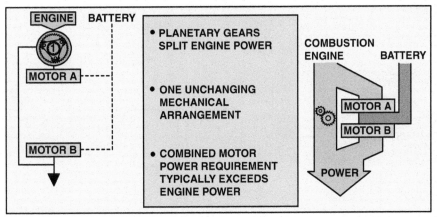

FIGURE 15–19 The high-voltage battery current can be fed to both electric motors to propel the vehicle.

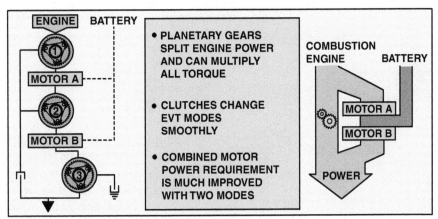

FIGURE 15–20 The electric motors can be used to assist the gasoline engine to provide additional torque for rapid acceleration.

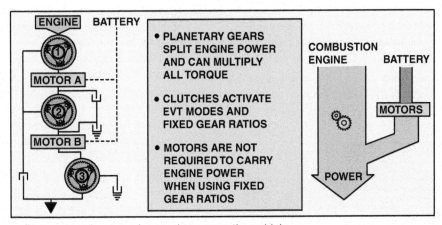

FIGURE 15–21 The gasoline engine alone can be used to power the vehicle.

Drive Motor/Generator Control Module (DMCM) system. The DMCM cooling system includes:

- The DMCM coolant surge tank,
- DMCM surge tank pressure cap,
- DMCM cooling pumps, and
- Hybrid cooling radiator and the Drive Motor/Generator Control Module (DMCM).

The DMCM cooling system uses a 50–50 pre-mixed DEX-COOL™ coolant and de-ionized water.

TECH TIP

Raise the Hood to Keep the Engine Running

When the hood is raised, the engine will remain running and will not try to enter into the idle stop mode. This makes it easy when service work that requires the engine to be kept running is being performed.

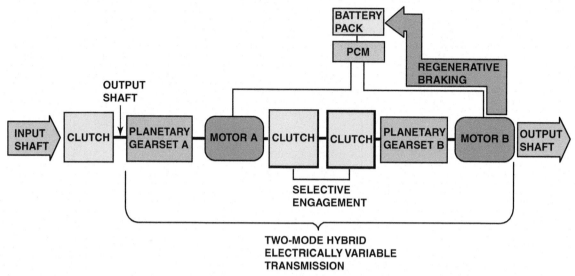

FIGURE 15–22 The two-mode hybrid also operates on electric power alone during deceleration (regenerative braking).

CHEVROLET VOLT

GENERAL DESCRIPTION The 2011+ Chevrolet Volt is an extended range electric vehicle based on the Chevrolet Cruze platform. ● **SEE FIGURE 15–23.**

Major features of the Volt include:

- A 346-volt lithium-ion 435 lb (197 kg) battery pack that has 16 kW-h (16,000 watt-hours) of electrical power.

- A 1.4 liter four-cylinder gasoline engine (premium fuel required) that produces 84 HP and 92 lb-ft of torque.

- The Volt is capable of being powered using battery power alone for 25 to 50 miles depending on conditions and driving style.

- The gasoline engine is started only to extend the range once the state-of-charge of the battery pack is reduced to 25% to 35%.

FIGURE 15–23 The Chevrolet Volt is a small four door vehicle that is based on the Chevrolet Cruze platform.

FOUR PHASES OF OPERATION There are four phases of operation of the Chevrolet Volt, including the following:

1. In the low-speed electric vehicle mode the vehicle is powered up to about 40 MPH (65 km/h) using electrical power from the high-voltage battery to the larger of the two electric motors inside the transaxle assembly.

2. Above about 40 MPH, the second smaller electric motor starts to help power the vehicle, which reduces the speed of the larger electric motor. The two motors connect to the planetary gearset inside the transaxle and their combined torque is applied to the drive wheels.

3. The vehicle operates using electric power alone until the state-of-charge (SOC) of the high-voltage battery drops to about 30% . At this time the gasoline engine will start, which drives the smaller electric motor so it becomes a generator to keep the high-voltage battery at about 30% SOC (25% to 35%).

4. At highway speeds, the gasoline engine helps power the vehicle. Using the gasoline engine to help power the vehicle at higher speeds allows the large electric motor to operate slower thereby increasing its efficiency.

VOLT HIGH-VOLTAGE BATTERY PACK The high-voltage battery pack in the Chevrolet Volt is located under the center console and under the rear seat. ● **SEE FIGURE 15–24.**

The battery pack is kept cool by using a separate cooling system. The system has a coolant pump and reservoir with a 5 PSI pressure cap. ● **SEE FIGURE 15–25.**

When the high-voltage battery pack drops to about 30% SOC, the gasoline engine is turned on to maintain a certain level of battery charge. However, the engine is not able to fully charge the high-voltage battery pack. To fully charge the high-voltage battery, the vehicle must be plugged into to an electrical outlet. ● **SEE FIGURE 15–26** (smart phone photo).

Normal battery usage includes two modes.

- **Charge Depleting Mode.** During the charge depleting mode, the vehicle is operating in electric vehicle (EV)

FIGURE 15–24 The high-voltage battery pack is housed between the seat under the center console and under the rear seat. The orange high-voltage disconnect plug is shown in this cutaway model and is located under the console package tray.

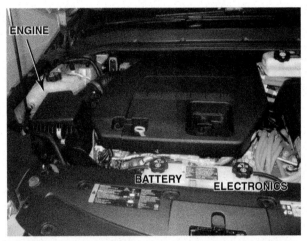

FIGURE 15–25 The engine cooling system uses a 20 PSI pressure cap and the cooling systems for the battery and the electronic use 5 PSI caps.

FIGURE 15–26 A smart phone can be used to link On-Star in the Chevrolet Volt, which can send state-of-charge and estimated range information.

mode only. All power needed to propel the vehicle, and for heating and cooling is provided by the high-voltage battery. The range of EV mode can vary from 25 to 50 miles depending on the weather and driving conditions.

- **Charge Sustaining Mode.** In charge sustaining mode, the gasoline engine is cycled on and off as needed to keep the battery state-of-charge at the 25% to 35% level. The driver has no control over when the engine starts or stops. ● **SEE FIGURE 15–27.**

ENGINE MAINTENANCE MODE Engine operation in the Chevrolet Volt is carefully monitored because the engine may not run for many days or even weeks if driven in electric vehicle mode. The engine maintenance mode is needed because

- Fuel can age and old fuel can cause problems with proper engine operation.
- The engine needs to be kept lubricated to prevent rust and corrosion of internal engine parts.

To address these concerns the controller is capable of performing the following functions:

1. **Fuel weathering.** The powertrain control module keeps track of the amount of fuel used during each drive cycle and calculates the percentage of new and old fuel that is in the fuel tank. If the age of the fuel is determined to be a concern, the driver will be notified that the engine will likely be started to use some of the fuel. It may require several drive cycles for the fuel to be used so that even though the vehicle is used only in electric vehicle mode, it will use some gasoline to maintain fresh fuel in the system. This condition will be rarely used and the gasoline life monitor will attempt to keep the fuel in the tank so that it is less than a year old.

2. **Engine Lubrication.** To help keep the mechanical parts of the gasoline engine at peak operating efficiency the powertrain control module will perform the following actions if the engine has not run for an extended period.

   - Power the actuators such as the electronic throttle control (no engine operation).
   - Engine spin without fuel.
   - Engine spin with fuel and spark (too lean to cause the engine to actually start).
   - Engine start to purge contaminates from the oil and condensate from the exhaust.

These modes will be very rare and used only if the vehicle is used in electric vehicle mode for many days or weeks.

CHARGING THE VOLT The Chevrolet Volt comes equipped with a charging cable that is stored in the rear compartment which can be used to recharge the vehicle from a 110- to 120-volt outlet (Level 1). ● **SEE FIGURE 15–28.**

The standard connector built into the left front fender of the vehicle can also be used to charge the vehicle from a 220- to 240-volt (Level 2) charging station or outlet.

For technical service information on General Motors hybrid electric vehicles, visit *www.gmtechinfo.com.*

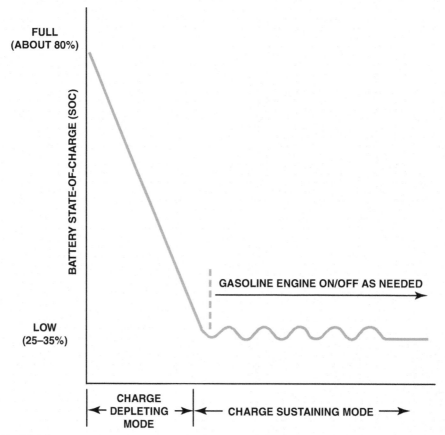

FIGURE 15–27 After the Volt has been charged it uses the electrical power stored in the high-voltage battery to propel the vehicle and provide heating and cooling for 25 to 50 miles (40 to 80 km). Then the gasoline engine starts and maintains the SOC between 25% and 35%. The gasoline engine cannot fully charge the high-voltage batteries but rather the vehicle has to be plugged in to provide a higher SOC level.

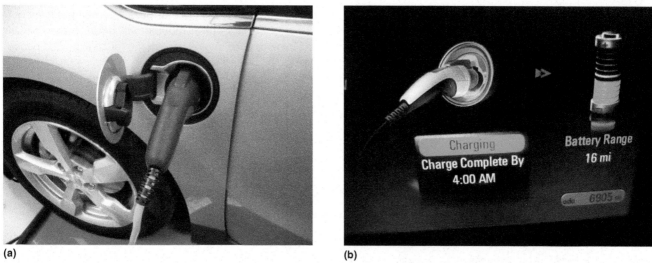

(a)
(b)

FIGURE 15–28 (a) The Chevrolet Volt is charged using a standard SAE 1772 connector using either 110 or 220 volts. (b) After connecting the charging plug, a light on the top of the dash turns green and the dash display shows the estimated time when the high-voltage battery will be fully charged and the estimated current range using battery power alone.

1. The General Motors parallel hybrid truck (PHT) uses three conventional VRLA 12-volt batteries connected in series to provide 36 volts (42 volts charging).

2. The flywheel alternator starter (FAS) is used to start the gasoline engine, provide torque smoothing, and generate electrical energy for the 120-volt outlets.

3. The PHT has four auxiliary power outlets (APOs)—two at the base of the rear seat and two in the bed of the truck.

4. The Saturn, Buick, and Chevrolet Malibu hybrid vehicles use a Belt Alternator Starter (BAS) system and 36-volt NiMH or 115-volt Li-ion battery packs.

5. The General Motors two-mode hybrid electric vehicle uses two 60-kW electric motors inside the transmission and can power the vehicle using electrical energy alone.

6. The two-mode hybrid vehicle is a full (strong) hybrid and uses a 300-volt NiMH battery pack located under the rear seat.

7. The Chevrolet Volt is an extended range electric vehicle that uses a 16-kW lithium-ion battery and a four-cylinder gasoline engine to help propel the vehicle and to keep the high-voltage battery at about 25% to 35% state-of-charge to extend the driving range of the vehicle.

REVIEW QUESTIONS

1. How is the General Motors parallel hybrid truck able to supply 120 volts AC to the auxiliary power outlet?

2. What type of hybrid vehicle is the GM PHT truck, and what are its capabilities?

3. How does the electrohydraulic power steering (EHPS) work?

4. How does the Belt Alternator Starter (BAS) system work?

5. How does the two-mode hybrid system work?

CHAPTER QUIZ

1. The batteries used in the General Motors parallel hybrid truck are _____.
   a. 300-volt NiMH
   b. Three 12-volt valve-regulated lead-acid
   c. 36-volt NiMH
   d. 144-volt D-cell-size NiMH

2. In a General Motors parallel hybrid truck, where is the electric motor (FAS)?
   a. Attached to the crankshaft at the rear of the engine
   b. Belt driven at the front of the engine
   c. Inside the transmission assembly
   d. At the output of the transmission

3. Which statement(s) is/are true about the auxiliary power outlets (APOs)?
   a. Two outlets are inside the cab of the truck.
   b. Two outlets are in the bed of the truck.
   c. Each outlet provides 120 volts AC.
   d. All of the above.

4. The General Motors mild (assist) hybrid system uses what type of motor/generator?
   a. Induction type motor located between the engine and the transmission
   b. A belt operated motor/generator
   c. A motor/generator located inside the transmission/transaxle
   d. A conventional but larger than normal alternator and starter

5. How is the high-voltage battery recharged in a Chevrolet Volt?
   a. By plugging the vehicle into an electrical outlet
   b. By running the engine
   c. Can be charged using the gasoline engine or by plugging it into an outlet
   d. By using a special high-voltage battery charger at a shop or dealer only

6. What type of battery pack is used in the Saturn VUE and Chevrolet Malibu BAS hybrid?
   a. 300-volt NiMH
   b. Three 12-volt valve-regulated lead-acid
   c. 36-volt NiMH
   d. 144-volt D-cell-size NiMH

7. The Saturn VUE and Chevrolet Malibu hybrid electric vehicles (BAS) are capable of which of the following?
   a. Idle stop
   b. Regenerative braking
   c. Powering the vehicle from a stop using electric power only
   d. Both a and b are correct

8. Where are the electric motors in the two-mode hybrid vehicle?
   a. Belt driven at the front of the engine
   b. Inside the transmission housing
   c. At the rear of the engine
   d. At the rear (output shaft) of the transmission

9. The batteries used in the GM two-mode hybrid vehicles are _____.
   a. 300-volt NiMH
   b. Three 12-volt valve-regulated lead-acid
   c. 36-volt NiMH
   d. 144-volt D-cell-size NiMH

10. Two technicians are discussing the two-mode hybrid vehicle. Technician A says that the two modes are idle stop and regenerative braking. Technician B says that the trucks are full (strong) hybrids capable of operating on battery power alone. Which technician is correct?
    a. Technician A only
    b. Technician B only
    c. Both technicians A and B
    d. Neither technician A nor B

chapter 16

FUEL CELLS AND ADVANCED TECHNOLOGIES

OBJECTIVES: **After studying Chapter 16, the reader will be able to:** • Explain how a fuel cell generates electricity. • Discuss the advantages and disadvantages of fuel cells. • List the types of fuel cells. • Explain how ultracapacitors work. • Discuss alternative energy sources.

KEY TERMS: • Electrolysis 253 • Energy carrier 253 • Fuel cell 253 • Fuel-cell hybrid vehicle (FCHV) 254 • Fuel-cell stack 255 • Fuel-cell vehicle (FCV) 254 • Homogeneous charge compression ignition (HCCI) 263 • Hydraulic power assist (HPA) 262 • Low-grade heat 257 • Membrane electrode assembly (MEA) 255 • Plug-in hybrid electric vehicle (PHEV) 264 • Polymer electrolyte fuel cell (PEFC) 254 • Proton exchange membrane (PEM) 254 • Specific energy 253 • Ultracapacitor 258

FUEL-CELL TECHNOLOGY

BACKGROUND A **fuel cell** is an electrochemical device in which the chemical energy of hydrogen and oxygen is converted into electrical energy. The principle of the fuel cell was first discovered in 1639 by Sir William Grove, a Welsh physician. In the 1950s, National Aeronautics and Space Administration (NASA) put this principle to work in building devices for powering space exploration vehicles. Fuel cells are being developed to power homes and vehicles while producing low or zero emissions. ● **SEE FIGURE 16–1.**

PARTS AND OPERATION The chemical reaction in a fuel cell is the opposite of **electrolysis.** Electrolysis is the process in which electrical current is passed through water in order to break it into its components, hydrogen and oxygen. While energy is required to bring about electrolysis, this same energy can be retrieved by allowing hydrogen and oxygen to reunite in a fuel cell. While hydrogen can be used as a fuel, it is *not* an

energy source. Instead, hydrogen is only an **energy carrier,** as energy must be expended to generate the hydrogen and store it so it can be used as a fuel.

HYDROGEN-POWERED BATTERY A fuel cell is a hydrogen-powered battery. Hydrogen is an excellent fuel because it has a very high **specific energy** when compared to an equivalent amount of fossil fuel. One kilogram (kg) of hydrogen has three times the energy content as one kilogram of gasoline. Hydrogen is the most common element on earth, but it does not exist by itself in nature.

HYDROGEN SOURCES This is because its natural tendency is to react with oxygen in the atmosphere to form water (H_2O). Hydrogen is also found in many other compounds, such as natural gas or crude oil. In order to store hydrogen for use as a fuel, different processes must be undertaken to separate it from these materials. ● **SEE FIGURE 16–2.**

FIGURE 16–1 Ford Motor Company has produced a number of demonstration fuel-cell vehicles based on the Ford Focus.

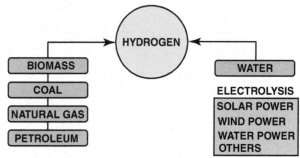

FIGURE 16–2 Hydrogen does not exist by itself in nature. Energy must be expended to separate it from other, more complex materials.

ADVANTAGES OF A FUEL CELL

A fuel cell can be used to move a vehicle by generating electricity to power electric drive motors, as well as powering the remainder of the electrical system of the vehicle. Advantages include the following:

- Because they are powered by hydrogen and oxygen, fuel cells by themselves do not generate carbon emissions such as CO_2. Instead, their only emissions are water vapor and heat, and this makes the fuel cell an ideal candidate for a ZEV (zero-emission vehicle).

- A fuel cell is also much more energy-efficient than a typical internal combustion engine. While a vehicle powered by an internal combustion engine (ICE) is anywhere from 15% to 20% efficient, a fuel-cell vehicle can achieve efficiencies upward of 40%.

- Fuel cells have very few moving parts and have the potential to be very reliable. Vehicle manufacturers have spent many years and millions of dollars in order to develop a low-cost, durable, and compact fuel cell that will operate satisfactorily under all driving conditions. ● **SEE FIGURE 16–3.**

A **fuel-cell vehicle (FCV)** uses the fuel cell as its only source of power, whereas a **fuel-cell hybrid vehicle (FCHV)** would also have an electrical storage device that can be used to power the vehicle. Most new designs of fuel-cell vehicles are now based on a hybrid configuration due to the significant increase in efficiency and driveability that can be achieved with this approach. ● **SEE FIGURE 16–4.**

DISADVANTAGES OF FUEL CELLS

While major automobile manufacturers continue to build demonstration vehicles and work on improving fuel-cell system design, no vehicle powered by a fuel cell has been placed into mass production. There are a number of disadvantages of fuel cells, including:

- High cost
- Lack of refueling infrastructure
- Safety perception
- Insufficient vehicle range
- Lack of durability

FIGURE 16–3 The Mercedes-Benz B-Class fuel-cell car was introduced in 2005.

FIGURE 16–4 The Toyota FCHV is based on the Highlander platform and uses much of Toyota Hybrid Synergy Drive (HSD) technology in its design.

- Cold weather starting problems
- Insufficient power density

All of these problems are being actively addressed by researchers, and significant improvements are being made. Once cost and performance levels meet that of current vehicles, fuel cells may be adopted as a mainstream technology.

FUEL-CELL TYPES

There are a number of different types of fuel cells, and these are differentiated by the type of electrolyte that is used in their design. Some electrolytes operate best at room temperature, whereas others are made to operate at up to 1,600°F.

The fuel-cell design that is best suited for automotive applications is the **Proton Exchange Membrane (PEM).** A PEM fuel cell must have hydrogen for it to operate, and this may be stored on the vehicle or generated as needed from another type of fuel. There are several types of fuel cells, and except for the PEM type, however, most of the others are most suitable for use as power generating units.

● **SEE CHART 16–1** for a comparison of the types of fuel cells and their most common uses.

PEM FUEL CELL OPERATION

The Proton Exchange Membrane fuel cell is also known as a **Polymer Electrolyte Fuel Cell (PEFC).** The PEM fuel cell is known for its lightweight and compact design, as well as its ability to operate at ambient temperatures.

This means that a PEM fuel cell can start quickly and produce full power without an extensive warm-up period. The PEM is a simple design based on a membrane that is coated on both sides with a catalyst such as platinum or palladium.

- There are two electrodes, one located on each side of the membrane. These are responsible for distributing hydrogen and oxygen over the membrane surface, removing waste heat, and providing a path for electrical current flow.

FUEL-CELL TYPES				
	PEM (Polymer Electrolyte Membrane)	**PAFC (Phosphoric Acid Fuel Cell)**	**MCFC (Molten Carbonate Fuel Cell)**	**SOFC (Solid Oxide Fuel Cell)**
Electrolyte	Sulfonic acid in polymer	Orthophosphoric acid	Li and K carbonates	Yttrium-stabilized zirconia
Fuel	Natural gas, hydrogen, methanol	Natural gas, hydrogen	Natural gas, synthetic gas	Natural gas, synthetic gas
Operating Temp (F) (C)	176–212°F 80–100°C	360–410°F 180–210°C	1100–1300°F 600–700°C	1200–3300°F 650–1800°C
Electric Efficiency	30–40%	40%	43–44%	50–60%
Manufacturers	Avista, Ballard, Energy Partners, H-Power, International, Plug Power	ONSI Corp.	Fuel Cell Energy, IHI, Hitachi, Siemens	Honeywell, Siemens-Westinghouse, Ceramic
Applications	Vehicles, portable power units, small stationary power units	Stationary power units	Industrial and institutional power units	Stationary power units, military vehicles

CHART 16–1

Types and details of fuel cells, including those most suitable to stationary power generation rather than for use in a vehicle.

- The part of the PEM fuel cell that contains the membrane, catalyst coatings, and electrodes is known as the **Membrane Electrode Assembly (MEA).**

- The negative electrode (anode) has hydrogen gas directed to it, while oxygen is sent to the positive electrode (cathode). Hydrogen is sent to the negative electrode as H_2 molecules, which break apart into H ions (protons) in the presence of the catalyst. The electrons (e) from the hydrogen atoms are sent through the external circuit, generating electricity that can be used to perform work.

- These same electrons are then sent to the positive electrode, where they rejoin the H ions that have passed through the membrane and have reacted with oxygen in the presence of the catalyst. This creates H_2O and waste heat, which are the only emissions from a PEM fuel cell. ● **SEE FIGURE 16–5.**

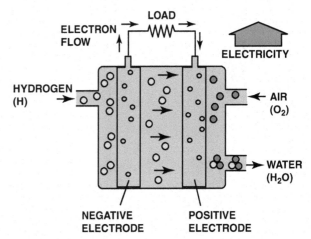

FIGURE 16–5 The polymer electrolyte membrane only allows H^+ ions (protons) to pass through it. This means that electrons must follow the external circuit and pass through the load to perform work.

FUEL-CELL STACKS A single fuel cell by itself is not particularly useful, as it will generate less than 1 volt of electrical potential. It is more common for hundreds of fuel cells to be built together in a **fuel-cell stack.** In this arrangement, the fuel cells are connected in series so that total voltage of the stack is the sum of the individual cell voltages. The fuel cells are placed end-to-end in the stack, much like slices in a loaf of bread. Automotive fuel-cell stacks contain upward of 400 cells in their construction. ● **SEE FIGURE 16–6.**

The total voltage of the fuel-cell stack is determined by the number of individual cells incorporated into the assembly. The current-producing ability of the stack, however, is dependent on the surface area of the electrodes. Since output of the fuel-cell stack is related to both voltage and

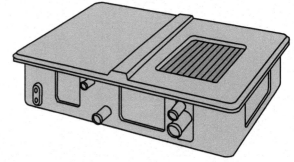

FIGURE 16–6 A fuel-cell stack is made up of hundreds of individual cells connected in series.

TECH TIP

CO Poisons the PEM Fuel-Cell Catalyst

Purity of the fuel gas is critical with PEM fuel cells. If more than 10 parts per million (ppm) of carbon monoxide is present in the hydrogen stream being fed to the PEM anode, the catalyst will be gradually poisoned and the fuel cell will eventually be disabled. This means that the purity must be "five nines" (99.999% pure). This is a major concern in vehicles where hydrogen is generated by reforming hydrocarbons such as gasoline, because it is difficult to remove all CO from the hydrogen during the reforming process. In these applications, some means of hydrogen purification must be used to prevent CO poisoning of the catalyst.

current (voltage × current = power), increasing the number of cells or increasing the surface area of the cells will increase power output. Some fuel-cell vehicles will use more than one stack, depending on power output requirements and space limitations.

DIRECT METHANOL FUEL CELLS

PURPOSE AND FUNCTION High-pressure cylinders are one method of storing hydrogen onboard a vehicle for use in a fuel cell. This is a simple and lightweight storage method, but often does not provide sufficient vehicle driving range. Another approach has been to fuel a modified PEM fuel cell with liquid methanol instead of hydrogen gas. ● SEE FIGURE 16–7.

OPERATION Methanol is most often produced from natural gas and has the chemical formula CH_3OH. It has a

FIGURE 16–8 A direct methanol fuel cell can be refueled similar to a gasoline-powered vehicle.

higher-energy density than gaseous hydrogen because it exists in a liquid state at normal temperatures and is easier to handle since no compressor or other high-pressure equipment is needed. This means that a fuel-cell vehicle can be refueled with a liquid instead of high-pressure gas, which makes the refueling process simpler and produces a greater vehicle driving range. ● SEE FIGURE 16–8.

DISADVANTAGES Unfortunately, direct methanol fuel cells suffer from a number of problems, not the least of which is the corrosive nature of methanol itself. This means that methanol cannot be stored in existing tanks and thus requires a separate infrastructure for handling and storage. Another problem is "fuel crossover," in which methanol makes its way across the membrane assembly and diminishes performance of the cell. Direct methanol fuel cells also require much greater amounts of catalyst in their construction, which leads to higher costs. These challenges are leading researchers to look for alternative electrolyte materials and catalysts to lower cost and improve cell performance.

NOTE: Direct methanol fuel cells are not likely to see service in automotive applications. However, they are well suited for low-power applications, such as cell phones or laptop computers.

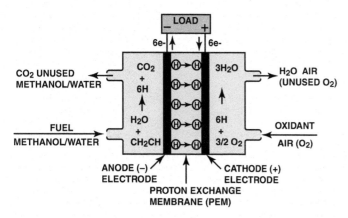

FIGURE 16–7 A direct methanol fuel cell uses a methanol/water solution for fuel instead of hydrogen gas.

? FREQUENTLY ASKED QUESTION

What Is the Role of the Humidifier in a PEM Fuel Cell?

The polymer electrolyte membrane assembly in a PEM fuel cell acts as conductor of positive ions and as a gas separator. However, it can perform these functions effectively only if it is kept moist. A fuel-cell vehicle uses an air compressor to supply air to the positive electrodes of each cell, and this air is sometimes sent through a humidifier first to increase its moisture content. The humid air then comes in contact with the membrane assembly and keeps the electrolyte damp and functioning correctly.

FUEL-CELL VEHICLE SYSTEMS

FUEL-CELL HUMIDIFIERS Water management inside a PEM fuel cell is critical. Too much water can prevent oxygen from making contact with the positive electrode; too little water can allow the electrolyte to dry out and lower its conductivity. The amount of water and where it resides in the fuel cell is also critical in determining at how low a temperature the fuel cell will start, because water freezing in the fuel cell can prevent it from starting. The role of the humidifier is to achieve a balance where it is providing sufficient moisture to the fuel cell by recycling water that is evaporating at the cathode. The humidifier is located in the air line leading to the cathode of the fuel-cell stack. ● **SEE FIGURE 16–9.**

Some newer PEM designs manage the water in the cells in such a way that there is no need to pre-humidify the incoming reactant gases. This eliminates the need for the humidifier assembly and makes the system simpler overall.

FUEL-CELL COOLING SYSTEMS Heat is generated by the fuel cell during normal operation. Excess heat can lead to a breakdown of the polymer electrolyte membrane, so a liquid cooling system must be utilized to remove waste heat from the fuel-cell stack. One of the major challenges for engineers in this regard is the fact that the heat generated by the fuel cell is classified as **low-grade heat**. This means that there is only a small difference between the temperature of the coolant and that of the ambient air. Heat transfers very slowly under these conditions, so heat exchangers with a much larger surface area must be used. ● **SEE FIGURE 16–10.**

Fortunately, it is possible to generate methanol from biomass and wood waste. Methanol made from renewable resources is carbon neutral, because no extra carbon is being released into the atmosphere than what was originally absorbed by the plants used to make the methanol.

In some cases, heat exchangers may be placed in other areas of the vehicle when available space at the front of the

engine compartment is insufficient. In the case of Toyota FCHV, an auxiliary heat exchanger is located underneath the vehicle to increase the cooling system heat-rejection capacity. ● **SEE FIGURE 16–11.**

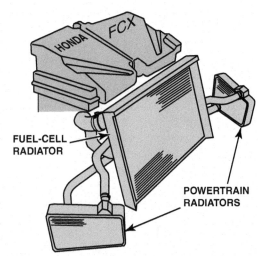

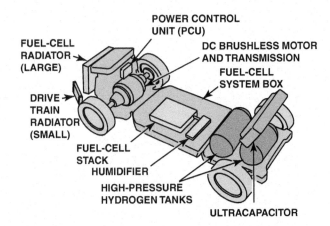

FIGURE 16–9 Powertrain layout in a Honda FCX fuel-cell vehicle. Note the use of a humidifier behind the fuel-cell stack to maintain moisture levels in the membrane electrode assemblies.

FIGURE 16–10 The Honda FCX uses one large radiator for cooling the fuel cell, and two smaller ones on either side for cooling drivetrain components.

FIGURE 16–11 Space is limited at the front of the Toyota FCHV engine compartment, so an auxiliary heat exchanger is located under the vehicle to help cool the fuel-cell stack.

An electric water pump and a fan drive motor are used to enable operation of the fuel-cell cooling system. These and other support devices use electrical power that is generated by the fuel cell and therefore tend to decrease the overall efficiency of the vehicle.

AIR SUPPLY PUMPS Air must be supplied to the fuel-cell stack at the proper pressure and flow rate to enable proper performance under all driving conditions. This function is performed by an onboard air supply pump that compresses atmospheric air and supplies it to the fuel cell positive electrode (cathode). This pump is often driven by a high-voltage electric drive motor.

FUEL-CELL HYBRID VEHICLES

PURPOSE AND FUNCTION Hybridization tends to increase efficiency in vehicles with conventional drivetrains, as energy that was once lost during braking and otherwise normal operation is instead stored for later use in a high-voltage battery. This same advantage can be gained by applying the hybrid design concept to fuel-cell vehicles. Whereas the fuel cell is the only power source in a fuel-cell vehicle, the fuel-cell hybrid vehicle (FCHV) relies on both the fuel cell and an electrical storage device for motive power. Driveability is also enhanced with this design, as the electrical storage device is able to supply energy immediately to the drive motors and overcome any "throttle lag" on the part of the fuel cell.

SECONDARY BATTERIES All hybrid vehicle designs require a means of storing electrical energy that is generated during regenerative braking and other applications. In most FCHV designs, a high-voltage nickel-metal hydride (NiMH) battery pack is used as a secondary battery. This is most often located near the back of the vehicle, either under or behind the rear passenger seat. ● **SEE FIGURE 16–12.**

The secondary battery is built similar to a fuel-cell stack, because it is made up of many low-voltage cells connected in series to build a high-voltage battery.

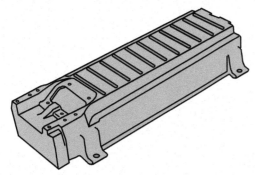

FIGURE 16–12 The secondary battery in a fuel-cell hybrid vehicle is made up of many individual cells connected in series, much like a fuel-cell stack.

ULTRACAPACITORS

PURPOSE AND FUNCTION An alternative to storing electrical energy in batteries is to use ultracapacitors. A capacitor is best known as an electrical device that will block DC current but allow AC to pass. However, a capacitor can also be used to store electrical energy, and it is able to do this without a chemical reaction. Instead, a capacitor stores electrical energy using the principle of electrostatic attraction between positive and negative charges.

PARTS AND OPERATION Ultracapacitors are built very different from conventional capacitors. **Ultracapacitor** cells are based on double-layer technology, in which two activated carbon electrodes are immersed in an organic electrolyte. The electrodes have a very large surface area and are separated by a membrane that allows ions to migrate but prevents the electrodes from touching. ● **SEE FIGURE 16–13.**

Charging and discharging occurs as ions move within the electrolyte but no chemical reaction takes place. Ultracapacitors can charge and discharge quickly and efficiently, making them especially suited for electric assist applications in fuel-cell hybrid vehicles.

Ultracapacitors that are used in fuel-cell hybrid vehicles are made up of multiple cylindrical cells connected in parallel. ● **SEE FIGURE 16–14.**

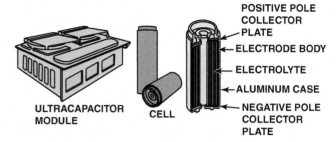

FIGURE 16–13 The Honda ultracapacitor module and construction of the individual cells.

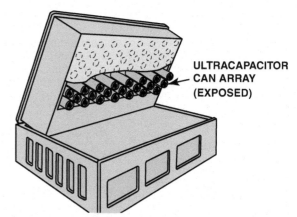

FIGURE 16–14 An ultracapacitor can be used in place of a high-voltage battery in a hybrid electric vehicle. This example is from the Honda FCX fuel-cell hybrid vehicle.

This results in the total capacitance being the sum of the values of each individual cell. For example, ten 1.0-farad capacitors connected in parallel will have a total capacitance of 10.0 farads. Greater capacitance means greater electrical storage ability, and this contributes to greater assist for the electric motors in a fuel-cell hybrid vehicle.

ADVANTAGES Ultracapacitors have excellent cycle life, meaning that they can be fully charged and discharged many times without degrading their performance. They are also able to operate over a wide temperature range and are not affected by low temperatures to the same degree as many battery technologies.

DISADVANTAGES The one major downside of ultracapacitors is a lack of specific energy, which means that they are bested suited for sudden bursts of energy as opposed to prolonged discharge cycles. Research is being conducted to improve this and other aspects of ultracapacitor performance.

FUEL-CELL VEHICLE TRANSAXLES

PURPOSE AND FUNCTION Some fuel-cell hybrid vehicles use a single electric drive motor and a transaxle to direct power to the vehicle. It is also possible to use wheel motors to drive individual wheels. While this approach adds a significant amount of unsprung weight to the chassis, it allows for greater control of the torque being applied to each individual wheel. ● **SEE FIGURE 16–15.**

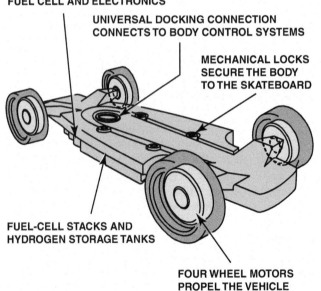

HEAT VENTS TO DISSIPATE HEAT GENERATED BY THE FUEL CELL AND ELECTRONICS

UNIVERSAL DOCKING CONNECTION CONNECTS TO BODY CONTROL SYSTEMS

MECHANICAL LOCKS SECURE THE BODY TO THE SKATEBOARD

FUEL-CELL STACKS AND HYDROGEN STORAGE TANKS

FOUR WHEEL MOTORS PROPEL THE VEHICLE

FIGURE 16–15 The General Motors "Skateboard" concept uses a fuel-cell propulsion system with wheel motors at all four corners.

Aside from the hydrogen fueling system, fuel-cell hybrid vehicles are effectively pure electric vehicles in that their drivetrain is electrically driven. Electric motors work very well for automotive applications because they produce high torque at low RPMs and are able to maintain a consistent power output throughout their entire RPM range. This is in contrast to vehicles powered by internal combustion engines, which produce very little torque at low RPMs and have a narrow range where significant horsepower is produced.

ICE-powered vehicles require complex transmissions with multiple speed ranges in order to accelerate the vehicle quickly and maximize the efficiency of the ICE. Fuel-cell hybrid vehicles use electric drive motors that require only a simple reduction in their final drive and a differential to send power to the drive wheels. No gear shifting is required and mechanisms such as torque converters and clutches are done away with completely. A reverse gear is not required either, as the electric drive motor is simply powered in the opposite direction. The transaxles used in fuel-cell hybrid vehicles are extremely simple with few moving parts, making them extremely durable, quiet, and reliable. ● **SEE FIGURE 16–16.**

FUEL-CELL TRACTION MOTORS Much of the technology behind the electric drive motors being used in fuel-cell vehicles was de-eloped during the early days of the California ZEV mandate. This was a period when battery-powered electric vehicles were being built by the major vehicle manufacturers in an effort to meet a legislated quota in the state of California. The ZEV mandate rules were eventually relaxed to allow other types of vehicles to be substituted for credit, but the technology that had been developed for pure electric vehicles was now put to work in these other vehicle designs.

The electric traction motors used in fuel-cell hybrid vehicles are very similar to those being used in current hybrid electric vehicles. The typical drive motor is based on an AC synchronous design, which is sometimes referred to as a DC brushless motor. This design is very reliable as it does not use a commutator or brushes, but instead has a three-phase stator and a permanent magnet rotor. ● **SEE FIGURE 16–17.**

An electronic controller (inverter) is used to generate the three-phase high-voltage AC current required by the motor. While the motor itself is very simple, the electronics required to power and control it are complex.

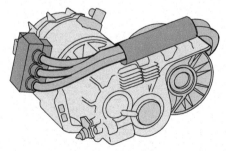

FIGURE 16–16 The electric drive motor and transaxle assembly from a Toyota FCHV. Note the three orange cables, indicating that this motor is powered by high-voltage three-phase alternating current.

FIGURE 16–17 Drive motors in fuel-cell hybrid vehicles often use stator assemblies similar to ones found in Toyota hybrid electric vehicles. The rotor turns inside the stator and has permanent magnets on its outer circumference.

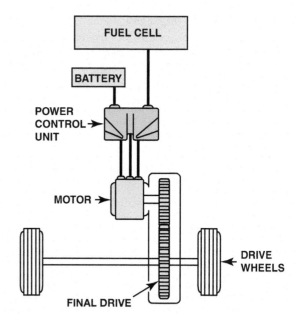

FIGURE 16–19 Toyota's FCHV uses a power control unit that directs electrical energy flow between the fuel cell, battery, and drive motor.

Some fuel-cell hybrid vehicles use a single electric drive motor and a transaxle to direct power to the vehicle. It is also possible to use wheel motors to drive individual wheels. While this approach adds a significant amount of unsprung weight to the chassis, it allows for greater control of the torque being applied to each individual wheel.

FUEL CELL POWER CONTROL UNITS The drivetrain of a fuel-cell hybrid vehicle is controlled by a power control unit (PCU), which controls fuel-cell output and directs the flow of electricity between the various components. One of the functions of the PCU is to act as an inverter, which changes direct current from the fuel-cell stack into three-phase alternating current for use in the vehicle drive motor(s). ● SEE FIGURE 16–18.

Power to and from the secondary battery is directed through the power control unit, which is also responsible for

- Maintaining the state-of-charge of the battery pack and
- Controlling and directing the output of the fuel-cell stack. ● SEE FIGURE 16–19.

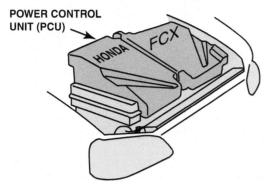

FIGURE 16–18 The power control unit (PCU) on a Honda FCX fuel-cell hybrid vehicle is located under the hood.

During regenerative braking, the electric drive motor acts as a generator and converts kinetic (moving) energy of the vehicle into electricity for recharging the high-voltage battery pack. The PCU must take the three-phase power from the motor (generator) and convert (or rectify) this into DC voltage to be sent to the battery. DC power from the fuel cell will also be processed through the PCU for recharging the battery pack.

A DC-to-DC converter is used in hybrid electric vehicles for converting the high voltage from the secondary battery pack into the 12 volts required for the remainder of the vehicle electrical system. Depending on the vehicle, 42 volts may also be required to operate accessories such as the electric-assist power steering. In fuel-cell hybrid vehicles, the DC-to-DC converter function may be built into the power control unit, giving it full responsibility for power distribution.

HYDROGEN STORAGE

PURPOSE AND FUNCTION One of the issues with fuel-cell hybrid vehicles is how to store sufficient hydrogen onboard to allow for reasonable vehicle range. Modern drivers have grown accustomed to having a minimum of 300 miles between refueling stops, a goal that is extremely difficult to achieve when fueling the vehicle with hydrogen. Hydrogen has very high energy content on a pound-for-pound basis, but its energy density is less than that of conventional liquid fuels. This is because gaseous hydrogen, even at high pressure, has a very low physical density (mass per unit volume). ● SEE FIGURE 16–20.

A number of methods of hydrogen storage are being considered for use in fuel-cell hybrid vehicles. These include high-pressure compressed gas, liquefied hydrogen, and solid storage in metal hydrides. Efficient hydrogen storage is one of

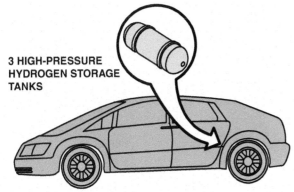

FIGURE 16–20 This GM fuel-cell vehicle uses compressed hydrogen in three high-pressure storage tanks.

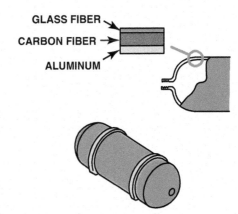

FIGURE 16–21 The Toyota FCHV uses high-pressure storage tanks that are rated at 350 bar. This is the equivalent of 5,000 pounds per square inch.

the technical issues that must be solved in order for fuel cells to be adopted for vehicle applications. Much research is being conducted to solve the issue of onboard hydrogen storage.

HIGH-PRESSURE COMPRESSED GAS Most current fuel-cell hybrid vehicles use compressed hydrogen that is stored in tanks as a high-pressure gas. This approach is the least complex of all the storage possibilities, but also has the least energy density. Multiple small storage tanks are often used rather than one large tank in order to fit them into unused areas of the vehicle. One drawback with this approach is that only cylinders can be used to store gases at the required pressures. This creates a good deal of unused space around the outside of the cylinders and leads to further reductions in hydrogen storage capacity. It is common for a pressure of 5,000 PSI (350 bar) to be used. ● **SEE FIGURE 16–21.**

Many newer systems use pressures as high as 10,000 PSI (700 bar) to increase the range of the fuel cell-powered vehicle. The tanks used for compressed hydrogen storage are typically made with an aluminum liner wrapped in several layers of carbon fiber and an external coating of fiberglass. In order to refuel the compressed hydrogen storage tanks, a special high-pressure fitting is installed in place of the filler neck used for conventional vehicles. ● **SEE FIGURE 16–22.**

There is also a special electrical connector that is used to enable communication between the vehicle and the filling station during the refueling process. ● **SEE FIGURE 16–23.**

The filling station utilizes a special coupler to connect to the vehicle high-pressure refueling fitting. The coupler is placed on the vehicle fitting, and a lever on the coupler is rotated to seal and lock it into place.

LIQUID HYDROGEN Hydrogen can be liquefied in an effort to increase its energy density, but this requires that it be stored in cryogenic tanks at −423°F (−253°C). This increases vehicle range, but impacts overall efficiency, as a great deal of energy is required to liquefy the hydrogen and a certain amount of the liquid hydrogen will "boil off" while in storage.

One liter of liquid hydrogen has only one-fourth the energy content of 1 liter of gasoline. ● **SEE FIGURES 16–24 AND 16–25.**

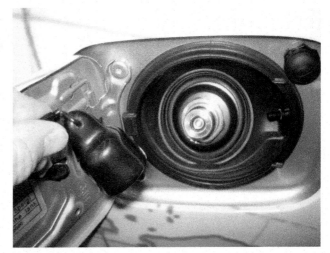

FIGURE 16–22 The high-pressure fitting used to refuel a fuel-cell hybrid vehicle.

FIGURE 16–23 Note that high-pressure hydrogen storage tanks must be replaced in 2020.

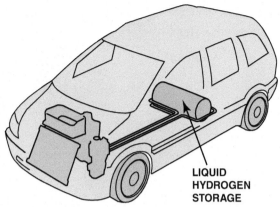

FIGURE 16–24 The GM Hydrogen3 has a range of 249 miles when using liquid hydrogen.

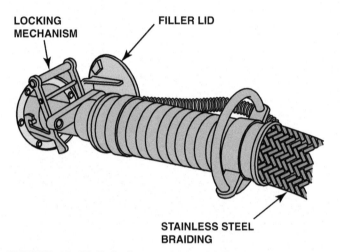

LOCKING MECHANISM

FILLER LID

STAINLESS STEEL BRAIDING

FIGURE 16–25 Refueling a vehicle with liquid hydrogen.

SOLID STORAGE OF HYDROGEN One method discovered to store hydrogen in solid form is as a metal hydride, similar to how a nickel-metal hydride (NiMH) battery works.

A demonstration vehicle features a lightweight fiber-wrapped storage tank under the body that stores about

TECH TIP

Hydrogen Fuel = No Carbon

Most fuels contain hydrocarbons or molecules that contain both hydrogen and carbon. During combustion, the first element that is burned is the hydrogen. If combustion is complete, then all of the carbon is converted to carbon dioxide gas and exits the engine in the exhaust. However, if combustion is not complete, carbon monoxide is formed, leaving some unburned carbon to accumulate in the combustion chamber. ● **SEE FIGURE 16–26.**

FIGURE 16–26 Carbon deposits, such as these, are created by incomplete combustion of a hydrocarbon fuel.

6.6 pounds (3.3 kg) of hydrogen as a metal hydride at low pressure. The vehicle can travel almost 200 miles with this amount of fuel.

- One kilogram of hydrogen is equal to 1 gallon of gasoline.
- Three gallons of water will generate 1 kilogram of hydrogen.

A metal hydride is formed when gaseous hydrogen molecules disassociate into individual hydrogen atoms and bond with the metal atoms in the storage tank. This process uses powdered metallic alloys capable of rapidly absorbing hydrogen to make this occur.

HYDRAULIC HYBRID STORAGE SYSTEM

TERMINOLOGY Ford Motor Co. is experimenting with a system it calls **Hydraulic Power Assist (HPA).** This system converts kinetic energy to hydraulic pressure, and then uses that pressure to help accelerate the vehicle. It is currently being tested on a four-wheel-drive (4WD) Lincoln Navigator with a 4.0-L V-8 engine in place of the standard 5.4-L engine.

PARTS AND OPERATION A variable-displacement hydraulic pump/motor is mounted on the transfer case and connected to the output shaft that powers the front drive shaft. The HPA system works with or without 4WD engaged.

- A valve block mounted on the pump contains solenoid valves to control the flow of hydraulic fluid.
- A 14-gallon, high-pressure accumulator is mounted behind the rear axle, with a low-pressure accumulator right behind it to store hydraulic fluid.
- The master cylinder has a "deadband," meaning the first few fractions of an inch of travel do not pressurize the brake system. When the driver depresses the brake pedal, a pedal movement sensor signals the control unit, which then operates solenoid valves to send hydraulic

fluid from the low-pressure reservoir to the pump. The pumping action slows the vehicle, similar to engine compression braking, and the fluid is pumped into the high-pressure reservoir.

- Releasing the brake and pressing on the accelerator signals the control unit to send that high-pressure fluid back to the pump, which then acts as a hydraulic motor and adds torque to the driveline.
- The system can be used to launch the vehicle from a stop and/or add torque for accelerating from any speed.

While the concept is simple, the system itself is very complicated. Additional components include:

- Pulse suppressors
- Filters
- An electric circulator pump for cooling the main pump/motor

Potential problems with this system include leakage problems with seals and valves, getting air out of the hydraulic fluid system, and noise. In prototype stages, the system demands different driving techniques. Still, this system was built to prove the concept, and the engineers believe that these problems can be solved and that a control system can be developed that will make HPA transparent to the driver. A 23% improvement in fuel economy and improvements in emissions reduction were achieved using a dynamometer set for a 7,000-pound vehicle. While the HPA system could be developed for any type of vehicle with any type of drivetrain, it does add weight and complexity, which would add to the cost.

TERMINOLOGY **Homogeneous Charge Compression Ignition (HCCI)** is a combustion process. HCCI is the combustion of a very lean gasoline air–fuel mixture without the use of a spark ignition. It is a low-temperature, chemically controlled (flameless) combustion process. ● **SEE FIGURE 16–27.**

HCCI combustion is difficult to control and extremely sensitive to changes in temperature, pressure, and fuel type. While the challenges of HCCI are difficult, the advantages include having a gasoline engine being able to deliver 80% of diesel efficiency (a 20% increase in fuel economy) for 50% of the cost. A diesel engine using HCCI can deliver gasoline-like emissions. Spark and injection timing are no longer a factor as they are in a conventional port-fuel injection system.

FUTURE OF HCCI While much research and development needs to be performed using this combustion process, it has been shown to give excellent performance from idle to mid-load, and from ambient to warm operating temperatures as well as cold-start and run capability. Because the engine operates only in HCCI mode at light throttle settings, such as during cruise conditions at highway speeds, engineers need to improve the transition in and out of the HCCI mode. Work is also being done on piston and combustion chamber shape to reduce combustion noise and vibration that is created during operation in the HCCI operating mode.

Ongoing research is focusing on improving fuel economy under real-world operating conditions as well as controlling costs.

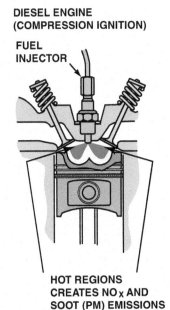

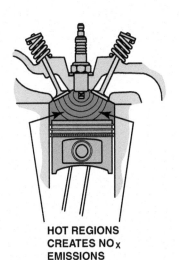
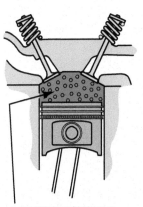

DIESEL ENGINE (COMPRESSION IGNITION)

FUEL INJECTOR

HOT REGIONS CREATES NO$_X$ AND SOOT (PM) EMISSIONS

GASOLINE ENGINE (SPARK IGNITED)

HOT REGIONS CREATES NO$_X$ EMISSIONS

HCCI ENGINE (HOMOGENEOUS CHARGE COMPRESSION IGNITION)

LOW-TEMPERATURE COMBUSTION RESULTS IN REDUCED EMISSIONS

FIGURE 16–27 Both diesel and conventional gasoline engines create exhaust emissions due to high peak temperatures created in the combustion chamber. The lower combustion temperatures during HCCI operation result in high efficiency with reduced emissions.

PLUG-IN HYBRID ELECTRIC VEHICLES

PURPOSE AND FUNCTION A **plug-in hybrid electric vehicle (PHEV)** is a hybrid electric vehicle that is designed to be plugged in to an electrical outlet at night to charge the batteries. By charging the batteries in the vehicle, it can operate using electric power alone (stealth mode) for a longer time, thereby reducing the use of the internal combustion engine (ICE). The less the ICE is operating, the less fuel is consumed and the lower the emissions. At the present time, plug-in hybrids are not offered by any major manufacturer but many conventional HEVs are being converted to plug-in hybrids by adding additional batteries.

ADVANTAGES Production plug-in hybrids are often able to get about twice the fuel economy of a conventional hybrid. Recharging will normally take place at night during cheaper off-peak hours. Counting fuel and service, the total lifetime cost of ownership will be lower than a conventional gasoline-powered vehicle.

DISADVANTAGES The extra weight of the batteries will be offset, somewhat, by the reduced weight of a smaller ICE. At highway speeds, fuel efficiency is affected primarily by aerodynamics, and therefore the added weight of the extra batteries is equal to one or two additional passengers and thus would only slightly reduce fuel economy. The owner also has to plug the vehicle in at night and remember to unplug it the next time the vehicle is used. This is something that would become a habit after a while but could present some problems to those not used to plugging a vehicle into an outlet when parked.

EMISSIONS There are emissions related to the production of electricity, which are called well-to-wheel emissions. These emissions, including greenhouse gases, are far lower than those of gasoline, even for the national power grid, which is 50% coal. Vehicles charging off-peak will use power from plants that cannot be turned off at night and often use cleaner sources such as natural gas and hydroelectric power. Plug-in hybrids could be recharged using rooftop photovoltaic systems, which would create zero emissions.

ELECTRIC VEHICLES (EV)

PURPOSE AND FUNCTION The future of electric vehicles depends on many factors, including:

1. The legislative and environmental incentives to overcome the cost and research efforts to bring a usable electric vehicle to the market.

2. The cost of alternative energy. If the cost of fossil fuels increases to the point that the average consumer cannot afford to drive a conventional vehicle, then electric vehicles (EVs) may be a saleable alternative.

3. Advancement in battery technology that would allow the use of lighter-weight and higher-energy batteries.

COLD WEATHER CONCERNS Past models of electric vehicles such as the General Motors electric vehicle (EV1) were restricted to locations such as Arizona and southern California that had a warm climate, because cold weather is a major disadvantage to the use of electric vehicles for the following reasons:

- Cold temperatures reduce battery efficiency.
- Additional electrical power from the batteries is needed to heat the batteries themselves to be able to achieve reasonable performance.
- Passenger compartment heating is a concern for an electric vehicle because it would require the use of resistance units or other technology that would reduce the range of the vehicle.

HOT WEATHER CONCERNS Batteries do not function well at high temperatures, and therefore some type of battery cooling must be added to the vehicle to allow for maximum battery performance. This would then result in a reduction of vehicle range due to the use of battery power needed just to keep the batteries working properly. Besides battery concerns, the batteries would also have to supply the power needed to keep the interior cool as well as all of the other accessories. These combined electrical loads represent a huge battery drain and reduce the range of the vehicle.

RECHARGING METHODS AND CONCERNS The distance an electric vehicle can travel on a full battery charge is called its range. The range of an electric vehicle depends on many factors, including:

- Battery energy storage capacity
- Vehicle weight
- Outside temperature
- Terrain (driving in hilly or mountainous areas requires more energy from the battery)
- Use of air conditioning and other electrical devices

Because electric vehicles have a relatively short range, charging stations must be made available in areas where these vehicles are driven. For example, when the state of California mandated the sale of zero-emission vehicles (ZEVs), charging stations were set up in many areas, usually in parking lots of businesses and schools. ● **SEE FIGURE 16–28.**

The parking spaces near the charging stations were designated for electric vehicles only and could be used for free to recharge electric vehicles. If electric vehicles are going to become widely used, charging stations will have to be established to allow the necessary recharging for trips to work and back home.

FIGURE 16–28 A typical electric vehicle charging station on the campus of a college in Southern California.

FIGURE 16–29 A conductive-type charging connector. This type of battery charging connector is sometimes called an AVCON connector, named for the manufacturer.

CHARGING METHODS When the state of California set up electric vehicle charging stations, both conductive- and inductive-type chargers were made available at each station.

- **Conductive Charging.** Conductive charging uses an electrical plug that makes physical contact with terminals in the vehicle. The charger can be powered by 110-volt AC, or most commonly 220-volt AC. ● **SEE FIGURE 16–29.** This type of charger connection is used on some Ford and Honda electric vehicles.

- **Inductive Charging.** Inductive charging is achieved by inserting a paddle-like probe into a charging receptacle (opening) in the vehicle. The charger is powered by 220-volt AC and does not make physical contact with the vehicle. ● **SEE FIGURE 16–30.**

An inductive charger paddle contains a coil of wire and the AC current from the charger flows through the winding, which creates a moving magnetic field around the paddle. Inside the charging receptacle of the vehicle is another coil of wire. The alternating magnetic field induces an AC voltage in the coil winding.

FIGURE 16–30 An inductive-type electric vehicle battery charger connector. This type of connector fits into a charging slot in the vehicle, but does not make electrical contact.

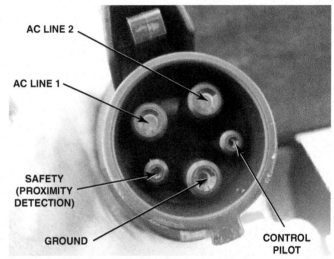

FIGURE 16–31 The SAE J 1772 plug is used on most electric and plug-in hybrid electric vehicles and is designed to work with Level 1 (110–120 volt) and Level 2 (220–240 volt) charging.

The electronics in the vehicle then changes the induced AC current into DC current to charge the batteries. Inductive-type chargers are used with the General Motors EV1, as well as Nissan and Toyota electric vehicles.

- **SAE Standard Plug.** Most electric (Nissan Leaf) and plug-in hybrid vehicles (Chevrolet Volt and Toyota Prius) use a standard plug. The standard plug meets the specification as designated by SAE standard J1772 (updated in 2009). ● **SEE FIGURE 16–31.**

CHARGING LEVELS There are three levels of chargers that can be used to charge a plug-in hybrid electric vehicle (PHEV) or electric vehicle (EV). The three levels include:

- **Level 1** Level 1 uses 110- to 120- volt standard electric outlet and is capable of charging a Chevrolet Volt extended range electric vehicle in 10 hours or more. The advantage is that there is little if any installation cost as most houses are equipped with 110-volt outlets and can charge up to 16 amperes.

- **Level 2** Level 2 chargers use 220 to 240 volts to charge the same vehicle in about 4 hours. Level 2 chargers can be added to most houses, making recharging faster (up to 80 amperes) when at home, and are the most commonly used charging stations available at stores and college. Adding a level 2 charging outlet to the garage for access can cost $2,000 or more depending on the location and the wiring of the house or apartment.

- **Level 3** Level 3 charging stations use 440 volts and can charge most electric vehicles to 80% charge in less than 30 minutes. This high charge rate may be harmful to battery life. Always follow the charging instructions and recommendations as stated in the owner's manual of the vehicle being charged. Level 3 chargers charge the vehicle using direct current (DC) at a rate up to 125 amperes. A Level 3 charger station can cost $50,000 or more, making this type of charger most suitable where facilities will be selling the service of rapidly charging the vehicle. ● **SEE FIGURE 16–32.**

? FREQUENTLY ASKED QUESTION

What Is NEDRA?

NEDRA is the National Electric Drag Racing Association, which holds drag races for electric-powered vehicles throughout the United States. The association does the following:

1. Coordinates a standard rule set for electric vehicle drag racing, to balance the needs and interests of all those involved in the sport.
2. Sanctions electric vehicle drag racing events to:
   - Make the events as safe as possible.
   - Record and maintain official records.
   - Maintain consistency on a national scale.
   - Coordinate and schedule electric vehicle drag racing events.
3. Promotes electric vehicle drag racing to:
   - Educate the public and about the awareness of electric vehicles while eliminating any misconceptions.
   - Encourage participation in electric vehicle drag racing.
   - Have fun in a safe and silent drag racing environment.

● **SEE FIGURE 16–33.**

FIGURE 16–32 A cutaway view of a Nissan Leaf electric vehicle showing the two charging connectors. Both of these connectors are located in the center of the vehicle in the front making plugging in the cable easy to access.

FIGURE 16–33 The motor in a compact electric drag car. This 8-inch-diameter motor is controlled by an electronic controller that limits the voltage to 170 volts to prevent commutator flash-over, yet provides up to 2,000 amperes. This results in an amazing 340,000 watts or 455 horsepower. The batteries used for the compact drag car include twenty 12-volt absorbed glass mat (AGM) batteries connected in series to provide 240 volts.

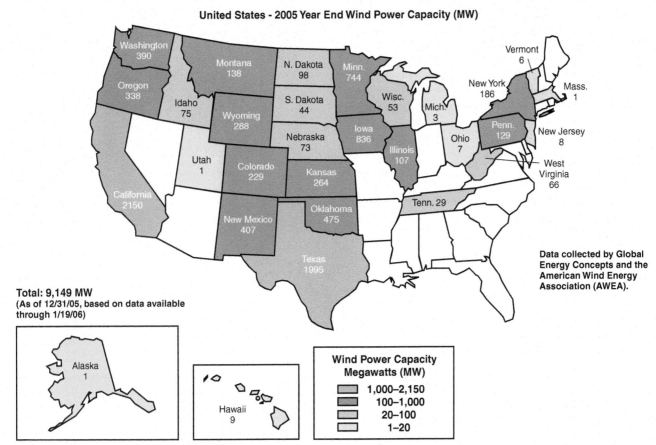

United States - 2005 Year End Wind Power Capacity (MW)

Washington 390
Montana 138
N. Dakota 98
Minn. 744
Vermont 6
New York 186
Mass. 1
Oregon 338
Idaho 75
Wyoming 288
S. Dakota 44
Wisc. 53
Mich. 3
Penn. 129
New Jersey 8
Utah 1
Colorado 229
Nebraska 73
Iowa 836
Illinois 107
Ohio 7
West Virginia 66
California 2150
Kansas 264
Tenn. 29
New Mexico 407
Oklahoma 475
Texas 1995

Data collected by Global Energy Concepts and the American Wind Energy Association (AWEA).

Total: 9,149 MW
(As of 12/31/05, based on data available through 1/19/06)

Alaska 1

Hawaii 9

Wind Power Capacity Megawatts (MW)
1,000–2,150
100–1,000
20–100
1–20

FIGURE 16–34 Wind power capacity by area. (Courtesy of U.S. Department of Energy)

WIND POWER

ADVANTAGES Wind power is used to help supplement electric power generation in many parts of the country. Because AC electricity cannot be stored, this energy source is best used to reduce the use of natural gas and coal to help reduce CO_2 emissions. Wind power is most economical if the windmills are located where the wind blows consistently above eight miles per hour (13 km/h). Locations include the eastern slope of mountain ranges, such as the Rocky Mountains, or on high ground in many states.

DISADVANTAGES Often, wind power is used as supplemental power in the evenings when it is most needed, and is allowed to stop rotating in daylight hours when the power is not needed. Windmills are usually grouped together to form wind farms, where the product is electrical energy. Energy from wind farms can be used to charge plug-in hybrid vehicles, as well as for domestic lighting and power needs.
● **SEE FIGURES 16–34 AND 16–35.**

FIGURE 16–35 A typical wind generator that is used to generate electricity.

HYDROELECTRIC POWER

Hydroelectric power is limited to locations where there are dammed rivers and hydroelectric plants. However, electricity can be and is transmitted long distances—so that electricity generated at the Hoover Dam can be used in California and other remote locations. Electrical power from hydroelectric sources can be used to charge plug-in hybrid electric vehicles, thereby reducing emissions that would normally be created by burning coal or natural gas to create electricity. However, hydroelectric plants are limited as to the amount of power they can produce, and constructing new plants is extremely expensive. ● **SEE FIGURE 16–36.**

FIGURE 16–36 The Hoover Dam in Nevada/Arizona is used to create electricity for use in the southwest United States.

SUMMARY

1. The chemical reaction inside a fuel cell is the opposite of electrolysis in that electricity is created when hydrogen and oxygen are allowed to combine in the fuel cell.

2. A fuel cell produces electricity and releases heat and water as the only by-products.

3. The major disadvantages of fuel cells include:
   • High cost
   • Lack of hydrogen refueling stations
   • Short range
   • Freezing-temperature starting problems

4. Types of fuel cells include PEM (the most commonly used), PAFC, MCFC, and SOFC.

5. Ultracapacitors are an alternative to batteries for the storage of electrical energy.

6. A gasoline-powered engine can be more efficient if it uses a homogeneous charge compression ignition (HCCI) combustion process.

7. Plug-in hybrid electric vehicles could expand the range of hybrid vehicles by operating on battery power alone.

8. The levels of charging include:
   • Level 1—110–120 volts
   • Level 2—210–220 volts
   • Level 3—440–480 volts

9. Wind power and hydroelectric power are being used to recharge plug-in hybrids and provide electrical power for all uses, without harmful emissions.

REVIEW QUESTIONS

1. How does a fuel cell work?
2. What are the advantages and disadvantages of fuel cells?
3. What are the uses of the various types of fuel cells?
4. How does an ultracapacitor work?
5. What are the advantages and disadvantages of using hydrogen?
6. What alternative power sources could be used for vehicles?

CHAPTER QUIZ

1. A fuel cell produces electricity from _____ and _____.
   a. Gasoline/oxygen
   b. Nitrogen/hydrogen
   c. Hydrogen/oxygen
   d. Water/oxygen

2. What are the by-products (emissions) from a fuel cell?
   a. Water
   b. CO
   c. CO_2
   d. Nonmethane hydrocarbon

3. Which type of fuel cell is the most likely to be used to power vehicles?
   a. PAFC
   b. MCFC
   c. PEM
   d. SOFC

4. Which liquid fuel could be used to directly power a fuel cell?
   a. Methanol
   b. Biodiesel
   c. Ethanol
   d. Unleaded gasoline

5. Which is not a function of an ultracapacitor?
   a. Can pass AC current
   b. Can be charged with DC current
   c. Discharges DC current
   d. Can pass DC current

6. Hydrogen is commonly stored at what pressure?
   a. 100,000 PSI
   b. 50,000 PSI
   c. 5,000 PSI
   d. 1,000 PSI

7. Hydrogen storage tanks are usually constructed from _____.
   a. Steel
   b. Aluminum
   c. Carbon fiber
   d. Both b and c

8. HCCI is a process that eliminates what parts or components in a gasoline engine?
   a. Fuel tank
   b. Battery
   c. Fuel injectors
   d. Ignition system

9. A plug-in hybrid is different from a conventional hybrid electric vehicle because it has _____.
   a. A built-in battery charger
   b. More batteries
   c. Li Ox batteries
   d. Bigger motor/generator

10. Which energy source(s) is (are) currently being used to help reduce the use of fossil fuels?
    a. Hydrogen
    b. Wind power
    c. Hydroelectric power
    d. Both b and c

chapter 17
HYBRID SAFETY AND SERVICE PROCEDURES

OBJECTIVES: **After studying Chapter 17, the reader will be able to:** • Safely de-power a hybrid electric vehicle. • Safely perform high-voltage disconnects. • Understand the unique service issues related to HEV high-voltage systems. • Correctly use appropriate personal protective equipment (PPE). • Perform routine vehicle service procedure on a hybrid electric vehicle. • Explain hazards while driving, moving, and hoisting a hybrid electric vehicle.

KEY TERMS: • ANSI 270 • ASTM 270 • CAT III 272 • DMM 271 • Floating ground 273 • HV 270 • HV cables 270 • IEC 271 • Lineman's gloves 270 • NiMH 275 • OSHA 270 • Service plug 274

HIGH-VOLTAGE SAFETY

NEED FOR CAUTION There have been electrical systems on vehicles for over 100 years. Technicians have been repairing vehicle electrical systems without fear of serious injury or electrocution. However, when working with hybrid electric vehicles, this is no longer true. It is now possible to be seriously injured or electrocuted (killed) if proper safety procedures are not followed.

Hybrid electric vehicles and all electric vehicles use **high-voltage (HV)** circuits that if touched with an unprotected hand could cause serious burns or even death.

IDENTIFYING HIGH-VOLTAGE CIRCUITS **High-voltage cables** are identified by color of the plastic conduit and include:

- **Blue or yellow.** 42 volts (not a shock hazard but an arc will be maintained if a circuit is opened)
- **Orange.** 144 to 600 volts or higher

☠ WARNING

Touching circuits or wires containing high voltage can cause severe burns or death.

HIGH-VOLTAGE SAFETY EQUIPMENT

RUBBER GLOVES Before working on the high-voltage system of a hybrid electric vehicle, be sure that high-voltage **lineman's gloves** are available. Be sure that the gloves are rated at least 1,000 volts and class "0" by ANSI/ASTM. The **American National Standards Institute (ANSI)** is a private, nonprofit organization that administers and coordinates the U.S. voluntary standardization and conformity assessment system. ASTM International, originally known as the **American Society for Testing and Materials (ASTM),** was formed over a century ago, to address the need for component testing in industry. The **Occupational Safety and Health Administration (OSHA)** requirements specify that the HV gloves get inspected every six months by a qualified glove inspection laboratory. Use an outer leather glove to protect the HV rubber gloves. Inspect the gloves carefully before each use. High voltage and current (amperes) in combination is fatal. ● **SEE FIGURES 17–1 AND 17–2.**

NOTE: The high-voltage insulated safety gloves must be recertified every six months to remain within Occupational Safety and Health Administration (OSHA) guidelines.

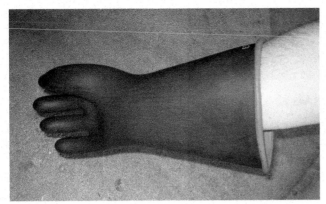

FIGURE 17–1 Rubber lineman's gloves protect the wearer from a shock hazard.

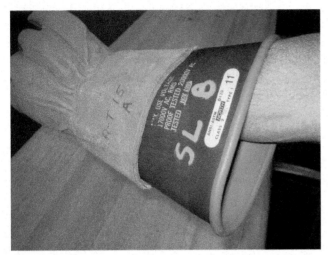

FIGURE 17–2 Wearing leather gloves over the lineman's gloves helps protect the rubber gloves from damage.

Before using the rubber gloves, they should be tested for leaks using the following procedure:

1. Roll the glove up from the open end until the lower portion of the glove begins to balloon from the resulting air pressure. Be sure to "lean" into the sealed glove to raise the internal air pressure. If the glove leaks any air, discard the gloves. ● **SEE FIGURE 17–3.**

2. The gloves should not be used if they show any signs of wear and tear.

☠ **WARNING**

Cables and wiring are orange in color. High-voltage insulated safety gloves and a face shield must be worn when carrying out any diagnostics involving the high-voltage systems or components.

FIGURE 17–3 Checking rubber lineman's gloves for pinhole leaks.

CAT III-RATED DIGITAL MULTIMETER Hybrid electric vehicles are equipped with electrical systems whose voltages can exceed 600 volts DC. A CAT III-certified **digital multimeter (DMM)** is required for making measurements on these high-voltage systems.

The **International Electrotechnical Commission (IEC)** has several categories of voltage standards for meter and meter leads. These categories are ratings for over-voltage protection and are rated CAT I, CAT II, CAT III, and CAT IV. The higher the category (CAT) rating, the greater the protection to the technician when measuring high-energy voltage. Under each category there are various voltage ratings.

CAT I Typically a CAT I meter is used for low-voltage measurements, such as voltage measurements at wall outlets in the home. Meters with a CAT I rating are usually rated at 300 to 800 volts. CAT I is for relatively low-energy levels, and while the voltage level to be high enough for use when working on a hybrid electric vehicle, the protective energy level is lower than what is needed.

? **FREQUENTLY ASKED QUESTION**

Is It the Voltage Rating That Determines the CAT Rating?

Yes and no. The voltages stated for the various CAT ratings are important but the potential harm to a technician due to the energy level is what is most important. For example some CAT II rated meters may have a stated voltage higher than a meter that has a CAT III rating. Always use a meter that has a CAT III rating when working on a hybrid electric vehicle. ● **SEE FIGURES 17–4 AND 17–5.**

FIGURE 17-4 Be sure to only use a meter that is CAT III-rated when taking electrical voltage measurements on a hybrid electric or electric vehicle.

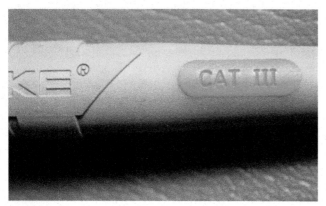

FIGURE 17-5 The meter leads should also be CAT III-rated when checking voltages on a hybrid electric vehicle.

CAT II A higher-rated meter that would be typically used for checking voltages at the circuit-breaker panel in the home. Meters with a CAT II rating are usually rated at 300 to 600 volts. CAT II rated meters have similar voltage ratings as the other CAT ratings, but the energy level of protection is higher with a CAT II compared to a CAT I.

CAT III **CAT III** is the minimum-rated meter that should be used for hybrid vehicles. Meters with a CAT III rating are usually rated at 600 to 1,000 volts and the highest energy level which is needed to protect the service technician.

CAT IV CAT IV meters are for clamp-on meters only. A clamp-on meter is used to measure current (amperes) in a circuit by placing the clamp around the wire carrying the current. If a clamp-on meter also has meter leads for voltage measurements, that part of the meter will be rated as CAT III.

INSULATION TESTER An electrical insulation tester, such as the Fluke 1587, is used to test for electrical continuity between the high-voltage wires or components and the body of the vehicle. If a hybrid electric vehicle has been involved in any type of collision or any other incident where damage could

occur to the insulation, the high-voltage system should be checked. An insulation tester is more expensive than a digital meter. This means that an individual service technician often does not purchase one, but any technician or service shop that works on hybrid electric vehicles should have one available.

EYE PROTECTION Eye protection should be worn when testing for high voltage, which is considered by many experts to be over 60 volts. Eye protection should include the following features:

1. Plastic frames (avoid metal frames as these are conductive and could cause a shock hazard)
2. Side shields
3. Meet the standard ANSI Z87.1

Most hybrid electric systems use voltages higher than this threshold. If the system has not been powered down or has not had the high-voltage system disabled, a shock hazard is always possible. Even when the high-voltage system has been disconnected, there is still high voltage in the HV battery box.

NOTE: Some vehicle manufacturers specify that full face shields be worn instead of safety glasses when working with high-voltage circuits or components.

SAFETY CONES Ford requires that cones be placed at the four corners of any hybrid electric vehicle when service work on the high-voltage system is being performed. They are used to establish a safety zone around the vehicles so that other technicians will know that a possible shock hazard may be present.

FIBERGLASS POLE Ford requires that a ten foot insulated fiberglass pole be available outside the safety zone to be used to pull a technician away from the vehicle in the unlikely event of an accident where the technician is shocked or electrocuted.

ELECTRIC SHOCK POTENTIAL

LOCATIONS WHERE SHOCKS CAN OCCUR Accidental and unprotected contact with any electrically charged ("hot" or "live") high-voltage component can cause serious injury or death. However, receiving an electric shock from a hybrid vehicle is highly unlikely because of the following:

1. Contact with the battery module or other components inside the battery box can occur only if the box is damaged and the contents are exposed, or the box is opened without following proper precautions.
2. Contact with the electric motor can occur only after one or more components are removed.
3. The high-voltage cables can be easily identified by their distinctive orange color, and contact with them can be avoided.
4. The system main relays (SMRs) disconnect power from the cables the moment the ignition is turned off.

LOCATIONS OF AUXILIARY BATTERIES ● SEE

CHART 17–1 for a summary of the locations of auxiliary batteries.
As a rule of thumb, the auxiliary battery is usually a flood-type if it is located under the hood and an AGM-type if it is in the trunk area.

WARNING

Power remains in the high-voltage electrical system for up to 10 minutes after the HV battery pack is shut off. Never touch, cut, or open any orange high-voltage power cable or high-voltage component without confirming that the high-voltage has been completely discharged.

TECH TIP

Silence Is NOT Golden

Never assume the vehicle is shut off just because the engine is off. When working with a Toyota or Lexus hybrid electric vehicle, always look for the **READY** indicator status on the dash display. The vehicle is shut off when the **READY** indicator is off.

The vehicle may be powered by:

1. The electric motor only.
2. The gasoline engine only.
3. A combination of both the electric motor and the gasoline engine.

The vehicle computer determines the mode in which the vehicle operates to improve fuel economy and reduce emissions. The driver cannot manually select the mode. ● **SEE FIGURE 17–6.**

FIGURE 17–6 The Ford Escape Hybrid instrument panel showing the vehicle in park and the tachometer on "EV" instead of 0 RPM. This means that the gasoline engine could start at any time depending on the state-of-charge of the high-voltage batteries and other factors.

TECH TIP

High Voltage Is Insulated From the Vehicle Body

Both positive and negative high-voltage power cables are isolated from the metal chassis, so there is no possibility of shock by touching the metal chassis. This design is called a **floating ground.**

A ground fault monitor continuously monitors for high-voltage leakage to the metal chassis while the vehicle is running. If a malfunction is detected, the vehicle computer will illuminate the master warning light in the instrument cluster and the hybrid warning light in the LCD display. The HV battery pack relays will automatically open to stop electricity flow in a collision sufficient to activate the SRS airbags.

HYBRID VEHICLE AUXILIARY BATTERY CHART		
VEHICLE	**AUXILIARY BATTERY TYPE**	**AUXILIARY BATTERY LOCATION**
Honda Insight Hybrid	Flooded lead acid	Underhood; center near bulkhead
Honda Civic Hybrid	Flooded lead acid	Underhood; driver's side
Honda Accord Hybrid	Flooded lead acid	Underhood; driver's side
Ford Escape Hybrid	Flooded lead acid	Underhood; driver's side
Toyota Prius Hybrid (2001–2003)	Absorbed glass mat (AGM)	Trunk; driver's side
Toyota Prius Hybrid (2004–2007)	Absorbed glass mat (AGM)	Trunk; passenger side
Toyota Highlander Hybrid	Flooded lead acid	Underhood; passenger side
Toyota Camry Hybrid	Absorbed glass mat (AGM)	Trunk; passenger side
Lexus RX 400h Hybrid	Flooded lead acid	Underhood; passenger side
Lexus GS 450h Hybrid	Absorbed glass mat (AGM)	Trunk; driver's side
Chevrolet/GMC Hybrid Pickup Truck	Flooded lead acid	Underhood; driver's side

CHART 17–1

As a rule of thumb, the auxiliary battery is usually a flood-type if it is located under the hood and an AGM-type if it is in the trunk area.

DE-POWERING THE HIGH-VOLTAGE SYSTEM

THE NEED TO DE-POWER THE HV SYSTEM During routine vehicle service work there is no need to go through any procedures needed to de-power or to shut off the high-voltage circuits. However, if work is going to be performed on any of the following components then service information procedures must be followed to prevent possible electrical shock and personal injury.

- The high-voltage (HV) battery pack
- Any of the electronic controllers that use orange cables such as the inverter and converters
- The air-conditioning compressor if electrically driven and has orange cables attached

To safely de-power the vehicle always follow the instructions found in service information for the exact vehicle being serviced. The steps usually include:

STEP 1 Turn the ignition off and remove the key (if equipped) from the ignition.

> **CAUTION:** If a push-button start is used, remove the key fob at least 15 feet (5 meters) from the vehicle to prevent the vehicle from being powered up.

STEP 2 Remove the 12-volt power source to the HV controller. This step could involve:
- Removing a fuse or a relay
- Disconnecting the negative battery cable from the auxiliary 12-volt battery

STEP 3 Remove the high-voltage (HV) fuse or **service plug** or switch.

> ☠ **WARNING**
>
> Even if all of the above steps are followed, there is still a risk for electrical shock at the high-voltage batteries. Always follow the vehicle manufacturer's instructions exactly and wear high-voltage gloves and other specified personal protective equipment (PPE).

COLLISION AND REPAIR INDUSTRY ISSUES

JUMP STARTING The 12-volt auxiliary battery may be jump started if the vehicle does not start. The 12-volt auxiliary battery is located under the hood or in the cargo (trunk) area of

---

? **FREQUENTLY ASKED QUESTION**

When Do I Need to De-Power the High-Voltage System?

During routine service work, there is no need for a technician to de-power the high-voltage system. The only time when this process is needed is if service repairs or testing is being performed on any circuit that has an orange cable attached. These include:

- AC compressor if electrically powered
- High-voltage battery pack or electronic controllers

The electric power steering system usually operates on 12 volts or 42 volts and neither is a shock hazard. However, an arc will be maintained if a 42-volt circuit is opened. Always refer to service information if servicing the electric power steering system or any other system that may contain high voltage.

---

some HEVs. Using a jump box or jumper cable from another vehicle, make the connections to the positive and negative battery terminals. ● **SEE FIGURE 17–7.**

On the 20041 Toyota Prius vehicles, there is a stud located under the hood that can be used to jump start the auxiliary battery, which is located in the truck. ● **SEE FIGURE 17–8.**

NOTE: The high-voltage (HV) battery pack cannot be jump started on most HEVs. One exception is the Ford Escape/Mercury Mariner hybrids that use a special "jump-start" button located behind the left kick panel. When this button is pushed, the auxiliary battery is used to boost the HV battery through a DC-DC converter.

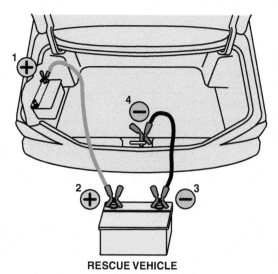

RESCUE VEHICLE

FIGURE 17–7 Jump starting a 2001–2003 Toyota Prius using a 12-volt supply to boost the 12-volt auxiliary battery in the trunk.

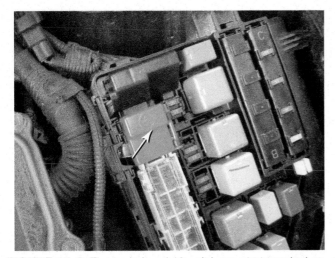

FIGURE 17–8 The underhood 12-volt jump-start terminal on this 20041 Toyota Prius has a red plastic cover with a "+" sign. The positive booster cable clamp will attach directly to the vertical metal bracket.

FIGURE 17–9 Using a warning cover over the steering wheel helps others realize that work is being performed on the high-voltage system and that no one is to attempt to start or move the vehicle.

MOVING AND TOWING A HYBRID

TOWING If a disabled vehicle needs to be moved a short distance (to the side of the road, for example) and the vehicle can still roll on the ground, the easiest way is to shift the transmission into neutral and manually push the vehicle. To transport a vehicle away from an emergency location, a flatbed truck should be used if the vehicle might be repaired. If a flatbed is not available, the vehicle should be towed by wheel-lift equipment with the front wheels off the ground (FWD hybrid electric vehicles only). Do not use sling-type towing equipment. In the case of 4WD HEVs such as the Toyota Highlander, only a flatbed vehicle should be used.

MOVING THE HYBRID VEHICLE IN THE SHOP After an HEV has been serviced, it may be necessary to push the vehicle to another part of the shop or outside as parts are ordered. Make sure to tape any orange cable ends that were disconnected during the repair procedure. Permanent magnets are used in all the drive motors and generators and it is possible that a high-voltage arc could occur as the wheels turn and produce voltage. Another way to prevent this is to use wheel dollies. A sign that says "HIGH VOLTAGE—DO NOT TOUCH" could also be added to the roof of the vehicle. Remove the keys from the vehicle and keep in a safe location. ● **SEE FIGURES 17–9 AND 17–10.**

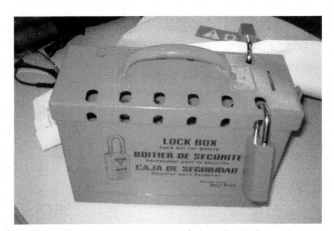

FIGURE 17–10 A lock box is a safe location to keep the ignition keys of a hybrid electric vehicle while it is being serviced.

? FREQUENTLY ASKED QUESTION

Will the Heat from Paint Ovens Hurt the High-Voltage Batteries?

Nickel-metal hydride (**NiMH**) batteries may be damaged if exposed to high temperatures, such as in a paint oven. The warning labels on hybrid vehicles specify that the battery temperature not exceed 150° F (66° C). Therefore be sure to check the temperature of any paint oven before allowing a hybrid electric vehicle into one that may be hotter than specified. Check service information for details on the vehicle being repaired.

REMOVING THE HIGH-VOLTAGE BATTERIES

PRECAUTIONS The HV battery box should always be removed as an assembly, placed on a rubber-covered work bench, and handled carefully. Every other part, especially the capacitors, should be checked for voltage reading while wearing HV rubber gloves. Always check for voltage as the components become accessible before proceeding. When removing high-voltage components, it is wise to use insulated tools. ● **SEE FIGURE 17–11.**

TECH TIP

High-Voltage Battery SOC Considerations

NiMH batteries do not store well for long lengths of time. After a repair job, or when the HV system has been powered down by a technician and powered up again, do not be surprised if a warning lamp lights, diagnostic trouble codes are set, and the MIL are illuminated. If everything was done correctly, a couple road tests may be all that is required to reset the MIL. The HV battery indicator on the dash may also read zero charge level. After a road test, the HV battery level indicator will most likely display the proper voltage level.

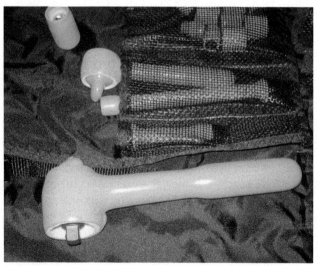

FIGURE 17–11 Insulated tools, such as this socket set, would provide an additional margin of safety to the service technician when working around high-voltage components and systems.

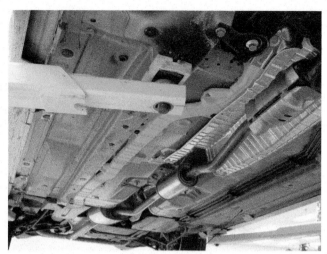

FIGURE 17–12 The high-voltage wiring on this Honda hybrid is colored orange for easy identification.

STORING THE HIGH-VOLTAGE BATTERIES If a hybrid is to be stored for any length of time, the state of charge of the HV batteries must be maintained. If possible, start the vehicle every month and run it for at least 30 minutes to help recharge the HV batteries. This is necessary because NiMH batteries suffer from self-discharge over time. High-voltage battery chargers are expensive and may be hard to find. If the HV battery SOC was over 60% when it was put into storage, the batteries may be stored for about a month without a problem. If, however, the SOC is less than 60%, a problem with a discharged HV battery may result.

HOISTING A HYBRID VEHICLE When hoisting or using a floor jack, pay attention to the lift points. Orange cables run under the vehicle just inside the frame rails on most hybrids. ● **SEE FIGURE 17–12.**

Some Honda hybrid vehicles use an aluminum pipe painted orange that includes three HV cables for the starter/generator and also three more cables for the HV air-conditioning compressor. If any damage occurs to any high-voltage cables, the MIL will light up and a no-start will result if the PCM senses a fault. The cables are not repairable and are expensive. The cables can be identified by an orange outer casing, but in some cases, the orange casing is not exposed until a black plastic underbelly shield is removed first.

HV BATTERY DISPOSAL The hybrid electric vehicle manufacturers are set up to ship NiMH battery packs to a recycling center. There is an 800 number located under the hood or on the HV battery pack that can be used to gain information on how to recycle these batteries.

Always follow the proper safety procedures, and then minor service to hybrid vehicles can be done with a reasonable level of safety.

ROUTINE SERVICE PROCEDURES

DIAGNOSIS PROCEDURES Hybrid electric vehicles should be diagnosed the same as any other type of vehicle. This means following a diagnostic routine, which usually includes the following steps:

STEP 1 Verify the customer concern.

STEP 2 Check for diagnostic trouble codes (DTCs). An enhanced or factory level scan tool may be needed to get access to codes and sub-codes.

STEP 3 Perform a thorough visual inspection. If a DTC is stored, carefully inspect those areas that might be the cause of the trouble code.

STEP 4 Check for technical service bulletins (TSBs) that may relate to the customer concern.

STEP 5 Follow service information specified steps and procedures. This could include checking scan tool data for sensors or values that are not within normal range.

STEP 6 Determine and repair the root cause of the problem.

STEP 7 Verify the repair and clear any stored diagnostic trouble codes unless in an emission testing area. If in an emission test area, drive the vehicle until the powertrain control module (PCM) passes the fault and turns off the malfunction indicator lamp (MIL) thereby allowing the vehicle to pass the inspection.

STEP 8 Complete the work order and record the "three Cs" (complaint, cause, and correction). ● **SEE FIGURE 17–13.**

OIL CHANGE Performing an oil change is similar to changing oil in any vehicle equipped with an internal combustion engine.

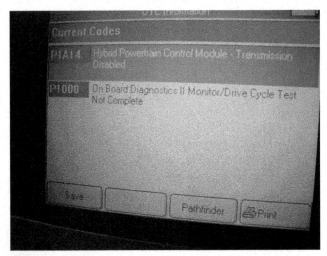

FIGURE 17–13 A scan tool display showing two hybrid-related faults in this Ford Escape hybrid.

FIGURE 17–14 Always use the specified viscosity of oil in a hybrid electric vehicle not only for best fuel economy but also because of the need for fast lubrication because of the engine (idle) stop feature.

However, there are several items to know when changing oil in a hybrid electric vehicle including:

- **Use vehicle manufacturer's recommended hoisting locations.** Use caution when hoisting a hybrid electric vehicle and avoid placing the pads on or close to the orange high-voltage cables that are usually located under the vehicle.

- **Always use the specified oil viscosity.** Most hybrid electric vehicles require either:

    SAE 0W-20

    SAE 5W-20

    Using the specified oil viscosity is important because the engine stops and starts many times and using the incorrect viscosity not only can cause a decrease in fuel economy but also could cause engine damage. ● **SEE FIGURE 17–14.**

- **Always follow the specified procedures.** Be sure that the internal combustion engine (ICE) is off and that the "READY" lamp is off. If there is a smart key or the vehicle has a push-button start, be sure that the key fob is at least 15 feet (5 meters) away from the vehicle to help prevent the engine from starting accidentally.

COOLING SYSTEM SERVICE Performing cooling system service is similar to performing this service in any vehicle equipped with an internal combustion engine. However, there are several items to know when servicing the cooling system on a hybrid electric vehicle including:

- **Always check service information for the exact procedure to follow.** The procedure will include the following:

    1. **The specified coolant.** Most vehicle manufacturers will recommend using premixed coolant because using water (half of the coolant) that has minerals could cause corrosion issues.

A Bad Day Changing Oil

A shop owner was asked by a regular customer who had just bought a Prius if the oil could be changed there. The owner opened the hood, made sure the filter was in stock (it is a standard Toyota filter used on other models), and said yes. A technician with no prior knowledge of hybrids drove the warmed-up vehicle into the service bay. The internal combustion engine never started, as it was in electric (stealth) mode at the time. Not hearing the engine running, the technician hoisted the vehicle into the air, removed the drain bolt, and drained the oil into the oil drain unit. When the filter was removed, oil started to fly around the shop. The engine was in "standby" mode during the first part of the oil change. When the voltage level dropped, the onboard computer started the engine so that the HV battery could recharge. The technician should have removed the key to keep this from happening. Be sure that the "ready" light is off before changing the oil or doing any other service work that may cause personal harm or harm to the vehicle if the engine starts.

2. **The specified coolant replacement interval.** While this may be similar to the coolant replacement interval for a conventional vehicle, always check to be sure that this service is being performed at the specified time or mileage interval.

3. **The specified precautions.** Some Toyota Prius HEVs use a coolant storage bottle that keeps the coolant hot for up to three days. Opening a coolant hose could cause the release of this hot coolant and can cause serious burns to the technician.

4. Always read, understand, and follow all of the service information instructions when servicing the cooling system on a hybrid electric vehicle.

AIR FILTER SERVICE Performing air filter service is similar to performing this service in any vehicle equipped with an internal combustion engine. However, there are several items to know when servicing the air filter on a hybrid electric vehicle including:

1. Always follow the service information recommended air filter replacement interval.

2. For best results use the factory type and quality air filter.

3. Double-check that all of the air ducts are securely fastened after checking or replacing the air filter.

AIR-CONDITIONING SERVICE Performing air-conditioning system service is similar to performing this service in any vehicle equipped with an internal combustion engine. However, there are several items to know when servicing the air-conditioning system on a hybrid electric vehicle including:

1. Many hybrid electric vehicles use an air-conditioning compressor that uses high voltage from the high-voltage (HV) battery pack to operate the compressor either all of the time, such as many Toyota/Lexus models, or during idle stop periods, such as on Honda hybrids.

2. If the system is electrically driven, then special refrigerant oil is used that is nonconductive. This means that a separate recovery machine should be used to avoid the possibility of mixing regular refrigerant oils in with the oil used in hybrids.

3. Always read, understand, and follow all of the service information instructions when servicing the air-conditioning system on a hybrid electric vehicle.

STEERING SYSTEM SERVICE Performing steering system service is similar to performing this service in any vehicle equipped with an internal combustion engine. However, there are several items to know when servicing the steering system on a hybrid electric vehicle including:

1. Check service information for any precautions that are specified to be followed when servicing the steering system on a hybrid electric vehicle.

2. Most hybrid electric vehicles use an electric power steering system. These can be powered by one of two voltages:

   - **12 volts**—These systems can be identified by the red or black wiring conduit and often use an inverter that increases the voltage to operate the actuator motor (usually to 42 volts). While this higher voltage is contained in the controller and should not create a shock hazard, always follow the specified safety precautions and wear protective high-voltage gloves as needed.

   - **42 volts**—These systems use a yellow or blue plastic conduit over the wires to help identify the possible hazards from this voltage level. This voltage level is not a shock hazard but can maintain an arc if a circuit carrying 42 volts is opened.

BRAKING SYSTEM SERVICE Performing braking system service is similar to performing this service in any vehicle equipped with an internal combustion engine. However, there are several items to know when servicing the braking system on a hybrid electric vehicle including:

1. Check service information for any precautions that are specified to be followed when servicing the braking system on a hybrid electric vehicle.

2. All hybrid electric vehicles use a regenerative braking system, which captures the kinetic energy of the moving vehicle and converts it to electrical energy and is sent to the high-voltage battery pack. The amount of current produced during hard braking can exceed 100 amperes. This current is stored in the high-voltage battery pack and is then used as needed to help power the vehicle.

3. The base brakes used on hybrid electric vehicles are the same as any other conventional vehicle except for the master cylinder and related control systems. There is no high-voltage circuits associated with the braking system as the regeneration occurs inside the electric drive (traction) motors and is controlled by the motor controller.

4. The base brakes on many hybrid vehicles are often found to be stuck or not functioning correctly because the brakes are not doing much work and can rust.

NOTE: Always check the base brakes whenever there is a poor fuel economy complaint heard from an owner of a hybrid vehicle. Often when a disc brake caliper sticks, the brakes drag but the driver is not aware of any performance problems but the fuel economy drops.

TIRES Performing tire-related service is similar to performing this service in any vehicle equipped with an internal combustion engine. However, there are several items to know when servicing tires on a hybrid electric vehicle including:

1. Tire pressure is very important to not only the fuel economy but also on the life of the tire. Lower inflation pressure increases rolling resistance and reduces load carrying capacity and tire life. Always inflate the tires to the pressure indicated on the door jamb sticker or found in service information or the owner's manual.

2. All tires create less rolling resistance as they wear. This means that even if the same identical tire is used as a replacement, the owner may experience a drop in fuel economy.

3. Tires can have a big effect on fuel economy. It is best to warn the owner that replacement of the tires can and often will cause a drop in fuel economy, even if low rolling resistance tires are selected.

4. Try to avoid using tires that are larger than used from the factory. The larger the tire, the heavier it is and it takes more energy to rotate, resulting in a decrease in fuel economy.

5. Follow normal tire inspections and tire rotation intervals as specified by the vehicle manufacturer.

FIGURE 17–15 This 12-volt battery under the hood on a Ford Fusion hybrid is a flooded cell type auxiliary battery.

AUXILIARY BATTERY TESTING AND SERVICE

Performing auxiliary battery service is similar to performing this service in any vehicle equipped with an internal combustion engine. However, there are several items to know when servicing the auxiliary battery on a hybrid electric vehicle including:

1. Auxiliary 12-volt batteries used in hybrid electric vehicles are located in one of two general locations.
   - **Under the hood**—If the 12-volt auxiliary battery is under the hood it is generally a flooded-type lead–acid battery and should be serviced the same as any conventional battery. ● **SEE FIGURE 17–15.**
   - **In the passenger or trunk area**—If the battery is located in the passenger or trunk area of the vehicle, it is usually of the absorbed glass mat (AGM) design. This type of battery requires that a special battery charger that limits the charging voltage be used.

2. The auxiliary 12-volt battery is usually smaller than a battery used in a conventional vehicle because it is not used to actually start the engine unless under extreme conditions on Honda hybrids only.

3. The 12-volt auxiliary battery can be tested and serviced the same as any battery used in a conventional vehicle.

4. Always read, understand, and follow all of the service information instructions when servicing the auxiliary battery on a hybrid electric vehicle.

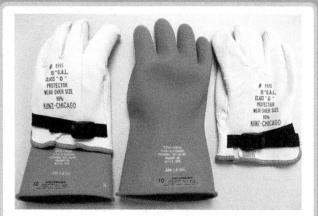

1 The cuff of the rubber glove should extend at least 1/2 inch beyond the cuff of the leather protector.

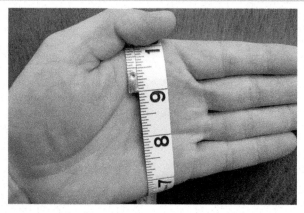

2 To determine correct glove size, use a soft tape to measure around the palm of the hand. A measurement of 9 inches would correspond with a glove size of 9.

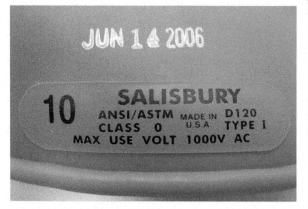

JUN 1 4 2006

10 **SALISBURY**
ANSI/ASTM MADE IN D120
CLASS 0 U.S.A. TYPE I
MAX USE VOLT 1000V AC

3 The glove rating and the date of the last test should be stamped on the glove cuff.

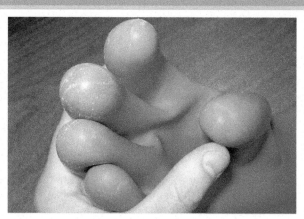

4 Start with a visual inspection of the glove fingertips, making sure that no cuts or other damage is present.

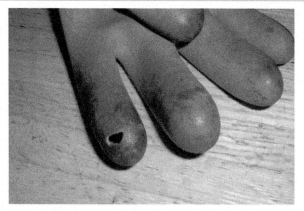

5 The damage on this glove was easily detected with a simple visual inspection. Note that the rubber glove material can be damaged by petroleum products, detergents, certain hand soaps, and talcum powder.

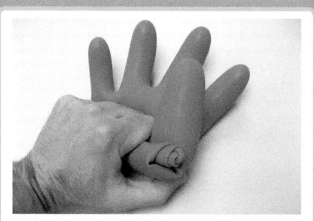

6 Manually inflate the glove to inspect for pinhole leaks. Starting at the cuff, roll up the glove and trap air at the finger end. Listen and watch carefully for deflation of the glove. If a leak is detected, the glove must be discarded.

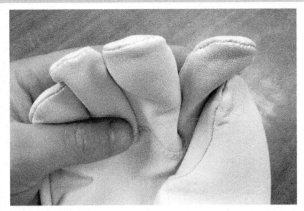

7 Petroleum on the leather protector's surfaces will damage the rubber glove underneath.

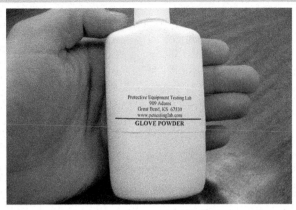

8 Glove powder (glove dust) should be used to absorb moisture and reduce friction.

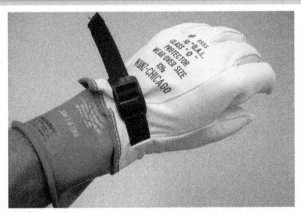

9 Put on the gloves and tighten the straps on the back of the leather protectors.

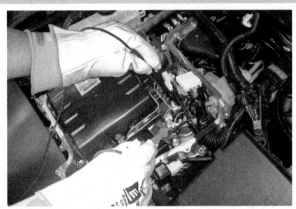

10 Technicians MUST wear HV gloves and leather protectors whenever working around the high-voltage areas of a hybrid electric vehicle.

11 HV gloves and leather protectors should be placed in a canvas storage bag when not in use. Note the ventilation hole at the bottom of this bag.

12 Make sure that the rubber gloves are not folded when placed in the canvas bag. Folding increases mechanical stress on the rubber and can lead to premature failure of the glove material.

1. Personal protective equipment (PPE) for work on hybrid electric vehicles includes the wearing of high-voltage rubber gloves rated at 1,000 volts or more worn with outer-leather gloves to help protect the rubber gloves.

2. A digital meter that meets CAT ill standards should be used when working around the high-voltage section of a hybrid electric vehicle.

3. Safety glasses and a face shield should be worn whenever working around the high-voltage circuits of a hybrid electric vehicle.

4. The high-voltage system can be shut off at the battery pack by simply being certain that the ignition is off. Disconnecting the 12-volt battery is additional security that the highvoltage circuits are de-powered.

5. When servicing a hybrid electric vehicle, always observe safety procedures.

REVIEW QUESTIONS

1. What are the recommended items that should be used when working with the high-voltage circuits of a hybrid electric vehicle?

2. What actions are needed to disable the high-voltage (HV) circuit?

3. What are the precautions that service technicians should adhere to when servicing hybrid electric vehicles?

CHAPTER QUIZ

1. Rubber gloves should be worn whenever working on or near the high-voltage circuits or components of a hybrid electric vehicle. Technician A says that the rubber gloves should be rated at 1,000 volts or higher. Technician B says that leather gloves should be worn over the high-voltage rubber gloves. Which technician is correct?
   a. Technician A only
   b. Technician B only
   c. Both Technicians A and B
   d. Neither Technician A nor B

2. A CAT- III- certified DMM should be used whenever measuring high-voltage circuits or components. The CAT III rating relates to _____.
   a. High voltage
   b. High energy
   c. High electrical resistance
   d. Both a and b

3. All of the following will shut off the high voltage to components and circuits, except _____.
   a. Opening the driver's door
   b. Turning the ignition off
   c. Disconnecting the 12-volt auxiliary battery
   d. Removing the main fuse, relay, or HV plug

4. If the engine is not running, Technician A says that the high-voltage circuits are de-powered. Technician B says that all high-voltage wiring is orange-colored. Which technician is correct?
   a. Technician A only
   b. Technician B only
   c. Both Technicians A and B
   d. Neither Technician A nor B

5. Which statement is false about high-voltage wiring?
   a. Connects the battery pack to the electric controller
   b. Connects the controller to the motor/generator
   c. Is electrically grounded to the frame (body) of the vehicle
   d. Is controlled by a relay that opens if the ignition is off

6. What routine service procedure could result in lower fuel economy, which the owner may discover?
   a. Using the wrong viscosity engine oil
   b. Replacing tires
   c. Replacing the air filter
   d. Either a or b

7. Two technicians are discussing jump starting a hybrid electric vehicle. Technician A says that the high-voltage (HV) batteries can be jumped on some HEV models. Technician B says that the 12-volt auxiliary battery can be jumped using a conventional jump box or jumper Which technician is correct?
   a. Technician A only
   b. Technician B only
   c. Both Technicians A and B
   d. Neither Technician A nor B

8. What can occur if a hybrid electric vehicle is pushed in the shop?
   a. The HV battery pack can be damaged
   b. The tires will be locked unless the ignition is on
   c. Damage to the electronic controller can occur
   d. High voltage will be generated by the motor/generator

9. Nickel-metal hydride (NiMH) batteries can be damaged if exposed to temperatures higher than about _____.
   a. 150°F (66°C)   b. 175°F (79°C)
   c. 200°F (93°C)   d. 225°F (107°C)

10. How should nickel-metal hydride (NiMH) batteries be disposed?
    a. In regular trash
    b. Call an 800 number shown under the hood of the vehicle for information
    c. Submerged in water and then disposed of in regular trash
    d. Burned at an EPA-certified plant

chapter 18
FIRST RESPONDER PROCEDURES

OBJECTIVES: **After studying Chapter 18, the reader will be able to:** • Follow first responder standard operating procedures. • Identify a hybrid electric vehicle. • Safely de-power a hybrid electric vehicle. • Safely handle spills from a hybrid electric vehicle. • Discuss first responder issues involving alternative-fuel vehicles.

KEY TERMS: • Cut lines 288 • Double cut method 288 • Hazmat 289 • Hot stick 285 • Incident 283 • International Fire Service Training Association (IFSTA) 288 • National Fire Academy (NFA) 288 • National Fire Protection Association (NFPA) 288 • Personal protective equipment (PPE) 283 • Standard operating guidelines (SOG) 283 • Standard operating procedures (SOP) 283

HYBRID ELECTRIC VEHICLE INCIDENTS

Incidents involving a hybrid electric vehicle (HEV) could include the following:

1. Vehicle crash
2. Fire
3. Crash and fire
4. Submerged or partially submerged vehicle

FIRST RESPONDER PROCEDURES

SOP/SOG Whenever first responders approach an incident, they do not know for sure what they will find or how to handle the situation. The best approach for first responders is to follow **standard operating procedures (SOP)** also called **standard operating guidelines (SOG).** SOP/SOG procedures and guidelines are used to ensure that everyone in the department perform common tasks in a specific manner.

All standard operating procedures specify that human life should be considered the highest priority over any property damage. In other words, save the occupants first and/or do not put the lives of first responders in danger to save a vehicle or other property from harm. Standard operating procedures also include the use of the proper **personal protection equipment (PPE)** including:

- Protective clothing including helmet with face shield
- Self contained breathing apparatus (SCBA)

- High-voltage gloves, including leather protective gloves over the rubber insulated gloves
- Have insulated tools available if possible in the event that tools are needed. ● **SEE FIGURE 18–1.**

VISUAL ANALYSIS When approaching the scene of an **incident,** the first consideration is always the safety of people including:

- Occupants of the vehicle
- First responders
- Others in the area

If the initial visual evaluation of the scene indicates that a hybrid electric vehicle may be involved, then check the vehicle to confirm that it is a hybrid.

FIGURE 18–1 Insulated tools should be used, if possible, when tools are needed to free an occupant or perform removal of battery cables of a hybrid electric vehicle.

EMBLEMS. To confirm whether a vehicle is a hybrid, look for the word "HYBRID" on the rear, front, or side of the vehicle. Except for the Honda Insight and the Toyota Prius, there is very little difference in the exterior or interior appearance of hybrids, compared to those of their gasoline-only counterparts. ● **SEE FIGURE 18–2.**

ORANGE-COLORED CABLES. Orange cables under the hood, or orange shielding bolted to the underside of the vehicle indicates that the vehicle is a hybrid electric vehicle. If a hybrid badge or label is not visible (due to damage for example), the presence of orange cables under the hood or orange shielding under the vehicle would also identify the vehicle as an HEV. Electrical energy flows between the high-voltage battery module and the motor through either two or three heavy-duty orange cables. In some hybrid vehicles, high-voltage cables also deliver current to the air conditioning (A/C) compressor (if equipped). The high-voltage cables are routed under the vehicle between the battery box and the engine compartment inside sturdy orange plastic protective shields. ● **SEE FIGURE 18–3.**

FIGURE 18–2 Most hybrid electric vehicles (HEVs) can be identified by emblems on the front, side or rear of the vehicle.

FIGURE 18–3 A hybrid electric vehicle can often be identified by looking for orange-colored cables under the hood, as well as other markings on the engine cover.

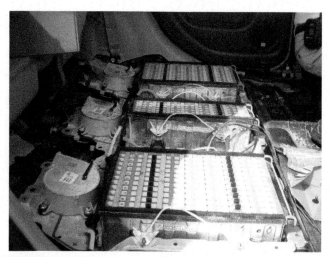

FIGURE 18–4 A Toyota Highlander hybrid battery pack located under the rear seat.

12-VOLT AUXILIARY BATTERY. The locations of a conventional lead–acid 12-volt battery generally include:

- Under the hood
- In the trunk
- Under the vehicle, attached to the frame

In most HEVs, this battery also provides power to the high-voltage battery control systems. Disconnecting or cutting the negative cables to the battery may be necessary in some emergency situations.

HIGH-VOLTAGE BATTERY. The electric motor is powered by a high-voltage battery module. The high-voltage battery modules are in plastic containers, which are then placed in a sturdy metal box. ● **SEE FIGURE 18–4.**

 ? FREQUENTLY ASKED QUESTION

How Can the Battery Be Disconnected if It Is under the Vehicle?

Some vehicles have the 12-volt auxiliary battery under the vehicle or behind panels that have to be removed to gain access to the battery terminals or cable. In these cases the vehicle manufacturer specifies that the correct procedure to follow to de-power the high-voltage circuit is to remove a fuse or relay. Instead of trying to locate a fuse that may not be readily seen as being the correct one to remove, the suggested approach is to remove all fuses and relays. Many hybrid electric vehicles use more than one fuse panel or relay center. It is best to check the first responder vehicle information to be sure. This way the 12-volt power is removed from the high-voltage controller and the high voltage is retained in the battery pack.

What Do the Colors of Cables Mean?

Hybrid electric vehicles are equipped with plastic conduit to cover and protect the electrical cables. This plastic conduit is color coded to help identify the potential risk. The colors and their meaning include:

- **Black**—12-volt cable. Not a shock hazard but can power airbags and pretensioners.
- **Red**—12 volts
- **Blue**—42 volts. Not a shock hazard but could maintain an arc if the circuit is opened. Is used for some electric power steering systems and mild hybrid vehicles such as the GM Belt-Alternator Starter (BAS) system.
- **Yellow**—42 volts. Not a shock hazard but could maintain an arc if the circuit is opened (cut). Usually used for electric power steering.
- **Orange**—144 to 600 volts or higher. Shock hazard and could cause severe burns or death. ● **SEE FIGURE 18–5.**

FIGURE 18–5 Blue cables under the hood of a General Motors mild hybrid electric vehicle.

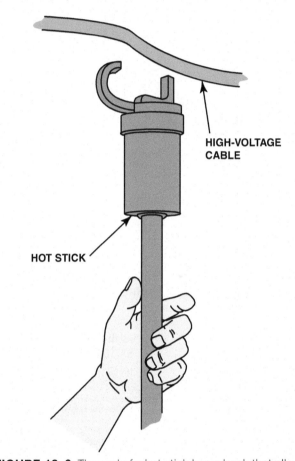

FIGURE 18–6 The end of a hot stick has a hook that allows first responders to grab and move high-voltage cables without being shocked because the pole is made from fiberglass, which is an insulator.

All components inside the battery box are completely insulated and isolated from the vehicle body. For maximum safety, the high-voltage battery box is positioned directly behind the seat-backs or under the rear seat where it is well-protected from potential damage in a collision.

Small quantities of a highly alkaline liquid electrolyte, which is corrosive to human tissue, are used in the manufacture of the nickel-metal hydride (NiMH) battery cells. However, in the finished cells, electrolyte is absorbed into the battery separator and sealed in a metal case, and any leakage would be extremely rare. Moreover, the electrolyte is nonflammable, nonexplosive, and creates no hazardous fumes or vapors in normal operating conditions.

HOT STICK Whenever approaching a hybrid electric vehicle, one option that can be used by first responders is the hot stick. A **hot stick** is a long tool used to pull high-voltage lines away from buildings or vehicles. ● **SEE FIGURE 18–6.** This may or may not be available to first responders and could be used to move orange cables out of the way to get access to an occupant.

SHEPHERD'S HOOK Some vehicle manufacturers specify that a long pole with a large lop on one end be used to grab a person and remove them from high voltage. This tool is commonly referred to as a shepherd's hook and is made from non-electrical-conducting fiberglass.

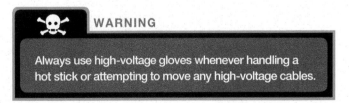

☠ WARNING

Always use high-voltage gloves whenever handling a hot stick or attempting to move any high-voltage cables.

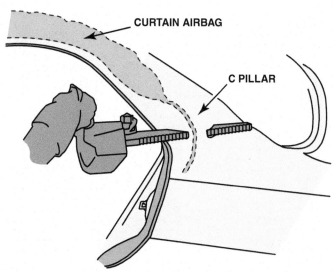

FIGURE 18–7 Use caution when cutting roof pillars because the curtain airbags could be deployed.

AIRBAGS AND TENSIONERS All hybrids have front airbags and front seat belt pretensioners. Most hybrid electric vehicles also have side airbags for front-seat occupants, and many are equipped with side curtain airbags as well. These systems all use pyrotechnic devices with a deactivation time (after 12-volt power is disconnected) of up to 3 minutes. To reduce the risk of injury during the deactivation period, the following steps are recommended:

■ Keep out of the path of an undeployed front airbag, and do not cut into the center of the steering wheel or dashboard where the front airbags are stored.

■ Do not cut into the rear (C) pillar where the side curtain inflator is stored. ● **SEE FIGURE 18–7.**

 **WARNING**

Extreme heat (320°F to 356°F [160°C to 180°C]) can cause unintended airbag inflation. Follow recommended procedures to avoid possible injury from a deploying airbag or inflator.

ELECTRIC SHOCK POTENTIAL

LOCATIONS OF SHOCK HAZARDS Unprotected contact with any electrically charged ("hot" or "live") high-voltage component can cause serious injury or death. However, receiving an electric shock from a hybrid vehicle is highly unlikely because of the following:

1. Contact with the battery module or other components inside the battery box can occur only if the box is damaged and the contents are exposed, or the box is opened without following proper precautions.

2. Contact with any electric motor or device that has high voltage, such as the air conditioning compressor that operates using high voltage and is identified by having orange electrical conduit.

3. The high-voltage cables can be easily identified by their distinctive orange color, and contact with them can be avoided.

4. The system main relays (SMRs) disconnect power from the cables the moment the ignition is turned off.

● **SEE CHART 18–1** for a summary of the locations of the 12-volt auxiliary battery and high-voltage battery and safety switch/plug.

MAKE MODEL (YEARS)	AUXILIARY 12-VOLT BATTERY LOCATION	HV BATTERY PACK LOCATION (VOLTAGE)	HV SAFETY SWITCH/PLUG LOCATION
Cadillac Escalade (2008+) (Two mode)	Under the hood; driver's side	Under second-row seat (300 volts)	Under second-row seat; passenger side
Chevrolet Malibu (2008+)	Under the hood; driver's side	Mounted behind rear seat under vehicle floor (36 volts)	Located on the side of the battery pack behind rear seat.
Chevrolet Silverado (2004–2008) (PHT)	Under the hood; driver's side	Under second-row seat (42 volts)	Rear passenger side behind cover
Chevrolet Tahoe (Two mode)	Under the hood; driver's side	Under second-row seat (300 volts)	Under second-row seat; passenger side
Chrysler Aspen (2009)	Quick disconnect plug under the hood; driver's side of air cleaner. Battery under driver's side door under vehicle	Under rear seat; driver's side (288 volts)	Under the front of rear seat; driver's side

CHART 18–1

A summary chart showing where the 12-volt and high-voltage batteries and shut-off switch/plugs are located.

MAKE MODEL (YEARS)	AUXILIARY 12-VOLT BATTERY LOCATION	HV BATTERY PACK LOCATION (VOLTAGE)	HV SAFETY SWITCH/PLUG LOCATION
Dodge Durango (2009)	Quick disconnect plug under the hood; driver's side of air cleaner. Battery under driver's side door under vehicle	Under rear seat; driver's side (288 volts)	Under the front of rear seat; driver's side
Ford Escape (2005+)	Under the hood on driver's side	Cargo area in the rear under carpet (300 volts)	Under rear carpet, round orange switch on passenger side
GMC Sierra (2004–2008) (PHT)	Under the hood; driver's side	Under second-row seat (42 volts)	Rear passenger side behind cover
GMC Yukon (2008+) Two Mode	Under the hood; driver's side	Under second-row seat (300 volts)	Under second-row seat; passenger side
Honda Accord (2005–2007)	Under the hood; driver's side	Behind rear seat (144 volts)	Switch on battery pack behind rear seat
Honda Civic (2003+)	Under the hood; driver's side	Behind rear seat (144 volts–158 volts 2006+)	Switch on battery pack behind rear seat
Honda Insight (1999–2005)	Under the hood; center under windshield	144 volts; under hatch floor in the rear	Under hatch carpet, remove small plate in center
Honda Insight (2010+)	Under the hood; driver's side	144 volts; under floor behind rear seat	Switch on battery pack behind rear seat
Lexus GS450h (2007+)	In the trunk; driver's side behind interior panel.	Trunk behind rear seat (288 volts)	No high-voltage disconnect; disconnect 12-volt battery to de-power the HV system
Lexus LS 600 (2006+)	In the trunk; driver's side behind interior panel.	Trunk behind rear seat (288 volts)	No high-voltage disconnect; disconnect 12-volt battery to de-power the HV system
Lexus RX400h (2006–2009)	Under the hood on the passenger side	Under the second-row seat (288 volts)	Under second-row seat; driver's side behind an access panel
Mercury Mariner (2005+)	Under the hood on driver's side	Cargo area in the rear under carpet (300 volts)	Under rear carpet, round orange switch on passenger side
Nissan Altima (2007+)	Trunk; driver's side	Behind rear seat (245 volts)	Trunk area; passenger side of high-voltage battery pack
Saturn AURA Hybrid (2007+)	Under the hood on the driver's side	Behind the rear seat; under the vehicle floor (36 volts)	Located on the side of the battery pack behind rear seat.
Saturn VUE Hybrid (2007+)	Under the hood on the driver's side	Behind the rear seat; under the vehicle floor (36 volts)	Located on the side of the battery pack behind rear seat.
Toyota Camry Hybrid (2007+)	Trunk on the passenger side	Behind the rear seat; under the vehicle floor (245 volts)	Remove IGCT #2 10 Amp (red) fuse from underhood fuse panel on driver's side
Toyota Highlander Hybrid (2006–2009)	Under the hood on the passenger side	Under the second-row seat (288 volts)	Under second-row seat; driver's side behind an access panel
Toyota Prius (2001–2003)	In the trunk on the driver's side	Behind rear seat (274 volts)	Remove IGCT relay from underhood fuse panel on passenger side; near windshield
Toyota Prius (2004–2009)	In the trunk on the driver's side	Behind rear seat (201 volts)	Remove HEV 20 Amp (yellow) fuse from the underhood fuse panel on the driver's side
Toyota Prius (2010+)	In the trunk on the driver's side	Behind rear seat (201.6 volts)	Remove HEV 20 Amp (yellow) fuse from the underhood fuse panel on the driver's side

CHART 18-1 (CONTINUED)

DANGEROUS CONDITIONS The high-voltage (orange) cables can be hot whenever:

- The ignition switch is on.
- The engine has been turned off by the auto idle stop feature.
- The air conditioner is on in vehicles that use an electric drive A/C compressor.

NOTE: The only condition common to all three situations in which the cables can be "hot" is that the ignition is on. Therefore, when the ignition switch is off, electric current cannot flow into the high-voltage cables because the system main relays that control the high voltage are turned off when the ignition is off.

EMERGENCY RESPONSE

FOLLOW STANDARD OPERATING PROCEDURES (SOP)
On arrival, emergency responders should follow standard operating procedures (SOP) for vehicle incidents. Standard operating procedures usually include the following steps:

STEP 1 **Identify the vehicle** as soon as possible to determine if it is a hybrid electric vehicle.

STEP 2 **Disable the vehicle** by performing the following:
- Remove the ignition key or fob.
- Move the key or fob at least 15 feet away from vehicle in case it is a smart key that can keep the vehicle powered up if near the vehicle.
- Verify that the "READY" light is off (if equipped).
- Place the transmission in PARK or Neutral.
- Approach the vehicle from the side; avoid walking in the front or rear of the vehicle if possible.

STEP 3 **Stabilize the vehicle.** Chock the wheels and set the parking brake if possible.

    CAUTION: Do not place cribbing (blocks) under the high-voltage power cables, exhaust system, or fuel system.

STEP 4 **Access the occupants.** Use normal removal procedures as required such as:
- Pull steering column forward and away from the occupant.
- Cut front pillar.
- Remove (peel) the roof.
- Door removal/displacement. Doors can be removed by conventional rescue devices such as hand, electric, and hydraulic tools.
- Dashboard displacement.
- Rescue lift airbags. Responders should not place cribbing or rescue lift airbags under the high-voltage power cables, exhaust system, or fuel system.

STEP 5 **Turn the ignition off.** Turning the ignition off and moving the key or key fob away from the vehicle will disable the high-voltage system.

STEP 6 **Disconnect or cut the 12-volt battery cables.**

What Are Cut Lines?

Cut lines are dashed or dotted lines printed on yellow tape that is wrapped around the positive and/or negative 12-volt battery cables showing the first responder where the cable should be cut to disable the 12-volt electrical system. Only some hybrid electric vehicles have these cut lines marked on the battery cables. The double cut method is preferred using insulated cutters. A **double cut method** means that after making the first cut on a battery cable, then move about 2 inches and make another cut so cables will not make contact if jarred. When the 12 volts are cut, the high-voltage system is de-powered and no high voltage should be in any of the orange cables except at the battery pack itself. ● **SEE FIGURE 18–8.**

FIGURE 18–8 The dotted lines on the battery cables indicate where first responders should cut the 12-volt battery cables, which will de-power the high-voltage system.

FIRE

FOLLOW SOP/SOG Approach and extinguish a fire using proper vehicle firefighting practices as recommended by **National Fire Protection Association (NFPA), International Fire Service Training Association (IFSTA),** or the **National Fire Academy (NFA).** Water (or foam if available) has been proven to be a suitable extinguishing agent. Perform a fast, aggressive fire attack. Use large amounts of water. Attack teams may not be able to identify the vehicle as being a hybrid until the fire has been knocked down and overhaul operations have commenced. A dry powder or CO_2 fire extinguisher can also be used if water is not readily available.

NOTE: If a fire occurs in the high-voltage battery pack, the incident commander will have to decide whether to pursue an offensive or defensive attack.

OFFENSIVE FIRE ATTACK Flooding the high-voltage (HV) battery pack, located in the cargo area, with large amounts of water at a safe distance will effectively control the HV battery pack fire by cooling the adjacent NiMH battery modules to a point below their ignition temperature. Any remaining modules that are not extinguished by the water will burn themselves out.

DEFENSIVE FIRE ATTACK If the decision has been made to fight the fire using a defensive attack, the fire attack crew should pull back a safe distance and allow the NiMH battery modules to burn out. During this defensive operation, fire crews may utilize a water stream or fog pattern to protect exposures or to control the path of smoke.

HAZMAT ISSUES

Hybrid vehicles contain the same common automotive fluids used in other vehicles. These fluids and chemicals may be considered **hazardous materials (hazmat).**

12-VOLT AUXILIARY BATTERY Conventional 12-volt batteries used in hybrid electric vehicles are lead–acid type. If a 12-volt battery is damaged, liquid electrolyte could spill. This mild sulfuric acid solution can be neutralized using baking soda.

HIGH-VOLTAGE (HV) BATTERIES The high-voltage NiMH battery electrolyte is a caustic alkaline (pH 13.5) that is corrosive to human tissues. The electrolyte, however, is absorbed in the separator material and will not normally spill or leak out even if a battery module is cracked. A catastrophic crash that would breach both the metal battery pack case and the plastic battery module would be a rare occurrence. Similar to using baking soda to neutralize a lead–acid battery electrolyte spill, a dilute boric acid solution or vinegar is used to neutralize a NiMH battery electrolyte spill.

Handle NiMH electrolyte spills using the following personal protective equipment (PPE):

- Splash shield or safety goggles
- Rubber, latex, or nitrile gloves
- Apron suitable for alkaline materials
- Rubber boots

Neutralize NiMH electrolyte using a boric acid solution or vinegar: boric acid solution—5.5 ounces boric acid to 1 gallon of water (800 grams boric acid to 20 liters water).

OTHER HAZARDS There are no unusual hazards if a hybrid electric vehicle is involved in a fire. It should be noted, however, that extremely high temperatures (320°F to 356°F [160°C to 180°C]) can cause airbag modules to deploy.

SUBMERGED OR PARTIALLY SUBMERGED VEHICLE

If a hybrid electric vehicle is submerged, the system main (high-voltage) relays cut off high voltage to all systems except the batteries themselves. The relays are opened by the circuit that monitors any electrical connection between the high-voltage system and the body (ground). Therefore, there should not be a shock hazard involving a submerged hybrid electric vehicle. Treat a submerged hybrid electric vehicle as a normal incident. It will not usually be known if the vehicle is a hybrid electric vehicle until it has been removed from the water.

Follow these steps to handle a hybrid electric vehicle that is fully or partially submerged in water:

STEP 1 Remove the occupants.

STEP 2 Remove vehicle from the water.

STEP 3 Drain water from the vehicle if possible.

NOTE: There is no risk of electric shock from touching the body or the framework of the vehicle whether in or out of the water.

ALTERNATIVE-FUEL VEHICLE ISSUES

IDENTIFICATION OF ALTERNATIVE-FUEL VEHICLES It is often impossible for first responders to be able to identify a vehicle as being powered by an alternative fuel besides gasoline. When approaching any vehicle incident, the standard operating procedures should be followed and proceed to save human life first and property second.

TYPES OF VEHICLE FUELS Most vehicles including hybrid electric vehicles use gasoline for a fuel. Gasoline is very flammable and can become explosive. However, first responders often cannot determine if a vehicle uses an alternative fuel until the fire has been extinguished.

Some types of alternative fuels and their concerns to first responders include:

- **Methanol alcohol**—Some flexible fuel vehicles were made in the 1990s that were able to use methanol (methyl alcohol) or gasoline. If the vehicle was using methanol and it caught fire, this can be a very serious situation because a methanol fire cannot be seen. Look for heat coming from the vehicle and use large amounts of water to cool the fire and dilute the fuel. ● **SEE FIGURE 18–9.**
- **Ethanol or E85 (85% ethanol; 15% gasoline)**—Treat as a normal vehicle fire as this type of fuel does show a yellow flame when burning, similar to gasoline.

FIGURE 18–9 A methanol fuel pump is rarely seen. Methanol is seldom used as a fuel, but it is commonly used as an industrial solvent.

FIGURE 18–10 A vehicle designed to use compressed natural gas (CNG) will usually be equipped with a blue CNG label.

- **Propane (LPG)**—Propane is stored in steel tanks and could explode if heated. Use large amounts of water and direct the water so as to force the fire away from the propane tank.
- **CNG (compressed natural gas)**—Vehicles designed to use CNG are usually identified by a blue CNG sticker. However, some vehicles such as the Honda Civic GX do not have any external identification that may help first responders know that the vehicle has a high-pressure composite storage tank. If a CNG-powered vehicle is involved in a fire, use lots of water and direct the water so that the flames are being forced away from the rear of the

vehicle where the storage tank is usually located. ● **SEE FIGURE 18–10.**

- **Diesel or biodiesel**—Vehicles using diesel or biodiesel fuel should be treated the same as if they were using gasoline as a fuel. No special precautions are needed, and the lower volatility of diesel fuel makes it less flammable than gasoline.
- **Fuel-cell vehicles**—A fuel-cell vehicle uses hydrogen stored in a high-pressure tank. If a fuel-cell vehicle is on fire, follow standard operating procedures and use water or a fire extinguisher to reduce the fire. If hydrogen is released through a safety release valve, it is lighter than air and will rise. A fire in the fuel cell itself could release toxins from the plastics and other chemicals.

SUMMARY

1. Any incident involving a hybrid electric or alternative-fuel vehicle should be treated following standard operating procedures (SOP).
2. Identification of the hybrid electric vehicle includes:
   - Emblems
   - Orange cables
3. The wiring conduit colors and their meaning include:
   - Black—12 volts
   - Red—12 volts
   - Yellow—42 volts
   - Blue—42 volts
   - Orange—144 to 600 volts or higher
4. To de-power the high-voltage system, the 12-volt auxiliary battery must be disconnected. Use the double cut method for best results.
5. Cut lines are often marked on the 12-volt battery cable to indicate where they should be cut to disable the 12-volt system, which in turn de-powers the high-voltage system.
6. The location of the high-voltage battery and 12-volt battery can vary according to make, model, and year of

vehicle. High-voltage batteries are located at the rear either under or behind the rear seat. The 12-volt auxiliary battery can be located either under the hood or in the trunk area.

7. The steps involved in the event of an incident with a hybrid electric vehicle include:
   - **STEP 1**—Identify the vehicle.
   - **STEP 2**—Disable the vehicle.
   - **STEP 3**—Stabilize the vehicle.
   - **STEP 4**—Access the occupants.
   - **STEP 5**—Turn off the ignition.
   - **STEP 6**—Disconnect or cut the 12-volt battery cables.
8. In the event of a fire with a hybrid electric vehicle, follow standard operating procedures.
9. Most hybrid electric vehicles do not create any hazardous materials that are not commonly found in any other incident involving conventional vehicles.
10. Treat any vehicle using alternative fuels as a normal incident and yet extra water should be directed to keep flames from getting to storage tanks (LPG or CNG).

1. What is the meaning of the various colors of wiring?

2. What steps should be followed when dealing with an incident involving a hybrid electric vehicle?

3. How should a fire involving an alternative-fuel vehicle be handled?

CHAPTER QUIZ

1. What is the highest priority when following standard operating procedures?
   a. Save or protect human life
   b. Protect vehicle from damage
   c. Extinguish the fire
   d. Rescue animals

2. What personal protective equipment (PPE) should be used when responding to an incident that could involve a hybrid electric vehicle?
   a. Helmet with face shield
   b. Self contained breathing apparatus (SCBA)
   c. High-voltage linesman's gloves
   d. All of the above

3. How would a first responder be able to identify a hybrid electric vehicle?
   a. Emblems on the front, side, or rear of the vehicle
   b. Orange-colored cables
   c. Blue-colored cables
   d. All of the above

4. A fire involving a hybrid electric vehicle should be extinguished using _____.
   a. Water or a fire extinguisher
   b. Large amounts of water only
   c. Dry chemical fire extinguisher only
   d. CO_2 fire extinguisher only

5. What is the color of the cables for the 12-volt auxiliary battery?
   a. Blue
   b. Yellow
   c. Red or black
   d. Orange

6. What color wires or cable represent a shock hazard?
   a. Yellow
   b. Red or black
   c. Orange
   d. Blue

7. The 12-volt auxiliary battery is located where?
   a. Under the hood
   b. Under the second-row seat
   c. In the trunk
   d. Either a or c

8. Why should 12-volt battery cables be double cut?
   a. To prevent the possibility of the cut ends from coming in contact
   b. To prevent the high voltage from arcing
   c. To be sure the circuit has been cut
   d. All of the above

9. If the electrolyte from a high-voltage battery is spilled, what should be used to neutralize it?
   a. Baking soda
   b. Vinegar or boric acid
   c. Water
   d. CO_2

10. Which alternative fuel burns with an invisible flame?
    a. Ethanol (E85)
    b. Propane
    c. Methanol
    d. CNG

HYBRID ELECTRIC VEHICLE GENERIC OBD II DIAGNOSTIC TROUBLE CODES

P0A00	Motor electronics coolant temperature sensor circuit
P0A01	Motor electronics coolant temperature sensor circuit range/performance
P0A02	Motor electronics coolant temperature sensor circuit low
P0A03	Motor electronics coolant temperature sensor circuit high
P0A04	Motor electronics coolant temperature sensor circuit intermittent
P0A05	Motor electronics coolant pump control circuit/open
P0A06	Motor electronics coolant pump control circuit low
P0A07	Motor electronics coolant pump control circuit high
P0A08	DC/DC converter status circuit/open
P0A09	DC/DC converter status circuit low
P0A0A	High-voltage system interlock circuit
P0A0B	High-voltage system interlock circuit performance
P0A0C	High-voltage system interlock circuit low
P0A0D	High-voltage system interlock circuit high
P0A0E	High-voltage system interlock circuit intermittent
P0A0F	Engine failed to start
P0A10	DC/DC converter status circuit high
P0A11	DC/DC converter enable circuit/open
P0A12	DC/DC converter enable circuit low
P0A13	DC/DC converter enable circuit high
P0A14	Engine mount control A circuit/open
P0A15	Engine mount control A circuit low
P0A16	Engine mount control A circuit high
P0A17	Motor torque sensor circuit
P0A18	Motor torque sensor circuit range/performance
P0A19	Motor torque sensor circuit low
P0A1A	Generator control module
P0A1B	Drive motor "A" control module
P0A1C	Drive motor "B" control module
P0A1D	Hybrid powertrain control module
P0A1E	Starter/generator control module
P0A1F	Battery energy control module
P0A20	Motor torque sensor circuit high
P0A21	Motor torque sensor circuit intermittent
P0A22	Generator torque sensor circuit
P0A23	Generator torque sensor circuit range/performance
P0A24	Generator torque sensor circuit low
P0A25	Generator torque sensor circuit high
P0A26	Generator torque sensor circuit intermittent
P0A27	Hybrid battery power off circuit
P0A28	Hybrid battery power off circuit low
P0A29	Hybrid battery power off circuit high
P0A2A	Drive motor "A" temperature sensor circuit
P0A2B	Drive motor "A" temperature sensor circuit range/performance
P0A2C	Drive motor "A" temperature sensor circuit low
P0A2D	Drive motor "A" temperature sensor circuit high
P0A2E	Drive motor "A" temperature sensor circuit intermittent
P0A2F	Drive motor "A" over temperature
P0A30	Drive motor "B" temperature sensor circuit
P0A31	Drive motor "B" temperature sensor circuit range/performance
P0A32	Drive motor "B" temperature sensor circuit low
P0A33	Drive motor "B" temperature sensor circuit high
P0A34	Drive motor "B" temperature sensor circuit intermittent
P0A35	Drive motor "B" over temperature
P0A36	Generator temperature sensor circuit
P0A37	Generator temperature sensor circuit range/performance
P0A38	Generator temperature sensor circuit low
P0A39	Generator temperature sensor circuit high
P0A3A	Generator temperature sensor circuit intermittent
P0A3B	Generator over temperature
P0A3C	Drive motor "A" inverter over temperature
P0A3D	Drive motor "B" inverter over temperature
P0A3E	Generator inverter over temperature
P0A3F	Drive motor "A" position sensor circuit

P0A40	Drive motor "A" position sensor circuit range/performance	P0A6A	Drive motor "B" phase V current low
P0A41	Drive motor "A" position sensor circuit low	P0A6B	Drive motor "B" phase V current high
P0A42	Drive motor "A" position sensor circuit high	P0A6C	Drive motor "B" phase W current
P0A43	Drive motor "A" position sensor circuit intermittent	P0A6D	Drive motor "B" phase W current low
P0A44	Drive motor "A" position sensor circuit overspeed	P0A6E	Drive motor "B" phase W current high
P0A45	Drive motor "B" position sensor circuit	P0A6F	Generator phase U current
P0A46	Drive motor "B" position sensor circuit range/performance	P0A70	Generator phase U current low
P0A47	Drive motor "B" position sensor circuit low	P0A71	Generator phase U current high
P0A48	Drive motor "B" position sensor circuit high	P0A72	Generator phase V current
P0A49	Drive motor "B" position sensor circuit intermittent	P0A73	Generator phase V current low
P0A4A	Drive motor "B" position sensor circuit overspeed	P0A74	Generator phase V current high
P0A4B	Generator position sensor circuit	P0A75	Generator phase W current
P0A4C	Generator position sensor circuit range/performance	P0A76	Generator phase W current low
P0A4D	Generator position sensor circuit low	P0A77	Generator phase W current high
P0A4E	Generator position sensor circuit high	P0A78	Drive motor "A" inverter performance
P0A4F	Generator position sensor circuit intermittent	P0A79	Drive motor "B" inverter performance
P0A50	Generator position sensor circuit overspeed	P0A7A	Generator inverter performance
P0A51	Drive motor "A" current sensor circuit	P0A7B	Battery energy control module requested MIL illumination
P0A52	Drive motor "A" current sensor circuit range/performance	P0A7C	Motor electronics over temperature
P0A53	Drive motor "A" current sensor circuit low	P0A7D	Hybrid battery pack state of charge low
P0A54	Drive motor "A" current sensor circuit high	P0A7E	Hybrid battery pack over temperature
P0A55	Drive motor "B" current sensor circuit	P0A7F	Hybrid battery pack deterioration
P0A56	Drive motor "B" current sensor circuit range/performance	P0A80	Replace hybrid battery pack
P0A57	Drive motor "B" current sensor circuit low	P0A81	Hybrid battery pack cooling fan 1 control circuit
P0A58	Drive motor "B" current sensor circuit high	P0A82	Hybrid battery pack cooling fan 1 performance/stuck off
P0A59	Generator current sensor circuit	P0A83	Hybrid battery pack cooling fan 1 stuck on
P0A5A	Generator current sensor circuit range/performance	P0A84	Hybrid battery pack cooling fan 1 control circuit low
P0A5B	Generator current sensor circuit low	P0A85	Hybrid battery pack cooling fan 1 control circuit high
P0A5C	Generator current sensor circuit high	P0A86	14-volt power module current sensor circuit
P0A5D	Drive motor "A" phase U current	P0A87	14-volt power module current sensor circuit range/performance
P0A5E	Drive motor "A" phase U current low	P0A88	14-volt power module current sensor circuit low
P0A5F	Drive motor "A" phase U current high	P0A89	14-volt power module current sensor circuit high
P0A60	Drive motor "A" phase V current	P0A8A	14-volt power module current sensor circuit intermittent
P0A61	Drive motor "A" phase V current low	P0A8B	14-volt power module system voltage
P0A62	Drive motor "A" phase V current high	P0A8C	14-volt power module system voltage unstable
P0A63	Drive motor "A" phase W current	P0A8D	14-volt power module system voltage low
P0A64	Drive motor "A" phase W current low	P0A8E	14-volt power module system voltage high
P0A65	Drive motor "A" phase W current high	P0A8F	14-volt power module system voltage performance
P0A66	Drive motor "B" phase U current	P0A90	Drive motor "A" performance
P0A67	Drive Motor "B" phase U current low	P0A91	Drive motor "B" performance
P0A68	Drive motor "B" phase U current high	P0A92	Hybrid generator performance
P0A69	Drive motor "B" phase V current		

U0110	Lost communication with drive motor control module A	P1431	Battery module overheating
U0111	Lost communication with battery energy control module A	P1432	Battery cell overheating
U0119	Lost communication with fuel-cell control module	P1433	Battery module deterioration
U0120	Lost communication with starter/generator control module	P1435	Charge/discharge balance problem
U0286	Lost communication with radiator anti-tamper device	P1436	Motor power inverter (MPI) module overheating
U0287	Lost communication with transmission fluid pump module	P1437	Motor power inverter (MPI) module short circuit
U0288	Lost communication with DC-to-AC converter control module A	P1440	IMA system problem
U0289	Lost communication with DC-to-AC converter control module B	P1443	High-voltage contactor/bypass contactor stays activated
U0291	Lost communication with gear shift module B	P1444	High-voltage short circuit
U0292	Lost communication with drive motor control module B	P1445	Bypass contactor problem
U0293	Lost communication with hybrid powertrain control module	P1446	Battery module individual voltage input deviation
U0294	Lost communication with powertrain control monitor module	P1447	Battery module deterioration
U0295	Lost communication with AC-to-AC converter control module	P1448	Intelligent power unit (IPU) module fan problem
U0296	Lost communication with AC-to-DC converter control module A	P1449	Battery module overheating
U0297	Lost communication with AC-to-DC converter control module B	P1449	Battery cell overheating
U0298	Lost communication with DC-to-DC converter control module A	P1449	Battery module deterioration
U0299	Lost communication with DC-to-DC converter control module B	P1553	Battery module temperature sensor 1 signal circuit low input
U029A	Lost communication with hybrid battery pack sensor module	P1554	Battery module temperature sensor 1 signal circuit high input
U0588	Invalid data received from transmission fluid pump module	P1555	Battery module temperature sensor 2 signal circuit low input
U0589	Invalid data received from DC-to-AC converter control module A	P1556	Battery module temperature sensor 2 signal circuit high input
U058A	Invalid data received from DC-to-AC converter control module B	P1557	Battery module temperature sensor 3 signal circuit low input
U0592	Invalid data received from gear shift module "B"	P1558	Battery module temperature sensor 3 signal circuit high input
U0593	Invalid data received from drive motor control module "B"	P1559	Motor commutation sensor A circuit low input
U0594	Invalid data received from hybrid powertrain control module	P1560	Motor commutation sensor A circuit high input
U0595	Invalid data received from powertrain control monitor module	P1561	Motor commutation sensor B circuit low input
U0596	Invalid data received from AC-to-AC converter control module	P1562	Motor commutation sensor B circuit high input
U0597	Invalid data received from AC-to-DC converter control module "A"	P1563	Motor commutation sensor C circuit low input
U0598	Invalid data received from AC-to-DC converter control module "B"	P1564	Motor commutation sensor C circuit high input
U0599	Invalid data received from DC-to-DC converter control module "A"	P1566	Motor commutation sensor signal problem
U059A	Invalid data received from DC-to-DC converter control module "B"	P1567	Cylinder position signal circuit problem
U059B	Invalid data received from hybrid battery pack sensor module	P1569	Battery cell temperature signal circuit problem
		P1570	Battery module individual voltage problem
		P1571	Motor commutation sensor voltage problem
		P1573	DC-DC converter temperature signal circuit problem
		P1574	Battery module temperature signal circuit problem
		P1575	Motor power inverter (MPI) module voltage problem
		P1580	Battery current circuit problem

P1585	Motor current signal circuit problem
P1586	Motor power inverter (MPI) module current signal/battery current signal circuit problem
P1587	Motor power inverter (MPI) module current signal circuit low input
P1588	Motor power inverter (MPI) module current signal circuit high input
P1589	Motor power inverter (MPI) module current signal circuit problem
P1590	Motor current U phase signal circuit low voltage
P1591	Motor current U phase signal circuit high voltage
P1592	Motor current V phase signal circuit low voltage
P1593	Motor current V phase signal circuit high voltage
P1594	Motor current W phase signal circuit low voltage
P1595	Motor current W phase signal circuit high voltage
P1629	Motor control module (MCM) internal circuit malfunction
P1633	ECM signal circuit problem
P1634	Motor power inverter (MPI) module signal circuit
P1636	Motor power inverter (MPI) module problem
P1637	Motor control module (MCM) internal circuit malfunction
P1638	Motor control module (MCM) internal circuit malfunction
P1673	MCM relay stays activated

TOYOTA HYBRID OBD II DIAGNOSTIC TROUBLE CODES

P3000	Abnormal signal input from battery ECU
P3009	Insulation resistance of high-voltage component is low
P3011	Battery block 1 becomes weak
P3012	Battery block 2 becomes weak
P3013	Battery block 3 becomes weak
P3014	Battery block 4 becomes weak

P3015	Battery block 5 becomes weak
P3016	Battery block 6 becomes weak
P3017	Battery block 7 becomes weak
P3018	Battery block 8 becomes weak
P3019	Battery block 9 becomes weak
P3020	Battery block 10 becomes weak
P3021	Battery block 11 becomes weak
P3022	Battery block 12 becomes weak
P3023	Battery block 13 becomes weak
P3024	Battery block 14 becomes weak
P3030	Disconnection between battery and ECU
P3056	Battery current sensor circuit malfunction

FORD HYBRID OBD II DIAGNOSTIC TROUBLE CODES

P1A03	Drive motor A shutdown circuit
P1A04	Generator shutdown circuit
P1A05	Desired engine speed signal
P1A06	Vehicle mode signal
P1A07	Inverter high-voltage performance
P1A08	Generator mode signal
P1A0A	Immediate shutdown signal
P1A0C	Hybrid powertrain control module—engine disabled
P1A0D	Hybrid powertrain control module—generator disabled
P1A0E	Hybrid powertrain control module—motor disabled
P1A0F	Hybrid powertrain control module—vehicle disabled
P1A10	Hybrid powertrain control module—battery disabled
P1A13	Hybrid powertrain control module—regenerative braking disabled
P1A14	Hybrid powertrain control module—transmission disabled

appendix 2
NATEF TASK LIST

GLOSSARY

720° cycle The number of degrees of crankshaft rotation required to complete the four-stroke cycle.

ABS Antilock Braking System. ABS prevents wheel lockup when braking, giving the car better stability in slippery conditions.

AC motor An electric motor that is powered by AC (alternating current).

AC synchronous motor An electric motor that uses a three-phase stator coil with a brushless permanent magnet rotor. Another term for DC brushless motor.

Accumulator An A/C system component that is used to accumulate liquid refrigerant from the evaporator and allow only gas to continue on to the compressor. Accumulators are typically found in orifice tube (OT) systems.

Acidic A chemical compound that produces a pH of less than 7 when dissolved in water. Acidic is the opposite of alkaline.

ACIM AC Induction Motor. See definition for *Induction motor*.

ACM Active Control Engine Mount. ACMs are computer controlled and are designed to dampen unusual vibrations during ICE start/stop.

Active fuel management A General Motors terms for the cylinder deactivation system used on some V-8 engines.

AFV Alternative Fuel Vehicle.

AGM battery Absorbed Glass Mat. AGM batteries are lead-acid batteries, but use an absorbent material between the plates to hold the electrolyte. AGM batteries are classified as valve-regulated lead-acid (VRLA) batteries.

Ah Ampere-Hour. A battery capacity rating.

Air–fuel ratio The ratio of air to fuel in an intake charge as measured by weight.

AKI Antiknock Index. The octane rating posted on a gas pump, which is the average of the RON and MON octane ratings.

Alkaline battery A battery that uses an alkaline (pH greater than 7) electrolyte solution.

ANC Active Noise Control. ANC is a function of the vehicle's sound system, and is designed to generate sound pulses that "cancel" undesirable noises from the engine compartment.

Anhydrous ethanol Ethanol that has no water content.

ANSI American National Standards Institute.

Antifreeze A liquid such as ethylene glycol or propylene glycol that is used to lower the freezing point of the ICE coolant. Antifreeze also raises the coolant boiling point and contains inhibitors to prevent rust and corrosion inside the cooling system.

APO Auxiliary Power Outlet. 120V AC electrical outlets located on a vehicle such as the GM Parallel Tybrid Truck or Ford Escape Hybrid.

APP Accelerator Pedal Position sensor. Also known as an Accelerator Pedal Sensor (APS).

APS Accelerator Pedal Sensor. Also known as an Accelerator Pedal Position (APP) sensor.

Armature The rotating unit inside a DC generator or starter, consisting of a series of coils of insulating wire wound around a laminated iron core.

Assist hybrid A type of hybrid electric vehicle that is able to assist the ICE in propelling the vehicle but is not capable of using electric power alone.

ASTM American Society for Testing and Materials.

Atkinson cycle An internal combustion engine design that limits the effective intake stroke in order to maximize the engine's expansion ratio. Atkinson-cycle engines produce less horsepower than Otto-cycle designs, but are more efficient overall.

AT-PZEV Advanced Technology Partial-Zero-Emission Vehicle.

Auxiliary battery The 12-volt battery in a hybrid electric vehicle.

B20 A blend of 20% biodiesel with 80% petroleum diesel.

BAS Belt-Alternator Starter system. A hybrid electric vehicle system that uses a motor-generator connected to the ICE through an accessory drive belt.

Base brakes The conventional friction brakes (drum or disc) on a vehicle.

Battery module A number of individual cells (usually 6) connected in series. NiMH cells produce 1.2 volts, so most NiMH battery modules produce 7.2 volts.

Battery vent The external air intake vent for the battery cooling system in a Ford Escape hybrid.

BAS Belt-Alternator-Starter. A term used to describe a parallel hybrid design that utilizes a belt-driven motor-generator to provide idle stop and limited traction assist.

BCM Battery Condition Monitor Module. On Honda HEVs, the BCM is responsible for providing information on high-voltage battery condition to other modules on the vehicle network.

Belt-and-pulley CVT A continuously-variable transmission (CVT) that utilizes a belt with two variable-width pulleys to achieve an infinite number of gear ratios.

BEV Battery Electric Vehicle.

BHP Brake Horsepower. BHP is horsepower as measured on a dynamometer.

Bin number An EPA rating indicating the "dirtiness" of a vehicle's emissions. A low Bin rating (i.e., Bin 3) is considered to be very clean, where higher Bin numbers indicate higher emission levels.

Bi-Directional Testing A type of testing that is performed using a scan tool that allows the technician to control parts of the vehicle or the engine in order to test if it can be controlled.

BJB Battery Junction Box. The power distribution box located near the battery in the ICE compartment.

Blend door An air mix valve located in the air distribution box of a vehicle HVAC system. The blend door is responsible for "blending" air from the A/C evaporator with warm air from the heater core to deliver air at the proper temperature at the outlet ducts.

Blower motor An electric motor used to move air through the vehicle's HVAC system.

Boost converter An electronic component that increases voltage from a DC power source. Toyota's THS II system utilizes a boost converter to increase electric drive motor efficiency.

BPP Brake Pedal Position sensor.

Brake Any device that is designed to slow or stop the mechanism to which it is attached to.

Brushless motor An electric motor that does not use brushes or a commutator. Instead, brushless motors are typically constructed with permanent magnets in the rotors and are powered by three-phase alternating current.

BTU British Thermal Unit. A measure of heat energy. One BTU of heat will raise the temperature of one pound of water one Fahrenheit degree.

Bypass tube A tube located in the ICE water jacket that allows coolant to bypass the radiator and be sent directly to the water pump inlet when the thermostat is closed.

CA Cold Ampere rating. A battery rating performed at 32° F.

CAA Clean Air Act. Federal legislation passed in 1970 that established national air quality standards.

Cabin filter A filter located in the air intake of a vehicle's HVAC system. A cabin filter prevents particulate matter from entering the cabin air space.

CARB California Air Resources Board. Responsible for developing air quality standards for the State of California.

Carbohydrates A chemical compounds that store energy and contain carbon, hydrogen, and oxygen atoms.

Carbon An element found in all organic materials. Carbon combines with oxygen to form carbon monoxide (CO) and carbon dioxide (CO_2).

Carbon dioxide (CO_2) A colorless, odorless, nonflammable gas produced during the combustion process. Considered to be a greenhouse gas and a direct contributor to global warming.

Carbon footprint The net amount of carbon emitted into the atmosphere through processes such as combustion and so on. Burning of fossil fuels is considered to have a large carbon footprint.

Carbon monoxide (CO) A colorless, odorless, and highly poisonous gas formed by the incomplete combustion of gasoline.

Carbonated water Water containing dissolved carbon dioxide. The carbon dioxide remains in solution when under pressure and is released when its container is opened to the atmosphere. Soft drinks get their "fizz" from carbonated water.

CAT III An electrical measurement equipment rating created by the International Electrotechnical Commission (IEC). CAT III indicates the lowest level of instrument protection that should be in place when performing electrical measurements on hybrid electric vehicles.

Catalytic cracking Breaking hydrocarbon chains using heat in the presence of a catalyst.

Cd Coefficient of drag. A measure of the aerodynamic efficiency of a vehicle's body design.

Cell An individual segment of a battery which includes a negative electrode, a positive electrode, and the electrolyte solution. Batteries are made up of a number of cells connected in series.

Cellulosic biomass Biomass feedstock such as agricultural and industrial plant wastes.

Cellulose ethanol Ethanol produced from biomass feedstock such as agricultural and industrial plant wastes.

Cetane number (rating) A diesel fuel rating that indicates how easily the fuel can be ignited.

Change of state The process where a material absorbs or releases heat energy to change between solid, liquid, and gaseous states.

Charge indicator A hydrometer built into one battery cell that gives a visual indication of the battery's state-of-charge.

Cloud point A temperature point where the wax in diesel fuel starts to crystalize.

CNG Compressed Natural Gas.

Coal-to-liquid (CTL) A refining process where coal is converted to liquid fuel.

Coefficient of drag A calculation of the amount of aerodynamic drag created by a vehicle's body. A higher coefficient of drag indicates more wind resistance created by the vehicle.

Cold cranking amperes (CCA) The number of amperes that can be supplied by the battery at 0° F for 30 seconds while the battery maintains a voltage of at least 1.2 volts per cell.

Commutator The name for the copper segments of the armature of a starter or DC generator. The revolving segments of the commutator collect the current from or distribute it to the brushes.

Compressor An A/C system component that is responsible for compressing refrigerant vapor and circulating refrigerant through the system.

Compression ratio The ratio of the volume in the engine cylinder with the piston at bottom dead center (BDC) compared to the volume at top dead center (TDC).

Condenser An A/C system component that rejects heat from the refrigerant and causes it to change from a gas to a liquid.

Conductance The plate surface area in a battery that is available for chemical reaction. Battery condition can be assessed using a measurement of its conductance.

Coolant heat storage system A system used on the 2nd generation Toyota Prius that stores hot coolant in order to warm the ICE prior to a cold start.

Coolant recovery reservoir An external storage tank for the ICE cooling system. Collects coolant as the ICE warms up and supplies coolant to the system as the ICE cools down.

COP Coil-on-Plug. This term describes ignition systems where each spark plug has its own coil assembly mounted directly over top of it. Also known as coil-over-plug, coil-by-plug, or coil-near-plug ignition.

CR Compression Ratio.

Cracking A refinery process where hydrocarbons with high boiling points are broken into hydrocarbons with low boiling points.

Creep aid A function of some hybrid electric vehicles that keeps the vehicle's base brakes applied briefly after the ICE leaves idle stop mode to allow for smooth starts.

Crossflow A radiator that is designed so the coolant flows through it horizontally.

CTL Coal-to-liquid. See definition for *Coal-to-liquid*.

Cut line Places marked on low-voltage electrical cable in a hybrid electric vehicle that should/can be cut by a first responder to disable the high-voltage circuits.

Cycle life The number of times a battery can be charged and discharged without suffering significant degradation in its performance.

Cylinder deactivation A phase of internal combustion engine operation where the valves of certain cylinders are disconnected from the valve train and remain closed. This allows the ICE to operate on fewer cylinders for greater fuel economy and efficiency.

Cylindrical cell A battery cell that is constructed similar to a D cell.

DC-to-DC converter An electronic component found in a hybrid electric vehicle that converts high-voltage DC to 12-volts DC for charging the auxiliary battery.

DC brushless motor An electric motor that uses a 3-phase stator coil with a brushless permanent magnet rotor. Another term for AC synchronous motor.

DC motor An electric motor powered by direct current (DC). DC motors typically utilize brushes and a commutator on a wire-wound armature.

Deep cycling Discharging a battery completely and then recharging it. Most battery technologies do not tolerate deep cycling.

Degas bottle A reservoir mounted at the highest point in the cooling system. Allows for coolant expansion/contraction and prevents air from being entrained in the coolant. Also known as a surge tank.

Detonation Abnormal combustion that is caused by a spontaneous explosion of air–fuel mixture in the combustion chamber. Also known as *spark knock*.

DFCO Deceleration Fuel Cut-off. An engine control function that cuts fuel to the ICE cylinders when the vehicle is decelerating.

DI Distillation Index. A rating of a fuel's volatility and how well it evaporates in cold temperatures.

DIC Driver Information Center. The instrument panel readout on a GM vehicle that provides extra information about vehicle operation and diagnostics.

Dielectric The material used to separate the two conductive plates in a capacitor.

Diesohol Standard #2 diesel fuel combined with up to 15% ethanol.

Differential A mechanical device that allows one wheel of a drive axle to turn at a different speed from the wheel on the opposite side.

Direct drive A drivetrain mechanism that turns the output shaft at the same speed as the input shaft. A direct drive has a gear ratio of 1:1.

Displacement The total volume displaced or swept by the cylinders in an internal combustion engine.

Distillation The process of purification through evaporation and then condensation of the desired liquid.

Distillation curve A graph that plots the temperatures at which the various fractions of a fuel evaporate.

DMM Digital Multimeter. A digital multimeter is capable of measuring electrical current, resistance, and voltage.

Downflow A radiator design in which coolant flows vertically (top to bottom).

Driveability index (DI) A number that is achieved by using the distillation curve temperatures to arrive at a number that indicates how well a gasoline will perform in an engine.

Drive-by-wire Another term for Electronic Throttle Control (ETC).

Drive Motor/Generator Control Module (DMCM) The term used by General Motors to describe the two-mode hybrid cooling system.

Dry charged Emptying the electrolyte from a fully charged lead-acid battery in order to store or ship it. Dry-charged batteries are refilled with electrolyte before being put back into service.

Dry ice Frozen carbon dioxide. Dry ice exists at a temperature at or below −78° C.

E10 A motor fuel blend of 10% ethanol and 90% gasoline.

E85 A motor fuel blend of 85% ethanol and 15% gasoline.

ECB Electronically Controlled Braking system. The system used on Toyota HEVs that controls the operation of the vehicle's base brakes and regenerative braking systems.

eCVT Electronic Continuously Bariable Transmission. An electric motor is used in conjunction with a planetary gearset to provide an infinite number of gear ratios.

E-diesel Standard #2 diesel fuel combined with up to 15% ethanol. Also known as diesohol.

EHPS Electro-Hydraulic Power Steering. A 42-volt assist unit that provides pressurized fluid for power steering and brakes in a GM Parallel Hybrid Truck.

EI Electronic Ignition. An SAE term for an ignition system that does not use a distributor.

Electric secondary fluid pump An electrically driven auxiliary pump used in automatic transmissions for hybrid electric vehicles. This pump is energized when the ICE is in idle stop mode to maintain transmission pressures.

Electrical noise Electrical interference sometimes caused by the arcing of brushes on the commutator in a DC motor.

Electrode A solid conductor through which current enters or leaves a substance, such as a gas or liquid.

Electrolysis The process where electric current is passed through water in order to break it into hydrogen and oxygen gas.

Electromagnetics The science or application of electromagnetic principles.

Electromagnetism A magnetic field created by current flow through a conductor.

EM Electric Machine. A term used to describe any device that converts mechanical energy into electrical energy or vice versa.

EMI Electromagnetic Interference. An undesirable electronic signal. It is caused by a magnetic field building up and collapsing, creating unwanted electrical interference on a nearby circuit.

Energy carrier Any medium that is utilized to store or transport energy. For example, hydrogen is an energy carrier because energy must be used to generate hydrogen gas that is used as a fuel.

Energy recirculation A term used to describe the Toyota THS-II system's ability to propel the vehicle using either MG1 or MG2 depending on which is most efficient at the time.

EPA Environmental Protection Agency. A department of the federal government that is responsible for the development and enforcement of environmental regulations in the United States.

EPAS Electric Power Assist Steering. Also known as EPS (Electric Power Steering).

EPS Electric Power Steering. Also known as EPAS (Electric Power Assist Steering).

ERFS Electronic Returnless Fuel System. A fuel delivery system that does not return fuel to the tank. Instead, the fuel pump speed is controlled electronically to adjust pressure and flow according to engine demand.

ETBE Ethyl Tertiary Butyl Ether. ETBE is an oxygenated fuel that is used as a gasoline additive to enhance its burning characteristics.

ETC Electronic Throttle Control. The intake system throttle plate is controlled by a servo motor instead of a mechanical linkage. Also known as drive-by-wire.

Ethanol Grain alcohol that is blended with gasoline to produce motor fuel. Also known as Ethyl Alcohol.

Ethyl alcohol See definition for *Ethanol*.

Ethylene glycol A refined petroleum product that is mixed with water to produce ICE coolant. Lowers the coolant freezing point, raises its boiling point, and is highly toxic.

EV Electric Vehicle. A term used to describe battery-powered vehicles.

Evaporator An A/C system component that absorbs heat from the air in the vehicle's passenger compartment.

Evaporator drain An outlet at the bottom of the evaporator housing that allows condensed water to flow out of the passenger compartment.

Fan clutch A device used to control the speed of the radiator fan. Typically used with belt-driven fans.

FAS Flywheel Alternator Starter. A term used to describe the motor-generator located between the ICE and the transmission on a GM Parallel Hybrid Truck.

FFV Flex-Fuel Vehicle. Flex-fuel vehicles are capable of running on straight gasoline or gasoline/ethanol blends.

Final Drive The term used to describe the differential in a front wheel drive transaxle.

Fischer-Tropsch A refining process that converts coal, natural gas, or other petroleum products into synthetic motor fuels.

Flex Fuel A term used to describe a vehicle that is capable of running on straight gasoline or gasoline–ethanol blends.

Floating ground An electrical system where neither the power nor ground circuits are connected to a chassis or body ground.

Flooded cell batteries A battery cell with electrodes immersed in liquid electrolyte.

Flux Magnetic lines of force.

F = ma The formula used to determine the force required to accelerate an object. Force is expressed in Newtons, mass is in kilograms, and acceleration in meters per second^2.

Force The amount of effort required to cause an object to accelerate. Force can be expressed in pounds or Newtons.

Four-stroke cycle An internal combustion engine design where four strokes of the piston (two crankshaft revolutions) are required to complete one cycle of events. The four strokes include intake, compression, power, and exhaust.

FTD Fischer-Tropsch Diesel process. See definition for *Fischer-Tropsch*.

FTP Federal Test Procedure.

Fuel cell An electrochemical device that converts the energy stored in hydrogen gas into electricity, water, and heat.

Fuel-cell hybrid vehicle (FCHV) A vehicle that uses a fuel cell to create electricity and also uses an electrical storage device such as a high-voltage battery that can be used to power the vehicle.

Fuel cell vehicle (FCV) A vehicle that is powered directly from the electrical power generated by a fuel cell.

Fuel cell stack A collection of individual fuel cells "stacked" end-to-end, similar to slices of bread.

Fuel compensation sensor A sensor used in flex-fuel vehicles that provides information to the PCM on the ethanol content and temperature of the fuel as it is pumped through the fuel delivery system.

Full hybrid A hybrid electric vehicle that utilizes high voltages (200 volts and above) and is capable of propelling the vehicle using "all-electric" mode at low speeds. Also known as a "strong" hybrid.

Fungible A term used to describe a product, such as gasoline or electricity, that can be intermixed regardless of source because it is interchangeable and identical in physical properties.

FWD Front-Wheel Drive.

G A letter used to represent the force of gravity.

G force The amount of force applied to an object by gravity.

Gasoline Refined petroleum product that is used primarily as a motor fuel. Gasoline is made up of many different hydrocarbons and also contains additives for enhancing its performance in an ICE.

Gassing Gasses released from a battery during the charging and discharging process. Gassing levels increase as battery temperature increases.

GDI Gasoline Direct Injection. A fuel injection system design where gasoline is injected directly into the combustion chamber.

Gear ratio For a transmission or drive axle, the number of turns of the input shaft required to produce 1 turn of the output shaft.

Gel battery A lead-acid battery with silica added to the electrolyte to make it leak proof and spillproof.

Generation mode A mode of operation in hybrid electric vehicles that uses engine power to generate electricity for charging the high-voltage battery.

Generator motor A term used to describe the smaller electric machine in a Ford Escape Hybrid transmission.

GFD Ground-Fault Detection. A diagnostic function used to monitor the auxiliary power outlets in a GM Parallel Hybrid Truck.

GHG An abbreviation for Greenhouse gas. A greenhouse gas is any gas that tends to increase the heat retention in the earth's atmosphere. Two examples of greenhouse gases are carbon dioxide and methane.

Global warning An overall increase in the earth's temperature. Global warming is thought to be caused by an increased concentration of greenhouse gases in the earth's atmosphere.

Grain alcohol See definition for *Ethanol*.

Green zone The area of the tachometer face on a Ford Escape Hybrid that indicates the vehicle is operating in "all-electric" or "stealth" mode.

Greenhouse gas See definition for *GHG*.

Grid The lead-alloy framework (support) for the active materials of an automotive battery.

GTL Gas-to-Liquid. A refining process where natural gas is converted into liquid fuel.

HCCI See Homogeneous-Charge Compression Ignition below.

HCM Hybrid Control Module. The module in a GM Parallel Hybrid truck that is responsible for all vehicle hybrid functions.

Heat exchanger A device such as a radiator or condenser that is used to absorb or reject heat from a fluid passing through it.

Heat sink A device used to dissipate heat from electronic components.

Heater core A cooling system component that is responsible for transferring heat from the ICE coolant to the air flowing into the passenger compartment.

Helper pump An electric water pump used to circulate coolant through a hybrid electric vehicle's heater core when the ICE is in idle stop mode.

HEV Hybrid Electric Vehicle. Describes any vehicle that uses more than one source of propulsion.

HOAT Hybrid Organic Acid Technology. A corrosion inhibitor additive with reduced silicate content. Used in Ford and Chrysler extended-life coolants.

Homogeneous-charge compression ignition A low-temperature combustion process that involves air–fuel mixtures being burned without the use of spark ignition.

Horsepower A unit of power equivalent to 33,000 foot-pounds per minute. One horsepower equals 746 W.

HOV lane High-Occupancy Vehicle lane. Sometimes known as the "carpool" lane on urban highway systems.

hp Horsepower.

HPA See Hydraulic Power Assist.

HV High Voltage. Applies to any voltage above 50 volts.

HV battery High-Voltage Battery. Hybrid electric vehicles use NiMH battery packs that are rated up to 330 volts DC.

HV cables Vehicle cables that carry high voltage.

HVTB High-Voltage Traction Battery. The high-voltage battery in a Ford Escape Hybrid.

Hybrid Abbreviated version of Hybrid Electric Vehicle (HEV).

Hybrid synergy drive The term used by Toyota to describe their hybrid electric vehicle system.

Hydraulic power assist A hybrid vehicle configuration that utilizes hydraulic pumps and accumulators for energy regeneration.

Hydrocarbons Any compound made up of hydrogen and carbon atoms. Examples of hydrocarbons include propane, butane, and methane.

Hydrocracking A refinery process that converts hydrocarbons with a high boiling point into ones with low boiling points. Hydrocracking is done using a catalyst in a hydrogen atmosphere.

Hydrometer An instrument used to measure the specific gravity of a liquid. A battery hydrometer is calibrated to read the expected specific gravity of battery electrolyte.

Hygroscopic The tendency of a liquid to absorb moisture from the surrounding air.

IAT Inorganic Additive Technology. The corrosion inhibitor used in most green-colored ICE coolants.

ICE Internal Combustion Engine.

IEC International Electrotechnical Commission.

Idle stop mode A phase in hybrid electric vehicle operation where the internal combustion engine shuts off during idle operation. The ICE typically restarts the moment the brake pedal is released.

IGBT Insulated Gate Bipolar Transistors. IGBTs are the primary switching devices for the inverter in a hybrid electric vehicle.

ILSAC International Lubricant Standardization and Approval Committee. Responsible for development of the ILSAC standard for motor oil performance.

IMA Integrated Motor Assist. Describes the motor-generator located between the ICE and the transmission on Honda hybrid electric vehicles.

Impeller The mechanism in a water pump that rotates to produce coolant flow.

Induction motor An AC motor in which electromagnetic induction is used to generate a magnetic field in the rotor without the need for brushes. Also known as an AC asynchronous motor.

Inertia The tendency of an object to resist changes in motion. An object at rest tends to stay at rest, and an object in motion tends to stay in motion unless acted on by an outside force.

Internal resistance The resistance to current flow that exists inside the battery. Battery condition can be assessed using an internal resistance measurement.

IOD Ignition Off Draw. The measure of the amount of current that is being discharged for the battery with the ignition off. Also called *parasitic draw*.

Ion-sensing ignition An electronic ignition system that uses the spark plug as a sensor to determine camshaft position, misfire, and knock.

IPCC Intergovernmental Panel on Climate Change.

IPM Interior Permanent Magnet. Describes the arrangement of the permanent magnets on the inside of the rotor shell in an AC synchronous electric motor.

IPU Intelligent Power Unit. Describes the collection of modules responsible for control of the motor-generator in the Honda IMA system.

Irradiance The amount of solar radiation reaching the earth's surface.

ISO International Standards Organization.

i-VTEC Intelligent Variable Valve Timing and Lift Electronic Control. A system used to control the valve train on some Honda vehicles.

Kinetic energy The energy of motion. Any object (or mass) in motion has kinetic energy.

kW Abbreviation for kilowatt, a measure of power. One kilowatt is 1,000 watts, and 746 watts is equivalent to one horsepower.

Kyoto Protocol An agreement reached among most of the world's industrialized nations for limiting the production of carbon dioxide and other greenhouse gases in an effort to avert climate change.

Left-hand rule A method of determining the direction of magnetic lines of force around a conductor. The left-hand rule is used with the electron flow theory (– flowing to +).

Lenz's law The relative motion between a conductor and a magnetic field is opposed by the magnetic field of the current it has induced.

LEV Low Emission Vehicle.

Lineman's gloves Type of gloves worn by technicians when working around high-voltage circuits. Usually includes a rubber inner glove rated at 1,000 volts and a protective leather outer glove when used for hybrid electric vehicle service.

Load tester A device for applying a heavy current load to a battery in order to assess its current-producing ability.

Lodestone A type of iron ore that exists as a magnet in its natural state.

LPG Liquefied Petroleum Gas. Another term for propane.

M-85 Internal combustion engine fuel containing 85% methanol and 15% gasoline.

Magnetism A form of energy that is recognized by the attraction it exerts on other materials.

Major thrust surface The side of an engine cylinder that receives the greatest thrust or force from the piston during the power stroke.

Mass A measure of the amount of material contained in an object. Gravity acts on a mass to give it weight.

MCA Marine cranking amperes. A type of battery rating performed at 32° F.

MCM Motor Control Module. The module in a Honda HEV that controls the operation of the IMA unit.

MDM Motor Drive Module. The module in a Honda HEV that controls the flow of current to and from the IMA unit. The MDM is controlled by the MCM (Motor Control Module).

MEA See Membrane Electrode Assembly below.

Medium hybrid A hybrid electric vehicle design that utilizes "medium" voltage levels (between 50 and 200 volts). Medium hybrids use regenerative braking and idle stop but are not capable of starting the vehicle from a stop using electric mode.

Membrane electrode assembly The part of the PEM fuel cell that contains the membrane, catalyst coatings, and electrodes.

Metal hydride A hydrogen storage alloy used in the negative electrode of a NiMH cell.

Methanol Wood alcohol that is blended with gasoline to produce motor fuel. Also known as Methyl Alcohol. Methanol is poisonous as well as highly corrosive to fuel system parts.

Methyl alcohol See *Methanol*.

Micro-hybrid drive A term used to describe belt alternator starter (BAS) and other mild hybrid systems.

Mild hybrid A hybrid electric vehicle design that utilizes regenerative braking and idle stop but cannot propel the vehicle in electric-only mode. A mild hybrid drive typically operates below 50 volts.

Miller cycle A four-stroke cycle engine design that utilizes the Atkinson cycle along with a forced induction system such as a supercharger.

Motoring mode A phase of BAS hybrid vehicle operation where the motor-generator cranks the ICE to start it.

MRFS Mechanical Returnless Fuel System. A returnless fuel delivery system design that uses a mechanical pressure regulator located in the fuel tank.

MTBE Methyl Tertiary Butyl Ether. MTBE is an oxygenated fuel that is used as a gasoline additive to enhance its burning characteristics.

MTG Methanol-to-Gasoline. A refining process where methanol is converted into liquid.

MTHF Methyltetrahydrofuron. A component of P-series non-petroleum-based fuels.

National Fire Academy (NFA) An organization devoted to fire fighter training.

Nernst cell Another name for a conventional oxygen sensor is a Nernst cell, named for Walther Nernst, 1864–1941, a German physicist known for his work in electrochemistry.

NGV Natural Gas Vehicle.

NiMH Nickel Metal Hydride. A battery design used for the high-voltage batteries in most hybrid electric vehicles.

Nitrogen An inert gas that comprises approximately 78% of the earth's atmosphere.

NLEV National Low-Emission Vehicle.

Nominal voltage The approximate voltage of a fully charged battery cell.

Nomograph A type of graph that shows various speeds of components under various conditions.

OAT Organic Acid Technology. A corrosion inhibitor additive containing no silicates or phosphates. Used in DEX-COOL and some other extended-life coolants.

Octane rating A measure of the antiknock characteristics of a motor fuel.

ODS Ozone Depleting Substances. These include CFCs (chlorofluorocarbons) such as R-12 refrigerant and halons used in fire extinguishers.

Offset crankshaft The ICE crankshaft is offset from the centerline of the cylinders to reduce internal friction.

Open circuit voltage The measured voltage across a battery's terminals with no current being drawn from the battery.

Open-loop A phase of computer-controlled engine operation where air–fuel mixture is calculated in the absence of oxygen sensor signals. During open loop, calculations are based primarily on throttle position, engine RPM, and engine coolant temperature.

Organic A term used to describe anything that was alive at one time.

OSHA Occupational Safety and Health Administration. OSHA is the main federal agency responsible for enforcement of workplace safety and health legislation.

OT Orifice Tube. Refers to an A/C system design that uses an orifice tube as an expansion device.

Overdrive In a transmission or drive axle, when the input shaft turns slower than the output shaft. A gear ratio of 0.87:1 is considered to be an overdrive gear ratio because only 0.87 turns of the input shaft will result in 1 full turn of the output shaft.

Oxygen A colorless, odorless gas that is a direct supporter of combustion. Earth's atmosphere contains approximately 21% oxygen.

Oxygenated fuels Fuels such as ETBE or MTBE that contain extra oxygen molecules to promote cleaner burning. Oxygenated fuels are used as gasoline additives to reduce CO emissions.

Ozone A toxic, oxidizing gas formed by the combination of hydrocarbons (HC) and NO_x in the presence of sunlight. Ozone is a major component of smog.

PAG Polyalkylene Glycol. A type of refrigerant oil used in most R-134a A/C systems.

Parallel-hybrid design A hybrid vehicle design where the electric machine (or other source of energy) assists the ICE to propel the vehicle.

Parasitic load test A test used to determine the amount of current being drawn from a battery with everything turned off.

PCU Power Control Unit. The assembly that contains the MDM and DC-to-DC converter in a Honda hybrid electric vehicle.

Peak oil A term used to describe the peak of worldwide oil production.

PDU Power Drive Unit. An electronic component that controls all functions of an electric motor.

PEFC Polymer Electrolyte Fuel Cell. Another term for PEM fuel cell.

PEM Proton Exchange Membrane fuel cell. A low-temperature fuel cell known for fast starts and relatively simple construction.

Permeability The measure of a material's ability to conduct magnetic lines of force.

Petrodiesel Another term for petroleum diesel, which is ordinary diesel fuel refined from crude oil.

Petroleum   Another term for crude oil. The literal meaning of petroleum is "rock oil."

pH   A measure of the acidity or alkalinity of a material. A pH of 7 is neutral, higher than 7 is alkaline, and lower than 7 is acidic.

Phase-change liquid   A fluid used to transfer heat efficiently from electronic components. The components are immersed in the fluid, which changes from a liquid to a vapor as it absorbs heat.

PHEV   Plug-in Hybrid Electric Vehicle.

PHT   Parallel Hybrid Truck. A term used to describe the Chevrolet Silverado/GMC Sierra hybrid pickup truck.

PID   Parameter Identification. The information found in the vehicle datastream as viewed on a scan tool.

Ping   The metallic noise made by an ICE when abnormal combustion takes place in its cylinders.

Planetary gearset   A simple mechanism made up of a ring gear, a planet carrier, and a sun gear. A single planetary gearset can be used to achieve a reduction, a direct drive, an overdrive, or a reverse.

Plate   An electrode in a prismatic battery. Each battery cell is made up of a group of positive plates interleaved with a group of negative plates.

Plate strap   A strap used to connect common plates in a battery cell.

Plenum chamber   The air distribution box in a vehicle HVAC system.

Plug-in hybrid   A hybrid electric vehicle utilizing batteries that can be recharged by plugging into a household electrical outlet.

PM   Particulate Matter. PM can be made up of any airborne liquid or solid, and its concentration is regulated by both CARB and the EPA.

Pole   The point where magnetic lines of force enter or leave a magnet.

Polymer electrolyte fuel cell   Another term for Proton Exchange Membrane fuel cell. (See definition for *PEM*.)

Positive temperature coefficient (PTC)   A term used to describe when the electrical resistance increases as the temperature increases.

Power   The rate of doing work. Measured in horsepower or kilowatts.

Power-assist mode   A phase of hybrid vehicle operation where the ICE is assisted by the electric machine (or other source of energy) to propel the vehicle.

Power drive unit (PDU)   The PDU controls all functions of the motor, whether it is producing torque to drive the vehicle or is being used as a generator to charge the batteries during regenerative braking.

Power split CVT   A continuously variable transmission that manages power input from an ICE and two motor-generators.

Powertrain control module (PCM)   The SAE standard term used to describe the computer that controls the engine and often the transmission.

Pressure cap   A device used to maintain and limit pressure in the ICE cooling system.

Pressure drop   A decrease in pressure that takes place across a restriction. This principle is key to the operation of an expansion device in an A/C system.

Primary battery   Non-rechargeable battery.

Principal end   The end of the engine that the flywheel is attached to.

Prismatic cell   A battery cell made with flat plates.

Proton exchange membrane (PEM)   See definition for *PEM*.

PTC heater   An electric heater that operates on the principle of positive-temperature coefficient, where electrical resistance of the heater increases as temperature increases.

PTO   Power Take Off. A PTO is typically located near a transmission final drive and is used to provide power to a rear drive axle or other mechanism.

Pumping losses   The energy lost due to restrictions in the ICE's air intake system.

Pure plant oil (PPO)   A term used in Europe to describe straight vegetable oil.

PVV   Pressure Vent Valve. A valve located in the fuel tank to prevent overpressure due to the thermal expansion of the fuel.

PWM   Pulse Width Modulation. The control of a device by varying the on-time of the current flowing through the device.

PZEV   Partial Zero-Emission Vehicle.

Quiet mode   A term used to describe when a strong (full) hybrid electric vehicle is powering the vehicle.

R-134a   A refrigerant used in the A/C systems of most domestic vehicles built since 1994.

Radiator   A cooling system component used to dissipate heat from the coolant to the surrounding air.

Radiator hose   A flexible hose used to transfer coolant between the various cooling system components.

RBS   Regenerative Braking System. A hybrid electric vehicle system that allows vehicle kinetic energy to be converted into electrical energy for charging the high-voltage battery.

Receiver-drier   An A/C system component used to filter and remove moisture from liquid refrigerant on the high side of the system.

Recombinant battery   A battery design that does not release gasses during normal operation. AGM batteries are known as recombinant batteries.

Reduction   A drivetrain mechanism designed to decrease speed and increase torque. A gear ratio of 3.56:1 would be considered to be a reduction because the input shaft must turn 3.56 times in order to achieve 1 turn of the output shaft.

Refractometer   A device used to measure battery state of charge by allowing light to pass through an electrolyte sample.

Refrigerant   A fluid used in A/C systems to absorb, transfer, and release heat energy.

Regen   An abbreviated term for Regenerative Braking.

Regeneration   The process of retrieving, storing, and reusing energy that would otherwise be lost.

Regenerative braking   A hybrid vehicle function that recovers kinetic energy while the vehicle is decelerating and stores it for later use.

Reluctance   The resistance to the movement of magnetic lines of force.

Reserve capacity   The number of minutes that a battery is able to provide 25 amperes of current to a vehicle's electrical system and still maintain a minimum voltage of 1.75 volts per cell.

Resolver A speed sensor that utilizes three coils to determine rotor position.

RFG Reformulated Gasoline. RFG has oxygenated additives and is refined to reduce both the lightest and heaviest hydrocarbon content from gasoline in order to promote cleaner burning.

RGB Regenerative Braking.

Right-hand rule A method of determining the direction of the magnetic lines of force in a current-carrying conductor. The right-hand rule is used with conventional current flow theory (+ flowing to –).

Rotor In a hybrid electric vehicle the rotor is the rotating part of the electric motor and is usually constructed on permanent magnets.

RVP Reid vapor Pressure. A measure of the volatility of gasoline (how easily it evaporates).

RWD Rear Wheel Drive.

Scroll compressor An A/C compressor design known for its efficiency and excellent NVH characteristics.

Secondary battery Rechargeable battery.

Semi-closed loop A phase of computer-controlled engine operation where lean air–fuel mixtures are used to maximize fuel economy.

Senseless DC motor An AC synchronous electric motor that does not require a rotor position sensor for operation.

Separator In a battery, non-conducting, porous, thin materials used to separate positive and negative plates.

Series circuit An electrical circuit that provides only one path for current to flow.

Series-hybrid design A hybrid vehicle design in which there is no mechanical connection between the ICE and the drive wheels. Instead, the ICE drives a generator that is used to produce electricity for recharging the high-voltage battery and for propelling the vehicle through an electric motor.

Series–parallel hybrid A hybrid vehicle design that can operate both as a series hybrid, a parallel hybrid, or both series and parallel at the same time.

Service plug A high-voltage electrical disconnect device on hybrid electric vehicles. The service plug should always be disconnected whenever working on a hybrid electric vehicle's high-voltage circuits.

Servomotor The actuator in an electronic throttle control (ETC) system. Located in the ETC throttle body.

SFI Sequential Fuel Injection. A fuel injection system where injectors are pulsed individually instead of in groups.

SGCM Starter Generator Control Module. The module in a GM Parallel Hybrid Truck that controls the current to and from the integrated starter generator.

SLA Sealed Lead-Acid battery. One term used to describe a sealed valve-regulated battery.

SLI battery The battery that is responsible for starting, charging, and lighting in a vehicle's electrical system.

Smartkey A brand name of a key that transmit a signal to allow the engine to operate without actually being required to be plugged into the vehicle.

Smog Air pollution made up of ozone and very small particulate matter. A combination of the terms "smoke" and "fog."

SMR System Main Relay. The high-voltage disconnect relays used in Toyota HEVs.

SOC State-of-Charge. Expressed as a percentage, this refers to the charge level of a battery.

Solid state A term used to describe electronic components that have no moving parts.

Soot Particulate matter emitted by diesel engines.

Spark knock See *detonation*.

Specific energy The energy content of a battery relative to the mass of the battery. Specific energy is measured in Watt-hours per kilogram (W-h/kg).

Specific gravity The ratio of the weight of a given volume of a liquid divided by the weight of an equal volume of water.

SPM Surface Permanent Magnet. A type of rotor in an AC synchronous electric motor that places the magnets on its outside circumference.

Squirrel-cage rotor A rotor design utilized in AC induction motors. The conductors in the rotor are made in the shape of a squirrel cage.

State-of-charge The degree or the amount that a battery is charged. A fully charged battery would be 100% charged. Abbreviated as SOC.

Stator The stationary coil winding of a generator or electric motor. AC synchronous and AC induction motor-generators use 3-phase stators, meaning there are 3 separate coil windings in the stator.

Stoichiometric The ideal air–fuel ratio, where all of the fuel combines with all of the oxygen and burns completely.

Straight vegetable oil (SVO) A term used to describe vegetable oil which is a triglyceride with a glycerin component.

Stratosphere The earth's upper atmosphere. Most of the earth's ozone is located in the stratosphere.

Strong hybrid Another term for "full hybrid" (see definition for *full hybrid*).

Subliming The process of a material changing directly from a solid into a gas, skipping the liquid phase completely.

Sulfation Permanent damage in a lead-acid battery caused by the hardening of lead sulfate on the battery plates. Sulfation takes place when a lead-acid battery is discharged for an extended period of time.

Surface charge A "false" charge that exists on the battery plates when a vehicle is first turned off.

Surge tank See definition for *degas bottle*.

SULEV Super Ultra Low-Emission Vehicle.

SUV Sport Utility Vehicle.

SVR Sealed Valve-Regulated lead-acid battery.

Switchgrass A feedstock for ethanol production that requires very little energy or fertilizer to cultivate.

Syncrude Crude oil generated from coal or natural gas through synthetic processes such as Fischer-Tropsch.

Syn-gas Synthesis gas generated by a reaction between coal and steam. Syngas is made up of mostly hydrogen and carbon monoxide and is used to make methanol. Syngas is also known as *town gas*.

Synthetic fuel Fuels generated through synthetic processes such as Fischer-Tropsch.

TAME Tertiary Amyl Methyl Ether. TAME is an oxygenating fuel and is used as a gasoline additive similar to ETBE or MTBE.

Tank-to-wheel efficiency The percentage of energy stored in a vehicle's fuel that is converted into useful mechanical energy.

TCC Torque Converter Clutch. Used to lock the turbine to the housing, thus producing a direct drive through the torque converter assembly.

TCM Transmission Control Module. The electronic control module that is responsible for the operation of the vehicle's transmission or transaxle.

TDC Top Dead Center. The highest point of piston travel in the ICE cylinder.

TEL Tetra Ethyl Lead. TEL was used as an antiknock additive in gasoline. TEL was phased out in favor of more benign additives such as ethanol.

Thermistor An electronic device that changes resistance with temperature.

Thermoelectric switch An electrical switch designed to actuate at a specified temperature.

Thermostat A device used in a cooling system to regulate coolant temperature. The thermostat directs flow either to the water pump inlet or the radiator depending on coolant temperature.

THS Toyota Hybrid System. Two generations of THS have been produced thus far, and these are known as THS I and THS II.

Tier A level of environmental regulation created by the EPA. Tier 1 is gradually being phased out in favor of stricter Tier 2 regulations.

TLEV Transitional Low-Emission Vehicle.

Top tier gasoline Gasoline with a higher detergent content than that specified by the US. EPA.

Torque Twisting force. Torque is measured in pound-feet or Newton-meter.

TRAC Traction Control. A function of the vehicle antilock brake system that enables application of the brake on wheels that have lost traction.

Traction battery The term used to describe the high-voltage battery used to power the drive (traction) motor of a hybrid or electric vehicle.

Traction motor A motor-generator in a hybrid electric vehicle that is responsible for propelling or assisting the ICE in propelling the vehicle.

Troposphere The earth's lower atmosphere. The layer above the troposphere is known as the stratosphere.

TXV Thermostatic Expansion Valve. An A/C system component that acts as a refrigerant expansion device.

UCG Underground Coal Gasification.

ULEV Ultra Low-Emission Vehicle.

ULEV II Ultra Low-Emission Vehicle certified under the Phase II LEV standard.

ULSD Ultra Low Sulfur Diesel. Diesel fuel with a maximum sulfur content of 15 parts per million.

Ultracapacitor A specialized capacitor technology with increased storage capacity for a given volume.

Ultraviolet (UV) radiation A spectrum of radiation emitted by the sun that is mostly absorbed in the earth's upper ozone layer. Ultraviolet radiation is a major contributor to health issues such as cataracts and skin cancer.

Used cooking oil (UCO) Used oil which may or may not be pure vegetable oil.

UVA Ultraviolet radiation from the sun that is not absorbed by the ozone layer and is not damaging to biological organisms.

UVB Ultraviolet radiation from the sun that is only partially absorbed by the ozone layer. UVB can cause damage to biological organisms.

UVC High-energy ultraviolet radiation that is almost completely absorbed by the ozone layer.

Vapor lock A lean condition caused by vaporized fuel in the fuel system.

Variable fuel sensor See definition for *compensation sensor*.

VCM Variable Cylinder Management. A function of some Honda HEVs that allows some ICE cylinders to be disabled in order to enhance regenerative braking action.

VDIM Vehicle Dynamic Integrated Management. A vehicle stability control system used on Lexus HEVs.

V-FFV Virtual Flexible Fuel Vehicle. This fuel system design does not use a fuel compensation sensor and instead uses the vehicle's oxygen sensor to adjust for different fuel compositions.

VI Viscosity Index. An index of the change in a motor oil's viscosity between hot and cold extremes.

VIN Vehicle Identification Number.

Volatility A measure of how easily a fuel evaporates. Volatility is measured using RVP, or Reid Vapor Pressure.

VRLA battery Valve Regulated Lead-Acid battery. A sealed battery that is both spill proof and leak proof. AGM and gelled electrolyte are both examples of VRLA batteries.

VSC Vehicle Stability Control. An electronic stability control system used on Lexus HEVs.

VTEC Variable Valve Timing and Lift Electronic Control. A valvetrain control system developed by Honda Motor Company to enhance engine output and efficiency over a wide RPM range.

VVT-i Variable Valve Timing with Intelligence. A Toyota ICE control system that allows for variable intake valve timing.

Waste vegetable oil (WVO) Oil that is used and can include animal or fish oils from the cooking process.

Water jacket The coolant passages surrounding an ICE which are used to absorb and transfer heat away from the ICE assembly.

Water pump A mechanical device responsible for circulating coolant through a liquid cooling system.

Water valve An electrically operated valve used in Toyota's coolant heat storage system that directs coolant flow between the ICE, the heater core, and the coolant storage tank.

Well-to-tank efficiency The percentage of energy contained in unrefined fuel that is delivered for storage in a vehicle's fuel tank.

Well-to-wheel efficiency The percentage of energy contained in unrefined fuel that is converted into useful mechanical energy.

Wide-band oxygen sensor An oxygen sensor design that is capable of detecting actual air–fuel ratios. This is in contrast to a conventional oxygen sensor that only changes voltage when a stoichiometric air–fuel ratio has been achieved.

Wood alcohol See definition for *Methanol*.

Work Force exerted over a distance.

WWFC World Wide Fuel Charter. A fuel quality standard developed by vehicle and engine manufacturers in 2002.

ZEV Zero-Emission Vehicle. This rating is typically only achieved by battery-powered vehicles or those powered by fuel cells.

Zone valve An electrically operated valve for controlling refrigerant flow in A/C systems with multiple evaporators.

INDEX